The Essential
Distributed Objects
Survival Guide

The Essential Distributed Objects Survival Guide

Robert Orfali • Dan Harkey • Jeri Edwards

JOHN WILEY & SONS, INC.

New York   Chichester   Brisbane   Toronto   Singapore

Publisher: Katherine Schowalter
Editor: Theresa Hudson
Managing Editor: Frank Grazioli
Text Design & Composition: Robert Orfali, Dan Harkey, and Jeri Edwards

Library of Congress Cataloging-in-Publication Data:

Orfali, Robert.
    The essential distributed objects survival guide / Robert Orfali, Dan Harkey, Jeri Edwards
        p.   cm.
    Includes index.
    ISBN 0-471-12993-3

   Additional CIP Data available upon request.

Printed in the United States of America
10 9 8 7 6 5 4 3 2 1

Foreword

by Zog the Martian

Captain Zog

Greetings, Earthlings! I'm Zog, the captain of the Martian team. My team and I first visited earth over a year ago to understand what client/server is all about. During that visit, we discovered the **Essential Client/Server Survival Guide** and found it to be absolutely vital in our mission to explore this new technology. So we were very excited to hear about **The Essential Distributed Objects Survival Guide** by the same authors. We returned to earth to explore this new technology and pick up a copy of the book. It was just what we were looking for.

So what did I like about this book? It felt like it was talking directly to me and to my crew in a friendly voice. That's very important when you're from a foreign planet. We like books that are painless, fun to read, and contain good Martian humor. We were apprehensive at first about objects. Here at Mars, we're still trying to figure out how to use client/server, and then here comes this new technology called distributed objects. As it turns out, the timing was perfect. We now believe that objects are the only way to build our intergalactic client/server webs. Yes, we will be connected to the Internet. Hopefully, our CORBA-compliant components will be able to talk to yours.

We really like this component stuff—we want our objects to be smart from the very start and play in suites. We were disappointed to find out that you earthlings are still at war with each other over component technologies. Can't you have a single infrastructure? All this CORBA/OpenDoc versus COM/OLE stuff can really be confusing. Which component standard should we build on? This Survival Guide provides a very complete, in-depth coverage of CORBA, OpenDoc, and COM/OLE. We haven't seen anything like it in your earthling bookstores. We appreciated its coverage of other object technologies—including OpenStep, Taligent, and Newi. We like to fully understand our options.

This latest Survival Guide is another masterpiece from the authors. The Soapboxes really helped us understand the issues and what the latest earthling debates are all about. We like to hear strong opinions instead of just sterilized information. The artwork and cartoons are absolutely wonderful. I like to see pictures of myself in books (and especially on the cover). The ubiquitous scenarios show how objects really interact with each other. It's not that inert boring stuff you read in the textbooks. It makes objects come to life.

In summary, this Survival Guide gave us a comprehensive tour of distributed object technology and components. We now have a better idea of how to use this technology in practical Martian situations. The personal touch was great; it felt like we had our own private tour. I cannot recommend this book enough to my fellow Martians. Through this foreword, I highly recommend this book to you Earthlings. If I can understand components, so can you.

Zog

Preface

Objects: A Revolution Within the Revolution

Client/server computing has created a deep paradigmatic shift in our industry. It's replacing monolithic mainframe applications with applications split across client and server lines. The client—typically a PC—provides the graphical interface, while the server provides access to shared resources—typically a database. Distributed objects are a paradigm shift within a paradigm shift—they're a new client/server revolution within the client/server revolution. Objects break-up the client and server sides of an application into smart components that can play together and roam across networks.

Why Another Revolution?

So why is there another client/server revolution when the first one is still in full swing? The answer—as usual—is newer and better hardware and the demand for applications that match the new hardware. The first client/server revolution was driven by new hardware—PCs and Ethernet LANs forever changed the way we interact with our applications. Gone are the green-screen uglies associated with terminal-attached mainframes. Instead, we have GUIs. There's no way to turn back the clock.

The second client/server revolution is also being fueled by advances in hardware. This time, Wide Area Networks (WANs) are breaking the proximity barriers associated with Ethernet LANs. Millions of us are getting a firsthand taste—thanks to the Internet, CompuServe, and America Online—of the joys of intergalactic networking. We will soon want a lot more. We won't be satisfied with just navigating through information and chatting; we will want to conduct our business on these networks. Money will start changing hands. People will either transact directly or through their electronic agents. In the age of intergalactic transactions, there's no going back to single-server, departmental client/server LANs. Mosaic has changed that forever.

So, the second era of client/server is being driven by very high speed, low-cost, wide-area bandwidth. The telephone companies and WAN providers are getting ready to unleash almost unlimited bandwidth—they're wiring the entire planet for fiber optic speeds. In addition, network-ready PCs running commodity multi-threaded operating systems—such as OS/2 Warp Connect and Windows 95—are now capable of running as both clients and servers.

This means that we may soon have millions of servers interconnected across the planet at ten times LAN speeds. This is the good news. The bad news is that our existing client/server infrastructure is geared for single-server departmental LANs; it cannot cope with the new intergalactic demands—millions of servers and applications that can spawn trillions of distributed transactions. Distributed objects are our only hope for dealing with the new client/server infrastructure requirements.

Why Distributed Objects?

A distributed object is essentially a *component*. This means it's a blob of self-contained intelligence that can interoperate across operating systems, networks, languages, applications, tools, and multivendor hardware. Without stealing the punchline from this Survival Guide, we can say that distributed objects—when packaged as *components*—provide the only middleware that can make client/server computing really work at an intergalactic level.

This Survival Guide is not an academic exercise on the wonders of objects. For the first time in the 22-year history of objects, we have true intergalactic standards for building object components that are interoperable, transactional, secure, and self-managing. We also have standards that allow these components to play in *suites*—on the desktop or across the enterprise. The industry even has two "standards" to choose from: COM/OLE from Microsoft and CORBA from the OMG (augmented by OpenDoc from CI Labs). And we are starting to see applications and products that build on these standards.

Building Applications With Components

Distributed objects and components will change the way we architect, develop, package, distribute, license, and maintain our software. The component is a unit of packaging, distribution, and maintenance. It's also a unit of deployment on the intergalactic network. A component does not operate in a vacuum. It lives on a distributed object bus—for example, CORBA or COM. The component derives its system smarts from the bus. It is architected to work with other components from the very start. In fact, the object buses are now adding new services that components can inherit at build time or even at run time to achieve higher levels of collaboration with other independent components.

This intelligent infrastructure makes it easier to develop and assemble independent components. It lowers the barriers to entry and changes the economics of software. Components bring the fun back to software development. Smaller ISVs will find it easier to create components for the functions they do best without having to reinvent the entire infrastructure. The object bus provides a unified systems architecture that can be of tremendous help to IS shops and system integrators. Finally, components will help lower the costs of software development and maintenance for regular software houses. Consumers also win because they can control when to upgrade their software with add-on components to get more customized systems.

The beauty of all this is that a single object bus can support components that run in the same process as well as components that run across an intergalactic network. It's one bus that really scales. You can use it for both standalone applications and intergalactic ones. In addition, the applications we can create are unlike any we've seen before. Component agents will watch for network events and act on their own to submit transactions or gather data. Components will come together in real time to create a one-time application tailored for a particular customer. New applications—some yet to be imagined—will generate millions of new transactions daily. These include electronic travel agencies, health-care portfolio managers, financial agents, shopping mavens, and career managers. These applications can transact for you in all kinds of intergalactic electronic bazaars that specialize in every known form of trading.

What This Survival Guide Covers

This book explains distributed objects and components in depth. It consists of six parts—each one can almost be read independently. We'll give you a short description of what the parts cover. If you find the terminology too foreign, then by all means read the book to find out what it all means.

■ **Part 1** starts with an overview of what objects can do for client/server. We compare distributed objects with competing client/server application environments—including SQL databases, TP Monitors, and Groupware. If you come from a client/server background, this discussion will help you understand what the distributed object fuss is all about. In this part, we also explain what objects are and when an object is a component. We provide a very comprehensive description of the benefits of components and their attributes. Components do more than just client/server—they change the nature of computing, especially on the desktop.

- **Part 2** covers the CORBA object bus and system-level object services in great detail. If you're not interested in all the low-level details, the first chapter provides a birds-eye view of CORBA.

- **Part 3** covers business objects and application-level frameworks—including CORBA frameworks, OpenDoc, OLE, Taligent, OpenStep, and Newi. Of course, the most important of these frameworks are currently OLE and OpenDoc. But the rest of the frameworks also have important features that you should know about. Many of these features may eventually be merged with either OLE or OpenDoc.

- **Part 4** covers OpenDoc in depth. We go over all the features of its compound document application-level framework.

- **Part 5** covers COM/OLE in depth. We cover both OLE's object bus—called COM—and its compound document application-level framework.

- **Part 6** helps you narrow down your options. We try and bring it all together and speculate on where it's all going.

This book contains a detailed overview of CORBA, OpenDoc, and COM/OLE. If this is not enough, we include a bibliography and pointers on where to go for more information.

How to Read This Book

As we recommend in all our books, the best way to approach this Survival Guide is to ask your boss for a one-week, paid sabbatical to go sit on a beach and read it. Tell him or her that it's the cheapest way to revitalize yourself technically and find out all there is to know about distributed objects, components, OpenDoc, CORBA, OLE, Taligent, and OpenStep. Once you sink into that comfortable chair overlooking the ocean, we think you'll find the book a lot of fun—maybe even downright relaxing. You won't get bored; but if you do, simply jump to the next part until you find something you like. You can jump to any part of the book and start reading it. We recommend, however, that you carefully go over the cartoons so that you have something to tell the boss back at the office.

What Are the Boxes For

We use shaded boxes as a way to introduce concurrent threads in the presentation material. It's the book version of multitasking. The Soapboxes introduce strong opinions or biases on some of the more controversial topics of distributed object computing (see the next Soapbox). Because the discipline is so new and fuzzy, there's lots of room for interpretation and debate—so you'll get lots of Soapboxes that are just another opinion (ours). The Briefing boxes give you background or tutorial type information. You can safely skip over them if you're already familiar with a topic. The Detail boxes cover some esoteric area of technology that may not be of interest to the general readership. Typically, the same readers that skip over the briefings will find the details interesting (so you'll still get your money's worth). Lastly, we use Warning boxes to let you know where danger lies—this is, after all, a Survival Guide.

Who Is This Book For?

This book is for anybody who's associated with the computer industry and needs to understand where it's heading. Within three years we will all be involved with objects and components in some form or another—as users, assemblers, integrators, system developers, and component developers. All new software will be built using components.

If you have very little time to spare (or little interest in the technical details), we suggest that you take the *scenic route*. It includes all of Part 1, the first chapter of Part 2, and all of Parts 3 and 6. Look for the scenic route signs at the beginning of these chapters and in the Table of Contents. This will let you postpone reading the more technical chapters, but you will still have a solid overview of distributed objects and components, their standards, and the key products.

How Does This Survival Guide Compare With Our Previous Book?

Our previous book, the **Essential Client/Server Survival Guide** (Wiley, 1994) provides an overview of the entire field of client/server computing—including NOSs, SQL databases, TP Monitors, groupware, system management, tools, and distributed objects. This Survival Guide starts out where the other one leaves off. It focuses entirely on distributed objects and components. We felt there was a lot more to say about distributed objects than we could cover in the previous Survival Guide. If you read our previous book, you'll notice that we borrowed about 50 pages from it to make this one stand on its own. If you did not read the previous Survival Guide, Chapter 1 reviews the main ideas we developed there.

Some of the ideas in this Survival Guide appeared in articles we published over the last 10 months in major trade publications—including **BYTE**, **Datamation**, **Object Magazine**, **Dr. Dobb's Journal**, and others. We're grateful to the senior editors of these magazines for providing us a forum to develop our ideas. However, we felt we could not tell the distributed components story—including CORBA, OpenDoc, and OLE—in articles that average 10 pages or less. These component technologies are like a giant tidal wave that's heading our way to reshape our industry. They deserve a bit more scrutiny than what you read in a fast-paced magazine article. So we finally decided we had to write this Survival Guide to get this story off our chests. We wrote it. Now it's in your hands—totally unabridged.

We hope you enjoy the reading, the cartoons, and the Soapboxes. Drop us a line if you have something you want to "flame" about. We'll take compliments too. We're relying on word-of-mouth to let people know about the book, so if you enjoy it, please spread the word. Finally, we want to thank you, as well as our Martian friends, for trusting us to be your guides.

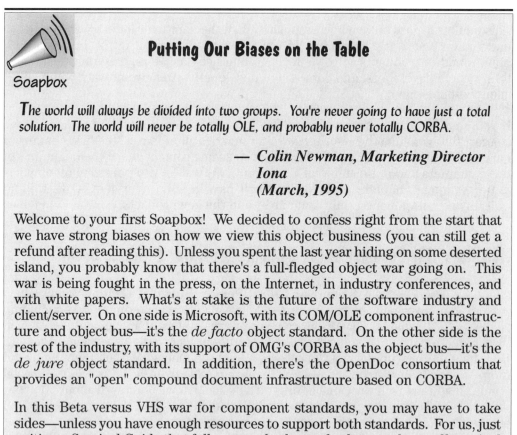

Putting Our Biases on the Table

Soapbox

The world will always be divided into two groups. You're never going to have just a total solution. The world will never be totally OLE, and probably never totally CORBA.

— *Colin Newman, Marketing Director*
Iona
(March, 1995)

Welcome to your first Soapbox! We decided to confess right from the start that we have strong biases on how we view this object business (you can still get a refund after reading this). Unless you spent the last year hiding on some deserted island, you probably know that there's a full-fledged object war going on. This war is being fought in the press, on the Internet, in industry conferences, and with white papers. What's at stake is the future of the software industry and client/server. On one side is Microsoft, with its COM/OLE component infrastructure and object bus—it's the *de facto* object standard. On the other side is the rest of the industry, with its support of OMG's CORBA as the object bus—it's the *de jure* object standard. In addition, there's the OpenDoc consortium that provides an "open" compound document infrastructure based on CORBA.

In this Beta versus VHS war for component standards, you may have to take sides—unless you have enough resources to support both standards. For us, just writing a Survival Guide that fully covers both standards was a huge effort. And it takes a lot more effort to develop and support code that runs on two standards. Our industry can at most support two standards. But, we briefly cover Taligent, Newi, and OpenStep just to give you an idea of what else is happening in distributed objects. We also show how these highly creative "alternate standards" are starting to merge with the big two. However, the emphasis in this book is on the "big two": CORBA/OpenDoc and COM/OLE. Both of these standards are here to stay. Neither will disappear soon. And we may have to live with both for a very long time; but it won't be easy.

We believe that CORBA is much better than COM/OLE, at least technically. We also feel more comfortable with a *de jure* standard that's not controlled by a single company. Microsoft—like the old IBM—is trying to single-handedly control standards. It believes it can define a homogeneous world where all the important standards will be theirs. But we believe that this single-system view of the world just doesn't work in the case of components, which—by definition—must be heterogeneous, multiplatform, open, interoperable, and supported by multiple vendors. It's best to do this with *de jure* and open standards. OLE may become "Microsoft's SAA."

You may hear from naysayers that CORBA—with its 500+ members—is "designed by committee" and that it may be best to have a single vendor do the whole design. This is not the case. Some standard bodies have rightfully acquired a bad name. However, CORBA is almost a labor of love by some of the best object technologists in the business. The CORBA standards move fast and are very creative. As you'll see in this Survival Guide, CORBA compromises typically give us the best of two technologies. Let's face it: Objects are still an art form. It takes a lot of collective brain power to figure out how to build an infrastructure for heterogeneous distributed components.

We challenge the naysayers to say that OLE is better technically than CORBA. On the contrary, CORBA is at least two years ahead of OLE/COM in creating a heterogeneous, distributed, component infrastructure. And OpenDoc is better than OLE as a compound document framework. Microsoft has just too many legacy APIs to bring forward. You'll be able to judge these things for yourself when you read this book.

Despite our CORBA bias, this Survival Guide contains one of the most complete technical descriptions of COM/OLE anywhere. We tried very hard to keep our opinions in Soapboxes (like this one). Also, we believe that OLE is here to stay because of its close integration with Windows. So you might as well learn it. This Survival Guide contains over 160 pages on COM/OLE—including many comparisons with CORBA and OpenDoc.

In addition to our own opinions, we also include lots of quotes from industry people on this object war. It seems everybody has something to say about this important issue. So we wanted you to hear from them, too. The bad news is that we have fewer quotes this time from non-industry people such as Bob Dylan and Lao Tzu. So now that we got our biases out on the table, let's move forward with this Survival Guide. ❑

Acknowledgments

It's impossible to thank all the hundreds of people that helped us with this book. But, we'll give it a try:

- To Cynthia McFall and Cliff Reeves for giving Bob and Dan a home with the object group in Austin, even though we work from the San Francisco Bay Area. Cynthia was there when we needed her. We also thank Dave Brandt and Dell Rieth for their ongoing support.

- To the technical people in different companies who helped us make some sense out of this difficult topic—including Mike Blevins, Kathy Bohrer, Grady Booch, Kraig Brockschmidt, Frank Campagnoni, Guylaine Cantin, Rick Cattell, Dan Chang, Phil Chang, Ed Cobb, Mike Conner, Bill Culman, Richard Finkelstein, Ira Forman, Jim Gray, Jed Harris, Pete Homan, Ivar Jacobson, Ralph Johnson, Johannes Klein, Charly Kleissner, Wilfried Kruse, Christina Lau, Kevin Leong, Geoff Lewis, Mary Loomis, Hari Madduri, Tom Mowbray, Annrai O'Toole, Mark Phillips, Kurt Piersol, Mike Potel, Tony Rego, John Rymer, Harold Sammer, Roger Sessions, Oliver Sims, Richard Soley, Chris Stone, Bruce Tate, David Taylor, Lou Thomason, John Tibbetts, Robert Tycast, Robert Vasaly, Don Vines, John Vlissides, Sara Williams, Tony Williams, and Dave Wilson.

- To the senior editors in the major trade publications who gave us a chance to develop an early version of this story—including Dick Conklin, Marie Lenzi, Kevin Strehlo, Jon Udell, Ray Valdes, and Alan Zeichick. Some of these editors wrote their own distributed object story.

- To the marketing directors and product managers who fed us with up-to-the-minute information on their latest and greatest products—including Michael Barton, Lydia Bennett, Anthony Brown, Dianne Copenhaver, Scott Hebner, Chris Hyrne, Larry Perlstein, and Keith Wescourt.

- To Dave Pacheco for creating the wonderful technical illustrations in this book (the cartoons are still by Jeri).

- To our tireless copy editor, Larry Mackin.

- To the people at Wiley that had to deal with our pickiness—including Terry Canela, Frank Grazioli, Terri Hudson, Bob Ipsen, Ellen Reavis, and Katherine Schowalter. We also thank our previous editor Diane Littwin.

- To the more than 100,000 readers who read our previous books. Without your continued support we couldn't write these books.

Contents at a Glance

Contents

Part 2. CORBA: The Distributed Object Bus 43

Chapter 8. CORBA Services: Persistence and Object Databases . 139

Chapter 9. CORBA Services: Query and Relationships 165

Chapter 10. CORBA Services: System Management and Security 183

Chapter 11. CORBA Commercial ORBs 203

Part 3. Frameworks for Business Objects and Components 217

Chapter 17. Taligent's CommonPoint: Frameworks Everywhere. . 297

Chapter 18. NeXT's OpenStep and Portable Distributed Objects . 313

Part 5. OLE/COM Under the Hood 425

Chapter 25. COM: OLE's Object Bus 429

List of Boxes

Part 1
Client/Server With
Distributed Objects

An Introduction to Part 1

No self-respecting computer scientist can look in the mirror each day without confronting the reality of object technology.

— *Dr. Ted Lewis*
IEEE Computer Magazine
(April, 1995)

First, we would like to extend our warmest greetings to our Martian friends. We're glad that you're back to visit us. You probably want to know what these distributed objects have to do with client/server computing. You won't be disappointed. Distributed objects are the latest revolution within the ongoing client/server revolution. But the reach of these objects extends much further than client/server. Distributed objects—especially when packaged as *components*—promise to overhaul the way we design, develop, package, distribute, and maintain *all* software. When an overhaul of this magnitude takes place, it tends to create many winners and losers. This Survival Guide will help you understand your options.

Part 1 starts out with a vision of the *intergalactic era* of client/server. This vision is close to being the new reality. The current *Ethernet era* of client/server—which began about 10 years ago—is coming to an end. It's being replaced by intergalactic webs created by the abundance of low-cost bandwidth. The distributed object bus provides the essential middleware that will help propel this intergalactic era. Objects that live on this bus are called *components*. They are independently packaged objects that can operate across languages, operating systems, networks, and tools. These components are ultimately blobs of distributed intelligence. They know how to cooperate with other such blobs to create systems that are smarter and more agile than anything we have today.

We start Part 1 by introducing the intergalactic era. Then we explain the role of objects in this new era and how they compete with existing client/server application environments—including SQL databases, TP Monitors, and groupware. After whetting your appetite, we go over what a distributed object is. You'll discover that distributed objects are essentially software components. You'll also discover that our industry currently has two competing "standards" for creating component infrastructures: CORBA/OpenDoc and COM/OLE. Both of these standards will eventually let you create supersmart components that can roam on intergalactic networks and collaborate with other components across desktops or the enterprise. So welcome to this exciting new world. Hopefully, you'll find components to be profitable, fun, and productive.

Chapter 1

Objects:
The Next
Client/Server
Revolution

---

*O*bjects are closer than you think.

— *Steve Jobs, CEO NeXT*
(February, 1995)

The next generation of client/server systems will inevitably be built using distributed objects. This chapter will tell you why. If you're like most of us—just starting to feel comfortable with your Ethernet departmental LAN and local database server—you may not want to hear this: Our industry is poised for a second client/server revolution. Fasten your seat belts because this second revolution promises to be just as traumatic as the one we just went through when client/server applied a giant chainsaw to mainframe-based monolithic applications and broke them apart into client and server components.

Today our industry stands at a new threshold brought on by: 1) the exponential increase of low-cost bandwidth on Wide Area Networks—for example, the Internet and CompuServe; and 2) a new generation of network-enabled, multithreaded desktop operating systems—for example, OS/2 Warp and Windows 95. This new threshold marks the beginning of a transition from *Ethernet* client/server to *intergalactic* client/server that will result in the irrelevance of proximity. The center of gravity is shifting from single-server, LAN-based departmental client/server to a post-scarcity form of client/server where every machine on the global "information highway" can be both a client and a server.

INTERGALACTIC CLIENT/SERVER COMPUTING

The big insight for the next ten years is this: What if digital communications were free? The answer is that the way we learn, buy, socialize, do business, and entertain ourselves will be very different.

> — **Bill Gates, Chairman**
> **Microsoft**
> **(January, 1995)**

Fiber optics is taking us from a modest to an almost infinite bandwidth, with nothing in between. New information and entertainment services are not waiting on fiber in the home; they are waiting on the imagination.

> — **Nicholas Negroponte, Author**
> **Being Digital**
> **(Knopf, 1995)**

When it comes to intergalactic client/server applications, the imagination is at the controls. The promise of high-bandwidth at very low cost has conjured visions of an information highway that turns into the world's largest shopping mall. The predominant vision is that of an electronic bazaar of planetary proportions—replete with boutiques, department stores, bookstores, brokerage services, banks, and travel agencies. Like a Club Med, the mall will issue its own electronic currency to facilitate round-the-clock shopping and for business-to-business transactions. Electronic agents of all kinds will be roaming around the network looking for bargains and conducting negotiations with other agents. Billions of electronic business transactions will be generated on a daily basis. Massive amounts of multimedia data will also be generated, moved, and stored on the network.

Obviously what we're describing is not the Internet as we know it today—there is a lot more to this vision than just surfing through hypertext webs of HTML-tagged information. We're talking about transaction rates that are thousands of times larger than anything we have today. In addition, these transactions are going to be more long-lived and complex. The data these transactions operate on will also be more complex and rich in multimedia content. Of course, we're not just talking about the Internet. This technology will also be used on small "i" Internets—including LANs, interbusiness networks, and private wide-area networks.

What Client/Server Software Is Needed?

The information highway will generate a higher volume of transactions than anything has to date...

> — *Bill Gates, Chairman*
> *Microsoft*
> *(January, 1995)*

The volume low-risk Internet transactions will triple to $750 million-plus in 1995 and balloon to $100 billion-plus by 1998/99.

> — *Meta Group*
> *Business on the Internet*
> *(January, 1995)*

Some key technologies are needed at the client/server application level to make all this happen, including:

■ ***Rich transaction processing***. In addition to supporting the venerable flat transaction, the new environment requires nested transactions that can span across multiple servers, long-lived transactions that execute over long periods of time as they travel from server to server, and queued transactions that can be used in secure business-to-business dealings. Most nodes on the network should be able to participate in a secured transaction; superserver nodes will handle the massive transaction loads.

■ ***Roaming agents***. The new environment will be populated with electronic agents of all types. Consumers will have personal agents that look after their interests; businesses will deploy agents to sell their wares on the network; and sniffer agents will be sitting on the network, at all times, collecting information to do system management or simply looking for trends and gathering statistics. Agent technology includes cross-platform scripting engines, workflow, and an environment that allows agents to live on any machine on the network.

■ ***Rich data management***. This includes active multimedia compound documents that you can move, store, view, and edit in-place anywhere on the network. Again, most nodes on the network should provide compound document technology—for example, OLE or OpenDoc—for doing local document management. Superservers will provide repositories for storing and distributing massive numbers of documents. Of course, this environment must also be able to support existing record-based structured data including SQL databases.

■ *Intelligent self-managing entities*. With the introduction of new multi-threaded, high-volume, network-ready, desktop operating systems—such as OS/2 Warp and Windows 95—we anticipate a world where millions of machines can be both clients and servers. However, we can't afford to ship a system administrator with every $99 operating system. To avoid doing this, we need distributed software that knows how to manage and configure itself and protect itself against threats.

■ *Intelligent middleware*. The distributed environment must provide the semblance of a single system image across potentially millions of hybrid client/server machines. The middleware must create this Houdini-sized illusion by making all servers on the global network appear to behave like a single computer system. Users and programs should be able to dynamically join and leave the network and discover each other. You should be able to use the same naming conventions to locate any resource on the network. You should be able to talk to any resource without worrying about the underlying protocol stacks or transport medium.

This is a tall order of requirements. Can our client/server infrastructure—conceived to meet the needs of the single-server Ethernet era—meet the new challenges? Is our client/server infrastructure ready for intergalactic prime time? Can our existing middleware deal with millions of machines that can be both clients and servers? We answer these questions in the next section.

WHO WILL LEAD THE NEXT CLIENT/SERVER REVOLUTION?

It is obvious that new types of applications will live on the intergalactic network. These applications will be created, deployed, and managed differently from the way we do it today in the Ethernet single-server era. Today, there are four competing paradigms (and technologies) for developing new client/server applications: SQL databases, TP Monitors, Groupware, and Distributed Objects. You can use all four technologies to create very complete client/server applications. All provide tools to help you develop client/server applications (some more than others). And they each introduce their favorite form of middleware for client/server interactions. And to complicate matters, the four paradigms are starting to encroach on each other's turf. For example, they can all manage processes, data, and middleware.

In our book, **Essential Client/Server Survival Guide** (Wiley, 1994), we explained the technology base for these competing client/server application paradigms, and then we fearlessly picked a winner.[1] The winner we picked in our previous book and in the **BYTE Magazine** article was, of course, client/server with distributed objects—which is why we wrote the book you're now reading. We now very briefly

---

[1] Also see our more recent article on the same topic: "Intergalactic Client/Server Computing," Orfali, Harkey, and Edwards, **BYTE Magazine** (April, 1995).

7

summarize why we picked distributed objects instead of the competing solutions. You can read the details in our other publications.

Client/Server With SQL Databases

At present the majority of existing client/server-based software is to be found in the area of databases, and it is here that the greatest challenge to any corporation currently lies.

— *Richard Finkelstein, President*
Performance Computing

SQL database servers are the dominant model for creating client/server applications today. SQL started out as a declarative language for manipulating data using ten simple commands. However, as SQL applications moved to more demanding client/server environments, it became clear that the management of data alone was not enough. There was also a need to manage the functions that manipulated the data. Various benchmarks demonstrated that submitting SQL commands on the network resulted in poor performance. This performance can be greatly improved by encapsulating SQL commands in a procedure that resides on the same server as the database. The procedure is invoked by clients via an RPC-like call (see Figure 1-1). This mechanism is sometimes referred to as *TP lite* or *stored procedures*. A stored procedure is formally a named collection of SQL statements and procedural logic that is compiled, verified, and stored in the server database.

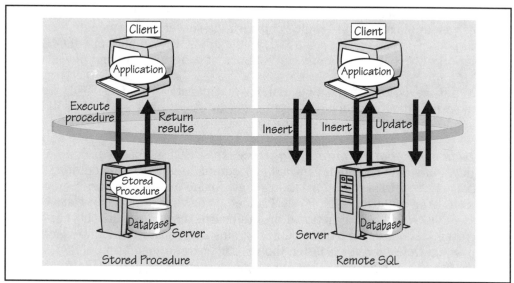

Figure 1-1. Stored Procedures Versus Networked SQL.

SQL Standards Lag Implementations

Sybase pioneered the concept of stored procedures in 1986. Today, virtually all SQL vendors provide some form of stored procedure. Over time, SQL vendors introduced other procedural extensions to SQL—including *triggers* and *rules*. These procedural extensions are used to enforce data integrity; to perform system maintenance; and, primarily, to create the server side of an application's logic. The problem, of course, is that all the procedural extensions to SQL are totally non-standard. No two vendor implementations are alike. The language for describing the stored procedures and their functionality varies from one vendor to the next. And there is no standard way to pass or describe the parameters. As a result, stored procedures lock you into proprietary vendor implementations. In addition, stored procedures provide very minimal transaction support.

Because SQL standards always seem to lag behind vendor implementations—by at least five years—almost anything that's interesting in database client/server technology is non-standard. This includes database administration, data replication, stored procedures, user-defined data types, the client APIs, and the formats and protocols on the network. So the best you can do in heterogeneous database environments is to create a loose federation of databases that operate at the least common denominator level—typically dynamic SQL. These arrangements—called *Federated Databases*—predominate the SQL client/server landscape.

Why SQL Can't Hack It

On the plus side, the SQL model of client/server makes it is very easy to create client/server applications in single-vendor/single-server environments. In these environments, you can easily create SQL applications using a plethora of GUI tools. Most importantly, SQL feels familiar to millions of programmers and power users.

So why did we write off the SQL database application model? SQL database servers—even when they include stored procedures—cannot provide a solid intergalactic middleware foundation for the following reasons:

- *SQL is very poor at managing processes*. SQL manages processes using highly non-standard extensions and procedural languages. In addition, an SQL server either buries the application's logic inside a stored procedure or inside an SQL front-end tool—like Power Builder. Programs are second-class citizens in the SQL world. Transactional programs are third-class citizens. And don't even think about using SQL to run programs that must interact transactionally across multiple servers. So even though the current generation of SQL servers was able to manage processes on single servers, it cannot scale to multiple servers.

■ *SQL middleware is non-standard*. SQL from different vendors does not interoperate. There's no standard wire protocol for exchanging intervendor SQL messages across networks.

■ *SQL is not suitable for managing rich data*. SQL is based on simple data types; it is not suitable for managing complex data types or data that's spread across multiple servers (especially heterogeneous ones). Yes, SQL will continue to play a role in the intergalactic era, but mostly as a store of legacy data. SQL itself will be encapsulated with object wrappers—for example, OLE DB and the CORBA persistence service. Most new data will follow the object model using either the SQL3 object extensions or pure object databases.

To summarize, SQL is too proprietary and data-centric to provide the next generation intergalactic client/server bus.[2]

Client/Server With TP Monitors

My transaction hopes are pinned on the impact of the distribution of processing—when it is realized that data is not everything and that process is just as important.

— Jim Gray, Author
Transaction Processing
(Morgan Kaufmann, 1993)

Transaction Processing Monitors (TP Monitors) have solid credentials—they've been used for many years to keep the biggest of "Big Iron" running. In the mainframe world, a TP Monitor is sold with every mission critical database. The mainframe folks realized many moons ago that you can't create mission-critical applications without managing the programs (or processes) that operate on data. TP Monitors were born to manage processes and to orchestrate programs. They do this by breaking complex applications into pieces of code called *transactions*. Using these transactions, a TP Monitor can get pieces of software that don't know anything about each other to act in total unison. This is obviously a very desirable function in intergalactic client/server environments that must deal with billions of daily transactions running anywhere on the network on thousands of servers.

---

[2] On a personal note, SQL was very good to your authors over the last ten years. We used it very effectively to create single-server client/server applications. We even wrote a very fat book on how to write client/server programs using SQL. But we don't believe SQL has what it takes to create multiserver applications.

What Does a TP Monitor Do?

TP Monitors were introduced to run classes of applications that could service thousands of clients. They do this by providing an environment that interjects itself between the remote clients and the server resources. By interjecting themselves between clients and servers, TP Monitors can manage transactions, route them across systems, load-balance their execution, and restart them after failures. A TP Monitor can manage transactional resources on a single server or across multiple servers, and it can cooperate with other TP Monitors in federated arrangements.

TP Monitors also provide a "great funneling act" that helps the operating system and server resource managers deal with large numbers of clients. The top part of Figure 1-2 shows an operating system having to deal with a 1000 clients without the help of a TP Monitor. If each client were given all the resources it needed, even the largest mainframe server would fall on its knees. Luckily, not all the clients require all the resources at the same time. However, when they do require it, they want their service immediately. So, instead of giving each client a dedicated process, the TP Monitor prestarts a pool of shared server processes and waits for clients to request a service. When a client request comes in, the TP Monitor hands it to the first available process in the shared server pool. After the client completes, the server process can be reused by another client. By removing this process-per-client requirement, the TP Monitor allows server applications to service very large number of clients; the operating system can stay up (see bottom half of Figure 1-2).

Why Are TP Monitors Such a Well-Kept Secret?

Obviously, TP Monitors can be very useful in intergalactic client/server environments—they manage transactions and processes and they provide upward scalability. Compared to SQL databases, TP Monitors did not do very well during the Ethernet era of client/server. TP Monitor vendors were slow to adapt to the new paradigm and did a very poor job explaining what they had to offer. Their packaging was also poor—they did not understand the shrink-wrap market realities. And, TP Monitors are probably an overkill for the single-server/single-vendor, departmental-sized applications that predominate the Ethernet era.

Even though the modern client/server incarnations of TP Monitors have played a very minor role in the Ethernet client/server era, they seem to have what it takes to play in the intergalactic client/server era. In fact, it wouldn't be far fetched to assume that every machine on the network will have a TP Monitor to represent it in global transactions. Under the control of a TP Monitor, a transaction can be managed from its point of origin—typically on the client—across one or more servers, and then back to the originating client. When a transaction ends, all the

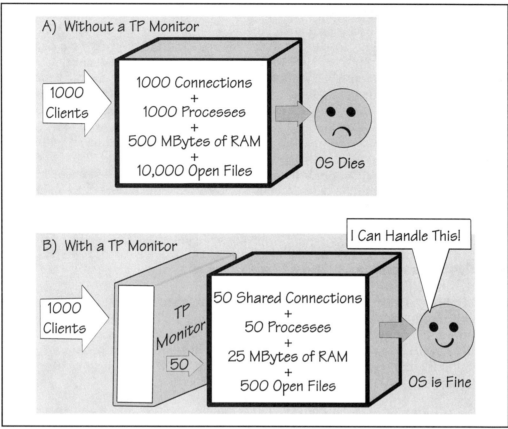

Figure 1-2. Why a Server Operating System Needs a TP Monitor.

parties involved are in agreement as to whether it succeeded or failed. The transaction becomes the contract that binds the client to one or more servers.

Will TP Monitors Morph Into ORBs?

So why are we writing off TP Monitors? We're not writing them off. *Au contraire,* we believe that the next generation TP Monitor is called an *Object Request Broker (ORB).* TP Monitors will simply morph into the distributed object infrastructure. The TP Monitor vendors were heavily involved in creating the standards for the CORBA *Object Transaction Service.* Consequently, they laid the groundwork to marry objects with transactions. This time around, object TP Monitors will be packaged for the mass market.

What Do TP Monitors Do for Objects?

In pure CORBA implementations, objects can appear from anywhere at any time. However, under the control of a TP Monitor, objects can be managed in a *predictable* manner. For example, a TP Monitor can prestart objects, manage their life cycle, and provide transaction-level authorization. TP Monitors do not like to be surprised. They like to be in control of their environment. In contrast, pure objects are totally anarchistic. The marriage of objects and TP Monitors will create some interesting new patterns. We usually recommend that you use today's crop of TP Monitors to help you transition into the world of distributed objects. This is because TP Monitors use a *three-tiered*, client/server architecture—which means the process is separated from the data and the user interface. This architecture is in some ways similar to distributed objects. In addition, TP Monitors are more robust than the ORBs that are on the market today.

What Do Distributed Objects Do for TP Monitors?

Objects allow TP Monitors to work with transactional middleware provided by standard off-the-shelf Object Request Brokers (ORBs). The ORBs will be incorporated into commodity desktop operating systems such as OS/2 Warp, Windows 95, and Macintosh. For the first time TP Monitor vendors will not be providing the transactional middleware themselves. Better yet, they will be working with mainstream middleware that works on both clients and servers.

Objects also make it easier for TP Monitors to create and manage rich transaction models—such as nested transactions and long-lived transactions (or workflow). Instead of managing dumb monolithic applications, TP Monitors will become frameworks for managing smart components. Once TP Monitors and components figure out how to play together, they can literally perform magic. In addition, the distributed object infrastructure provides TP Monitors with myriads of standard services—including metadata, dynamic invocations, persistence, relationships, events, naming, component factories, versioning, licensing, security, change management, collections, and many others. These are services TP Monitor vendors will not have to recreate. If this terminology doesn't make any sense, please bear with us—you'll know exactly what it all means by the time you finish reading this Survival Guide.

Client/Server With Groupware

Groupware is a collection of technologies that allow us to represent complex processes that center around collaborative human activities. It builds on five foundation technologies: multimedia document management, workflow, e-mail, conferencing, and scheduling. Groupware is not another downsized mainframe technology—it's genuinely a new model of client/server computing. Groupware collects highly unstructured data—including text, images, faxes, mail, and bulletin boards—and organizes it in a nebulous thing called a *document*. The documents can then be viewed, stored, replicated, and routed anywhere on the network. The multimedia document is to Groupware what a table is to an SQL database: It's a basic unit of management. Groupware excels in the art of document database management. Groupware makes good use of e-mail—it's the communication middleware of choice. E-mail is one of the easiest ways for electronic processes to communicate with humans. Its store-and-forward nature is a good match for the way businesses sometimes work—asynchronously. You don't have to respond to a sender until you're ready. With over 60 million globally interconnected electronic mailboxes, e-mail is becoming quite ubiquitous.

Lotus Notes: The Archetypical Groupware Product

The best way to appreciate what makes Groupware technology so different is to look at Lotus Notes—the premier Groupware product in the industry. The secret of Lotus Notes' success is that it creates a whole that is much more than the sum of its parts. Figure 1-3 shows the components of Lotus Notes. Like all good Groupware, Notes makes good use of e-mail and does client/server document database management. But what makes Notes so revolutionary is the built-in technology it provides for the widespread replication of these databases. Notes uses replication as a means to disseminate (or broadcast) information across geographically distributed locations. What happened to locking and data integrity—the darlings of SQL databases? Notes doesn't care—it was more important to get the information out. Now that's revolutionary! Notes Release 3 introduced a level of version control that provides adequate protection for document-centric applications but it's not recommended for situations that require highly concurrent and immediate updates.

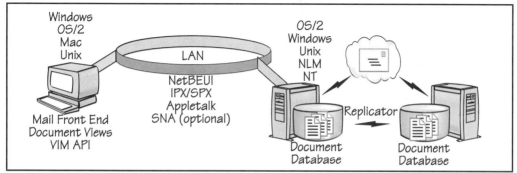

Figure 1-3. The Components of Lotus Notes.

Workflow: Process Management for Groupware

Process management via *workflow* is another revolutionary aspect of Groupware. Workflow is used to automatically route events (and work) from one program to the next in structured or unstructured client/server environments (see Figure 1-4). Some workflows may be fuzzy and not understood well; others are deterministic and highly repetitive. Modern workflow software can do both well; it can also create electronic renditions of real-world collaborative activity. Work can be routed along any type of topology that's common to human communications. You can create sequential routes, parallel routes (alternate paths), routes with feedback loops (for example, rework), circular routes, and many others. A good workflow package lets you specify acceptance criteria for moving work from one operation to the next along a route. So, workflow brings the information to the people (and programs) who can act on it. It can also coordinate existing software and track processes to make sure the work gets done by the right people.

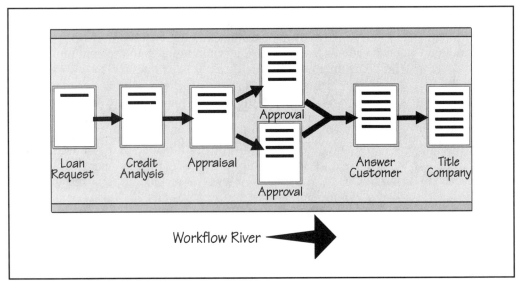

Figure 1-4. Managing Processes via Workflows.

Why Groupware Middleware Can't Hack It

Groupware provides many of the components we need for creating intergalactic client/server applications. Groupware technology is also starting to encroach on its competitors' turf. For example, Lotus Notes—via DataLens—can access information that's stored in SQL databases; it also lets SQL applications access Notes data via ODBC APIs. A new generation of tools—for example, *Lotus VIP*—integrates GUI building client facilities with data that can be accessed from both document or

SQL databases. Groupware demonstrates how synergy is obtained by combining different technologies on client/server networks. The result is a flexible technology that adapts to the way people do business in both structured and ad-hoc settings.

So why are we writing off Groupware? Of course, we're not writing off the function Groupware provides—we will need it more than ever in the world of online electronic commerce. But, we are writing off the middleware foundation on which the present generation of Groupware is built. It is proprietary and does not scale well to the world of rich transactions. In addition, Groupware does not play well with legacy applications; its middleware cannot subsume it. We believe that Groupware itself will be subsumed by distributed objects. Objects provide a much more robust middleware foundation for providing Lotus Notes-like functions. Perhaps IBM purchased Lotus Notes to recreate its function using object components (for example, OpenDoc) and a distributed object bus (for example, CORBA).

Client/Server With Distributed Objects

The problem with software, other than being a medieval art form, is that everything we build today is monolithic.

> — *Steve Mills, General Manager of Software*
> *IBM*
> *(March, 1995)*

As we said earlier, client/server has applied a giant chainsaw to centralized mono-lithic applications, slicing them into two halves. Unfortunately, with the technology we just described, you simply wind up with two monoliths instead of one: one running on the client and another running on the server. SQL databases, TP Monitors, and visual builder tools help you get some leverage and let you deploy your applications more quickly. But, by and large, today's client/server applications remain difficult to build, manage, and extend.

Distributed objects change this. With the proper packaging and infrastructure, objects will help subdivide today's monolithic client/server applications into self-managing components that can play together and roam across networks and operating systems. Component-like objects allow us to create client/server systems by assembling "live blobs of intelligence and data" in an infinite number of lego-like arrangements. These components represent the ultimate form of client/server distribution and prepare us for a near future when millions of machines—mostly desktops—will be both clients and servers.

The Benefits of Distributed Objects

Object technology has the ability to revolutionize client/server computing because it makes software easier and faster to develop for programmers, easier to use for users, and easier to manage for system administrators.

> — *Ronald Weissman, Director*
> *NeXT*

Distributed object technology is extremely well-suited for creating flexible client/server systems because the data and business logic are encapsulated within objects, allowing them to be located anywhere within a distributed system. The granularity of distribution is greatly improved. Distributed objects have the inherent potential to allow granular *components* of software to plug-and-play, interoperate across networks, run on different platforms, coexist with legacy applications through object wrappers, roam on networks, and manage themselves and the resources they control. Objects are inherently self-managing entities. Objects should allow us to manage very complex systems by broadcasting instructions and alarms. You can modify or change any object without affecting the rest of the components in the system or how they interact (Figure 1-5 shows some of these benefits).

Why This Sudden Interest in Distributed Objects?

We still need to answer the question: Why is there this renewed interest in the 20-year old object technology? The technology is now ripe. And we can't build the type of applications we need with any other technology. Also, our industry has now created the foundation for a distributed object infrastructure that includes an object software bus and the technology for components that can plug-and-play on this bus. Monolithic applications are monolithic because they're built as a whole. The object bus and component infrastructure make it unnecessary to build information systems from scratch. They let us create whole applications from parts.

However, distributed objects (and components) by themselves are not enough to get us there. They need to be packaged as components that can play together in *suites*. These suites combine the best in client/server and distributed object technology. They allow us to "build to order" entire information systems by assembling off-the-shelf object components. We will be able to assemble—in record time—highly flexible client/server applications tailored to a customer's needs. The components may be shipped in preassembled suites, where all the pieces are known to work together to perform a specific task. We anticipate that components and the

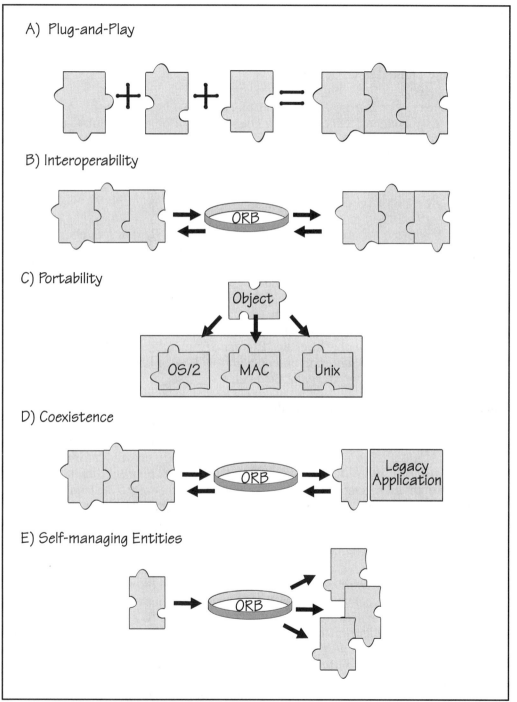

Figure 1-5. The Benefits of Distributed Objects.

client/server suites that integrate them will create vast new opportunities for ISVs, system integrators, and in-house IS developers.

This Time the Standards Came First

When it comes to standards, distributed objects have a leg up over the competitive client/server approaches. Since 1989, a consortium of object vendors—the *Object Management Group (OMG)*—has been busily specifying the architecture for an open software bus on which object components written by different vendors can interoperate across networks and operating systems. Today, the OMG boasts over 500 member companies, and the object bus is well on its way to becoming the "mother of all client/server middleware."

The object bus provides an *Object Request Broker (ORB)* that lets clients invoke methods on remote objects either statically or dynamically. If a component interface is already defined, you can bind your program to a static stub to call its methods; otherwise, you can discover how the interface works at run time by consulting an OMG-specified Interface Repository. In late 1994, the OMG approved a set of specifications—called CORBA 2.0—that define a TCP/IP based Inter-ORB backbone. CORBA 2.0 also specifies an optional inter-ORB communication service based on OSF's DCE. The new Interface Repository specification defines extensions that allow components to generate universal global IDs for their interfaces to ensure that they are unique at the intergalactic level.

The OMG bus is extended with modular add-on *object services*, each specified by leading industry experts in a software middleware area. Each add-on provides an essential object service for the bus. This is the ultimate in modular bus design. The OMG has currently defined standards for how objects are created, stored, defined, and named on the bus. OMG also defined an event service that lets objects communicate in loosely-coupled arrangements. It recently finalized additional CORBA-based object services—including transactions, externalization, concurrency control, relationships, query, licensing, and others. When they are ready, these services can incrementally be added to CORBA-compliant buses.

The OMG created important alliances to make sure its standards are universal. The *International Standards Organization (ISO)* announced it will sanction all the OMG standards by reference. The OMG-defined persistent service is closely aligned with the *ODMG-93* specifications for object databases. OMG standards are typically endorsed by *X/Open* as part of the *Common Application Environment (CAE)* Specification.[3] CORBA object transaction services can interoperate with X/Open defined procedural transactions. The OMG is also working with the X/Open *SysMan* group on ORB-based system management interfaces—including security. In addition, *Component Integration Laboratories (CI Labs)*—a consortium of companies that's doing OpenDoc—picked CORBA as its object model for intercomponent communications. Both Taligent and OpenStep are providing CORBA gateways for their external object communications. Finally, even Microsoft approached OMG—in late 1994—with a proposal for an "official" OLE to CORBA gateway. But OLE will remain the industry's "other object standard." The good news is that we *only* have two major competing standards to contend with: CORBA/OpenDoc and COM/OLE.

So it looks like the object community may have its act together to create a universal object infrastructure that can meet the demands of the intergalactic client/server era. Distributed objects with the proper component packaging and infrastructure may provide the ultimate building blocks for creating client/server solutions—including suites of cooperating business objects.

Are Objects Ready for Client/Server Prime Time?

By 1997/98, object technology will become the predominant paradigm for conceptualizing, building, and using applications; providing integration of legacies into client/server; extended interoperability via CORBA; and advanced information synthesis via unified "objectories" for structured and unstructured information and workflow.

> *— Meta Group*
> *Evaluating Systems Integrators*
> *(January 31, 1995)*

In all honesty, the current generation of CORBA 1.2 compliant ORBs is not ready for intergalactic prime time. We believe that CORBA 2.0 and the new object services—including transactions, concurrency, life cycle, naming, and persistence—must be implemented in commercial ORBs before the technology can take off. The good news is that—in this case—the standards are ahead of the commercial offerings. The other piece of good news is that ORBs and the object component infrastructure will be integrated with high volume desktops—such as OS/2 Warp, Windows 95, and Mac. Both OLE and OpenDoc are built on top of ORBs and will be freely distributed with desktop OSs. This means distributed objects will be more ubiquitous (and freely available) than any other form of client/server middleware.

Once object technology takes off, it will subsume all other forms of client/server computing—including TP Monitors, Database, and Groupware. Distributed objects

---

[3] X/Open is an independent, worldwide, open systems organization. Its strategy is to combine various standards into a comprehensive integrated systems environment called CAE, which currently contains an evolving portfolio of practical APIs. X/Open supports its specifications with an extensive set of conformance tests that a product must pass to obtain the X/Open trademark (the XPG brand).

can do it all, and better. Objects will help us break large monolithic applications into more manageable multivendor components that live and coexist on the intergalactic bus. They are also our only hope for managing the millions of software entities that will live on intergalactic networks. We offer Figure 1-6 as the answer to the question: Which way client/server? The Ethernet era of client/server saw a file-centric application wave followed by a database-centric wave; TP Monitors and Groupware generated minor ripples. Distributed objects are the next big wave. We believe that distributed objects are essential for making the intergalactic client/server vision real.

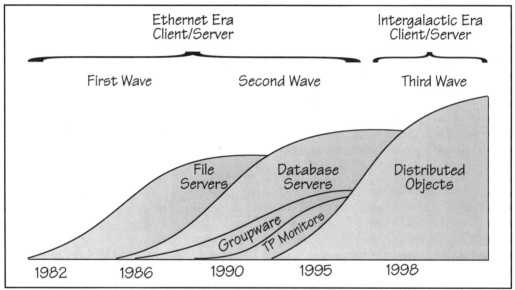

Figure 1-6. The Waves of Client/Server.

Chapter 2

From Distributed Objects To Smart Components

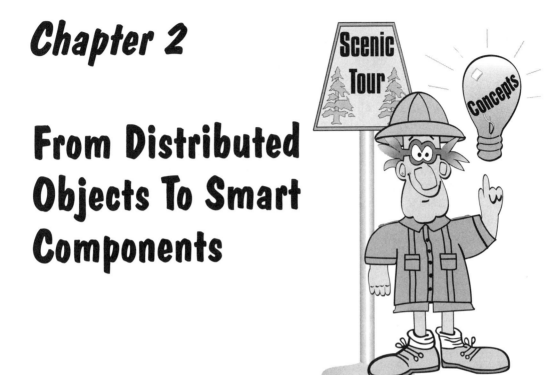

General industry consensus is that the ultimate goal is to have component-based systems capable of operating in distributed heterogeneous computing environments. Loosely bound and highly configurable components will be able to accommodate continuous changes such as the rapid creation and destruction of virtual enterprises.

— Richard Barnwell, Architect
Software 2000, Inc.
(June, 1995)

A "classical" object—of the C++ or Smalltalk variety—is a blob of intelligence that encapsulates code and data. Classical objects provide wonderful code reuse facilities via inheritance and encapsulation. However, these classical objects only live within a single program. Only the language compiler that creates the objects knows of their existence. The outside world doesn't know about these objects and has no way to access them. They're literally buried in the bowels of a program.

In contrast, a *distributed object* is a blob of intelligence that can live anywhere on a network. Distributed objects are packaged as independent pieces of code that can be accessed by remote clients via method invocations. The language and compiler used to create distributed server objects are totally transparent to their clients. Clients don't need to know where the distributed object resides or what operating system it executes on; it can be on the same machine or on a machine that sits across an intergalactic network. Distributed objects are smart pieces of software that can message each other transparently anywhere in the world. Distributed objects can interrogate each other—"tell me what you do." Distributed objects are very dynamic—they come and go and move around.

When we talk about distributed objects, we're really talking about independent software *components*. These are smart pieces of software that can play in different networks, operating systems, and tool palettes. A component is an object that's not bound to a particular program, computer language, or implementation. Objects built as components provide the right "shapes" for distributed applications. They are the optimal building blocks for creating the next generation of distributed systems. In this chapter, we first explain what an object is. Then we go over the attributes that make components out of ordinary objects.

OBJECTS AND DISTRIBUTED OBJECTS

Everybody can resonate with objects—managers, 3-year olds, and superprogrammers. Object-oriented technology appeals to all these different camps...

> — **Jim Gray**
> **(February, 1995)**

Objects has to be one of the most bastardized, hackneyed, and confusing terms in the computer industry. Everyone claims to have them.

> — **Kraig Brockschmidt, Author**
> **Inside OLE 2, Second Edition**
> **(Microsoft Press, 1995)**

By now, anybody associated with computers knows that objects are wonderful—we simply can't live without them. Smalltalk can be used to create GUI front-ends, C++ is the only way to write code, and the literature is full of articles on the wonders of encapsulation, multiple inheritance, and polymorphism. Objects for the last 20 years have been promising us code reuse and higher levels of software productivity. Software methodologists tell us objects can cure almost any software ill—as long as we faithfully follow "the methodology *du jour*." Note that traditional methodologies treat functions and data as separate; object methodologies, on the other hand, view them as an integrated whole. An object describes both the behavior and information associated with an entity.

More recently, objects have become the darling of the *Business Process Reengineering (BPR)* crowd. These folks discovered that objects map very well to the way businesses are organized. They use objects to simulate, describe, and analyze the business process. Finally, these folks also discovered that business objects can naturally emulate their real-world counterparts in different domains.

As a result of all this interest, objects are starting to boom. Datapro estimates the general object marketplace to be growing at 67% annually; it expects it to become a $4 billion market by 1997. But there's still more to this story.

Distributed Objects

The potential of distributed objects is what causes your authors to "resonate," as Jim Gray would put it. We are particularly interested in how object technology can be extended to deal with the complex issues that are inherent in creating robust, single-image, client/server systems. The key word is *systems*—or how objects work together across machine and network boundaries to create client/server solutions. We're not going to rehash the marvels of Object-Oriented Programming (OOP) methodologies, Smalltalk, and C++ because we assume you've heard about them all before. We're moving on to the next step: objects in client/server systems. This is the area where objects will realize their greatest potential and growth; in the process, they will become the new "mainstream computing model." Distributed objects are in the fortunate position of being able to build on the strong language and methodological foundations of classical objects. But distributed objects introduce a whole new ball game. They have the potential of creating a $50 billion software industry by the turn of this century (especially when components are factored in).

Object Magic

Most people involved in the computer industry believe objects to be a "good thing." An object is an encapsulated chunk of code that has a name and an interface that describes what it can do. Other programs can invoke the functions the interface describes or simply reuse the function itself. Objects should let you write programs faster by incorporating large chunks of code from existing objects—this is called *inheritance*. In addition, an object typically manages a resource or its own data. You can only access an object's resource using the interface the object publishes. This means objects *encapsulate* the resource and contain all the information they need to operate on it.

Objects let you package software capabilities into more manageable (and useful) chunks. You can scale objects by composing them from other objects. Eventually, you can create objects that model real-world entities—called *business objects*. The basic concepts of object technology are the same, regardless of the level of abstraction an object provides. System objects and business objects all provide three magical properties: *encapsulation, inheritance,* and *polymorphism.* These are the properties that provide the behavior and benefits you typically associate with an object. You must understand these three magical properties in order for objects (and their component extensions) to make sense. The next Briefing box provides the world's shortest tutorial on objects.

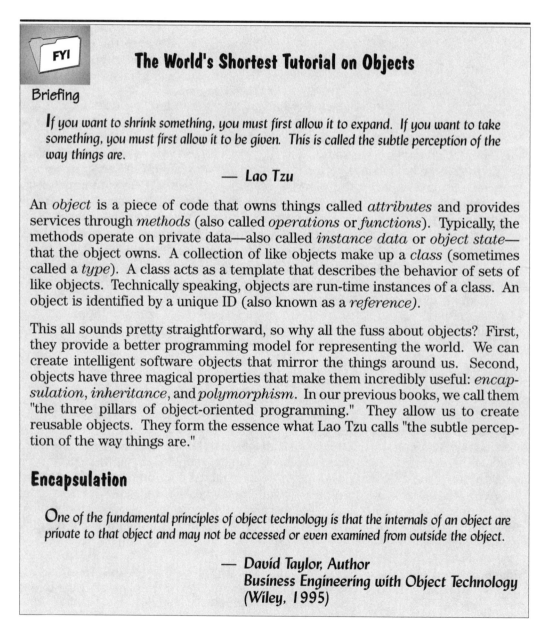

The World's Shortest Tutorial on Objects

Briefing

If you want to shrink something, you must first allow it to expand. If you want to take something, you must first allow it to be given. This is called the subtle perception of the way things are.

— Lao Tzu

An *object* is a piece of code that owns things called *attributes* and provides services through *methods* (also called *operations* or *functions*). Typically, the methods operate on private data—also called *instance data* or *object state*—that the object owns. A collection of like objects make up a *class* (sometimes called a *type*). A class acts as a template that describes the behavior of sets of like objects. Technically speaking, objects are run-time instances of a class. An object is identified by a unique ID (also known as a *reference).*

This all sounds pretty straightforward, so why all the fuss about objects? First, they provide a better programming model for representing the world. We can create intelligent software objects that mirror the things around us. Second, objects have three magical properties that make them incredibly useful: *encapsulation, inheritance,* and *polymorphism.* In our previous books, we call them "the three pillars of object-oriented programming." They allow us to create reusable objects. They form the essence what Lao Tzu calls "the subtle perception of the way things are."

Encapsulation

One of the fundamental principles of object technology is that the internals of an object are private to that object and may not be accessed or even examined from outside the object.

— David Taylor, Author
Business Engineering with Object Technology (Wiley, 1995)

Encapsulation means "don't tell me how you do it; just do it." The object does this by managing its own resources and limiting the visibility of what others should know. In this sense, objects are self-contained atoms. An object publishes a public *interface* that defines how other objects or applications can interact with it (see Figure 2-1). An object also has a private component that implements the methods. The object's implementation is *encapsulated*—that is, hidden from the public view. Instance data can be declared private—usually, the default—or public. Private instance data can only be accessed by methods of the class. Public instance data, on the other hand, is part of the published external interface. The public methods and instance data are the permanent interface between the object and the outside world. Old methods must continue to be supported when an object changes. The public interface is a binding contract between the class providers and their clients.

	Instance
○ Method 1	Data
○ Method 2	
○ Method 3	
○ Method 4	
○ Method 5	

Figure 2-1. The First Pillar of OO Wisdom: Class Encapsulation.

Polymorphism

A *true living object can be replaced.*

— **Christine Comaford, Columnist**
PC Week

Polymorphism is a high-brow way of saying that the same method can do different things, depending on the class that implements it. Looking at Figure 2-2, you can see polymorphism in action (hit the accelerator on a Corvette and on a Volvo, and then compare notes). Objects in different classes receive the same message yet react in different ways. The sender does not know the difference; the receiver interprets the message and provides the appropriate behavior. Polymorphism lets you view two similar objects through a common interface; it eliminates the need to differentiate between the two objects. Polymorphism is the underlying principle behind the object-style user interfaces. You can click on any visual object or drag-and-drop it. Polymorphism is also the mechanism that allows subclasses (see next paragraph) to override an inherited method—and "do their own thing"—without affecting the ancestor's methods.

Figure 2-2. The Second Pillar of OO Wisdom: Polymorphism.

Overloading is a variant of polymorphism that lets you define different versions of a method, each with different parameter types.

Inheritance

Children classes can enhance the behavior of their parents. And if parental behavior is enhanced, it is to the benefit of the children.

> — **Steve Jobs, CEO**
> **NeXT**
> **(February, 1995)**

Inheritance is the mechanism that allows you to create new child classes—known as *subclasses* or *derived* classes—from existing parent classes. Child classes inherit their parent's methods and data structures. You can add new methods to a child's class or override—that is, modify—inherited methods to define new class behaviors. The parent's method is not affected by this modification. You use inheritance to extend objects; it means "everything in that object plus...."

Some object models support *single inheritance*—a class has exactly one parent class. Others support *multiple inheritance*—a class can have more than one direct parent. *Abstract classes* are classes whose main purpose is to be inherited by others. *Mixins* are classes whose main purpose is to be multiply inherited by others. They're typically partial classes that cannot stand alone. Mixins must be combined with other classes in order to function. If you do it carefully, multiple inheritance can help you reuse code very effectively. Together, abstract classes and mixins are sometimes known as *base classes*—this means other classes inherit from them. As in real-life family inheritances, class inheritances are controlled by the parents. This means that providers of base classes can establish the rules about what aspects of their classes they will let their children inherit.

Figure 2-3 shows a typical *class hierarchy* tree—start with a generic "car" class and derive from it Volvos or Corvettes. Note that the arrows in the class hierarchy point upward from a class to its parent class—the idea is that classes must know their parent class, but not vice versa. A class hierarchy can introduce many levels of hierarchy. If the hierarchy becomes too deep, you may have to restructure it (object people call it *refactoring* the hierarchy). To eliminate code redundancy, you should move common functions to the top of the class hierarchy. You do this by simply moving common code from the derived classes into a common ancestor class.

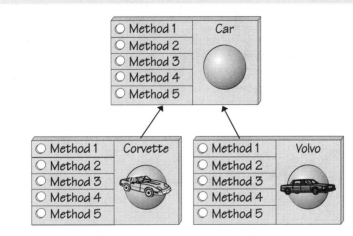

Figure 2-3. The Third Pillar of OO Wisdom: Inheritance and Subclassing.

Frameworks and Class Libraries

The three pillars of OO provide the foundation for creating, assembling, and reusing objects. The first generation of OO relied on *class libraries* to package objects for reusability. A more promising approach is to use object *frameworks*. These are preassembled class libraries that are packaged to provide specific functions. Frameworks will make it easier to assemble objects; they raise the level of abstraction. We cover frameworks in more detail in Part 3.

Object Binding

Binding refers to the linking of the software interface between two objects. If the binding is *static* both client and server have an interface that is determined at compile or build time. *Dynamic binding*—also known as *late binding*—occurs when a message is sent. It requires objects to have an agreed-upon way of determining the shape of the interface at send time. Late binding lets you create very flexible systems with code you can select at run time. This lets you replace code dynamically and introduce new functions without recompiling existing software.

Object Relationships

According to David Taylor, objects relate to each other in one of three basic ways: 1) *specialization*, in which classes are defined as special cases of each other; 2) *collaboration*, in which objects send messages to each other to request services; and 3) *composition*, in which objects are constructed out of other objects. Taylor's list provides a good start. We will also be seeing other patterns of collaboration throughout this book. Note that an object that contains other objects is called a *composite* object. A composite object holds *references* to the objects it contains instead of containing the object itself. An object can be contained in multiple composite objects. ❑

COMPONENTS: THE GRAND PRIZE OF OBJECTS

Object technology failed to deliver on the promise of reuse...What role will object-oriented programming play in the component-software revolution that's now finally under way?

— **Jon Udell, Senior Technical Editor**
BYTE Magazine
(May, 1994)

Components are standalone objects that can plug-and-play across networks, applications, languages, tools, and operating systems. Distributed objects are, by definition, components because of the way they are packaged. In distributed object systems, the unit of work and distribution is a component. The distributed object infrastructure must make it easier for components to be more autonomous, self-managing, and collaborative. However, note that not all components are objects. Nor are they all distributed. For example, an OLE custom control (or OCX) is a component that is neither an object nor distributed.

Component technology—in all its forms—promises to radically alter the way software systems are developed. For example, distributed objects allow us to put together complex client/server information systems by simply assembling and extending components. The goal of object components is to provide software users and developers the same levels of plug-and-play application interoperabilty that are available to consumers and manufacturers of electronic parts or custom integrated circuits.

The Driving Force Behind Components

It's really getting harder and harder for us to keep up with the amount of resources needed to develop applications today. Up to 80% of application resources go into capabilities that are ancillary to what really makes our product stand out.

> — *Randell Flint, President*
> *Sundial Systems*
> *(January, 1995)*

The component revolution is being driven from the desktop, where vendors are realizing that to be profitable, they must quickly rearchitect their existing applications and suites into components. Today's desktop applications are monolithic and over-bloated. They contain every possible feature you might use—whether or not you really want them. Most of us use less than 10% of an application's features— the rest of the features simply add complexity and bulk. We must wait—it seems forever—to get the new features we really need in the form of new upgrades or replacements. This is because vendors must bring forward all the hundreds of product features with every new release, leading to long and costly development cycles. Vendors take the "shotgun" approach because they don't know which features you need, and they try to be all things to all people.

These feature-heavy, bloated, monolithic applications are very costly for vendors to upgrade and maintain. Each change challenges the fragile integrity of the monolith and requires long regression cycles (and resources). Maintaining these applications is no picnic either. The smaller *Independent Software Vendors (ISVs)* face these same problems but even more acutely. They have much more limited resources to throw at them.

To give you an idea of the magnitude of the problem, consider that it took WordPerfect just under 14 developer years to upgrade their product from version 3 to version 4. However, it took 250 developer years to move the same product from version 5 to version 6. If things continue at this rate, it could cost them as many as 4,464 developer years to move the product to version 8. WordPerfect realized that the monolithic approach to application development is simply no longer feasible; it is now rearchitecting the product using OLE and OpenDoc components. Microsoft is experiencing the same phenomenon. For example, the size of Excel went from 4 MBytes in 1990, to over 16 MBytes today. Microsoft is looking at OLE components to improve the situation. Lotus has a similar story. It shipped 1-2-3 shipped on one floppy in 1982; today 1-2-3, requires 11 MBytes of disk space to install. Lotus is looking at both OLE and OpenDoc to fix the problem.

Components to the Rescue

Objects have been freed from the shackles of a particular language or platform. Programmers have been liberated from the confines of one compiler or family of class libraries. Objects can be everywhere, working together and delivering a new world of opportunity to the next generation of systems architectures.

> — Martin Anderson, Chairman
> Integrated Objects
> (June, 1995)

Object-oriented programming has long been advanced as a solution to the problems we just described. However, objects by themselves do not provide an infrastructure through which software created by different vendors can interact with one another within the same address space—much less across address spaces, networks, and operating systems. The solution is to augment classical objects with a standard component infrastructure.

OpenDoc and OLE are currently the leading component standards for the desktop; CORBA provides a component standard for the enterprise. CORBA and OpenDoc complement each other—OpenDoc uses CORBA as its object bus. These new component standards will change the economics of software development. Monolithic applications—both on the desktop and in the enterprise—will be replaced with component suites. Here's how this new technology will affect you:

- *Power users* will find it second nature to assemble their own personalized applications using off-the-shelf components. They will use scripts to tie the parts together and customize their behavior.

- *Small developers and ISVs* will find that components reduce expenses and lower the barriers to entry in the software market. They can create individual components with the knowledge that they will integrate smoothly with existing software created by larger development shops—they do not have to reinvent all the functions around them. They can get fine-grained integration instead of today's "band-aid" integration. In addition, they get faster time to market because the bulk of an application is already there.

- *Large developers, IS shops, and system integrators* will use component suites to create (or assemble) enterprise-wide client/server applications in record time. Typically, about 80% of the function they need will be available as off-the-shelf components. The remaining 20% is the value-added they provide. The client/server systems may be less complex to test because of the high reliability of the pretested components. The fact that many components are black boxes reduces the overall complexity of the development process. Com-

ponents—especially of the CORBA variety—will be architected to work together in intergalactic client/server networks (Parts 2 and 3 provide more details).

- **Desktop vendors** will use components to assemble applications that target specific markets (for example, "WordPerfect for Legal Firms"). Instead of selling monster suites—packed with everything but the kitchen sink—at rock-bottom prices, they will be able to provide their consumers with what they really need. Increased customization and more malleable products will create new market segments. Consumers will not be at the mercy of the long product release cycles to get new functions. They can buy add-on functions—in the form of components—when they need it.

In summary, components reduce application complexity, development cost, and time to market. They also improve software reusability, maintainability, platform independence, and client/server distribution. Finally, components provide more freedom of choice and flexibility.

When Can We Expect These Components?

The transition to component-based software will change the way we buy and build systems and what it means to be a software engineer.

— *Dave Thomas, President*
Object Technology International
(March, 1995)

By 1997, most new software will be developed (or assembled) using components. According to *Strategic Focus*, 25% of developers are already building component software today. This number climbs abruptly to include 66% of all developers by the end of 1996.[1] This means that in less than two years, two out of three developers will have adopted the component approach (see Figure 2-4).

If this forecast is correct, then the software industry is now at the same point where the hardware industry was about 23 years ago. At that time, the first integrated circuits (ICs) were developed to package discrete functions into hardware. ICs were wired together on boards to provide more complex functions. These boards were eventually miniaturized into ICs. These new and more powerful ICs were wired together on new boards, and so on. We should experience the same spiral with software. A component is what Brad Cox calls a *software IC. Frameworks* are the boards we plug these components into. The object bus provides the backplane. Families of software ICs that play together are called *suites*. You should be able to

---

[1] Source: **Strategic Focus** (January, 1995).

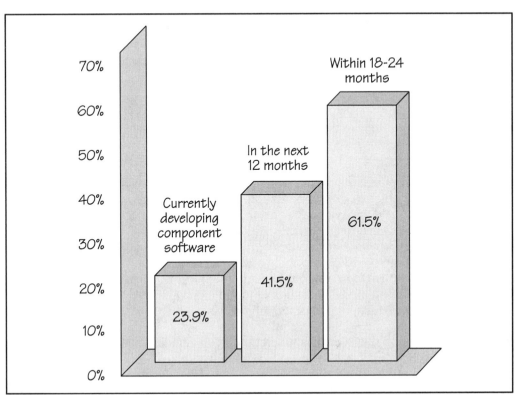

Figure 2-4. When Developers Plan to Start Developing With Components (Source: Strategic Focus, January 1995).

purchase your software ICs—or components—through standard part catalogs. According to Gartner Group, components will foster the emergence of three new markets: 1) the component market itself, 2) a market for component assembly tools, and 3) a market for custom applications developed using components.[2]

So, the million-dollar question is: Why didn't this happen any sooner? Why did we have to wait 23 years to follow the footsteps of our cousins, the hardware engineers? Yes, it's true that for almost 20 years the software industry has been talking about reuse, objects, and methodologies that would get us out of the crises of the day. The difference this time is that we have two standards to choose from: OpenDoc/CORBA and OLE/COM. Without standards, you cannot have components. So, it didn't happen sooner because our industry did not have the right component infrastructure or standards. We now have both.

---

[2] Source: **Gartner Group**, "Object Orientation for the Rest of Us" (March, 1995).

So, What Exactly Is a Component?

A component is a piece of software small enough to create and maintain, big enough to deploy and support, and with standard interfaces for interoperability.

> — *Jed Harris, President*
> *CI Labs*
> *(January, 1995)*

Components interoperate using language-neutral client/server interaction models. Unlike traditional objects, components can interoperate across languages, tools, operating systems, and networks. But components are also object-like in the sense that they support inheritance, polymorphism, and encapsulation. Note that some components—Ivar Jacobson calls them *black box* components—cannot be extended through inheritance. OLE components fall into the black box category. However, both CORBA and OpenDoc components support inheritance. As a result, they let you build either white box or black box components. A *white box* component is a component that behaves like a classical object.

Because components mean different things to different people, we will define the functions a *minimal* component must provide. In the next section, we expand our definition to include features that supercomponents must provide. Our definition of a component is a composite of what CORBA, OpenDoc, and OLE provide. Most of the earlier definitions of components were based on wish lists. Now that we have standards, we can use them to derive a definition. So, a minimalist component has the following properties:

- **It is a marketable entity.** A component is a self-contained, shrink-wrapped, binary piece of software that you can typically purchase in the open market.

- **It is not a complete application.** A component can be combined with other components to form a complete application. It is designed to perform a limited set of tasks within an application domain. Components can be fine-grained objects—for example, a C++ size object; medium-grained objects—for example, a GUI control; or coarse-grained objects—for example, an applet.

- **It can be used in unpredictable combinations.** Like real-world objects, a component can be used in ways that were totally unanticipated by the original developer. Typically, components can be combined with other components of the same family—called suites—using plug-and-play.

- **It has a well-specified interface.** Like a classical object, a component can only be manipulated through its interface. This is how the component exposes its function to the outside world. A CORBA/OpenDoc component also provides

an Interface Definition Language that you can use to invoke the component or inherit and override its functions. Note that the component's object-like interface is separate from its implementation. A component can be implemented using objects, procedural code, or by encapsulating existing code.

■ *It is an interoperable object.* A component can be invoked as an object across address spaces, networks, languages, operating systems, and tools. It is a system-independent software entity.[3]

■ *It is an extended object.* Components are *bona fide* objects in the sense that they support encapsulation, inheritance, and polymorphism. However, components must also provide all the features associated with a shrink-wrapped standalone object. These features will be discussed in the next section.

In summary, a component is a reusable, self-contained piece of software that is independent of any application.

---

[3] The term "interoperable object" was first coined by Ray Valdes in a special issue of **Dr. Dobb's Journal** on "Interoperable Objects" (January, 1995).

So, What Is a Supercomponent?

If the components come with a bad reputation, no one will use them. Therefore components must be of an extraordinary quality. They need to be well tested, efficient, and well documented...The component should invite reuse.

> — Ivar Jacobson, Author
> Object-Oriented Software Engineering
> (Addison-Wesley, 1993)

Supercomponents are components with added smarts. The smarts are needed for creating autonomous, loosely-coupled, shrink-wrapped objects that can roam across machines and live on networks. Consequently, components need to provide the type of facilities that you associate with independent networked entities— including:

- *Security*—a component must protect itself and its resources from outside threats. It must authenticate itself to its clients, and vice versa. It must provide access controls. And it must keep audit trails of its use.

- *Licensing*—a component must be able to enforce licensing policies including per-usage licensing and metering. It is important to reward component vendors for the use of their components.

- *Versioning*—a component must provide some form of version control; it must make sure its clients are using the right version.

- *Life cycle management*—a component must manage its creation, destruction, and archival. It must also be able to clone itself, externalize its contents, and move from one location to the next.

- *Support for open tool palettes*—a component must allow itself to be imported within a standard tool palette. An example is a tool palette that supports OLE OCXs or OpenDoc parts. A component that abides by an open palette's rules can be assembled with other components using drag-and-drop and other visual assembly techniques.

- *Event notification*—a component must be able to notify interested parties when something of interest happens to it.

- *Configuration and property management*—a component must provide an interface to let you configure its properties and scripts.

- **Scripting**—a component must permit its interface to be controlled via scripting languages. This means the interface must be self-describing and support late binding.

- **Metadata and introspection**—a component must provide, on request, information about itself. This includes a description of its interfaces, attributes, and the suites it supports.

- **Transaction control and locking**—a component must transactionally protect its resources and cooperate with other components to provide all or nothing integrity. In addition, it must provide locks to serialize access to shared resources.

- **Persistence**—a component must be able to save its state in a persistent store and later restore it.

- **Relationships**—a component must be able to form dynamic or permanent associations with other components. For example, a component can contain other components.

- **Ease of use**—a component must provide a limited number of operations to encourage use and reuse. In other words, the level of abstraction must be as high as possible to make the component inviting to use.

- **Self-testing**—a component must be self-testing. You should be able to run component-provided diagnostics to do problem determination.

- **Semantic messaging**—a component must be able to understand the vocabulary of the particular suites and domain-specific extensions it supports.

- **Self-installing**—a component must be able to install itself and automatically register its factory with the operating system or component registry. The component must also be able to remove itself from disk when asked to do so.

This list should give you a pretty good idea of the level of quality and functionality we expect from our components. The good news is that both OpenDoc/CORBA and OLE/COM already provide quite a few of these functions. Typical OpenDoc/CORBA implementations let you add this behavior to ordinary components via mixins at build time. Some CORBA implementations—for example, SOM—even let you insert this system behavior into binary components at run time. OLE lets you add the behavior at build time by composing components that consist of multiple interfaces; an outer component can then call the appropriate interfaces via a reuse technique called *aggregation*.

Business Objects: The Ultimate Components

Components will help users focus on tasks, not tools, just as a well-stocked kitchen lets you focus on preparing and enjoying great food and not on the brand of your ingredients.

— *Dave LeFevre, Novell/WordPerfect*
(January, 1995)

Distributed objects are by definition components. The distributed object infrastructure is really a component infrastructure. Programmers can easily get things to collaborate by writing code for the two sides of the collaboration. The trick, however, is to get components that have no previous knowledge of each other to do the same. To get to this point, you need standards that set the rules of engagement for different component interaction boundaries. Together, these different interaction boundaries define a distributed component *infrastructure*.

At the most basic level, a component infrastructure provides an object bus—the *Object Request Broker (ORB)*—that lets components interoperate across address spaces, languages, operating systems, and networks. The bus also provides mechanisms that let components exchange metadata and discover each other. At the next level, the infrastructure augments the bus with add-on *system-level services* that help you create supersmart components. Examples of these services include licensing, security, version control, persistence, suite negotiation, semantic messaging, scripting, transactions, and many others.

The ultimate goal is to let you create components that behave like *business objects*. These are components that model their real-world counterparts in some application-level domain. They typically perform specific business functions—for example, a customer, car, or hotel. These business objects can be grouped into visual suites that sit on a desktop but have underlying client/server webs.

So the ultimate Nirvana in the client/server components business are supersmart business object components that do more than just interoperate—they collaborate at the semantic level to get a job done. For example, roaming agents on a global network must be able to collaborate to conduct negotiations with their fellow agents. Agents are examples of business objects. The infrastructure provides application-level collaboration standards in the form of *application frameworks*. These frameworks enforce the rules of engagement between independent components and allows them to collaborate in suites.

Figure 2-5 shows the evolution of components from interoperability to collaboration. This evolution corresponds to the service boundaries of the component infrastructure. The component bus gives you simple interoperability; the system services give you supersmart components; and the application frameworks provide the application-level semantics for components to collaborate in suites.

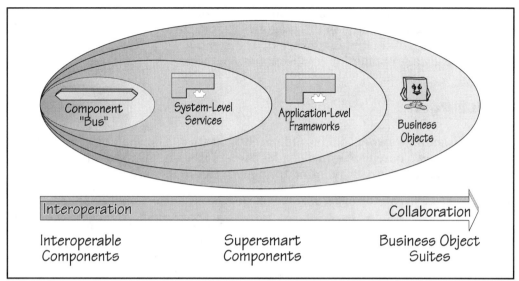

Figure 2-5. Component Evolution and Infrastructure Boundaries.

Your Guide to the Symbols Used in This Survival Guide

This section gives you a quick guide to the notation we use in this book. We're not trying to invent a new OO notation—Booch diagrams are just fine with us. However, we did take a few artistic liberties to make the notation more fun and intuitive for people that are looking at objects for the first time. So here's your quick guide to the symbols we use.

Objects and OLE Interfaces

Figure 2-6 shows the three symbols we use to denote objects and OLE interfaces. The ball-like icon denotes an object usually in some type of relationship—for

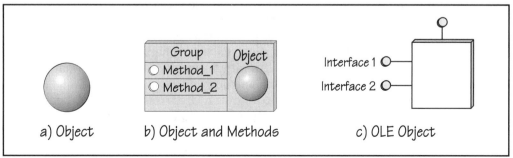

Figure 2-6. Objects and OLE Objects.

example, an object on a bus. The second symbol shows an object and its methods; sometimes we group methods in categories. The third symbol denotes an OLE object consisting of multiple interfaces. The symbol for an interface is a plug-in jack; it is really a grouping for a collection of methods.

A Class Hierarchy

Figure 2-7 shows a two-level class hierarchy. In this case, the object inherits its methods from two parent classes and adds a few of its own. We show the inheritance relationship as a thin arrow pointing from an object to its parent.

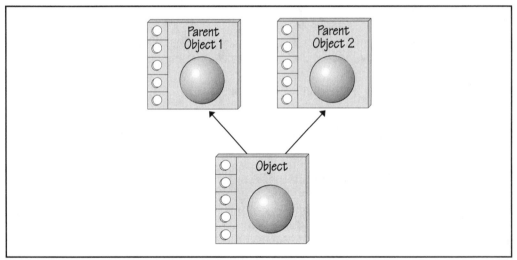

Figure 2-7. A Class Hierarchy and Inheritance.

Icons for Components, Frameworks, and ORBs

Figure 2-8 shows a miscellaneous set of icons we use for components, frameworks, and object buses. You'll see these icons everywhere. The component icon is the *component person*. Component people—they come in different genders, ages, and roles—are very social and they make great cartoon characters. The icon for a *framework* looks like a hardware board with a puzzle piece. The board is the framework; the puzzle piece is the extension you add to the framework. The *object bus* looks like a hardware bus; we use it to show an ORB or any medium that objects use to interoperate. The little balls are objects that hang off the bus.

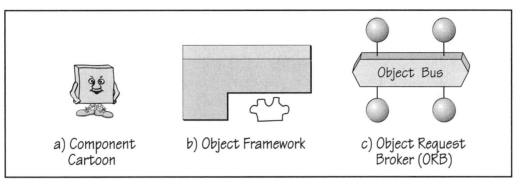

a) Component Cartoon   b) Object Framework   c) Object Request Broker (ORB)

Figure 2-8. Miscellaneous Icons: Component, Framework, and Object Bus.

Object Interaction Diagrams

An object-oriented program's run-time structure often bears little resemblance to its code structure. The code is frozen at compile-time; it consists of classes of fixed inheritance relationships. A program's run-time structure consists of rapidly changing networks of communicating objects. Trying to understand one from the other is like trying to understand the dynamism of living ecosystems from the static taxonomy of plants and animals, and vice versa.

> — **Erich Gamma et al., Authors**
> **Design Patterns**
> **(Addison Wesley, 1994)**

We use object interaction diagrams to trace the execution of a scenario that shows a run-time collaboration between objects (see Figure 2-9). An object is represented

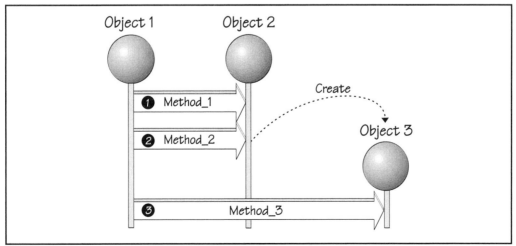

Figure 2-9. An Object Interaction Diagram for Object Scenarios.

by its icon and a vertical line that drops down from it. The thick horizontal arrows denote method invocations between objects. We use thin arrows to denote other types of interactions; for example, creating an object. The numbers denote the sequence of events; you will usually find an explanation in the text that goes along with a number (if it's very obvious, we skip the explanation). Note that time elapses from the top moving down.

The Component Road Map

The clearer the view of our dreams, the greater our cohesion.

> — *Carlos Castaneda*
> *The Art of Dreaming*

Now that we've developed a common vocabulary around objects and components, let's revisit the plan for this book. Our road map follows the component evolution path shown in Figure 2-5. Part 2 covers the CORBA object bus and system-level object services in great detail. Part 3 covers application-level frameworks—including CORBA frameworks and business objects, OpenDoc, OLE, Taligent, OpenStep, and Newi. Part 4 covers OpenDoc in depth. We go over all the features of its compound document application-level framework. Part 5 covers OLE/COM in depth. This part covers both OLE's object bus—called COM—and its compound document application-level framework. Part 6 helps you narrow down some of your options. We compare the component infrastructures, look at how they interoperate, and speculate on where it's all going.

Part 2
CORBA: The Distributed Object Bus

An Introduction to Part 2

Standards are more important for distributed objects than for any other technology in any other industry. Objects from one company must be able to communicate and cooperate with objects from other companies.

— *Roger Sessions, Author*
Object Persistence
(Prentice Hall, 1996)

This part is about the intergalactic CORBA object bus—a topic that should be dear to the hearts of our Martian friends. We're talking about a bus that lets objects communicate across enterprises, continents, and planets. Of course, this is really a loosely-coupled federation of buses that together provide this intergalactic reach. It's like the Internet. But this time it's an Internet done with objects for objects.

Because CORBA was designed for loose federations, you Martians will be able to run your own bus from Mars and interoperate with our webs of buses here on Earth. And we can even do better. What if we told you that in the near future, every laptop, car, and refrigerator will have its own CORBA bus? Yes, the same bus can provide standalone communications for objects that run within the same process—on a laptop—and still communicate with every other object in the galaxy. How's that for a bus that scales?

CORBA is the most important (and ambitious) middleware project ever undertaken by our industry. It is the product of a consortium—called the Object Management Group (OMG)—that includes over 500 companies representing the entire spectrum of the computer industry. The notable exception being Microsoft, which has its own competing object bus called the *Component Object Model (COM)*. For the rest of our industry, the next generation of middleware is CORBA.

What makes CORBA so important is that it defines middleware that has the potential of subsuming every other form of existing client/server middleware. In other words, CORBA uses objects as a unifying metaphor for bringing to the bus existing applications, while at the same time providing a solid foundation for a component-based future. The magic of CORBA is that the entire system is self-describing. In addition, the specification of the services are always separated from the implementation. This lets you incorporate existing systems within the bus.

CORBA was designed to allow intelligent components to discover each other and interoperate on an object bus. However, CORBA goes beyond just interoperability. It also specifies an extensive set of bus-related services for creating and deleting objects, accessing them by name, storing them in persistent stores, externalizing their states, and defining ad-hoc relationships between them. In late 1994, OMG also defined a comprehensive set of services for how objects meet transactions.

An Introduction to Part 2

CORBA lets you create an ordinary object and then make it transactional, lockable, and persistent by making the object multiply-inherit from the appropriate services. This means that you can design an ordinary component to provide its regular function and then insert the right middleware mix when you build it or create it at run time. So, welcome to the age of flexible "made to order" middleware. There is nothing like it for any other form of client/server computing.

Part 2 is about the CORBA object bus and the object system services that extend the bus. We start out with an overview of CORBA and what it does for intelligent components. In the overview, we cover the CORBA object model and the architecture that ties it all together. We follow this overview with chapters that cover the CORBA 2.0 object bus—including its services for static and dynamic method invocations, its architecture for intergalactic Object Request Brokers (ORBs), its self-describing metadata facilities, and many other bus-oriented details. Then we cover CORBA's sixteen object services. OMG has already adopted standards for eleven of these services—including object transactions and persistence; the other five are in the making. Finally, we go over some of the commercial CORBA products and tell you what's available today and what's coming down the pipe.

We hope our Martian friends will enjoy reading about this great intergalactic bus. It's really the most incredible piece of software plumbing ever created. If software plumbing could be visualized, the CORBA bus would dwarf other great engineering feats such as the Golden Gate bridge, the railways, and the air transportation system. Unfortunately, software buses are invisible—and therefore unsung. Without getting too poetic, we hope to surface some of the wonderful engineering and design work that went into CORBA in the next few chapters. We believe the CORBA bus will provide the underpinnings for a true components software industry and new forms of electronic commerce that may even exceed the economic impact of the airlines or railways. So, in this sense, CORBA may be one of the greatest engineering feats of our time (we would like to say the greatest but then we would have to turn this into a Soapbox). Happy reading.

Chapter 3

CORBA: A Bird's Eye View

If one vendor owns the distributed infrastructure, all others may be forced to pay a toll for its use.

— Dr. Ted Lewis
IEEE Computer Magazine
(April, 1995)

Our plan is to make the pie really big and take a little slice out of each transaction.

— Nathan Myhrvold, Microsoft Group VP
Time magazine (June, 1995)

The primary goal of the *Object Management Group (OMG)* is to create a truly open object infrastructure instead of a "toll road" controlled by a single company. Since 1989, the OMG has been busily defining a global bus for distributed components called the *Common Object Request Broker Architecture (CORBA)*. As we go to press, over 500 member companies have joined OMG which makes it the largest standards body in existence. The success of OMG may signify that our

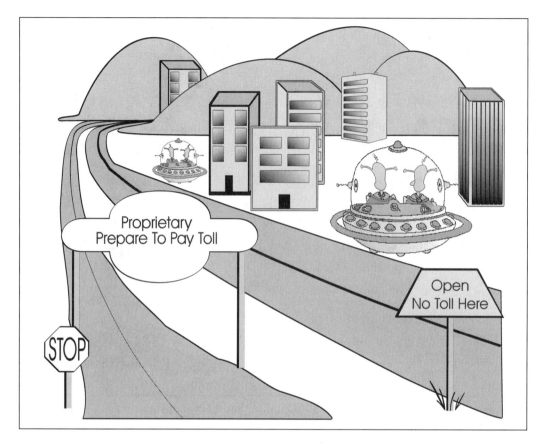

industry has voted for an open intergalactic object bus instead of a toll road. The CORBA object bus defines the shape of the components that live within it and how they interoperate. Consequently, by choosing an open bus, the industry is also choosing to create an open playing field for components.

Perhaps the secret to OMG's success is that it creates interface specifications, not code. The interfaces it specifies are always derived from demonstrated technology submitted by member companies. The specifications are written in a neutral *Interface Definition Language (IDL)* that defines a component's boundaries— that is, its contractual interfaces with potential clients. Components written to IDL should be portable across languages, tools, operating systems, and networks. And with the adoption of the CORBA 2.0 specification in December 1994, these components should be able to interoperate across multivendor CORBA object brokers.

Unfortunately, CORBA is not the only game in town. Microsoft is defining a rival standard for distributed objects called the *Common Object Model (COM)*—also known as *Network OLE*. CORBA is much further along than COM in defining a distributed object infrastructure. There are nearly a dozen CORBA 1.2 compliant object broker implementations on the market—including SOM from IBM, ORB Plus from HP, ObjectBroker from Digital, and Orbix from Iona. The COM specification is very preliminary—a final specification is expected in October 1995. By the time Network OLE ships (as part of Cairo), CORBA ORBs may be in their third generation. OLE and COM are covered in Parts 3 and 5 of this book.

This chapter presents a high-level overview of the OMG object model and its object services. We explain the elements of CORBA and how the pieces play together. This overview sets the stage for the more detailed chapters that follow. We explain the CORBA 2.0 object bus and object services in Part 2. We cover CORBA business objects and application frameworks in Part 3. It's really important that you get the "bird's eye" view of CORBA before jumping into the details.

DISTRIBUTED OBJECTS, CORBA STYLE

If objects are to be assembled, they must be compatible with one another. This is rarely a problem when writing a single program because all the objects are written in the same language, run on the same machine, and use the same operating system. But building entire information systems out of objects is quite a different matter. Objects have to interact with each other even if they are written in different languages and run on different hardware and software platforms.

> — **David Taylor, Author**
> **Business Engineering with Object Technology**
> **(Wiley, 1995)**

Clearly, we need standards for objects to interoperate in heterogeneous client/server environments. Fortunately, the industry anticipated this need, and the OMG was founded specifically to create distributed object standards before any major products were introduced—a truly amazing phenomenon in our industry. As a result, over 500 vendors (and corporate associate members) are working on CORBA-compliant software products. With CORBA 2.0, OMG has almost completed the definition of the plumbing for its distributed component infrastructure. With the major plumbing behind it, OMG is now shifting its focus to business objects and applications frameworks—OMG calls them "Common Facilities."

What Is a CORBA Distributed Object?

CORBA objects are blobs of intelligence that can live anywhere on a network. They are packaged as binary components that remote clients can access via method invocations. The language and compiler used to create server objects are totally transparent to clients. Clients don't need to know where the distributed object resides or what operating system it executes on. It can be in the same process or on a machine that sits across an intergalactic network. In addition, clients don't need to know how the server object is implemented. For example, a server object could be implemented as a set of C++ classes or it could be implemented with a million lines of existing COBOL code—the client doesn't know the difference. What the client needs to know is the interface its server object publishes. This interface serves as a binding contract between clients and servers.

Everything Is in IDL

OMG IDL is the best standard notation language available for defining component boundaries. It provides a universal notation for specifying APIs. IDL supports library function interfaces just as well as distributed objects across a network.

> — *Tom Mowbray et al., Authors*
> *The Essential CORBA*
> *(Wiley, 1995)*

As we said earlier, OMG uses *Interface Definition Language (IDL)* contracts to specify a component's boundaries and its contractual interfaces with potential clients. The OMG IDL is purely declarative. This means that it provides no implementation details. You can use IDL to define APIs concisely and it covers important issues such as error handling. IDL-specified methods can be written in and invoked from any language that provides CORBA bindings—currently, C, C++, and Smalltalk (Ada, COBOL, and Objective C are in the works). Programmers deal with CORBA objects using native language constructs. IDL provides operating system and programming language independent interfaces to all the services and components that reside on a CORBA bus. It allows client and server objects written in different languages to interoperate across networks and operating systems (see Figure 3-1).

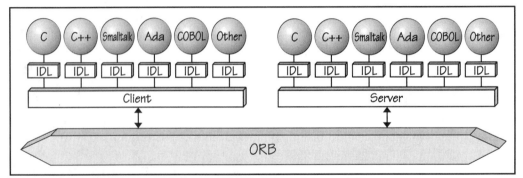

Figure 3-1. CORBA IDL Language Bindings Provide Client/Server Interoperability.

You can use the OMG IDL to specify a component's attributes, the parent classes it inherits from, the exceptions it raises, the typed events it emits, and the methods its interface supports—including the input and output parameters and their data types. The IDL grammar is a subset of C++ with additional keywords to support distributed concepts; it also fully supports standard C++ preprocessing features and pragmas.

The ambitious goal of CORBA is to "IDL-ize" all client/server middleware and all components that live on an ORB. OMG hopes to achieve this goal by following two steps: 1) it will turn everything into nails, and 2) it will give everyone a hammer.

■ The "nail" is the CORBA IDL. It allows component providers to specify in a standard definition language the interface and structure of the objects they provide. An IDL-defined contract binds the providers of distributed object services to their clients. For one object to request something from another object, it must know the target object's interface. The CORBA Interface Repository contains the definitions of all these interfaces. It contains the metadata that lets components discover each other dynamically at run time. This makes CORBA a self-describing system.

■ The "hammer" includes the set of distributed services OMG providers will supply. These services will determine which objects are on the network, which methods they provide, and which object interface adapters they support. The location of the object should be transparent to the client and object implementation. It should not matter whether the object is in the same process or across the world.

Does this all sound familiar? It should. We're describing the "object wave" of client/server computing; this time it's between cooperating objects as opposed to cooperating processes. The goal of this new wave is to create multivendor, multiOS, multilanguage "legoware" using objects. Vendors such as Sun, HP, IBM, Digital, Tandem, and NCR are all using CORBA as their standard IDL-defined interface into the object highway. The IDL is the contract that brings it all together.

CORBA Components: From System Objects To Business Objects

Objects can vary tremendously in size and number. They can represent everything down to the hardware or all the way up to entire design applications. How can we decide what should be an object?

> — *Erich Gamma et al., Authors*
> *Design Patterns*
> *(Addison Wesley, 1994)*

Notice that we've been using the terms "components" and "distributed objects" interchangeably. CORBA distributed objects are, by definition, components because of the way they are packaged. In distributed object systems, the unit of work and distribution is a component. The CORBA distributed object infrastructure makes it easier for components to be more autonomous, self-managing, and collaborative. This undertaking is much more ambitious than anything attempted by competing forms of middleware. CORBA's distributed object technology allows us to put together complex client/server information systems by simply assembling and extending components. Objects may be modified without affecting the rest of the components in the system or how they interact. A client/server application becomes a collection of collaborating components.

The ultimate "Nirvana" in the client/server components business are supersmart components that do more than just interoperate—they collaborate at the semantic level to get a job done. Programmers can easily get things to collaborate by writing code for the two sides of the collaboration. The trick, however, is to get components that have no previous knowledge of each other to do the same. To get to that point, you need standards that set the rules of engagement for different component interaction boundaries.

Figure 3-2 shows the progression of boundaries OMG is specifying to take us into the age of collaborative components. The most fundamental boundary is a global bus that allows client components to discover server components and invoke their methods. Next are the core object services that are needed by all components—including naming, persistence, life cycle, events, transactions, concurrency, relationships, and security. Horizontal and vertical Common Facilities define application-level frameworks for components to collaborate. Eventually, there are "business objects." These are end-user recognizable components that perform specific business functions and roles—for example, a customer, car, or hotel. Business objects can be grouped into visual suites that sit on a desktop but have underlying client/server webs. The end goal of the OMG is to create a collaborative client/server component environment.

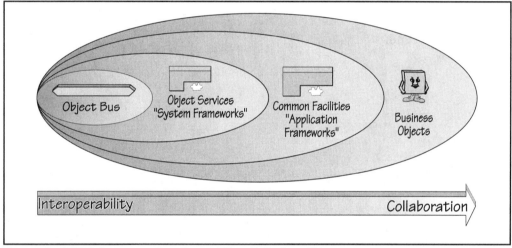

Figure 3-2. CORBA Components: From System Objects To Business Objects.

OMG'S OBJECT MANAGEMENT ARCHITECTURE

In the fall of 1990, OMG first published the *Object Management Architecture Guide (OMA Guide)*. It was revised in September 1992. The details of the Common Facilities were added in January 1995. Figure 3-3 shows the four main elements of the architecture: 1) *Object Request Broker (ORB)* defines the CORBA object bus; 2) *Common Object Services* define the system-level object frameworks that extend the bus; 3) *Common Facilities* define horizontal and vertical application frameworks that are used directly by business objects; and 4) *Application Objects* are the business objects and applications—they are the ultimate consumers of the CORBA infrastructure. This section provides a top-level view of the four elements that make up the CORBA infrastructure.

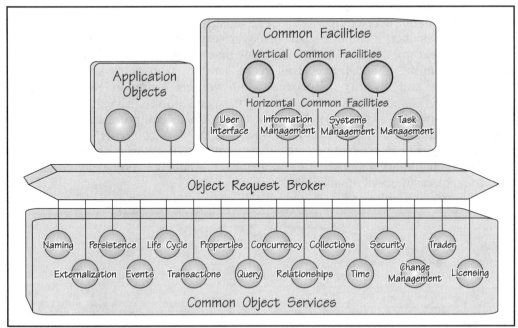

Figure 3-3. The OMG Object Management Architecture.

The Object Request Broker (ORB)

ORBs facilitate coarse-grained class reuse by providing a layer beneath the application but above the programming language, operating system, and hardware fray. In this middle ground, reuse grows and object technology blossoms.

— *John Gidman, Fidelity Investments*

The *Object Request Broker (ORB)* is the object bus. It lets objects transparently make requests to—and receive responses from—other objects located locally or remotely. The client is not aware of the mechanisms used to communicate with, activate, or store the server objects. The CORBA 1.1 specifications—introduced in 1991—only specified the IDL, language bindings, and APIs for interfacing to the ORB. So, you could write portable programs that could run on top of the nearly dozen CORBA-compliant ORBs on the market (especially on the client side). CORBA 2.0 specifies interoperability across vendor ORBs.

A CORBA ORB provides a very rich set of distributed middleware services. The ORB lets objects discover each other at run time and invoke each other's services. An ORB is much more sophisticated than alternative forms of client/server middleware—including traditional Remote Procedure Calls (RPCs), Message-Oriented Middleware (MOM), database stored procedures, and peer-to-peer services.[1] In theory, CORBA is the best client/server middleware ever defined. In practice, CORBA is only as good as the products that implement it.

To give you an idea of why CORBA ORBs make such great client/server middleware, we offer the following "short" list of benefits that every CORBA ORB provides:

- **Static and dynamic method invocations.** A CORBA ORB lets you either statically define your method invocations at compile time, or it lets you dynamically discover them at run time. So you either get strong type checking at compile time or maximum flexibility associated with late (or run-time) binding. Most other forms of middleware only support static bindings.

- **High-level language bindings.** A CORBA ORB lets you invoke methods on server objects using your high-level language of choice—currently C, C++, and Smalltalk. It doesn't matter what language server objects are written in. CORBA separates interface from implementation and provides language-neutral data types that make it possible to call objects across language and operating system boundaries. In contrast, other types of middleware typically provide low-level, language-specific, API libraries. And they don't separate implementation from specification—the API is tightly bound to the implementation, which makes it very sensitive to changes.

- **Self-describing system.** CORBA provides run-time metadata for describing every server interface known to the system. Every CORBA ORB must support an *Interface Repository* that contains real-time information describing the functions a server provides and their parameters. The clients use metadata to discover how to invoke services at run time. It also helps tools generate code "on the fly." The metadata is generated automatically either by an IDL-language precompiler or by compilers that know how to generate IDL directly from an OO language. For example, the MetaWare C++ compiler generates IDL directly from C++ class definitions (it also directly writes that information in the Interface Repository). To the best of our knowledge, no other form of client/server middleware provides this type of run-time metadata and language-independent definitions of all its services. As you will discover later in this book, business objects and components require all the late binding flexibility they can get.

- **Local/remote transparency.** An ORB can run in standalone mode on a laptop, or it can be interconnected to every other ORB in the universe (using CORBA 2.0's inter-ORB services). An ORB can broker interobject calls within a single

---

[1] For a basic overview of middleware concepts, please refer to our book, **Essential Client/Server Survival Guide** (Wiley, 1994).

process, multiple processes running within the same machine, or multiple processes running across networks and operating systems. This is all done in a manner that's transparent to your objects. Note that the ORB can broker among fine-grained objects—like C++ classes—as well as more coarse-grained objects. In general, a CORBA client/server programmer does not have to be concerned with transports, server locations, object activation, byte ordering across dissimilar platforms, or target operating systems—CORBA makes it all transparent.

■ ***Built-in security and transactions.*** The ORB includes context information in its messages to handle security and transactions across machine and ORB boundaries (more on that in later chapters).

■ ***Polymorphic messaging.*** In contrast to other forms of middleware, an ORB does not simply invoke a remote function—it invokes a function on a target object. This means that the same function call will have different effects, depending on the object that receives it. For example, a *configure_yourself* method invocation behaves differently when applied to a database object versus a printer object (also see following Briefing box).

Of course, CORBA also has its share of shortcomings. We explore all these shortcomings in a soapbox at the end of this chapter entitled "Is 1996 The Year of CORBA?"

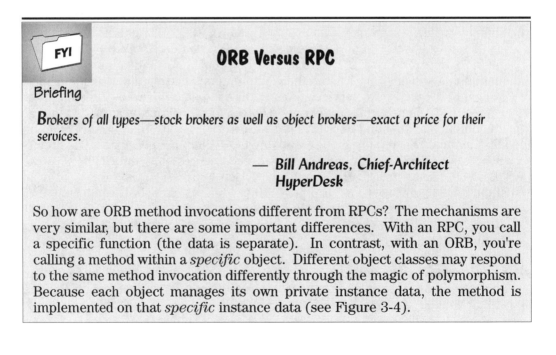

FYI

ORB Versus RPC

Briefing

*B*rokers of all types—stock brokers as well as object brokers—exact a price for their services.

— *Bill Andreas, Chief-Architect*
HyperDesk

So how are ORB method invocations different from RPCs? The mechanisms are very similar, but there are some important differences. With an RPC, you call a specific function (the data is separate). In contrast, with an ORB, you're calling a method within a *specific* object. Different object classes may respond to the same method invocation differently through the magic of polymorphism. Because each object manages its own private instance data, the method is implemented on that *specific* instance data (see Figure 3-4).

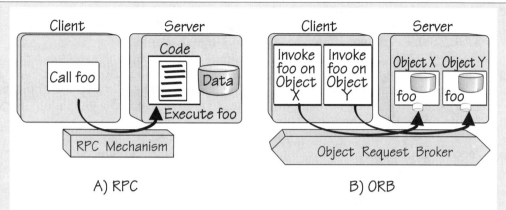

Figure 3-4. ORBs Versus RPC.

ORB method invocations have "scalpel-like" precision. The call gets to a *specific* object that controls *specific* data, and then implements the function in its own *class-specific* way. In contrast, RPC calls have no specificity—all the functions with the same name get implemented the same way. There's no differentiated service here.

Of course, some ORBs are built on top of an RPC service, so you end up paying a performance penalty for this "refined" level of service. It's worth every penny if you're taking advantage of new levels of distributed granularity provided by objects. Otherwise, you just bought yourself another layer of middleware—with all the costs and headaches that come with it. Note that within a single address space, ORBs are now targeting method resolution performance equivalent to C++ virtual function invocations (for example, this is SOM 3.0's target). If they achieve this low overhead, you will be able to use ORBs for very small grained objects as well as the larger ones. ❏

Object Services

CORBA *object services* are collections of system-level services packaged as components with IDL-specified interfaces. You can think of object services as augmenting and complementing the functionality of the ORB. You use them to create a component, name it, and introduce it into the environment. OMG has currently defined standards for eleven object services:

■ The ***Life Cycle Service*** defines operations for creating, copying, moving, and deleting components on the bus.

■ The ***Persistence Service*** provides a single interface for storing components persistently on a variety of storage servers—including Object Databases (ODBMSs), Relational Databases (RDBMSs), and simple files.

■ The ***Naming Service*** allows components on the bus to locate other components by name; it also supports federated naming contexts. The service allows objects to be bound to existing network directories or naming contexts—including ISO's X.500, OSF's DCE, and Sun's NIS.

■ The ***Event Service*** allows components on the bus to dynamically register or unregister their interest in specific events. The service defines a well-known object called an *event channel* that collects and distributes events among components that know nothing of each other.

■ The ***Concurrency Control Service*** provides a lock manager that can obtain locks on behalf of either transactions or threads.

■ The ***Transaction Service*** provides two-phase commit coordination among recoverable components using either flat or nested transactions.

■ The ***Relationship Service*** provides a way to create dynamic associations (or links) between components that know nothing of each other. It also provides mechanisms for traversing the links that group these components. You can use the service to enforce referential integrity constraints, to track containment relationships, and for any type of linkage among components.

■ The ***Externalization Service*** provides a standard way for getting data into and out of a component using a stream-like mechanism.

■ The ***Query Service*** provides query operations for objects. It's a superset of SQL based on the upcoming *SQL3* specification and the Object Database Management Group's (ODMG) *Object Query Language (OQL)*.

■ The ***Licensing Service*** provides operations for metering the use of components to ensure fair compensation for their use. The service supports any model of usage control at any point in a component's life cycle. It supports charging per session, per node, per instance creation, and per site.

■ The ***Properties Service*** provides operations to let you associate named values (or, properties) with any component. Using this service you can dynamically associate properties with a component's state. For example, a title or a date.

Two more services—security and time—are expected to be standardized in late 1995. And three more—trader, collections, and change management—should be available by the end of 1996. All these services enrich a component's behavior and provide the robust environment in which it can safely live and play.

Object Services: Build-to-Order Middleware

You should note that CORBA object services provide a unique approach for creating *build-to-order* middleware. It's unlike anything classical client/server systems provide today. With CORBA, component providers can develop their objects without any concern for system services. Then, depending on what the customer's needs are, the developer (or system integrator) can mix the original component with any combination of CORBA services to create the needed function. They do this by subclassing the original class, and then mixing it with the required object service classes via multiple inheritance. It's all done via IDL—no source code is needed. For example, you may develop a component called "car" and create a concurrent, persistent, and transactional version of car by multiply inheriting from the corresponding services.

In addition, some ORB vendors will take advantage of their metaclass CORBA extensions to let you create your mixins at object-creation time. A *metaclass* is a class that is also a run-time object. For example, IBM's SOM extends CORBA by treating classes as first-class objects. This means that you can create and customize new classes at run time. Object factories can use these metaclass facilities to compose a class at run time based on a client's request. You can create made-to-order classes by multiply-inheriting from existing object services. For example, the factory can take an ordinary component such as a "car" and make it transactional, lockable, and secure by multiply inheriting from existing object service classes. This approach is the ultimate form of made-to-order middleware. The beauty is that the original component provider may have known nothing about transactions, security, or locking. These services are dynamically added to the component at factory creation time based on the client's requirements.

If you don't like multiple inheritance, some ORB implementations let you add methods "on the fly" to existing classes. In particular, you can add *before* and *after* callbacks that are triggered before and after any ordinary method executes. You can use these before and after calls to call any of the existing CORBA services—or, for that matter, anything that lives on an ORB. You can even attach scripts to before/after triggers. For example, you can use a *before* trigger to obtain a lock from the concurrency service; you use the *after* trigger to release the lock.

By combining metaclass technology with CORBA services, you will be able to create "customize at the last minute" middleware environments for running particular components. It demonstrates the ultimate flexibility of objects. Most component developers will probably take a more conservative approach and create their mixins at compile time or via a tool at build time. In either case, it's still a lot more flexible than anything you can do with today's client/server middleware.

Object Services: The Roll-Out Road Map

Figure 3-5 shows the *Request For Proposal (RFP)* schedules that OMG is using to develop the object service specifications. OMG RFPs are requests for a technology. They result in responses from members on how to implement a particular standard. Members must base their responses on existing products or products that are in development (some proof of concept is needed). Usually an RFP is met by merging the responses obtained from several organizations. From the time the OMG issues an RFP, it takes about 12 to 16 months to obtain a working standard.

Table 3-1 provides more details. As you can see—*RFP1* also known as *Common Object Service Specification Volume 1 (COSS1)*—was adopted as an OMG standard in February 1994. COSS1 includes life cycle, naming, persistence, and event notification. *RFP2* (or COSS2) became an official OMG standard in December 1994. COSS2 includes transactions, concurrency, relationships, and externalization. The technical specifications for *RFP4* (or COSS4) were in their final form when this book went to press, but they were still not officially ratified. COSS4 includes query, licensing, and properties. *RFP3* was still being worked on when we went to press. It includes a very elaborate security service and a time service. *RFP5* was just issued; it includes trader, collections, and change management services. ORB products typically lag behind standards by about 12 to 16 months. So by the time you read this book, you should be expecting to see COSS1 and COSS2 services bundled with your ORBs.

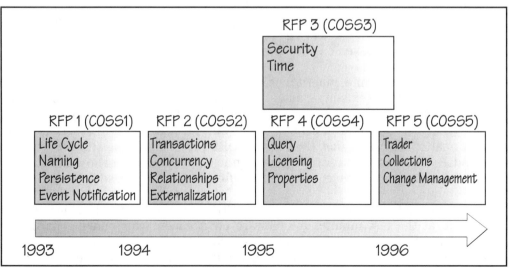

Figure 3-5. The OMG Road Map for Delivering Object Services.

Table 3-1. The OMG Road Map for Delivering Object Services.[1]

RFP	RFP Issue Date	OMG Adoption	Services
RFP1 (COSS1)	10/92	2/94	Life cycle, naming, persistence, and event notifications
RFP2 (COSS2)	7/93	12/94	Transactions, concurrency, relationships, and externalization
RFP3 (COSS3)	8/94	12/95 (estimate)	Security and time
RFP4 (COSS4)	6/94	10/95 (estimate)	Query, licensing, and properties
RFP5 (COSS5)	8/95 (estimate)	11/96 (estimate)	Trader, collections, and change management

[1]. We thank Dan Chang from the Object Services Task Force for helping us come up with these estimates.

Common Facilities

Common Facilities are collections of IDL-defined components that provide services of direct use to application objects. Think of them as the next step up in the semantic hierarchy. The two categories of common facilities—*horizontal* and *vertical*—define rules of engagement that business components need to effectively collaborate. There are four types of horizontal facilities: 1) *User Interface* in-place editing services similar to those provided by OpenDoc and OLE; 2) *Information Management* services—including compound document storage and data interchange facilities similar to those provided by OLE and OpenDoc; 3) *Systems Management* services that define interfaces for managing, instrumenting, configuring, installing, operating, and repairing distributed object components; and 4) *Task Management* services—including workflow, long transactions, agents, scripting, rules, and e-mail. The *vertical* facilities will provide IDL-defined interfaces for vertical market segments such as health, retail, telcos, and finance.

To give you a feel for where things stand, in October 1994 the OMG issued the Common Facilities *Request for Proposal 1 (RFP1)* to obtain technology submissions for compound documents—OpenDoc is the most likely candidate technology. It generally takes OMG about a year to adopt a technology after it issues an RFP. Based on the RFP schedules, it looks as if most of the Common Facilities may be completed by year-end 1996. When this happens, CORBA will provide IDL-interfaces for virtually every distributed service we know today (many will be IDL-ized versions of existing middleware).

Application/Business Objects

For years, we've talked about how information technology needs to be aligned with corporate strategy and tactics. Business objects offer a way to turn words into action. Literally.

> — John R. Rymer, Editor
> Distributed Computing Monitor
> (January, 1995)

Application Objects are components specific to end-user applications—we call them "Object Nirvana." You must define these objects using IDL if they are to participate in ORB-mediated exchanges. You typically build an application from a number of cooperating business components that play together in suites. Application objects, of course, build on top of services provided by the ORB, Common Facilities, and Object Services. The goal is for end users or system integrators to directly assemble these business objects into applications in ways that were totally unforeseen by their original designers. Application and business objects are work in progress. We expect OMG to complete this work by 1997. But, as we explain in Part 3, there are quite a few application frameworks that can help you build business objects today. So we will also cover in detail today's crop of application frameworks—including OpenDoc, OLE, Taligent, OpenStep, and Newi.

Is 1996 "The Year of the ORB"?

Soapbox

The fact that CORBA is a standard that people are using today dwarfs any potential shortcoming it may possess.

> — W. Roelandts, Manager
> HP's General Computer Systems
> (April, 1995)

In the early 1980s, a favorite industry pundit game was to predict the "Year of the LAN." After many false starts (and predictions), the year of the LAN finally arrived in 1986. It was the year when LANs were everywhere. This was also the year when pundits stopped talking about LANs—they had become a given. In this Soapbox, we want to talk about the "Year of the ORB." The question is really this: When will ORBs be ready for prime time? In our "fearless" forecast, we declare *late 1996 to be the year of the ORB*. We believe that by early 1997, ORBs will become ubiquitous. And we won't be talking about them any more. Read on to find out why.

The best way to support this prediction is to first look at what's missing from CORBA; when can we expect the missing pieces; and what, if any, are the showstoppers for the technology. We also have a surprise in the bag; it will prove beyond doubt that 1996 (or early 1997) is the year of the ORB. The good news on the CORBA front is that our list of shortcomings is much shorter this time than the one we put together in our previous book, **Essential Client/Server Survival Guide**. But there's still some bad news on the CORBA front:

■ *Commercial ORBs are slow and inefficient.* This first generation of CORBA ORBs is totally unsuited for mission-critical client/server environments. Most of today's ORBs don't perform any garbage collection, load-balancing or concurrency control. None of the CORBA servers on the market can deal with millions of fine-grained objects—they just don't scale. In addition, there are no fault-tolerant servers for ORBs. Note that objects are inherently very scalable and can easily be replicated to provide fault tolerance. The problem is that on the server side, existing commercial ORBs are not on par with TP Monitors, ODBMSs, or even RDBMSs—they're not mature server products. Of course, this will change soon. One of your authors is working on a line of mission-critical "Serverware" for CORBA ORBs.

■ *Where's MOM?* MOM stands for *Message-Oriented Middleware*. It provides asynchronous message queues on both the client and server sides. MOM allows clients and servers to function at their own designated times and speeds without necessarily being simultaneously active. ORBs must provide MOM services to support mobile users and to facilitate communications in heterogeneous environments. The OMG Common Facilities task force is currently working on a MOM RFP to introduce messaging and queuing classes into CORBA.

■ ***The server code is not very portable.*** The CORBA specification does not sufficiently define all the interfaces required to write portable server code. In contrast, the specification to write fully portable clients is complete. OMG is aware of this shortcoming and is starting to work on a solution.

■ ***Standard CORBA does not support metaclasses.*** The ability to treat classes as first-class objects is very important for business objects and customizable middleware. We went over some of the miracles that meta-classes can perform in the Object Services section. In Part 3, you'll discover that the run-time flexibility provided by metaclasses is an absolute necessity for business objects. It would be nice to see OMG standardize on the SOM metaclasses (or something equivalent) to create a level playing field for all vendors. Currently, SOM-based CORBA vendors have an edge over their competitors because of SOM's support for metaclasses. The bad news is that these SOM metaclass implementations are not portable across CORBA ORBs, which is a real shame.

■ ***IDL needs to support semantic-level extensions.*** The OMG IDL needs to provide extensions for semantic message structures that are similar to those provided by Newi and OpenDoc (see Part 3). The idea is that components should be able to interact with each other at the semantic level. CORBA IDL should provide "glue" to deal with mismatches between what a client component expects and what a server component provides. In other words, a flexible self-describing form of messaging is needed. You will understand what we mean when you get to the Newi and OpenDoc chapters. The OMG Common Facilities task force is starting to address this issue.

Are any of these items showstoppers? The only major showstopper is the first item on our list—the lack of robust commercial implementations. The rest of the issues are also important, and also need solutions. But without robust server implementations, ORBs will never be able to displace other forms of client/server middleware or application environments. In our opinion, OMG has created a nice set of standards (with the noted deficiencies). The ball is now in the vendors' court. They must deliver commercial implementations that are robust enough to satisfy the client/server mainstream. The first truly robust ORBs will probably be delivered by TP Monitor vendors in 1996. We predict that the next generation of TP Monitors will be called ORBs. You should note that TP Monitor vendors helped define the CORBA Object Transaction Service. They are very aware of the synergy between ORBs and classical transaction processing environments.

So are ORBs ready for prime time? They're getting there. You can use the current generation of ORBs in homogeneous environments to develop a better understanding of distributed object technology and encapsulate some of your key legacy applications with object wrappers. The current ORBs will help you create and manage a consistent set of distributed interfaces to all your important networked applications, tools, utilities, and medium-grained objects. The ORB becomes the "great integrator." However, heterogeneous object-oriented production applications with fine-grained distributed objects will come later. How much later?

We predict we will get these functions by late-1996, when CORBA 2.0-compliant ORBs hit the market. Typically, products lag standards by about 16 months. The relevant CORBA 2.0 standards—including the transactions and concurrency services—were passed in December 1994. So our 1996 assumption may be right on target. By then, we expect to see a new generation of ORBs with built-in CORBA-compliant transaction services. These are the ORBs that will ultimately revolutionize the way we do client/server computing.

There's More to This Story

Is our forecast built entirely on the delivery of robust technology? Not really—that would be too foolish. There's another wildcard on the horizon that will greatly accelerate the penetration of CORBA ORBs—it's called OLE. As you may recall, OLE is part of Windows 95. As a result, it is practically free. When Cairo ships in late 1996, OLE will be extended across networks. In other words, it will become an ORB. It's also a high-volume ORB that will compete head-on with CORBA. To meet the competition from OLE, we expect that over the next few years CORBA vendors will be bundling their ORBs with mass volume desktops—such as OS/2 Warp, Windows 95, and Macintosh. In fact, this is precisely what the OpenDoc consortium is planning to do.

As a result, we anticipate that sometime in 1996, industrial-strength CORBA ORBs will become ubiquitously available—they will be part of every shipping OS/2 Warp and Macintosh. In addition, Novell and CI Labs plan to make OpenDoc/CORBA available on Windows through some form of contamination (free downloads, preloads, and other "free" distribution programs). You can't beat free. So yes, 1996 will be the year of the ORB. If not, it will be early 1997. If it does not happen by then, it's good-bye CORBA. It means that OLE would have won the battle for the ORB. So by 1997, the world will either be fully populated with OLE ORBs or CORBA ORBs (or, in the worst case, by both). ❏

Chapter 4

CORBA 2.0:
The Intergalactic
Object Bus

Orb—A jeweled globe surmounted by a cross that is part of a sovereign's regalia and that symbolizes monarchical power and justice.

— **American Heritage Dictionary**

ORB—Putting down some pavement on the dirt road called distributed computing.

— **Chris Stone, President of OMG**

A CORBA 2.0 ORB provides more than just the basic messaging mechanisms needed by objects to communicate with one another across heterogeneous languages, tools, platforms, and networks. It also provides the environment for managing these objects, advertising their presence, and describing their metadata. A CORBA ORB is a self-describing object bus. With CORBA 2.0, an ORB can broker interactions between objects that reside within a single process (like a C++ program) as well as between objects that globally interact across multivendor ORBs and operating systems.

A CORBA 2.0 ORB is truly an intergalactic object bus. We consider it to be the "mother of all client/server middleware." This chapter describes the ORB mechanisms that have been available since CORBA 1.1 was introduced in 1991. We also cover the new CORBA 2.0 enhancements introduced in December 1994. CORBA 2.0 is a superset of CORBA 1.1. It adds multivendor ORB interoperability, ORB initialization services, and enhancements to the Interface Repository. You may also have heard the term CORBA 1.2, which is a very minor corrective revision of CORBA 1.1. We use CORBA 1.1 to refer to both CORBA 1.1 and 1.2.

WHAT EXACTLY IS A CORBA 2.0 ORB?

A request broker mediates interactions between client applications needing services and server applications capable of providing them.

— *Richard Adler, Coordinated Computing*
(April, 1995)

A CORBA 2.0 *Object Request Broker (ORB)* is the middleware that establishes the client/server relationships between objects. Using an ORB, a client object can transparently invoke a method on a server object, which can be on the same machine or across a network. The ORB intercepts the call and is responsible for finding an object that can implement the request, pass it the parameters, invoke its method, and return the results (see Figure 4-1). The client does not have to be aware of where the object is located, its programming language, its operating system, or any other system aspects that are not part of an object's interface. It is very important to note that the client/server roles are only used to coordinate the interactions between two objects. Objects on the ORB can act as either client or server, depending on the occasion.

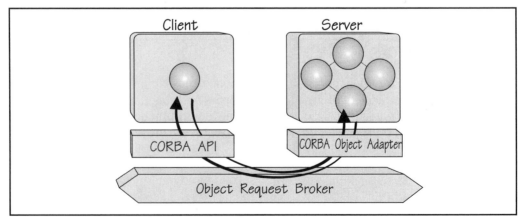

Figure 4-1. The Client/Server Request Using the ORB.

The Anatomy of a CORBA 2.0 ORB

Figure 4-2 shows the client and server sides of a CORBA ORB. The light areas are new to CORBA 2.0. Even though there are many boxes, it's not as complicated as it appears to be. This section provides the big picture of what these components do. We then go into more details in the sections that follow. The key is to understand that CORBA, like SQL, provides both static and dynamic interfaces to its services. This happened because the OMG received two strong submissions to its original ORB Request For Proposal (RFP): one from HyperDesk and Digital that was based on a dynamic API, and one from Sun and HP that was based on static APIs. The OMG told the two groups to come back with a single RFP that combined both features. The result was CORBA. The "Common" in CORBA stands for this two-API proposal, which makes a lot of sense because it gives us both static and dynamic APIs.

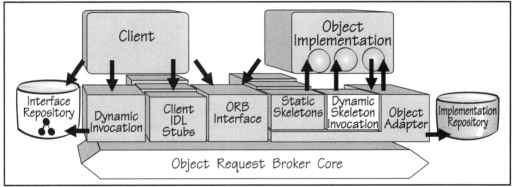

Figure 4-2. The Structure of a CORBA 2.0 ORB.

Let's first go over what CORBA does on the client side:

- ■ **The client IDL stubs** provide the static interfaces to object services. These precompiled stubs define how clients invoke corresponding services on the servers. From a client's perspective, the stub acts like a local call—it is a local *proxy* for a remote server object. The services are defined using IDL, and both client and server stubs are generated by the IDL compiler. A client must have an IDL stub for each interface it uses on the server. The stub includes code to perform *marshaling*. This means that it encodes (and decodes) the operation and its parameters into flattened message formats that it can send to the server. It also includes header files that enable you to invoke the method on the server from a higher-level language (like C, C++, or Smalltalk) without worrying about the underlying protocols or issues such as data marshaling. You simply invoke a method from within your program to obtain a remote service.

- *The Dynamic Invocation Interface (DII)* lets you discover the method to be invoked at run time. CORBA defines standard APIs for looking up the metadata that defines the server interface, generating the parameters, issuing the remote call, and getting back the results.

- *The Interface Repository APIs* allow you to obtain and modify the descriptions of all the registered component interfaces, the methods they support, and the parameters they require. CORBA calls these descriptions *method signatures*. The *Interface Repository* is a run-time database that contains machine-readable versions of the IDL-defined interfaces. Think of it as a dynamic metadata repository for ORBs. The APIs allow components to dynamically access, store, and update metadata information. This pervasive use of metadata allows every component that lives on the ORB to have self-describing interfaces. The ORB itself is a self-describing bus (see next Briefing box).

- *The ORB Interface* consists of a few APIs to local services that may be of interest to an application. For example, CORBA provides APIs to convert an object reference to a string and vice versa. These calls can be very useful if you need to store and communicate object references. The Details box on page 73 describes some of the ORB APIs.

The support for both static and dynamic client/server invocations—as well as the Interface Repository—gives CORBA a leg up over competing middleware. Static invocations are easier to program, faster, and self-documenting. Dynamic invocations provide maximum flexibility, but they are difficult to program; they are very useful for tools that discover services at run time.

 CORBA 2.0 Global Repository IDs

Briefing

With CORBA 2.0, ORBs provide global identifiers—called *Repository IDs*—to uniquely and globally identify a component and its interface across multivendor ORBs and repositories. The Repository IDs are system-generated unique strings that are used to maintain consistency in the naming conventions used across repositories—no name collisions are allowed. Repository IDs are generated via *pragmas* in IDL. The pragma specifies whether to generate them via DCE *Universal Unique Identifiers (UUIDs)* or via a user-supplied unique prefix appended to IDL-scoped names. The Repository ID itself is a string consisting of a three level name hierarchy. We cover the Interface Repository in greater detail in the next chapter. ❑

The server side cannot tell the difference between a static or dynamic invocation; they both have the same message semantics. In both cases, the ORB locates a server object adapter, transmits the parameters, and transfers control to the object implementation through the server IDL stub (or skeleton). Here's what CORBA elements do on the server side of Figure 4-2:

■ The **server IDL stubs** (OMG calls them *skeletons*) provide static interfaces to each service exported by the server. These stubs, like the ones on the client, are created using an IDL compiler.

■ The **Dynamic Skeleton Interface (DSI)**—introduced in CORBA 2.0—provides a run-time binding mechanism for servers that need to handle incoming method calls for components that do not have IDL-based compiled skeletons (or stubs). The Dynamic Skeleton looks at parameter values in an incoming message to figure out who it's for—that is, the target object and method. In contrast, normal compiled skeletons are defined for a particular object class and expect a method implementation for each IDL-defined method. Dynamic Skeletons are very useful for implementing generic bridges between ORBs. They can also be used by interpreters and scripting languages to dynamically generate object implementations. The DSI is the server equivalent of a DII. It can receive either static or dynamic client invocations.

■ The **Object Adapter** sits on top of the ORB's core communication services and accepts requests for service on behalf of the server's objects. It provides the run-time environment for instantiating server objects, passing requests to them, and assigning them object IDs—CORBA calls the IDs *object references*. The Object Adapter also registers the classes it supports and their run-time instances (i.e., objects) with the *Implementation Repository*. CORBA specifies that each ORB must support a standard adapter called the *Basic Object Adapter (BOA)*. Servers may support more than one object adapter.

■ The **Implementation Repository** provides a run-time repository of information about the classes a server supports, the objects that are instantiated, and their IDs. It also serves as a common place to store additional information associated with the implementation of ORBs. Examples include trace information, audit trails, security, and other administrative data.

■ The **ORB Interface** consists of a few APIs to local services that are identical to those provided on the client side.

This concludes our panoramic overview of the ORB components and their interfaces. Next, we'll dive one level deeper to get a more specific idea of what each of these elements do.

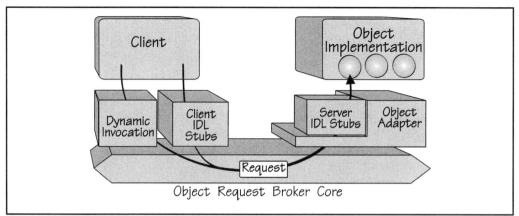

Figure 4-3. CORBA's Static and Dynamic Method Invocations.

CORBA Method Invocations: Static Versus Dynamic

Figure 4-3 shows the two types of client/server invocations that are supported by a CORBA ORB: static and dynamic. In both cases, the client performs a request by having access to an object reference (i.e., object ID) and invoking the method that performs the service (see the following Details box). The dynamic and static interfaces for performing the service satisfy the same request semantics.

Clients see the object interfaces through the perspective of a *language mapping*—or *binding*—that brings the ORB right up to the programmer's level. Client programs should be able to work without any source changes on any ORB that supports the language binding. They should be able to call any object instance that implements the interface. The implementation of the object, its object adapter, and the ORB used to access it is totally transparent to both static and dynamic clients.

The *static interface* is directly generated in the form of stubs by the IDL precompiler. It is perfect for programs that know at compile time the particulars of the operations they will need to invoke. The static stub interface is bound at compile time and provides the following advantages over the dynamic method invocation:

■ *It is easier to program*—you call the remote method by simply invoking it by name and passing it the parameters. It's a very natural form of programming.

■ *It provides more robust type checking*—the checking is enforced by the compiler at build time.

■ *It performs well*—a single API call is issued to the stub, which takes it from there.

■ *It is self-documenting*—you can tell what's going on by reading the code.

In contrast, the *dynamic* method invocation provides a more flexible environment. It allows you to add new classes to the system without requiring changes in the client code. It's very useful for tools that discover what services are provided at run time. You can write some very generic code with dynamic APIs. However, most applications don't require this level of flexibility and are better off with static stub implementations.

What's an Object Reference?

Details

An object reference provides the information you need to uniquely specify an object within a distributed ORB system—it's a unique name or identifier. The implementation of object references is not defined by the CORBA specification, which means it is implementation specific. Two CORBA-compliant ORBs may have different representations for object references. CORBA 2.0 now defines *Interoperable Object References (IOR)* that vendors must use to pass object references across heterogenous ORBs. So how do you maintain client/server program portability in such an environment? You maintain it by using language bindings to insulate your programs from the actual representation of the object references (see Figure 4-4).

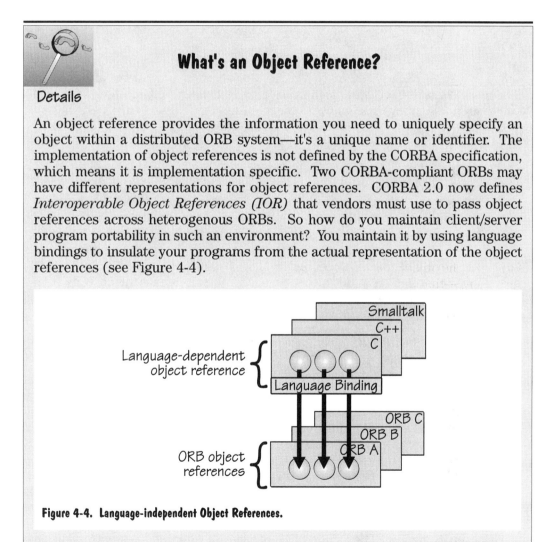

Figure 4-4. Language-independent Object References.

All ORBs must provide the same language binding to an object reference (usually referred to as an *object*) for a particular programming language. This means that the language provides the portability and allows you to reference objects that run on different ORBs from within your programs. What happens if your program is accessing object references on two different ORBs? According to CORBA, your programs should still work fine; it is up to the vendors to resolve any object reference conflicts that may be encountered by the client code.

How do the client programs obtain object references? They usually receive them from directories or invocations on other objects to which they have references. You can convert an object reference to a string-name that you can store in files. The string-name can be preserved or communicated by different means and then turned back into an object reference by the ORB that produced the string. CORBA defines two ORB interface functions—*object_to_string* and *string_to_object*—to help store, communicate, and retrieve object references. Client programs can use these two functions to obtain a string-name and convert it to an object reference, and vice versa. We also expect the OMG to get into the business of allocating "well-known object references." The CORBA 2.0 Initialization Service already includes a few well-known objects. We cover ORB initialization later in this chapter.

The ORB interface also defines some operations that you can invoke on any object reference. These operations are directly implemented by the ORB on the object reference. This means that they're not passed to the object implementation. You can invoke the ORB method *get_interface* on any object reference to obtain an Interface Repository object that provides type and metadata information for that object. You can invoke the ORB method *get_implementation* on any object reference to obtain an Implementation Repository object that describes the implementation of that object. You can invoke the ORB method *is_nil* on any object reference to test if an object exists. ❑

CORBA Static Method Invocations: From IDL to Interface Stubs

Figure 4-5 shows the steps you go through to create your server classes, provide interface stubs for them, store their definitions in the Interface Repository, instantiate the objects at run time, and record their presence with the Implementation Repository. Let's go through these steps one-by-one and see what's involved:

1. ***Define your object classes using Interface Definition Language (IDL).***
   The IDL is the means by which objects tell their potential clients what operations are available and how they should be invoked. The IDL definition language defines the types of objects, their attributes, the methods they export, and the method parameters. The CORBA IDL is a subset of ANSI C++ with additional constructs to support distribution. The IDL is purely a declarative language. It uses the C++ syntax for constant, type, and operation definitions, and it does

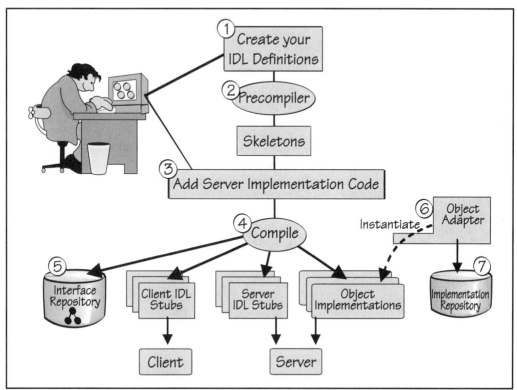

Figure 4-5. Defining Services: From IDL To Interface Stubs.

not include any control structures or variables (we cover CORBA IDL in the next chapter).

2. ***Run the IDL file through a language precompiler.*** A typical CORBA-compliant precompiler processes the IDL files and produces language *skeletons* for the implementation server classes.

3. ***Add the implementation code to the skeletons***. You must supply the code that implements the methods in the skeletons. In other words, you must create your server classes.

4. ***Compile the code***. A CORBA-compliant compiler is typically capable of generating at least four types of output files: 1) *import files* that describe the objects to an Interface Repository; 2) *client stubs* for the IDL-defined methods—these stubs are invoked by a client program that needs to statically access IDL-defined services via the ORB; 3) *server stubs* that call the methods on the server—they're also called *up-call interfaces*; and 4) the code that implements the server classes. The automatic generation of stubs frees developers from having to write them, and frees applications from dependencies on a particular ORB implementation.

5. ***Bind the class definitions to the Interface Repository.*** Typically, you use a utility to bind—or, if you prefer, compile—the IDL information in an Interface Repository that programs can access at run time (we cover the Interface Repository in the next chapter).

6. ***Instantiate the objects on the server.*** At startup time, a server *Object Adapter* may instantiate server objects that service remote client method invocations. These run-time objects are instances of the server application classes. CORBA specifies different Object Adapter strategies that are used to create and manage the run-time objects (more on this in later sections).

7. ***Register the run-time objects with the Implementation Repository.*** The Object Adapter records in the *Implementation Repository* the object reference and type of any object it instantiates on the server. The Implementation Repository also knows which object classes are supported on a particular server. The ORB uses this information to locate active objects or to request the activation of objects on a particular server.

The seven steps we just outlined are typical of most CORBA implementations. CORBA, of course, allows deviations. For example, it is not a requirement for IDL source code to be available, as long as the interface information is available in stub form or in an Interface Repository. You don't have to implement the server objects as classes as long as they're encapsulated by IDL stubs. The separation of the interface from the implementation enables you to incorporate existing (legacy) systems within an ORB environment.

CORBA Dynamic Method Invocations: A Step-By-Step Guide

CORBA's *Dynamic Invocation* APIs allow a client program to dynamically build and invoke requests on objects. The client specifies the object to be invoked, the method to be performed, and the set of parameters through a call or sequence of calls. The client code typically obtains this information from an *Interface Repository* or a similar run-time source. The dynamic invocation provides maximum flexibility by allowing new object types to be added to the distributed system at run time. Visual tools will use this API to create interfaces through point-and-click interactions with a user.

To invoke a dynamic method on an object, the client must perform the following steps (see Figure 4-6):

1. ***Obtain the method description from the Interface Repository.*** CORBA specifies about ten calls for locating and describing objects within the repository. After you locate an object, you issue a *describe* call to obtain its full IDL definition.

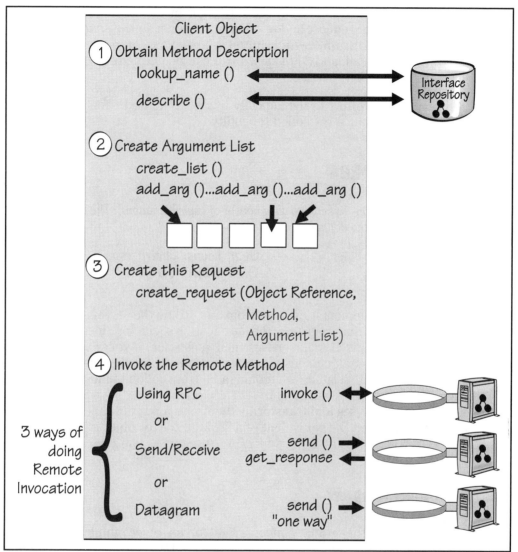

Figure 4-6. The CORBA Dynamic Invocation Interface.

2. **Create the argument list.** CORBA specifies a self-defining data structure for passing parameters, which it calls the *NamedValue list*. The list is created using the *create_list* operation and as many *add_arg* calls as it takes to add each argument to the list.

3. **Create the request.** The request must specify the object reference, the name of the method, and the argument list. The request is created using the CORBA *create_request* call.

4. ***Invoke the request.*** You can invoke a request in one of three ways: 1) the *invoke* call sends the request and obtains the results; 2) the *send* call returns control to the program, which must then issue a *get_response* or *get_next_response* call; and 3) the *send* call can be defined to be "oneway"; in this case, no response is needed.

As you can see, it takes effort to dynamically invoke a method. You're trading off complexity and performance for added flexibility.

The Server Side of CORBA

A *primary CORBA goal was to permit a wide variety of implementations. The specification does not rule out any of the different approaches to an ORB.*

> — *Geoff Lewis, Chairperson*
> *OMG Object Services*

What does an object implementation need from an ORB on the server side? It needs a server infrastructure that registers the application's classes, instantiates new objects, gives them unique IDs, advertises their existence, invokes their methods when clients request it, and manages concurrent requests for their services. If we want to get more sophisticated, we could add transaction management, load balancing, and fine-grained security to the list. In other words, we need a program that takes raw class libraries and transforms them into a multiuser server environment. We're talking about the equivalent of a TP Monitor for objects. So who does this type of work? The answer is the *Object Adapter*.

What's an Object Adapter?

The Object Adapter is the primary mechanism for an object implementation to access ORB services (see Figure 4-7). It provides a total environment for running the server application. Here are some of the services provided by the Object Adapter:

1. ***Registers server classes with the Implementation Repository.*** You can think of the Implementation Repository as a persistent store that the Object Adapter manages. Object Implementation classes are registered and stored in the Implementation Repository.

2. ***Instantiates new objects at run time***. The Object Adapter is responsible for creating object instances from the implementation classes. The number of instances created is a function of the incoming client traffic loads. The Adapter

is responsible for balancing the supply of objects with the incoming client demands.

3. ***Generates and manages object references***. The Object Adapter assigns references (unique IDs) to the new objects it creates. It's responsible for mapping between the implementation-specific and ORB-specific representations of object references.

4. ***Broadcasts the presence of the object servers.*** The Object Adapter may broadcast the services it provides on the ORB—or it may respond to directory type queries from the ORB core. It is in charge of letting the outside world know of the services it manages. Eventually, we expect to see some tight levels of integration with global directory services such as X.500.

5. ***Handles incoming client calls.*** The Object Adapter interacts with the top layer of the ORB core communication stack, peels off the request, and hands it to the interface stub. The stub is responsible for interpreting the incoming parameters and presenting them in a form that's acceptable to the object's method invocation.

6. ***Routes the up-call to the appropriate method.*** The Object Adapter is implicitly involved in the invocation of the methods described in the stubs (or the skeleton). For example, the Object Adapter may be involved in activating the implementation. And it can authenticate the incoming requests.

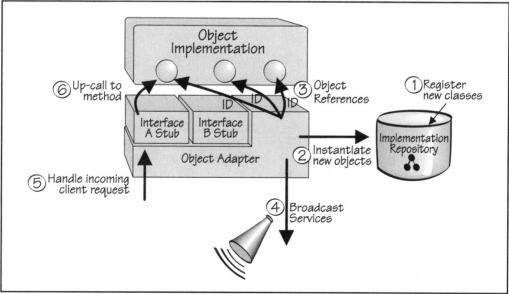

Figure 4-7. The Structure of a Typical Object Adapter.

BOA and Other Object Adapters

An *Object Adapter* defines how an object is activated. It can do this by creating a new process, creating a new thread within an existing process, or by reusing an existing thread or process. A server could support a variety of object adapters to satisfy different types of requests. For example, an Object Database (ODBMS) may want to implicitly register all the fine-grained objects it contains without issuing individual calls to the Object Adapter. In such a case, it doesn't make sense for an Object Adapter to maintain a per-object state. The ODBMS may want to provide a special-purpose Object Adapter that not only interfaces with the ORB core, but also meets its special requirements. However, OMG prefers not to see a proliferation of Object Adapter types. To avoid this proliferation, CORBA specifies a *Basic Object Adapter (BOA)* that "can be used for most ORB objects with conventional implementations."

CORBA requires that a BOA adapter be available in every ORB. Object implementations that use it should be able to run on any ORB that supports the required language bindings. CORBA requires that the following functions be provided in a BOA implementation:

- An Implementation Repository that lets you install and register an object implementation. It also lets you provide information describing the object.

- Mechanisms for generating and interpreting object references; activating and deactivating object implementations; and invoking methods and passing them their parameters.

- A mechanism for authenticating the client making the call. BOA does not enforce any specific style of security. It guarantees that for every object or method invocation, it will identify the client (or principal) on whose behalf the request is performed. What to do with this information is left to the implementation.

- Activation and deactivation of implementation objects.

- Method invocations through stubs.

BOA supports traditional and object-oriented applications. It does not specify how methods are packaged or located—this could be done through DLLs or a system call at startup that identifies the location of the methods. To get the widest application coverage, CORBA defines four activation policies that specify the rules a given implementation follows for activating objects. Think of them as scheduling policies. The four policies are: *shared server, unshared server, server-per-method*, and *persistent server.*

BOA Shared Server

In a *shared server* activation policy, multiple objects may reside in the same program (i.e., process). The BOA activates the server the first time a request is performed on any object implemented by that server (see Figure 4-8). After the server has initialized itself, it notifies BOA that it is prepared to handle requests by calling *impl_is_ready*. All subsequent requests are then delivered to this server process; BOA will not activate another server process for that implementation. The server handles one request at a time and notifies BOA via a *deactivate_obj* call when it finishes processing a request. When the process itself is ready to terminate, it notifies BOA by issuing a *deactivate_impl* call.

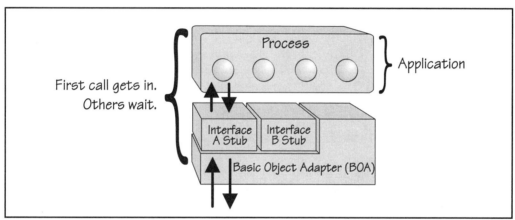

Figure 4-8. The BOA Shared Server Activation Policy.

BOA Unshared Server

In an *unshared server* activation policy, each object resides in a different server process. A new server is activated the first time a request is performed on the object (see Figure 4-9). When the object has initialized itself, it notifies BOA that it is prepared to handle requests by calling *obj_is_ready*. A new server is started whenever a request is made for an object that is not yet active, even if a server for another object with the same implementation is active. A server object remains active and will receive requests until it calls *deactivate_obj*.

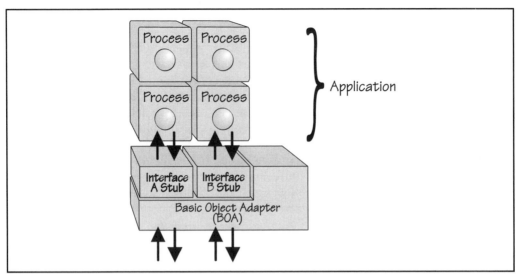

Figure 4-9. The BOA Unshared Server Activation Policy.

BOA Server-per-Method

In a *server-per-method* activation policy, a new server is always started each time a request is made. The server runs only for the duration of the particular method (see Figure 4-10). Several server processes for the same object—or even the same method of the same object—may be concurrently active. A new server is started

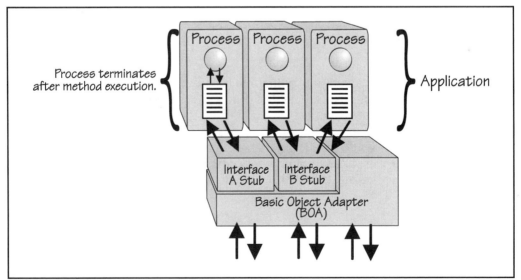

Figure 4-10. The BOA Server-per-Method Activation Policy.

for each request, so it's not necessary for the implementation to notify BOA when an object is ready or deactivated. BOA activates a new process for each request, whether or not another request for that operation or object is active at the same time.

BOA Persistent Server

In a *persistent server* activation policy, servers are activated by means outside BOA (see Figure 4-11). BOA may start the server application, which then notifies BOA that it's ready to accept work by means of an *impl_is_ready* call. BOA treats all subsequent requests as shared server calls; it sends activations for individual objects and method calls to a single process. If no implementation is ready when a request arrives, an error is returned for that request.

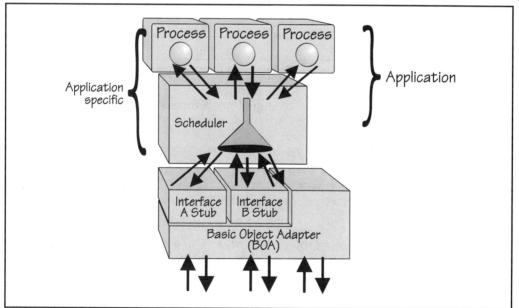

Figure 4-11. The BOA Persistent Server Activation Policy.

CORBA 2.0 Initialization—Or How Does a Component Find Its ORB?

How does a component first discover its ORB? CORBA 1.1 left this as an exercise for the ORB vendors. The results were non-portable solutions. CORBA 2.0 fixes this problem by defining a set of initialization APIs that allow an object to bootstrap itself into an ORB's environment. These APIs allow components to discover their

ORB, BOA, Interface Repository, and a set of well-known object services. In essence, the initialization service provides a barebones naming service that allows objects to find the services they need to function on an ORB.

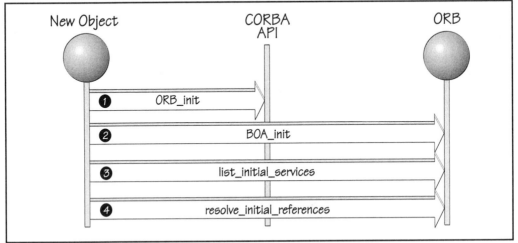

Figure 4-12. CORBA 2.0 Initialization Service—Or, How Does a Component Find Its ORBs?

Figure 4-12 shows the typical calls an object must invoke to bootstrap itself. Let's walk through this initialization scenario:

1. ***Obtain an object reference for your ORB.*** You issue the new CORBA API call *ORB_init* to inform the ORB of your presence and to obtain a reference to an ORB *pseudo-object.*[1] Note that we issued an API call and not a method invocation. To invoke a method you must first bootstrap yourself into the CORBA world.

2. ***Obtain a pointer to your Object Adapter.*** You invoke the method *BOA_init* on the ORB pseudo-object to tell the BOA you're there and to obtain its object reference (BOA is also a pseudo-object).

3. ***Discover what initial services are available.*** You invoke the method *list_initial_services* on the ORB pseudo-object to obtain a list of well-known objects—for example, the Interface Repository and the Naming Service. The well-known objects are returned in a list of string names.

4. ***Obtain object references for the services you want.*** You invoke the method *resolve_initial_references* to obtain object references for the services you

---

[1] A *pseudo-object* is an object that is created directly by an ORB but you can invoke it like any other object. The ORB itself is a pseudo-object and provides an interface to its services.

want. You're now a well-connected, first-class citizen on the CORBA ORB.

Note: An object can initialize itself in more than one ORB.

CORBA 2.0: THE INTERGALACTIC ORB

CORBA 1.1 was only concerned with creating portable object applications; the implementation of the ORB core was left as an "exercise for the vendors." The result was some level of component portability, but not interoperability. CORBA 2.0 added interoperability by specifying a mandatory *Internet Inter-ORB Protocol (IIOP)*. The IIOP is basically TCP/IP with some CORBA-defined message exchanges that serve as a common backbone protocol. Every ORB that calls itself CORBA-compliant must either implement IIOP natively or provide a "half-bridge" to it. Note: It's called a half-bridge because IIOP is the "standard" CORBA ORB. So any proprietary ORB can connect with the universe of ORBs by translating requests to and from the IIOP backbone.

CORBA 2.0: The Inter-ORB Architecture

The choice of ORB interoperability solutions does not impact application software. Interoperability is an issue between ORB vendors, not between vendors and users. Few, if any, developers will ever be involved in programming with GIOPs and ESIOPs.

> — Tom Mowbray et al., Authors
> The Essential CORBA
> (Wiley, 1995)

Even though few application developers need to worry about how ORBs interoperate, it is interesting to understand the mechanics. So despite what Mowbray says, we'll dive into CORBA 2.0 interoperability. Figure 4-13 shows the elements of the CORBA 2.0 inter-ORB architecture. Here's a description of what each of these elements provide:

■ The ***General Inter-ORB Protocol (GIOP)*** specifies a set of message formats and common data representations for communications between ORBs. The GIOP was specifically built for ORB-to-ORB interactions. It is designed to work directly over any connection-oriented transport protocol. GIOP defines seven message formats that cover all the ORB request/reply semantics. No format negotiations are needed. In most cases, clients send a request to objects immediately after they open a connection. The *Common Data Representation (CDR)* maps data types defined in OMG IDL into a flat networked message representation. The CDR also takes care of inter-platform issues such as byte

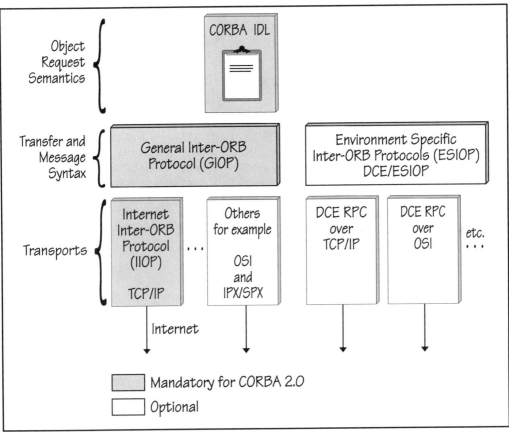

Figure 4-13. The CORBA 2.0 Inter-ORB Architecture.

ordering (no byte swapping is needed) and memory alignments (also see next Briefing box).

■ The *Internet Inter-ORB Protocol (IIOP)* specifies how GIOP messages are exchanged over a TCP/IP network. The IIOP makes it possible to use the Internet itself as backbone ORB through which other ORBs can bridge. It was designed to be simple and provide "out of the box" interoperation for TCP/IP based ORBs. The GIOP may be mapped to different transports in the future. To be CORBA 2.0 compatible, an ORB must support GIOP over TCP/IP (or connect to it via a half-bridge). Note that both the IIOP and DCE/ESIOP have built-in mechanisms for implicitly transmitting context data that is associated with the transaction or security services. The ORB takes care of passing these requests without your application's involvement. Better yet, this information can also be passed across heterogenous CORBA ORBs via bridges. The CORBA 2.0 standard does a good job specifying the location of this context data in an ORB-generated message.

■ The ***Environment-Specific Inter-ORB Protocols (ESIOPs)*** are used for "out of the box" interoperation over specific networks. CORBA 2.0 specifies DCE as the first of many optional ESIOPs (pronounced "E-SOPs"). Like GIOP, DCE/ESIOP supports IORs using a DCE tagged profile (see next Briefing box). The DCE/ESIOP uses the GIOP CDR to represent OMG IDL data types over the DCE RPC. This means that DCE IDL is not required. Instead, OMG IDL and CDR types are mapped directly into DCE's native *Network Data Representation (NDR)*. The DCE ESIOP currently provides a robust environment for mission-critical ORBs. It includes advanced features such as Kerberos security, cell and global directories, distributed time, and authenticated RPC. DCE also lets you transmit large amounts of data efficiently and it supports multiple underlying transport protocols, including TCP/IP. Finally, with DCE you can use both connection and connectionless protocols for your ORB communications (also see the Soapbox, "Is It CORBA Versus DCE?" at the end of this chapter).

FYI

GIOP: Interoperable Object References

Briefing

GIOP also defines a format for *Interoperable Object References (IORs)*. An ORB must create an IOR (from an object reference) whenever an object reference is passed across ORBs. IORs associate a collection of *tagged profiles* with object references. The profiles describe the same object, but they each describe how to contact the object using a particular ORB's mechanism. More precisely, a profile provides self-describing data that identifies the ORB domain to which a reference is associated and the protocols it supports. ❏

CORBA 2.0: ORB-to-ORB Bridging

CORBA 2.0 provides the mechanisms needed for creating generic ORB-to-ORB bridges. Figure 4-14 shows an implementation of a stub-free bridge. The new *Dynamic Skeleton Interface (DSI)* is used to receive all outgoing requests; the *Dynamic Invocation Interface (DII)* is used to invoke the request on a destination ORB object. This late-binding technology is also well-suited for creating gateways to non-CORBA object buses such as Microsoft's OLE/COM. We will have more to say about it when we cover CORBA/COM gateways in Part 6.

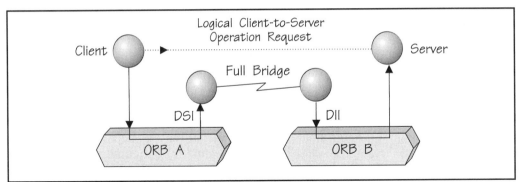

Figure 4-14. Generic ORB-to-ORB Bridging Using CORBA 2.0's Dynamic Facilities.

Federated ORBs

You can use inter-ORB bridges and IIOPs to create very flexible topologies via federations of ORBs. Figure 4-15 shows an IIOP backbone with various proprietary ORBs feeding into it via half-bridges. Note the presence of the DCE ESIOP. You can segment ORBs into domains based on administrative needs, vendor ORB implementations, network protocols, traffic loads, types of service, and security concerns. Policies on either side of the fence may conflict, so you can create firewalls around the backbone ORB via half-bridges. CORBA 2.0 promotes diversity and gives you total mix-and-match flexibility, as long as you use IIOP for your global backbone.

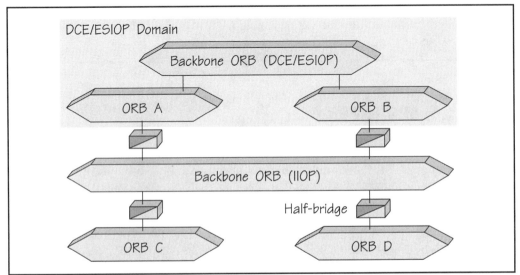

Figure 4-15. An Intergalactic Federation of Multivendor ORBs.

Is It CORBA Versus DCE?

Soapbox

CORBA did not build on anything from DCE; they are reinventing the wheel.

> — *David Chappell, Keynote Speaker*
> *DCE Developer's Conference*
> *(April, 1995)*

Many of us believed that ultimately, CORBA would build on top of DCE. We never dreamed that inter-ORB backbones would be built on anything but DCE. The choice of IIOP as the inter-ORB protocol was extremely traumatic for us DCE supporters. We felt that the DCE/ESIOP should have gotten, at the very least, equal billing with IIOP; it should have been a mandatory part of CORBA 2.0. Well, we didn't win this vote. So is DCE really on a collision course with CORBA? Should the DCE camp focus its energy on object DCE, provide an OO IDL for DCE, and forget CORBA? Or better yet, why not just use Microsoft's COM/OLE as the object foundation for DCE and completely forget CORBA?

Before answering these questions, we have a confession to make: We've grown to like IIOP over the last few months. Yes, we like the idea of using the Internet as a backbone for ORBs. IIOP will eventually transform the Internet into a CORBA bus; it's a nice evolutionary migration plan. IIOP is also a lightweight, easy-to-install ORB. Consequently, it's ideal for the Small Office Home Office (SOHO) market. So hats off to the people that brought us IIOP (sorry we didn't see the light earlier).

So what about DCE? Well, it's there. IBM, Digital, Tandem, and HP will support it on their ORBs. And you can use the DCE/ESIOP to create your ORB backbones. DCE will interoperate very nicely with IIOP because both sides follow the CORBA object model. So we can have our cake and eat it too: the Internet and secure industrial-strength ORBs.

Creating a new object model on top of DCE—as some have suggested—is totally ridiculous. The world needs another object model like it needs a hole in its head. DCE is just a fancy RPC with security and a directory service. To create an object model on top of this RPC would require an effort of the same magnitude as CORBA. OSF can't repeat this enormous undertaking. Can you imagine recreating the dynamic invocations, Interface Repository, object adapters, and the various CORBA services—including transactions, events, relationships, security, persistence, query, and so on? CORBA is the collective product of the best minds in the object industry. It has an almost insurmountable head-start in distributed objects.

Is OLE the DCE Killer App?

Microsoft's strategy towards standards is like the Trojan horse. Believers welcomed Microsoft into the community believing that it would help DCE survive. Once in, however, it will alter the standard so that it is proprietary all but killing the open version of DCE.

> *— Gartner Group*
> *(January, 1995)*

But life isn't that simple. There's a company with very deep pockets that is trying to create a distributed object bus—of CORBA magnitude—on top of DCE. We're talking about Microsoft, which is becoming the great hope of the DCE avant-garde. Never mind the fact that Microsoft is creating a closed standard that's a far cry from the open systems idealism that drove the early DCE work. It doesn't seem to matter. Microsoft has the resources to attempt to recreate CORBA single-handedly on top of DCE. And this is the great hope of the purists that don't want their DCE to play second fiddle to IIOP or any other protocol. Of course, Microsoft is at least three years behind CORBA in its distributed objects quest. So the DCE purists can either wait for Microsoft to catch up, or they can learn how to coexist with IIOP.

DCE needs CORBA and CORBA needs DCE. DCE enhances CORBA with a mission-critical RPC infrastructure. CORBA enhances DCE with an open platform for objects. There's nothing wrong with bridges to IIOP—as long as both sides of the bridge use the same CORBA 2.0 object model. So even though we dearly love IIOP, we also believe that DCE/ESIOP is crucial to CORBA's success. CORBA needs the two. The magic of OMG is that it was able to synthesize competing technologies. For example, the OMG merged two warring submissions to give us both static and dynamic invocations. The CORBA 2.0 merger of DCE and IIOP falls into the same category—it gives us two complementary technologies for ORBs. So let's make the best out of this situation and move on to the more important stuff—like business objects. ❑

Chapter 5

CORBA Metadata: IDL and Interface Repository

Metadata is self-descriptive information that can describe both services and information. With metadata, new services can be added to a system and discovered at run time.

— *Tom Mowbray et al., Authors*
The Essential CORBA
(Wiley, 1995)

Metadata is the ingredient that lets us create agile client/server systems. An agile system is self-describing, dynamic, and reconfigurable. The system helps components discover each other at run time; it provides information that lets them interoperate. An agile system lets you write client software without hardcoding all calls to particular servers. Finally, it provides metadata information that application tools can use to create and manage components.

An agile system differentiates itself from a traditional client/server system by its pervasive use of *metadata* to consistently describe all available services, components, and data. Metadata allows independently developed components to dynamically discover each other's existence and to collaborate. The pervasive dissemination of metadata is a key ingredient in a distributed component infrastructure. Without it, you have a hardcoded client/server system with no flexibility.

CORBA is such an agile system. To be CORBA-compliant, any component you write must be self-describing. Every system-level object or service that lives on a CORBA bus must also be self-describing. Even the CORBA bus itself is self-describing. As a result, CORBA is a totally self-describing system. The CORBA metadata language is the *Interface Definition Language (IDL)*. The CORBA metadata repository is the *Interface Repository*. It's nothing more than a run-time database that contains the interface specifications of each object an ORB knows about. Think of the Interface Repository as a queryable and updatable run-time database that contains IDL-generated information.

The IDL precompiler and the Interface Repository are basic ORB services that are shipped with every CORBA-compliant ORB. The pervasive use of IDL and the Interface Repository makes CORBA more self-describing than any other form of client/server middleware. This chapter covers the CORBA IDL and the Interface Repository. We also cover in detail the new services CORBA 2.0 defines to make the Interface Repository metadata available across multivendor ORBs.

THE CORBA IDL: A CLOSER LOOK

Separating interfaces and implementations is critical for general interoperability across programming languages, object versions, executables, dynamic libraries, address spaces, and platforms.

— Richard Adler, Coordinated Computing
(March, 1995)

As we said in Chapter 3, the IDL is a contractual language that lets you specify a component's boundaries and its interfaces with potential clients. The CORBA IDL is language neutral and totally declarative. This means it does not define the implementation details. The IDL provides operating system and programming language independent interfaces to all services and components that reside on a CORBA bus.

What Does an IDL Contract Cover?

An IDL contract includes a description of any resource or service a server compo- nent wants to expose to its clients. Server components must support two kinds of clients: 1) run-time clients that invoke their services; and 2) developers who use IDL to extend an existing component's functions by subclassing. In both cases, IDL is required to specify the component's interfaces so that the implementation can be treated as a black box (or binary code).

You can use CORBA IDL to specify a component's attributes (or public variables), the parent classes it inherits from, the exceptions it raises, typed events, pragmas for generating globally unique identifiers for the interfaces, and the methods an interface supports—including the input and output parameters and their data types. The IDL grammar is a subset of C++ with additional keywords to support distrib- uted concepts; it also fully supports standard C++ preprocessing features.

The IDL is a descriptive language; it supports C++ syntax for constant, type, and operation declarations. However, IDL does not include any procedural structures or variables. Note that because it separates implementation from specification, IDL is a good notational tool for software architects. Most notational languages only provide descriptions of interfaces. In contrast, CORBA IDL provides a direct path between a software architecture—defined by its interfaces—and the compiled code that implements it. From IDL descriptions, a precompiler can directly generate client header files and server implementation skeletons. IDL also provides a great way to encapsulate low-level APIs and legacy software. Client/server architects will find CORBA IDL to be a very useful and versatile tool.

The Structure of the CORBA IDL

The Interface Repository contains metadata that is identical to the components you describe in IDL. In fact, the Interface Repository is simply an active database that contains compiled versions of the metadata information captured via IDL. So, before we jump into the structure of the Interface Repository, let's take a quick look at what's inside a CORBA IDL file (see Figure 5-1). Warning: This section contains some messy technical jargon. We provide an example in the next section that should make it all perfectly clear. So bear with us.

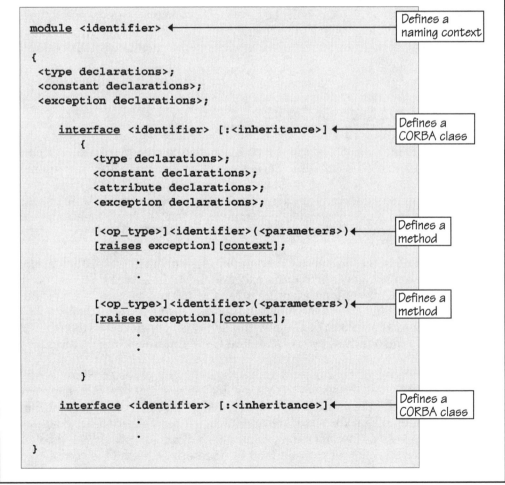

Figure 5-1. The Structure of a CORBA IDL File.

Figure 5-1 shows the main elements that constitute the CORBA IDL. Let's go over the pieces:

- **Modules** provide a namespace to group a set of class descriptions (or *interfaces* in OMG terminology). A module is identified by the keyword *module*. A module has a *scoped* name that consists of one or more *identifiers*. This means simple name strings. The identifiers are separated by the characters "::". So the main purpose of a module is to introduce an additional level of hierarchy in the IDL namespace.

- **Interfaces** define a set of methods (or *operations* in OMG terminology) that a client can invoke on an object. Think of it as a class definition, but without the implementation section. An interface can declare one or more *exceptions*, which indicate that an operation did not perform successfully. An interface may have *attributes*. These are values for which the implementation automatically creates *get* and *set* operations. You can declare an attribute read-only, in which case the implementation only provides the *get* function. An interface can be derived from one or more interfaces, which means IDL supports multiple inheritance. You define inheritance relationships using a syntax that's similar to C++'s.

- **Operations** is the CORBA-equivalent of a method. It denotes a service that clients can invoke. The IDL defines the operation's *signature*, which means the method's parameters and the results it returns. A parameter has a *mode* that indicates whether the value is passed from client to server (*in*), from server to client (*out*), or both (*inout*). The parameter also has a *type* that constrains its possible values. The *op_type* is the type of the return value. The method signature optionally defines the exceptions that a method *raises* when it detects an error. An optional *context* expression contains a set of attribute values that describe a client's context. It lets a client pass information to a server that describes its local environment.

- **Data types** are used to describe the accepted values of CORBA parameters, attributes, exceptions, and return values. These data types are named CORBA objects that are used across multiple languages, operating systems, and ORBs. CORBA supports two categories of types: *basic* and *constructed*. CORBA's basic types include short, long, unsigned long, unsigned short, float, double, char, boolean, and octet. CORBA's constructed types include enum, string, struct, array, union, sequence, and any. The *struct* type is similar to a C++ structure; it lets you create any complex data type using *typedefs* (meaning type definitions). The *sequence* type lets you pass a variable-size array of objects (you must still specify a maximum number of items that can be placed in a sequence). The *any* type is very useful in dynamic situations because it can represent any possible IDL data type—basic or constructed. This means you can use any to pass any type of information. Each CORBA IDL data type is mapped to a native data type via the appropriate language bindings.

The CORBA IDL is very complete and concise. The entire language is described in 36 pages.[1] This includes the definition of the IDL grammar and all the CORBA data types.

An IDL Example

Was that too much material to digest in one reading? The answer is probably yes. So let's see if we can help make it "perfectly clear" with a quick example. Let's create some IDL to describe the interfaces in Figure 5-2. In the figure, we define two new CORBA interfaces—**Dog** and **Cat**—in a module called *MyAnimals*. Figure 5-3 shows the IDL file that creates these two interfaces (or classes).

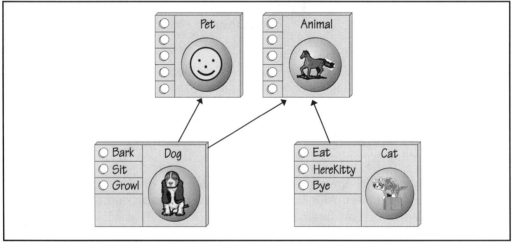

Figure 5-2. MyAnimals With Two Interfaces: Dog and Cat.

The MyAnimals IDL module listed in Figure 5-3 defines two interfaces: **Dog** and **Cat**. **Dog** is derived from the parent classes **Pet** and **Animal**. **Dog** has an attribute called *age* for which the implementation automatically provides *get* and *set* methods. **Dog** supports three methods (or operations): *Bark*, *Sit*, and *Growl*. It *raises* an exception when the dog is not in the mood to obey the master. **Cat** is derived from **Animal** and supports the methods: *Eat*, *HereKitty*, and *Bye* (of course, cats are also pets but we don't show it in the class hierarchy).

---

[1] See **CORBA: Architecture and Specification** (OMG, 1995). The CORBA references are listed in the back of this Survival Guide.

```
module MyAnimals
{
    /* Class Definition of Dog */
    interface Dog:Pet, Animal
    {
        attribute integer age;
        exception NotInterested {string explanation};

        void Bark(in short how_long)
            raises (NotInterested);

        void Sit(in string  where)
            raises (NotInterested);

        void Growl(in string  at_whom)
            raises (NotInterested);
    }

    /* Class Definition of Cat */
    interface Cat: Animal
    {
        void Eat();
        void HereKitty();
        void Bye();
    }
} /* End MyAnimals */
```

Figure 5-3. IDL Module MyAnimals With Two Interfaces: Dog and Cat.

Type Codes: CORBA's Self-Describing Data

CORBA defines *type codes* that represent each of the IDL-defined data types. You use these type codes to create self-describing data that can be passed across operating systems, ORBs, and Interface Repositories. Each type code has a globally unique Repository ID. Type codes are used in any CORBA situation that requires self-describing data. For example, they are used:

■ *By Dynamic Invocation Interfaces* to indicate the data types of the various arguments.

■ *By Inter-ORB Protocols*—including IIOP and DCE/ESIOP—to specify the data types of arguments within messages that get passed across ORBs and operating systems. So it serves as a canonical data representation.

■ *By Interface Repositories* to create ORB-neutral IDL descriptions.

■ *By the any data type* to provide a self-describing generic parameter.

The CORBA **TypeCode** interface defines a set of methods that let you operate on type codes, compare them, and obtain their descriptions (see Figure 5-4). For example, you can invoke a *content_type* operation on an array or sequence to obtain the element type they contain. Note that many of the operations are data type specific. For example, you can only invoke the member operations on structures, unions, and enumerated data types.

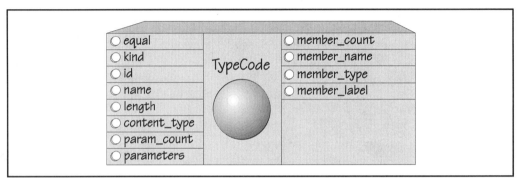

Figure 5-4. The CORBA TypeCode Interface.

THE CORBA 2.0 INTERFACE REPOSITORY

CORBA 2.0 greatly enhances the functions of the CORBA 1.1 Interface Repository and broadens its inter-ORB scope. It is now possible to create federations of Interface Repositories that operate across ORBs while maintaining the autonomy of local administrators. CORBA 2.0 introduces two new features that make this possible: 1) A set of new methods for *incrementally* updating the contents of an Interface Repository at run time, and 2) Globally unique *Repository IDs* that can be used in a distributed namespace. The good news for CORBA 1.1 programmers is that the interfaces for reading the contents of an Interface Repository are backward compatible. This section covers the Interface Repository in some detail. If it gets too detailed, just go into fast-forward mode to the next section.

What's an Interface Repository?

A CORBA 2.0 *Interface Repository* is an on-line database of object definitions. These definitions may be captured directly from an IDL-compiler or through the new CORBA Interface Repository write functions—CORBA doesn't care how the information gets there. The CORBA specification, however, does detail how the information is organized and retrieved from the repository. It does this creatively by specifying a set of classes whose instances represent the information that's in the repository. The class hierarchy mirrors the IDL specification. The result is a highly flexible object database that keeps track of collections of objects organized along the same lines as the IDL. Of course, all the objects in the repository are compiled versions of the information that's in an IDL source file.

Why Is an Interface Repository Needed Anyway?

An ORB needs to understand the definition of the objects it is working with. One way to get these definitions is by incorporating the information into the stub routines we introduced in the last chapter. The other way to get this information is through a dynamically accessible Interface Repository. What does an ORB do with the information in the repository? It can use the object definitions to do the following:

- *Provide type-checking of method signatures*. The parameter types are checked regardless of whether the request is issued using dynamic APIs or through a stub. Signatures define the parameters of a method and their type.

- *Help connect ORBs together*. A multi-ORB "federation" of Interface Repositories is used to translate objects that go across heterogeneous ORBs. Note that you must use the same Repository ID to describe these objects. The interfaces of these intergalactic objects must be defined in all ORB repositories.

- *Provide metadata information to clients and tools*. Clients use the Interface Repository to create "on the fly" method invocations. Tools—such as class browsers, application generators, and compilers—can use the information to obtain inheritance structures and class definitions at run time.

- *Provide self-describing objects*. You can invoke the *get_interface* method on any CORBA object to obtain its interface information (after that information is installed in the Interface Repository).

Interface Repositories can be maintained locally or managed as departmental or enterprise resources. They serve as valuable sources of metadata information on class structures and component interfaces. An ORB may have access to multiple Interface Repositories.

Interface Repository Classes: The Containment Hierarchy

The Interface Repository is implemented as a set of objects that represent the information in it. These objects must be persistent, which means they must be stored on a nonvolatile medium. CORBA groups the metadata into modules that represent naming spaces. The repository object names are unique within a module. CORBA defines an interface for each of its eight IDL structures:

- *ModuleDef* defines a logical grouping of interfaces. Like an IDL file, the Interface Repository uses modules to group interfaces and to navigate through groups by name. So you can think of a module as providing a namespace.

- *InterfaceDef* defines the object's interface; it contains lists of constants, type-defs, exceptions, and interface definitions.

- *OperationDef* defines a method on an object's interface; it contains lists of parameters and exceptions raised by this operation.

- *ParameterDef* defines an argument of a method.

- *AttributeDef* defines the attributes of an interface.

- *ConstantDef* defines a named constant.

- *ExceptionDef* defines the exceptions that can be raised by an operation.

- *TypeDef* defines the named types that are part of an IDL definition.

In addition to these eight interfaces that represent IDL structures, CORBA specifies a **Repository** interface that serves as the root for all the modules contained in a repository namespace. Each Interface Repository is represented by a global root repository object. Figure 5-5 shows the containment hierarchy for objects that belong to these interfaces (or classes). You'll notice that some of the objects—for example, instances of the **Repository** class—contain other objects. Some objects—for example, instances of the **ModuleDef** class—are both contained and containers. Finally, some objects—for example, instances of the **ExceptionDef** class—are always contained in other objects but don't contain objects of their own.

The Interface Repository Class Hierarchy

The CORBA Interface Repository architects noticed these containment hierarchies and defined three abstract superclasses—or classes that cannot be instantiated—called **IRObject**, **Contained**, and **Container** (see Figure 5-6). Notice that this figure shows an inheritance hierarchy as opposed to a containment hierarchy. All Interface Repository objects inherit from the **IRObject** interface, which is new to CORBA 2.0. This interface provides an attribute operation for identifying the actual type of an object as well as a *destroy* method. Objects that are containers inherit

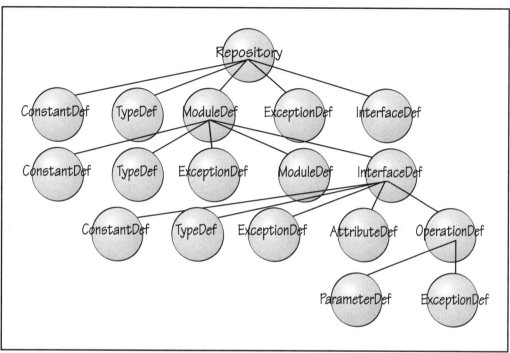

Figure 5-5. The Containment Hierarchy for the Interface Repository Classes.

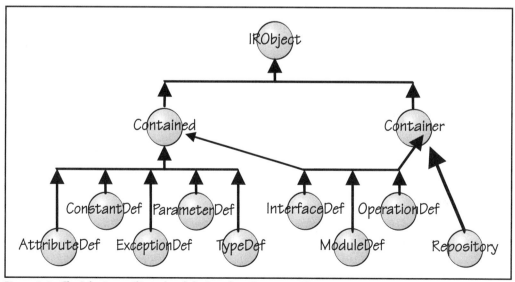

Figure 5-6. The Inheritance Hierarchy of the Interface Repository Classes.

navigation operations from the **Container** interface. The **Contained** interface defines the behavior of objects that are contained in other objects. All the repository classes are derived from **Container**, from **Contained**, or from both through multiple inheritance. This clever scheme allows the repository objects to behave according to their containment relationships (also see the next Details box).

The Interface Repository: A Closer Look

Details

Figure 5-7 shows a class hierarchy of the more important Interface Repository classes (and their interfaces). The rest of the classes simply inherit from these interfaces; they are not shown here. The Interface Repository classes provide operations which let you read, write, and destroy metadata that's stored in a repository. The *destroy* operation deletes an object from the repository; if you apply this operation on a container object, it will destroy all its contents. The **Contained** interface provides a *move* operation to remove an object from its current container and add it to a target container. The write, destroy, and move operations are new to CORBA 2.0.

You access Interface Repository metadata by invoking methods polymorphically on different object types. Because of this clever design, you can navigate and extract information from repository objects with only nine methods (see Figure 5-7). Five of these methods are derived from the ancestor classes **Container** and **Contained**. The other four methods are specific to the **InterfaceDef** and **Repository** interfaces. Here's a description of the read and navigation methods:

■ *Describe*—when you invoke this method on a target **Contained** object, it returns a Description structure containing the IDL information that "describes" the object.

■ *Lookup*—when you invoke this method on **Container** objects, it returns a sequence of pointers to the objects it contains.

■ *Lookup_name*—you invoke this method on a **Container** object to locate an object by name.

■ *Contents*—when you invoke this method on **Container** objects, it returns the list of objects directly contained or inherited by this object. You use this method to navigate through a hierarchy of objects. For example, you can start with a **Repository** object and list all the objects it contains, and so on.

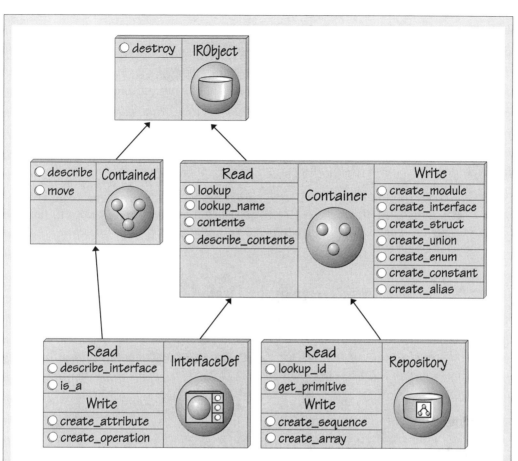

Figure 5-7. Interface Repository: The Top-Level Class Hierarchy and Interfaces.

■ *Describe_contents*—when you invoke this method on a **Container** object, it returns a sequence of pointers to the content descriptions of the objects it contains. This method combines the *contents* and *describe* operations. You can limit the scope of the search by excluding inherited objects or by looking for a specific type of object (for example, of type InterfaceDef).

■ *Describe_interface*—when you invoke this method on an **InterfaceDef** object, it returns a structure that fully describes the interface—including its name, Repository ID, version number, operations, attributes, and all the parent interfaces.

■ *Is_a*—when you invoke this method on an **InterfaceDef** object, it returns TRUE if the interface is identical to or inherits directly from an interface that you specify in an input parameter.

■ *Lookup_id*—you invoke this method on a **Repository** object to look up an object in a repository given its Repository ID.

■ *Get_primitive*—you invoke this method on a **Repository** object to obtain a reference on a primitive object. This means an immutable object type that is owned by the repository. Examples of primitive objects include object references, principals, base data types, and type codes.

Together, these method calls allow you to navigate through an Interface Repository. You can search through the namespaces of specific modules to look for objects that meet your search criteria. When you find an object, you use the *describe* method to retrieve the IDL information that defines it. Also, remember that **IRObject**, **Container,** and **Contained** are abstract classes, which means that you never deal with them directly. Instead, you invoke methods on Interface Repository objects that inherit their behavior from these abstract base classes.

How Do You Find an Interface in the First Place?

You can locate an object's interface in one of three ways:

1. ***By directly calling the ORB's Object::get_interface method.*** You can issue this call against any valid object reference. The call will return an **InterfaceDef** object that fully describes the object's interface. This method is useful when you encounter an object whose type you do not know at compile time.

2. ***By navigating through the module namespace using a sequence of names.*** For example, if you know the name of the interface you're after, you can start by looking for it in the root module of the repository. When you find the entry, invoke the method *InterfaceDef::describe_interface* to obtain the metadata that describes that interface.

3. ***By locating the InterfaceDef object that corresponds to a particular Repository ID.*** You do this by invoking the method *Repository::lookup_id*.

Once you obtain an **InterfaceDef** object, you can invoke its interfaces to obtain the metadata you need. You can then use this metadata to dynamically invoke methods on that object. ❑

Federated Interface Repositories

With the new CORBA 2.0 enhancements, we can now create intergalactic federations of Interface Repositories that operate across multiple ORBs. To avoid name collisions, these repositories assign unique IDs—called *Repository IDs*—to global interfaces and operations. You can use these Repository IDs to replicate copies of the metadata across multiple repositories and still maintain a coherent view across them. This means that the unique identity of an interface is preserved across ORB and repository boundaries. For example, with a global Repository ID, you can obtain some metadata on an interface from a local repository. You can then obtain additional metadata on that *same* interface from a remote repository.

To ensure that IDL definitions in various repositories do not contain any duplicates, CORBA 2.0 defines the following naming conventions:

■ *Scoped names* uniquely identify modules, interfaces, constants, typedefs, exceptions, attributes, operations, and parameters within an Interface Repository. A scoped name is made up of one or more identifiers separated by the characters "::".

■ *Repository IDs* globally identify modules, interfaces, constants, typedefs, exceptions, attributes, operations, and parameters. They are used to synchronize definitions across ORBs and Repositories.

The next section describes the mechanisms for creating these global Repository IDs.

What Does a Global Repository ID Look Like?

The *Repository ID* itself is a string consisting of a three level name hierarchy. CORBA 2.0 defines two formats for specifying global Repository IDs:

■ *Using IDL names with unique prefixes*. You create a Repository ID using an IDL name that consists of three components separated by colons ":". The first component is the string "IDL". The second component is a list of identifiers separated by "/" characters. The first identifier is a unique prefix, and the rest are the IDL identifiers that make up a scoped name. The third component consists of major and minor versions in decimal format separated by a period. For example, a valid Repository ID for the interface **Cat** in the module MyAnimals is "*IDL:DogCatInc/MyAnimals/Cat/:1.0*". In this case, *DogCatInc* is a unique prefix that denotes an organization. You can also use an Internet ID for a prefix (or any other unique name).

■ *Using DCE Universal Unique Identifiers (UUIDs)*. DCE provides a UUID generator that calculates a globally unique number using the current date and time, a network card ID, and a high-frequency counter. There's almost no chance for this algorithm to create duplicate UUIDs. The DCE format for the Repository

ID also consists of three components separated by colons ":". The first component is the string "DCE". The second component is a printable UUID. The third component is made up of a version number in decimal format. Note that there is no minor version. For example, a DCE Repository ID could look like, *"DCE:700dc500-0111-22ce-aa9f:1"*.

You can associate Repository IDs with IDL definitions in a variety of ways. For example, an installation tool might generate them for you. Or an IDL precompiler can generate them based on pragma directives that you embed in the IDL (see next Details box).

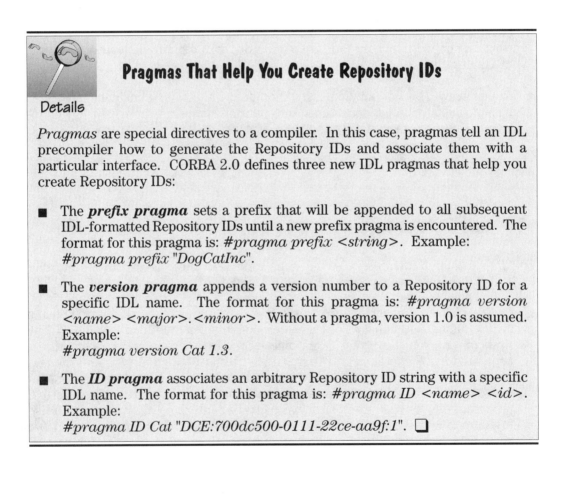

Pragmas That Help You Create Repository IDs

Details

Pragmas are special directives to a compiler. In this case, pragmas tell an IDL precompiler how to generate the Repository IDs and associate them with a particular interface. CORBA 2.0 defines three new IDL pragmas that help you create Repository IDs:

- The **prefix pragma** sets a prefix that will be appended to all subsequent IDL-formatted Repository IDs until a new prefix pragma is encountered. The format for this pragma is: *#pragma prefix <string>*. Example: *#pragma prefix "DogCatInc"*.

- The **version pragma** appends a version number to a Repository ID for a specific IDL name. The format for this pragma is: *#pragma version <name> <major>.<minor>*. Without a pragma, version 1.0 is assumed. Example: *#pragma version Cat 1.3*.

- The **ID pragma** associates an arbitrary Repository ID string with a specific IDL name. The format for this pragma is: *#pragma ID <name> <id>*. Example: *#pragma ID Cat "DCE:700dc500-0111-22ce-aa9f:1"*. ❑

Conclusion

A CORBA ORB comes with standard mechanisms for generating and managing metadata. You generate metadata that describe your components and their interfaces using IDL. The ORB's IDL precompiler automatically writes your IDL-defined metadata in an Interface Repository. From then on, you can update that metadata using the new Interface Repository write and update operations. Clients can query the Interface Repository; they can discover what interfaces are available and how to call them. You can use the same Interface Repository to store the description of components—ranging from very fine-grained system objects to business objects. It's all very regular. With CORBA 2.0, we have a solid specification for creating federated Interface Repositories that can operate across heterogeneous ORBs and operating systems.

We apologize for the heavy dose of technical material that you may have encountered in this chapter. But we felt it was important to give you this information. We wanted you to be aware of what the combination of IDL and Interface Repository can do for your client/server systems. There's some powerful stuff here. Now for the good news: This is the final chapter in which we cover the CORBA ORB. It's time to move on to bigger and better things. The CORBA object services are our next stop. Of course, these services live on the object bus and complement it. So you may still catch a glimpse of the CORBA bus every now and then.

Chapter 6

CORBA Services:
Naming,
Events, and
Life Cycle

Large lump development hinges on a view of the environment which is static and discontinuous; piecemeal growth hinges on a view of the environment which is dynamic and continuous.

— **Christopher Alexander et al., Authors**
The Oregon Experiment
(Oxford, 1975)

An ORB by itself does not have all it takes for objects to interoperate at the system level. The ORB is like a telephone exchange—it provides the basic mechanism for brokering object requests. All other services are provided by objects with IDL interfaces that reside on top of the ORB. The IDL and ORB provide the function of a "software bus"; the CORBA object services plug into this bus and augment it. The end-user object components make use of both the bus and its services.

CORBA's object services are designed to be mixed and matched. We'll do a bit of mix-and-matching ourselves in the way we present these services. Instead of grouping them by chronological order—for example, COSS1, COSS2, and so on—we group them by function. This chapter introduces the four most basic services

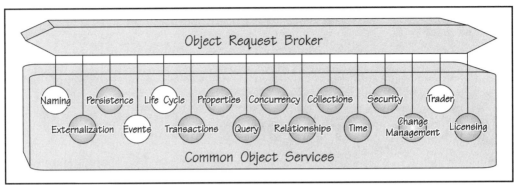

Figure 6-1. CORBA Object Services: Naming, Trader, Life Cycle, and Events.

you need to simply operate within an ORB environment: Naming, Trader, Life Cycle, and Events (the light services in Figure 6-1).

Why are these services basic? When objects first get started, they need to find other objects on the ORB. The CORBA *Naming Service* is like the telephone white pages for objects; it lets you find objects by name. The *Trader Service* (soon to be defined) is like the telephone yellow pages; it advertises object services and helps you find them. The *Life Cycle Service* deals with key existential issues—including life, death, and relocation; it lets you create objects, move them around, and destroy them. The *Event Service* provides asynchronous interactions between anonymous objects; you get notified when significant things happen on the ORB.

THE CORBA OBJECT NAMING SERVICE

The *Object Naming Service* is the principal mechanism for objects on an ORB to locate other objects. Names are humanly recognizable values that identify an object. The naming service maps these human names to object references. A name-to-object association is called a *name binding*. A *naming context* is a namespace in which the object's name is unique. Every object has a unique reference ID. You can optionally associate one or more names with an object reference. You always define a name relative to its naming context.

The Object Naming Service was originated by 15 companies that go under the name of JOSS, which stands for Joint Object Services Submission. It became an OMG standard in September 1993. The Naming Service does not try to reinvent the wheel. It was designed to transparently encapsulate existing name and directory services such as the DCE CDS, ISO X.500, or Sun NIS+.

The service lets you create naming hierarchies. Clients can navigate through different naming context trees in search of the object they want. Name contexts from different domains can be used together to create federated naming services for objects. A CORBA naming hierarchy does not require a "universal" root.

The Naming Service has no dependencies on other CORBA object services. But if your clients need to perform complex searches, you can register naming characteristics for your object with the *Properties Service*. Clients can then use the *Query Service* to look for object names with certain externally visible characteristics—for example, objects whose *time_last_modified* date is greater than 1/1/96.

What's in a CORBA Object Name?

You can reference a CORBA object using a sequence of names that form a hierarchical naming tree (see Figure 6-2). In the figure, each dark node is a naming context. An object's name consists of a sequence of names (or components) that form a *compound name*. Each component—except for the last one—is used to name a context. The last component is the object's *simple* name.

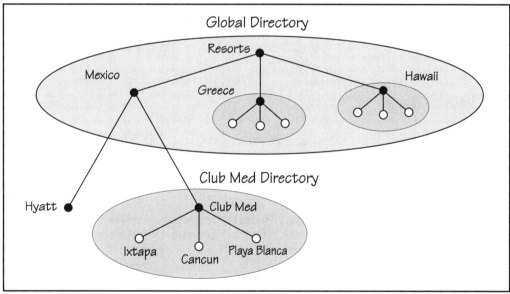

Figure 6-2. CORBA Objects Support Hierarchical Naming.

In Figure 6-3 we show a compound name that consists of a simple name—*Playa Blanca*—and three context names: *Club Med*, *Mexico*, and *Resorts*. The compound name defines a path for resolving context names until you get to the simple name. You can start from any context and use a sequence of names to resolve an object. To *resolve* a name means to find the object associated with the name in a given context. To *bind* a name is to create a name-to-object association for a particular context.

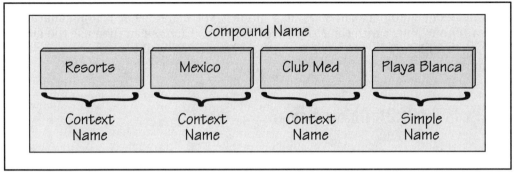

Figure 6-3. A Compound Name.

Each named component is a structure with two attributes: 1) *identifier* is the object's name string; 2) *kind* is a string in which you can put a descriptive attribute for your name—for example, a file type. The service designers prefer that you do not encode meanings directly into names. Instead, they want you to use the *kind* attribute to qualify names. The Naming Service does not interpret, assign, or manage these attributes in any way. They are used by higher levels of software.

How Does It Work?

Figure 6-4 shows the two interfaces **NamingContext** and **BindingIterator** that implement the Naming Service. Objects of **NamingContext** class contain a set of name-to-object bindings in which each name is unique. These objects may also be bound to names in other naming context objects to be part of a name hierarchy.

You invoke the *bind* method in the **NamingContext** interface to associate an object's name with a binding context. This is how you create a naming hierarchy. You invoke *unbind* to remove a name from a binding context. The *new_context* method returns the naming context. *Bind_new_context* creates a new context and binds it to a name you supply. The *destroy* method lets you delete a naming context.

You can find any named object using the *resolve* method; it retrieves an object bound to a name in a given context. The *list* method lets you iterate through a returned set of names (it returns a **BindingIterator** object). You iterate by invoking *next_one* and *next_n* on the returned **BindingIterator** object. You invoke *destroy* to free the iteration object.

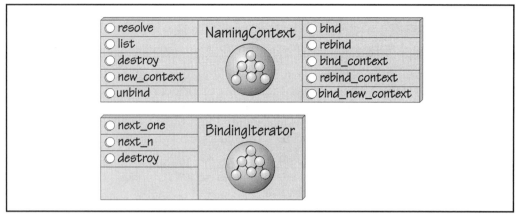

Figure 6-4. The Object Naming Service Interfaces.

In summary, the Object Naming Service defines interfaces that let you manage namespaces for objects, and query and navigate through them. The objects that provide these interfaces live on the ORB and can be implemented by encapsulating existing procedural naming services with CORBA wrappers. CORBA simply defines the interfaces to these services, not the implementation.

THE CORBA OBJECT TRADER SERVICE

When it is completed, the *Object Trader Service* will provide "matchmaking" services for objects. This service is part of *RFP5*. Consequently, we do not expect a final standard until mid-1996. This section is based on the description of the service that went out with the RFP5 bid. According to RFP5, a new service provider will first register its service with the trader. Then it will give it all the relevant information, including:

■ *An object reference.* This is the reference clients use to connect to the advertised service and invoke its operations.

■ *A description of the type of service offered.* This includes information on the names of the operations (or methods) to which the service will respond along with their parameters and result types. It also includes distinguishing attributes of the service and the trading context.

The trader object stores this information persistently. Clients can get in touch with the trader to find out what services are listed or to ask for a service by type—it's like the telephone yellow pages. The trader will find the best match for the client based on the context of the requested service and the offers of the providers. A matching service will have a type that matches the client's request. It can also have attributes; a client can specify search criteria for a service based on these attributes.

Traders from different domains can create federations. This lets systems in different domains advertise their services in a pool while maintaining control of their own policies and services. These loose federation of traders will provide electronic bazaars. We can't wait to see what type of commissions they're going to extract from us for their brokerage services. We just wanted you to know what's coming down the CORBA pipe. We have no interfaces to share with you as we go to press.

THE CORBA OBJECT LIFE CYCLE SERVICE

The *Object Life Cycle Service* provides operations for creating, copying, moving, and deleting objects. The Life Cycle Service was recently expanded so that all these operations can now handle associations between groups of related objects. This includes containment and reference relationships, as well as the enforcement of referential integrity constraints between objects. In accordance with CORBA's use of the Bauhaus principle (keep the services simple and single focused), you define these relationships using the *Relationship Service*. To be more precise, the Life Cycle Service provides interfaces that are derived from the Relationship Service.

A Compound Life Cycle Example

Let's walk through an example of how the life cycle operations are implemented on an object that has explicit associations with other objects. Figure 6-5 shows a document object that contains one or more page objects, which in turn contain multimedia and text objects. The document is stored in a folder object and *references* a catalog object that contains an entry for it. The Life Cycle Service maintains a graph of all these associations.

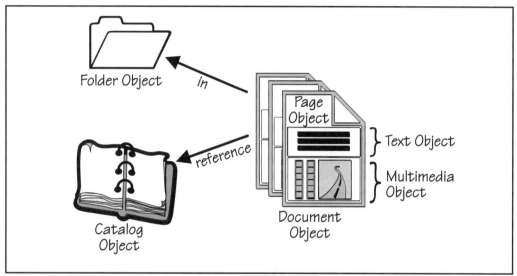

Figure 6-5. Object Life Cycle Services Must Handle Associated Objects.

A "deep move" causes the document to be moved with all its dependent objects (the pages and their contents); the reference in the catalog is updated; and the document gets removed from the source folder and gets inserted into the target folder (see Figure 6-6). Likewise, when the document is externalized to a file, all the objects it contains go with it. When the document is deleted, its page objects and the graphic objects they contain are also deleted. The references to the document are removed from both the catalog and the folder (see Figure 6-7).

The Life Cycle Interfaces

Clients have a simple view of Life Cycle operations. In the previous example, the clients simply invoke methods to *move* and *copy* the document object; all the associated objects are handled transparently. The Life Cycle Service is able to handle both simple containment and referential relationships.

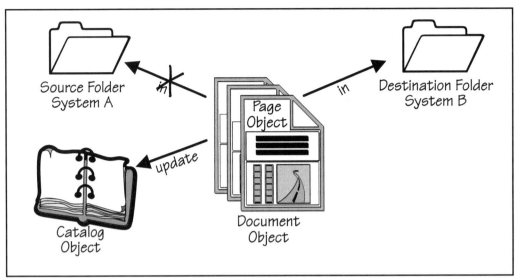

Figure 6-6. A "Deep" Move Handles All the Associations.

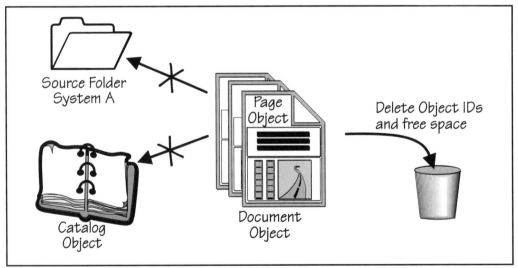

Figure 6-7. Delete Removes Objects and Dependents and Manages References.

To create a new object, a client must find a *factory* object (meaning an object that knows how to instantiate an object of that class), issue a *create* request, and get back an object reference. A client can also create an object by cloning an existing object with a *copy* operation. The factory objects must allocate resources, obtain object references, and register the new objects with the Object Adapter and Implementation Repository. When an object is copied across machines, the factory object on the target node is involved.

Figure 6-8 shows the three interfaces that provide the basic Life Cycle Service (more interfaces were recently added to support Compound Life Cycle and are described in the next section). The **LifeCycleObject** interface defines the *copy, move,* and *remove* operations; it provides the client's primary view of Life Cycle operations on target objects. The *copy* operation makes a copy of the object and returns an object reference; the *move* operation allows the object to roam to any location within the scope of the factory finder; and the *remove* operation deletes the object. The **FactoryFinder** defines an interface for finding factories. Because every object requires different resource information for its creation, it's impossible to define a single factory interface for all objects. The **GenericFactory** simply defines a general *create_object* operation.

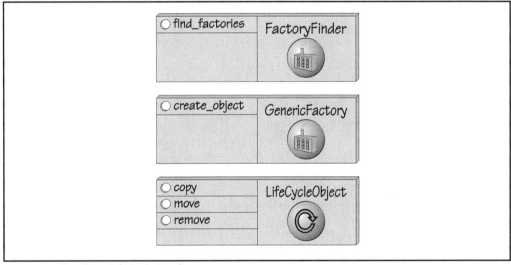

Figure 6-8. The Object Life Cycle Interfaces.

The Compound Life Cycle Interfaces

The Compound Life Cycle interfaces are a recent addendum to the Life Cycle Service. The addendum provides new interfaces that support deep copies, moves, and deletes (see Figure 6-9). The addendum adds a new factory interface called **OperationsFactory**, which creates objects of the class **Operations**. Notice that the **Operations** interface supports the same *copy, move,* and *remove* methods; it also adds a new method *destroy*.

The three classes **Node**, **Role**, and **Relationship** are derived from corresponding classes in the Relationship Service. They let you define relationships between objects that know nothing of each other. To define a relationship, you must associate a role with an object and then create relationships between these roles.

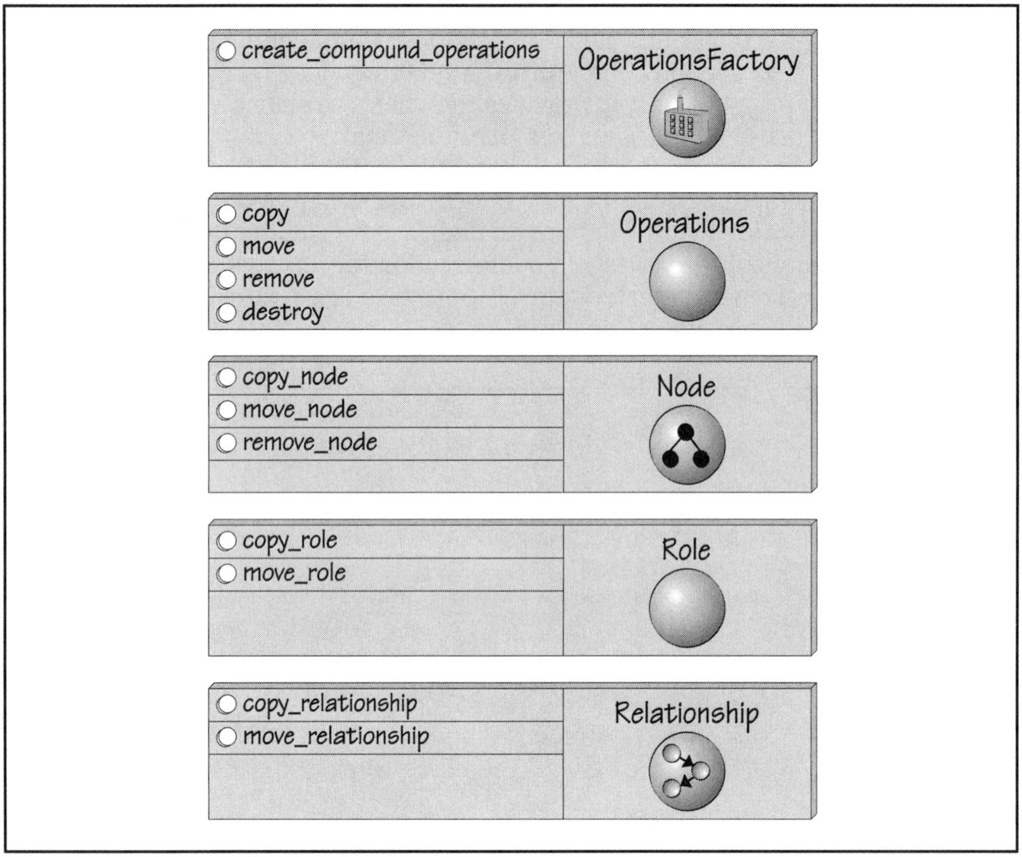

create_compound_operations	OperationsFactory

copy	Operations
move	
remove	
destroy	

copy_node	Node
move_node	
remove_node	

| copy_role | Role |
| move_role | |

| copy_relationship | Relationship |
| move_relationship | |

Figure 6-9. The Compound Life Cycle Interfaces.

Complex relationships can be expressed using graphs that keep track of nodes that form the relationship's web. What this all means is that when you invoke an operation—such as *copy, move, remove,* or *destroy*—you're performing it on group of related objects instead of a single object. You define the group using the Relationship classes. We explain these classes in more detail in Chapter 10, "CORBA Services: Query, Relations, and Externalization."

You should note that clients of the Life Cycle Service typically interact with the **LifeCycle** object we described in the previous section. If the object participates as a node in a graph of related objects, it will delegate the call to a service that implements the **Operations** interface. The caller must also pass an object reference for a **Node** object to indicate the starting node in a graph of related objects. The delegation mechanism hides most of the compound node complexities from clients. As far as the clients are concerned, they just say copy or move and all the magic occurs under the cover.

THE CORBA EVENT SERVICE

The *Event Service* allows objects to dynamically register or unregister their interest in specific events. An *event* is an occurrence within an object specified to be of interest to one or more objects. A *notification* is a message an object sends to interested parties informing them that a specific event occurred. Normally, the object generating the event doesn't have to know the interested parties. This is all handled by the Event Service, which creates a loosely-coupled communication channel between objects that don't know much about each other. Events are more loosely coupled than RPC but less loosely coupled than Message-Oriented Middleware (MOM).

Suppliers and Consumers of Events

The Event Service decouples the communication between objects. The service defines two roles for objects: *suppliers* and *consumers*. The suppliers produce events; the consumers process them via event handlers. Events are communicated between suppliers and consumers using standard CORBA requests. In addition, there are two models for communicating event data: push and pull. In the *push model*, the supplier of events takes the initiative and initiates the transfer of event data to consumers. In the *pull* model, the consumer takes the initiative and requests event data from a supplier. An *event channel* is an intervening object that is both a supplier and consumer of events. It allows multiple suppliers to communicate with multiple consumers asynchronously and without knowing about each other. An event channel is a standard CORBA object that sits on the ORB and decouples the communications between suppliers and consumers.

The event channel supports both the "push and pull" event notification models (see Figure 6-10):

- With the ***push model***, the supplier issues a *push* method invocation on the event channel object; the event channel, in turn, pushes the event data to the consumer objects. A consumer can stop receiving events by invoking the method *disconnect_push_consumer* on the event channel. The consumer invokes an *add_push_consumer* method on the event channel to register its interest in some event type.

- With the ***pull model***, the consumer issues a *pull* method invocation on the event channel object; the event channel, in turn, pulls the event data from the supplier. Using the *try_pull* method, the consumer can periodically poll for events. A supplier can stop accepting requests for supplying events by invoking a *disconnect_pull_supplier* method on the event channel. The supplier issues an *add_pull_supplier* method on the event channel to register its object reference and offer its services.

An event channel can communicate with a supplier using one style of communication, and it can communicate with a consumer using a different style of communication.

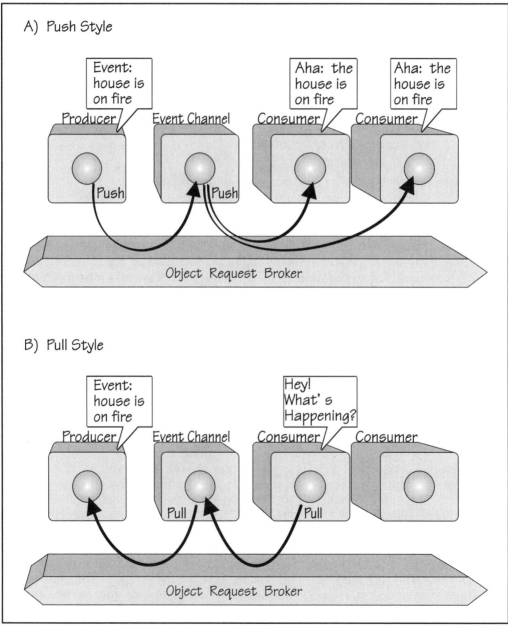

Figure 6-10. The Event Service: Push and Pull Styles.

The Event Channel

The generic event channel object does not understand the contents of the data it's passing. Instead, the producers and consumers agree on common event semantics. However, the Event Services also support a *Typed Event* model that allows applications to describe the contents of events using the IDL. The parameters passed must be input only; no information is returned. Typed events support both the pull and push models. Using the IDL, you can define special event types—for example, document or system management events. Consumers can then subscribe to a particular event type; typing becomes a powerful means of filtering event information. You can track the exact events you're interested in (it's a rifle instead of a shotgun).

The event interface supports multiple levels of service (for example, different levels of reliability). A persistent store of events may be supplied by the event channel object as part of its service (for example, some key events may be stored for up to a week or whatever). The event channels are *well-known* objects. They can serve as anchor points to help objects discover each other at run time. The consumers and suppliers of events use the standard CORBA IDL interfaces—no extensions are required.

In summary, the Event Service introduces a minimalist form of MOM communications into CORBA. It is minimalist because it doesn't support MOM-like message priorities, filters, transaction protection, reception confirmation, time-to-live stamps, or sophisticated queue management.[1] The event channel objects make it easier to develop groupware applications and to help objects discover each other. Event typing allows you to zoom-in on the events of interest. The fan-in and fan-out capabilities of event channel objects can serve as a broadcast or multicast system, which can help create online object bazaars. The Event Service is extremely useful; it provides a foundation for creating a new genre of distributed object applications.

Conclusion

We just concluded our first four CORBA object services—the tally is four down and twelve more to go. As you can see from this chapter, CORBA is defining a very useful set of services. When it's all done, CORBA will be able to recreate every conceivable form of client/server middleware using system-level objects (the CORBA services). Each service is carefully designed to do one thing well; it's as complicated as it needs to be. The services are typically divided into several distinct interfaces that provide different views for different kinds of clients of the service.

---

[1] CORBA is working on adding MOM capabilities to the event service.

For example, the Life Cycle Service exposes a set of interfaces to its regular clients as well as a set of delegation interfaces that service providers can use. More importantly, all the services are designed from the ground up to work together; they all use IDL and the CORBA bus.

Chapter 7

CORBA Services: Transactions and Concurrency

If we could combine the power of objects with the reliability of transactions, we would catapult commercial computing into a new era.

— *John Tibbetts and Barbara Bernstein*

Transactions are essential for building reliable distributed applications. So it should come as no surprise that transactions and distributed objects are getting married. OMG's newly adopted *Object Transaction Service (OTS)* defines IDL interfaces that let multiple distributed objects on multiple ORBs participate in atomic transactions—even in the presence of catastrophic failure. OTS optionally supports nested transactions. The support of nesting and inter-ORB transactions provides an object foundation for dealing with the complex world of multistep consumer-to-business and business-to-business transactions.

The *Concurrency Control Service* allows objects to coordinate their access to shared resources using locks. An object must obtain an appropriate lock from the service before accessing a shared resource. Each lock is associated with a single resource and a single client. The service defines several lock modes that correspond to different categories of access and multiple levels of granularity. This

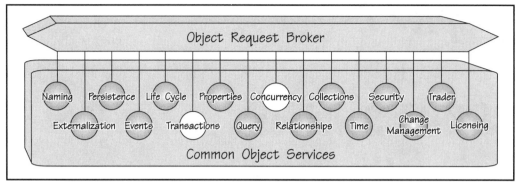

Figure 7-1. CORBA Object Services: Transactions and Concurrency Control.

service complements OTS by letting you obtain and release locks on transactional boundaries. This chapter covers both services (see Figure 7-1).

THE CORBA OBJECT TRANSACTION SERVICE

The *Object Transaction Service (OTS)* is possibly the most important piece of middleware for intergalactic objects. OTS does a superb job of marrying transactions with objects at the ORB level.[1] With OTS, ORBs provide a seamless environment for running mission-critical components. This feature alone gives ORBs a leg up over any competing form of client/server middleware. An ORB becomes the next-generation TP Monitor. In this section, we first go over what makes transactions so important. Then we introduce OTS.

What Is a Transaction?

The idea of distributed systems without transaction management is like a society without contract law. One does not necessarily want the laws, but one does need a way to resolve matters when disputes occur.

— Jim Gray

Transactions are more than just business events: They've become an application design philosophy that guarantees robustness in distributed systems. In an ORB

---

[1] OTS is the result of the work of some of the best technologists in the transaction processing business. The key architects were Pete Homan from Tandem; Ed Cobb, Tony Storey, and Ian Houston from IBM; Graeme Dixon from Transarc; Alan Snyder from SunSoft; Annrai O'Toole from Iona; and Brian Vetter from Tivoli.

environment, a transaction must be managed from its point of origin on the client, across one or more servers, and then back to the originating client. When a transaction ends, all parties involved agree as to whether it succeeded or failed. The transaction is the contract that binds the client to one or more servers. A transaction becomes the fundamental unit of recovery, consistency, and concurrency in a distributed object system. Of course, all participating objects must adhere to the transactional discipline; otherwise, a single faulty object can corrupt an entire system. In an ideal world, all distributed object interactions will be based on transactions.[2]

Transaction models define when a transaction starts, when it ends, and what the appropriate units of recovery are in case of failure. The flat transaction model is the workhorse of the current generation of TP Monitors (and other transactional systems). It is called *flat* because all the work done within a transaction's boundaries is at the same level. The transaction starts with *begin_transaction* and ends with either a *commit_transaction* or *abort_transaction* (see Figure 7-2). It's an all or nothing proposition—there's no way to commit or abort parts of a flat transaction. However, the newer transaction models—for example, *nested transactions*—provide a much finer granularity of control over the different threads that

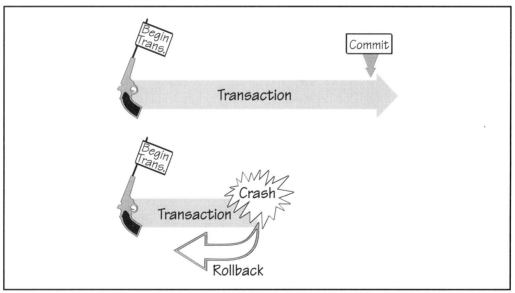

Figure 7-2. The Flat Transaction: An All-Or-Nothing Proposition.

---

[2] If you need more information on transactions, we recommend Jim Gray and Andreas Reuter's **Transaction Processing Concepts and Techniques** (Morgan Kaufmann, 1993). This 1000-page book is the Bible of transaction processing. If you want a lighter introduction, try our **Essential Client/Server Survival Guide** (Wiley, 1994). Our book covers transactions and TP Monitors in less than 100 pages.

constitute a transaction. The newer transaction models are attractive because they have the potential to better mirror their real world counterparts (see next Briefing box).

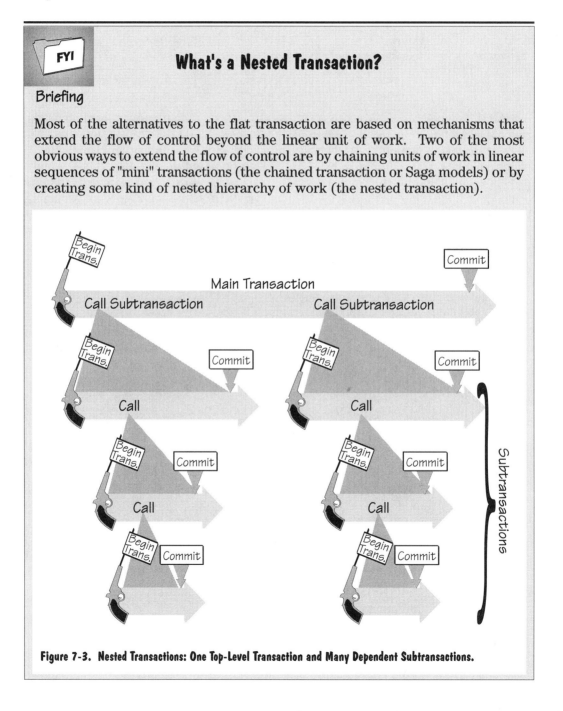

FYI

What's a Nested Transaction?

Briefing

Most of the alternatives to the flat transaction are based on mechanisms that extend the flow of control beyond the linear unit of work. Two of the most obvious ways to extend the flow of control are by chaining units of work in linear sequences of "mini" transactions (the chained transaction or Saga models) or by creating some kind of nested hierarchy of work (the nested transaction).

Figure 7-3. Nested Transactions: One Top-Level Transaction and Many Dependent Subtransactions.

Nested transactions provide the ability to define transactions within other transactions. They do this by breaking a transaction into hierarchies of "subtransactions," very much like a program is made up of procedures. The main transaction starts the subtransactions, which behave as dependent transactions. A subtransaction can also start its own subtransactions, making the entire structure very recursive. A subtransaction's effects become permanent after it issues a local commit and all its ancestors commit. If a parent transaction aborts, all its descendent transactions abort—regardless of whether they issued local commits.

Figure 7-3 shows a main transaction that starts nested transactions, which behave as dependent transactions. Each subtransaction can issue a commit or rollback for its designated pieces of work. When a subtransaction commits, its results are only accessible to the parent that spawned it. The main benefit of nesting is that a failure in a subtransaction can be trapped and retried using an alternative method, still allowing the main transaction to succeed. ❏

Object Transaction Service: Features

CORBA's OTS provides the following features:

■ ***Supports flat and nested transactions***. All OTS implementations must support flat transactions; nested transaction support is optional. In a nested environment, the flat transaction is the top-level transaction.

■ ***Allows both ORB and non-ORB applications to participate in the same transaction***. OTS lets you interoperate object transactions with procedural transactions that adhere to the X/Open DTP standard.

■ ***Supports transactions that span across heterogenous ORBs.*** Objects on multiple ORBs can participate in a single transaction. In addition, a single ORB can support multiple transaction services.

■ ***Supports existing IDL interfaces***. A single interface supports both transactional and non-transactional implementations. To make an object transactional, you use an ordinary interface that inherits from an abstract OTS class. This approach avoids a combination explosion of IDL variants that differ only in their transaction characteristics.

OTS is a well-designed, low-overhead service that should perform at least as well as an X/Open-compliant procedural transaction service.

The Elements of the Object Transaction Service

Figure 7-4 shows the elements of OTS. Objects involved in a transaction can assume one of three roles: *Transactional Clients*, *Transactional Servers*, or *Recoverable Servers*. Let's go over these roles and see what they each do:

■ *A transactional client* issues a set of method invocations that are bracketed by begin/end transaction demarcations. The calls within the bracket may be for both transactional and non-transactional objects. The ORB intercepts the begin call and directs it to the Transaction Service, which establishes a transaction context associated with the client thread. The client then issues method invocations on remote objects. The ORB implicitly tags the transaction context and propagates it in all subsequent communications among the participants in the transaction. The ORB also gets involved when the client issues a commit or rollback and notifies the Transaction Service. The client is oblivious to all this under-the-cover activity; it simply starts a transaction, issues its method invocations, and commits or rolls back the transaction.

■ *A transactional server* is a collection of one or more objects whose behavior is affected by the transaction but have no recoverable states or resources of their own. The ORB implicitly propagates the transaction's context whenever these objects call a recoverable resource. A transactional server does not participate in the completion of the transaction, but it can force the transaction to be rolled back.

■ *A recoverable server* is a collection of one or more objects whose data (or state) is affected by committing or rolling back a transaction. *Recoverable objects* are transactional objects with resources to protect. Examples of recoverable resources are transactional files, queues, or databases. Recoverable objects use *register_resource* method invocations to tell the Transaction Service that a recoverable resource has just joined the transaction whose context was propagated in the client call. In addition, recoverable objects provide methods that are used by a transaction coordinator (the *coordinator* is the transaction service) to orchestrate an ORB-mediated, two-phase commit protocol.

OTS is seamlessly integrated with the ORB mechanisms. It relies on the ORB to automatically propagate the transaction context. Notice that the scope of a transaction is defined by a *transaction context* that is shared by the participant objects. The transaction context is a pseudo-object that's maintained by the ORB for each ORB-aware thread. The context is null when there is no transaction associated with a thread. The transaction service manages and propagates the transaction context with help from the ORB.

OTS provides "IDL-ized" interfaces for the objects that make up the transaction service. So it is possible for clients and transactional objects to get more intimately involved in the details of the transaction propagation via explicit method invocations. However, most transactions will depend on the ORB to transparently do all the work using its built-in facilities. Fewer interventions means better performance.

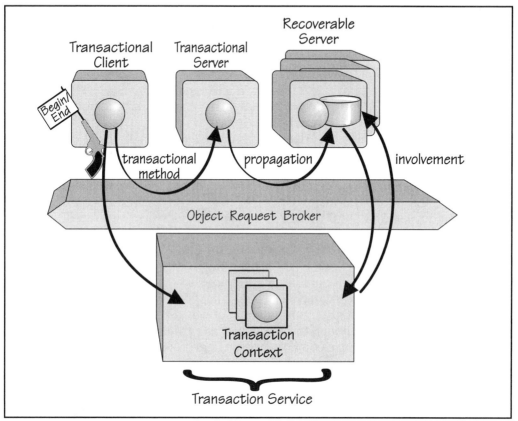

Figure 7-4. Object Transaction Service: Meet the Players.

The OTS Interfaces

Figure 7-5 shows the four key interfaces of OTS; we left out the minor ones. The following is a brief description of what each of these interfaces do:

■ **Current** defines a CORBA pseudo-object that makes it easy for clients to use OTS. Clients invoke *begin* and *commit* to start and end a transaction. The ORB will transparently propagate the context of the pseudo-object to the transaction service and to all participants in the transaction. The context contains an ID that uniquely identifies the transaction; it also contains status information. The client can invoke *rollback* to abort the transaction. It can *suspend* the transaction to stop propagating the context with each message; it can *resume* it when it wants the context to be propagated. *Get_control* returns a **Control** object that you can use to directly interact with the transaction service—a recoverable server typically invokes this method to obtain a reference to its transaction coordinator. A top-level transaction invokes *set_timeout* to define maximum elapsed time (in seconds) for its subtransactions to complete before it aborts them.

Coordinator is implemented by the transaction service. Recoverable objects use it to coordinate their participation in a transaction with the OTS. A server invokes *register_resource* to participate in a transaction. If it supports nested transactions, it instead invokes *register_subtran_aware*. It invokes *create_subtransaction* to create a nested transaction that's a child of the current transaction. It invokes *rollback_only* to abort the entire transaction. The *get_* and *is_* operations are useful to servers that need to explicitly control their participation in a transaction. The *hash_* operations return a handle to the current transaction. Before invoking *register_resource*, servers use the hashed value to quickly find out if the current resource is already registered.

Resource is implemented by a recoverable server object to participate in a *two-phase* commit protocol. OTS uses the two-phase commit protocol to coordinate a transaction's commit or abort across multiple server objects so that they either all fail or all succeed. To do this, OTS centralizes the decision to commit but gives each participant the right of veto. It's like a Christian wedding: You're given one last chance to back out of the transaction when you're at the altar. If none of the parties object, the marriage takes place.

In the first phase of a commit, OTS invokes *prepare* on all the participant resource objects. Each resource object returns in a parameter a "vote" value that is either vote_commit, vote_rollback, or vote_readonly. Based on the vote's outcome (everyone has veto power), the transaction service either issues *commit* or *rollback*. It can also issue a *forget* to a resource object that's fuzzy about its outcome. If the coordinator has only a single registered resource, it avoids the two-phase commit altogether and invokes *commit_one_phase* instead.

SubtransactionAwareResource is implemented by a recoverable server object with nested transaction behavior. Notice that this interface is derived from the **Resource** interface. It adds two new methods *commit_subtransaction* and *rollback_subtransaction*. These methods are invoked when subtransactions complete. Subtransaction aware server objects must first register with the **Coordinator** object by invoking *register_subtran_aware*.

You should also be aware of the existence of a **TransactionalObject** interface. This is an abstract class that defines no operations. What is it good for? It's actually a very

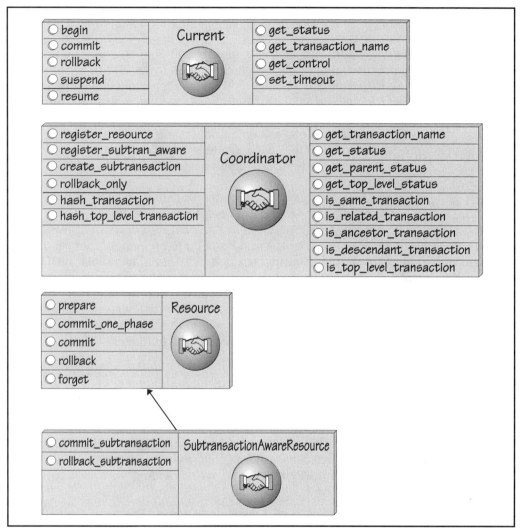

Figure 7-5. Object Transaction Service: The Key Interfaces.

important class. It serves as a marker objects use to indicate that they're transactional. To make your object transactional you simply inherit from the **TransactionalObject** class. The ORB will then propagate the transaction context associated with a client's thread whenever the client invokes any method on your object. Note that the ORB passes this context in a special field (the context field) that is totally transparent as far you're concerned. It's something ORBs do implicitly.

An Object Transaction Scenario

Are you getting overwhelmed with all these interfaces? As you know by now, our tradition in this book is to explain how interfaces are really used with an annotated scenario (too bad we can't animate a book). This next scenario will be fun. It's like going to a movie and seeing us squirm through these interface patterns. You get to sit back, relax, and munch on popcorn. Just look at the figure and the annotated text that comes with it. Then follow the numbers and read the explanations. Warning: We only do scenarios after we introduce a particularly heavy dose of interfaces; you don't get them all the time—they're hard work!

Figure 7-6 shows a scenario of a client doing a debit against one server object and a credit against another one. The example is "get a $100,000 dollars out of Jeri's account in Bank A and put it in your account in Bank B." You don't want this to fail, do you? The objects representing Bank A and Bank B are recoverable server objects that multiply inherit from the **Resource** class and the **TransactionalObject** abstract class (remember, this is the indicator that does nothing). We also show two transaction service objects that are instances of the **Current** and **Coordinator** classes. The client initiates this transaction across the two servers and issues a *commit* when it's done. Hopefully the money will get tucked away safely in your account. Here's the explanation that goes along with the numbers in the picture:

1. ***Client begins transaction.*** The client invokes *begin* on the **Current** pseudo-object. The ORB passes this information to the transaction service that maintains a **Current** object for each active transaction.

2. ***Client makes a debit on Bank A's object.*** The client invokes a *debit* method on an object in Bank A. This object implements the logic of the transaction (something you write) but it also inherits its behavior from the OTS classes **Resource** and **TransactionalObject**. So we're dealing with a recoverable resource object.

3. ***Bank A's recoverable object registers its resource.*** The recoverable server object first invokes the method *get_control* on the **Current** object (the shorthand notation is *Current::get_control*) to obtain a reference to the **Coordinator** object. Then it invokes *Coordinator::register_resource* to register with the coordinator object for this transaction. The coordinator keeps track of all the participants.

4. ***Client makes a credit on Bank B's object.*** The client invokes a *credit* method on an object in Bank B. This object implements the logic of the transaction (again, something you write) but also inherits its behavior from the OTS classes **Resource** and **TransactionalObject**. So we're dealing with a recoverable resource object.

5. ***Bank B's recoverable object registers its resource.*** It's a repeat of what Bank A's server just did.

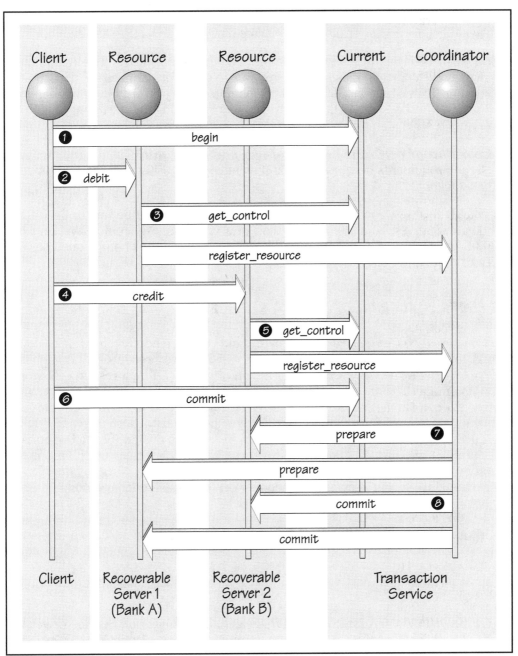

Figure 7-6. Object Transaction Service: A Two-Phase Commit Scenario.

6. ***Client issues a commit.*** The client invokes the method *Current::commit*. The ORB informs the transaction service that the transaction has ended.

7. ***Coordinator performs phase 1 of two-phase commit.*** The coordinator invokes each participant's *prepare* method to get a vote from all the participants on whether this transaction should be committed for posterity (i.e., you get your $100,000). Let's give this scenario a happy ending by assuming everyone returns a "vote_commit."

8. ***Coordinator performs phase 2 of two-phase commit.*** The coordinator tells all the participants to *commit*. You now have $100,000 more to spend in your bank account.

Are you all feeling richer, or just tired? It would have been better for Jeri if the coordinator had issued a rollback instead of a commit. She could have kept her $100,000. Luckily, our scenarios are only fiction. This happy ending concludes our OTS story.

THE CORBA CONCURRENCY CONTROL SERVICE

The *Concurrency Control Service* provides interfaces to acquire and release locks that let multiple clients coordinate their access to shared resources. The service does not define a *resource*. For example, an object could be a resource; it would then implement the Concurrency Control Service to let its clients access it concurrently. The Concurrency Control Service supports both transactional and non-transactional modes of operation. It was designed to be used with OTS to coordinate the activities of concurrent transactions. The design for the Concurrency Control Service originated from Transarc—a company that specializes in TP Monitors for nested transactions. Consequently, the service is tightly coupled to transactional locks and is even designed to work with nested transactions.

The Concurrency Control Service and Transactions

The client of the Concurrency Control Service can choose to acquire locks in one of two ways:

■ ***On behalf of a transaction.*** In this case, the Transaction Service drives the release of locks as the transaction commits or aborts. Typically, a transaction will retain all its locks until it completes.

■ ***On behalf of a non-transactional client.*** In this case, the responsibility for releasing locks lies with the client.

The Concurrency Control Service will ensure that both transactional and non-transactional clients serially access a resource. It doesn't matter to the service whether a lock was acquired by a transactional or non-transactional client. A lock is after all a lock.

Locks

A *lock* is a token that lets a client access a particular resource. The role of the Concurrency Service service is to prevent multiple clients from simultaneously owning locks to the same resource if their activities conflict. The service defines several lock modes that correspond to different categories of access—including *read, write, intention read, intention write,* and *upgrade*. An *upgrade* lock is a *read* lock that conflicts with itself. You use it to prevent deadlocks. For example, a deadlock occurs when multiple clients have *read* locks to a resource, and one of these clients requests a *write* lock. If, however, each client requests an *upgrade* lock followed by a *write* lock, the deadlock will not occur.

Locksets

The Concurrency Control Service does not define the granularity of resources that are locked. However, it defines a *lockset*, which is a collection of locks associated with a single resource. You must associate a lockset with each protected resource. For example, if an object is a resource, then it must internally create a lockset and maintain it. Locks are acquired on locksets. You can manage related locksets as a group.

The Concurrency Control Service defines a *lock coordinator* that manages the release of related locksets. For example, the coordinator can free all locks associated with a particular transaction when the transaction commits. In addition, the coordinator may manage the release of locks on behalf of a group of related transactions—for example, nested transactions.

Nested Transactions and Locking

The general rule is that transactions must not be able to observe partial effects of other transactions that might later abort. However, the Concurrency Control Service relaxes this rule for nested transactions. It will tolerate a certain level of *lock conflicts* within a nested transaction family. It can do this because nesting creates abort dependencies among parent/child transactions. If the parent aborts, all its subtransactions also abort. As a result, it doesn't matter if the child observes the partial effects of a parent transaction that may later abort because the child will also abort.

When a nested transaction requests a lock that is held by its parent, it becomes the new owner of the lock. When a nested transaction commits (or aborts), the Concurrency Control Service will automatically transfer ownership of all its locks to the parent transaction. A child transaction can acquire a lock on a resource locked by its parent; it can then drop that lock without causing its parent to lose its lock.

The Concurrency Control Interfaces

Figure 7-7 shows the four key interfaces that make up the Concurrency Control Service. The following is a very brief description of what each of these interfaces do:

■ **LocksetFactory** lets you create locksets. You invoke *create* to create a regular lockset or *create_transactional* to create a transactional lockset. To create new locksets that are related to existing locksets, you either invoke *create_related* or *create_transactional_related*. When locksets are "related," they release their locks together.

■ **Lockset** lets you acquire or release locks. You invoke *lock* to acquire a lock or block until it's free. If you don't want to block waiting, use *try_lock* instead; it returns control immediately if the lock is not available. You invoke *unlock* to release a lock. You invoke *change_mode* to change the mode on an individual lock. Finally, *get_coordinator* returns a lock coordinator object.

■ **TransactionalLockset** supports the same methods as **Lockset**. The difference is that you must now pass a parameter that identifies your transaction ID. This interface is only used by transactional objects that need to pass their transaction ID explicitly. In contrast, the **Lockset** interface implicitly uses the transaction context associated with the caller's thread. As a result, **Lockset** can support implicit transactional clients as well non-transactional clients (their transaction context is null).

■ *LockCoordinator* defines a single method called *drop_locks*. OTS invokes this method to release all locks held by a transaction when it commits or aborts.

This concludes the section on the Concurrency Control Service. As you can see, it's a straightforward locking system with built-in transactional support.

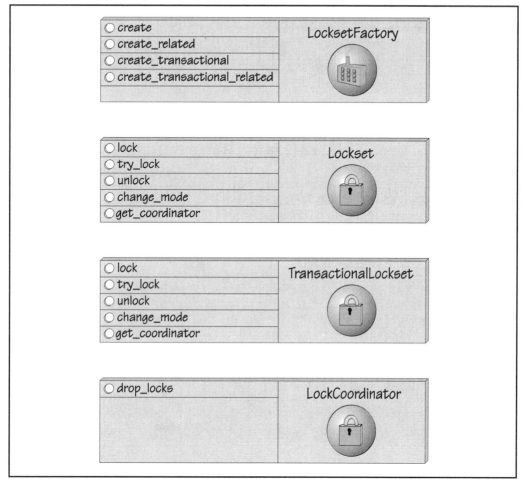

Figure 7-7. Concurrency Control Service: The Interfaces.

Conclusion

The marriage of ORB and TP Monitor technologies will create a new infrastructure that exploits the strengths of TP Monitors while providing a robust application development environment based on reusable objects. It's a truly superior client/server alternative.

> — *Edward E Cobb, IBM*
> *Senior Technical Staff Member*
> *Object Magazine (February, 1995)*

OK, we've covered two more services—the tally is now six down and ten more to go. But OTS was a particularly important service. As Ed Cobb notes, the marriage of objects and transactions can lead to some very potent client/server middleware. OTS is a service that can integrate other services. For example, the Concurrency Control Service releases locks on transaction boundaries. The Persistent Object Service could also use transaction boundaries to commit data changes in memory to a non-volatile store. So transactions become a generic unit of resource allocation.

In addition to being important at the system level, OTS will redefine the way we build our client/server middleware. For starters it will encourage developers to use transactions pervasively. Transactions are now part of the ORB. As a result, most objects that live on the ORB will be transactional. The ubiquitous use of transactions on the ORB will result in TP Monitors morphing into ORBs (or vice versa). This means that ORBs may very well be the next generation TP Monitor. What else would you expect from a service that was designed from scratch by the best TP Monitor people in the business?

Chapter 8

CORBA Services: Persistence and Object Databases

The next generation of software will consist of components tied into a huge variety of database products. For the first time, the Persistent Object Service (POS) provides a single client interface for storing objects—regardless of whether the object is stored in file systems, Bento containers, relational databases, or object databases.

— *Roger Sessions, Author*
Object Persistence
(Prentice Hall, 1996)

Unlike C++ objects, most distributed objects are persistent. This means they must maintain their state long after the program that creates them terminates. To be persistent, the object's state must be stored in a non-volatile datastore—for example, a database or file system. So, who controls the object's persistence? At one end, the *Object Database Management System (ODBMS)* vendors believe that object persistence is totally transparent. An ODBMS magically moves your object between memory and disk to meet your usage needs. All you see is a single-level store of objects. At the other end of the spectrum are those of us with terabytes of existing data. We need a way to get data from our existing stores into objects (and vice versa). As a result, we may need to be more intimately involved with how to

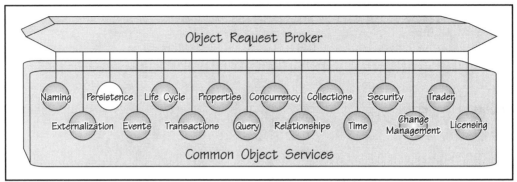

Figure 8-1. The Persistent Object Service.

access this data and associate it with an object's state. In the middle are those of us that save our data on flat files. All we may need is a streaming service that moves object data into and out of a file. This chapter covers a single CORBA service: *POS*, which stands for *Persistent Object Service* (see Figure 8-1). We also cover ODBMSs because they are so intimately related to object persistence. However, POS works with both relational and object databases.

THE CORBA PERSISTENT OBJECT SERVICE (POS)

The *Persistent Object Service (POS)* allows objects to "persist" beyond the application that creates the object or the clients that use it. The lifetime of an object could be relatively short or indefinite. POS allows the state of an object to be saved in a persistent store and restored when it's needed (see Figure 8-2). When the object is in local memory, you can access its data at native programming language speed.

What Is POS?

POS is the result of the merging of the IBM and SunSoft/ODBMS-vendor submissions to the OMG (see the next Soapbox). The merger resulted in a specification that can accommodate a variety of storage services—including SQL databases, ODBMSs, document filing systems (like Bento), and others (see Figure 8-3). POS defines the interface to data and persistent objects using IDL-defined interfaces. The implementations of the interface can be lightweight file systems or heavyweight full-featured SQL or Object Database systems. The idea was to create an open implementation that meets the different persistent storage requirements of objects—it encompasses the needs of large-grained objects (such as documents) as well as fined-grained objects (such as SQL table rows). So the main idea behind POS is a single object interface to multiple datastores.

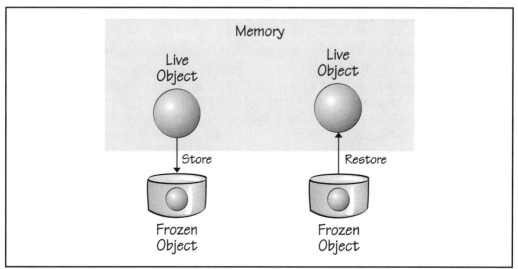

Figure 8-2. A Persistent Object Is Either Live or Frozen.

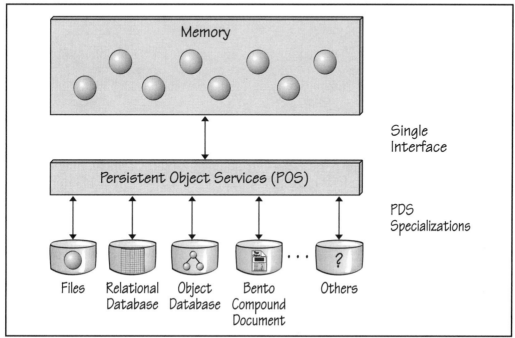

Figure 8-3. Persistent Objects: One Interface Multiple Datastores.

Single-Level Stores Versus Two-Level Stores

POS provides a single client interface for storing objects regardless of their persistent storage mechanism. POS can handle both *single-level stores* (for example, ODBMSs) and *two-level stores* (for example, SQL databases and simple file systems). In a single-level store, the client is not aware of whether the object is in memory or disk. It's one big virtual store—memory and persistent storage are the same thing. Although ODBMSs sometimes let you use transaction boundaries to flush a cache, they provide most of object storage management transparently. In contrast, two-level stores separate memory from persistent storage. The object must be explicitly staged from a database (or file) into memory, and vice versa.

Almost all the world's existing data is stored in two-level stores. In an ideal world, all objects would be stored in ODBMSs, which are single-level stores for objects. The beauty of ODBMSs is that they do not introduce an impedance mismatch between an object and its storage. ODBMSs provide the most direct path for storing objects. They also provide the best performance and most versatility. We cover ODBMSs in this chapter to give you an idea of where things are going. Remember, however, that POS is not limited to supporting ODBMSs. The whole point of POS is to provide datastore-independent persistence for objects. POS is database secular; it supports them all and lets you make the choice.

POS: The Client's View

Sometimes clients of an object need to control or assist in managing persistence. POS can accommodate different levels of client involvement. At one extreme, the service can be made transparent to client applications. This means the client is completely ignorant of the persistence mechanism; objects appear magically on demand from whatever state they're in. At the other extreme, client applications can use storage-specific protocols that surface all the details of the underlying persistence storage mechanism. Again, the idea is to accommodate different client needs. Some clients need a fine-grain level of control over their persistent store, and for others, ignorance is pure bliss.

The client makes the choice of how much persistent data management it wants. Note that this is a two-way street: Persistent objects can choose not to expose their persistence to clients. POS provides nine operations on three interfaces that clients use to control persistence. These interfaces do not abandon the principle of data encapsulation, but they give clients some of the visibility they may need. More specifically, they let the client decide when the persistent object is stored and restored.

POS: The Persistent Object's View

The *persistent object (PO)* is ultimately in charge of its persistence; it decides what datastore protocol to use and how much visibility to give its clients. The PO can also delegate the management of its persistent data to the underlying persistent services. Or, it can maintain a fine-grained control over all its interactions with the storage system. The PO can also inherit most of the function it needs to be persistent. At a minimum, a PO must collaborate with its datastores to translate its state into something the underlying service can handle.

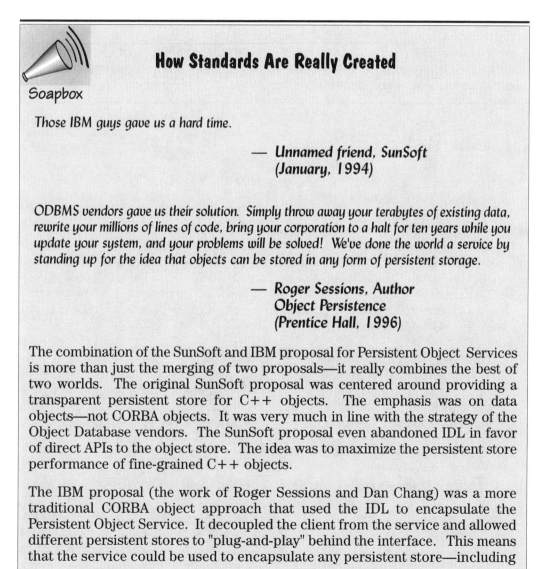

How Standards Are Really Created

Soapbox

Those IBM guys gave us a hard time.

> — *Unnamed friend, SunSoft*
> *(January, 1994)*

ODBMS vendors gave us their solution. Simply throw away your terabytes of existing data, rewrite your millions of lines of code, bring your corporation to a halt for ten years while you update your system, and your problems will be solved! We've done the world a service by standing up for the idea that objects can be stored in any form of persistent storage.

> — *Roger Sessions, Author*
> *Object Persistence*
> *(Prentice Hall, 1996)*

The combination of the SunSoft and IBM proposal for Persistent Object Services is more than just the merging of two proposals—it really combines the best of two worlds. The original SunSoft proposal was centered around providing a transparent persistent store for C++ objects. The emphasis was on data objects—not CORBA objects. It was very much in line with the strategy of the Object Database vendors. The SunSoft proposal even abandoned IDL in favor of direct APIs to the object store. The idea was to maximize the persistent store performance of fine-grained C++ objects.

The IBM proposal (the work of Roger Sessions and Dan Chang) was a more traditional CORBA object approach that used the IDL to encapsulate the Persistent Object Service. It decoupled the client from the service and allowed different persistent stores to "plug-and-play" behind the interface. This means that the service could be used to encapsulate any persistent store—including

SQL databases, Bento-like containers, file systems, or Object Databases. It's the standard OMG encapsulation stuff (hammer and nails).

The merger of the two proposals—an effort that lasted over six months—gave us the best of all worlds. This includes CORBA persistent objects with IDL interfaces, a wide choice of object store implementations, and fine-grained object performance. The Persistent Object Service again demonstrates that the CORBA technology selection process works. It seems to resolve the tension between opposing proposals to create something that's better than each individual proposal. Without the IBM counter-proposal, we would have ended up with a pure ODBMS approach. Now we have something that works with both ODBMSs and traditional two-level stores. Roger Sessions—now an independent consultant—wrote a whole book on how the POS standard was created. The book is must reading; it contains "techie" stuff laced with suspense and intrigue—a wonderful combination! □

The Elements of POS

Figure 8-4 shows the elements of the Persistent Object Service. Let's quickly review what they each do, starting from the top down:

■ ***Persistent Objects (POs)*** are objects whose state is persistently stored. An object can be made persistent by inheriting (via IDL) the **PO** class behavior. It must also inherit (or provide) a mechanism for externalizing its state when asked to do so by the underlying storage mechanism (via a "protocol"). Every persistent object has a *Persistent Identifier (PID)* that describes the location within a datastore of that object using a string identifier. Clients typically interact with the **PO** interface to control the object's persistence.

■ ***Persistent Object Manager (POM)*** is an implementation-independent interface for persistence operations. It insulates the POs from a particular Persistent Data Service. The POM can route PO calls to the appropriate Persistent Data Service by looking at information that's encoded in the PID. A Persistent Object Service has a single POM that typically sits between the objects and the Persistent Data Services. The POM is a router for datastores. It provides a uniform view of persistence in the system across multiple data services.

■ ***Persistent Data Services (PDSs)*** are interfaces to the particular datastore implementations. The PDSs perform the actual work of moving data between an object and a datastore. The PDSs must all implement the IDL-specified **PDS** interface. In addition, some PDSs may support an implementation-dependent *protocol*. This protocol provides a mechanism for getting data in and out of an object. Rick Cattel of SunSoft calls it a "conspiracy" between the object and a

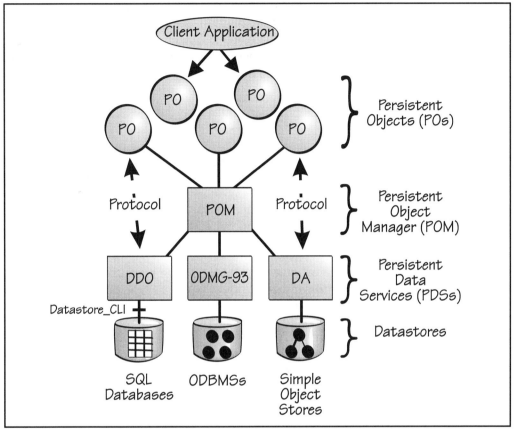

Figure 8-4. The Components of the OMG Persistent Object Service.

PDS. The conspiracy is straightforward between objects and ODBMSs. But it can be quite convoluted when it maps between objects and two-level stores—for example, SQL databases. POS currently specifies three protocols for creating these conspiracies: *Direct Attribute (DA)*, *Object Database Management Group (ODMG-93)*, and *Dynamic Data Object (DDO)*.

■ ***Datastores*** are the implementations that store an object's persistent data independently of the address space containing the object. Examples of datastores are ODBMSs, Posix files, Bento, and SQL databases. POS also provides a set of IDL-defined interfaces that encapsulate the *X/Open Callable Level Interface (CLI)*; it's called the *Datastore_CLI*. This CLI provides an API-like interface to SQL databases; it combines Microsoft's ODBC and Borland's IDAPI.[1]

---

[1] If these terms are unfamiliar to you, please refer to our book **Essential Client/Server Survival Guide** (Wiley, 1994). We cover SQL and the CLI in some detail.

In a nutshell, POS defines three levels of abstraction that hide different storage implementations. For most client applications, the persistence mechanism will be totally transparent. If you need to control your object's persistence, use the **PO** interface. Of course, the object is responsible for storing and restoring its state. You simply tell it when to do so using the **PO** interface.

POS Protocols: The Object-PDS Conspiracy

The **POM** router provides a generic interface that allows different PDSs to plug-and-play transparently. Datastores provide a single interface to **POM** called the **PDS** interface. In addition, they provide datastore-specific protocols. These are the conspiracies that let an object expose its data to a datastore. Think of it as an agreement between object providers and the PDS implementors on how to get data in and out of an object.

Roger Sessions suggests that if all objects use the stream protocol (it is part of the CORBA *Externalization Service*), then two-level store PDSs only need to support one conspiracy. This conspiracy is between the PDS and the streams to which an object externalizes (and internalizes) its persistent state. We are not aware of the performance implications of streaming. You typically use streams to externalize data to a file or to another process. But is it the most efficient mechanism for an object to exchange data with an SQL database? Perhaps Roger can answer this question (we cover the streaming protocol in Chapter 10).

Excluding streams, POS defines three implementation-specific protocols for moving data between an object and different PDSs:

■ **The Direct Access (DA)** protocol is the basis of the original SunSoft proposal; it provides direct access to persistent data using an IDL-like Data Definition Language (see next Briefing box).

■ **The ODMG-93** protocol provides direct access from C++ using an ODMG-specific Data Definition Language (DDL). We cover ODMG in the Object Database section of this chapter.

■ **The Dynamic Data Object (DDO)** protocol is a datastore-neutral representation of an object's persistent data; it defines a structure that contains all the data for an object. You can use this protocol to dynamically describe an object's data without going through IDL. Clients can use DDOs (with the Datastore_CLI) to formulate dynamic SQL queries. DDO is the basis for the original IBM proposal (from Dan Chang of IBM). Several commercial implementations use DDO to access data from relational databases via the Datastore_CLI. For example, the IBM Visual Age C++ visual builder uses DDO and the

Datastore_CLI to access SQL databases. DDO is no panacea. But there's no panacea for mapping between objects and SQL databases; every approach requires some messy mapping constructs. Visual tools make it easier. We cover the Datastore_CLI later in this chapter.

To summarize, protocols simply map between object and datastore views of data (for example, between an object and SQL tables). ODBMSs use a superset of the OMG IDL to describe their objects; they represent objects in a very straightforward way (there is no impedance mismatch). Consequently, ODBMSs and objects have minimal conspiracies. This is not the case for SQL databases and other non-object stores—their impedance mismatch with objects is large. As a result, it takes a quite a bit of "conspiring" to smooth the exchange path between the two. But this is a small price to pay to bring the bulk of the world's data into the object domain.

The Direct Attribute "Conspiracy"

Briefing

The *Direct Attribute (DA)* protocol defines a conspiracy that lets an object directly access a PDS. It's meant to support very "fine-grained" objects that are comparable in size and complexity to typical C++ data structures. The design is the brainchild of the Object Database vendors and SunSoft. It's an upwardly compatible subset of the Object Database Management Group (ODMG) standard that we cover later in this chapter. The DA protocol allows CORBA-compliant object applications to easily upgrade to ODBMSs as their object storage needs evolve.

The DA protocol uses an IDL-like *Data Definition Language (DDL)* to define persistent data. It also employs an IDL-like language binding approach to provide client API support from within C and C++. To provide compatibility with ODBMSs, access to persistent data is done using native programming language operations. For example, C and C++ data structures can be accessed using the dot notation. The DDL only supports data structures defined in CORBA 1.1; the only collection data type supported is an IDL sequence—an element array of variable length. In contrast, ODBMSs support a wide range of container types (more on that later).

To store an object's persistent state, the designer of a CORBA object implementation first uses the DA DDL to describe the object's persistent state as one or more data object interfaces. Each data object provides persistent storage for the list of attributes defined by its interface. A schema is a group of data objects that define the persistent storage for an application. The schema bindings are created by a standalone DDL precompiler.

DA Clusters

A datastore may service many schemas (or applications); each is given its own cluster of storage (see Figure 8-5). You make changes to data within a cluster using transactions. However, a cluster store can only deal with single-user transactions. The DA protocol is based on the idea that only an object should access its private state. Concurrency control is achieved via private ORB calls between objects. The DA protocol does not support fine-grained concurrent access to persistent data; this functionality is provided by a full-fledged ODBMS. However, DA supports concurrent activity on different clusters—they're treated as totally independent databases that share a physical store. Each cluster is isolated from the concurrent changes occurring elsewhere in the datastore. ❏

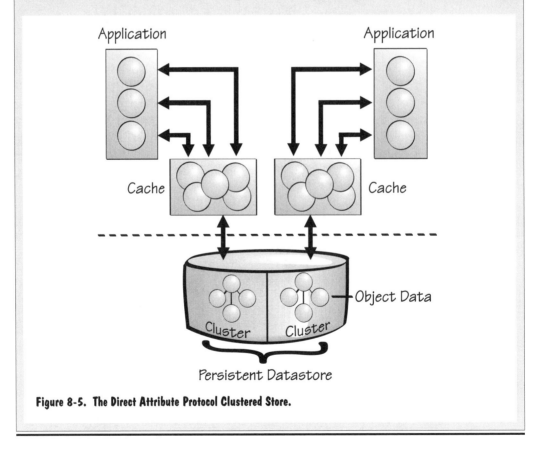

Figure 8-5. The Direct Attribute Protocol Clustered Store.

The POS Interfaces

Figure 8-6 shows the six required interfaces that provide the Persistent Object Service. Clients only need to be aware of the factories and the **PO** and **PID** interfaces. Also notice that **PO**, **POM**, and **PDS** provide the same set of functions, but at different levels of abstraction. Let's go over these interfaces:

■ **PIDFactory** lets you create a *Persistent Object ID (PID)* three different ways. Every object must have a PID to store its data persistently. The PID describes where the underlying data for an object lives.

■ **POFactory** provides a single operation *create_PO* that lets you create an instance of a persistent object.

■ **PID** provides a single operation *get_PIDString* that returns a string version of the PID.

■ **PO** provides five operations that let a client externally control the persistent object's relationship with its persistent data. You invoke *store* to get the state data out of the object into the datastore location designated by a PID. *Restore* does the reverse. All persistent objects are derived from the **PO** interface.

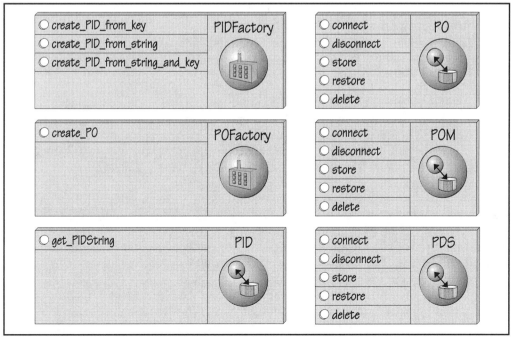

Figure 8-6. The Persistent Object Service Interfaces.

- **POM** provides five operations that a persistent object uses to communicate with its underlying datastore; these are the same operations a persistent object exposes to its clients.

- **PDS** provides five operations that a **POM** uses to communicate with its underlying datastore; these are the same operations a persistent object exposes to its clients. The **PDS** is ultimately the interface that moves data between the object and the datastore. To plug a new datastore into the Persistent Object Service, all you need to do is specialize the **PDS** and **PID** interfaces (and work out the protocols).

Most of these operations are self-explanatory. The main idea here is that **POMs** mediate between multiple datastores.

The POS CLI Interfaces

The POS CLI interfaces encapsulate the X/Open CLI, IDAPI, and ODBC functions. These three database interface standards let you access relational databases, XBase file systems, and even hierarchical databases. The POS CLI allows objects to access these databases via ORBs using IDL-defined interfaces. POS prefers that you avoid going directly to the CLI even if it's via an ORB. Instead, it wants you to use the higher-level persistent object interface. The CLI is meant to be used by PDSs to get to the data. However, if you're an ODBC fan, you should know this interface is available on ORBs using CORBA's POS.

CLI (it used to be called SAG) is an X/Open standard that is being merged with the SQL3 specification. Microsoft promised to make ODBC conform to CLI at some future date. The POS CLI is a superset that covers both ODBC and CLI. You can use the select/cursor CLI operations alone when there is no Query Service. These interfaces hook into the Query Service when it exists. Actually, the Query Service uses the POS CLI to query about persistent objects. As a result, the Query Service does not have to repeat what the Persistence Service provides—for example, schema mapping, datastore access, and so on.

Figure 8-7 shows the four key interfaces that constitute the POS CLI (we do not show three minor interfaces). The **Datastore_CLI** interface is the workhorse that provides most of the operations. Typically, you first create a **Connection** object and set the appropriate options. Then you open a connection to the datastore by invoking *connect*. To store an object, you invoke *add_object* or *update_object*. You invoke *retrieve_object* to restore an object. *Select_object* lets you retrieve sets of objects that match certain keys from the datastore. You can navigate a select's result set using a **Cursor** object (if necessary, get the mapping information first). The CLI is a recoverable object; it participates in an OTS transaction via *transact*.

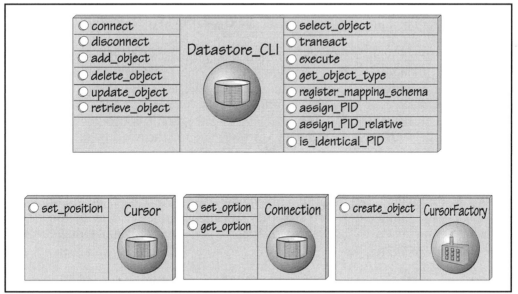

Figure 8-7. POS: The Four Key POS CLI Interfaces.

You can invoke a command or stored procedure in the database using *execute*. Finally, you invoke *delete_object* to delete an object.

OBJECT DATABASE MANAGEMENT SYSTEMS

*T*he biggest problem with relational databases is that they deal with an intermediate level of data abstraction. Users want to browse the real world and record the transactions of an enterprise...This requires adding a new schema, a higher-level application programming interface. The way we're doing this [in Oracle8] is by decomposing the data from the object and storing it in two-dimensional tables.

— *Larry Ellison, CEO of Oracle*
(May, 1993)

Object Database Management Systems (ODBMSs) provide a client/server architecture that is significantly different from *Relational Database Management Systems (RDBMSs)*. ODBMSs take a revolutionary approach to shared data that's totally centered on the management of persistent objects. We encountered some of this technology in the OMG Persistent Object Service. Today, the ODBMS vendors claim they can provide efficient client/server access to fine-grained objects. In late 1993, the major ODBMS vendors released their *ODMG-93* standard. They produced the final ODMG-93 v1.1 revision in early 1994. The standard is intended to become the SQL of the ODBMS world. Of course, with a common standard, the market for ODBMSs may take off like its SQL-based RDBMS counterpart.

So, will ODBMSs replace RDBMSs in the same way relational vendors replaced their hierarchical predecessors ten years ago? This is one of the questions we'll try to answer in this chapter (in a Soapbox, of course). But just to give you a preliminary idea, the Cowen Market Research firm believes the market for ODBMSs will grow to $430 million by 1997. In contrast, the RDBMS market is expected to grow to $6.8 billion in 1997.[2] According to Gartner Group, the worldwide market for ODBMSs was less than $72 million in 1994. The numbers show that ODBMSs will grow very fast; however, their market size is dwarfed by RDBMSs. ODBMSs will grow in areas like multimedia, object repositories, and groupware—the next wave of client/server technology. The RDBMS vendors won't sit still either. All the major relational vendors have declared that they will incorporate support for objects as it's being defined in the SQL3 standard. According to Larry Ellison, Oracle8 will be fully object-based.

In this section, we first look at what an ODBMS is and what it does well. We look at it through the composite technology that's provided by five small but very dynamic ODBMS vendors (together, they own over 90% of the object database market). Then we go over the ODMG-93 standard that was created by these five vendors—incidentally, they all pledged to make their products ODMG-compliant. We'll look at how ODMG-93 compares with OMG's Object Services and SQL3. As part of living dangerously, we end the chapter with a Soapbox on RDBMSs versus ODBMSs.

What's an ODBMS?

We define an ODBMS to be a DBMS that integrates database capabilities with object-oriented programming language capabilities. An ODBMS makes database objects appear as programming language objects, in one or more existing programming languages.

> — *Rick Cattel, Chairman*
> *ODMG-93 Committee*

An ODBMS provides a persistent store for objects in a multiuser client/server environment. The ODBMS handles concurrent access to objects, provides locks and transaction protection, protects the object store from all types of threats, and takes care of traditional tasks such as backup and restore. What makes ODBMSs different from their relational counterparts is that they store objects rather than tables. Objects are referenced through *Persistent Identifiers (PIDs)*, which uniquely

---

[2] Source: **Cowen Research Report**, "Object Development Strategies" (September 15, 1993).

identify objects, and are used to create referential and containment relationships between them. ODBMSs also enforce encapsulation and support inheritance. The ODBMS combines object properties with traditional DBMS functions such as locking, protection, transactions, querying, versioning, concurrency, and persistence.

Instead of using a separate language like SQL to define, retrieve, and manipulate data, ODBMSs use class definitions and traditional OO language (usually C++ and Smalltalk) constructs to define and access data. The ODBMS is simply a multiuser, persistent extension of in-memory language data structures (see Figure 8-8). In other words, the client is the C++ program; the server is the ODBMS—there are no visible intermediaries like RPCs or SQL. The ODBMS integrates database capabilities directly into the language.

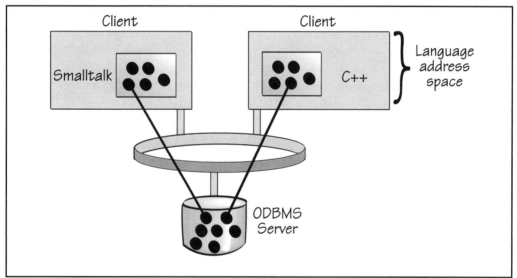

Figure 8-8. ODBMS: An Extension to OO Language Data Structures.

Of course, not everything is transparent to the language. By necessity, the ODBMS introduces extensions to the OO language such as container classes and operations that help you navigate through the containers. The ODMG-93 specification includes a full-blown *Object Manipulation Language (OML)* that supports queries and transactions. In an attempt to make the data-definition language neutral, ODMG-93 specifies a generic *Object Definition Language (ODL)*. As a result, the ODBMS, like SQL, requires a precompiler to process the object definitions, language extensions, and queries. The output of the compiler, like SQL plans, must also be linked to the ODBMS runtime. So we've come full circle.

What's an ODBMS Good For?

Rather than trying to mangle the data or tear it apart and put it into relational tables, obviously it was best to store those objects in their natural form.

> — *Jonathan Cassell, IS Manager*
> *Granite Construction*
> *(July, 1995)*

ODBMSs are perfect fits for users whose data isn't simple enough to line up in relational tables. For a long time, ODBMSs were an area of great interest to academicians and OO researchers. The earliest commercial ODBMSs made their appearance in 1986 with the introduction of Servio and Ontos. The three firms that currently lead the industry today—Object Design (ODI), Versant, and Objectivity—all entered the market in 1990. The ODBMS vendors first targeted applications that dealt with complex data structures and long-lived transactions—including computer-aided design, CASE, and intelligent offices. With the emergence of multimedia, groupware, and distributed objects, the esoteric features of ODBMSs are now becoming mainstream client/server requirements. ODBMS technology fills the gap in the areas where relational databases are at their weakest—complex data, versioning, long-lived transactions, nested transactions, persistent object stores, inheritance, and user-defined data types.

Here's a list of the features that were pioneered by the ODBMS vendors (see Figure 8-9):

- **Freedom to create new types of information.** ODBMSs give you the freedom to create and store any data type using standard object descriptions. The data type is part of the object class definition. You can easily store arbitrarily complex data structures in an ODBMS (like container hierarchies). In contrast, traditional databases offer a limited number of hard-wired data types; complex structures must be converted into artificially "flattened" table representations.

- **Fast access.** ODBMSs keep track of objects through their unique IDs. A search can move directly from object to object without the need for tedious search-and-compare operations using foreign keys and other associative techniques.

- **Flexible views of composite structures.** ODBMSs allow individual objects to participate in a multiplicity of containment relationships, creating multiple views of the same objects. Objects can maintain pointers to other objects in a very recursive manner; there's no limit to the different container relationships that you can create. A container typically maintains references to object IDs as opposed to the objects themselves—it's a form of *linking* as opposed to *embedding*.

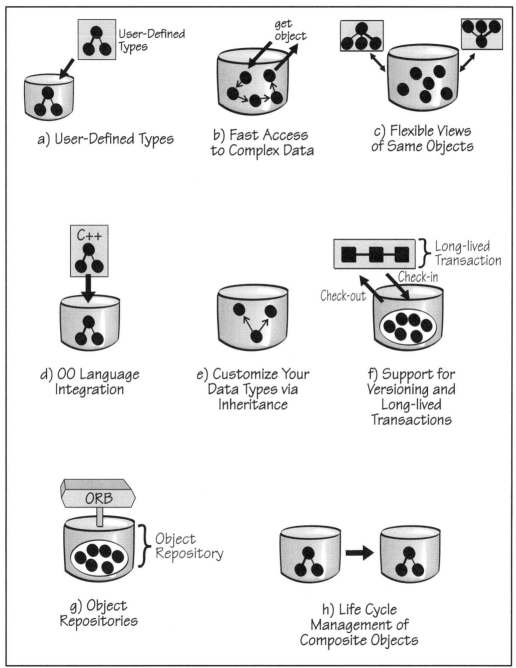

Figure 8-9. The Eight Wonders of ODBMS.

- ***Tight integration with object-oriented languages.*** ODBMSs present themselves as persistent extensions of the OO language's in-memory data structures. This allows them to minimize the impedance mismatch between programs and data while maintaining the strong encapsulation features that are inherent in OO languages. OO programmers should find an ODBMS to be a natural extension of their paradigm. ODBMSs provide the fastest and most direct access to objects they store; they also do a good job of preserving the characteristics of these objects. In contrast, RDBMSs require multiple transformations to represent the complex in-memory data structures of an OO language in tabular form. Relational systems can store objects, but they must first break them down into chunks and flatten them into structures that can fit in tables. SQL people, of course, may think that chasing corporate data via in-memory C++ pointers is a travesty. (We'll resume this discussion in the Soapbox.)

- ***Support for customizable information structures using multiple inheritance.*** The ODBMS data types are defined using object classes. This means that any class can be subclassed to create custom structures that meet exceptional data needs. In addition, the ODBMS lets you mix desirable characteristics from different classes and combine them using multiple inheritance. So the ODBMS extends the concept of object reuse through inheritance to the database.

- ***Support for versioning, nesting, and long-lived transactions.*** Many commercial ODBMSs (including ObjectStore, Ontos, and Objectivity) support nested transactions and versioning for long-duration transactions. Objects can be grouped in configurations and managed as one transaction. ODBMSs are most popular in engineering design applications that require the management of complex documents. A typical Computer Aided Design (CAD) system also depends on version control to track the progressively more enhanced versions of an engineering design. Because of their long involvement with CAD, ODBMSs have perfected the art of versioning and long-lived transactions. ODBMSs have introduced the concept of *configurations*—meaning a collection of objects that are managed as a locking and versioning unit. CAD users typically *check out* a configuration of objects from the ODBMS, work on it, and *check in* their configuration as a new version.

- ***Repositories for distributed objects.*** ODBMSs provide natural multiuser repositories for run-time objects. We believe the ODBMS vendors have a huge lead in providing solutions for concurrent access to large numbers (in the millions) of fine-grained objects with ACID protection. Eventually, ODBMSs will provide true stores for *roaming objects* (a la General Magic's Telescript product); they serve as object servers for roaming objects—think of them as object Hiltons.

- *Support for life cycle management of composite objects.* ODBMSs have also perfected the art of managing composite objects as a unit. For example, you can assemble, disassemble, copy, store, restore, move, and destroy composite objects. The ODBMS automatically maintains the relationships between the parts and treats the aggregate as a single component. This is also a result of their long involvement with CAD.

In summary, ODBMS vendors have had the luxury of being able to create pure object databases without being encumbered by debt to history. As a result, they were able to provide some missing pieces of technology needed to create the new generation of multimedia intensive databases with flexible data types. An ODBMS has the advantage over a relational database of knowing the overall structure of a complex object (like a document) and sometimes its behavior (or methods) as well; it can refer to any constituent object by its ID. In contrast, RDBMS vendors are attempting to provide object technology (with SQL3) by using a hybrid approach that decomposes the data from the object and then stores it in tables. This is an area where relational databases are at a disadvantage, but we'll defer that discussion to the Soapbox, too.

ODBMS Client/Server Implementations

ODBMS technology is clearly mature enough for major products, though the momentum for object-database vendors is much slower than analysts predicted.

> — *Frank Hayes*
> *Information Week*
> *(July 17, 1995)*

There are several architectural alternatives to implementing ODBMSs on client/server networks. The effects of the architecture show up in various ways, even though the underlying programming model is the same. Mary Loomis—a leading ODBMS architect—defines two basic approaches for splitting the application between ODBMS clients and servers:

- The *object server* balances the load between the client and the server. The client and server communicate by moving objects from the server's persistent store to the client's memory (see Figure 8-10). Clients request objects by specifying their Persistent IDs. The client component manages the object in the local memory; the server provides a multiuser ODBMS with transaction protection and locking. The unit of locking is an object. Methods can be executed on either the client or the server, depending on the location of the object. The processing of queries is done on the server.

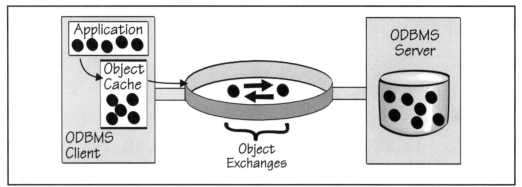

Figure 8-10. ODBMS Object Server Architecture.

■ The **page server** is a fat client approach that treats the ODBMS as a shared multiuser virtual memory store. The server pulls pages off the disk and moves them to the client's memory cache (see Figure 8-11). There are no persistent object IDs. All the intelligence and the object model are on the client. The page server locks pages, not objects. The methods are executed on the client where the object's logic resides. Queries are processed on the client, requiring the movement of candidate objects to the client's address space before applying selection criteria.

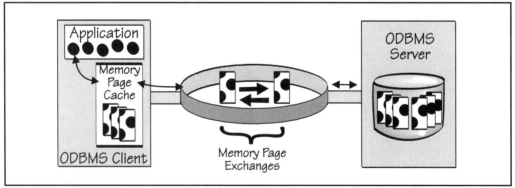

Figure 8-11. ODBMS Page Server Architecture.

We believe the object server is the better implementation. It allows objects to be moved to where they're needed. The access can be made transparent to the application (but it's done via RPCs). In contrast, a page server application needs to be aware of the distribution of objects across database systems. References within a single database are transparently traversed using C++ pointers. However, references across databases require the use of remote functions or RPCs. This means that objects cannot be moved around to improve performance without changes to the application's code.

ODMG-93: The Lingua Franca for ODBMS

The ODMG-93 standard is the ODBMS answer to SQL. The standard is the result of work done by the *Object Database Management Group (ODMG)*—a consortium that includes all the major ODBMS vendors. The ODMG is a working subgroup of the OMG and intends to submit its standard to both ISO and ANSI. In theory, the adoption of ODMG-93 should allow applications to work with ODBMSs from any of the major vendors. Today, most of the ODMG vendors are shipping systems that are compliant with large subsets of the specification. The ODMG members have committed to bring their systems into *full* compliance within 18 months of the publication of the standards document. Unfortunately, as we go to press, this hasn't happened yet.

ODMG-93 and CORBA

ODMG-93 is an extension of the CORBA Persistent Object Service that defines how to implement a protocol that provides an efficient *Persistent Data Service (PDS)* for fine-grained objects. The standard uses the OMG object model as its basis. The ODBMS's role in an ORB environment is to provide concurrent access to persistent stores capable of handling millions of fine-grained objects. To do this, the OMG refers to a special PDS protocol called ODMG-93. This protocol supplements the IDL-defined RPC invocations with direct API calls to the objectstore for faster access to data.

The ODBMS vendors are also actively promoting within the CORBA ORB committee a *Library Object Adapter (LOA)* that provides direct API access via the ORB to specialized high-speed APIs. ODMG-93 states that the ODBMS vendors would like CORBA to standardize on a specialized version of LOA called the *Object Database Adapter (ODA)*. Figure 8-12, adapted from ODMG-93, shows the differences among BOA, LOA, and ODA—yes, more TLAs (three-letter acronyms) you can use to impress the folks back home.

The ODA should provide the ability to register subspaces of object identifiers with the ORB instead of all the millions of objects that are stored in the ODBMS. From the client's point of view, the objects in the registered subspace appear just as any other ORB-accessible objects. The ODA should allow for the use of direct access—as in the LOA—to improve the performance of ORB/ODBMS applications. To summarize, the ODBMS vendors are pushing CORBA to be more flexible when it comes to dealing with applications that manage millions of fine-grained objects. The Persistent Object Service specification indicates that OMG got the message. But it remains to be seen if OMG will extend this new permissiveness to the ORB itself.

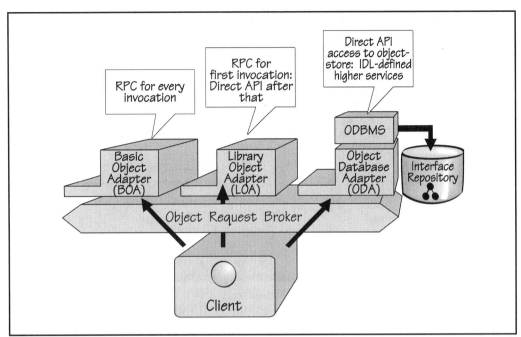

Figure 8-12. ODMG-93: ODBMS as Object Manager on an OMG ORB.

The Elements of ODMG-93

The ODMG-93 standard consists of three major components (see Figure 8-13):

- ■ *Object Definition Language (ODL)*—ODMG-93 uses the OMG IDL as its data definition language. ODL is a "clean" superset of IDL in the sense that it defines elements that are not in IDL, such as collection classes and referential relationships. The ODL lets you describe metadata independently of the programming language. The ODL is processed through a precompiler, which generates stubs that get linked to the ODBMS and the client language (C++ or Smalltalk). ODL provides interface and data definition portability across languages and ODBMS vendor platforms.

- ■ *Object Query Language (OQL)*—ODMG-93 defines a SQL-like declarative language for querying and updating database objects. It supports the most commonly used SQL SELECT structures, including joins; it does not support SQL INSERT, UPDATE, or DELETE (it uses C++ or Smalltalk extensions for this). ODMG-93 purposely did not use the SQL3 semantics for objects because of "limitations in its data model and because of its historical baggage." However, as you will read in the next chapter, OQL and SQL3 may converge. The OMG Query Service tries to bring the best of both worlds together. OQL provides

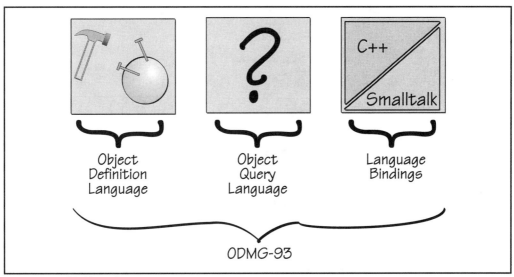

Figure 8-13. ODMG-93 Components.

high-level primitives to query different collections of objects—including *sets*, which means unordered collections with no duplicates; *bags*, which means unordered collections with duplicates; and *lists*, which are ordered collections. OQL also supports structures in queries—a very powerful construct.

■ *C++ and Smalltalk language bindings*—ODMG-93 defines how to write portable C++ or Smalltalk code that manipulates persistent objects. The standard defines C++ *Object Manipulation Language (OML)* extensions. The C++ OML includes language extensions for OQL, iterations for navigating through containers, and transaction support. The ODMG-93 people do not believe exclusively in a "universal" Data Manipulation Language (a la SQL). Instead, they propose "a unified object model for sharing data across programming languages, as well as a common query language." According to ODI's Tom Atwood, "The OML should respect the syntax of the base language into which it is being inserted. This enables programmers to feel they are writing in a single integrated programming language that supports persistence." In theory, it should be possible to read and write the same ODBMS from both Smalltalk and C++, as long as the programmer stays within the common subset of supported data types.

Figure 8-14 shows the steps involved in using an ODMG-compliant ODBMS. The process is very similar to the CORBA IDL, except that the stub bindings are for an ODBMS and the OO Language application that manipulates persistent objects.

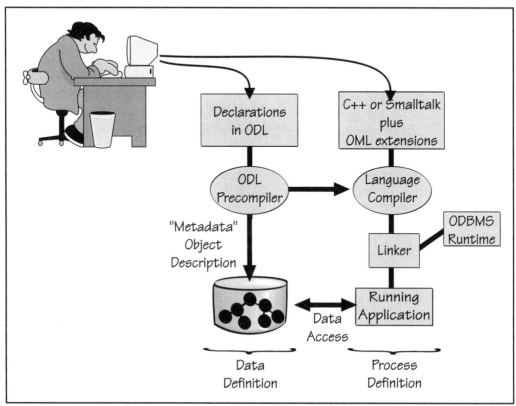

Figure 8-14. The ODMG-93 Process.

So, What's Wrong With ODBMSs?

*P*ure ODBMSs are mere pretenders to the DBMS throne.

> — **Dr. Michael Stonebraker, Professor**
> **University of California at Berkeley**
> **(February, 1994)**

Stonebraker notes that pure ODBMSs still lack functionality in the areas of complex search, query optimizers, and server scalability. Furthermore, many ODBMSs run their products in the same address space as user programs. This means that there is no protection barrier between a client application and the ODBMS. In addition, ODBMSs have a minuscule market penetration when compared to relational DBMSs. The debate continues in the following Soapbox.

The Future of Database: Object or Relational?

Soapbox

Object Mania has taken over the industry. Proponents of object orientation are heralding object databases and ODBMSs as a cure for the purported weakness of relational technology. Poppycock...Applying object orientation directly and indiscriminately at the database level reintroduces problems that took the relational approach two decades to get rid of.

> — Fabian Pascal, Author
> **Understanding Relational Databases**
> **(Wiley, 1994)**

Among users, few doubts remain that ODBMS will ultimately be the successor to RDBMS...In the imagery of the poet William Blake, the young god of revolution Orc has begun to age into the icy tyrant Urizen—keeper of the law and standards.

> — Thomas Atwood, Chairman
> Object Design

We can have our cake and eat it, too! The point is to marry the two technologies instead of throwing mud at each other...It would be a great shame to walk away from the experience gained from more than 20 years of solid relational research and development.

> — Chris Date

Date and Pascal both acknowledge that current SQL database implementations have weaknesses; however, they both feel the relational model per se can handle the problems that ODBMSs solve. The power of ODBMS can be approximated in the relational world using nested relations, domains (or user-defined encapsulated data types) and a more powerful set-oriented language than SQL. These features can do the job without chasing after object pointers or manipulating low-level, language-specific, record structures. We don't have to mitigate the associative powers of relational theory. Developers won't have to resort to manual methods to maximize and reoptimize application performance—setting the clock back. Date believes that a domain and an object type are the same; the solution is for relational vendors to extend their systems to include "proper domain support."

The ODBMS people feel that there's more to this than just extending the relational model. In fact, they've rejected the SQL3 extensions as being insufficient (a truce is in the making). ODBMS diehards believe that they're creating better plumbing for a world where information systems will be *totally* object-based. Relational databases are an impedance mismatch in a plumbing consisting of ORBs, object services, OO languages, and OO frameworks. A pure ODBMS is exactly what's needed. Why keep extending a legacy foundation like SQL with BLOBs, stored procedures, and user-defined types? They prefer to stick to objects all the way and sometimes borrow a few things from SQL (such as queries). They're also recreating the multiuser robust foundation that includes locking, transactions, recovery, and tools.

Of course, we're talking about David and Goliath here. SQL databases are the current kings of the hill. They have the big development budgets and wide commercial acceptance that ranges from MIS shops to the low end of the client/server market. Will the king of the hill be deposed because ODBMSs do objects better? It remains to be seen. But as Esther Dyson puts it, "Using tables to store objects is like driving your car home and then disassembling it to put it in the garage. It can be assembled again in the morning, but one eventually asks whether this is the most efficient way to park a car." ❏

Chapter 9

CORBA Services: Query and Relationships

Distributed objects do not float in space; they are connected to one another.

> — *CORBA COSS Specification*
> *(March, 1995)*

In this chapter, we cover three relatively new CORBA services: *Query, Relationships*, and *Collections* (see Figure 9-1). These services let you discover, create, and manipulate relationships between objects. They also let you manipulate multiple objects as a group.

THE CORBA QUERY SERVICE

The CORBA *Object Query Service*—adopted in early 1995—is the result of a joint submission by nine vendors—including the major ODBMS vendors, Sybase, IBM, SunSoft, and Taligent. In essence, the service lets you find objects whose attributes meet the search criteria you specify using a query. You should note that queries have no access to an object's internal state. This means they do not violate an

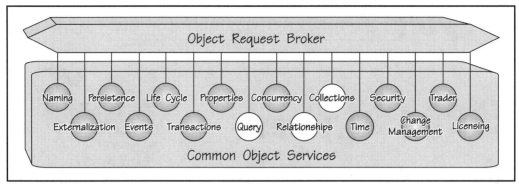

Figure 9-1. CORBA Services: Query, Collections, and Relationships.

object's encapsulation; you can hide your object's internal data structures and expose only what you want the public to see.

You can formulate an object query using one of the following languages: ODMG-93's Object Query Language (OQL), SQL (with object extensions), or a subset of these two languages. The OMG is working with the SQL3 ANSI X3H2 committee and the ODMG to create a single query language for objects.[1] A single query language makes it easier for queries to interoperate across servers; it also gives you a common language for writing queries.

Federated Queries

We designed the Query Service to let you query and manipulate any CORBA object— transient or persistent, concrete or meta, local or remote, individually or in a collection. If there is one object service that can utilize and unify all object services together with the ORB, the Query Service is it.

> — *Dan Chang, Object Architect*
> *IBM*
> *(June, 1995)*

The Query Service can either directly execute a query or delegate it to some other *query evaluator.* For example, the service can use the native query facilities of a relational or object database to execute a nested query. The Query Service combines the query results from all the participating query evaluators and returns the final results to the caller. This means you can use the Query Service to

---

[1] ODMG's OQL provides full object query capabilities and contains almost all of the SQL-92 query language as a subset. OQL is available today.

coordinate loose federations of native query managers. The beauty is that each database can use its own optimized search engine while participating in a global search.

Collections for Manipulating Query Results

When you execute a query, the service returns a *collection* of objects that satisfy the search criteria you specify via a *select* operation. Note that CORBA uses the term "query" in its broader connotation. A CORBA query does more than just let you find objects; it also lets you manipulate a *collection* of objects. The collection is returned by the query—it's the result. The Query Service treats the collection itself as an object. It defines operations that let you manipulate and navigate a collection. It also lets you add and remove collection members.

Query Service: The Collection Interfaces

The Query Service provides a "minimalist" collection service to let you manipulate the results of a query (see Figure 9-2). This minimalist service consists of three interfaces:

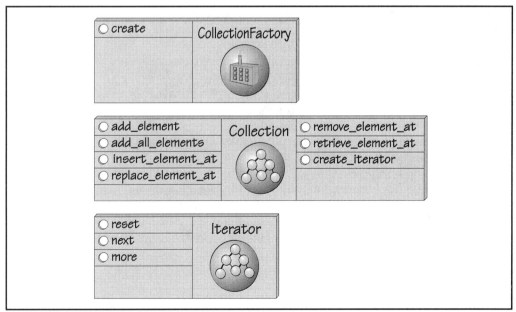

Figure 9-2. Query Service: The Collection Interfaces.

■ **CollectionFactory** defines a single *create* operation. You invoke this operation to create a new instance of an empty collection.

■ **Collection** defines operations that let you *add, replace, retrieve,* and *remove* members of a collection. You invoke *add_all_elements* to add all the elements from a source collection to your collection. *Insert_element_at* lets you add an element in a particular position. *Create_iterator* lets you create a movable pointer to navigate the collection.

■ **Iterator** defines three operations that let you traverse a collection. *Reset* points to the start of a collection. *Next* increments the iterator's position. *More* lets you test if there are elements left in the iteration. The method returns true if there are more elements that you can access in a collection; it returns false if you've reached the end of a collection.

These three interfaces may serve as base classes for the future CORBA *Collection Service*, which we cover later in this chapter.

Query Service: The Query Interfaces

The Query Service provides a framework consisting of five interfaces for dealing with the preparation and execution of a query (see Figure 9-3).[2] Here's what these interfaces do:

■ **QueryEvaluator** defines an operation to *evaluate* a query. This operation executes the query using the query language you specify (or a default). A database system is an example of a **QueryEvaluator** object; it manages an implicit collection of persistent objects.

■ **QueryManager** is a more powerful form of **QueryEvaluator**. It also lets you *create* a **Query** object.

■ **Query** defines four operations that you can perform on an instance of a query. Every query is represented by a **Query** object. *Prepare* lets you compile a query and prepare it for execution. *Execute* lets you execute a compiled query. *Get_status* lets you determine the preparation/execution status of the query. *Get_result* lets you obtain the result of a query.

---

[2] The Query Service also defines an interface called **QueryLanguageType** and six classes derived from it to represent a classification of query languages. These interfaces do not provide any operations. They just use IDL to represent a query language type hierarchy.

- **QueryableCollection** does not introduce new operations. Instead it inherits its function from the interfaces **QueryEvaluator** and **Collection**. Objects of this class evaluate a query on members of a particular collection. Note that any collection member can itself be an object of this class. This means that you can have an infinite number of nested subqueries.

You can extend these four interfaces (via inheritance) to provide additional functions. For example you can extend the **Query** interface to provide a general-purpose result browser that keeps track of successive results. Note that the base Query Service consists of only two interfaces: **QueryEvaluator** and **QueryableCollection**.

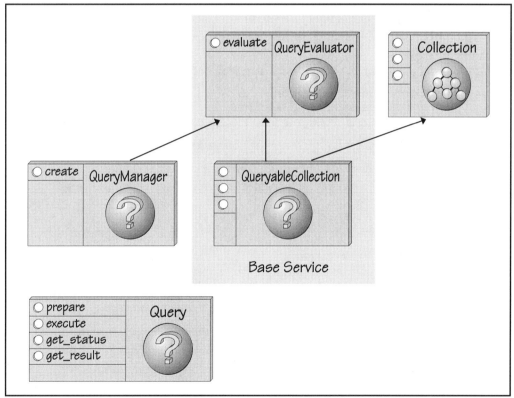

Figure 9-3. Query Service: The Query Interfaces.

A Simple Query Scenario

It's time to go over a couple of scenarios that show how these interfaces play together. We'll start out with the simplest possible query scenario, using an object that implements the **QueryableCollection** interface. Remember, this is an object that knows how to execute a query over a collection of objects it controls. Here are the steps you follow to issue a query and iterate through the result (see Figure 9-4):

1. *Submit the query.* You invoke *evaluate* on the **QueryableCollection** object to execute the query. You pass it parameters that include the query statement and the language you used to express the query (OQL or SQL). The target object executes the query and returns the results in a collection that it controls.

2. *Create a pointer for navigating the results.* You invoke *create_iterator* to create a new iterator. The iterator is automatically reset to point to the beginning of the collection that contains the query results.

3. *Read the first element in the collection.* You invoke *retrieve_element_at* to read the object (or a row expressed as a CORBA "any" type) that the iterator is pointing at.

4. *Point to the next object in the collection.* You invoke *next* to point to the next object or row in the collection.

Loop on the last two steps until you read all the objects that are returned by the query. You're done.

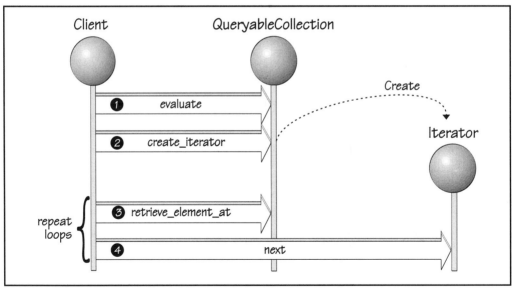

Figure 9-4. A Simple Query Scenario.

A More Complex Query Scenario

Because queries can be complex and resource demanding, there are times when you may want finer control over the processing of a query. In particular, you may want to: 1) use a graphical query picker to construct the query; 2) precompile and save the query to reexecute it at a later time; 3) execute the query asynchronously—this lets you do something else and then come back and check the results of the query later; and 4) check the status of a long-running query to decide whether to continue or abort.

To obtain these finer levels of control, you must use a **QueryManager** object and an associated **Query** object. The **QueryManager** controls a set of collections that you may query. It will assign your query (and the collection against which it executes) to a particular **Query** object. You can interact with this **Query** object to control the execution of your query. The scenario in Figure 9-5 shows the steps you must follow:

1. **Create a Query object.** You invoke *create* on an object that supports the **QueryManager** interface to create a new **Query** object. The **QueryManager** then creates a new **Query** object and returns its object reference (so that you can call it directly).

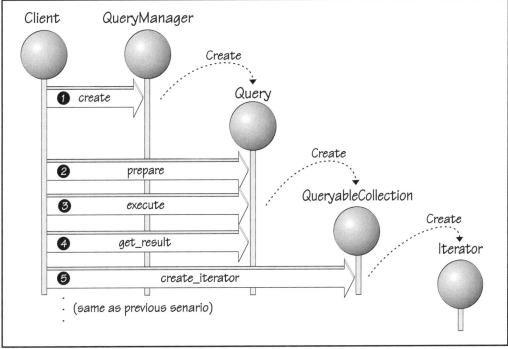

Figure 9-5. A More Complex Query Scenario.

2. ***Precompile the query.*** You invoke *prepare* on the **Query** object to precompile (and store) the query for later execution. The parameters you pass include the query expression and the language you used to express the query (OQL or SQL).

3. ***Execute the query.*** You can execute a precompiled query as many times as you like (perhaps using a different set of search parameters each time). You do this by invoking *execute* on a **Query** object (the object maintains the context of a query that you previously prepared). In our scenario, the **Query** object places the results of a query in a **QueryableCollection** object. The **QueryManager** typically owns all the collection objects in a domain.

4. ***Obtain the result of the query.*** You invoke *get_result* to make sure the query executed successfully. The call will typically return the object reference of a collection object that contains the results of the query.

5. ***Iterate through the results.*** You follow the same steps as in the previous scenario to iterate through the returned collection of objects (or table rows).

This concludes our second query scenario. You should now have a better picture of how these interfaces play together. The trick is to understand that there are different levels of query service available to you. You should also understand how collections can help you process the results of a query.

THE CORBA COLLECTION SERVICE

Collections let you manipulate objects in a group. You typically apply collection operations on groups instead of the individual objects they contain. Examples of collections are *queues, stacks, lists, arrays, trees, sets,* and *bags.* Each of these collection types exhibit behaviors that are specific to the collection. For example, here are some of the operations you can invoke on a set: add a new member, test for equality, test for emptiness, union, intersection, and so on. Some collections are ordered; others use keys to identify the elements. Finally, some collections keep track of object references; others simply collect data types (for example, rows in a table collection).

The purpose of the CORBA *Collection Service* is to provide a uniform way to create and manipulate the most common collections. Once CORBA defines IDL for these common collection classes, we expect that you will be able to acquire multiple substitutable implementations from the supplier community. For example, we expect to see CORBA IDL-ized versions of a variety of collection classes—including the Taligent C++ collections, the ANSI C++ Standard Template Library (STL), ODMG collections, Rogue Wave, and others. If this happens, you will never have to reinvent operations for manipulating stacks, queues, sets, and so on. Note that the Collection Service was issued as part of RFP5 (in mid-1995). So don't hold your breath waiting for implementations—we don't expect any before year-end 1996.

How does the Collection Service relate to the collection interfaces that were introduced by the Query Service? The Query Service only supports a minimalist collection service. It defines top-level collection interfaces. We expect the Collection Service to subclass these interfaces for different types of collections. So you can start using this minimalist collection service now until you get the real thing.

THE CORBA RELATIONSHIP SERVICE

Applications are built out of existing objects that are connected together.

— CORBA COSS Specification
(March, 1995)

Real-world objects never exist in isolation. They form a myriad of relationships with other objects. These relationships come and go. Relationships can be static, spontaneous, dynamic, and ad hoc. Distributed objects (and components) must be able to model their real-world counterparts. You should be able to dynamically create and keep track of relationships between objects that are not relationship-aware. You should be able to do this without changing or recompiling objects when they are brought into new relationships.

The CORBA *Relationship Service* allows components and objects that know nothing of each other to be related. It lets you do this without changing existing objects or requiring that they add new interfaces. In other words, the service lets you create dynamic relationships between immutable objects. The service keeps track of the relationships between objects; the related objects are not even aware that they are part of a relationship.

Why a Relationship Service?

Without a relationship service, your objects would have to keep track of their relationships using ad-hoc pointers. For example, an object could maintain a collection of references to all its related objects. It would need to keep track of the type of the relationship and its attributes.

This ad-hoc solution—using object references—is not very appealing or useful. Object references are unidirectional. It is very difficult to navigate a relationship that's maintained by a set of ad-hoc pointers. You can't easily export your ad-hoc pointers to other objects that need to understand and navigate the relationship. For example, you may need to pass to a deep copy service an object relationship graph so that it can understand which related objects it must copy or move. Most importantly, without a Relationship Service, you cannot create relationships between objects "on the fly." Hardcoded relationships between objects won't get you very far in a dynamic component environment. The bottom line is that you need a Relationship Service.

What Exactly Is a Relationship?

Real-world objects are always involved in relationships. For example, consider the book you're reading. Here are some of the relationships in which it is involved (see Figure 9-6):

- *Ownership relationships* between people and books. A person *owns* a book; a book is *owned* by one or more persons. In the ownership relationship instance shown, you own this book (and we thank you for it).

- *Containment relationships* between books and parts. A book *contains* parts; a part is *contained in* a book. In the containment relationship instance shown, this book contains parts on CORBA, Frameworks, OLE, and OpenDoc.

- *Reference relationships* between books. A book *references* other books; a book is *referenced by* one or more books. In the reference relationship instance shown, this book references our other book, **Essential Client/Server Survival Guide**—what braggarts we are!

- *Authoring relationships* between books and authors. A book is *written by* one or more authors; an author *writes* a book. In the authoring relationship instance shown, this book was authored by Bob, Dan, and Jeri.

- *Employment relationships* between companies and people. A company *employs* one or more persons; a person is *employed* by one or more companies. In the relationship instance shown, Jeri works for Tandem Computers; Dan and Bob work for IBM (when they're not writing books).

A *relationship* is defined by a set of *roles* that two or more objects play (roles are denoted by the dark bubbles). For example, in an employment relationship, a company plays an *employer* role and a person plays an *employee* role. A single object can play different roles in different relationships. For example, Jeri is an employee and an author. A *degree* refers to the number of required roles in a relationship. All the relationships we've shown in the figure are *binary*—they are of degree two. *Cardinality* defines the maximum number of relationships in which a role is involved. For example, a book has a many-to-one containment relationship with parts (the cardinality is unbounded); but a part is contained in only one book (its cardinality is one).

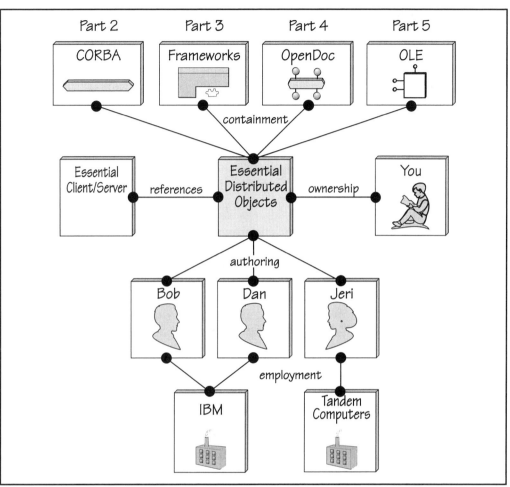

Figure 9-6. A Graph of Related Objects.

A relationship can have one or more *attributes*. For example, we could add a *job_title* attribute to the employment relationship. A relationship can also support method invocations that return information. Note that the attributes and methods of a relationship are totally independent of the objects they represent. You can think of the relationship as introducing its own independent semantics. A set of related objects form a *graph*. The objects themselves are *nodes* in the graph; the relationships form the *edges*. Figure 9-6 shows a graph of related objects (each object is a node in the graph).

Levels of Relationship Service

The Relationship Service defines generic interfaces that let you associate roles and relationships with existing CORBA objects. You can then traverse them (in any direction) using very sophisticated graph interfaces. The service maintains the relationships between the related objects. It also defines two specific relationships: *containment* and *references*. The service lets you create relationships of arbitrary degree and cardinality; it will enforce the degree and cardinality constraints and detect violations. The service treats relations, roles, and graphs as first-class CORBA objects. As a result, you can extend their function by subclassing. You can also pass around graphs that describe related objects to interested parties.

The beauty of the CORBA Relationship Service is that it lets you create arbitrary relations between objects that are totally unaware of relationships. You can do this without changing the implementation of the existing objects. The service lets you surround existing objects with a web of relationship objects that you put together piece by piece. The service defines interfaces that let you construct and navigate these relationship webs (node by node). The interfaces of the Relationship Service are grouped into three categories: *base*, *graph*, and *specific*. We go over these three categories in the next three sections.

Relationship Service: The Base Interfaces

The base relations interfaces define operations that let you create **Role** and **Relationship** objects and navigate the relationships in which a role participates (see Figure 9-7). We also show them inheriting from an **IdentifiableObject** interface that lets you test two CORBA object references for equality. This is a very generic object service that should have been part of the ORB interface; instead, it ended up in the Relationship Service (at least you know where to find it). The interfaces are grouped into two modules called *CosObjectIdentity* and *CosRelationships*. Here's what these interfaces do:

- **IdentifiableObject** provides a single operation *is_identical* that returns true if two CORBA objects are identical. The Relationship Service requires this object identity operation for the objects it defines.

- **RelationshipFactory** defines a *create* operation that lets you create an instance of a relationship. You pass the factory a sequence of named roles that represent the related objects in the newly created relationship. The factory, in turn, informs each of the **Role** objects of the newly created relation by invoking their *link* operation.

- **RoleFactory** defines a *create_role* operation that lets you associate a role with a CORBA object you pass as a parameter.

- **Relationship** defines a single operation that lets you *destroy* a relationship. The roles are *unlinked* by the operation before the relationship is destroyed.

- **Role** defines operations that let you navigate relationships in which a role participates and to link a role to a relationship. You invoke *get_other_role* to get to the related role in a relation; you invoke *get_other_related_object* to get the related object at the other end. You invoke *get_relationships* to obtain the relationships in which a role participates (see next bullet). You invoke *destroy_relationships* to free the role from all the relationships in which it participates. You invoke *destroy* to destroy a role that is not participating in any relationships. *Check_minimum_cardinality* returns true if a role satisfies its minimum cardinality constraints. *Link* is used by factories to link a role into a relationship. *Unlink* is used by the *destroy* operation to remove a role from a relationship.

- **RelationshipIterator** lets you iterate through additional relationships in which a **Role** participates. An iterator object is returned when you invoke *Role::get_relationships*.

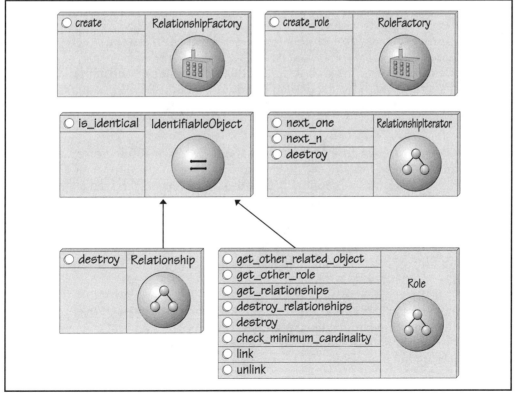

Figure 9-7. Relationship Service: The Base Interfaces.

Relationship Service: Graphs of Related Objects

As we explained earlier, a graph is a set of nodes and edges. The *nodes* are the related objects; the *edges* are the relationships. A node can support one or more roles. The graph interfaces let you describe and traverse graphs (see Figure 9-8). Most of these interfaces are self-explanatory, but let's quickly go over the most important ones:

- **Node** associates an object with its roles. It provides operations that let you add and remove roles. The *roles_of_type* operation lets you query for roles of a particular type.

- **Traversal** lets you navigate through a graph of related objects starting at a **Node** object that you specify.

- **TraversalCriteria** lets you associate rules in the form of callback functions to determine what relationship/node should be visited next. The operations of this object are invoked by the **Traversal** object.

- **Role** is derived from **CosRelationships::Role**. It provides a new operation called *get_edges*. This operation returns a role's view of its relationships either in the form of a structure or an iterator of type **EdgeIterator**.

- **EdgeIterator** provides two operations that let you iterate through the relationships associated with a role. It also provides a self-destructing operation called *destroy*. You create and obtain an **EdgeIterator** object when you invoke *Role::get_edges*.

As you can see, these graph interface objects can be very useful. For example, you can use them to describe all the objects (and relationships) shown in Figure 9-6. You can then ship a graph object that describes these objects (as well as the objects themselves) to a remote destination where the relationships can be recreated and traversed. You do all this without modifying the related objects or their attributes. They're not in the least way aware that they are part of a graph of related objects. It's magic! The graph interfaces are used by the Life Cycle Service to implement deep copies and moves. They are also used by the Externalization Service to stream a group of related objects.

We anticipate that system integrators and IS shops will be the primary users of this service. Relationships offer them a standard way to define ad-hoc ensembles made of multiple components. They will be able to attach roles to different components and connect them via graphs. This is one way for them to assemble a component suite (or ensemble).

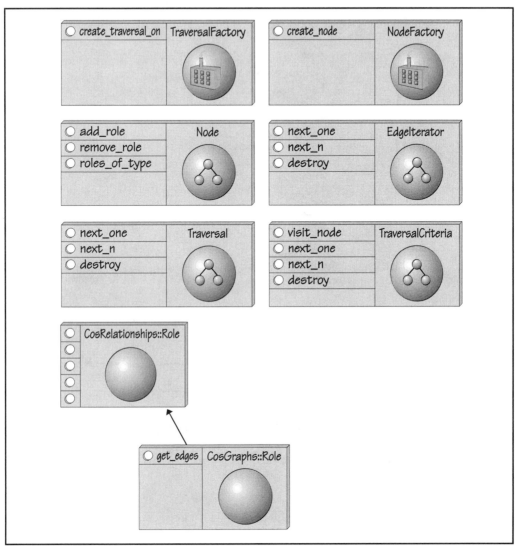

Figure 9-8. Relationship Service: The Graph Interfaces.

Relationship Service: The Containment and Reference Relationships

Containment and *reference* are very common relationships. Consequently, the Relationship Service provides a standardized set of interfaces for both these relationships (see Figure 9-9). You can use these interfaces as a model for how to create your own relationships (for example, authoring, employment, family, friends, and so on).

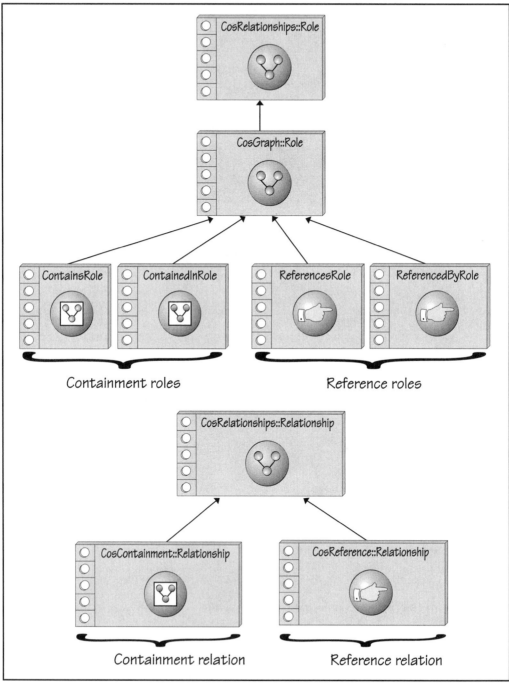

Figure 9-9. Relationship Service: The Containment and Reference Relationships.

Notice in the figure that these two relationships do not introduce any new operations. They are simply derived from the existing Relationship Service interfaces. These derived interfaces define CORBA IDL types for all the roles and relationships that are specific to containment and reference. The derived attributes let you define the degree of each relation. The containment relation defines a *ContainsRole* and a *ContainedInRole*. Likewise, the references relation defines a *ReferencesRole* and a *ReferencedByRole*. Both these relations are binary (of degree 2). The factories will enforce these constraints when you create new instances of these relationships.

Conclusion

This concludes another three CORBA services—the tally is now ten down and six more to go. CORBA is an extremely ambitious undertaking; it covers the entire field of distributed object computing. The three services we presented in this chapter are extremely important in their own right. We could write an entire book describing the fun things you could do with just these three services. The marriage of object queries with collections is absolute dynamite. And you can use the Relationship Service in countless situations involving independently developed components. For example, you could use that service to create workflows, enforce referential integrity, describe compound documents, and create object containers of all types. But we've got to move on.

Chapter 10

CORBA Services: System Management and Security

Never deploy a component you cannot manage.

> — *An old system manager's tale*
> *(July, 1995)*

This is the last chapter on CORBA services. We've grouped all six remaining services under the umbrella of system management (it's as good a catch-all classification as we could find). We will be covering the following services: *Security, Licensing, Time, Change Management, Properties,* and *Externalization* (see Figure 10-1). With the exception of Externalization and Properties, these services let you manage an object's distributed environment. Externalization lets you write an object's contents into a stream so that you can exchange it or move it around. It complements the Persistence and Life Cycle Services. Properties is a very useful service. It lets you dynamically associate attributes with shrink-wrapped components at run time. You can then manage these attributes independently from the objects they describe. We will cover these six CORBA services in their order of completion in the standards process.

Part 2. CORBA: The Distributed Object Bus

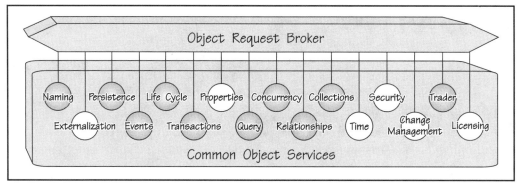

Figure 10-1. CORBA System Management Services.

THE CORBA EXTERNALIZATION SERVICE

Streams are quite fascinating because they can be used for so many purposes. It will be virtually impossible to develop a serious object which does not support the streamable interface.

> — **Roger Sessions, Author**
> **Object Persistence**
> **(Prentice Hall, 1996)**

The *Externalization Service*—originally from Taligent—defines interfaces for externalizing an object to a stream and internalizing an object from a stream. Most programmers are already familiar with the power and simplicity of streams. A *stream* is a data holding area with an associated cursor. A *cursor* is a mobile pointer that moves forward and backward as you write and read data to and from a stream. The data holding area can be in memory, on a disk file, or across a network. You can't tell the difference. You *externalize* an object to a stream to transport it to a different process, machine, or ORB. You *internalize* the object when you need to bring it back to life at its new destination.

Stream Power

In a sense, externalizing and then internalizing an object is similar to copying it using the Life Cycle Service. The difference is that externalization and internalization break the copy into two steps: 1) You copy the object to a stream; 2) You copy from the stream into the final destination object. This two-step process lets you export the object outside of its ORB environment. You do not create a new object until the stream is internalized somewhere else. Streams become an import/export medium for objects. As opposed to a Life Cycle copy the Externalization Service stops along the way—by breaking a move or copy operation into two steps. It gives you a chance to do something with the intermediate results

Streams let you copy and move objects. They also let you pass objects by value in a parameter (today, CORBA only lets you pass objects by reference in a method call). Roger Sessions predicts that every object will be streamable. If this happens, streams will become the universal protocol for getting data into and out of objects. Every Persistent Data Service will only need to translate from streams to their own persistent store mechanism.

Externalization Service: The Base Interfaces

Figure 10-2 shows the six interfaces that provide the core Externalization Service. The client's view of externalization is very simple. A client creates (or locates) a **Stream** object and passes it one or more objects to be externalized. You create a stream by invoking a **StreamFactory**. You can also create a file-based stream by invoking **FileStreamFactory**. You then invoke *externalize* to request that the object write itself to a stream. You can also write several objects to the same stream as follows: 1) invoke *begin_context*; 2) invoke *externalize* for each object you want to store in the stream; and 3) invoke *end_context*. You invoke the same *externalize* call to store a simple object or a graph of related objects.

When the **Stream** object receives an *externalize* invocation, it turns around and invokes the *externalize_to_stream* method on the target object's **Streamable** interface. All streamable objects must implement this interface (typically as a mixin using multiple inheritance). The streamable object calls the **StreamIO** operations to read or write its state to or from that stream. This interface is implemented by the Stream Service; it provides operations to write and read—to and from a stream—all the IDL data types. It also lets you read and write related objects using the *write_graph* and *read_graph* operations. The **Stream** object either directly implements the **StreamIO** interface or passes an object reference to it when it calls the streamable object.

To internalize an object from a stream, the client invokes *internalize* on a **Stream** object. The **Stream** object must locate (or create) a **Streamable** object that can internalize its state from a stream; it uses the **StreamableFactory** interface to create the object. The stream then invokes the streamable object's *internalize_from_stream* method. Of course, the streamable object uses the **StreamIO** interface to read the stream contents. Does it sound complicated? It really isn't. We'll back our claim with a little scenario.

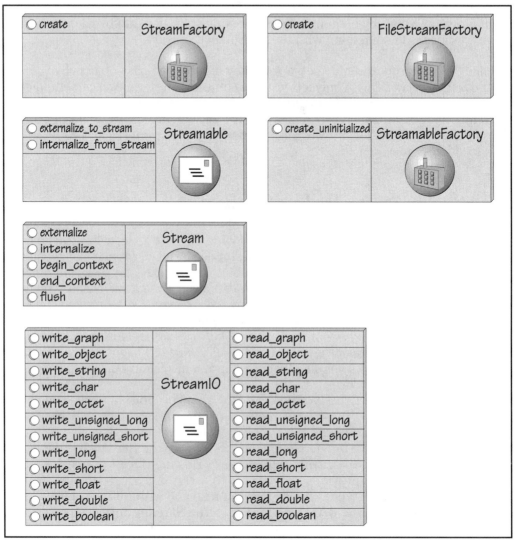

Figure 10-2. Externalization Service: The Base Interfaces.

A Stream Scenario

The scenario in Figure 10-3 demonstrates how objects are externalized and internalized using streams. Let's walk through the steps:

1. ***Client obtains a Stream object***. The client invokes *StreamFactory::create* to obtain a new **Stream** object.

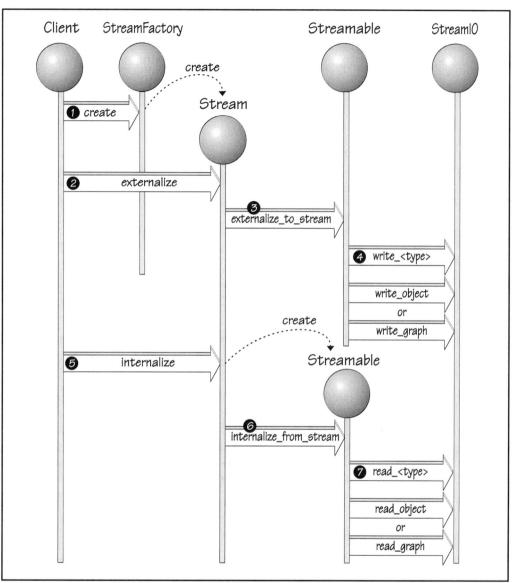

Figure 10-3. Scenario: Object Externalization and Internalization Via Streams.

2. ***Client tells stream to externalize an object.*** The client invokes *Stream::externalize* and passes it the object reference to be externalized (Note: this object must support the **Streamable** interface).

3. ***Stream tells the streamable object to externalize itself.*** The stream invokes *Streamable::externalize_to_stream* to tell the object to externalize itself to stream.

4. *Object writes its contents to stream*. The object uses the **StreamIO** *write_<type>* operations to write its data contents. It invokes *write_object* to stream embedded objects. A streamable object may also participate as a node in a graph of related objects. This means it may be connected to other objects via the Relationship Service. Connected objects invoke *write_graph* to let the stream service coordinate the externalization of the graph of related objects with the help of the Relationship Service.

5. *Later, the client needs to internalize the stream*. You can store the externalized form of an object inside a stream for arbitrary amounts of time. You can even transport it to an outside ORB. When you're ready to internalize the object, you invoke *Stream::internalize*. The **Stream** object looks inside the stream for a key that helps it locate a factory that can create an object with an implementation that matches the object in the stream.

6. *Stream tells the streamable object to internalize itself*. The stream invokes *Streamable::internalize_from_stream* to tell the object to internalize itself to stream.

7. *Object reads its contents from the stream*. The object uses the **StreamIO** *read_<type>* operations to read its data contents. It invokes *read_object* to read embedded objects. If the streamable object is a node within a graph of related objects, it invokes *read_graph* to let the stream service coordinate the internalization of the related objects with the help of the Relationship Service.

The Externalization Service also defines a *Standard Stream Data Format* that lets you exchange streams across dissimilar networks, operating system platforms, and storage implementations. This standard stream representation uses self-describing IDL data type formats as well as headers that describe the types of objects that are contained within the stream. The **StreamIO** object is responsible for encoding the data within a stream using this canonical representation and for recreating a stream's contents.

THE CORBA OBJECT LICENSING SERVICE

As desktop networking increases, control of component usage becomes more difficult. Components will "leak" into organizations from external sources and be propagated quickly via networks and "sneakernet."

— *Gartner Group*
(February, 1995)

For the component market to evolve in a manageable fashion, license management software will have to grow to include component licensing. And components will have to be written to automatically register with license managers. The CORBA *Licensing Service*—originally from Gradient, Digital, and IBM—meets these requirements. It should be dear to the heart of all component providers. The service lets you meter the use of your components and charge accordingly. Traditional licensing mechanisms—for example, site licensing and node-locked licensing—do not play well in the world of distributed ORB-based components. We need more flexible mechanisms for metering the use of our components and charging for their usage.

What Does the Licensing Service Do?

The Licensing Service lets you enforce a wide range of licensing options to fit your business needs. For example, you can provide a grace period to let potential new users test-drive your components, you can ensure that a license is always available to high-priority customers, you can allow multiple components to be used with a single license, and so on. The Licensing Service separates the "I want to be controlled" requirements of a component from the "how am I to be controlled" requirements that deal with policy. A component notifies the service when it wishes to be controlled without getting into the details of how the control is enforced.

The Licensing Service can collect component usage metrics. This helps you determine which components are "shelfware" and which are actively being used. All licenses must have start/duration and expiration dates. You should also be able to assign some licenses to specific users, collections of users, or organizations. The service makes sure that when a licensed component is being used, the component and the licensing server are continuously aware of each other's existence. Finally, the Licensing Service must be a secured server resource. You don't want a Trojan horse (or an imposter licensing system) to give away free licenses to your components. You also don't want to let outsiders tamper with the usage database.

Licensing Service Interfaces

A component market must protect itself from copying and distribution of good components without reimbursement.

> — *Dr. Ivar Jacobson, Author*
> *Object-Oriented Software Engineering*
> *(Addison-Wesley, 1993)*

The Licensing Service consists of two interfaces (see Figure 10-4) that provide all the operations a component needs to license-protect itself. The component uses

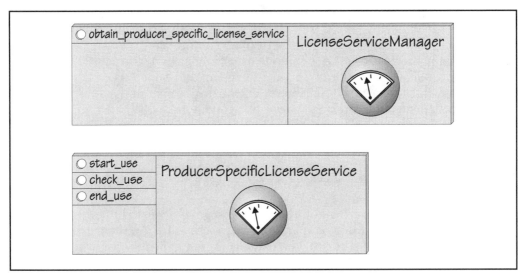

Figure 10-4. The Licensing Service Interfaces.

these interfaces to let the service monitor know when it's being used (including by whom and for how long). Let's go over these two interfaces and explain what they do:

- **LicenseServiceManager** is like a minibroker for locating license services that implement specific policies. It will connect you with a service that's suitable for your component. The interface supports a single operation with a very long name: *obtain_producer_specific_license_service*. This operation returns an object reference for a particular license service. Note that a "producer" is your licensed component. It's the intellectual property you produced and for which you want to be compensated.

- **ProducerSpecificLicenseService** provides three operations that do all the work. Your licensed component invokes *start_use* when it's first used. You must pass in a parameter all the necessary information associated with the user of the component. The component invokes *end_use* when it stops being used. It invokes *check_use* periodically when it's being used to let the service know the connection with the customer is still live. The service may check for license expiration time and return a message to that effect. How does the component know when to invoke a *check_use*? It knows by either polling at an interval specified by the server, or by asynchronously receiving an event notification from the server telling it to issue a *check_use*.

All the operations between the component and the service are protected by a poor man's authentication mechanism called a *challenge* (it's an in/out parameter that serves as an authentication key in the message). The license server must return the proper challenge result to authenticate itself to the licensed component. We expect these challenges to be replaced by the ORB's security service when it becomes available.

A Licensing Scenario

The scenario in Figure 10-5 demonstrates how a licensed-protected component interacts with the Licensing Service. Let's walk through the steps:

1. ***Obtain an object reference for a licensing service***. Every license-protected component must obtain an object reference to a licensing service that implements a policy that suits the component provider. You do this by invoking *obtain_producer_specific_license_service* on the **LicenseServiceManager**.

2. ***Notify the licensing service when a client starts using your component***. You must determine what it means to use your component and how you want to get paid for it. At one extreme, you may want to charge for each method invocation. At the other extreme, you may want to charge for a connection to a collection of objects. In any case, you invoke *start_use* to tell the licensing service that your component is being used. You must pass it the name of your component, its version, and the object reference for a callback event notification. In addition, you must pass it a user context that is used by the service to determine how to deal with the user of your component—for example, you might

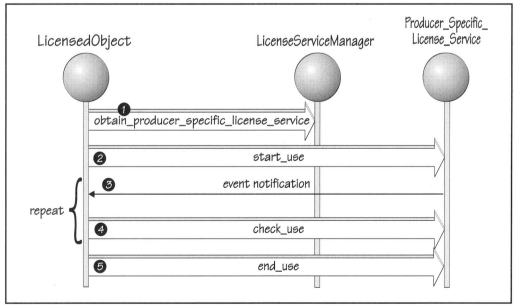

Figure 10-5. Scenario: How A License Protected Component Interacts With the Licensing Service.

want to ask these two important questions: Is the user's license still valid? How should the user be charged for the use of your component? You will receive from the service instructions on how to proceed in the *action_to_be_taken* returned parameter.

3. ***Licensing service sends your component an event notification***. The licensing service tells your component that it's time to perform a *check_use*. It does this using the CORBA Event Service. Alternatively, the component could have issued *check_uses* at server-specified checking intervals.

4. ***Issue a check_use***. You invoke *check_use* to tell the licensing service that your component is still being used. The call returns instructions from the licensing service. You must issue *check_use*—either when requested to do so via an event or at regular intervals. This is how the licensing server and your component are continuously made aware of each other's existence when the component is in use.

5. ***Inform the licensing service when your component is no longer being used***. You invoke *end_use* to tell the licensing service the user (or client) stopped using your component. This how the meter gets turned off.

In summary, your component must inform the service when it is first used, when it is still in use, and when it stops being used.

THE CORBA OBJECT PROPERTY SERVICE

The *Property Service*—originally from Taligent, SunSoft, and IBM—lets you dynamically associate named attributes with a shrink-wrapped component. You can define these dynamic attributes (or properties) at run time without using IDL. Then you can associate them with an object that already exists. Once you define these properties, you can give them names, get and set their values, set their access modes, and delete them. In contrast, you can only get and set an IDL-defined attribute. You cannot create an attribute "on the fly", set its mode, or delete it.

Properties are essentially typed named values that you can dynamically associate with an object outside the IDL type system. For example, you should be able to add an archive property to an existing document at run time and mark the document as ready to be archived. The archive information is associated with the object, but it's not part of the object's type.

Property Service Interfaces

The Property Service consists of six interfaces; four of these are factories and iterators. The two main interfaces are **PropertySet** and **PropertySetDef** (see

Figure 10-6). **PropertySetDef** is a subclass of **PropertySet**; it provides additional operations that let you manipulate and control a property's mode.

The Property Service defines four mutually exclusive property *modes*: 1) *normal* means there are no restrictions to the property; 2) *read-only* means clients can read and delete the property but not update it; 3) *fixed-normal* means the property can be modified but not deleted; and 4) *fixed-readonly* means the property can only be read. You can think of these modes as metadata that define the constraints on a property. Every object that supports the Property Service must implement either the **PropertySet** or **PropertySetDef** interfaces. Let's go over the operations these two interfaces define:

■ **PropertySet** defines ten operations that let you define, delete, enumerate, and check for the existence of properties. It provides *get* operations for reading property values and their metadata. It also provides "batch" operations that let you deal with sets of properties as a whole. These are the operations whose names end in "s". Note that a property consists of a name (a string), a value (of type any), and a mode.

■ **PropertySetDef** defines eight operations that let you control and modify the property modes. You can manipulate these modes either individually or in batches.

It's easy to associate a property with an object and then manipulate it either individually or in a batch. The experience with SNMP and CMIP has taught the industry that it's important to be able to manipulate properties in groups, especially in distributed environments. The Properties Service lets you do this very well; it also provides interfaces to iterate through groups of properties.

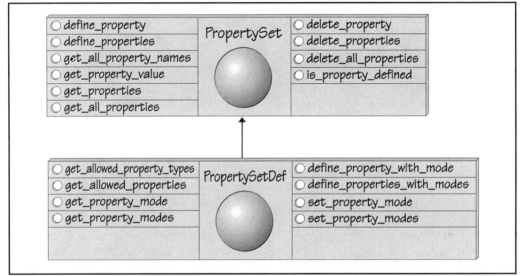

Figure 10-6. The Two Key Property Service Interfaces.

THE CORBA OBJECT TIME SERVICE

Maintaining a single notion of time is important for ordering events that occur in distributed object systems. So how does an ORB keep the clocks on different machines synchronized? How does it compensate for the unequal drift rates between synchronizations? How does it create a single-system illusion that makes all the different machine clocks tick to the same time? The *Object Time Service* is the obvious answer.

As we go to press, OMG has still not completed the Object Time Service—it's part of RFP3. Based on some early input, we expect the service to address the problem of distributed time using the following complementary techniques:

■ It could periodically synchronize the clocks on every machine in the network. The service could have an agent on each machine—DCE calls it a *Time Clerk*— that asks global *Time Servers* for the correct time and adjusts the local time accordingly. The agent may consult more than one Time Server, and then calculate the probable correct time and its inaccuracy based on the responses it receives. The agent can upgrade the local time either gradually or abruptly.

■ It could introduce *inaccuracy factors* to compensate for unequal clock drifts that occur between synchronizations. You can configure the local time agents to know the limits of their local hardware clock. They can maintain a count of the inaccuracy factor and return it to an invocation that asks for the time. The time agent requests a resynchronization after the local clock drifts past an inaccuracy threshold.

■ It could introduce *time server* objects that answer queries about the time. Following the DCE model, an ORB could provide at least three time servers; one (or more) must be connected to an external time provider. The time servers query one another to adjust their clocks. The external time provider may be a hardware device that receives time from a radio or a telephone source. If no such source is available, the system administrator's watch may suffice. The commonly used time format in the industry is the *Coordinated Universal Time (UTC)* standard, which keeps track of time elapsed since the beginning of the Gregorian calendar—October 15, 1582. This time is adjusted using the Greenwich time zone differential factor (for example, –5 hours in New York City).

By the time you read this book, OMG will have defined its Time Service. We are confident much of it will be along the lines we just described. After all, there is only so much you can do with distributed time.

THE CORBA OBJECT SECURITY SERVICE

Security is a pervasive object service that affects every aspect of distributed object computing (see next Briefing box). In April 1994, OMG issued an elaborate "White

Paper on Security" that describes a security model for distributed objects. OMG then issued RFP3 in June 1994, making it clear that responders should address the issues raised in the White Paper. In March 1995, OMG received three strong submissions on security all of which address the issues in the White Paper. Consequently, OMG approved an extension to the submission deadline in return for a merger of the three proposals.

As we go to press, there is still no official OMG Security Service, but it was getting close. We expect the Security Service to be finalized by the end of 1995. The good news is that all three submissions are superior to any existing client/server security system. We hope the final outcome will be even better by combining the best in the three submissions. This section gives you a sampling of the general ideas that were brought up in the White Paper and the three submissions. It is not based on the final specification. Note that the *Security Service* is more than a set of interfaces; it includes models of how users, programmers, and administrators think of security.

Are Distributed Objects Less Secure?

Briefing

Distributed objects face all the security problems of traditional client/server systems—and more. The client/server environment introduces new security threats beyond those found in traditional time-shared systems. In a client/server system, you can't trust any of the client operating systems on the network to protect the server's resources from unauthorized access. And even if the client machines were totally secure, the network itself is highly accessible. You can never trust information in transit. Sniffer devices can easily record traffic between machines and introduce forgeries and Trojan horses into the system. This means the servers must find new ways to protect themselves without creating a fortress mentality that upsets users. In addition to these threats, distributed objects must also be concerned with the following added complications:

■ *Distributed objects can play both client and server roles*. In a traditional client/server architecture, it is clear who is a client and who is a server. Typically, you can trust servers, but not clients. For example, a client trusts its database server, but the reverse is not true. In distributed object systems, you cannot clearly distinguish between clients and servers. These are just alternate roles that a single object can play.

■ ***Distributed objects evolve continually.*** When you interact with an object, you're only seeing the tip of the iceberg. You may be seeing a "facade" object that delegates parts of its implementation to other objects; these delegates may be dynamically composed at run time. Also, because of subclassing, the implementations of an object may change over time, without the original programmer ever knowing or caring.

■ ***Distributed objects interactions are not well understood***. Because of encapsulation, you cannot fully understand all the interactions that take place between the objects you invoke. There is too much "behind the scenes" activity.

■ ***Distributed object interactions are less predictable***. Because distributed objects are more flexible and granular than other forms of client/server systems, they may interact in more ad-hoc ways. This is a strength of the distributed object model, but it's also a security risk.

■ ***Distributed objects are polymorphic***. Objects are flexible; it is easy to replace one object on the ORB with another that abides by the same interfaces. This makes it a dream situation for Trojan horses; they can impersonate legitimate objects and thus cause all kinds of havoc.

■ ***Distributed objects can scale without limit.*** Because every object can be a server, we may end up with millions of servers on the ORB. How do we manage access rights for millions of servers?

■ ***Distributed objects are very dynamic.*** A distributed object environment is inherently anarchistic. Objects come and go. They get created dynamically and self-destruct when they're no longer being used. This dynamism is, of course, a great strength of objects, but it could also be a security nightmare.

To maintain a single system illusion, every trusted user (and object) must be given transparent access to all other objects. How is this done when every PC poses a potential threat to network security? Will system administrators be condemned to spend their working lives granting access level rights to objects— one at a time—for each individual object on each server across the enterprise?

The good news is that many of these problems can be solved by moving the security implementation into the CORBA ORB itself. The ORB must manage security for a range of systems from trusted domains (within a single process or machine) to intergalactic inter-ORB situations. Components that are not responsible for enforcing their own security are easier to develop, administer, and port across environments. In addition, moving security inside the ORB can minimize the performance overhead. ❑

What Is ORB-Based Security?

The three security proposals in front of the OMG build security into the ORB itself (see Figure 10-7). They all provide better than C2 security for distributed objects. C2 is a government security standard for operating systems that requires users and applications be authenticated before gaining access to any operating system resource. To obtain C2 certification on a network, all clients must provide an authenticated user ID, all resources must be protected by access control lists, audit trails must be provided, and access rights must not be passed to other users that reuse the same items. Let's go over the security mechanisms an ORB must provide to meet (and even beat) C2 level security on the network.

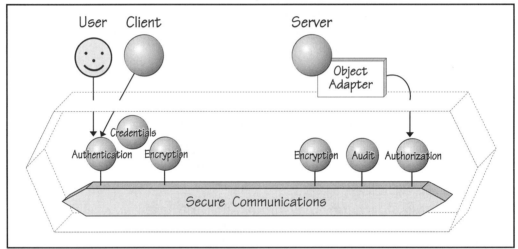

Figure 10-7. CORBA Security Is Built Into the ORB.

Authentication: Are You Who You Claim to Be?

In timeshared systems, the operating system does authentication by using passwords. ORBs must do better than that. Any hacker with a PC and network sniffer knows how to capture a password and reuse it. OK, so let's encrypt the password. Oh boy! Who is going to manage the secret keys and all that good stuff? Luckily, ORBs have an answer: trusted third-party authenticators (for example, Kerberos) that let objects prove to each other that they are who they claim to be. It's a bit like two spies meeting on a street corner and whispering the magical code words that establish the "trust" relationship. Both parties obtain the magic words separately from the trusted third party. The result is that a user—called a *principal*—is authenticated once by the ORB and given a role, select rights, and a security clearance. This means that the principal only has to log on once regardless of the number of objects it uses.

Authentication results in a unique *authenticated ID* that cannot be changed by an object; only the authentication server can change it. The authenticated client can access any server object from anywhere—including hotel rooms, offices, homes, and cellular phones—using a single signon. How's that done? With ORB-propagated *context security*. You simply log on once, get authenticated, and then obtain a set of security tickets (also called tokens) for the objects with which you want to communicate. All this activity is conducted "under-the-cover" by the ORB's security mechanisms. No password is stored in the login script on the client, and no telephone callbacks are required. It doesn't get any easier, as long as you can remember your password.

The authenticated ID that's automatically propagated by the ORB—as part of a caller's *context*—also serves the following purposes: 1) it makes clients (or users) accountable for their actions; 2) it lets a server determine which resources a user can access; 3) it uniquely identifies the originator of a message; 4) it helps service providers determine who to charge for the use of a service; and 5) it serves as a privilege that can be delegated by a server to its helper objects.

Authorization: Are You Allowed to Use This Resource?

Once clients are authenticated, the server objects are responsible for verifying which operations the clients are permitted to perform on the information they try to access (for example, a payroll server may control access to salary data on a per-individual basis). Servers use *Access Control Lists (ACLs)* and a derivation called *Capability Lists* to control user access. ACLs can be associated with any computer resource. They contain the list of names (and group names) of principals and the type of operations they are permitted to perform on each resource. You should be able to have multiple ACL policies in an ORB. The ORB can implement some of the policies; the server object can implement the others.

In a distributed object system, an object is typically the unit of access control. However, you may also want to control access at a lower level of granularity by making each method of an object a controlled resource. To make it easier on the administrator, you may want less granularity, and you may want to provide controls on collections of objects instead of individual objects or methods. In addition, it requires a lot more overhead to run an access control check on every method for every object. So the tradeoff is between having very fine levels of granular security controls that objects can provide and having an explosion of objects and subjects in your access control lists.

Audit Trails: Where Have You Been?

Audit services allow system managers to monitor ORB events, including attempted logons and which servers or objects are used. Audit services are a piece of the arsenal needed by system managers to detect intruders in their own organizations. For example, they can monitor all the network activity associated with a suspect client workstation (or user). Knowing an audit trail exists usually discourages insiders from tampering with servers using their own logon, but they can do it under somebody else's logon.

Non-Repudiation: Was This Message Tampered With?

Non-repudiation has become a hot topic in electronic commerce circles. It means that neither party can deny in a court of law that they were involved in a client/server interaction. An ORB must provide safeguards that protect all parties from false claims that data was tampered with or not sent or received. In other words, the ORB must provide the electronic equivalent of a sealed envelope. The information must be protected against corruption or replay. To do this, the ORB must provide the sender with proof of delivery and the receiver with proof of a sender's identity. You don't want the data in an electronic fund transfer to be intercepted and rerouted from your account to somebody else's.

ORBs can provide at least two mechanisms for dealing with these type of situations: 1) *Encryption* allows two principals to hold a secure communication, and 2) *Cryptographic checksums*—a less extreme solution—ensures that data is not modified as it passes through the network. All three RFP submissions make it possible for ORBs to use standard industry encryption and electronic signature mechanisms such as RSA's Cryptoki, OSF's Kerberos, Internet's GSS, NetWare 4.X, and NIS+. [1]

Other Security Issues

In addition to providing an ORB-based solution for the issues we just described, the three security proposals make strong provisions for the following: inter-ORB security, federated security domains, trusted domains, protection boundaries, and

---

[1] The first submission from SunSoft is based on a working implementation of their new distributed object operating system called *Spring*. The second submission from Tivoli, HP, and IBM marries distributed object security with existing security systems. The third very strong submission is from nine companies—including AT&T, Digital, Novell, ICL, Tandem Computers, Expersoft, Groupe Bull, Siemens Nixdorf, and Odyssey Research.

coexistence with existing standards and security mechanisms. They also deal with the issue of how to assign access list protection to millions of objects. More importantly, all these proposals make it possible to provide security for components that know nothing of security and have no security interfaces. This makes it easy to port components across environments that support different security mechanisms.

THE CORBA OBJECT CHANGE MANAGEMENT SERVICE

Change Management is another service that should be dear to the heart of component providers. It lets you track different versions of your components (and their interfaces) as they evolve; it will also maintain their evolution history. You will be able to maintain versions of individual components as well as their interfaces and implementations. It's certainly a service that's vital for the creation of a true components industry.

The Change Management Service will ensure that an object instance uses a consistent implementation version. For example, an old version of an object instance will use an old implementation version, and so on. You'll be able to find object versions by name. The version will be directly encoded in an object reference. This means that you can invoke several versions of the same object at the same time. A version may also have a context associated with it—for example, demo, test, and release. The default is always the latest version.

Interface versions will be tracked by the IDL and Interface Repository. You can create new versions of objects explicitly—for example, by invoking *CreateVersion*,

or implicitly—for example, when a long transaction commits. The service will be able to track snapshots of a mutually consistent collection of components (or a compound object). It will also maintain change reasons as well as backward and forward deltas from a periodic baseline. The service will let you *checkout* a version of a component, *checkin* a modified version, and so on.

This is all good stuff. Don't you wish you had it today? Unfortunately, this service is part of RFP5, which was just being issued as we went to press. So it won't be available until the end of 1996 (or later). In the meantime, you may want to consider some ORB-specific form of versioning. For example, SOM implements a proprietary IDL-based form of versioning today.

Conclusion

This concludes our presentation of the CORBA services. The tally is sixteen down with no more to go. The message we want to leave you with is that CORBA services represent the cutting edge of distributed object technology and client/server middleware. Most of this technology comes from advanced research projects such as SunSoft's Spring (a next generation distributed object OS), Taligent's state-of-the-art frameworks, and advanced projects at IBM, HP, Digital, ICL, Tandem, Novell, Groupe Bull, AT&T, Siemens, and others. In addition, it represents the work of small but highly innovative companies such as Tivoli, Gradient, Iona, Expersoft, Visual Edge, and many others. Some people may call it "design by committee." However, we see it as the most ambitious cross-company effort ever attempted. This is what it takes to create the next generation of intergalactic middleware. No company alone can ever hope to duplicate this effort.

Chapter 11

CORBA Commercial ORBs

---

*T*he CORBA products of today are in a situation analogous to the early days of Ethernet products; the vendors are building to a common standard, and they are actively working towards interoperability with CORBA 2.0.

— Tom Mowbray et al., Authors
The Essential CORBA
(Wiley, 1995)

In this chapter, we look at the top six commercial CORBA ORBs. At this stage of the game, it's too early to pick winners. The CORBA market is still in its infancy. Everyone is trying to figure out how to use these ORBs. The ORBs themselves are still very experimental. And, they will all go through major product upgrades in the next six months. Given all this, our choice of the "top six" is very arbitrary. Anyway, the six ORBs we're going to cover are Iona's Orbix, IBM's SOM, Digital's ObjectBroker, Sun's DOE, HP's ORB Plus (or ORB+), and Expersoft's XShell. We left out several good ORBs, but this representative sample should give you an idea of what's currently available and what's coming down the road very shortly.

If all these ORBs are CORBA-compliant, what's there to discuss? It turns out there's quite a bit of ground to cover. We first go over the features these ORBs provide today. We also look at what's in the pipeline for early 1996. We also briefly cover the underlying architectures on which these ORBs are built. Even though they all follow the CORBA object model, most of the ORB implementations are radically different. For example, some vendors build their ORBs on RPCs, others write directly to the transport layer, and so on. Finally, we go over the CORBA extensions these ORBs provide. These non-standard features can be extremely useful but they lock you into a vendor's implementation.

Ideally, we would have liked to run some benchmarks on these ORBs to give you some hard numbers on how they compare. Unfortunately, the benchmark we are developing is still work in progress (we expect it to be in our next book). Also, these ORBs are all going through major performance upgrades, so any performance numbers are bound to change. In addition to raw performance, the benchmark should look at other factors—including scaling, load-balancing, garbage collection, fault-tolerance, resource consumption, ease-of-installation, ease-of-management, availability of tools, and so on.

IONA'S ORBIX

Iona has become the leading third-party Windows-based object request broker.

> — *Timothy O'Brien*
> *Distributed Computing Monitor*
> *(July, 1994)*

Iona is a small Irish company that was established in 1991. The founders came from Groupe Bull and the Distributed Systems Group at Trinity College, Dublin. Orbix is a light-weight ORB that was built from scratch to the CORBA specifications. Orbix 1.0 shipped in 1993; Orbix 2.0 shipped in 1995. The current product provides a C++ binding for CORBA and is supported on multiple operating systems. Major enhancements to Orbix 2.0 are in the works. Two releases are expected—one in late 1995, and the other in early 1996.

Even though Iona is a small company, it has strong alliances with Sun. SunSoft owns a part of Iona; it plans to use Orbix as an extension of DOE on non-Sun platforms. Iona has a strong alliance with ODI, which plans to use Orbix as the ORB for its ObjectStore ODBMS. Iona is also working on integrating Orbix with Novell's Tuxedo TP Monitor. If it succeeds, Tuxedo will provide process management and load balancing for Orbix objects.

Orbix Architecture

Orbix is implemented as a pair of libraries—one for the client and one for the server. It also includes an activation daemon on the server that provides the BOA function. This daemon uses a CORBA Implementation Repository database to launch server objects based on their activation policy. The entire Orbix system is implemented in C++ and is very portable. It was compiled with several compilers—including Microsoft C++ and various Unix C++ compilers.

Orbix uses TCP/IP as its transport layer. It builds on sockets (WinSock on the Windows platform). It also supports the ONC-RPC (the SUN RPC). Orbix provides a transport-layer encapsulator that shields applications from the underlying transports. Using this encapsulator, Iona demonstrated an implementation of Orbix that uses ATMI—Novell's Tuxedo TP Monitor messaging protocol—as its underlying transport. Tuxedo complements Orbix by providing load-balancing and transaction management. Iona also demonstrated a prototype of Orbix that uses the *Reliable Computing Environment* from Isis as its underlying protocol. Isis complements Orbix by letting you replicate objects for high availability; it also provides a robust network operating system.

Orbix 2.0's Current CORBA Support

Orbix 2.0 is based on CORBA 1.2. It provides all the CORBA 1.2 ORB functionality—including an Interface Repository, Implementation Repository, IDL precompiler, and Basic Object Adapter (BOA). It supports both CORBA's static and dynamic method invocations. Orbix provides language bindings for C and C++; the C++ bindings are slightly different from the CORBA specification, but they will be compliant by the time your read this. Currently, Orbix runs on the following platforms: Windows 3.X, Windows NT, Sun Solaris, SunOS, HP-UX, IBM AIX, Novell UnixWare, SGI IRIX, SCO Unix, and Digital Unix and Ultrix.

Orbix's CORBA Support in Early 1996

Iona's two major upgrades of Orbix will provide CORBA 2.0 support and some key CORBA services (Iona does not provide any CORBA services today).[1] Here are the upgrades you should be expecting:

---

[1] Some of the information on product futures in this chapter was obtained from an advanced copy of a report by John Rymer to be published in the **Distributed Computing Monitor**.

- **CORBA 2.0 support**—including Interface Repository upgrades, IIOP, DSI, and ORB initialization; it does not include support for the DCE/ESIOP.

- **CORBA services**—including Naming, Events, Transactions, and Life Cycle.

- **CORBA language bindings**—including Smalltalk IDL bindings.

- **Additional platform support**—including OS/2, Macintosh, and Windows 95.

Orbix's CORBA Extensions

Iona provides C++ class libraries that act as a framework for programming in CORBA. For example, Orbix encapsulates CORBA's Dynamic Invocation Interface with C++ classes that provide a stream-based interface—this lets you assemble and invoke a dynamic method using familiar stream-like calls.

Orbix also provides a non-standard construct called *filters*. You can use filters to extend the ORB's functionality (or customize it). For example, you can use filters to add authentication, tracing, or a threads package to the Orbix ORB. A filter is simply a mechanism that lets you attach one or more *callback* functions to different ORB events. You can attach a filter to an operation request or reply. Filters are instances of classes derived from the abstract **Filter** class. Filters can form a linked list—this lets you pass the event to the next filter in the chain, and so on.

Iona complements filters on the client side with *smart proxies*. A *proxy* in ORB-terminology is a piece of code that represents a server object on the client side—it runs in the same address space as the client. Regular proxies provide local/remote transparency by intercepting a local call for a server object, which they then marshal to the remote server. The Iona "smart" proxy lets you add filters to a regular proxy so that you can customize the behavior of the client to suit your needs. For example, you can add a filter to cache a request or respond to it locally to cut down the network traffic. You can also use smart proxies to accept callbacks from a server. This means the server can call the client whenever it wants via its agent—the smart proxy.

DIGITAL'S OBJECTBROKER

Digital's ObjectBroker started life as the *Application Control Architecture Services (ACAS)*. ACAS was redesigned to be CORBA-compliant in 1993 and renamed ObjectBroker. ObjectBroker runs on over a dozen platforms; it is also closely aligned with Microsoft's OLE/COM. Digital claims that a future release of ObjectBroker will be able to support both the CORBA and OLE/COM object models.

This remains to be seen. ObjectBroker 2.5 has a strong presence in financial establishments and in Digital shops. New releases of ObjectBroker are scheduled starting in late 1995.

ObjectBroker Architecture

ObjectBroker is layered on top of sockets; it runs on top of either TCP/IP or DECnet. Future releases will support the DCE RPC and Microsoft's COM. In addition to CORBA, Digital also supports the old ACAS proprietary APIs. Digital will support a queueing system—DECmessageQ—that provides asynchronous ORB messaging in 1996. It will also provide authentication services using DCE and Kerberos in 1996.

ObjectBroker 2.5's Current CORBA Support

ObjectBroker 2.5 provides all the CORBA 1.2 functionality—including an Interface Repository, Implementation Repository, IDL Precompiler, and Basic Object Adapter (BOA). It supports both CORBA's static and dynamic method invocations. Object-Broker 2.5 provides language bindings for C and supports the CORBA Naming Service. Currently, ObjectBroker 2.5 runs on the following platforms: Windows 3.X, Windows NT, Macintosh, OS/2, Tandem NonStop Kernel, OpenVMS, Sun Solaris, SunOS, HP-UX, IBM AIX, Tandem Integrity, SGI IRIX, and Digital Unix and Ultrix.

ObjectBroker's CORBA Support in 1996

Digital plans major upgrades for ObjectBroker starting in late 1995. Here's what you should be expecting:

- **CORBA 2.0 support**—including Interface Repository upgrades, IIOP, DSI, DCE/ESIOP, and ORB initialization.

- **CORBA services**—including Events and Life Cycle (the rest of the CORBA services won't be available until 1997). Digital may provide a Trader service based on the DCE directory services in 1996.

- **CORBA language bindings**—including C++.

- **Additional platform support**—including Windows 95, MVS, and OS/400.

IBM'S SOM

SOM just gets us plumbing. We spent a lot of time up front getting out a couple releases of this stuff to make sure we have a good understanding of the infrastructure before we get to the killer, which is component software...our approach to that is OpenDoc.

> — *Larry Loucks, VP of Software*
> *IBM PSP*
> *(March, 1995)*

IBM's *System Object Model (SOM)*—currently available in a product called *SOM-objects 2.1*—is probably the most important CORBA ORB on the market because of its close relationship with OpenDoc. SOM provides OpenDoc's underlying CORBA-compliant object bus. As an integral part of OpenDoc, SOM will ship with every copy of OS/2 Warp, Macintosh, and AIX. CI Labs (and Novell) will also distribute SOM freely on all versions of Windows through a "contamination" process. This means SOM will become the first high-volume CORBA ORB.

SOM has been part of OS/2 since 1992; it provides the object infrastructure on which the Workplace Shell is built. Every visible object you see on the OS/2 Warp desktop is a SOM object. This makes the Workplace Shell the most widely used CORBA application. It provides living proof that CORBA can manage objects on a desktop as well as on intergalactic networks. The design target of SOM 3.0—due late 1995 (or early 1996)—is to provide C++ virtual function speeds for fine-grained objects that operate within a single process. It must also provide "better than RPC" performance for remote objects.

SOM Architecture

The design point for SOM is to support very fine-grained objects that run in a single process at C++ speeds as well as medium-grained components that live on intergalactic ORBs. In addition, SOM is designed to be totally modular and replaceable. Most of SOM uses SOM itself to achieve this level of modularity. You can replace or extend nearly everything in SOM—including transports, client proxies, the BOAs, and so on. This is because the entire SOM system is built using SOM classes, which are themselves first-class objects (more on this later).

SOM provides a transport-layer encapsulation framework that currently supports TCP/IP, IPX/SPX, and NetBIOS. Using this framework, the SOM ORB can easily be extended—in future releases—to support wireless transports, the DCE RPC, and Message Queues (MOM).

SOM's Object Model Extensions and Other Features

With SOM, you can add virtual functions or even refactor the class hierarchy dynamically.

— *Tom Pennello, VP of MetaWare*
(May, 1994)

SOM uniquely extends CORBA with a *Metaclass Framework* that allows you to treat classes as first-class objects or *metaclasses*. This means that you can compose classes "on the fly" at run time. SOM lets you dynamically compose a class by following these steps: 1) create a new class; 2) inform the new class object of its parents using the *somInitMIClass* method; 3) add new methods to the class or override inherited methods; and 4) invoke *somClassReady* to inform the SOM registry that a new class was constructed.

In addition, SOM lets you create objects that inherit from a **SOMMBeforeAfter** metaclass. This inherited metaclass lets you precede each method invocation on an ordinary object with a call to a *BeforeMethod* method. And you can follow the execution of each method with a call to an *AfterMethod*. You can override the before and after methods with your own implementations to enhance a class's behavior. For example, you can provide a before method to grab locks on behalf of an object; you can then use an after method to release the locks you previously acquired. You can use the same technique to route the call to a "delegate" object, to call a security server, to log a method in a trace file, or to call a licensing server. You can do all this at run time without modifying the original class.

The SOM Metaclass Framework is extremely useful. It lets you dynamically create components from existing components. And it lets you tailor existing components for a given environment by automatically inserting system behavior into binary object classes. We can imagine object factories using these techniques to insert system behavior into new components, on-demand. For example, an object factory should be able to combine a regular component's binaries with extended binaries that provide persistence, concurrency, licensing, security, and transaction support. Of course, the problem is that the metaclass framework is SOM-proprietary. As we mentioned in an earlier chapter, it would be wonderful if CORBA defined a standard metaclass framework; SOM would make an excellent submission.

SOM 2.1's Current CORBA Support

SOM 2.1 is based on CORBA 1.2. It provides all the CORBA 1.2 ORB functionality—including an Interface Repository, Implementation Repository, IDL Precompiler, and Basic Object Adapter (BOA). It supports both CORBA's static and dynamic method invocations. SOM provides language bindings for C and C++; the C++ bindings are slightly different from the CORBA specification (but they're being upgraded). Currently, SOM 2.1 runs on the following platforms: Windows 3.X, OS/2, AIX, Macintosh, and MVS.

SOM provides several object services today—including Persistence, Collections, and Events—but they're not CORBA-compliant (CORBA-compliant versions are expected in SOM 3.X). SOM also provides a *Replication Framework* that lets you replicate objects. You can use this framework to create object-based groupware applications. You can also use it to load-balance objects across servers.

SOM's CORBA Support in 1996

IBM is planning a series of major upgrade of SOM starting in late 1995 or early 1996. The press calls these new upgrades SOM 3.X (or Distributed SOMobjects 3.X). The SOM 3.X family is expected to provide a rich offering of CORBA services and eventually full CORBA 2.0 support. Here are the upgrades you should be expecting:

- **CORBA 2.0 support**—including Interface Repository upgrades, IIOP, DSI, and ORB initialization. The DCE/ESIOP is expected late 1996 (or early 1997).

- **CORBA services**—including Events, Persistence, Life Cycle, Transactions, Concurrency Control, and Externalization. These services are expected in early 1996 (more may come later). SOM 3.X also intends to offer security based on DCE and ORB-based system management based on Tivoli.

- **CORBA language bindings**—SOM will upgrade its C++ bindings to CORBA standards. It will also provide IDL bindings for Smalltalk and OO COBOL.

- **Additional platform support**—including OS/2 PowerPC, Windows 95, Windows NT, Tandem NonStop Kernel, OS/400, and some Unix platforms.

EXPERSOFT'S XSHELL

I really can't conceive of a true information superhighway that is not based on distributed objects.

— *David Porreca, President*
Expersoft
(February, 1995)

Expersoft (spelled without a "t") is a small company founded in 1989 by client/server experts. The company released an early ORB in 1991. They shipped their first CORBA-compliant ORB—XShell 3.0—in the middle of 1994. XShell 3.5 shipped in mid-1995. A new release is expected in early 1996 (or late 1995). At this time XShell will be renamed *PowerBroker*. XShell's claim to fame is that it was picked as the Anderson Consulting ORB in a much publicized bake-off. XShell was also quite influential in the design of UNO—the proposal that lead to the CORBA 2.0 IIOP.

XShell 3.5's Current CORBA Support

XShell provides an integrated object solution that includes naming, Kerberos security, tools, and TP Monitor integration. The ORB proper is almost CORBA 1.2 compliant; it does not support the dynamic invocation interface or provide an Interface Repository. These features are due in late 1995. The ORB only supports C bindings; C++ and Smalltalk support are due in late 1995. XShell only supports TCP/IP. It runs on Windows NT, Sun Solaris, HP-UX, AIX, and SGI IRIX.

XShell (or PowerBroker): CORBA Support in 1996

The next version of XShell—due in late 1995—should introduce the missing CORBA 1.2 features and support for five CORBA services: Naming, Events, Life Cycle, Persistence, and Externalization. Transactions, Concurrency, and Relationships are expected in mid-1996. In late 1995, XShell may be the first ORB on the market to fully support CORBA 2.0. This is not too surprising considering that much of the IIOP technology originated from Expersoft in the first place. The only additional platform XShell is expected to support is Windows 95. Finally, Expersoft is working on some new innovations such as asynchronous messaging, replicated namespaces, and facilities for adding methods to objects at run time.

SUN'S DISTRIBUTED OBJECTS EVERYWHERE (DOE)

Sun's *Distributed Objects Everywhere (DOE)* was announced in 1993. However, Sun only shipped *Early Developer Release (EDR)* toolkits of DOE to selected customers. DOE Release 1 is scheduled to ship very early in 1996 (or late 1995). Sun was very influential in developing the CORBA specifications. DOE is an integral part of Sun's revolutionary software vision. This vision includes a CORBA-compliant operating system called *Spring*. Sun's vision also includes a fully integrated object application environment based on OpenStep and DOE. Sun has assembled an impressive team of object technologists to realize its vision.

Sun's Current CORBA Support

The current EDR toolkit is an early version of the final product SunSoft will ship in early 1996 (or late 1995). EDR provides a CORBA 1.2 ORB that supports C and C++ language bindings. EDR uses object handles to route object requests between DOE daemons that reside on each node. The object handle contains an internal object ID, routing information, and implementation information. EDR is one of the first implementations of threads on the Sun platform. EDR supports the CORBA Naming and Event services. It also provides an early version of the Relationship and Properties services. These two services formed the basis for the Sun submissions to OMG. Note that EDR does not support multiple inheritance; it only supports single interface inheritance.

Sun's CORBA Support in 1996

Sun's DOE 1—expected in early 1996—will be based on CORBA 1.2. A second release—expected in mid-1996—will provide CORBA 2.0 support. Sun has no plans to support the DCE/ESIOP or Smalltalk language bindings. The first release of DOE will include the following CORBA services: Naming, Events, Life Cycle, and Persistence. The second release will include Transactions, Concurrency Control, Externalization, Licensing, and Query. DOE will run primarily on Sun platforms using TCP/IP as its underlying protocol. Sun depends on Iona to provide a multiplatform distributed object solution. Remember that Sun has purchased a stake in Iona.

HP'S ORB PLUS

Like Sun's DOE, HP's *ORB Plus* (also known as *ORB+*) is only available in toolkit form. The toolkit will be enhanced and relaunched as ORB Plus 2.0 in the first quarter of 1996. HP was very influential in the development of the CORBA specification. We speculate that they may have delayed making ORB Plus widely available to deliver an "industrial-strength" ORB based on DCE. HP is also working on the integration of the OpenStep and Taligent application environments with its ORB. ORB Plus 1.0—only available in toolkit form—is a CORBA 1.2 ORB that runs on top of the DCE RPC and TCP/IP. It only runs on HP-UX. This early version only supports C++ bindings.

HP's CORBA Support in 1996

ORB Plus 2.0 (due in early 1996) will mark HP's grand entry into the CORBA market. HP may attempt to compensate for its late entry by providing the first

CORBA 2.0 compliant ORB on top of a DCE RPC foundation. HP plans to provide an ORB that is integrated with the DCE security, RPC, and directory services. ORB Plus will support IPX/SPX in addition to TCP/IP. A full DCE/ESIOP is expected later in 1996. HP will also distinguish itself by providing a full set of CORBA services in 1996—including Naming, Events, Life Cycle, Persistence, Transactions, Relationships, Externalization, Licensing, and Query (missing is Concurrency Control). On the downside, HP only plans to support ORB Plus on the HP-UX server platform; it will provide client code for Windows 95, Windows NT, AIX, and Solaris.

WHO DID WE LEAVE OUT?

When the OMG was founded, there was a feeling that it would attract maybe 20 members. Today membership stands at more than 500.

> — *Lydia Bennett, Director of Marketing*
> *Object Management Group*
> *(June, 1995)*

OMG publishes a long directory of CORBA-compliant object products. We couldn't cover them all in this chapter. So in addition to the ORBs we covered here, you may want to look at the following CORBA-compliant ORBs: AT&T's *Cooperative Frameworks*, Black and White Software's *UIM/X*, ILOG's *BROKER*, NetLinks *ORBitize*, Object-Oriented Technologies *Distributed Object Management Environment (D.O.M.E.)*, NEC's *NEC-ORB*, ICL's *Distributed Application Integration System (DAIS)*, and PostModern Computing's *ORBeline*. The resources section in the back of this Survival Guide provides information on how to reach these vendors.

CONCLUSION AND SOME PARTING COMMENTS

It is from these CORBA vendors that a new, robust, and highly distributed world of information technology will grow.

> — *John Slitz, IBM VP (Ex-VP of OMG)*
> *(March, 1994)*

You should only use the current generation of ORBs to familiarize yourself with writing client/server applications using CORBA. We do not think the current products are ready for client/server prime time (see Soapbox on page 62, Is 1996 "The Year of the ORB"?). However, as you can see from this chapter, all the key vendors are about to introduce major new releases of their current ORB products. So by the time you read this book, the market may be flooded with new industri-

al-strength ORBs that can better handle the needs of client/server production environments.

How do you pick an ORB in this brave new world? First and foremost, make sure the ORB is compatible with the CORBA architecture we described in this long part. Then look at the services it provides and the platforms it supports. If you use OpenDoc, your first choice will be SOM; if you're a Sun shop, your first choice will be DOE and Orbix; and so on. Finally, you'll need some benchmarks to compare the products. You should compare features such as performance, garbage collection, tools, ease-of-management, and so on.

If you decide to pick a "fly-by-night" vendor's ORB, make sure not to use any proprietary extensions. If you do use the proprietary features, then make sure to encapsulate them with your own portable IDL interfaces. This means that you should use IDL to create your own wrappers instead of depending on the vendor's APIs.

What happens if you want to change ORBs midstream? In the past, this would have cost you dearly in terms of time and effort. The good news is that the new CORBA ORBs are getting more "CORBA-compliant." CORBA 2.0 closed many of the loopholes. The client side of CORBA is fairly portable if you use IDL and standard language bindings. The server side of CORBA is less portable, but the loopholes are being closed there, too. The newer CORBA services have fewer ambiguities in them and can be implemented in a more standard fashion. Earlier services— particularly Naming, Life Cycle, and Persistence—have lots of loopholes; they're open to fuzzy interpretations by vendors. So be careful. The X/Open CORBA branding "test suites" should help protect you from these different vendor interpretations. Make sure to request X/Open compliance certification from your vendors.

Aside from these caveats, it looks like CORBA is ready to explode in a big way. The infrastructure that we described in this long part is irresistible. It's the fastest way to develop intergalactic components and client/server applications. When you buy into CORBA, you're getting more than just an object bus. You get a complete infrastructure for creating smart distributed components. CORBA is inevitable. The basic standards are almost complete; you can add the new services piecemeal when they show up (it's all very modular). The products are starting to look like the architecture and the standards. If you've been on the sidelines sitting this out waiting for the right moment, this may be the right time for you to make the leap (especially if the new crop of products meet your expectations).

Part 3
Frameworks for
Business Objects
and Components

The Framework Orchestra

I want my freedom and independence.

What do you think we are? A jazz quartet?

Framework

An Introduction to Part 3

The information system of the future will take the form of a swarm of business objects engaging in numerous patterns of collaboration. A business object is the information system's mirror image of an object from the business world.

— Rob Prins, CYCLADE Consultants
(June, 1995)

You Martians are going to find this part really exciting. We cover business objects, which are components that the average Martian can immediately recognize and identify with—for example, space ships, moon rocks, Earthlings, and utility bills. These components are products that you can sell and profit from. They are also objects that behave "just as the real world does." They can be used and assembled in very unpredictable combinations, just like their real-world counterparts. So Part 3 is what object technology is all about—which is to create information systems that mimic the business world and introduce new paradigms for social and intergalactic computing.

Business objects build on top of an object bus and system-level components like the ones we described in Part 2. In addition, they require frameworks that define patterns of collaboration between them. The most valuable business objects do not live in isolation. They are able to collaborate with other business objects and components to create ensembles that their developers had never planned for or imagined. These collaborations are ad hoc and dynamic. They take place in environments that are sometimes simulations of real-world situations. For example, components can be assembled in *places* that look like offices, theaters, shopping malls, and even cities. The place defines the rules of engagement for intercomponent collaborations. Components within a place are very smart—they're "place savvy." So who assembles these places? They're assembled by end users, system integrators, IS shops, and even other developers.

Did we have too much espresso? Does it suddenly sound like you're reading a science fiction book? Hardly. This part covers five real products—including OpenDoc, OLE, Taligent, OpenStep, and Newi. All these products let you build components that are like business objects. They all provide frameworks that define the patterns of engagement for these components. They all provide unifying metaphors for bringing together components. And they even provide tools to help you build and deploy these components. You can take back with you some of these products to Mars and get started today.

But are there standards for these business objects? Unfortunately, the "real" standards are in the making—the OMG is putting together a very complete architecture for business objects and frameworks. In the meantime, there are *de facto* standards such as OLE, OpenDoc, and OpenStep. Some of these *de facto* standards—the ones built around industry consortia—may become part of CORBA. Are the existing products complete? They're complete enough for you to get started.

This area is too dynamic and creative to ever be completed. Products will evolve to become CORBA-compliant when the real standards come of age.

Can these products be used to create client/server systems? With the possible exception of Newi and OpenStep, most of these products are not ready for client/server prime time. But they're all moving in that direction. And soon components will revolutionize the way we build and use client/server systems. You can create client/server systems with components today if you're willing to do some hacking—for example, you can combine SOM/CORBA with OpenDoc or Newi.

Of course, the toughest question is: Which of these component technologies do you choose? As always, our advice is to stay with the standards—especially when it comes to distributed components. However, in this case, the standards are not yet in place. So our fallback advice is to stay with whichever products have $100 million already invested in them. According to Jim Gray, this much investment automatically creates a standard. Given this rule of thumb, your choices definitely include OLE and OpenDoc and perhaps even Taligent and OpenStep. That didn't help too much—we only lost Newi and it has some very creative technology.

Maybe a few mergers will occur and cut down our choices. Hmmm, let's see. Our guess is that Taligent and Newi may end up in the OpenDoc/CORBA camp. Open-Step may be combined with Sun's Distributed Objects Everywhere (DOE), which is also in the CORBA camp. So, in the long run, two object models will battle it out—Microsoft's OLE versus CORBA/OpenDoc (with help from Newi, Taligent, and OpenStep). Regardless of our prediction, we encourage you to read all of Part 3 and come up with your own conclusions. The technology behind OpenStep, Taligent, and Newi is too wonderful (and relevant) to skip over.

The plan for Part 3 is to first introduce the concept of frameworks and how they handle intercomponent collaboration. To understand what's coming down the pipe, we next look at what the OMG is doing in the area of business objects and frameworks. OMG also provides a very good reference model that will help you understand the rest of Part 3. Next, we will look at a particular framework called the *compound document framework*. Compound documents currently provide a unifying metaphor for desktop components. But they can also be used by servers to ship to their clients dynamic storefronts and to deploy roaming agents and route workflow across an intergalactic network. Finally, we come to the fun part—the products that make all this happen. Each of these products have unique new technologies that contribute to our understanding of business objects and intercomponent collaborations.

Part 3 is really where the action is today. The industry has almost finished defining the distributed object plumbing. It's time to begin creating component-based systems that will allow us to reap the benefits. The frameworks and collaboration patterns that we describe in Part 3 will collectively change the way distributed (and

An Introduction to Part 3

desktop) applications are created, used, and maintained. It will make creating intergalactic client/server applications fun. And it will open up tremendous new opportunities. We hope you enjoy reading it as much as we enjoyed writing it.

Chapter 12

Object Frameworks: An Overview

---

*F*rom the beginning, an important promise of object technology was to make software behave just as the real world does.

— **John R. Rymer, Editor**
Distributed Computing Monitor
(January, 1995)

So what does it take to create components that behave "just as the real world does"? The intergalactic object bus and system services provide a good start—they allow any component to talk to any other component. But, what do these components say to each other after they connect? What rules of engagement do they follow to start acting like "real-world" objects? What kind of semantic infrastructure do they need? And, how do we build, deploy, and maintain these type of components?

To answer these questions, we introduce a nebulous concept called *frameworks*. Because it's nebulous, it can mean different things to different people. In general, a framework provides an organized environment for running a collection of objects. It also provides tools that let you construct components that are willing to play by the framework's rules of engagement. With an object bus, anything goes. In contrast, with frameworks you get organized anarchy: "Everything goes as long as you play by the framework's rules."

Frameworks can offer simple "patterns" that guide the collaboration of objects so that they can start to model their real-world counterparts. The frameworks also provide a way for these components to exchange semantic-level *metadata* or self-describing data. The metadata allows loosely coupled components to dynamically discover each other's services and behaviors at run time. The better frameworks introduce a minimum number of rules, constructs, and metaphors so that components can use them consistently. Simple constructs encourage independent components to interact in myriads of ways unplanned by their developers.

The end goal is to let us dynamically assemble webs of components without being constrained by how a developer imagined they would be used. We cannot predict how these components will be combined, just like we can't predict the different ways in which real-world objects are combined and used. The better frameworks define simple collaboration patterns and metaphors that let us create *flexible* arrangements. We should be able to put together very complex systems by combining basic business object components—the complexity is in the organization, not the components.

In Part 3, we're interested in frameworks that define the rules of engagement for business-size object components. Of course, you can also use frameworks to create system-level objects and components. However, we will not spend too much time on these low-level frameworks because we expect to get these services from ORB vendors. But, a system-level framework can be valuable if it lets us extend the function it provides. Otherwise, it's just a "black box" service that sits on the bus.

We start this chapter by explaining what a framework is and what problems it solves. We compare frameworks with procedural APIs and object-oriented class libraries. Then we explain the relationship between frameworks and design patterns. Finally, we compare frameworks with white box components.

FRAMEWORKS OVERVIEW

The framework dictates the architecture of your application...A framework designer gambles that one architecture will work for all applications in a domain...The framework's contribution is the architecture it defines.

> — **Erich Gamma et al., Authors**
> **Design Patterns**
> **(Addison-Wesley, 1994)**

In this section, we define frameworks, explain what they do, and what benefits they provide. You'll discover that frameworks embody the patterns of collaboration between components at run time. Frameworks let you build families of components—called *suites*—that share a consistent design and implementation. As a result, framework-created components are easier to maintain and appear more consistent to their users. On the other hand, a framework locks you into a design and takes away some of your creative freedom.

What Are Object Frameworks?

Design is hard. One way to avoid the act of design is to reuse existing designs.

> — **Dr. Ralph Johnson, University of Illinois**
> **(April, 1995)**

In their 1991 article, "Reusing Object-Oriented Designs," Ralph Johnson of the University of Illinois and Vincent Russo of Purdue offer this widely accepted definition of frameworks:

> "An abstract class is a design for a single object. A framework is the design of a set of objects that collaborate to carry out a set of responsibilities. Thus frameworks are larger scale designs than abstract classes. Frameworks are a way to reuse high-level design."

Still confused? Let's try an explanation from Taligent's 1993 White Paper:

> "Frameworks are not simply collections of classes. Rather, frameworks come with rich functionality and strong wired-in interconnections between object classes that provide an infrastructure for the developer."

The "wired-in" interconnections among the classes are meant to provide the right level of abstraction to the consumer of the framework. Think of a framework as a fully debugged software subsystem that you can customize to create your own applications. It's like buying a hardware board instead of individual chips (see Figure 12-1). But unlike a hardware board, the "software board" can be extended and further customized to fit your needs.

The newer frameworks define the rules of engagement for "wiring" components together so that they can play in suites. In these new environments an individual component is like a hardware *Integrated Circuit (IC)*; the framework provides the board; and the ORB provides the backplane. We must learn from the hardware business this important lesson: Individual components are not very interesting but components that you can wire together are like gold. Frameworks help us integrate software components.

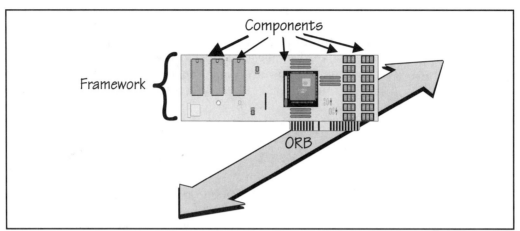

Figure 12-1. A Hardware Analogy for Frameworks.

How Frameworks Work

Frameworks obey the Hollywood principle: "Don't call us, we'll call you."

— *Dr. Dave Wilson, Framework Consultant*
(March, 1995)

So how do your components interact with a framework? First, you tell it which key events you want to personalize. Then you provide the code that handles those

events. The framework will then call your code when that event occurs; your code doesn't call the framework. Your programs don't have to worry about structure, flow of execution, and calls to system-level API libraries; the framework does it all for you. All your code does is wait to be called by the framework (see Figure 12-2).

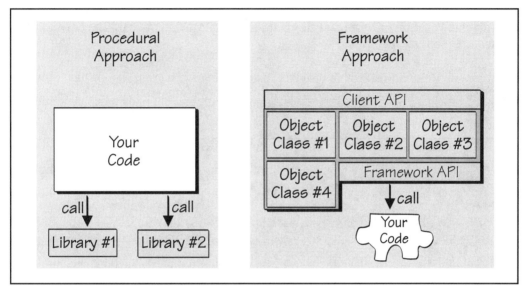

Figure 12-2. Procedural Versus Framework Approaches to Developing Code.

Because frameworks define the architecture of your applications, it's important to work with frameworks that are as flexible and extensible as possible. Unlike traditional operating systems, the newer frameworks are very malleable. If you don't like a particular part of the subsystem, just change it. You can also customize a framework by replacing some of its classes with your own. You do this using traditional object-oriented approaches such as multiple inheritance and method overrides. Of course, frameworks can also play tricks and change their underlying structure to take advantage of new hardware (or software) in a manner that's totally transparent to your software.

What else can frameworks do? They integrate well with other frameworks. Most distributed object environments will end up consisting of layers of frameworks that cooperate with each other. Going back to the hardware analogy, hardware boards can be plugged into a motherboard (a board with a system bus) to interoperate with other hardware boards and create a system. For example, a system could consist of a motherboard with a microprocessor, a LAN Adapter card, a memory card, and a printer card. Frameworks do the same for software.

But where's the software motherboard? How do frameworks in separate address spaces communicate with one another? The framework "software motherboard" consists of two mechanisms:

■ The framework service interface provides a set of APIs that are simple abstractions of the services provided by each framework. We show in Figure 12-3 that interface as a layer on top of the frameworks. A CORBA-compliant framework would use IDL-specified interfaces.

■ An inter-framework object request broker is used to pass the requests across address spaces. Figure 12-3 shows the software bus (the broker) that carries the traffic across frameworks. A CORBA environment would use regular ORBs.

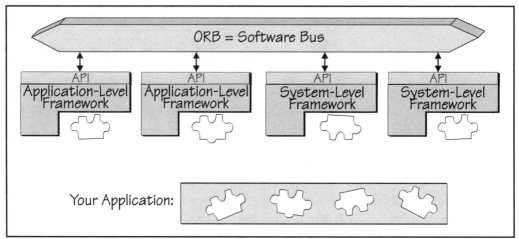

Figure 12-3. An Application in the Era of Frameworks.

But aren't we going back to APIs and procedural calls? No, because most of the code you write runs within individual frameworks (the little puzzle pieces in the figure). These little puzzle pieces of code are invoked directly by the framework. The APIs are used to invoke services on other frameworks where you may also have some code (another little puzzle piece).

Key Benefits of Object Frameworks

In a sense, a framework is a microarchitecture...It provides the highest level of reuse in a complex system.

— Grady Booch, Rational
(March, 1995)

You may have already surmised that frameworks provide a very powerful approach for creating complex systems. Here's a list of the advantages frameworks provide:

- *A prefabricated infrastructure*. Frameworks reduce coding, debugging, and testing by providing working subsystems. This is code that you don't have to write yourself.

- *Architectural guidance*. Frameworks are wired and ready to go. All you need to know is where the hooks are and then tap into them to extend the system's behavior. You don't have to plow through thick manuals that describe APIs. And if you're an object-oriented programmer, you won't have to spend half your time shopping for classes, providing the interconnections between classes, discovering which methods are available, and then trying to figure out which ones need to be called and in which order. Frameworks hide all this complexity by providing a higher level of abstraction.

- *Less monolithic applications*. Frameworks encourage you to write small pieces of applications that plug into their appropriate frameworks. When you need a function in another framework, you simply call that piece of the application that runs there (or the framework itself). Instead of writing one monolithic application, you write little pieces of custom code that run in different frameworks.

- *A foundation for a software components industry*. Well-designed frameworks allow third-party software companies to provide parts or entire components that can be assembled or modified by end users or system integrators.

- *Reduced maintenance*. Frameworks provide the bulk of the code that goes into applications. So your maintenance costs should be substantially reduced. Because of inheritance, when a framework bug is fixed or a new feature is added, the benefits are immediately available to derived classes.

The overall benefit of frameworks is that they enable a very high level of code and design reuse in the development of complex systems. They also provide the environment in which like-minded components can collaborate to get things done. The main weakness of frameworks is that they limit your flexibility—your component must live within the constraints imposed by the framework.

Frameworks, APIs, or Class Libraries?

The line of code that costs the least is the line of code you don't write.

— *Steve Jobs*

Yes, you've heard it before. Structured programming, then OO class libraries, were supposed to save the world from programming drudgery. None were a panacea. Why are frameworks any different? Table 12-1 provides a quick summary of the features that distinguish frameworks from procedural API programming and object-oriented class libraries.

Table 12-1. Comparing Frameworks, OO Class Libraries, and Procedural APIs.

Feature	Frameworks	OO Class Libraries	Procedural APIs
Application model	Frameworks are the application. The frameworks handle all the control flow.	You must create the control flow of the application and the glue that ties the different class libraries together.	You must create the control flow of the application and the logic that invokes the APIs. The system knows nothing about your code.
Application structure	Multiple cooperative frameworks.	Single monolithic application consisting of class libraries.	Single monolithic application linked to API libraries.
How are services obtained?	The frameworks are the service.	By inheriting function from the class libraries.	By calling API libraries.
How is the system customized?	The frameworks call your code. You can subclass parts of frameworks.	By subclassing or creating new classes.	By writing new code and calling additional APIs.
Granularity of control	Medium. You can only subclass parts of frameworks.	High. You can subclass any class.	High. You can write everything from scratch.
Abstraction of services	High. Hides complexity. Automates standard features. You program by exception.	Low. Hides APIs but creates its own layer of complexity. You must determine which methods are available to call and in which order.	Very low. You need to deal with raw APIs and determine the order in which to call them.
How much code do you write?	Very little.	A Medium amount.	A lot.
Maintenance costs	Low.	Medium.	High.

Table 12-1. Comparing Frameworks, OO Class Libraries, and Procedural APIs. (Continued)

Feature	Frameworks	OO Class Libraries	Procedural APIs
Reduced complexity	Yes. You write small pieces of code within multiple frameworks. Frameworks call you only when necessary. Frameworks provide architectural guidance.	No. You must shop for classes and develop the program. You must integrate the different class libraries.	No. You must develop the entire program and understand how the APIs work together.
Client/Server support	High. Using inter-framework communications.	Low. You must use the native OS's interprocess communications.	Low. You must use the native OS's interprocess communications.
Time to develop an application	Low.	Medium. Depends on class reuse.	High.
Code reuse	Very high.	High. The classes gets reused.	Medium. Some functions get reused.
Is the model familiar?	No.	Somewhat.	Yes.

Procedural Frameworks: Look Ma, No Objects

Frameworks are not the only way to reuse architectures. Application environments such as Lotus Notes and TP Monitors—for example, CICS, Tuxedo, and Pathway—have always provided built-in architectures with default behaviors. These environments save application developers time and effort. They let you create applications without necessarily using the underlying operating system directly. So in this sense these environments are framework-like. So what's the difference? The difference is that Lotus Notes and TP Monitors are black boxes. You cannot modify or extend whatever comes out of the box. If you like the function these application environments provide, then you're in luck. Otherwise, you must recreate the entire function yourself. In contrast, you can extend and modify object frameworks to suit your needs. They don't lock you in an all-or-nothing proposition.

Note that not all frameworks are object-based. Many of the middleware services—including transports, NOSs, and transactions—can be provided using procedural frameworks. Why do we need procedural frameworks? Because the bulk of existing system code was written without the faintest notion of objects. DCE, for example, consists of more than two million lines of procedural legacy code. It will take some time to rewrite DCE into a workable object framework. In other cases, object frameworks are still being crafted. For example, we expect vendors to provide TP Monitor frameworks on top of the CORBA transaction services sometime in 1996. In the interim, we have procedural TP Monitor frameworks.

Procedural frameworks are very useful. They encapsulate heterogeneous services with CORBA-defined interfaces. Figure 12-4 shows an example of a SOM encapsulated procedural framework. Each framework provides configuration and installation support for its services. In addition, frameworks register their services with a CORBA-compliant Interface Repository that lets applications discover which services are available and how to invoke them at run time. The Operating System only has to load the framework itself and handle version control.

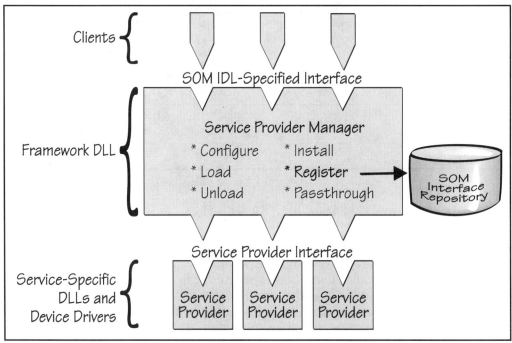

Figure 12-4. The Elements of a Procedural Framework.

Procedural frameworks are very useful as object wrappers. They allow us to transition to objects gradually from the existing base of legacy system software. The object wrappers make the legacy code appear object-like to the object-oriented programs, tools, and frameworks. So what do procedural frameworks lack? Their two major limitations are: 1) they don't allow you to modify the service itself using subclassing (for example, you won't be able to modify DCE); and 2) they are still API-based. So procedural frameworks are a cross between application environments like TP Monitors and pure object frameworks.

FRAMEWORKS FOR BUSINESS OBJECTS AND COMPONENTS

In the near future, framework providers will gradually move closer and closer to business object frameworks.

> — John R. Rymer, Editor
> Distributed Computing Monitor
> (January, 1995)

Today, most frameworks shipped are for system-level objects. Many of these frameworks are associated with programming environments and GUIs. Examples of these frameworks are Rogue Wave, ObjectWorks, MacApp, Galaxy, zApp, and OWL. But what's the state of frameworks for business objects and components? The answer is that these frameworks are off to a good start. The catalyst for this development is *compound document* frameworks. Compound documents provide a powerful metaphor for integrating desktop components. They start out where CORBA stops. The newer frameworks—for example, OpenDoc, OLE, and Taligent—use compound documents as their integration metaphor for components.

Meet the Players

Today's leading business-object frameworks are *OLE/COM* from Microsoft and *OpenDoc/CORBA* from CI Labs. Other contenders are *OpenStep* from NeXT (and partners), *CommonPoint* from Taligent (and partners), and *Newi* from Integrated Objects—a joint venture of IBM and Softwright based in England. You can use all these framework-based products to create the first generation business objects and components. Many of these frameworks include powerful graphical builders for creating and assembling components. In addition, CORBA is defining a set of frameworks for business objects on top of another set of frameworks called the *Common Facilities*. But until the CORBA business object standards materialize, these shipping frameworks are only game in town (see next Soapbox).

Types of Frameworks

In addition to compound document frameworks, you should expect to see many types of specialized frameworks that provide vertical business functions. For example, you may see CORBA-based frameworks for banking, health, retail, or manufacturing. You may even see CORBA frameworks that encapsulate a single business object—for example, a customer, competitor, supplier, doctor, or nurse. We also expect specialized multiuser server frameworks—for example, CORBA

Soapbox

Disposable Components

Until very recently, object-oriented software was just as obtuse and impenetrable as its predecessors.

> — *John R. Rymer, Editor*
> *Distributed Computing Monitor*
> *(January, 1995)*

The frameworks we describe in the next chapters—including Taligent, OpenDoc, OLE, OpenStep, and Newi—represent the "cutting edge" in object technology. They all provide environments for creating and running ensembles of collaborating business objects. So why do we call them first generation frameworks? Because this technology is still in its infancy. We have a lot to learn about how components play together in suites. And, how we are going to deploy and maintain these components. In addition, most of these frameworks—with the exception of Newi—are currently desktop-centric. We still don't have solid frameworks for servers. One of your authors is developing a whole product line of server frameworks—called *Serverware*—so you know they're just around the corner!

We also anticipate that alliances will change the mix and architecture of the current products—especially the more vanguard ones that predate the standards. For example, Newi pioneered the concept of business objects, but being at the cutting edge means their frameworks are not standards-based. Given IBM's stake in the company, it seems plausible that Newi may gravitate toward the OpenDoc/CORBA standard. The same can be said of Taligent. NeXT already has a toe in CORBA because of its alliance with Sun.

We recommend you start developing components using these frameworks now, but anticipate that things will change. It's easy to create and assemble components using visual builders and frameworks. If you can create a component in matter of days, you can dispose of it and try again when something better comes along. So don't think in terms of posterity. Instead, think in terms of disposable components. Our general rule is: If it's easy, then it's ready for prime time. The corollary is: If it's that easy, then it's disposable. So you're constantly introducing new technology by rapidly creating and deploying disposable components. Of course, you should always stay on top of the "strategic standards" because they offer more permanence and scalabilty. ❏

frameworks that encapsulate legacy data, long-lived transactions, workflow, or publish-and-subscribe. Of course, the OLE community is also working on similar ideas.

Dave Wilson of Personal Concepts (with suggestions from Jack Grimes of Taligent) has come up with the following classification for frameworks:

■ **Base frameworks** provide a set of customizable services in some general domain—for example, Microsoft Foundation Classes (MFC) or an inventory control framework.

■ **Derived frameworks** provide specialized services for a very narrow domain—for example, a property framework.

■ **Mixin frameworks** add additional properties or behavior to an existing framework—for example, a security framework.

■ **Integration frameworks** combine the services of multiple frameworks to make them easier to use—for example, Taligent's wrapper frameworks.

The terminology Dave Wilson uses in his seminars may be slightly different from the way we described it. But the general idea is that there are different ways to look at these frameworks. At this stage, any taxonomy will do. Everything is still very fluid.

Frameworks and Design Patterns

A pattern describes a problem which occurs over and over again in our environment, and then describes the core of the solution to the problem, in such a way that you can use this solution a million times over, without ever doing it the same way twice.

> — **Christopher Alexander et al., Authors**
> **A Pattern Language**
> **(Oxford, 1977)**

Design patterns are descriptions of communicating objects and classes that are customized to solve a general design problem in a particular context. One person's pattern can be another person's building block.

> — **Erich Gamma et al., Authors**
> **Design Patterns**
> **(Addison-Wesley, 1994)**

Christopher Alexander, an architect, developed the idea of "patterns" to describe buildings and towns. His pattern language starts by explaining how the world should be broken into nations and nations into smaller regions. He then goes on to explain how to arrange roads, parking, shopping, homes, and so on. Gamma et al. are the authors of a book on design patterns for objects—an idea that's currently very much in vogue within the object community. You may notice from their quotes that there is an overlap between "object patterns" and "frameworks." In fact, one of the authors of **Design Patterns** is the same Ralph Johnson who popularized frameworks. So, what's going on? Are object patterns a new name for frameworks?

According to Gamma et al., a design pattern is not a framework, and vice versa. Here are the differences they list:

- ***Design patterns are smaller architectural elements than frameworks.*** A framework can contain several design patterns but the reverse is never true (see Figure 12-5).

- ***Design patterns are more abstract than frameworks.*** You can embody frameworks in code and use them directly. In contrast, design patterns must be implemented each time they're used—they're just code examples.

- ***Design patterns are less specialized than frameworks.*** Frameworks always have a particular application domain. In contrast, you can use design patterns in any kind of application. Examples of design patterns are object *factories*, *iterators*, *mediators*, *proxies*, and *bridges*.

Frameworks are what we need to get to business objects and more intelligent components. Design patterns may be used to document certain elements of the framework design. For example, all compound document frameworks have a pattern for doing data transfers. In our opinion, what makes frameworks particularly useful is that they create integrating metaphors for components. They also

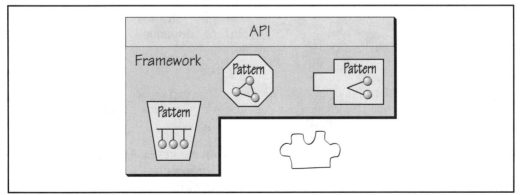

Figure 12-5. Frameworks, Patterns, and Objects.

define types of collaborations among components. In other words, frameworks provide a complete environment for creating component *ensembles* or *suites*.

Quiz: Framework or White Box Component?

It's now time for a little quiz and a short story that goes with it. Once upon a time, your authors created an OpenDoc part called a "Smiley Face" that does exactly what it says (see Figure 12-6). We want to get rich fast, so we think about splurging and buying a full color ad where we let the world know that Smiley is available for only $5—you get the binary for the part and the SOM Interface Definition Language (IDL), but no source code. Anyone that buys our Smiley Face can use it "as is" or extend it using SOM—remember, we provide the IDL. If you were to extend our part—say by making it frown—you could resell your "Frowney Face" for $10 and join us in Tahiti.

So, here's the million-dollar question: *Is Smiley a component or a framework?* Sad to say, we don't have a definitive answer. Smiley is certainly a component. But, because we provide IDL, you can extend Smiley using inheritance—so it could be a framework. We consider Smiley to be a "white box" component—meaning it is a component that can be extended to provide new behavior. There is obviously some overlap between a white box component and a framework. In our minds, the key difference is that frameworks are typically sold only to developers; components are sold to end users, integrators, or developers.

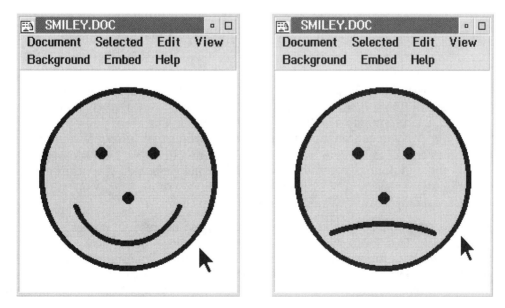

Figure 12-6. Smiley and Frowney.

Like frameworks, white box components make it possible for scripters, IS shops, or component providers to extend existing components and personalize their behavior. At a minimum, a white box component is "tinkerable," which means that an end user or scripter can customize its behavior. Typically, the white box component provides a property editor that allows an end user to customize the component's appearance or associate scripts with events such as a menu item selection. Programmers can customize components by registering callback functions for a particular event. The more sophisticated white box components are packaged with a CORBA-compliant IDL file that describes the classes and methods that a programmer can subclass and override. OpenDoc, for example, uses SOM to package components in binary executable files and yet allows them to be extended via the IDL; you don't have to provide the source code.

However, most components will be sold to the end user as black boxes, meaning that they cannot be tinkered with past a minimum level of property editing. The heavy tinkering will be done by IS shops, suite providers, and system integrators. Regardless of who does what, we have the technology to create components—white box or black box—and frameworks.[1]

Class Libraries, Frameworks, and Components

An object makes no sense on its own except as part of a larger framework, pattern, or class library.

— Ian Graham, Author
Migrating to Object Technology
(Addison-Wesley, 1995)

Chris Hyrne from Taligent has suggested to us a model for describing the difference between class libraries, frameworks, and components (see Figure 12-7). In the Hyrne model, components are the easiest to assemble, but they're essentially black boxes. Typically, you can change a component's properties using a visual property editor. And you can tinker a bit with the component's behavior by attaching scripts to events the component fires—it's like using Visual Basic. At the other extreme, class libraries are hard to use, but you can do anything you want with them.

---

[1] Note that OLE components are always "black boxes" because OLE does not support inheritance. This led some industry analysts to equate components with lack of inheritance. For example, in an August 1994 report titled **Components Are Not Top of the Class**, Gartner writes: "A component can only be used as is. If it does not perform the required task, it can only be modified by changing its source code. Components do not inherit from one another." Of course, this is not always true. OpenDoc/CORBA components can be extended through inheritance, if you provide IDL.

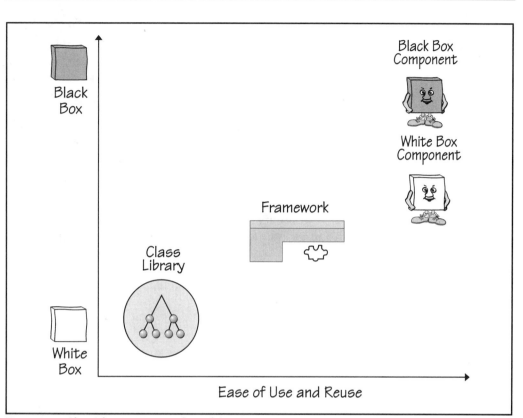

Figure 12-7. Class Libraries, Frameworks, and Components.

Frameworks are somewhere in the middle. Don't forget that you use class libraries and frameworks to create components in the first place. Also, frameworks provide a run-time environment for components.

Conclusion

We envision two levels of component assembly. One is an object builder environment in which rather technical people build abstract frameworks. The other is an environment in which business programmers develop applications using visual assembly tools.

— Vi Boudreau, Director
ITT Advanced Technology Center
(January, 1995)

Frameworks provide integrating metaphors and environments for creating and running components. They enforce the rules of engagement between components, as defined by the framework's metaphor. Because frameworks are fashionably fuzzy, you can use them to describe all types of constructs. In this book, a framework is a set of cooperating classes that make up a reusable design. You cannot just use one class from a framework—you must use them all. But you can customize the behavior of the framework in various ways. At run time the framework is typically in control. It creates objects when it needs them and calls methods when it thinks they should be called. Some of the methods a framework calls are the ones you provide to customize the framework's behavior.

Frameworks are our best hope for creating intelligent components that behave like business objects. They improve our ability to deal with the complexity of distributed object systems and collaborating components. Eventually, most components will live within one or more frameworks. A continuum of object frameworks—from the very simple to the very powerful—is coming our way. We will go over the major frameworks for components in the next few chapters—including CORBA, OpenDoc, Taligent, OpenStep, OLE/COM, and Newi. But first we revisit CORBA to understand what a business object is and where the standards are heading.

Chapter 13

CORBA's Frameworks and Business Objects

> *While we will continue to focus on "plumbing" issues, we're also now able to expand our focus to include areas of concern to end users and technology consumers such as Common Facilities, Application Objects—business objects and application frameworks—and vertical applications such as Finance, Manufacturing, and so on.*
>
> — **Chris Stone, President of OMG**
> **(May, 1995)**

With much of the basic plumbing behind it, the Object Management Group (OMG) is working on the CORBA infrastructure for *business object* components that behave "just as the real world does." Actually, this was OMG's goal from day one. But the first six years were spent defining the intergalactic object bus and its system services. In January 1995, OMG published a CORBA architecture called *Common Facilities* that defines the frameworks that will be needed to create *business objects*. Using these frameworks, business objects can be grouped into visual suites that sit on a desktop but have underlying client/server webs. The end goal of the OMG is to create a collaborative client/server business object environment. It's the ultimate middleware.

To get there, we need the core object bus (and services) and frameworks that define the high-level rules of engagements for business object components. The OMG will define both horizontal and vertical Common Facilities that can be used by business objects—also known as *application objects*. It is also working on a reference model for business objects. In this chapter, we first go over OMG's working definition of a business object. Then we cover the vertical and horizontal Common Facilities that define the frameworks for these business objects to collaborate.

BUSINESS OBJECTS

The changes caused by a shift to business objects will be huge. Business objects seek to allow for mass-produced solutions instead of following today's practice of relying on custom-built software for most solutions...That change has already begun and, over time, will be sweeping in its effects.

> — John R. Rymer, Editor
> *Distributed Computing Monitor*
> *(January, 1995)*

Business objects provide a natural way for describing application-independent concepts such as customer, order, competitor, money, payment, car, patient, and the like. They encourage a view of software that transcends tools, applications, databases, and other system concepts. John Rymer expects "business objects and component software to change the economics of software and many development practices during the next two to three years." The ultimate promise of object technology and components is to provide these medium-grained components that behave more like "the real world does." Of course, somebody must first define the rules of engagement for these components to play, which is where the OMG comes into the picture.

So What Is a Business Object Anyway?

A business object is a representation of a thing active in the business domain, including at least its business name and definition, attributes, behavior, relationship, and constraints. A business object may represent, for example, a person, place, or concept.

> — OMG, BOMSIG
> *(October, 1994)*

According to OMG's *Business Object Management Special Interest Group (BOMSIG)*, a business object is an application-level component you can use in unpredictable combinations. A business object is by definition independent of any single application. Post-monolithic applications will consist of suites of business objects—the application simply provides the environment to execute these business objects. In other words, a business object is a component object that represents a "recognizable" everyday life entity. In contrast, system-level components represent entities that make sense only to information systems and programmers—they're not something an end user recognizes.

In a high-rise building, everyone's ceiling is someone else's floor until you get to the penthouse. Then the sky is your ceiling. You may think of the business object as the penthouse of components. According to the BOMSIG definition, these top-level

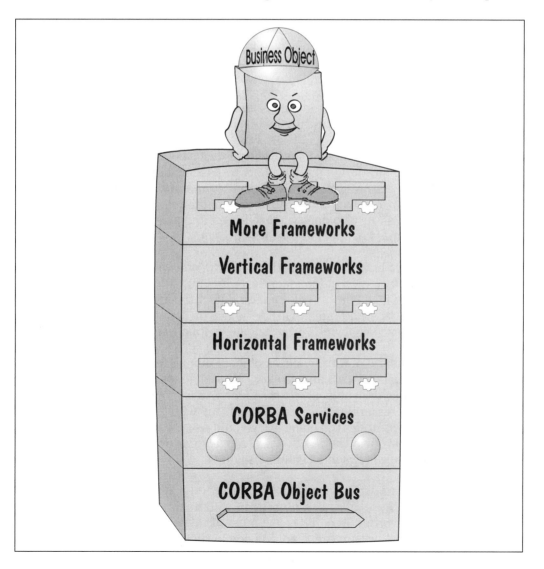

objects are recognizable to the end user of a system. The size of the object maps to "business" things like cars or tax forms. The word business is used in a very loose sense. A business object is a self-contained *deliverable* that has a user interface, state, and knows how to cooperate with other separately developed business objects to perform a desired task.

Cooperating Business Objects

A *group of business objects can form an information system only if they become a system and interact with each other.*

— **Rob Prins, CYCLADE Consultants**
(June, 1995)

Business objects will be used to design systems that mimic the business processes they support. In the real world, business events are seldom isolated to a single business object. Instead they typically involve clusters of objects. To mimic their real-world counterparts, business objects must be able to communicate with each other at a semantic level. You can capture and describe these object interactions using most of the popular design methodology tools—including Ivar Jacobson's *use cases*, Ian Graham's *task scripts*, Grady Booch's *interaction diagrams*, and Jim Rumbaugh's *event trace* diagrams. All these methodologies use some form of scenario diagrams to show who does what to whom and when. These scenarios can document the full impact of specific business events.

Business objects must have late and flexible binding and well-defined interfaces so that they can be implemented independently. A business object must be capable of recognizing events in its environment, changing its attributes, and interacting with other business objects. Like any CORBA object, a business object exposes its interfaces to its clients via IDL and communicates with other objects using the ORB.

Figure 13-1 shows a suite of four business objects that are part of a car reservation system: *customer, invoice, car,* and *car lot.* Note that *car lot* is a business object that contains other business objects—cars. Clearly, these four business objects have some agreed upon semantics for communicating with each other to perform business transactions. Under the cover, they could use the CORBA Object Transaction Service to synchronize their actions. They also know how to share a single window to display their views in a seamless manner.

So how is this different from a traditional application? With very little work, you can reuse some of these business objects in another application context. For example, a *car sales* program could reuse most of these objects, especially if they were designed to work with more than one semantic suite. For example, the car,

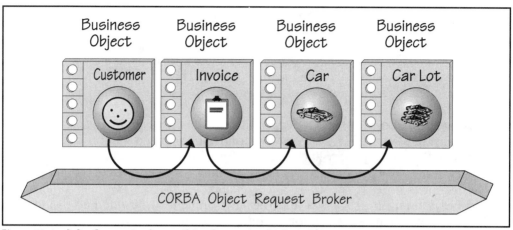

Figure 13-1. A Car Reservation System Using Cooperating Business Objects.

customer, and invoice objects could support multiple views to handle different business situations. In the extreme, the business objects could be specialized through inheritance to take into account the particularities of the car sales business. As you'll see in the next section, a business object is not a monolithic entity. It is factored internally into a set of cooperating objects that can react to different business situations. Business objects are highly flexible.

The Anatomy of a Business Object

Business objects directly represent the model of the enterprise, and this model becomes part of the information system. Every person, place, thing, event, transaction, or process in the business can be represented by an active object in the information system.

— **Cory Casanave, OMG Director**
(June, 1995)

As we go to press, the BOMSIG is working on the final touches of its *Business Application Architecture*. So far it is a variation of the *Model/View/Controller (MVC)* paradigm. MVC is an object design pattern used to build interfaces in Smalltalk and in almost every GUI class library. MVC consists of three kinds of objects. The *model* represents the application object and its encapsulated data. The *view* represents the object visually on the screen. And the *controller* defines the way the user interface reacts to user input and GUI events.

In the BOMSIG model, a business object also consists of three kinds of objects (see Figure 13-2):

■ ***Business objects*** encapsulate the storage, metadata, concurrency, and business rules associated with an active business entity. They also define how the object reacts to changes in the views or model.

■ ***Business process objects*** encapsulate the business logic at the enterprise level. In traditional MVC systems, the controller is in charge of the process. In the BOMSIG model, short-lived process functions are handled by the business object. Long-lived processes that involve other business objects are handled by the business process object—it's a specialization of the business object that handles long-lived processes and the environment at large. For example, it knows how to handle a workflow or long-lived transaction. The process object typically acts as the glue that unites the other objects. For example, it defines how the object reacts to a change in the environment. This type of change may be caused by the execution of a business transaction or by an incoming message from another business object. Note that some business objects may be entirely process-oriented and not associated with specific data or presentations.

■ ***Presentation objects*** represent the object visually to the user. Each business object can have multiple presentations for multiple purposes. The presentations communicate directly with the business object to display data on the screen. And sometimes they communicate directly with the process object. BOMSIG also recognizes that there are non-visual interfaces to business objects.

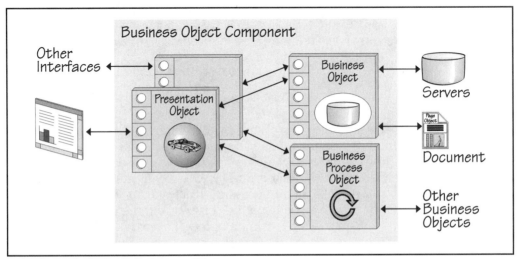

Figure 13-2. The Anatomy of a Business Object.

A typical business object component consists of a business object, one or more presentation objects, and a process object. Note that these entities act as a body. The underlying division of labor between the various objects is transparent to the users and clients of the business object. A business object also interacts with servers and system-level objects but, again, in a totally encapsulated manner. The user only sees the *aggregate* business object. And clients of the object only deal with IDL-defined interfaces that are exposed by the aggregate business object (see next Briefing box).

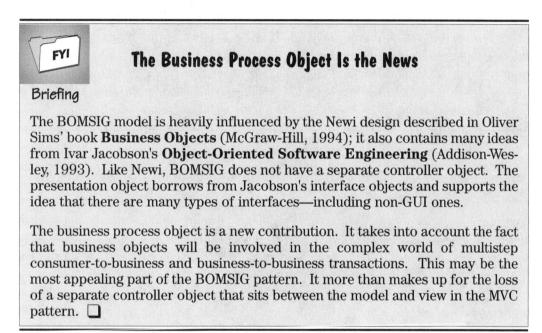

FYI

The Business Process Object Is the News

Briefing

The BOMSIG model is heavily influenced by the Newi design described in Oliver Sims' book **Business Objects** (McGraw-Hill, 1994); it also contains many ideas from Ivar Jacobson's **Object-Oriented Software Engineering** (Addison-Wesley, 1993). Like Newi, BOMSIG does not have a separate controller object. The presentation object borrows from Jacobson's interface objects and supports the idea that there are many types of interfaces—including non-GUI ones.

The business process object is a new contribution. It takes into account the fact that business objects will be involved in the complex world of multistep consumer-to-business and business-to-business transactions. This may be the most appealing part of the BOMSIG pattern. It more than makes up for the loss of a separate controller object that sits between the model and view in the MVC pattern. ❏

The Anatomy of a Client/Server Business Object

Typically, a business object—like a car—may have different presentation objects spread across multiple clients. The business object and the process object may reside in one or more servers. The beauty of a CORBA-based architecture is that all the constituent objects have IDL-defined interfaces and can run on ORBs (see Figure 13-3). So it does not matter if the constituent objects run on the same machine or on different machines (ORBs provide local/remote transparency). As far as clients are concerned, they're still dealing with a single business object component even though it may be factored into objects running in different machines.

A well-designed business object builds on the CORBA services. For example, you can use the concurrency and transaction services to maintain the integrity of the

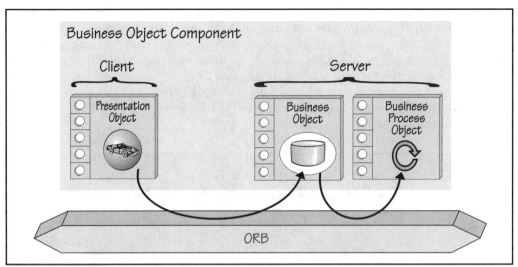

Figure 13-3. The Anatomy of a Client/Server Business Object.

business object's state. The ORB gives you these services for free, so you might as well use them.

As we go to press, we don't have enough information about how client/server splits within business objects will perform. But we know of many well-funded projects that are working along these lines. Newi and NeXT have done useful work in this area but they do not use CORBA ORBs.

CORBA'S COMMON FACILITIES

In large systems, we find clusters of abstractions built in layers on top of one another. At any given level of abstraction, we find meaningful collections of objects that collaborate to achieve some higher-level behavior.

— *Grady Booch, Author*
Object-Oriented Analysis and Design
(Benjamin-Cummings, 1994)

So where do the OMG business objects get their collaborative smarts? The smarts come from the underlying framework's rules of engagement, common data formats, and architecture boundaries. These frameworks define the stable design points for the system and how business objects interoperate. As technology evolves, you can add, update, and remove business objects while the frameworks remain stable. In other words, frameworks transcend the life cycles of individual business objects.

The CORBA *Common Facilities* are the newest area of OMG standardization—they represent the higher level component frameworks that complete the CORBA vision for interoperability.

What Are CORBA Common Facilities?

Common Facilities will provide richness and application-level focus to the ensemble of OMG technologies. Whereas ORB and Object Services are fundamental technologies, Common Facilities extend these technologies up to the application developer and ISV level. Common Facilities may become the most important area of OMG standards because it is the level most developers will utilize.

— *Thomas Mowbray, Chairman*
OMG Common Facilities
(May, 1995)

The CORBA *Common Facilities* are collections of IDL-defined frameworks that provide services directly useful to business objects (see white area in Figure 13-4). Think of them as the next step up in the semantic hierarchy. The two categories of Common Facilities—horizontal and vertical—define the rules of engagement that

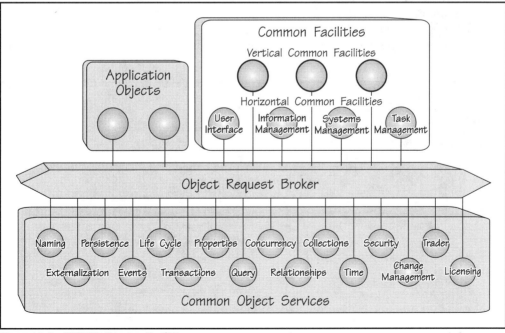

Figure 13-4. CORBA's Common Facilities.

are needed by business components to effectively collaborate. There are four types of *horizontal* facilities: *user interface, information management, systems management,* and *task management.* In addition, there are vertical facilities that will provide IDL-defined interfaces and frameworks for specialized vertical market segments such as health, retail, and finance.

Any service that's common across multiple vertical facilities is a good candidate for a horizontal facility. In addition, the boundaries separating the Common Facilities from application objects or from the system-level object services are not cast in concrete—they reflect the current state of object technology. The Common Facilities will build on top of the CORBA object services. And where it's feasible, the Common Facilities will extend the primitive object services into richer interfaces that directly address the needs of ISVs and applications.

The CORBA User Interface Common Facility

The *User Interface* Common Facility deals with *compound document* technology and in-place editing services similar to those provided by OpenDoc and OLE (see Figure 13-5). The idea is to provide a framework for sharing and subdividing a display window so that different components can share the screen's visual real estate in a seamless way. Obviously, it takes some strict rules of engagement to achieve this level of visual integration. But without these protocols, we can never get components developed by different vendors that know nothing of each other to look like they're all part of the same application. The visual protocols must resolve issues such as: visual geometry management, the distribution of interface events to

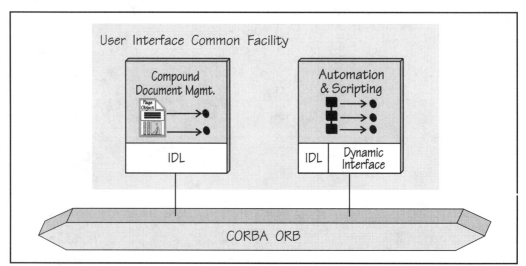

Figure 13-5. The User Interface Common Facility.

the right component, and sharing resources (for example menus and tool bars). A component must be able to embed other components within it and also be able to edit its contents in-place without leaving the window.

We'll have a lot more to say about compound documents in the OLE and OpenDoc chapters. The most likely candidate technology for OMG's compound document framework is OpenDoc. It was submitted to OMG by Apple and CI Labs in response to RFP1. Microsoft chose not to submit OLE—probably because it does not want the OLE standard to be controlled by an outside body like OMG.

The User Interface Common Facility also deals with scripting. This late-binding technology is essential for agents, workflow, and long-lived transactions. Because scripting languages use late-binding mechanisms—as opposed to binding at compile time—you can create and attach scripts "on the fly" to components and compound documents. This technology—called *automation*—is used by system integrators, IS shops, and power users to create dynamic collaborations between components. The facility will define semantic events—a form of application-level messaging—that can be used by a scripting language to coordinate the actions of component suites.

Using a scripting language, you should be able to invoke any IDL-specified CORBA service. The scripting language hooks into the CORBA bus using the dynamic invocation facility. For example, you should be able—via scripts—to create, copy, delete, and move objects using the CORBA life cycle service. You could advertise an object using the trader and naming services, again using a script. And you should be able to write scripts to find objects using the query service, and so on. Scripting and automation will make the ORB and all its services available to the masses of "authorized" end users. We cover automation, scripting, and agents in the OLE and OpenDoc chapters.

The CORBA Information Management Common Facility

The *Information Management* Common Facility includes compound document storage and data interchange facilities similar to those provided by OLE and OpenDoc. It also defines standards that components use to encode and represent their data, to define and exchange metadata, and to model information (see Figure 13-6). Clearly, OMG is not going to define all these facilities from scratch. Instead, it will pick a set of existing standards and provide the IDL and framework definitions to "CORBA-tize" them. For example, the OpenDoc Bento standard was submitted by Apple and CI Labs in response to RFP1's request for a compound document storage and data interchange facility. Bento is a mature technology that's available in over 100 products—including Lotus 1-2-3.

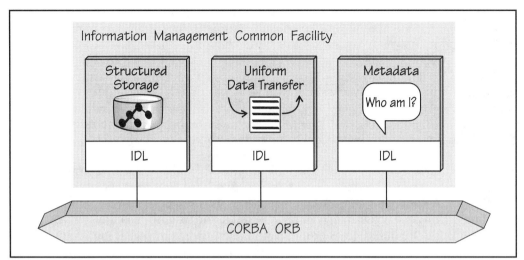

Figure 13-6. The Information Management Common Facility.

Metadata is particularly important in a distributed component environment. It is used to describe both services and information. With metadata, new services and components can dynamically join a system and be discovered at run time. Metadata is what makes systems dynamic and introspective. The OMG Interface Repository is a store of *service metadata*—it describes interfaces. *Information metadata* can supplement the Interface Repository by describing the structure and access procedures for data. This helps components search effectively for information and discover how to retrieve the contents. Information metadata is also used to define the access constraints that will be required by various service providers for billing, privacy, and security reasons.

The CORBA System Management Common Facility

Our idea was to build management applications around an ORB instead of network management protocols. So in 1989, we began working on a distributed object framework for managing applications.

> — **Todd Smith, Chief Scientist**
> **Tivoli Systems**
> **(February, 1995)**

The *System Management* Common Facility includes interfaces and services for managing, instrumenting, configuring, installing, operating, and repairing distributed object components. For a distributed component to be managed, it must implement IDL-defined management interfaces. The system management framework defines the following interfaces:

- **Instrumentation**—lets you collect information on a component's workload, responsiveness, throughput, consumption of resources, and so on.

- **Data collection**—lets you collect information on historical events related to a component. Any component may have a history—meaning a log of events. The data collection interface allows a managing workstation to query that log.

- **Quality of service**—lets you select the level of service a component provides in areas such as availability, performance, reliability, and recovery.

- **Security**—lets you manage the security system itself. It is distinct from the CORBA Security Service that implements the security mechanisms.

- **Event management**—lets you generate, register, filter, and forward event notifications to management applications. It builds on the CORBA Event Service.

- **Scheduling**—lets you schedule repetitive tasks and associate event handlers with events. For example, you can schedule the execution of a task when an event fires or a timer pops.

- **Instance tracking**—lets you associate objects with other managed objects that are subject to common policies.

The most likely candidate technology for these services is X/Open's new *SysMan* standard. SysMan itself is based on the *Tivoli Management Environment (TME)*, which provides a CORBA-based distributed system management framework (see Figure 13-7). TME 2.0 provides a set of CORBA-based technologies and services to create, maintain, and integrate distributed system management applications.

Tivoli and CORBA

TME consists of *Tivoli/Enterprise Console*, *Tivoli Management Framework (TMF)*, and a set of core management services. Tivoli/Enterprise is a desktop management console that collects management events and provides a rules-based technology for automating management operations and event processing. TMF includes basic services for handling user-defined policies, scheduling tasks, instance tracking, instrumentation, and security. TMF also provides a set of system management classes (in the form of mixins) that managed and managing objects can multiple inherit from and customize.

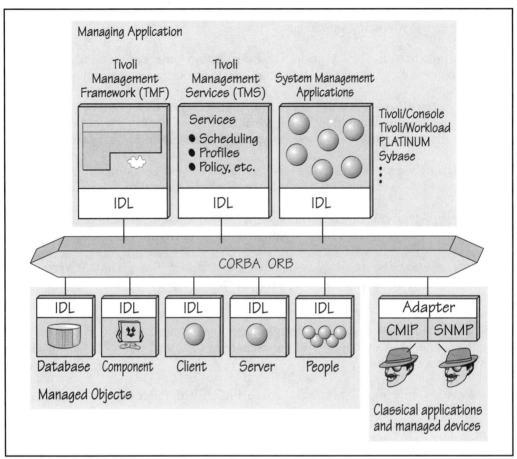

Figure 13-7. The Tivoli Management Environment (TME).

Tivoli has an active OEM program to license TME. Participants include IBM, Sybase, Informix, Sun, Unisys, Siemens-Rolm, and others. Tivoli and IBM will provide TME-based object-management services as part of SOM 3.X. Tivoli will be available on all major platforms—including Unixes, NetWare, OS/2, Windows NT, DOS, Windows, and so on. Tivoli is providing adapters to other system management platforms—including OpenView, SunNet Manager, NetView, NetWare Management System, Sybase, and Oracle. TME is the *de facto* and *de jure* (via X/Open) system management standard for CORBA ORBs. The most OMG can do is ratify the X/Open standard and make it more coherent in certain areas. So, for all practical purposes, systems management for ORBs is mostly here today—it's called Tivoli (see next Soapbox).

System Management: Why Objects Are the Answer

Soapbox

A *network-management system is limited by the capabilities of the network-management protocol and by the objects used to represent the environment to be managed.*

> — *William Stallings, Author*
> *SNMP, SNMPv2, and CMIP*
> *(Addison-Wesley, 1993)*

Warning: This Soapbox is filled with system management acronyms and four-letter words. If you understand them, everything will make sense. Otherwise, either skip this Soapbox or look up these acronyms in an introductory text such as Stallings' or our book, **Essential Client/Server Survival Guide** (Wiley, 1994). Sorry for the inconvenience, but there's no way we can do justice to SNMP and CMIP in this Soapbox.

We believe CORBA provides a modern and natural protocol for representing managed entities, defining their services, specifying instance data, and invoking methods via an ORB. You can use the CORBA Interface and Implementation Repositories to discover and dynamically invoke methods on these managed objects at run time. The managed objects can directly call the managing station when they have something significant to report (in contrast, SNMP relies mostly on polling). The CORBA event service is ideal for distributing asynchronous system management events. And the CORBA object services provide a ton of useful functions that would have to be reinvented by SNMP or OSI's CMIP (life cycle, naming, transactions, persistence, and so on). Using CORBA, distributed system management becomes just another service on the ORB. Objects can manage themselves. Management applications provide views on collections of self-managing objects.

The *Simple Network Management Protocol (SNMP)*—today's predominant management protocol—is too limiting for the requirements of total systems management. It needs to be replaced. This means that in the next few years we'll be experiencing a large migration to more sophisticated management software. The three contenders for replacing SNMP are SNMP2, OSI's CMIP, and CORBA. All three require more memory and smarter processors than SNMP. So the question is: Which one do you choose? In our opinion it should be CORBA. SNMP2 and CMIP are both antiques and incredibly clumsy to program. MIBs are an anachronism in the age of IDL and object persistent stores. They require that management applications interact with a very large number of low-level attributes that they manipulate through *get* and *set*. SNMP2 does not allow you to register operations on managed objects; CMIP does this very clumsily. We feel the "simple" SNMP was a wonderful, basic protocol that solved many real problems in the age of scarcity and simple network management. But now that we're moving to total systems management, the sooner the world moves away from SNMP, SNMP2, and CMIP and replaces them with CORBA, the better off system management will be.

Table 13-1 compares the features of SNMP, SNMP2, CMIP, and CORBA. SNMP and SNMP2 place a minimum amount of event-emitting logic in the agents so that the managed nodes are simple. The smarts are in the managing station. As a result, traps (or events) are infrequently used, and the managing station must poll the agents to find out what's happening. In contrast, CMIP and CORBA are event driven, which means the agents are smarter; the managing station doesn't have to poll as much. As a result, a CORBA managing station can handle a much larger number of managed objects.

In general, CMIP or CORBA are better suited for the management of large, complex, multivendor networks than SNMP. Of course, SNMP's simplicity allows it to be deployed on more devices, which, in turn, makes it easier to manage large networks. The designers of SNMP understood these trade-offs very well. They opted for the least common denominator approach and were willing to live with the consequences. SNMP2 makes the same architectural trade-offs as SNMP. Looking at the comparison table, we're not so sure SNMP is still the way to go. Systems management operational costs are just too high—the design point has shifted. We need smarter systems management software that knows how to deal with smarter objects anywhere on the intergalactic network. We believe CORBA is the answer to the distributed systems management nightmare. ❑

Table 13-1. Comparing SNMP, SNMP2, CMIP, and CORBA Objects.

Feature	SNMP	SNMP2	CMIP	CORBA Objects
Installed base	Huge	Small	Small	Very small
Managed objects per managing station	Small	Small	Large	Large
Management model	Manager and agents	Manager and agents	Manager and agents	Communicating objects
View of managed objects	Simple variables organized in MIB trees	Simple variables organized in MIB trees	Objects with inheritance defined in MIBs	Objects with IDL defined interfaces, attributes, and multiple inheritance

Table 13-1. Comparing SNMP, SNMP2, CMIP, and CORBA Objects. (Continued)				
Feature	**SNMP**	**SNMP2**	**CMIP**	**CORBA Objects**
Manager/agent interactions	Polling. Infrequent traps	Polling. Infrequent traps	Event driven	Event driven
Explicit manager to agent command invocations	No	No	Yes	Yes
Security	No	Yes	Yes	Yes
Manager-to-manager exchanges	No	Yes	Yes	Yes
Bulk transfers	No	Yes	Yes	Yes
Create/delete managed objects	No	No (but can add table rows)	Yes	Yes
Communication model	Datagram	Datagram	Session-based	ORB
Standards body	Internet	Internet	ISO	OMG, X/Open
Approximate memory requirements (in KBytes)	40-200	200-500	300-1000	300-2000

The CORBA Task Management Common Facility

The *Task Management* Common Facility provides a framework for managing workflows, long transactions, agents, scripting, rules, and task automation (see Figure 13-8). The framework includes a semantic messaging facility that defines high-level messages used to communicate task-oriented requests (typically originated by user transactions). A *task* can be composed of a single operation—for example, an ad-hoc query—or sequences of operations—for example, a workflow. The *information object* can be a simple structure—for example, an e-mail message—or a complex structure such as a compound document. *Operations* are atomic units of work invoked on information objects.

Agents consist of information objects and an associated script that knows what to do with the information and how to deal with the environment. The agent infrastructure consists of *static agents* and *mobile agents*—also known as *roaming agents*. Static agents assist their clients with solving a problem—for example, a personal mail sorting valet. Mobile agents are "intelligent messages" that contain data and scripts. The scripts know what to do with the data and how to interpret a workflow.

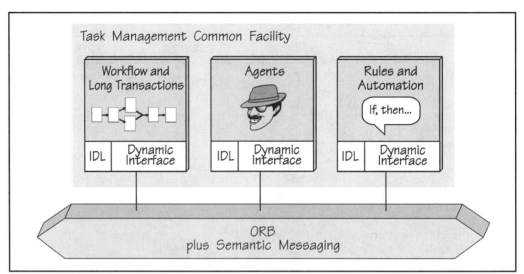

Figure 13-8. The Task Management Common Facility.

The CORBA *agenting infrastructure* will address a number of end-user and developer problems in the emerging information highway. It will help offload repetitive tasks from end users, and it will support electronic commerce and mobile computing. For example, a roaming agent can help you plan a trip, get the best accommodations, and then bill your account. The agent infrastructure relies on semantic messaging on top of the ORB. The *semantic messages* define the vocabulary agents use to communicate content and to perform administrative tasks. The messages contain both the nouns that describe contents of the message and the verbs that define the operations.

The CORBA agenting infrastructure will provide capabilities for agents to *advertise* their services and for *subscribers* to register for these services. *Broker* agents know how to recruit other agents to create task forces. The broker knows how to delegate or *forward* work to agents it has recruited for a job. In addition, mobile agents will have *home agencies*. An *agency* provides a script engine, an execution environment, and a registration database. Mobile agents will register themselves with their home agencies and have *visitor privileges* with other agencies. Because agencies are active entities, they may be grouped in different ways. For example, several agencies may be part of a group where one agency plays the role of a *receptionist*. So it's possible to create a virtual network of agencies. The CORBA agenting infrastructure will define the open protocols that let agencies communicate with agents, their brokers, and other agencies.

Rules management provides facilities for specifying *event-condition-action* rules in a declarative language and for managing and executing these rules. OMG will most likely provide an IDL-based rules specification language. It will also define the environment for CORBA-compliant rules execution engines. Of course, the idea is that you should be able to execute any CORBA service from within the rules language. This is not unlike the requirement placed on CORBA scripting languages. In fact, you can probably specify and execute most simple rules using scripts. More sophisticated rule engines must be able to support forward and backward chaining, certainty factors, and the maintenance and exchange of rules.

Automation is the underlying technology used by scripting systems or any clients that need to dynamically access a component's functions or content data. You can use automation to manipulate user visible objects that are larger grained than the typical ORB object. For example, a client could use the automation facilities to manipulate a document or a spreadsheet cell within that document. Server objects will typically expose—via automation—enough of their capabilities so that they may be driven by scripts or macros. Automation requires late binding, which can be provided using CORBA's dynamic method invocation and the dynamic skeleton interface. In addition, automation introduces a need for *object specifiers*, which let you describe an object within a context without specifying a concrete object reference. For example, in a document context, an object specifier could be the "last character of the last paragraph on the second page."

The CORBA Vertical Market Common Facilities

The hype touting the future as one in which you can buy individual business objects on the market will never materialize because such business objects will need substantial reworking before they fit your object web. Instead, people are now beginning to talk about industry-vertical frameworks that provide an integral set of business objects, together with their interconnecting web.

— *Rob Prins, CYCLADE Consultants*
(June, 1995)

The vertical facilities will provide IDL-defined interfaces and standards for component interoperability for vertical market segments such as health, retail, and finance. Most vertical market frameworks will be defined by industry SIGs using OMG's "fast track" process. Using this process, a member company can submit an unsolicited proposal to OMG for adopting a particular ORB-based industry framework. Note that it must be a commercialized technology. If there are no serious objections, a standard can be adopted in about 6 months. In contrast, the traditional *Request For Proposal (RFP)* process takes 12 to 16 months. The following is a sampling of CORBA-based vertical frameworks that are in development:

- **■** *CORBA for Document Imaging.* This includes image document stores that can move and copy BLOBs, index them, and so on. The imaging framework builds on CORBA's life cycle, query, security, persistence, transaction, relationships, and concurrency services. In addition, image metadata can be advertised via the trader service. The imaging framework can also make use of horizontal Common Facilities—including data interchange, compound documents, and automation.

- **■** *CORBA for Information Superhighways.* This framework uses CORBA as a backbone for the information superhighway. It uses CORBA-based facilities for advertising, metering, billing, monitoring, resource discovery, brokering, trading, intelligent agenting, and electronic commerce.

- **■** *CORBA for Computer Integrated Manufacturing (CIM).* This framework uses CORBA to componentize and integrate the various manufacturing functions—including process control, work-in-process tracking, quality control, CAD, labor management, inventory management, and so on. The idea is to create very "agile" manufacturing lines using distributed object technology. This framework builds on top of every CORBA service and horizontal facility.

- **■** *CORBA for Distributed Simulations.* This framework can be used for simulations of air traffic control, business scenarios, video games, and other such applications. The idea is that you can configure a simulation by choosing

CORBA components, specifying their connections, and providing them with "adaptation" data. You can start and stop components, ask them for their status, assign them unique roles, and control their environment. The simulation is a dance of the components.

■ **CORBA for Oil and Gas Exploration.** This framework controls the processes for finding and recovering natural resources. It involves a large quantity of data, complex algorithms, and long-term data storage.

■ **CORBA for Accounting.** This framework provides a distributed accounting system that includes business transactions, money exchanges, payroll, purchasing, and sales.

This is only a partial list of frameworks. By the time you read this, we expect that the list will have grown much longer. There are groups within the OMG already working on CORBA for Health and CORBA for Telcos. Your authors are aware of many company-specific CORBA frameworks that are under development in several key industries.

When Can You Expect These Common Facilities?

We expect the CORBA 2.0 ORB and Object Services to be incorporated into commercial ORBs starting in late 1995. However, the CORBA business objects and Common Facilities are work in progress. The Common Facilities Task Force— established in December 1993—is the third permanent OMG task force (after the ORB task force and the Object Services task force). In January 1995, the task force released the *Common Facilities Architecture* that we described in this chapter. It also published a road map that establishes a schedule for the adoption of this technology (see Figure 13-9).

In October 1994, the OMG issued the *Common Facilities Request for Proposal 1 (RFP1)* to obtain technology submissions for compound documents—both OpenDoc and Fresco are candidate technologies. It generally takes OMG about a year to adopt a technology after it issues an RFP. Based on the RFP schedules, it looks like most of the Common Facilities (as described here) may be completed by September 1996. When this happens, CORBA will provide IDL-interfaces for virtually every distributed service we know today (many are IDL-ized versions of existing standards).

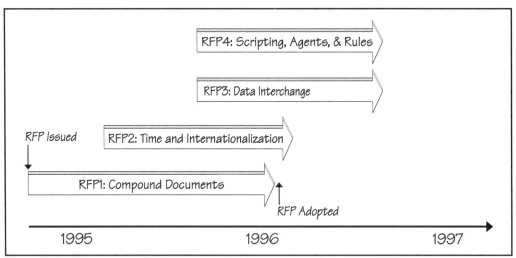

Figure 13-9. The Common Facilities Road Map Schedule.

Conclusion

This chapter is more about vision than product. Business objects are CORBA's vision of component nirvana. OMG has been patiently assembling the foundation on which this vision is being built. If you can't wait, there are many CORBA-based frameworks that you can use right now to provide some of the functions described in this chapter. For example, you can use OpenDoc for compound document management and Tivoli for systems management. Using these existing frameworks should provide you with a "head start" until the standards activities follow their course.

Chapter 14

Compound Documents: The Desktop Framework

---

*T*he real lure of this compound document technology is component software. It promises the ability to "roll your own" application by simply placing components together in a standard document that knows how to handle them.

> — David Linthicum
> Open Computing
> (January, 1995)

By late 1996, compound documents will become the dominant framework for deploying components on the desktop and across the enterprise. They will provide the mass channel for selling millions of components. The "document" metaphor may be the breakthrough we've been awaiting. It provides an intuitive way to group related objects, display them seamlessly in a window, store them in a shared file, and ship them across networks to other desktops or to servers. In addition, the document maintains persistent client/server links that let these embedded components extract data from servers anywhere in the enterprise. So the document becomes the universal client—the ultimate front-end to servers. In fact, servers can ship compound documents directly to their clients to create storefronts for their services. It's like shipping Mosaic on steroids. This chapter covers the fundamentals of compound documents. In later chapters, we introduce the real products—including OpenDoc, OLE, Taligent, OpenStep, and Newi.

COMPOUND DOCUMENTS: WHY ALL THE FUSS?

A *compound document* is nothing more than a metaphor for organizing collections of components—both visually and through containment relationships. It's an integration framework for visual components. The document is essentially a collection site for components and data that can come from a variety of sources. Because documents are so familiar, they create a very natural paradigm for the large-scale introduction of objects "for the masses." For most users, their first interaction with objects will be through these compound documents.

The Borderless Desktop

Compound documents are "places" where components live. The desktop itself is in the process of becoming a giant compound document that integrates in a "borderless" manner applications and operating system services. Did we have too much espresso? Perhaps, but if you think about it, OLE is an integral part of Windows 95. And OpenDoc will be shipped with every copy of OS/2 Warp and Macintosh. Both OpenDoc and OLE are frameworks for creating compound documents and managing components that live within these documents. Eventually, every object that appears on a desktop—in Windows, OS/2 Warp, or Mac—will be a component. Most of these components will be able to contain other components.

So the modern desktop simply becomes a giant container of components some of which are containers of other components, and so on. Components can be moved via drag-and-drop from the desktop to any visual container (and vice versa) to fit a user's needs for working "space." But isn't that the same as moving files into desktop folders? Yes, except that the visual components that are being moved around are more intelligent than anything that lives on today's desktops. In addition, they know how to collaborate with other components to share visual real estate and storage. Instead of seeing boxes within boxes, you will see something that looks more like a visual tapestry. It's really a self-organizing tapestry made up of intelligent components.

Documents Come in All Shapes

A compound document is primarily a visual container. With newer compound document technologies—such as OpenDoc—these containers can have irregular shapes. With irregular shapes, we can create container/component combinations that are bounded only by the imagination. For example, it's easy to imagine containers that look like airplane bodies, stadiums, garden plots, cities, shopping malls, and so on. You will be able to create applications by dragging components from palettes and dropping them into containers. It's just like a game of *SimCity*, except that each of these components is live and can directly interact with a user (see Figure 14-1). The beauty is that these components can be supplied by different vendors that know nothing of each other. Note that containers themselves are also components—they too can be embedded inside other components. So everything is very recursive.

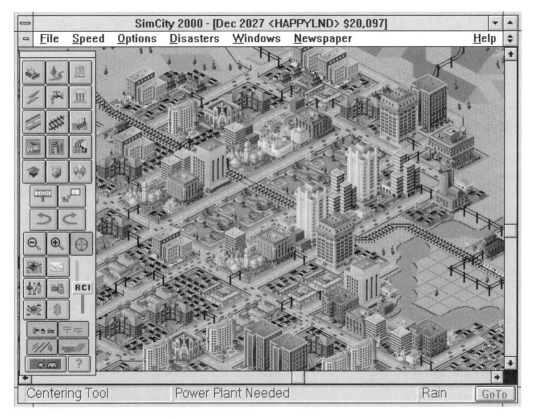

Figure 14-1. If SimCity Were a Compound Document.

A Home for All Data Types

Compound document data is more than the vanilla text of spreadsheets and paper documents. Data can be anything—including movies, sounds, animation, controls, networked calendars, and virtual folders. Each new kind of medium that is developed—video, sound, animation, simulation, and so on—can be represented by a component in a document. Database access components can feed visual information to users and to other components. For example, using scripts you can feed the data to a spell-checker component or a data-trend analysis component. Of course, all these components must have agreed upon data structures.

Compound documents can accept new kinds of data at run time because the data content is managed by the component that owns the data. In contrast, a traditional application restricts the types of data that can go into a document to the data types that are known by the application at compile time. If a new type of content becomes available, the application has no way to incorporate it into a document. You must modify and recompile a traditional application to incorporate new data types.

In-Place Editing

Switching among visual components within a document or across documents is much less intrusive than switching between conventional applications. You can immediately edit any content *in-place* without having to launch and execute different applications to create and assemble data. In-place editing allows the component to bring its editing tools to the container—including menus, toolbars, adornments, and small child windows. Instead of the user going to the program that manipulates data, the program comes to the container.

You no longer need to manually manage the various file formats that make up a compound document—all the pieces are now held in one place. The software that manipulates the document is hidden. You're manipulating parts of a document instead of switching between applications. The compound document either contains the data for its components or maintains links to data that's stored elsewhere. So you never have to visually leave the document—everything is right there.

Shippable Documents

By 1997 enterprise business documents will become the primary paradigm for capturing corporate information, challenging the dominance of record-oriented data. Compound document technology will become the overall framework for managing various non-record oriented information.

— Meta Group

Compound documents make it easier for developers to share storage for their separately developed components. And they make it easier for users to exchange documents. Documents can be printed, edited, shared, viewed, annotated, and circulated for review. You can pull data into the documents from several sources using client/server relationships. You can use a compound document to route work from one machine to the next. The routed document can contain data for the work-in-process, the user interface elements, and scripts that make the document intelligent. When the document lands on a workstation, an embedded script can log on the user and show the portions of the document that match the user's capabilities. A script can also decide where a document goes next.

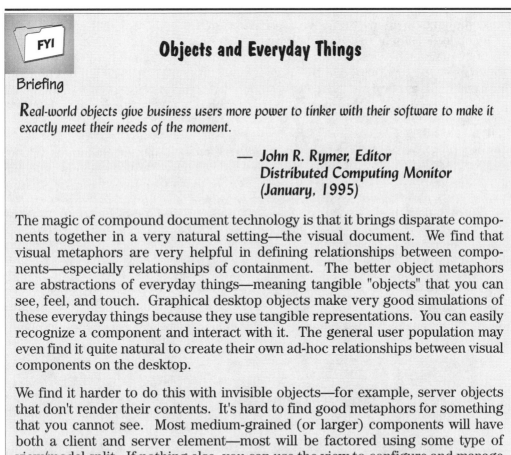

FYI

Objects and Everyday Things

Briefing

Real-world objects give business users more power to tinker with their software to make it exactly meet their needs of the moment.

— *John R. Rymer, Editor*
Distributed Computing Monitor
(January, 1995)

The magic of compound document technology is that it brings disparate components together in a very natural setting—the visual document. We find that visual metaphors are very helpful in defining relationships between components—especially relationships of containment. The better object metaphors are abstractions of everyday things—meaning tangible "objects" that you can see, feel, and touch. Graphical desktop objects make very good simulations of these everyday things because they use tangible representations. You can easily recognize a component and interact with it. The general user population may even find it quite natural to create their own ad-hoc relationships between visual components on the desktop.

We find it harder to do this with invisible objects—for example, server objects that don't render their contents. It's hard to find good metaphors for something that you cannot see. Most medium-grained (or larger) components will have both a client and server element—most will be factored using some type of view/model split. If nothing else, you can use the view to configure and manage the component. So the desktop will offer the user interface and increasingly the integration capability for enterprise components. You can store part of the model data locally but the bulk of it will typically reside in superservers. We also anticipate the increasing use of roaming objects. These are components that move between machines carrying with them—inside a compound document, of course—their user interface and state. ❑

THE COMPOUND DOCUMENT FRAMEWORK

The whole point of a compound document is to be able to mix the types of content, and to create the boundaries that sort out where one kind of content ends and another begins. This must all be done without the parts losing either their identities or boundaries.

— **Kurt Piersol, OpenDoc Architect**
Apple Computers

The compound document framework provides the protocols that let the component managing a document communicate with the components that own objects within the document. The protocols must also let these components effectively share resources such as a document file or a window on the screen. The trick is to make these protocols general enough to allow independently developed components, with no prior knowledge of each other, to discover each other's existence and collaborate at run time.

Figure 14-2 shows the constituent technologies of a compound document framework. Notice that the framework builds on top of an existing object bus and core object services. It provides four value-added services to its components: *visual layout, structured storage, scripting/automation,* and *uniform data transfer.* This section provides a brief introduction to these technologies. We cover them more extensively in the product chapters.

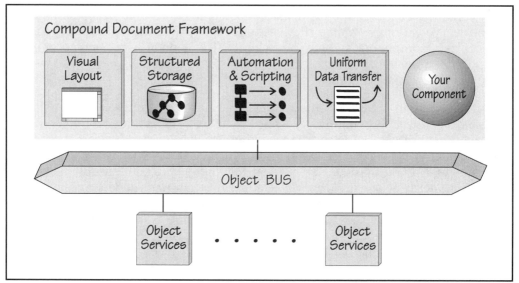

Figure 14-2. The Compound Document Framework.

Document Layout

The *document layout* service defines the rules of engagement that allow independently developed components to share the container's window. Using the container as the mediator, components must cooperate to produce a seamless-looking document for the end user. Remember, the word "document" is used in the SimCity sense. Containers activate the components that are embedded within a document and allocate to each a piece of the visual real estate. The components display their data in the area they're given and interact with the user.

Containers distribute events to their components and notify them when anything of interest happens within their surroundings. The container also arbitrates the use of shared resources—for example, a shared menu bar. A container must be able to accept a component that's dropped within its boundaries and figure out what to do with it. Embedded components negotiate with their containers for additional screen real estate if they need it.

Structured Storage

A traditional document is a monolithic block of data—inside a file—controlled by a single application. In contrast, a compound document consists of many smaller blocks of content data, each block is controlled by its own software component. The compound document provides the protocols that keep the components from corrupting the common document in which they live.

Compound documents must be able to partition a single file into storage compartments that can be allocated to individual components. Each component gets to store whatever data it wants within its storage. They're called compound documents because they can hold different kinds of data. When a compound document is first opened it knows how to find and activate the components that manipulate the data. A component, in this case, is the data plus the code that manipulates the data. The container never touches or manipulates data that belongs to its embedded components.

Structured storage is the technology that creates a "file system within a file" by providing a layer of indirection on top of existing file systems. Each component is given a directory-like structure to organize and describe the contents of its storage; the data itself is stored in streams. These streams must be able to accommodate tiny records as well as giant BLOBs of data—for example, a full-feature movie like *Gone With the Wind*.

The data in a compound document can come from a variety of sources, including foreign components and SQL databases. The container provides the appropriate hooks to activate the foreign components that are associated with the separate data elements. It does this by directly embedding the foreign data within a document or by maintaining pointers—or *links*—in the document to the external data sources. In either case, the document is still editable by various applications; each sees its data in native format.

Scripting and Automation

*T*he interconnection and specialization of application-level components are now referred to as scripting...Of course, scripting is programming but we don't want to tell all those end users that they've actually been programming, do we?

> — **Dave Thomas, President**
> **Object Technology International**
> **(March, 1995)**

Scripting—also called *automation*—is a major feature of the compound document component model. Scripts allow users to customize their applications. In compound document situations, they allow power users and scripters to create custom relationships between components in the document using standard document-editing facilities. Scripts allow programmers and system integrators to create client/server relationships that use the document metaphor for client front-ends. They also let you create smart documents.

Attached scripts can let a document track each time it is read or written. The document can notify its owners via e-mail each time their document is read. The script can also control what's being displayed in a document based on a user's authority. The script could request a password, validate digital signatures, and consult with an authentication server and a capabilities database before letting you see parts of the document. A smart document can adjust itself to your tastes. Scripts can also dynamically pull in content; for example, you could use a script to query a data warehouse to pull in data.

Scripts and compound documents complement each other very nicely. The document houses various scripts and invokes them when certain events fire—for example, when you open or close a document. In return, scripts protect the document and provide the intelligence that makes it self-sufficient. The result of marrying these two technologies are intelligent self-managing documents. You can also use this technology to create mobile components that roam over networks and do all kinds of useful work. For the first time, we have off-the-shelf technology that lets us create and deploy truly self-sufficient objects. A compound document can contain a component's state, data, intelligence, and user interface.

Uniform Data Transfer

Compound documents must be able to exchange data and components with their surroundings. *Uniform data transfer* provides a single data interchange mechanism that you can use with a variety of protocols—including clipboard cut-and-paste, drag-and-drop, and linking. The uniform data transfer mechanism must be capable of exchanging traditional data content as well as entire components—including components that are embedded within them. You can think of this as a form of "deep" copy or move.

Conclusion

Compound documents provide a framework and visual metaphor for organizing components. They provide negotiation protocols through which embedded components merge their user interface elements into the container's window space and share a document file. Embedded scripts add intelligence to the document and protect it from threats. Because the desktop operating systems themselves are becoming compound document frameworks, they will provide a mass market for components that play by the new rules of engagement. Remember, these rules of engagement are over and above those provided by the underlying object bus and services. Compound documents introduce a higher level of collaboration.

Compound documents are particularly attractive because they provide a powerful metaphor for integrating components. Compound document frameworks let you visualize the components, store them in a common file, exchange them via data transfers, and extend them using scripts and automation. In addition, everything is built on an object bus that allows these components to play in intergalactic networks and to be packaged in language-independent dynamic libraries.

Of course, the price of living within a framework is that you must accept the constraints (and rules of engagement) that it imposes to accrue the benefits. It's an all-or-nothing proposition. The constraints imposed by a compound document framework include its protocols for sharing a common file, negotiating for visual real estate, and exchanging information with the outside world. Components are no longer free standing. They live within the document. And they also use the container as an intermediary to receive events, share resources, and communicate with each other. In return, components achieve higher levels of visual collaboration and can be distributed via mass market channels. It's a classic trade-off.

Compound documents are also a key technology for enterprise client/server systems. Servers can ship flexible front-ends (for example, a storefront) to their services using compound documents. In addition, you can use compound documents to package and ship across networks all types of self-contained components—including roaming agents, mobile components, and workflow. So welcome to this brave new world. We cover *OLE* and *OpenDoc*—the two *de facto* standards for compound documents—in later chapters. We also cover NeXT's *OpenStep*, Taligent's *CommonPoint*, and Integrated Objects' *Newi*.

Chapter 15

The OpenDoc Component Model

OpenDoc is a bigger threat to Microsoft than its friends at the justice department. It's an angry Judge Stanley Sporkin written in C++.

> — *Editorial*
> *MacWEEK*
> *(March, 1995)*

OpenDoc is a component software architecture implemented as a set of cross-platform classes and services. The component model is a pure rendition of the compound document paradigm. Components in the OpenDoc world are called *parts*. Parts live within compound documents. You can't have free-floating OpenDoc components. All OpenDoc components must be associated with a compound document. An OpenDoc part consists of data stored in compound documents—including text, graphics, spreadsheets, and video—plus a *part editor* that manipulates this data. An OpenDoc document is a user-organized collection of parts.

PARTS: COMPONENTS, OPENDOC STYLE

OpenDoc is similar in scope and function to OLE, but it comes from CI Labs rather than Microsoft. The *Components Integration Lab (CI Labs)* was formed in September 1993 by Apple, IBM, Novell, Oracle, Taligent, SunSoft, WordPerfect, and Xerox. The purpose of this "open" industry consortium is to establish, promote, and certify OpenDoc and related compound document technologies. CI Labs technology will eventually integrate multimedia, three-dimensional models, text, graphics and other types of information in any application.

OpenDoc defines the rules of engagement for parts to coexist in compound documents and to share visual real estate. It also provides an elaborate scripting model that lets parts collaborate via scripts. The OpenDoc runtime—packaged as IDL-defined CORBA classes—provides a cross-language and cross-platform compound document environment.

OpenDoc Meets CORBA

If you come from the world of CORBA, an OpenDoc part is nothing more than a CORBA object with desktop smarts. OpenDoc extends the CORBA ORB to the desktop. Parts within a desktop can use a CORBA ORB to collaborate with other desktop parts and to access server objects wherever they reside. The ORB provides transparent access to remote components and CORBA services such as security, transactions, and naming. But before we get into these client/server collaborations, let's first go over the OpenDoc component model and see how it complements and extends CORBA.

OPENDOC'S CONSTITUENT TECHNOLOGIES

OpenDoc is similar to OLE in its intent but offers more features, support for object messaging across networks, a more elegant user interface convention, and support for multiple platforms. OpenDoc components can also interoperate with OLE components.

— *John R. Rymer, Editor*
Distributed Computing Monitor
(January, 1995)

OpenDoc uses the familiar document metaphor for visually organizing components on the desktop. OpenDoc parts are medium-grained objects. Jed Harris, President of CI Labs, defines an OpenDoc part as a piece of software "small enough to create and maintain, big enough to deploy and support, and with standard interfaces for interoperability." Parts can represent almost any type of data—including text, movies, sound clips, clocks, calendars, spreadsheets, and data types that haven't yet been invented. All these parts are concurrently active within the same document, which is why they're sometimes called "living, breathing documents" or, to be less dramatic, just "compound documents."

OpenDoc defines the rules of engagement for parts to: 1) seamlessly share screen real estate within a window; 2) store their data within a single container file; 3) exchange information with other parts via links, clipboards, and drag-and-drop; 4) coordinate their actions via scripts, semantic events, and CORBA method invocations; and 5) interoperate with other desktop component models—for example, OLE and Taligent. Figure 15-1 shows OpenDoc's constituent technologies and how they relate. The CORBA-compliant *System Object Model (SOM)* is from IBM. The rest of the technologies—including *Bento, Uniform Data Transfer, Compound Document Management*, and the *Open Scripting Architecture (OSA)*—are from Apple.

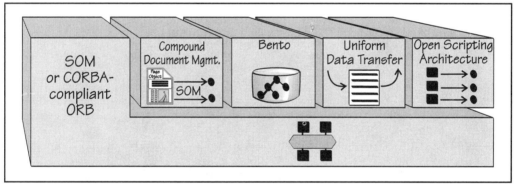

Figure 15-1. OpenDoc's Constituent Technologies.

In addition, Novell is distributing *ComponentGlue*, an interface and library that provide seamless interoperability between OLE and OpenDoc for Windows. Taligent will also provide a seamless interoperability layer between OpenDoc parts and its own component model. You will also be able to construct portable OpenDoc parts using Taligent's application frameworks and tools. In this chapter, we provide a brief overview of OpenDoc's constituent technologies. We cover the gory details in Part 4.

SOM

SOM provides local and remote interoperability for OpenDoc parts (i.e., components). SOM is a language-independent, CORBA-compliant ORB that lets objects communicate in a single address space or across address spaces on the same machine or across networks. Because SOM is included with every OpenDoc runtime, a part developer can access any service on any CORBA-compliant ORB. This literally opens up a universe of possibilities.

SOM is also a component packaging technology. It allows OpenDoc developers to package their parts in binary format and ship them as DLLs. SOM's support for multiple inheritance—both implementation and interface—makes it possible for developers to derive new OpenDoc parts from existing ones. They do this by subclassing an existing OpenDoc part via IDL and then either reusing or overriding the method implementations delivered in the DLL binaries. SOM also provides some form of version control. In addition, SOM allows developers to add methods to existing parts without impacting the programs that use them. We cover SOM and the OpenDoc object model in Chapter 20, "OpenDoc and SOM: The Object Model."

Bento

Bento—named after Japanese plates with compartments for different foods—defines a container format that you can use in files, network streams, clipboards, and so on. A Bento file container allows applications to store and retrieve collections of objects in a single structured file, along with their references—or links—to other objects.

The Bento container format is platform neutral; it can store any type of data. In a Bento document, each object has a persistent ID that moves with it from system to system. Bento also supports references between objects in different documents. If there are several drafts of a document, Bento only stores the incremental changes. This makes it easy to maintain different versions of the same document.

The Bento design is optimized for document interchanges. A Bento container is an excellent carrier for exchanging compound documents between applications running on different platforms. You can also use Bento to move groups of objects with their attached scripts, which makes it a very good foundation technology for roaming agents. We cover Bento in much more detail in Chapter 22, "OpenDoc: Bento and Storage Units."

Uniform Data Transfer

The OpenDoc storage APIs provide *Uniform Data Transfer* across and within applications. The same method invocations used for document storage can also be used to transfer data and parts via drag-and-drop, copy and paste, and linking. The data can be represented in a variety of formats. OpenDoc lets you move entire parts and the parts they embed in one operation. In addition to data transfer, linking adds notification calls that dynamically refresh the transferred information. We cover uniform data transfer in detail in Chapter 23, "OpenDoc: Uniform Data Transfer."

Compound Document Management

Compound Document Management defines the protocols that allow parts to share a visual space and coordinate their use of shared resources such as keyboard entries, menus, and the selection focus. *Parts* are the fundamental building block in OpenDoc. Every document has a top-level (or root) part in which all other parts are embedded. A part can contain other parts. *Frames* are areas of the display that represent a part. They also represent the part in the negotiations for space during the layout of a document.

Parts are associated with *part editors*. These are the active elements that handle the part's data and interact with the user. An OpenDoc component is the combination of the part editor and its data. You can select at run time an editor that will work with a particular part type. OpenDoc encourages vendors to provide part viewers that can be freely distributed with a document. The viewer lets you display the part but not alter the contents. We cover OpenDoc's compound document model in Chapter 21, "OpenDoc: The Compound Document Model."

Open Scripting Architecture

The *Open Scripting Architecture (OSA)* is an extension of the Macintosh's *Apple Events*. OSA lets parts expose their contents via semantic events that any OSA-compliant scripting language can invoke. The commands sent via these semantic events operate on an *object specifier* that identifies in a natural manner objects the user sees on a screen (or within some other context). And because we're dealing with objects, the commands are polymorphic. For example, "next" can mean the next cell or the next word, depending on the type of part that receives the command. Note that an object specifier describes things the user sees. This description gets translated by OSA into the actual object reference.

A scriptable part must be prepared to provide at run time the list of objects it contains and the operations it supports. OpenDoc can deliver event messages from the scripting system to the parts. Scripting lets you coordinate the interaction between parts. OpenDoc also lets you attach scripts to semantic events. This makes an OpenDoc part "tinkerable," which means that a user-written script can be triggered when a semantic event fires. By intercepting the event, the script can modify the part's behavior.

In addition, OpenDoc parts can be designed to be *recordable*. In this case, the part editor intercepts every incoming action, converts it into a semantic event, and then resends the event to itself—this is called a *bottleneck*. You can use bottlenecks to check for attached scripts and to record all events. The recorded events can be converted to your preferred OSA scripting language and replayed at a later time. We cover OpenDoc's OSA in much more detail in Chapter 24, "OpenDoc: Automation and Semantic Events."

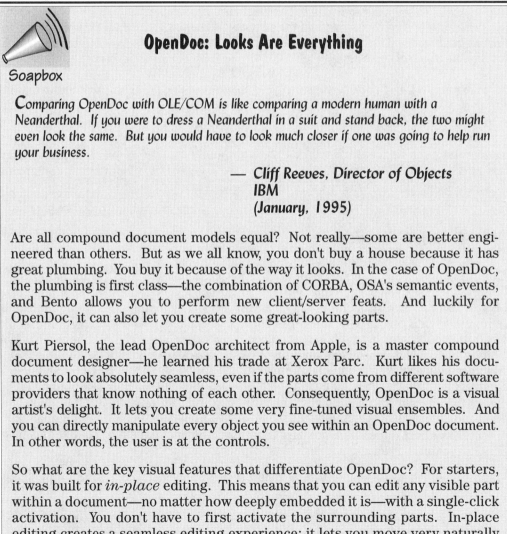

OpenDoc: Looks Are Everything

Soapbox

Comparing OpenDoc with OLE/COM is like comparing a modern human with a Neanderthal. If you were to dress a Neanderthal in a suit and stand back, the two might even look the same. But you would have to look much closer if one was going to help run your business.

— Cliff Reeves, Director of Objects
IBM
(January, 1995)

Are all compound document models equal? Not really—some are better engineered than others. But as we all know, you don't buy a house because it has great plumbing. You buy it because of the way it looks. In the case of OpenDoc, the plumbing is first class—the combination of CORBA, OSA's semantic events, and Bento allows you to perform new client/server feats. And luckily for OpenDoc, it can also let you create some great-looking parts.

Kurt Piersol, the lead OpenDoc architect from Apple, is a master compound document designer—he learned his trade at Xerox Parc. Kurt likes his documents to look absolutely seamless, even if the parts come from different software providers that know nothing of each other. Consequently, OpenDoc is a visual artist's delight. It lets you create some very fine-tuned visual ensembles. And you can directly manipulate every object you see within an OpenDoc document. In other words, the user is at the controls.

So what are the key visual features that differentiate OpenDoc? For starters, it was built for *in-place* editing. This means that you can edit any visible part within a document—no matter how deeply embedded it is—with a single-click activation. You don't have to first activate the surrounding parts. In-place editing creates a seamless editing experience; it lets you move very naturally from part to part within a document. It's the next generation of Object-Oriented User Interfaces (OOUIs).

With OpenDoc, the distinction between a part and a document is purposely blurred. For example, if you drag an icon representing a closed document from the desktop (or a palette) into an open document, a copy of the transferred document immediately becomes an embedded part. Likewise, if you drag a part (or frame) from an embedded document and drop it on the desktop, a copy of that part immediately becomes a separate document represented by an icon.

Another important visual feature in OpenDoc's repertoire is the support of irregularly shaped parts. This means that not all parts must be rectangular. Irregular parts help reinforce the seamless look. You can create parts that look more like their real-life counterparts. The parts seamlessly fit together and give the appearance they were all created by the same application. For example, a container part could be shaped like an airplane body—a highly irregular shape— and populated with other irregularly shaped parts that represent passengers, crew, and luggage. Other examples of irregular container parts are donut-shaped stadiums, cruise-ship floor plans, office layouts, and garden plots. All these containers can be filled with interesting looking parts.

So, perhaps it is this pretty face that will differentiate OpenDoc from OLE with end users, not its great client/server plumbing. Of course, we're more interested in the plumbing capabilities of OpenDoc then in its pretty face. After all, this book is about distributed objects and their plumbing. ❏

OPENDOC: WHO SHIPS WHAT?

OpenDoc is the "rest of the world's" response to Microsoft's OLE. It even encapsulates its archenemy, OLE.

> — **David Linthicum, Open Computing**
> **(January, 1995)**

CI Labs was given the mandate to make the OpenDoc source code available to the industry. The idea was to create an open playing field for desktop component software by placing all the relevant standards and the associated plumbing in the public domain. CI Labs relies on its sponsors to distribute the OpenDoc runtimes across multiple platforms. The OpenDoc runtimes are freely available from Novell on Windows, Apple on Mac, and IBM on OS/2. IBM is also working on Unix versions of OpenDoc. IBM plans to ship OpenDoc with every copy of OS/2. Apple will ship it with every Mac. And Novell will distribute OpenDoc on Windows through a "contamination" process. This means that Novell will make OpenDoc freely available on bulletin boards, preload it on PCs running Windows, and make the runtime freely available to part distributors. Note that OLE 2 is distributed in the same manner on Windows 3.1. So it looks like the OpenDoc camp will do everything they can to make OpenDoc as ubiquitous as OLE but on more platforms.

COMPONENTGLUE: OPENDOC BECOMES OLE AND VICE VERSA

A myth confronting developers is that they must choose between OLE and OpenDoc. This is simply not true. OpenDoc can be seen as an abstraction layer on top of OLE. We've abstracted all your OLE 2 integration nightmares. When you write an OpenDoc part editor, it is also a first-class OLE object.

> — Chris Andrew, Novell
> Project Lead of OpenDoc for Windows
> (February, 1995)

OpenDoc was designed from the very start with OLE compatibility in mind. Novell's *ComponentGlue* provides a bidirectional gateway between OpenDoc and OLE. This means that an OpenDoc container sees an OLE object as an OpenDoc part, and vice versa. The ComponentGlue translation layer provides a direct map between OLE and OpenDoc compound document APIs. When you write to the OpenDoc APIs, you automatically get an OLE container/server that runs on NT and Windows 95—Win16 will come later.

In contrast to ordinary CORBA/OLE gateways that only provide communication mappings, ComponentGlue provides a deep translation layer between OLE and OpenDoc. It provides full two-way compatibility between OLE objects and Open-Doc parts. It lets OpenDoc parts appear as OLE objects to the Windows Registry; and OLE objects—including OCXs—appear as OpenDoc parts to the OpenDoc binder. With ComponentGlue, you can embed OpenDoc parts in OLE documents and you can embed OLE objects in OpenDoc documents.

ComponentGlue lets an OpenDoc document contain both parts and OLE objects, and vice versa. Within such documents, a user can drag-and-drop, cut and paste, and even link data between OLE and OpenDoc components. Parts and OLE objects can exchange data using the same drag and drop, clipboard, and link facilities. OpenDoc parts and OLE documents can share the same Bento file containers or Windows *DocFiles*. Further, ComponentGlue maps between OLE's automation services and OpenDoc's semantic events. This means you can control both OLE and OpenDoc components with scripts written in either OLE-compliant or OSA-compliant scripting languages.

Novell claims that OpenDoc with ComponentGlue makes it easier to develop OLE containers and servers—including OCXs. And Microsoft provides its seal of Windows 95 approval to OLE components developed using OpenDoc. Note that Novell only provides ComponentGlue on Windows and the Mac. However, the technology is part of the OpenDoc architecture and can be adapted to other platforms. In theory, ComponentGlue could let users view (but not edit) OLE objects embedded within an OpenDoc document on platforms that do not have native Microsoft OLE support, such as OS/2 or Unix. In practice, it remains to be seen.

WHAT OPENDOC DOES FOR CLIENT/SERVER SYSTEMS

OpenDoc component technology introduces new opportunities for the creation of client/server systems. OpenDoc brings the CORBA bus into the desktop, making it the hub of all interprogram communications. You can use the same object model to connect enterprise objects as well as medium-grained visual objects that reside on a common desktop. It's all very consistent. It now becomes possible to repackage monolithic desktop applications into parts that can plug-and-play together on the same desktop or across the network.

Client/Server, OpenDoc Style

From a client/server viewpoint, an OpenDoc document acts as a central integration point for multiple sources of data that reside on different servers (see Figure 15-2). Parts can be linked to corporate databases, workflow managers, image repositories, e-mail, or the local spreadsheet. The document is the client/server application. It acts as a repository of client/server relationships or "links" to external data sources and remote functions. End users can assemble these applications by simply opening an OpenDoc container document and dragging parts into it. They can lay out live parts within a visual document just like we do today with page layout programs. Creating an application becomes a paste and layout job—no programming is required. Power users, IS shops, and system integrators can create more sophisticated client/server systems by writing OpenDoc scripts that orchestrate complex interpart collaborations.

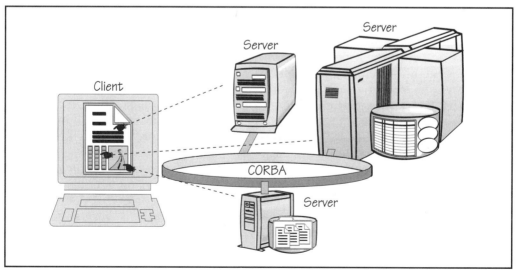

Figure 15-2. OpenDoc Document As a Central Integration Point for Client/Server Links.

It's easy to imagine other metaphors for visual containers into which parts can be dragged, dropped, rearranged, and manipulated to suit a user's needs. Examples of OpenDoc containers are business forms, airplanes, database front-ends, floor plans, desktops, garden plots, and any visual representation that you can use as a container of parts. We anticipate that software providers will provide "designer containers" to complement the parts business; parts and containers will work together "hand in glove." For example, an airline container can be populated with parts representing seats, passengers, crew, luggage, and so on.

Live OpenDoc documents can be saved, shipped across networks to different platforms, and reopened later with the same client/server links. Remember that we're talking about live multimedia documents with application intelligence and links to external data sources. You can move these roaming compound documents—combined with a workflow manager—from place to place to reflect a business process within and across enterprises.

In summary, OpenDoc will encourage new levels of direct manipulation on the desktop. End users will be able to create custom applications by choosing a container and populating it with active parts that live on the desktop or on servers anywhere on the network. Imagine being able to access multiple data sources and business objects through multiple client/server connections from within a single visual container or document. Kurt Piersol, the Apple Computers OpenDoc architect, calls it "an entire information system in a document."

How OpenDoc Enhances CORBA

OpenDoc also provides component enhancements over and above what CORBA provides today, including:

- **Reference counts**. OpenDoc objects maintain counts of who is using them. This helps the system release memory when components are no longer in use.

- **Named Extension Suites**. OpenDoc allows components to create named suites of services called *extensions*. A client can ask a component if it supports a particular named suite of functions and obtain a reference to it—extensions are objects. These extensions allow groups of parts to act like a suite. For example, a part can support an "airline reservation" extension. All the parts that belong to the airline reservation extension will share common semantics, protocols, and metadata that are registered with CI Labs. OpenDoc extensions will form the basis for collaborative desktops consisting of "very smart" parts that act like horizontal suites, vertical suites, or client/server suites.

- *Component versioning*. SOM provides proprietary extensions to the CORBA IDL for keeping track of major and minor versions. Because OpenDoc part editors are packaged using SOM, they can keep track of their version/release numbers. In addition, you can use Bento drafts to provide versioning on a document's data.

- *Property editors*. OpenDoc provides GUI interfaces—property dialog boxes or notebooks—for updating a component's properties and scripts at run time. This allows components to be inspected and modified by power users and system integrators.

- *Semantic messaging*. OpenDoc's OSA complements the CORBA messaging model by introducing a vocabulary of verbs and object specifiers that let clients manipulate the contents of server parts at the semantic level. It's a form of dynamic messaging. The messages are created "on the fly" at run time. However, unlike CORBA's dynamic method invocations, you do not invoke a method on an object reference on the server. Instead, the semantic message contains an *object specifier* that describes in human terms what the user sees—meaning the content objects on the screen. The messaging system resolves these "content descriptions" into target objects—ones that have unique object references. OpenDoc's semantic messaging provides the basis for language-independent scripting. It is also a general purpose client/server semantic messaging system that can be used by all types of business objects and smart components. Semantic messages are grouped into named suites that are, of course, tracked by CI Labs.

- *Scriptable components*. OpenDoc's parts are scriptable. This allows end users and system integrators to quickly assemble ensembles of components and integrate them using scripts. Scripts makes it easy to combine components from different sources into custom solutions.

Conclusion

CI Labs has a very good chance of wrestling this away from Microsoft. Everybody in the industry is starting to figure out that whatever money they've got in their pockets Microsoft wants to take it out...It looks like OpenDoc is fundamentally a sounder architecture because OLE is a horror show.

> — **Will Zachmann, President**
> **Canopus Research**
> **(January, 1995)**

OpenDoc is a good piece of compound document technology that complements CORBA very nicely. The marriage of OpenDoc and CORBA will let us create a new generation of client/server systems based on components. Servers will be able to ship to their clients Bento documents loaded with components. These components will provide customized front-ends to servers anywhere on the intergalactic network. With OpenDoc's support of irregular shapes, these client front-ends are only limited by the imagination.

However, it takes more than good technology for OpenDoc to succeed. CI Labs and its partners must also: 1) create a very strong parts business—this includes channels for selling parts around an architecture that defines part suites for every known industry; 2) provide superior OpenDoc tools for creating and assembling parts that run on multiple platforms (see Soapbox); and 3) define an architecture and the semantic events for client/server enterprise parts (i.e., distributed Open-Doc). CI Labs must drive all these efforts to provide an open playing field. If these conditions are met, CI Labs and its member companies may be able to contain OLE on the Windows desktop. And even there, they may be able to encapsulate OLE behind a layer of OpenDoc ComponentGlue. If they don't meet the challenge, OLE may win the battle for desktop components. Microsoft will then use the desktop as a springboard to win client/server components and the enterprise object bus.

Questions to Ask Your OpenDoc Providers

Soapbox

For you to succeed with OpenDoc, the system and part vendors must provide an infrastructure for parts and the right application tools. Here's a set of questions to ask your favorite OpenDoc vendor:

- How will OpenDoc handle cross-platform parts? How will common rendering be done across Windows, OS/2, Mac, and Unixes? Which scripting language should I use across these platforms?

- What cross-platform tools are available for part construction and assembly? Will these tools support OpenDoc parts in their palettes? Will they support OLE OCXs? Will they support component partitioning across client/server boundaries? Will they support server components on CORBA ORBs?

- How will the parts be distributed, certified, and maintained? Who will certify part suites—including client/server suites? Who do I call when a part breaks? Who do I call when a suite of multivendor parts doesn't perform as advertised?

- Who do I call when an OpenDoc-wrapped OLE component doesn't perform: Microsoft or CI Labs? ❑

Chapter 16

OLE/COM: The Other Component Standard

Many years from now, a Charles Darwin of computerdom might look back and wonder how the Microsoft Windows APIs evolved into an object-oriented operating system.

— **Kraig Brockschmidt, Author**
Inside OLE 2, Second Edition
(Microsoft Press, 1995)

If CORBA is the industry's leading standard for components, then Microsoft's *Object Linking and Embedding (OLE)* is the *de facto* "other standard." What makes OLE so important? Microsoft. Everything it is doing and will do is based on OLE. Windows itself is morphing into OLE. Or, if you prefer, OLE is the object-oriented foundation of Windows. By the time Cairo ships, all of Windows will be OLE. So what does this have to do with distributed objects? It may come as a surprise, but OLE is built on top of an ORB called the *Component Object Model (COM)*. Even though COM is currently a single machine ORB, Microsoft plans to carry COM— and most of today's OLE—in toto to Cairo. OLE and COM on Cairo will provide the basis for Microsoft's future distributed computing environment. Windows 95 will participate as a client.

OLE FOR THE ENTERPRISE

For us, the key to the kingdom in terms of Microsoft's growth in the next year is the large business enterprise computing.

> — *Roger Henien, Microsoft Senior VP*
> *(May, 1995)*

Microsoft is saying some pretty wild stuff about how they understand the enterprise and how OLE will be usable for production work.

> — *Roy Schulte, Gartner Group*
> *(May, 1995)*

In May 1995, Microsoft announced an "OLE everything" strategy for the enterprise. Over the next few years, Microsoft plans to deliver *OLE DB*, *OLE Transactions*, *OLE Team Development*, and *Network OLE* (also known as COM). Even highly successful Microsoft "standards" like ODBC are being tossed out in favor of OLE DB. Microsoft plans to release specifications for these new OLE interfaces by the end of 1995. Products incorporating these extensions won't be available until late 1996 or 1997. So don't hold your breath waiting.

Microsoft sees the "Enterprise" as a key market in the next few years. They roughly divide their areas of focus into four: Desktop, Home, Information Highway, and Enterprise. Microsoft foresees a world with 300,000,000 PCs. This leads them to conclude that there will be a market for at least 10,000,000 servers. Thus the enterprise market is not seen as fundamentally different from other markets in which they have entered and prospered. In their words, "it is high volume, high profit, and fun."

WHAT IS OLE?

The first thing you must know about OLE is that its name—"Object Linking and Embedding"—is misleading. OLE is more than just a compound document technology—it's a complete environment for components that competes head-on with CORBA and OpenDoc. Like CORBA, OLE is building a set of common services that allow these components to collaborate intelligently. Like CORBA, OLE covers the entire component spectrum—from fine-grained objects to coarse-grained existing applications. Unlike CORBA, OLE does not currently address the needs of distributed components—it's a big hole that will take a long time to fill. OLE will evolve in two directions: 1) compound documents will provide the framework for the visual components that live on the desktop; and 2) COM will provide the object bus and services.

OLE: A Short History

In 1990, Microsoft introduced OLE 1 technology as its basic strategy for integrating multiple applications and multimedia data types within a compound document framework. OLE 1 was a clumsy and slow protocol built on top of DDE. When an application was launched from within a compound document, it was given its own window and the data it needed was copied into its address space. There was no way for the application to directly access the document.

OLE 2, introduced in 1993, fixed many of these shortcomings with a new object-encapsulation technology called the *Component Object Model (COM)*. All of OLE 2 is built on top of COM—it's the heart of OLE. OLE 2 grew beyond the boundaries of compound documents into a much more generic object service architecture. The lion's share of OLE still belongs to compound documents. In late 1994, Microsoft added a new custom control architecture—also known as OCX— to the compound document model. An OCX is the OLE version of a generic part that plugs into the compound document framework.

OLE Is OLE

You may have noticed that OLE is no longer given a version number.

> — **Kraig Brockschmidt, Author**
> **Inside OLE 2, Second Edition**
> **(Microsoft Press, 1995)**

According to Microsoft's Kraig Brockschmidt, OLE will no longer be given a version number. The reason for this change is that the name OLE 2 implies that there will be an OLE 3. This is not the case any more. According to Kraig, "new features and technologies can be added to OLE within the existing framework." For example, OCXs were released a year after the original release of OLE 2, but OLE was not given a new version number—although some people now call it OLE 2.1. New OLE interfaces will simply be buried within new releases of Windows or new releases of Microsoft's Visual C++.

What this means is that OLE is not a separate product—it is the Windows operating system. Windows will evolve into a giant collection of OLE interfaces, with COM providing the underlying object bus and services. All system services—including the new file system—will be written as COM objects. The compound document model becomes the Windows desktop. It will contain objects a user sees and manipulates. Because everything is written on top of COM, anyone can extend the base operating system or the compound document user interface. For example,

OCXs can extend the Windows GUI, and lower-level COM components can extend the Windows persistent store.

The Vision: The Framework Is Windows

The ultimate OLE/COM vision is for Windows to become a large framework for running and deploying OLE objects. This can potentially create a huge market for OLE/COM objects. Of course, we're not there yet. There's also some strong competition on the horizon. Microsoft's OLE won't be the only compound document object framework for Windows. OpenStep, Taligent, and OpenDoc are all being ported to Windows. They will directly compete with OLE to provide the next object-oriented user interface on Windows as well as the underlying object services.

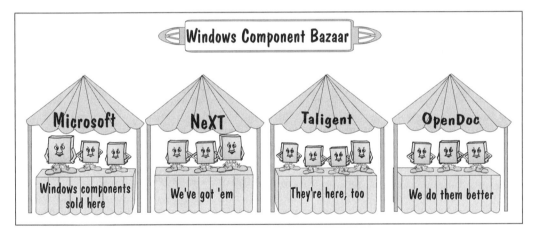

OpenStep, Taligent, and OpenDoc have many advantages over OLE. All three provide portable object environments that run on other operating systems. All three have dazzling user interfaces with very high levels of visual integration that make Windows 95 look pale in comparison. In addition, OpenDoc uses CORBA as its underlying object bus, which means it can seamlessly connect desktop objects with enterprise objects. Taligent and NeXT may follow suit. So Microsoft can be in for some real competition if these specialized object vendors—meaning NeXT, Taligent, and CI Labs—can provide better objects than OLE on Windows (as well as on other platforms). Who said object wars weren't exciting?

OLE: Interfaces Everywhere

OLE consists of a number of "interfaces" as well as Win32-style APIs. OLE interfaces are similar in concept to CORBA's—they define a set of related functions.

An *interface* defines a contract between components. An OLE component can support one or more interfaces. COM provides an interface negotiation protocol that lets clients acquire pointers—at run time—to the interfaces a component supports. Programmers can write their own interfaces using COM's *Interface Definition Language (IDL)*. COM also provides an *Object Description Language (ODL)* for describing these interfaces to a *Type Library*. This is the COM equivalent of a CORBA Interface Repository. Clients can discover dynamically which interfaces an object supports and what parameters they require. Like CORBA, COM provides both static and dynamic method invocations.

As we go to press, OLE consists of about 90 interfaces—each one supports on the average about 6 member functions. In addition, the OLE/COM library provides about 120 Win32-style APIs. This means that OLE introduces about 660 new function calls (over and above Win32). Some of these interfaces are simply abstract classes with no implementation. They only define the interface contract. The component implementor must provide the code that implements the interface. This can be quite a bit of work. Microsoft provides tools to help alleviate some of the burden (we cover OLE tools later). In addition to the Microsoft-defined interfaces, you can create your own interfaces—OLE calls them *custom* interfaces. You can also provide components that replace the ones Microsoft ships, as long as you match their interface contracts.

So, What Is an OLE Component?

An OLE component is defined by a *class* that implements one or more interfaces and a *class factory*—this is the interface that knows how to produce a component instance of that class. Unlike an OpenDoc part, an OLE component is not a predefined self-contained unit. All OpenDoc parts have the same basic interfaces, but they can also support extensions. In contrast, an OLE component is a group of interfaces. It requires many interfaces to make an OLE component reach the same level of sophistication as an OpenDoc part.

In late 1994, Microsoft introduced *custom controls* (or OCXs) that have a set of predefined interfaces (a la OpenDoc part). An OCX is a well-defined medium-grained component that is packaged like an OpenDoc part. However, OCXs still lack some of the function in OpenDoc parts. For example, an OCX cannot embed other parts—OLE containers do that. So an OCX is a set of contracts between an OLE visual component and its container. Of course, these contracts must be implemented by the OCX provider.

In summary, COM lets you access existing OLE interfaces, customize them through OCXs, or create your own. Like CORBA, COM supports components of all sizes:

fine-grained, medium-grained, and large-grained. An OCX is a medium-grained component. OLE containers are large-grained, application-size components.

OLE'S CONSTITUENT TECHNOLOGIES

Like OpenDoc, OLE uses the familiar document metaphor for visually organizing components on the desktop. Like OpenDoc, OLE defines the rules of engagement for OCXs and other visual components to share screen real estate within a single window and to store their data within a single container file. Like OpenDoc, OLE provides interfaces that let components exchange information with other components via links, the clipboard, and drag-and-drop. And like OpenDoc, OLE provides automation support that lets components coordinate their actions via automation scripts.

Figure 16-1 shows OLE's constituent technologies and how they relate. Notice that the figure is almost a replica of the one you saw in the OpenDoc chapter, but the names of the technologies have changed. The object bus is COM instead of SOM/CORBA. Structured storage is provided by compound files instead of Bento. OLE has its own model for doing automation and scripting. Even the uniform data transfer models are different. And, as you can expect, OLE and OpenDoc have very different compound document design points—OLE does not currently support irregular shaped parts, and it has limited in-place editing. As a result, OLE components don't look as if they're all part of the same application—they lack the visual continuity OpenDoc provides. In this chapter, we provide a brief overview of OLE's constituent technologies. We'll leave the gory details for Part 5.

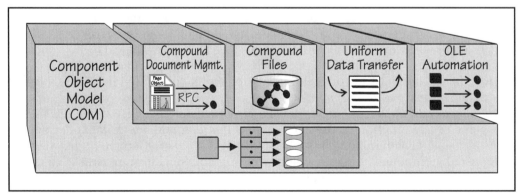

Figure 16-1. OLE's Constituent Technologies.

The Component Object Model (COM)

COM is a first step toward distributed objects, but it attempts to reinvent many of the mechanisms successfully addressed by CORBA...Unfortunately, COM represents a major fragmentation of distributed object technology.

> — Dr. Thomas Mowbray, Principal Scientist
> MITRE
> (December, 1994)

But one might certainly argue that having a single financially strong leader that owns the standard is more likely to ensure that it is clear-cut and not a product of committee think.

> — David Sarna, Columnist
> Datamation
> (February 15, 1995)

COM specifies interfaces between component objects within a single application or between applications. COM, like CORBA, separates the interface from the implementation. Like CORBA, it provides APIs for dynamically discovering the interfaces an object exports and how to load and invoke them. Like CORBA, COM requires that all shared code be declared using object interfaces (Microsoft even provides two proprietary interface languages: the IDL and the ODL). Unlike CORBA, COM only provides local RPC facilities—it's called a *Lightweight RPC (LRPC)* because it does not support remote method invocations or distributed objects.

COM's object model does not support multiple inheritance. Instead, a COM component can support multiple interfaces. COM uses the multiple interface capability to provide reuse through a technique called *aggregation*. It's a fancy name for a component that encapsulates the services of other components. Clients call the encapsulating component, which in turn calls the contained component (or puts it directly in touch with the client). What all this means, is that the COM environment is inherently flat. "Inheritance" is achieved through a web of pointers that link or aggregate different interfaces.

COM defines interfaces for object factories and provides a rudimentary component licensing mechanism. It also provides a local directory service based on the Windows Registry. A COM client asks for the services of a component by passing a unique *Class identifier (CLSID)*, the COM *Service Control Manager (SCM)*— also known as "Scum"—locates a server using the Registry and tells it to create an instance of that component by invoking the class factory interface.

COM provides a rudimentary event service called *connectable objects*. The event source is an ODL-defined *outgoing* interface—OLE components support both outgoing and incoming interfaces. The consumer of the event—also called a *sink*—is an incoming interface. The COM connectable object service allows sinks to directly register with sources their interest in an event—this is called an *advisory* connection.

Finally, COM requires that every OLE component implement the **IUnknown** interface. This interface is used by clients to discover at run time the interfaces a component provides and then connect with them. **IUnknown** also defines two methods that help components do garbage collection via reference counting. The two methods—*AddRef* and *Release*—let components increment and decrement a reference counter every time a client connects to an interface or releases it. When the reference count of a component goes to zero, you can safely delete it from memory—this is COM's version of component life cycle management. Figure 16-2 shows the anatomy of a COM (or OLE) component. We cover COM in a lot of detail in Chapter 25, "COM: OLE's Object Bus."

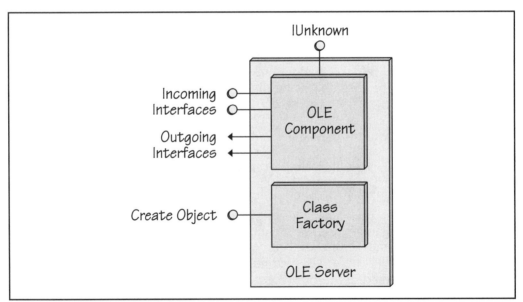

Figure 16-2. The Anatomy of a COM Component.

OLE's Automation and Scripting Services

OLE's Automation and Scripting services allow *server* components to be controlled by automation clients (also called automation *controllers*). An automation controller is typically driven by a scripting language or from a tool such as Visual Basic. Automation is based on OLE's dynamic invocation facilities called *dispatchable interfaces*. Like CORBA's dynamic method invocations, OLE's dynamic dispatch allows a client to invoke a method or manipulate a property through a late-binding mechanism. A dispatch ID is passed to an *invoke* method that resolves which method to call at run time.

Of course, automation clients must discover at run time what interfaces an automation server provides. This includes the methods an interface supports and the types of parameters that are required by each method. It also includes the properties a component exposes to its clients. Clients can obtain all this information at run time from *Type Libraries*—the OLE equivalent of a CORBA Interface Repository. How is this information entered in Type Libraries in the first place? You create it using an Object Definition Language (ODL) file that describes the interfaces. You can get the scoop on OLE automation by reading Chapter 26, "OLE: Automation, Scripting, and Type Libraries."

OLE's Uniform Data Transfer

Like OpenDoc, OLE provides a generalized intercomponent data transfer mechanism that can be used in a wide range of situations and across a variety of media. Data can be exchanged using protocols such as the clipboard, drag-and-drop, links, or compound documents. The exchanged data can be dragged and then pasted or dropped into the same document, a different document, or a different application. The actual data transfer can take place over shared memory or using storage files. Asynchronous notifications can be sent to a linked client when source data changes. OLE's uniform data transfer provides a single interface for transferring data that works with multiple protocols. We cover uniform data transfers in Chapter 27, "OLE: Uniform Data Transfer."

OLE's Structured Storage and Persistence Services

OLE's Structured Storage System provides a file system within a file. The current implementation of this architecture is called *compound files* (previously known as *DocFiles*). Compound files create a "file within a file" by introducing a layer of indirection on top of existing file systems. With Cairo, compound files will become the actual file system. Compound files break a file into a collection of *storages* (or directories) and *streams* (or raw data values). This internal directory system can be used to organize the contents of a document. OLE allows components to control their own storage in the compound document. The directories describe the streams; the hierarchical structure makes it easy for OLE objects to navigate within the document. Compound files provide some rudimentary transaction facilities for committing information to storages or restoring their previous states.

OLE also provides a set of interfaces that allow a client to communicate with a *persistent* object. These interfaces define the capabilities of a persistent object. At one end, a persistent object may know nothing about structured storage; it only knows how to store and manipulate its state in a regular file. At the other end, an object knows how to navigate the storages of a compound file. In the middle are objects that only know how to manipulate a single stream. In OLE, the client creates an object and then hands it a persistent store that contains state information. The object then initializes its state by reading the storage object. The client can also ask the object to write its state to storage.

OLE provides a persistent naming service called *monikers*. A moniker is an intelligent name that can be bound to some persistent data. All monikers have the same interface, but they can have different binding algorithms to find the data that's associated with a name. The binding algorithm is defined by the Class ID that implements the moniker. For example, monikers can serve as aliases (or nicknames) for a remote file, an item within a file, or a SQL query that extracts data from a relational database. We cover compound files, persistent objects, and monikers in Chapter 28, "OLE: Structured Storage and Monikers."

OLE's Compound Document Service

> **W**hen you think of OLE, probably the first thing that comes to mind is compound documents.
>
> — Chris Weiland et al.
> Windows Tech Journal

OLE's compound document service defines the interfaces between a *container* application and the *server* components that it controls. In this case, a server is a visual component that "serves" a container. The container/server interfaces define protocols for activating the servers and editing their contents "in-place" within the container's window. The container applications manage storage and the window for displaying a compound document's data. Each server component controls its own data. You can use the container/server relationship to visually integrate data of different formats, such as bitmaps or sound clips. The server data is *embedded* if it is stored within the container's compound document. It is *linked* if it is stored in another container's file. OLE only allows embedded servers to be edited or activated in-place.

OCXs are a special kind of server. They combine OLE automation and compound document technology to create very flexible container/server relationships. OCXs are embedded servers that support in-place editing. More importantly, OCXs use automation to expose their methods and properties to their containers. The containers also use automation to receive event notifications from OCXs whenever anything of interest happens. In addition, a container maintains *ambient* properties that inform OCXs of their surroundings. OCXs can use this information to blend with the document and other OCXs. The container, of course, exposes its ambient properties using automation. You can get all the details on OCXs and compound documents in Chapter 29, "OLE: Compound Documents and OCXs."

OLE TOOLS AND FOUNDATION CLASSES

As long as Microsoft is writing the rules—like the OLE standard—tools from the same company are going to enjoy an edge over others (for example, Borland).

— Mike Maddox, Unisys World
(March, 1995)

As you may tell from this chapter, OLE is massive. If we haven't convinced you yet, read Part 5. In any case, Microsoft realized early on that programming in OLE was not going to be a picnic. Consequently, they developed tools to make it easier for programmers to develop OLE-compliant components. These tools include a C++ class framework called the *Microsoft Foundation Classes (MFC)*, *Visual C++ 2.X (VC++)*, and *Visual Basic 4.0 (VB)*. Additional tools are available from Borland and other vendors. For example, Borland provides an MFC-like C++ class framework for OLE called *ObjectComponentsFramework (OCF)*. Borland also plans to support OCXs in its new *Delphi* tool.

The language of choice for OLE development is C++ because it maps nicely to the way OLE interface pointers are implemented (they're like the *vtables* C++ compilers generate). We briefly review MFC and VC++ to give you an idea of what OLE tools can do for you. Of course, tools are a moving target. Be sure to check the "tool du jour" before you start using one.

Microsoft Foundation Classes (MFC)

MFC is Microsoft's premier C++ class library for Windows development. It's a framework in the sense that it uses a *document/view* paradigm to structure Windows applications. Documents derived from the MFC class **CDocument** are used to store and encapsulate data. Views derived from the MFC class **CView** render the data and respond to the user. MFC 3.0 is said to include around 20,000 lines of prewritten and pretested 32-bit OLE code. Most of this code simply encapsulates the OLE interfaces with C++ classes. MFC supports OLE automation, compound documents, and controls. Note that MFC does not support all the functions that are in the raw OLE APIs—for example, MFC does not support monikers, persistent objects, connectable objects, type libraries, control containers, and so on. The benefit of using MFC over the raw OLE APIs is that you can use C++ multiple inheritance to derive new functions. And you can port the code you write to multiple platforms—including Win16, Win32, and Mac. MFC is also licensed by other C++ compiler vendors—including Watcom, MetaWare, and Symantec.

Microsoft Visual C++

Visual C++ (VC++) is Microsoft's premier visual builder tool for creating OLE components. VC++ provides a graphic environment for creating OLE applications on top of MFC 3.0 and the OLE *Custom Control Development Kit (CDK)*. Both MFC and the CDK are included with VC++ 2.X. The VC++ *AppStudio* lets you create and edit views, dialog boxes, bitmaps, icons, menus, and other resources. *Wizards* help you organize your classes and develop an application. The *AppWizard* generates a skeleton application as a starting point. The *ControlWizard* lets you create a new OLE OCX and test aspects of the control as you develop it. The *ClassWizard* lets you create new classes by inheriting from other MFC classes. It shields you from requiring intimate knowledge of the MFC class hierarchy. It also supports OLE OCX features such as event handling, and it lets you link user interface events to the code that handles these events. Note that ClassWizard only lets you create a new class that's derived from existing MFC classes.

Conclusion

Building an object-oriented system requires a tremendous amount of plumbing, and to the best of my knowledge Microsoft hasn't done that.

> — Joe Guglielmi, CEO of Taligent
> (December, 1994)

The facilities not in today's OLE, especially cross-system connections, will be supported directly and natively from the operating system, not as a stick-on.

> — David Sarna, Columnist
> Datamation
> (February 15, 1995)

It's clear that Microsoft is creating an entire distributed object foundation around OLE and COM. OLE is an integral part of Windows 95. You just can't ignore it. In distributed objects, COM is about two to three years behind CORBA. Even on the desktop, OLE's compound document technology is not as good as OpenDoc's—one problem is that Microsoft has too much "legacy" code to accommodate on existing interfaces. Objects are really a new paradigm. It will be very costly for Microsoft to break down its existing monolithic application code base into medium-grained components. The move to components will be much less costly for vendors that do not have a large legacy code base to protect.

The best OMG and Microsoft can do—short of having Microsoft give up COM for CORBA, or vice versa—is to create a single two-way gateway specification between CORBA and COM. This is exactly what OMG, with help from Microsoft, is trying to accomplish—if they can figure how to target the distributed version of COM that's still not fully specified. So OMG is currently specifying two gateway standards between CORBA and COM: one that targets local COM, and a later one that targets distributed COM.

Interoperability between OLE's non-distributed COM and CORBA is a snap—implementations are available from IBM, Iona, Candle, Visual Edge and Digital. Eventually COM and CORBA will interoperate. But because they have dissimilar object models, the components will never be able to fully collaborate across object environments. Each model will have its own rules of engagement. Component providers will most likely have to choose between OpenDoc/CORBA versus OLE/COM on the client, and between CORBA versus COM/Cairo on the server side. It won't be an easy decision, which is why we wrote this book. We continue this discussion in Parts 4 and 5. And we cover CORBA/OLE gateways in depth in Chapter 30, "Which Component Model?"

Chapter 17

Taligent's CommonPoint: Frameworks Everywhere

---

*N*early everything in the real world can be described in terms of conceptual frameworks...Everything, that is, except software. It's as if programmers have to grow the food, build the store, stock the shelves, and invent a monetary system each time they want to buy groceries.

> — *Mike Potel et al., Authors*
> *Inside Taligent Technology*
> *(Addison-Wesley, 1995)*

What would a product that made uncompromising use of object technology look like? The answer is Taligent's CommonPoint. Taligent Inc. was founded in 1992 by IBM and Apple (HP joined later). Its purpose was to extend the boundaries of object technology. Three years later, this extremely well-funded start-up gave birth to *CommonPoint*—an object purist's dream come true. Whether the mainstream of computing is ready for CommonPoint is another question. You'll have to wait for a soapbox to get the answer. But let's first try to understand what CommonPoint really is. CommonPoint introduces dozens of new technologies that push the boundaries of components and objects in the right direction. The three that we find most useful are:

- ■ ***Pervasive integrated frameworks***. CommonPoint consists of a web of over 100 collaborating frameworks. These frameworks provide an extensive set of platform-independent application and system services. You can create some very portable applications by inheriting functions from the various frameworks.

- ■ ***People, Places, and Things.*** This is the new CommonPoint desktop. It was designed to extend the familiar desktop paradigm to include *places* where *people* work with *things*. *People, Places, and Things* is a simulation of real-world environments—it's like a game of virtual reality that lets you interact with your extended workplace (and other shared environments).

- ■ ***Highly collaborative compound documents***. CommonPoint components inherit their behavior from a "common DNA"—the frameworks. As a result, they can achieve some very fine levels of collaboration. CommonPoint's compound document frameworks set the bar for what you can do with compound documents.

In this chapter, we briefly cover these CommonPoint features to give you a feeling for what Taligent technology is all about and how it relates to other object models—including CORBA, OpenDoc, and OLE.

INTEGRATED FRAMEWORKS

The quickest way to understand CommonPoint is to look at Figure 17-1. As you can see CommonPoint provides two things:

- ■ ***A portable application environment*** that sits between your application and the underlying operating systems—Taligent calls it an *application systems layer;* and

- ■ ***A new desktop*** called *People, Places, and Things*. Note that CommonPoint 1.0 only includes a small subset of the new desktop. The full implementation will be included in CommonPoint 1.1 (it will beta in late 1995).

CommonPoint lives on top of existing operating systems; it does not replace them. The CommonPoint desktop uses its own graphics engine (for portability reasons) but lives within an existing desktop. For example, "CommonPoint for OS/2 Warp" runs within the Workplace Shell. You should be able to drag-and-drop objects from the Workplace Shell to *People, Places, and Things,* and vice versa.

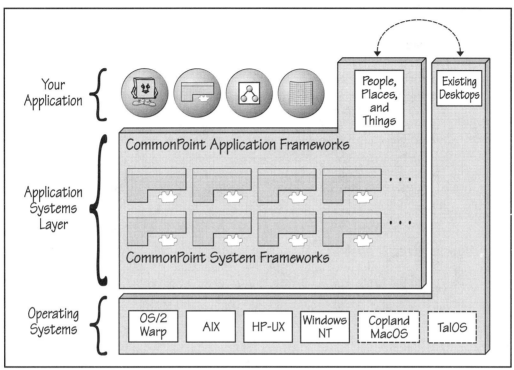

Figure 17-1. Where CommonPoint Fits in the Scheme of Things.

So What's an Application System Anyway?

*T*aligent has created a new category of system software called an application system.

> — *Mike Potel et al., Authors*
> *Inside Taligent Technology*
> *(Addison-Wesley, 1995)*

An *application system* is simply an environment that isolates your applications from the underlying operating system. It lets you port your software to any operating system that the application system supports. In the case of Common-Point, the target is any 32-bit desktop that supports preemptive multitasking—including OS/2, NT, Windows 95, AIX, and HP-UX. CommonPoint will later support the new microkernel-based MacOS, code named *Copland*. CommonPoint provides its own graphics engine and system services. As a result, CommonPoint only needs to target the underlying file system and the tasking facilities to run on an operating system. In other words, porting CommonPoint itself should be relatively easy.

So what makes an "application system" different from Lotus Notes, CICS, Tuxedo, Smalltalk, and so on? The dividing lines aren't entirely clear. TP Monitors, Lotus Notes, and Smalltalk allow developers to create applications without necessarily using the underlying operating system directly. They also provide an architected environment with default behaviors that save application developers time and effort. The difference is that CommonPoint does it in a more object-oriented fashion. It uses an integrated web of OO frameworks to create this common environment. As a result, the CommonPoint application system is more malleable than the alternatives—frameworks let you subclass the environment and customize it to meet your various needs. Even the CommonPoint tools are built as frameworks. If you like the concepts behind object frameworks, then CommonPoint is the way to go first class. You develop your application once using CommonPoint, and then port it to all the major desktops with a simple recompile.

Frameworks Everywhere

> *Virtually everything that is implemented as a library in a traditional operating system is implemented as a framework in the CommonPoint application system.*
>
> — *Mike Potel et al., Authors*
> *Inside Taligent Technology*
> *(Addison-Wesley, 1995)*

The beta version of CommonPoint includes over 100 frameworks that declare about 2,000 public classes and about 27,000 member functions. These frameworks are organized into three main groups: *application*, *system services*, and the *cpProfessional* development environment (see Figure 17-2). The Taligent frameworks contain a considerable amount of code for interframework collaborations. This means that the various frameworks are not isolated from each other. Let's go over what these frameworks provide:

■ *Application frameworks* consist of about 65 frameworks that provide desktop functions and embeddable data types. The more important desktop frameworks are: 1) *Documents*, which consists of about 8 frameworks that implement compound documents; 2) *Workspace*, which implements meeting rooms, business cards and other elements of People, Places and Things; and 3) *User Interface*, which consists of about 12 frameworks that implement controls, dialogs, and drag-and-drop. Other frameworks are for 2-D and 3-D graphics, Unicode text, text editing, time, internationalization, printing, scanning, and so on.

■ *System service frameworks* consist of about 38 frameworks that provide enterprise, foundation, and operating system services. The enterprise frameworks include *data access* to access SQL databases using ODBC or DRDA; *caucus* for group collaborations; *remote objects* for CORBA, DCE, and Taligent

RPC access; and *system management*, which includes licensing and authentication. The foundation frameworks include *notifications* (and events) and *object storage*, which consists of five frameworks that support archiving, persistence, collections, and streams. Finally, the OS services frameworks encapsulate communications, file services, memory management, interprocess communications, DLLs, and multitasking.

■ *cpProfessional frameworks* consist of a set of portable tools that make it easier to create and maintain applications using frameworks. Tools are essential because programming languages don't support frameworks. Those of us that joined the Taligent early adopter program know firsthand how difficult it is to develop framework applications without tools. The *cpProfessional* environment makes it easier. It provides an integrated development environment that supports rapid prototyping, a graphic visualizer that shows you framework and class relationships, and browsers that you can customize. The *cpConstructor* is a user interface builder that lets you visually lay out forms using a palette of

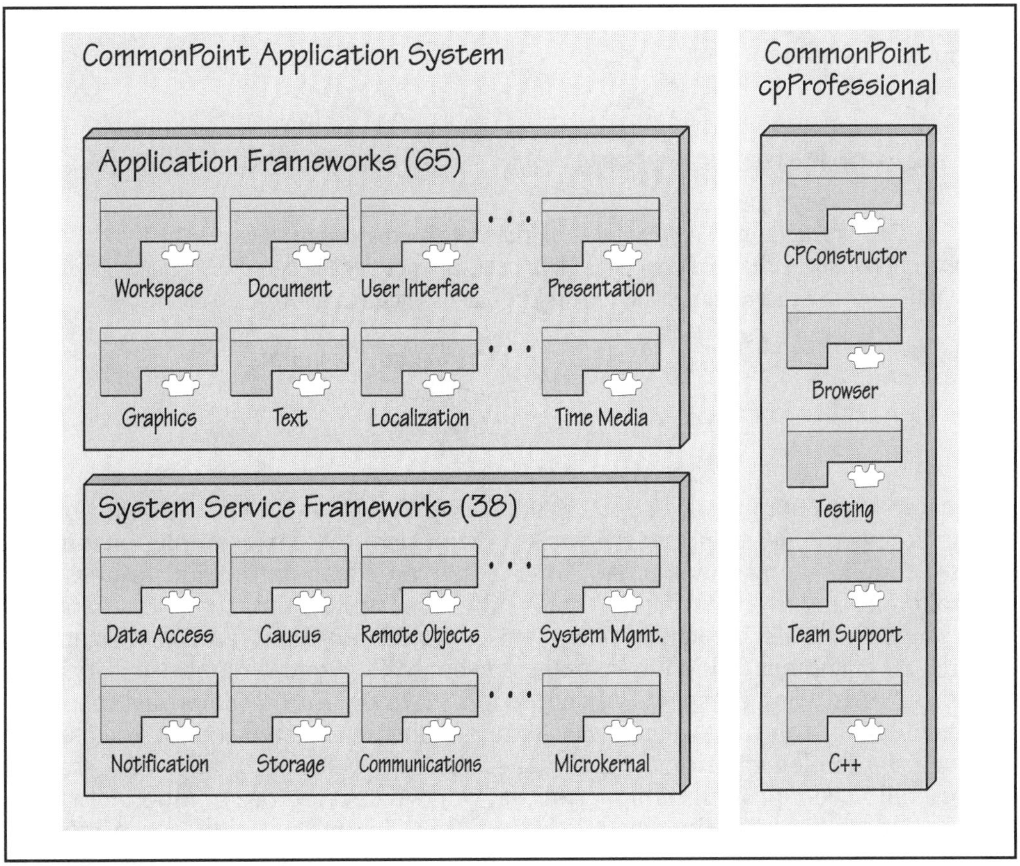

CommonPoint Application System

CommonPoint cpProfessional

Application Frameworks (65)

Workspace   Document   User Interface   · · ·   Presentation

Graphics   Text   Localization   · · ·   Time Media

System Service Frameworks (38)

Data Access   Caucus   Remote Objects   · · ·   System Mgmt.

Notification   Storage   Communications   · · ·   Microkernal

CPConstructor

Browser

Testing

Team Support

C++

Figure 17-2. The CommonPoint Frameworks.

visual parts. An inspector lets you view and edit the attributes of an object and the actions associated with it. A previewer lets you see the forms as they will appear in an application.

Every Taligent framework has two interfaces: 1) the *service* interface that lets you call framework functions; and 2) the *customization API* that lets you subclass the framework and extend its function. Taligent frameworks are highly integrated with each other. You inherit that integration when you subclass from these frameworks. This is an important benefit because it gives you a very fine level of semantic integration between components. Taligent sometimes call this effect "Common DNA."

PEOPLE, PLACES, AND THINGS

Taligent's *People, Places, and Things* is a new user interface model for the desktop. It's an *Object-Oriented User Interface (OOUI)* for a client/server desktop. It lets you directly manipulate visual objects that represent resources anywhere on the network—just like we manipulate local desktop resources using OS/2, Mac, or Windows 95. The interface also encourages collaborations between people that are working on a common task.

How the New Metaphor Works

You read its brochures and you yawn. You ruminate on the technical jargon such as "application frameworks" and your eyes glaze over. But you see the damn thing demonstrated and you start to believe that Taligent may just have something with its CommonPoint.

> — **Don Crabb, Columnist**
> **MacWeek**
> **(May, 1995)**

The underlying metaphor of *People, Places, and Things* is that all tasks performed on the connected desktop involve working with *people*—for example, customers, friends, suppliers, and coworkers. These people are located in various *places*—for example, meeting rooms, offices, homes, libraries, auditoriums, or parks. Specialized *things*—or tools, if you like—help you communicate, work, and play; examples include fax machines, telephones, pens, erasers, yellow markers, post-it notes, and bulletin boards. Some aspects of the *People, Places, and Things* metaphor are implemented in the first release of CommonPoint; each subsequent release will enhance the implementation further. The concepts behind *People, Places, and Things* will have a profound impact on the way we develop our component suites. So it's important to read the next few pages, even if you don't plan to use Taligent. In a sense, the Taligent desktop is a continuation of the advanced user interface work started at Xerox Parc, but it takes that work to the next level.

Places

People don't exist in the ether, they exist in Places.

> — *Mike Potel et al.*
> *Dr. Dobb's Journal*
> *(January, 1995)*

Today's user interfaces are centered around a primitive place that represents the familiar desktop. The desktop acts as a container for trashcans, folders, documents, and the like. In contrast, CommonPoint consists of *multiple* places that represent collaborative environments based on real-world models. These places let you organize shared information and tasks in meaningful contexts. You can create a place environment and customize its behavior to reflect the needs of a particular task. For example, you can create an auditorium place to deliver a seminar online. Like their real-world counterparts, places can have different *rules*. For example, if you visit an electronic store, you must pay for the items you purchase. Some places will only let you in with the proper invitation or credentials. If you go into an online auditorium, you must sit quietly and listen until the question-and-answer period starts. Online theaters will of course require that you purchase a ticket before you enter.

In CommonPoint, a place environment is represented by an icon. You double-click on the icon to get to a place. The system also provides a map to other places (see bottom right-hand corner of Figure 17-3). You can use this map to navigate

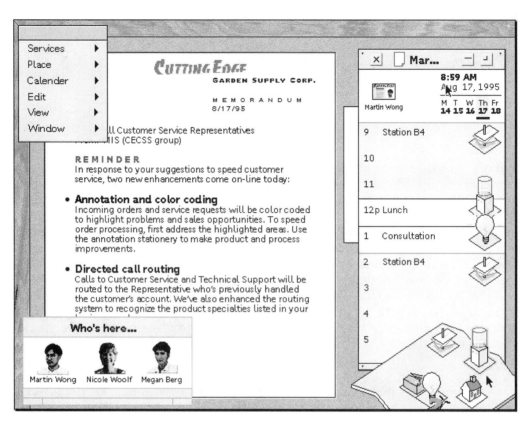

Figure 17-3. The CommonPoint Desktop: People, Places, and Things.

between places and discover what's happening on the intergalactic network. The system encourages you to visit places and meet people. For example, if you need an obscure article, you can visit the online library and talk to a librarian. You can choose to give others access to the places you create, or you can keep them private. You can advertise the existence of a new place on a bulletin board. Places are designed to handle scalable numbers of people. For example, an auditorium can hold hundreds of people. A classroom can limit the attendance to ten students. Examples of larger places are auditoriums, help desks, retail stores, mass media broadcast facilities, libraries, and town halls.

You can represent places as postcards, as well as icons on a map. You can also customize your own places and provide customized navigation tools—typically in the form of maps. You can protect places using security mechanisms and access control. For example, visitors may be asked to present some form of identification, credentials, invitations, reservations, or tickets. You can also meter the usage of a CommonPoint place. For example, you can track hourly charges, number of

visitors, items sold, items added, and so on. These metering artifacts will facilitate electronic commerce.

You can subclass from the *workspace* frameworks to provide your own specialized places. In addition, the *caucus* frameworks provide a collaborative whiteboard and document replication system that let multiple users work together within a single place (or workspace). Places are a powerful metaphor around which we can design new types of client/server software. The place is a visual front-end for shared resources on servers. Note that compound documents also use the places metaphor—the document is a place.

People

People are humans that live, work, shop, and visit places. CommonPoint represents people using metaphors such as business cards. *Collections* of people are represented using metaphors such as electronic phone books, group icons, mailing lists, organization charts, and so on. The different representations encapsulate the information that different programs need to work with people. For example, you can drop a business card on a database query form to extract more information on a potential customer. You can then call that customer by dragging the business card and dropping it on a telephone object. Both the telephone and the query know how to extract information they need from the business card. A business card represents a unique person.

The *workspace framework* provides standard people data types that all frameworks can inherit or query. Just like in real life, a person can delegate an electronic credential. For example, you can delegate your role or signature when you're away by shipping a signature or approval stamp. And, just like in real life, you can use a business card to let others know who you are when you visit their places. Again, the people metaphor is very useful. The same effect can be accomplished within compound documents by creating people components and a suite of protocols that related components understand. Of course, CommonPoint makes it easier to create these components because it builds their behavior directly inside a framework.

Things

Things represent all kinds of useful metaphors—including cursor tools, appliances, desktop elements, and business aids. Here's a list of common things you can expect to find in the CommonPoint user interface:

- **Desktop things** include folders, trash cans, stationery pads, sticky notes, proxy icons for representing objects, and so on.

- **Appliances** include telephones, fax machines, scanners, printers, answering machines, in and out boxes, cameras, recorders, data compressors, map makers, alarm clocks, and projectors. Appliances are objects that encapsulate some real-world appliance.

- **Cursor tools** include pencils, markers, erasers, approval stamps, highlighters, color pickers, and flags for national language translations. For example, you can drop a Japanese flag on English text to translate the text to Japanese and the currency to yen. Note that cursor tools are also a CommonPoint innovation. The idea is that you have a *global tool* palette that is decoupled from specific components or applications. The "global" tools are globally available to all applications on the CommonPoint desktop. You don't have to reinvent the same tools for each program. For example, a global tool designed to work on editable text works on all editable text in the system. Of course, all editable text programs must inherit their behavior from the CommonPoint *text editing* framework.

- **Business things** include forms, reports, invoices, ballots, routing slips, magazines, movies, business cards, credit cards, money, catalogs, personal organizers, agents, calendars, invoices, and so on.

You can combine the various CommonPoint "desktop things" with things on existing desktops to achieve maximum desktop integration. So the user experience of "things" may vary slightly from one operating system to another. For example, CommonPoint on OS/2 may use the Workplace Shell's shredder. This means it won't look exactly like CommonPoint on the Mac. According to Taligent, these slight deviations should not affect the portability of applications (they will provide the glue code that makes it right).

COMPOUND DOCUMENTS, COMMONPOINT STYLE

Some of the aspects of *People, Places, and Things* are implemented in the first release of CommonPoint using the underlying compound document, workspace, and caucus frameworks. These frameworks work together so that places built with compound documents are automatically capable of being shipped and shared by multiple users across a network. These powerful collaborative capabilities demonstrate what can really be accomplished with compound document technology. In this section, we explain the CommonPoint compound document model. Then we explain how it integrates with OpenDoc in particular.

Shared Documents

CommonPoint is the first implementation of a distributed, collaborative compound document framework. It lets you ship replicas of a document to multiple desktops; it then automatically synchronizes any updates across all documents. In addition, CommonPoint provides a collaborative whiteboard that lets distributed users share the cursor. They can observe in real time what they're each doing to the document. To provide this capability, the *compound document* framework is closely tied to the *shared document* framework, which in turn is built on the *caucus* framework. The caucus framework broadcasts commands issued on one document to all other documents registered in the same collaboration session. These documents can be on different computers running on different operating systems. This mechanism lets you collaborate on a single document with a group of people and see the results of a change any of them makes instantaneously. By only shipping commands, the caucus framework uses bandwidth efficiently during updates. Note that the initial broadcast of the replicas may be quite expensive.

CommonPoint ships with a *CSpace* document that serves as a sample of how compound documents are shared. You create a CSpace document by tearing off a piece of CSpace stationery. Then you ship it to all the people that will collaborate in a session. The *participants* window lets you see the people who are currently participating in a session. Any object you place in CSpace automatically appears in the shared document for all participants. Whomever starts working on an object first can edit that object. You can edit other objects simultaneously. All the copies of a CSpace document automatically reflect the same updates during the collaboration session.

The Taligent Compound Document Model

Taligent implements its compound document framework using a design pattern that extends the Model/View/Controller (MVC) paradigm. In CommonPoint, a compound document component manages relationships between four objects (see Figure 17-4):

■ A **presentation**, like an MVC view, represents how a component's data is displayed and handled. The presentation object is derived from the *presentation* framework. The rendering of the presentation is performed using the *interface* frameworks—one of these frameworks lets you create view objects. However, the easiest way to create your views is to use cpConstructor—the visual layout tool. It's better to let cpConstructor deal with all these frameworks.

■ A **model**, like its MVC counterpart, encapsulates a component's data. The model object is derived from the compound document framework.

■ A **selection** identifies a discrete portion of the model's data. It represents the portion of the model the user has currently selected. The selection object is derived from the compound document framework.

■ A **command** performs an action on a selection. The action is typically something the user does to the data. The command object is also derived from the compound document framework.

As you can see, the compound document framework only deals with the way a document stores and manipulates data. The presentation and interface frameworks deal with how the component is viewed. The components you create using the compound document framework inherit many other capabilities—including cut-and-paste, drag-and-drop, linking, embedding, and in-place editing.

Taligent/OpenDoc Interoperability

Taligent is a founding member of CI Labs. So the million-dollar question is: How will CommonPoint and OpenDoc components play together? According to Taligent, the two will play together very well in the following areas:

■ **Mutual embedding.** This means you can drag an OpenDoc part and embed it in a Taligent document, and vice versa. You will be able to view and manipulate OpenDoc parts in-place within a CommonPoint frame the same way you do it within OpenDoc.

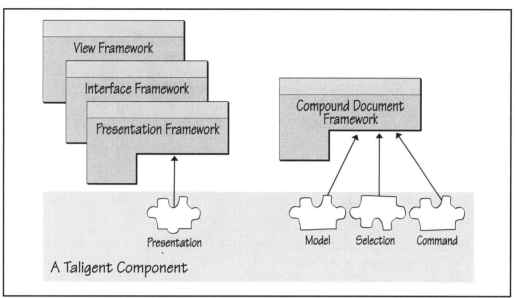

Figure 17-4. The CommonPoint Compound Document Framework.

■ *Common user interface policies.* Taligent has been tracking the OpenDoc user interface guidelines and uses them in its own compound document framework. For example, it uses the OpenDoc conventions for part activation, selection, and in-place editing.

■ *Bento framework.* Taligent plans to subclass a Bento framework from its compound document framework. This means that Taligent and OpenDoc can share and exchange documents using Bento.

■ *Open Scripting Architecture (OSA).* Taligent plans to support OSA-compliant scripting systems. This means that Taligent and OpenDoc components will be able to interact via semantic events. It also means that you can drive components in both systems from within a single script.

■ *SOM and CORBA support.* Taligent plans to support SOM for communicating over a CORBA bus and between components. It also plans to use SOM as a component packaging technology. And even more importantly, Taligent (with help from IBM) is investigating the use of SOM as its internal object model.

■ *CommonPoint as an OpenDoc tool.* Developers can use CommonPoint to develop multiplatform OpenDoc parts. IBM and Taligent demonstrated this capability at Spring/Comdex 1995. Of course, these parts will require part of the Taligent environment, which adds to the run-time costs. However, if you can afford the added memory, you can build some supersmart OpenDoc parts using

CommonPoint. Remember, the smarts come from all the "common DNA." So it's a trade-off between smarter components and more memory.

Most of these features are expected in CommonPoint 1.1. They will be provided by a set of *interoperability frameworks* that will also support OLE. In many ways, OpenDoc and OLE components make it easier for CommonPoint users to interact with existing desktops. The compound documents on both sides of the divide help create a unifying metaphor. In addition, OpenDoc and OLE can be a rich source of components for *People, Places, and Things* (also see next Soapbox).

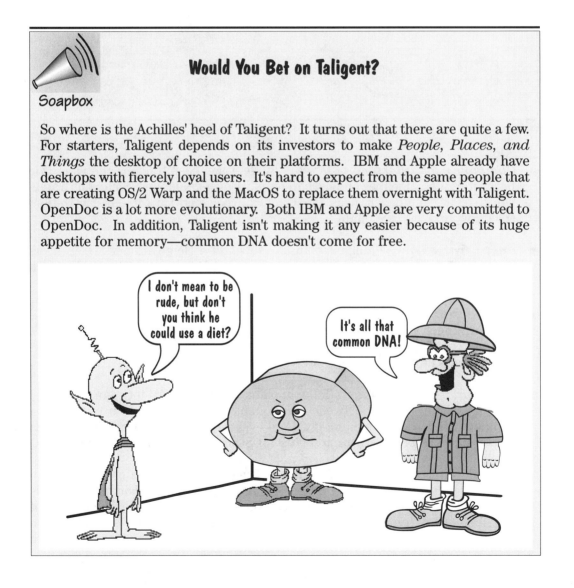

Would You Bet on Taligent?

Soapbox

So where is the Achilles' heel of Taligent? It turns out that there are quite a few. For starters, Taligent depends on its investors to make *People, Places, and Things* the desktop of choice on their platforms. IBM and Apple already have desktops with fiercely loyal users. It's hard to expect from the same people that are creating OS/2 Warp and the MacOS to replace them overnight with Taligent. OpenDoc is a lot more evolutionary. Both IBM and Apple are very committed to OpenDoc. In addition, Taligent isn't making it any easier because of its huge appetite for memory—common DNA doesn't come for free.

Ironically, Taligent's best bet may be to market CommonPoint on Windows 95, making it a *de facto* object standard. Taligent can compete with NeXT, OLE, and OpenDoc to become the object platform of choice for Windows. If Taligent wins that battle, it can become the Microsoft of objects. It would automatically become the object platform of choice on OS/2 Warp, Macintosh, and the Unixes. Where have we heard this story before? Here's a hint: his first name is Steve and he's considered to be a visionary (see the next chapter).

How can Taligent win against OLE? One scenario is that the price of memory drops dramatically and end users fall in love with components after they see OLE in action. Because end users always want more, they start asking for components that behave more like real-life objects. Both OpenDoc and OLE are two years behind because they haven't worked out the mechanics of their component suites. So enter Taligent with *People, Places, and Things*. For users, it's love at first sight. Developers also love it because it requires less coding; it also lets them create totally portable components that can run on OS/2 Warp, Mac, Windows NT, and the Unixes. So in this scenario, Taligent can win the desktop object war.

To win the enterprise, Taligent has to do more with CORBA. Having a closed object model may help on the desktop, but it doesn't help on the enterprise. No problem. With the desktop in its pocket, Taligent can afford to let the rest of the world have a few crumbs. Of course, Taligent can choose to use CORBA as its object bus and build frameworks for CORBA services. If this happens, then Taligent can also play in the enterprise.

So what are the odds of this happening? It's hard to say at this point. Currently, Taligent is a strong contender for the collaborative desktop; it has a huge head start. Taligent's two main competitors are OLE and OpenDoc. If OLE and OpenDoc can recreate *People, Places, and Things* using standard suites of components, then Taligent will simply become another tool for making OpenDoc parts. However, if it takes OLE and OpenDoc a large dose of "common DNA" to recreate this type of behavior, then Taligent has a good head start and may become the component standard.

Can OpenDoc and OLE meet the Taligent challenge? In May 1995, Claris demonstrated its *Visual Suite* for OpenDoc at the Apple World-Wide Developers Conference. Based on what we saw, it took a fair amount of work to get the pieces to look like CommonPoint. It can certainly be done, but it would help if CI Labs played a more active role in defining OpenDoc horizontal and vertical suites using the *places* concept. Until this happens in a big way, we're not ready to write off Taligent. In any case, there will always be room for Taligent at the high end of the component market. Some people will always buy Rolls Royces. ❑

Conclusion

You can never actually make things easier in software. You can only shift the burden of complexity from one place to another.

> — **Larry Tesler, Object Guru**
> **Apple Computers**

Taligent seems to be more than happy to absorb "the burden of complexity" and remove it from your shoulders. In return, your applications must learn to live within the web of frameworks Taligent defines. If you play by the Taligent rules, your components can painlessly participate in *People, Places, and Things* and join the 21st century. The alternative is to accomplish the same thing using more conventional compound document frameworks like OLE or OpenDoc. Of course, it will take some time before OpenDoc and OLE can build all the common DNA that is needed for their component suites to behave like *People, Places, and Things*. So if you're in a hurry to get there, you may want to consider CommonPoint (but make sure to read the previous Soapbox first).

Chapter 18

NeXT's OpenStep and Portable Distributed Objects

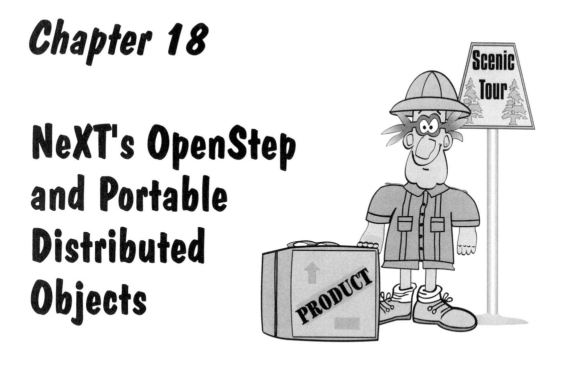

Objects are very dynamic—they can come and go.

> — *Steve Jobs, CEO*
> *NeXT*
> *(February, 1995)*

OpenStep is another multivendor initiative with the goal of "creating an open, high-volume portable standard for object-oriented computing." OpenStep focuses on the rapid development of distributed object business applications. The technology for OpenStep comes from NeXT, and it has the distinction of being the oldest distributed object platform. Because it was first, the OpenStep object bus called *Portable Distributed Objects (PDO)* is in direct competition with CORBA and COM. OpenStep plans to have gateways to both CORBA and OLE's COM. In addition to the object bus, OpenStep provides object services—such as persistence, a portable GUI class library, and an add-on client/server tool. OpenStep does not support the compound document model. An OpenStep component is an application that lives within the OpenStep framework.

WHO IS DOING WHAT WITH OPENSTEP?

After many false starts, NeXT learned an important lesson: How to separate its software offerings and make the pieces more portable. As a result, OpenStep is a flexible offering. You can use it as a client platform for objects, a server platform, or both. And with some tweaking, the client environment can even be made to work with a CORBA bus—in addition to PDO. NeXT hopes to make the OpenStep object framework ubiquitous so that it can concentrate on tools and enterprise objects.

OpenStep in the Unix World

In November 1993, Sun and NeXT formed the OpenStep initiative—Sun also bought a piece of NeXT. OpenStep is now the object client platform of choice for SunSoft's *Distributed Objects Everywhere (DOE)*—a CORBA-compliant ORB on Solaris. SunSoft is integrating OpenStep with DOE and the Solaris desktop. In June 1994, Digital joined the OpenStep initiative, and it is now porting OpenStep to its OSF/1 Unix platform. In addition, OpenStep will be integrated with Digital's *ObjectBroker* 3.0—another CORBA-compliant ORB. OpenStep is also being ported to HP-UX, where it will compete with the Taligent and Smalltalk object environments.

OpenStep may become the client platform of choice for objects on major Unix platforms. And it may even become a CORBA client of choice on these platforms. What about the Unix server? You can use OpenStep as a server platform on NEXTSTEP, Solaris, and Digital's OSF/1. PDO also provides a portable server environment for objects—you can port PDO without the client environment. Today, PDO is in direct competition with CORBA. However, by the time you read this book, NeXT may have announced a product to integrate PDO with CORBA.

OpenStep in the Windows World

NeXT cannot become a "high-volume" object vendor by simply going after the Unix desktop. So it is now porting OpenStep to Windows 95 and Windows NT, where it will compete head-on with OLE, OpenDoc, and Taligent to become the object platform of choice for Windows. NeXT even hopes to beat Microsoft to the punch by establishing PDO as a distributed OLE standard. Figure 18-1 shows how you can use a COM/PDO gateway to distribute OLE traffic across networks. Of course, this scenario assumes that PDO on Windows ships before Microsoft delivers Network OLE. With OpenStep, NeXT hopes to become the Microsoft of objects. After reading this chapter, you can decide for yourself what the odds are. Of course, you will get a Soapbox with our opinions.

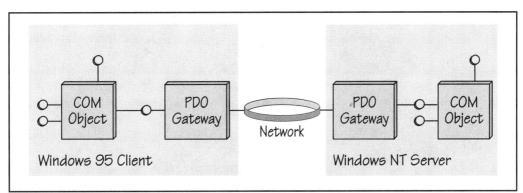

Figure 18-1. Distributing OLE With Portable Distributed Objects (PDO).

WHAT IS OPENSTEP?

The OpenStep interface consists of about 150 core classes that conform to the NEXTSTEP 3.2 interfaces. The class specifications are freely available on *ftp.next.com*. Figure 18-2 shows the three constituent technologies of OpenStep: *Application Framework*, *Display PostScript*, and *Portable Distributed Objects (PDO)*. In addition, we show two add-on packages that build on top of OpenStep: the NEXTSTEP *Developer* tools and *Enterprise Objects Framework*. The tools let you easily create client front-ends and "enterprise objects"—they're the Visual Basic of PDO objects. Enterprise Object Framework is a persistence service that stores an object's data in relational or object databases.

PDO and Objective C

PDO provides the OpenStep object bus—it's the ORB that defines the object model. PDO consists of *Foundation classes* and an object run-time environment. The OpenStep object model is intimately associated with NeXT's *Objective C* and its run-time facilities—the Objective C compiler is bundled with PDO. Objective C is a superset of ANSI C that provides language extensions for distributed objects and object classes (a la Smalltalk). The class model only supports single inheritance.

All Objective C classes are derived from a base class called **NSObject**. This class provides its derived classes with a framework for creating, initializing, deallocating, comparing, and archiving objects. It also allows you to query a class object about its methods and its position in the class hierarchy. Finally, it allows objects to forward—or *delegate*—method invocations to other objects. **NSObject** provides the object model for PDO and Objective C.

You can mix Objective C, C, and C++ statements within a single source file—a C++ method can invoke an Objective C object, and vice versa. However, only Objective

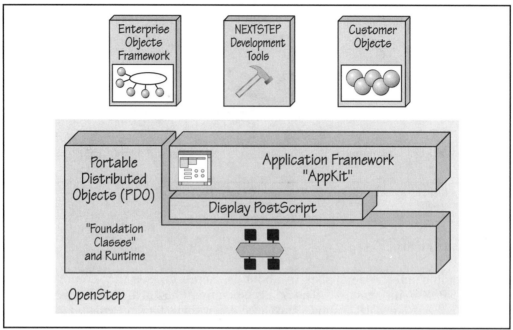

Figure 18-2. The OpenStep Frameworks.

C calls can be distributed across networks or address spaces. This means that an Objective C object cannot call a C++ object across program or machine boundaries. The remote extensions of Objective C provide ORB-like messaging facilities for PDO objects.

PDO: The Distribution Service

PDO clients and servers communicate over networks by sending ordinary Objective C messages. PDO isolates communicating objects from the underlying transport mechanisms. To make a distributed object publicly available, a server program must first *vend* the object. Vending is done using the **NSConnection** class. This class provides methods to instantiate a server and register it with a network name server—a portable version of the *Mach Network Name Server*.

To use an object that has been vended, a client looks up the server object and stores a handle to it in a local *proxy* object. All proxy objects are instances of the **NSproxy** class, which represents remote objects in a local process. Proxy objects use specialized subclasses to repackage a method invocation and send it to the remote object. Objective C also allows you to send an object—by value—as a parameter in a message. This lets you ship an object to a client to cut down on network traffic.

PDO: Where's the ORB?

The Objective C language is the ORB. This means that any object on this ORB must be written in Objective C to communicate across address spaces and networks. It also means that the ORB is not language neutral—Objective C is the language for PDO objects. A PDO object is an Objective C object. We will use the terms Objective C and PDO objects interchangeably.

NeXT and its partners are submitting Objective C to the ANSI standards committee. The OpenStep APIs will be submitted to X/Open for standardization. NeXT and partners are also creating CORBA language bindings for Objective C that will be submitted to OMG. Perhaps it will take a CORBA ORB to enable Objective C, Smalltalk, and C++ objects to communicate across address spaces and machine boundaries.

PDO: The Dynamic Object Model

Like SOM and Smalltalk, Objective C allows clients to extend and customize classes at run time—meaning after they are compiled. You can modify or extend existing classes by adding new methods without recompiling or restarting the applications that use these classes. Because a PDO class is itself an object, it can return class information. For example, you can ask a PDO class object for its version number and whether it declares specific methods. NeXT calls this feature object "introspection"; SOM and Smalltalk provide similar features. Clients can discover at run time the parameters a PDO method supports; CORBA objects use an Interface Repository to provide the same type of service. Like its CORBA counterpart, a PDO object can discover the run-time interfaces a server object provides, and then dynamically invoke methods on that server.

PDO: Delegation

PDO objects support event notifications (or callbacks) using a technique called *delegation*. At run time, a *delegate* object can attach itself to certain methods in a source object. The source object discovers through introspection that it has a delegate; it then calls the delegate's methods at key points during the execution of its own methods. Delegation lets you develop classes whose objects can be customized at run time. If a delegate is not present, the object behaves as usual. The delegate lets you tinker with an object's behavior during certain actions.

PDO: Garbage Collection and Reference Counting

Objective C provides automatic garbage collection by reclaiming memory after an event associated with an object executes. This means that all OpenStep objects are temporary by default. An object can persist longer than the current event in the event-loop by sending a *retain* message; it must be balanced with a *release* message when it no longer needs to stay in memory. The retain message increments a *reference count* and release decrements it. The object is released from memory when its reference count goes to zero.

PDO: The Foundation Classes

The *Foundation Classes* extend the Objective C language by providing new functions and a set of base object classes. The package consists of about 52 Objective C classes that provide the following functions:

- **General utilities** include classes that support Unicode strings, reference counting, collections, managing user default information, and a Btree-based associative search service.

- **Object persistence** includes classes that support a transactional file store, an archiver that stores and retrieves an object's persistent state to/from a file, and a serialization/deserialization service for writing and reading properties to/from a file.

- **Distributed services** include classes that manage connections between objects and proxies for remote objects. You can use the **NSInvocation** class to dynamically invoke methods. The **NSMethodSignature** class lets you query a remote object for the descriptions of the methods it supports and their parameters.

- **Events and notifications** include a **NSNotification** class that provides a way to transmit asynchronous events between objects. A notification object notifies its subscribers—called *listeners*—when an event occurs. Objects of the class **NSNotificationCenter** maintain lists of listeners.

- **Encapsulation services** include classes that encapsulate operating system functions to make the Objective C application programs more portable. This includes classes that support threads, exception handling, semaphores, memory management, timers, time zones, and calendar/date/time.

PDO: The Server Package

PDO can be carved out of OpenStep to provide a GUI-less server environment. This makes it easy for server vendors to port PDO to their platforms. Most server vendors support the C-language, so all they must do is port the foundation classes, the object runtime, and the Objective C precompiler.

The Application Framework

The *Application Framework* is a refinement of the core user interface classes that have been shipping for more than seven years as part of NEXTSTEP. The framework consists of about 70 Objective C classes that support event-driven windowing interfaces and their associated objects. In addition to standard GUI elements—such as scroll bars, cursors, buttons, sliders, tear-off menus, windows, and panels—the Application Framework includes a set of high-level objects for:

- Managing events
- Linking data across applications
- Imaging and device-independent printing and faxing
- Creating hierarchical browsers
- Manipulating, editing, and spell-checking multifont text

All these services are implemented as Objective C classes. Consequently, nearly every object in the Application Framework is extensible through subclassing. Elements that do not allow themselves to be subclassed can provide hooks for dynamic customization at run time. For example, they can use delegates.

Display PostScript

Display PostScript provides the OpenStep device-independent imaging model. It ensures that what is on the screen is what is printed on color or black and white PostScript printers—to the best of the printer's physical capabilities. OpenStep also includes screen support for scalable PostScript fonts. It provides a set of Objective C classes that encapsulate the PostScript services and receive notifications of the execution status of PostScript command sequences.

Application Development Tools

NeXT and partners will make available—as a companion product—an OpenStep version of the *NEXTSTEP Developer* tool suite. These tools will include language support for applications written in Objective C, C, and C++. In addition, they will include the following set of integrated tools:

- ***Project Builder***, a tool for managing, building, debugging, and maintaining software projects—including their files and resources.

- ***Interface Builder***, a rapid prototyping tool and visual editor that lets you associate method invocations with GUI events. The tool includes a visual form layout tool and facilities for subclassing existing objects. It also provides a graphical palette of objects. Third parties can provide their own palettes of custom objects. Or, they can add objects to existing palettes.

■ *Object Editor*, a tool for managing the interactions between objects in a program. Programmers use Interface Builder to define the messages objects may send each other.

■ *Class browser*, a tool for displaying class hierarchies and for creating subclasses of existing classes.

The *NEXTSTEP Developer V3* tool suite also includes a graphical debugger, a database kit, 3D graphics, and a set of prebuilt objects and controls. We expect the OpenStep toolkit to provide an equivalent set of functions.

The Enterprise Objects Framework

The most significant problem that developers face when using object-oriented programming environments with relational databases is the difficulty of matching static, two-dimensional data structures with the extensive flexibility afforded by objects. The benefits of objects are often negated by the programming restrictions that come with accessing relational databases within an object-oriented application.

> — **Charly Kleissner, Director of OpenStep**
> **NeXT**
> **(May, 1995)**

The *Enterprise Objects Framework* product provides a bridge between the "pure" OpenStep object model and existing relational database products—Sybase and Oracle are supported in the current release. NeXT takes the approach of storing an "enterprise" object's state in a relational (or object) database but implementing the methods as first-class Objective C objects.

In a sense, NeXT implements a Model/View/Controller separation. The business logic is implemented in its own object—as opposed to being buried in a screen or in a database stored procedure. An *interface layer* provides a mechanism for displaying data, while an *access layer* provides data access methods to storage engines (see Figure 18-3). A *data source* protocol provides a generic object interface to data. The information that describes the mapping between the relational world and the objects is stored in a *model* file.

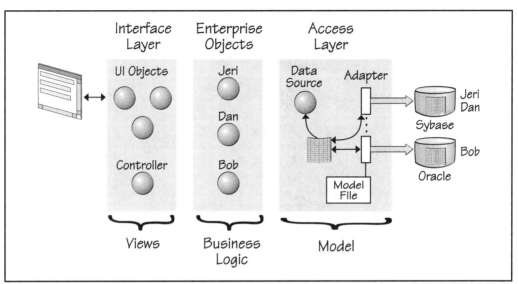

Figure 18-3. Enterprise Object Framework: Three-Tier Client/Server.

A data source provides the protocols by which you can access stored data, regardless of how the data is actually stored—for example, you could store it in a relational database or a flat-file system. Client objects interact with all data sources in the same way. The interface layer consists of a *controller* and the user interface objects. The controller coordinates the values displayed in the user interface with its enterprise objects. The user interface objects display data from enterprise objects. The access layer provides *adapters* for different data stores.

The Enterprise Objects Framework uses *snapshots* of the database data to implement its concurrency control mechanisms. An update strategy determines how updates should be made in the face of concurrent changes by others. The default update methodology uses optimistic locking, which assumes that the data won't be changed by others. But it checks this assumption before writing changes back to the database. The access component performs this check by comparing the data in a snapshot with the data in the database. An exception is raised if differences for the relevant attributes are detected.

The framework also provides a flexible buffering mechanism that determines when changes in the user interface are actually applied to the enterprise objects. The system keeps a stack of undo operations, which may be applied before the changes are actually committed to the database. It would be wonderful to have some TPC-like benchmarks to compare the performance of business functions implemented with objects with their stored procedure and TP Monitor counterparts. The best part of the framework is that it is tightly coupled to the NEXTSTEP Interface Builder (see Figures 18-4 and 18-5).

Palette of UI Objects

Application Window

Application Menu

Connecting a UI Object to an Enterprise Object

File Window

Palette of UI Objects

Figure 18-4. Constructing an OpenStep Client/Server Application With Interface Builder.

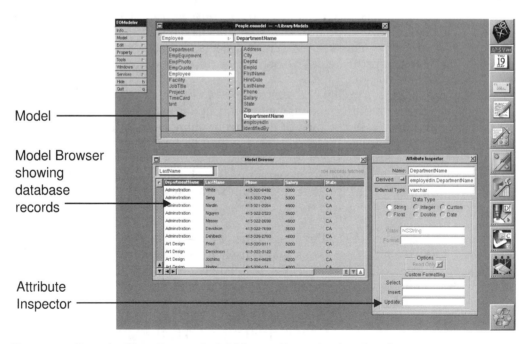

Model

Model Browser showing database records

Attribute Inspector

Figure 18-5. Enterprise Objects Framework: Model Browser Showing Database Records.

Dear Steve, Please Drop the Plumbing

Soapbox

If there is such a thing as technical justice, NeXT would own objects and OS/2 Warp would own the desktop.

— Anonymous

Of course, both NeXT and OS/2 Warp are still around and kicking hard, which is why we wrote this chapter. Because NeXT was first, it had to create an ORB in the form of language extensions. NeXT also invented its own object language, services, and tools. The result is a superbly integrated environment where all the pieces work together. NeXT has gone past the basic plumbing issues and now has a mature object technology that you can use to create the client and server parts of an object application. Of course, the environment to run these objects required more memory than the "high-volume" desktop market could afford. But all this is changing—the high-volume desktop OS market is ready for objects and may soon be able to afford the memory required by NeXT.

So can NeXT win the object war? In our opinion—and this is a Soapbox—NeXT must decide which piece of the object pie it wants to win and go after it. But it can't have the whole pie. So here's our humble advice to Steve Jobs:

Dear Steve,

Drop PDO and the Foundation Framework—they're no match for CORBA as an enterprise object bus. And, there's no money to be made in object plumbing—there are only headaches and bottomless expenses. So use an off-the-shelf CORBA ORB such as Sun's DOE, IBM's SOM, or Iona's Orbix.

Drop Objective C. There's no money to be made supporting yet another object language. Use C++ with SOM and you'll get all the same benefits without the headaches. If you don't like C++, use Smalltalk with CORBA—it will also give you the same results.

Without the burdens of an object bus and your private object language, you can now focus on modernizing the Application Framework. It needs to be wrapped with CORBA IDL to make it language neutral and open. It also needs to support compound document services and scripting. We suggest that you join CI Labs and get that technology from OpenDoc. It will complement your offering very nicely and help you play your stuff on multiple platforms.

You have great client/server tools, but they need to support industry standards (and also de facto ones). For example, your palette must be able to accept OpenDoc parts and OLE OCXs. In addition, any OpenStep component must be able to play within an OpenDoc or OLE container—this is the technology you'll get from CI Labs. By the way, tell CI Labs to adopt your Application Framework and tools. It will make OpenDoc a lot more competitive against OLE.

So, Dear Steve, now that you have CORBA and OpenDoc for plumbing, you can fully concentrate on "OpenStep for Windows" (don't forget OS/2 Warp and Mac). You can show Bill Gates and the world what a real killer desktop looks like. And your cool tools will make Visual C++ and Visual Basic look like antiques. The high volume object desktop is yours if you can focus your energy and creativity on winning it. Let someone else do the plumbing.

Sincerely,
Bob, Dan, and Jeri

Chapter 19

Newi: Cooperative Business Objects

---

*C*ooperative Business Objects (CBOs) are real things. Like other real things, they can be mixed and matched to suit user requirements—with no developer intervention necessary. You take an entity-like thing such as customer and that's what you deliver—a customer object all by itself. You get a whole customer and nothing but the customer ready to run and use!

> — *Oliver Sims, Author*
> *Business Objects*
> *(McGraw-Hill, 1994)*

Oliver Sims is the designer of the *New World Infrastructure (Newi)*—a framework whose sole purpose is to create and run business objects. Newi—shipped by Integrated Objects in 1994—is the first of a new generation of products that focus on the delivery of late-bound business objects. Newi calls them *Cooperative Business Objects (CBOs)*. CBOs are shaped and packaged as business objects—meaning something an end user can recognize. Examples of CBOs are a customer, a product, an order form, and an account.

CBOs follow a model/view separation, which means that the presentation of the business object is separated from its business logic and data. This makes it possible for you to distribute CBOs across client/server boundaries. In addition, CBOs are designed to work transactionally with distributed shared resources. Newi provides an ORB (and framework) that tie these business objects together into business processes across local and wide area networks.

Newi has been under development since 1990; it is now a mature product on Windows, OS/2, Unix, and OS/400. The product has already achieved some successes in the European finance and utilities sectors. It is now growing a customer base in communications, retail, and manufacturing. Because Newi was there first, it had to create its own ORB and object services. Future releases of Newi will be more integrated with CORBA/SOM and OpenDoc. Integrated Objects is a joint venture of IBM and Softwright. The company is an active member of OMG; its two architects are among the key drivers of BOMSIG. Newi is the closest product incarnation of the BOMSIG vision. It is living proof that you can use business objects in enterprise environments to create production-strength client/server applications. This chapter helps you understand the underlying architecture that makes it possible.

NEWI'S BUSINESS OBJECTS

Applications are bounded, introverted, and do not naturally speak to each other. The time has come to think of a new shape of deliverable...business objects as units of delivery to the user community.

> — *Martin Anderson, Chairman*
> *Integrated Objects*
> *(June, 1995)*

The business object as the unit of implementation for an information system is unbeaten as a strategy for arriving at the most desirable modular form.

> — *Rob Prins, CYCLADE Consultants*
> *(June, 1995)*

The Newi vision is simple: Design a business object, build a business object, and deliver a business object. Then let users and system integrators use business objects in any combination that suits their needs. The Newi framework and ORB provide the middleware to enable these business objects (or CBOs) to be assembled dynamically without being constrained by what Oliver Sims calls, "the straightjacket of how the developer imagined and planned their use." As you will see in the next few sections, Newi takes loosely coupling to the extreme. Everything in the system is configurable and flexible.

What Is a CBO?

A Newi CBO is a software executable with the following attributes:

- ■ *It is the unit of delivery to end users*. The effective "shape" of this executable is an object that makes sense to end users. It can appear as an icon. You can view its contents by double-clicking on it (see Figure 19-1). A CBO has all the attributes of a software object, including inheritance and polymorphism. The CBO is a file that you can load and execute. For example, you could put a "customer" CBO all by itself on a diskette and send it to someone who could then use it (provided the Newi runtime is present).

- ■ *It can interact at run time with other CBOs in ad-hoc ways*. You should be able to assemble collections of CBOs in ways that are not preplanned by their developers. The interactions between CBOs are loosely-coupled and agreed upon at run time. Newi only requires objects to have an agreed-upon way of determining the shape of the interface at send time. Newi provides facilities that allow CBOs to exchange semantic data in self-defining messages that describe each data item.

- ■ *It can be developed independently from other CBOs*. A CBO is a language-neutral, self-contained entity. You build a CBO using languages such as C, C++, COBOL, RPG, or REXX. CBOs written in different languages can interact using the Newi ORB.

- ■ *It can be built by a business programmer.* You don't have to be a C++ guru to build a CBO. Of course, this implies the existence of CBO-building tools and a CBO framework.

CBOs Versus Compound Document Components

The CBO is the epitome of a free-standing, loosely-coupled, self-contained component. In contrast to compound document components, CBOs have no container application that handles the visual layout negotiations. They have no compound document shell that activates the CBOs and remembers their visual placement within a document. They have no dispatcher that helps route events to the proper embedded part. They have no arbiter that worries about which component is active

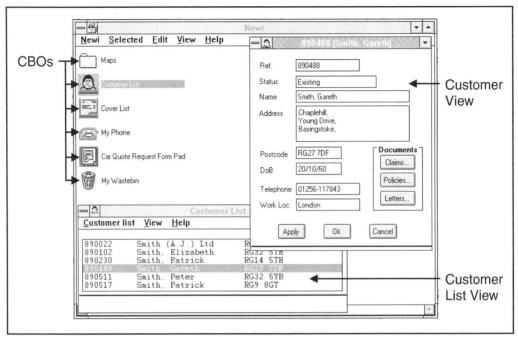

Figure 19-1. Newi: The Visual Representation of CBOs.

and who owns what shared user interface resource—for example, the menu bar. CBOs forego all these niceties so they can be independent.

So what form of visual consistency is provided by these highly independent CBOs? Or, what makes them look like they're part of the same application? Newi's model of visual integration is IBM's CUA'91 Object-Oriented User Interface (OOUI) specification. This is the same model that OS/2 Warp's Workplace Shell uses. The top level of a Newi business object is an icon. You can drag an object's icon and drop it on another object's icon to cause them to interact. The exact interaction is determined by the types of objects and how they react to drag-and-drop. Newi lets you directly manipulate a visual object by double-clicking on it to open its views. An object can have one or more views that represent its contents (or model). Objects can be grouped into folders. In summary, this 1991-vintage OOUI model has worked very well for OS/2 Warp and NeXT users. It is also the model used in Windows 95 (but not the previous versions of Windows).

So what does a compound document OOUI—like OpenDoc, OLE, and Taligent—do to make it even better? Simply put, compound documents provide the next level of technology for creating smarter visual objects. Compound documents are OOUIs on steroids. They provide a more integrated visual experience by allowing multiple components to seamlessly share a single window or visual container. You can edit a component in-place, regardless of how deeply embedded it is within other components. Components store their persistent data and visual state in a common document, allowing you to bring them back to life in the same state you left them in.

As a result, compound documents provide much better visual integration than Newi (or any existing desktop). Their embedded components appear within containers with seamless boundaries between them—just like you would expect from real-world objects. In contrast, Newi's containers can only be populated with icons. We will not repeat here all the wonders of compound documents; you should have gotten that already from the OpenDoc, OLE, and Taligent chapters. All we want to say here is that Newi provides better visual integration for independent components than most Windows 3.X applications. However, it is not on par with the visual integration that you can achieve with compound documents. So there's no free lunch. This is the price you pay for being an independent component—meaning a component that's not attached to a compound document framework. According to Integrated Objects, future releases of Newi will support the OpenDoc compound document model. If this happens, then this issue goes away (more on that later in this chapter).

THE NEWI ORB AND BUSINESS OBJECT FRAMEWORK

The Newi business object infrastructure consists of an ORB and its run-time frameworks and application development tools (see Figure 19-2). Because Newi was there first, it had to reinvent parts of CORBA. In the future, we expect that much of the Newi ORB and underlying services will use CORBA (more on that later in this chapter). Newi, however, introduces innovations that are beyond anything CORBA provides in the following areas: 1) message-time binding, 2) dynamic object hierarchies, 3) business object model/view separation. This section covers these Newi innovations in more depth.

The Newi ORB: Message-Time Binding

CBOs are executables that interact by sending messages to each other using the services of a Newi ORB. Newi, like CORBA, provides local/remote transparency and language independence. The ORB services let clients locate a recipient CBO (or start an instance of a CBO) anywhere on the Newi ORB. The Newi ORB can also bring persistent objects into memory whenever there's a message for them. Newi provides its own unique naming conventions for objects. Before you send a message to an object, you obtain a reference for the target object from the ORB using the following attributes: instance name, class name, and domain name. Newi lets you call an object that is not running. The ORB will bring the object into memory if it's persistently stored, or it will create a new instance of that class.

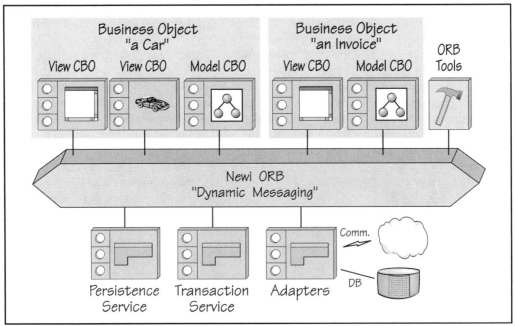

Figure 19-2. The Newi ORB and Object Services.

Unlike CORBA, Newi does not support static method invocations. It only supports dynamic method invocations on the client side and a form of "do-it-yourself" method resolution on the server side. Like CORBA, you can invoke a dynamic method either synchronously or post it asynchronously. Posting means that the calling object is not blocked waiting for the reply. Instead, it can specify which of its methods the response should invoke—in other words, Newi supports callbacks. Note that the receiver cannot tell the difference between a synchronous or asynchronous call.

Unlike CORBA, a Newi ORB does not support an Interface Definition Language (IDL) or an Interface Repository. Instead, Newi introduces *Semantic Data Objects (SDOs)*. These are self-describing message objects that a sender CBO constructs "on the fly." The method resolution is done within the receiving CBO. This process is similar to the CORBA dynamic invocation on the client side and the dynamic skeleton invocation on the server side. The difference is that there is no Interface Repository, shared data types, or type checking. But because of this loose binding arrangement, SDOs provide maximum flexibility for their business objects.

To invoke a method on a target CBO, a client asks the Newi ORB for a data "bucket" that it then fills with self-describing data—including semantic labels and the data itself. The ORB attaches the bucket to a message that includes the sender's ID and transmits it to the recipient. The receiving CBO must determine which method to invoke and hand the target method the data bucket. The target dips into the bucket and pulls out by name only the items it's interested in.

The sender and receiver must agree on the semantics of *labels* that describe the data—for example, date, price, or balance. If there are data type mismatches, the receiver CBO "does it right," which means that it converts the mismatched data into types that it can handle (Newi provides helper functions to automate the conversion). Because it knows the identity of the sender, the receiving CBO can choose to filter incoming requests and reject the ones it doesn't want to handle. If a receiving CBO cannot execute a method, it passes it to its parent class.

Newi achieves this level of loosely-coupled, *message-time* binding by leaving it up to the CBOs to work out standard agreements on the meaning (or semantics) of labels within the message. This is Newi's version of metadata. Other than that, almost anything goes. Communicating CBOs do not have to agree on the format of the message or the order of its contents. They only have to agree on the meaning of data that's passed between them. Newi helps out by providing macros for defining your methods, and for interpreting incoming messages.

Newi's Dynamic Object Hierarchies

Like SOM, Objective C, and Smalltalk, a Newi class is itself an object. The CBO class object provides a factory that's responsible for creating, restoring, and destroying CBO instances. Like CORBA, Newi separates interfaces from class implementation. This means that you can map several interfaces to one implementation. The unit of code reuse is the implementation not the class.

Newi lets you factor your class hierarchy dynamically at run time. This means that instead of having the compiler construct the class hierarchy, Newi builds the class hierarchy at run time from a CBO configuration file. This helps you create some very tailorable CBOs that you can configure to inherit from parent objects written in a variety of languages. Before you run any new object on a Newi ORB, you must first register its class. As part of the registration, you must provide the following information:

- ■ *The relationship between the CBO and its implementation*. You must assign a CBO a class name, icon, and implementation. A class uses the implementation that you specify. The interface for the implementation consists of the method names it supports. You must provide the name of the DLL or EXE that implements these methods.

- ■ *The parent class name*. This lets you establish the class hierarchy at configuration time.

■ *The relationship between a model and its views*. If your business object is visible, then you must associate one or more view CBOs with the model CBO. To do this you must provide the names of the view CBOs and the screen layout files that are used to display them (we explain what this means in the next section).

You must provide this information in a configuration file called NWI.CFG. Newi uses this information at run time to construct the CBO class hierarchy and model/view associations. You can change the class hierarchy or implementation by updating the configuration file. The system is very flexible and dynamic. Note that a CBO object only gets built when you create a particular instance of a class. At this time, Newi loads the DLL and brings the CBO to life.

Newi's Model/View Separation

What is new here is the idea of developing and producing independently executable objects rather than producing applications whose source code is organized on the basis of objects.

— Oliver Sims, Author
Business Objects
(McGraw-Hill, 1994)

You may have noticed in Figure 19-2 that a Newi business object is decomposed into a *model* CBO that you can associate with one or more *view* CBOs. This model/view separation decouples the "internals" of a business object from its user interface. Like everything in Newi, you can configure the model/view associations at run time using NWI.CFG. This means the binding is done as late as possible. To make it easier for you to develop these model/view CBOs, Newi provides two classes, **Model** and **View**, from which nearly all other objects are derived (see Figure 19-3).

A business object must have a model CBO and at least one view CBO. An object derived from the **Model** class manipulates data and state. The **Persistent Model** class provides a persistent version of the model class. Newi removes a persistent object from memory if there are no outstanding messages for it, and then saves its state. At this point, the object is in the *passive* state. Newi will reactivate the object (from its persistent store) whenever it must respond to a message. Non-persistent views and models are short-lived. Consequently, they are easier to manage; Newi only needs to instantiate these objects when they are first invoked and destroy them when they are no longer needed. Newi provides a **Container** class that can store a collection of objects persistently. The view object is the graphical representation of the data and what you can do with it. A **Container View** represents a collection of objects within a folder (or a window).

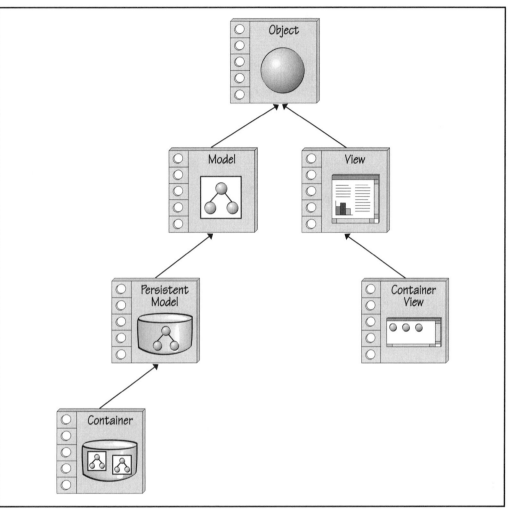

Figure 19-3. Newi's Base Class Hierarchy.

Newi's separation of model from view and its support of more than one view object per model is very useful in the following situations:

- ***Views and model provide a natural client/server split***. The ORB provides local/remote transparency, so it doesn't really matter where you run these CBOs. This means that you can run the views on a client machine and the model on a server. Or you can run them both on the same machine. You make that choice at configuration time.

- ***Views can serve different purposes***. You can use multiple views to restrict access to information or to show different facets of the same data. You can let users prototype and test drive different views and replace them with production versions when they're ready.

Figure 19-4 shows one small example of the model/view approach. We show a car business object that is built using a model CBO to represent the car data and three view CBOs that display: 1) a picture of the car, 2) service history, and 3) price and model features. You could be looking at all these views of the object simultaneously.

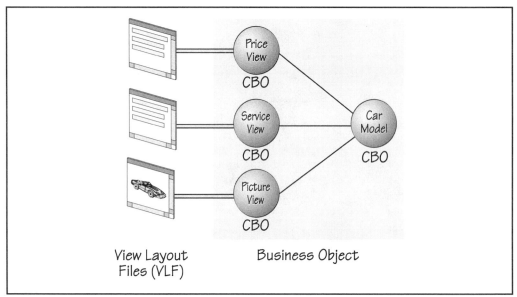

Figure 19-4. Newi: Views and Model.

View Layout Files

To help you create multiplatform views, Newi separates the layout of a view from the event handlers. To define the layout, you create a *View Layout File (VLF)* using Newi's semantic data service language. This is the same language that you use to describe the message contents. You can compile the user interface elements you describe using VLF to run on all the GUI platforms Newi supports—including Windows, OS/2, and others. VLF lets you describe the size and color of a window, the various controls that are embedded within it, and the placement and appearance of all text. You can also specify associations between a control's events and event-handling functions.

You can write the VLF file yourself, but a much quicker way is to use Newi's *View Capture* tool. This tool lets you create user interface controls on Windows and OS/2 using your resource editor or screen-painting tool. You then tell Newi to capture the controls in a window and append them to the VLF—it's as simple as doing a screen capture. Newi is also working on an interactive view editor that lets you build views by dragging controls from a palette.

After you create a VLF, you must associate it with a view CBO at configuration time. So once again, you have maximum flexibility because you can change the view at the very last moment without even going through a compile cycle. For example, you can edit the VLF file with a simple text editor to change text from English to French. When you're done, Newi interprets and targets it for the platform where your object appears.

Other Newi Frameworks and Tools

Newi has been used in production applications for a while. As a result, it provides the type of tools you would expect from a more seasoned platform. This includes tools for tracing, displaying, logging, and injecting messages on a Newi ORB. It also includes a class browser and an inspector called an *Object Bag*. As part of its run-time services, Newi provides platform-independent memory management, message routing, and adapters that interface to SQL databases and CICS TP Monitors. These adapters transform Newi messages into the corresponding SQL or CICS calls. The information in the SQL databases becomes part of the Newi model object.

Newi, OpenDoc, and SOM/CORBA

In March 1995, Integrated Objects announced that future versions of Newi will be integrated with OpenDoc and SOM/CORBA. More specifically, a Newi CBO will be packaged as an OpenDoc part. This will enable OpenDoc parts to take advantage of Newi features such as the model/view separation and semantic-level, inter-CBO interactions. Newi should make it easier to create OpenDoc client/server parts. Of course, Newi also benefits because its business objects will be able to reap all the advantages of a compound document framework—including seamless visual integration, Bento containers, uniform data transfers, and scripting.

The integration of Newi with SOM will provide a strong CORBA-based business object platform. Newi extends CORBA with its semantic message infrastructure and rich business object tools. CORBA brings to Newi an open ORB infrastructure, an Interface Repository, and all the system-level object services—including events, naming, persistence, relationships, and transactions. Newi can also use the SOM metaclass service for its object classes, which will help it converge with mainstream SOM and OpenDoc applications.

With CORBA 2.0, it's now possible for Newi to use standard ORB services to create and exchange semantic messages. Clients can create these semantic messages using the CORBA dynamic invocation service. On the server side, the message is received via the new CORBA 2.0 dynamic skeleton interface, which can accept any message and dynamically bind it to a method on a target object. Of course, the contents of the message are still pure Newi, which is a major benefit for business objects. When it moves to a CORBA foundation, Newi will become a perfect candidate technology for future OMG semantic messaging and business object RFPs (see next Soapbox).

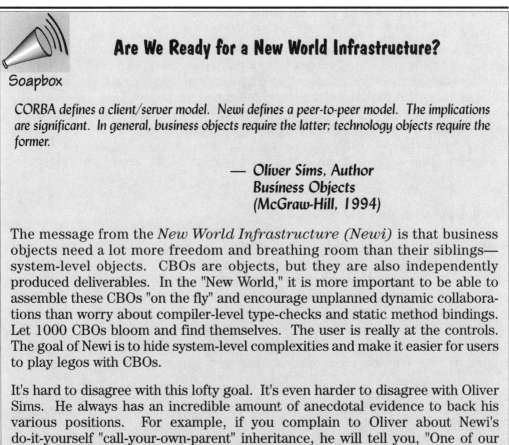

Are We Ready for a New World Infrastructure?

Soapbox

CORBA *defines a client/server model. Newi defines a peer-to-peer model. The implications are significant. In general, business objects require the latter; technology objects require the former.*

— **Oliver Sims, Author**
   Business Objects
   (McGraw-Hill, 1994)

The message from the *New World Infrastructure (Newi)* is that business objects need a lot more freedom and breathing room than their siblings—system-level objects. CBOs are objects, but they are also independently produced deliverables. In the "New World," it is more important to be able to assemble these CBOs "on the fly" and encourage unplanned dynamic collaborations than worry about compiler-level type-checks and static method bindings. Let 1000 CBOs bloom and find themselves. The user is really at the controls. The goal of Newi is to hide system-level complexities and make it easier for users to play legos with CBOs.

It's hard to disagree with this lofty goal. It's even harder to disagree with Oliver Sims. He always has an incredible amount of anecdotal evidence to back his various positions. For example, if you complain to Oliver about Newi's do-it-yourself "call-your-own-parent" inheritance, he will tell you, "One of our customers discovered that he could superclass across the network. He has a PC object whose superclass handles DB access; the superclass is actually on the server. We didn't plan this, but the loose binding and location transparency just allowed it to happen." What do you say to that? Awed silence. There's so much to learn in this area. Oliver's experience with living business object systems is extremely valuable. One of your authors spends about an hour digesting each note he receives from Oliver, even the shorter ones. The bottom line is that we're still trying to understand how much run-time freedom our customers really want and how they want it delivered.

However, we strongly disagree with Oliver's claim that CORBA is only a client/server model. Like Newi, a CORBA object can alternate between client and server roles. A client/server protocol is just a way to initiate an interaction between peers when one needs a service. It's also a defensive protocol—in its server role, an object must be able to handle concurrent requests from multiple clients and serialize access to shared resources. Of course, it's safe to say all this from a soapbox—with no Oliver in sight.

With the new dynamic skeleton interface, a CORBA 2.0 ORB can provide all the underlying plumbing Newi needs. So it's time for Newi to say farewell to their proprietary ORB and move their excellent semantic services on top of CORBA. The combination of Newi and CORBA will provide flexibility and autonomy for business objects within some form of "organized anarchy." For example, these objects will use an Interface Repository to discover metadata in a more organized way. Yes, it's a pain to keep these Interface Repositories current when configurations are continuously changing, but that's life! CORBA 2.0 now defines interfaces for updating these Interface Repositories even across global networks.

For us, an ideal component infrastructure needs to combine the strengths of Newi, OpenDoc, CORBA, and Taligent (and throw in some OpenStep tools). This combination gives us the best of worlds for business objects. Ahh, but can IBM fuse them together? Why IBM? As incredible as it may seem, IBM owns a piece of the action in each of these technologies (but, we'll spare you the "Dear Lou" letter). In any case, there seems to be a movement towards the mutual embedding of these components, with OpenDoc serving as the unifying compound document metaphor. Taligent will provide the technology for smart OpenDoc places; it will also provide *social computing* metaphors within these places. Newi will provide the client/server semantic glue (sorry, the "peer-to-peer" glue). If these great technologies come together, the "open component" camp will be able to field a business object environment that could really knock the wind out of OLE. ❑

Conclusion

Newi is the first product to tackle head-on the issues of business objects. The Newi architecture and frameworks evolved to meet the needs of business objects in live production environments. The primary lesson to be learned from the Newi experience is that late binding is important to business objects. The philosophy of Newi is that everything is configurable at run time—including class hierarchies, model/view associations, and messaging. You can compose CBOs "on the fly." And once you introduce CBOs in an environment, they can figure out how to collaborate with other CBOs with the help of metadata. So the message from the Newi front is: Late binding and dynamic discovery are absolute prerequisites for business objects (also see the previous Soapbox).

Part 4

OpenDoc

Under the Hood

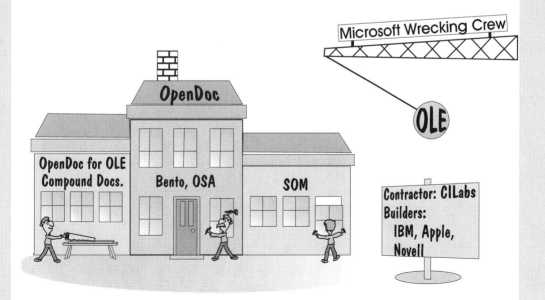

An Introduction to Part 4

The shift to a component desktop model presents a fundamental shift in application software...Many developers see compound document environments as the first really practical and valuable quasi frameworks available on top of desktop object models.

— *IDC*
Computer Industry Report
(December, 1994)

Part 4 is for diehards who really want to look at OpenDoc under the hood. We don't want to alarm our Martian friends: Don't worry—you can really read this part without incurring irreversible brain damage. The worst that can happen to you is that your brain may go numb from a severe overdose of OpenDoc details. If that happens, just take a few deep breaths and move on to the next chapter.

Obviously, we don't expect you all to turn into OpenDoc programmers. So why did we write this part? Because exploring the workings of OpenDoc in this level of detail can be very rewarding to anyone with an interest in interoperable components. Before components can play together in client/server suites, they must learn how to play together on the desktop.

Because of its superb component architecture, OpenDoc makes an excellent case study of how components—called *parts*—can interact at higher semantic levels. Independently developed OpenDoc components can seamlessly share a window on the screen, exchange content-based semantic messages, and store their contents within the same document file. A second major feature of OpenDoc is that parts are scriptable. This feature, along with the component architecture of OpenDoc, makes it easy to combine parts from different providers into custom solutions. Finally, OpenDoc is the first desktop component technology to use CORBA as its software bus.

The combination of OpenDoc and CORBA can lead to some highly attractive client/server applications. OpenDoc-style compound documents can revolutionize the way servers interact with their clients. For example, a server can ship to its clients specialized front-ends in the form of OpenDoc documents. These documents can contain visual "places" with parts that represent things and people that live within them. So with OpenDoc, servers can ship to their clients entire front-end environments in the form of visual places that plug into the desktop. These visual places can interact with servers using a CORBA ORB.

Scripting technology provides the basis for *roaming agents*. These agents are interpreted programs that carry their own environment (and state) with them. Roaming agents can execute on any machine in which they happen to land. OpenDoc documents are almost the perfect carriers for these roaming agents. This is because an OpenDoc document can store—in addition to part data—scripts that can be associated with the various parts or with the entire document. In the world of OpenDoc, a roaming agent is a document with its data and scripts.

The bottom line here is that OpenDoc introduces a new dimension in client/server component software. In the old days, when PCs were attached to servers, they played by the server rules. Today, the tables are turned—it's the servers that must learn to play by the client rules. Because OpenDoc builds on CORBA, components on the two sides of the client/server divide can interoperate as peers. However, server components must understand how to communicate semantically with their clients before they can perform this magic. So server providers must learn the rules of engagement by which clients play on the desktop. Then they too can join the party. For example, a server can learn how client components support scripting and provide the same interfaces.

Because of its clean architecture, OpenDoc is a textbook example of how component collaborations on the client are beginning to shape up. And, in the emerging world of components, we need all the textbook examples we can find on patterns of interaction and collaboration. So we strongly recommend that you invest the time to go through the next five chapters.

We first cover the OpenDoc object model—including SOM, the OpenDoc classes, and the programming model. Then we provide in-depth coverage of the four constituent technologies that make up OpenDoc: compound document services, Bento, uniform data transfer, and the Open Scripting Architecture. This is the OpenDoc model we introduced in Part 3, except that we go into the next layer of detail. So we hope you enjoy the diehard ride.

Chapter 20

OpenDoc and SOM: The Object Model

> *The OpenDoc standard, designed from the beginning as a network-ready architecture, will enable fine-grained components—parts in OpenDoc lingo—to travel the network and share information with other components across platforms.*
>
> — *Meta Group*
> *(December, 1994)*

This is the first of a five-chapter series in which we look at OpenDoc under the hood. In this chapter, we first go over the OpenDoc object model. Hopefully, much of this should be familiar to you because it's just an extension of the CORBA bus to the desktop (see Figure 20-1). SOM provides a packaging technology for OpenDoc components. It is also the ORB that lets these components interoperate on a CORBA bus. We also cover the OpenDoc class hierarchy and programming model. We want to answer these questions: How do you build a part editor? What OpenDoc run-time editors are available? How does a part find them? How does the surrounding OpenDoc environment interact with a part? And, how intrusive is the OpenDoc programming model?

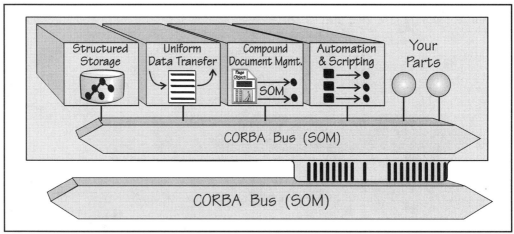

Figure 20-1. OpenDoc: The SOM Object Bus.

WHAT SOM BRINGS TO THE PARTY

SOM is one of the industry's first CORBA-compliant ORBs. It runs on OS/2, AIX, Windows, and Mac System 7. Over the next year, SOM is likely to appear on Novell's NetWare, IBM's OS/400 and MVS, Taligent, Tandem's NonStop Kernel, and on a multiplicity of Unix platforms. SOM allows objects written in different languages to communicate in the same address space, across address spaces, and across dissimilar OSs over networks. The interprocess communications mechanism is transparent to your programs.

OpenDoc and SOM

OpenDoc is a set of shared class libraries with IDL-defined platform-independent interfaces. The OpenDoc interfaces are compiled separately from an object's implementation using CORBA-compliant SOM skeletons. The OpenDoc runtime instantiates a set of CORBA objects; it uses SOM's language-neutral distributed dispatching standards for all its system, interpart, and client/server communications. SOM objects are dynamically bound, allowing new parts to be added to existing documents at any time.

IDL and SOM make it possible for part editors created with different compilers and in different programming languages to consistently communicate and pass parameters. SOM also includes a CORBA-compliant Interface Repository that makes the OpenDoc classes and their method descriptions available to clients at run time. Part editors can use the Interface Repository to dynamically discover and invoke any CORBA service at run time.

SOM: A Technology for Packaging Parts

Among other things, SOM provides a component packaging technology. In the case of OpenDoc, it allows software vendors to package their part editors in binary class libraries and ship them as DLLs. In addition, SOM supports implementation inheritance, which means that developers can subclass OpenDoc parts and either reuse or override their method implementations delivered in DLL binaries. This feature alone should help create a market for extendable parts, which means OpenDoc parts are sold as binary DLLs with an IDL and some documentation that explains how the part can be extended (also see next Briefing box).

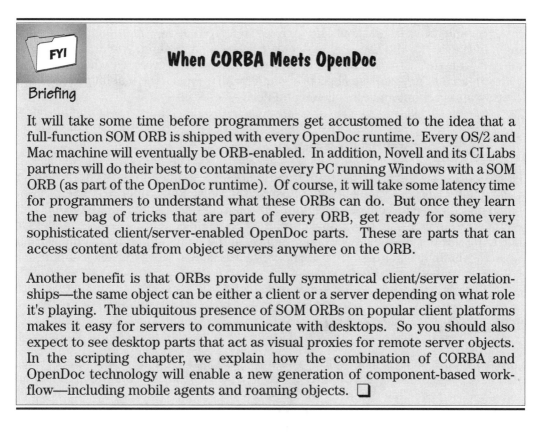

FYI

When CORBA Meets OpenDoc

Briefing

It will take some time before programmers get accustomed to the idea that a full-function SOM ORB is shipped with every OpenDoc runtime. Every OS/2 and Mac machine will eventually be ORB-enabled. In addition, Novell and its CI Labs partners will do their best to contaminate every PC running Windows with a SOM ORB (as part of the OpenDoc runtime). Of course, it will take some latency time for programmers to understand what these ORBs can do. But once they learn the new bag of tricks that are part of every ORB, get ready for some very sophisticated client/server-enabled OpenDoc parts. These are parts that can access content data from object servers anywhere on the ORB.

Another benefit is that ORBs provide fully symmetrical client/server relationships—the same object can be either a client or a server depending on what role it's playing. The ubiquitous presence of SOM ORBs on popular client platforms makes it easy for servers to communicate with desktops. So you should also expect to see desktop parts that act as visual proxies for remote server objects. In the scripting chapter, we explain how the combination of CORBA and OpenDoc technology will enable a new generation of component-based workflow—including mobile agents and roaming objects. ❏

SOM's CORBA-compliant *Interface Definition Language (IDL)* makes it possible for OpenDoc part editors to be distributed in a binary format, which means that the source code does not have to be provided. The IDL defines the interfaces a part supports without exposing the implementation. A client calling a SOM class has no built-in—or compiled—information about the entry points to that class. Instead, the method dispatch tables are computed and initialized at run time. Because these tables are computed at run time, a SOM class can be modified by refactoring the class hierarchy or by adding methods and instance data.

If a SOM class is modified and recompiled, it does not require the recompilation of all its derived classes and clients. This means that OpenDoc part editors can be independently extended, revised, or replaced and yet still work together. How does SOM perform this magic? It does it by providing a *release ordering* facility in the IDL that lets you to add new functions to a server class without having to recompile the client programs that use it.

The release ordering IDL facility is a powerful SOM feature that helps you maintain backward binary compatibility. As a component provider, all you need to do is list every method name introduced by your class and make sure you don't change the order in which you listed them. If you need to introduce new methods, simply add them to the end of the list. If you decide to remove a method, you must still leave its name on the list. Because of this flexibility, SOM overcomes what Microsoft refers to as the "fragile base class problem"—which means the inability to modify a class without recompiling its clients and derived classes.

THE OPENDOC PROGRAMMING MODEL

OpenDoc is a radical shift from traditional GUI applications; it introduces a component discipline to the design of user interfaces. Remember that an OpenDoc part consists of data and a part editor that manipulates the data. OpenDoc part editors are smaller than traditional applications. They neither have direct access to event queues nor do they own their windows and documents. A lot of this work is done for them by OpenDoc. In return, part editors must work in close cooperation with their fellow part editors.

ODPart: The Part Editor Class

To create an OpenDoc part editor, you must subclass **ODPart**—an abstract class that encapsulates the 60 methods that define a part's behavior. You provide the part behavior by overriding the methods that interest you. In typical framework fashion, OpenDoc calls your part editor when it needs something done. You can create a functional OpenDoc part by implementing as little as six methods. Your challenge is to anticipate which methods OpenDoc will call during the lifetime of your part.

At a minimum, a part must be able to allocate storage for its persistent data, initialize its data from a persistent store, draw its contents inside an area provided by its container, handle events, and externalize its data to a Bento persistent store.

To program a part, you first define the interface in an IDL source file (see the next Briefing box). Then you run the SOM precompiler on the IDL file, which produces an implementation skeleton for your class—it's a code skeleton for all the methods you defined in the IDL. Add the body of the implementation code to the skeleton. Then compile the class and create the part DLL.

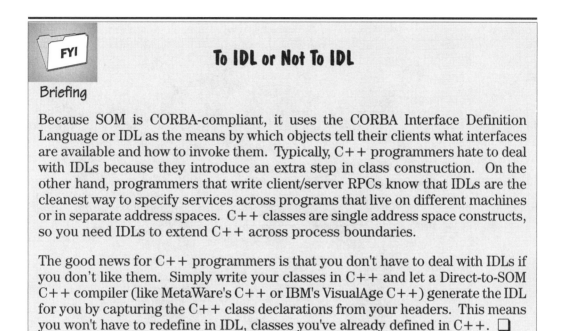

FYI

To IDL or Not To IDL

Briefing

Because SOM is CORBA-compliant, it uses the CORBA Interface Definition Language or IDL as the means by which objects tell their clients what interfaces are available and how to invoke them. Typically, C++ programmers hate to deal with IDLs because they introduce an extra step in class construction. On the other hand, programmers that write client/server RPCs know that IDLs are the cleanest way to specify services across programs that live on different machines or in separate address spaces. C++ classes are single address space constructs, so you need IDLs to extend C++ across process boundaries.

The good news for C++ programmers is that you don't have to deal with IDLs if you don't like them. Simply write your classes in C++ and let a Direct-to-SOM C++ compiler (like MetaWare's C++ or IBM's VisualAge C++) generate the IDL for you by capturing the C++ class declarations from your headers. This means you won't have to redefine in IDL, classes you've already defined in C++. ❏

The OpenDoc Class Hierarchy

The OpenDoc runtime is a collection of objects that belong to one of about 67 classes. A part editor interacts with these objects by invoking methods on them whenever it needs an OpenDoc service. Figure 20-2 shows a class hierarchy of OpenDoc's more important classes. As you can see, OpenDoc does not make too much use of inheritance—the class tree is relatively shallow by OO standards. And there's no multiple inheritance anywhere in that hierarchy. Why? The reason is that OpenDoc really encapsulates many unrelated groups of services. The main areas where inheritance make sense are for common functions such as reference counting, persistence, and extensions.

Figure 20-2 also shows that OpenDoc instantiates a substantial number of these objects to create its run-time environment. The rest of the objects are instantiated by a part editor when it needs a particular service. You'll get acquainted with most

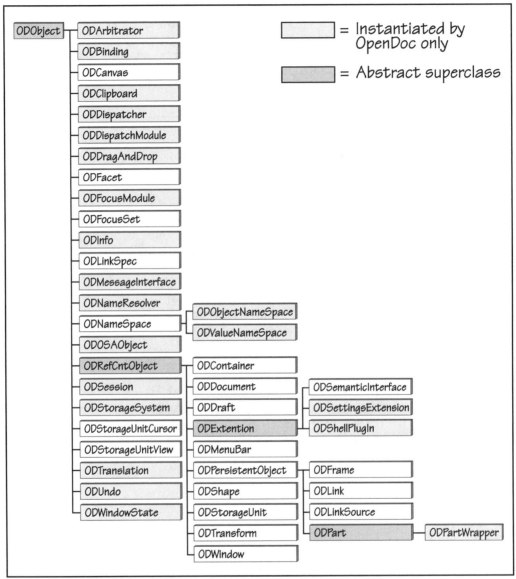

Figure 20-2. An Abbreviated OpenDoc Class Hierarchy.

of these classes by the time you get through the next four chapters. For component providers, the most important class is **ODPart**. Can you find it? This is the class you must customize via inheritance to provide your part editor's function. As you can see from the class hierarchy, a part editor is a persistent object that also supports reference counting. See the next Details box for a description of the methods **ODPart** supports.

Inside ODPart

Details

To create an OpenDoc part editor, you must subclass **ODPart**—an abstract superclass that encapsulates the 60 methods that define a part's behavior. **ODPart** serves as a template that embodies the structure and behavior of a generic part editor. The unique behavior of each part editor is created by subclassing **ODPart** and providing unique implementations of its pure virtual methods. Figure 20-3 shows all 60 methods that **ODPart** defines. As a convenience, we grouped the methods into 13 distinct functional categories. You should return to this figure while reading the remaining OpenDoc chapters; it will gradually start to make more sense.

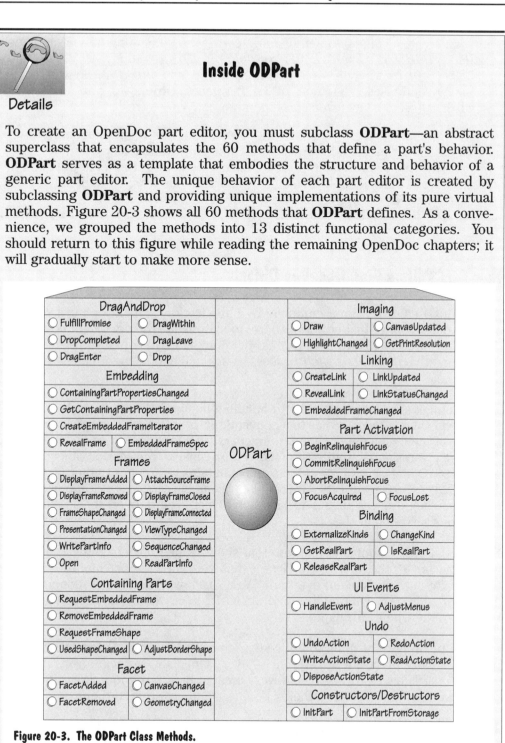

Figure 20-3. The ODPart Class Methods.

> You can create a simple non-embedding part by implementing only 5 methods: *InitPart, InitPartFromStorage, HandleEvent, Draw,* and *Externalize.* Note that *Externalize* is not one of the methods shown in Figure 20-3. So where does it come from? It's a method of **ODPersistentObject**—a parent class of **ODObject** (see the OpenDoc class hierarchy).
>
> The more sophisticated parts provide added behavior by implementing more methods, usually in related groups of function—for example, drag-and-drop. We recommend that you learn how to program in OpenDoc by first creating a simple part. For a code example of such a part, see our article "Building a SOM OpenDoc Part" in the March, 1995 issue of **Dr. Dobb's Journal**. ❏

How Part Editors Find OpenDoc Objects

Because part editors are not complete GUI applications, OpenDoc must provide a shared address space that editors can use to manipulate the document content and obtain services. OpenDoc provides this environment via a set of instantiated objects that belong to a *document shell* process. Each active document has its own shell process.

The document shell is responsible for handling document-wide operations. It's the closest equivalent OpenDoc has to a conventional application. OpenDoc creates an instance of the document shell environment whenever a document is opened. The shell then creates and initializes an **ODSession** object. The session object, in turn, instantiates OpenDoc *service* objects and maintains references to them. Parts find and gain access to most of the OpenDoc environment via the session object. Each document shell process has its own session object. Hanging off the session object are various service objects.

Figure 20-4 is a relationship diagram that shows which objects know about which other objects. It's the same set of classes that were shown in the hierarchy, but this time they're in a relationship diagram. We also show what type of functions these classes provide. You will find this diagram useful later when you're reading through the rest of the OpenDoc chapters.

For now, the important thing to notice in Figure 20-4 is that **ODSession** knows by name—or more precisely by reference—every OpenDoc service object. It's not a coincidence. Most of these objects were created by the session object in the first place. So, of course, it knows their references and how to find them.

The bottom line is that the session is an object that can help you find other objects. And it's a well-known object. So once you find the session, you can use it to find

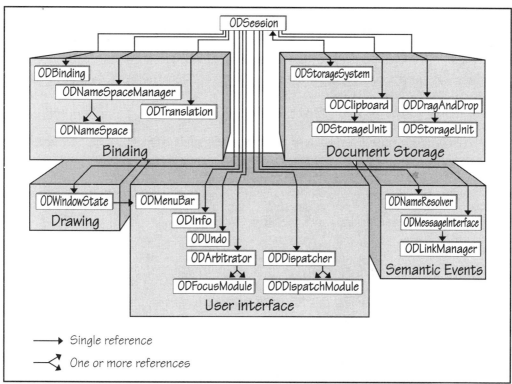

Figure 20-4. ODSession: The Mother of All Objects.

any other OpenDoc service object of interest. Think of it as a "yellow pages" for local OpenDoc objects. This is a good example of a design pattern that deals with the following vexing problem: How objects find references to other objects at run time. OpenDoc solves this problem with **ODSession**—a mini-directory object that serves two functions: 1) It creates new service objects when they're needed; 2) It knows where to find them.

How Intrusive Is the OpenDoc Programming Model?

OpenDoc is an object-oriented system. But, with some reengineering, existing applications can be retrofitted to work in the OpenDoc environment. Your programs—now called *part editors*—must be reengineered for an environment where they don't exclusively own the process, window, menu, event queue, or data file. Everything is shared with other parts.

The good news is that if you make it through this transition, you may find that programming with OpenDoc is not very intrusive. Here's why:

■ **You draw parts using the native platform's APIs.** However, instead of drawing to ordinary windows, you draw to part facets representing a part's real estate within a document window.

■ **You store data using ordinary streams.** Even though OpenDoc's Bento provides a very sophisticated object store, you can still read and write data using familiar streaming input/output commands.

■ **You process OpenDoc events using your platform's event queue.** The OpenDoc event model grafts itself nicely into the event queues of the platforms on which it runs.

■ **You use existing memory models.** OpenDoc may occasionally ask a part editor to free some memory; the editor can always say "no."

OpenDoc was designed to provide a cross-platform compound document architecture on top of platform-specific graphic systems and drawing interfaces. In addition, OpenDoc was designed for distributed interpart communications. All objects are instantiated via factories rather than programming language constructors. In addition, the system purposely minimizes the frequency of inter-library method calls.

OpenDoc Frameworks and Tools

Even though **ODPart** embodies the function needed for creating OpenDoc parts, it is still not a complete framework. A framework must also encapsulate the rendering mechanisms, scripting, and some of the application's logic. A framework is an all-or-nothing proposition. It creates an application skeleton based on a design philosophy. If you accept the framework's implementation, you are rewarded with large pieces of working code. On the downside, a framework locks you into an entire application design—you can't just pick and choose the pieces.

Most GUI frameworks—including OWL, MFC, and MacApp—use the model/view/controller split. Compound document architectures introduce new possibilities in framework design because the unit of construction is a granular component—for example, an OpenDoc part or OLE OCX. These components are bound to their containers and to each other through some very finely architected rules of engagement. All this opens up new opportunities in framework design. So keep your eyes open for new frameworks and tools that exploit these capabilities.

The OpenDoc community has at least two frameworks to choose from: one from Apple and one from IBM. Here's a short description of what they can do:

■ ***OpenDoc Development Framework (ODF)*** from Apple Computers builds on top of OpenDoc and the *Bedrock* rendering APIs. ODF-built parts can run on the Mac System 7 and Win32s (OS/2 Warp may come later). ODF does not include a visual builder. The philosophy of ODF is to provide programmers with recipes of prebuilt part editor functions that can be subclassed for their particular uses. For example, ODF can start you off with a simple part, an embedding part, or an embedding part that does scripting and linking. You then customize this prebuilt part to fit your needs.

■ ***OpenDoc Framework*** from IBM builds on top of OpenDoc and IBM's *Open-Class*—a cross-platform class library that provides rendering and other useful functions such as collections and database access. This framework will first target parts for the OS/2 and Windows environments (AIX and Mac come later). IBM's philosophy is to help developers build the part's contents—including the views and model. So it provides a set of smart parts that can be associated with very sophisticated views—including canvases, forms, and notebooks. These views can be populated with controls using geometry-independent layouts. IBM intends to integrate its OpenDoc framework with VisualAge C++.

The success of OpenDoc will depend on the quality of tools that vendors provide to make it easy to construct and assemble parts. OpenDoc has the potential of revolutionizing the application tool's market. We offer the following Soapbox as food for thought.

What to Look for in an OpenDoc Tool

Soapbox

Simply put, component-based application development is the process of building systems through the integration of prefabricated software modules, or application components Non-programmers may find that component application development empowers them to create their own application solutions, since most component applications are nearly codeless.

— David S. Linthicum
Application Development Trends
(January, 1995)

If you're like most of us, you will probably not want to program to the raw OpenDoc APIs—67 classes and 750 methods is just beyond the comprehension of mere programming mortals. The frameworks help, but they're not enough. What we really need are tools that allow us to visually construct OpenDoc parts and assemble them.

It's difficult to come up with a taxonomy of OpenDoc tools that covers all bases. There are different tools for different folks. But, for the sake of this discussion, here's a minimum set of basic features you should expect to find in a good OpenDoc tool:

- ■ ***A visual studio that helps you layout a part's views.*** The studio should let you create views by dragging controls and OpenDoc parts from a palette and dropping them where you want them. You should be able to customize the visual properties of the control and its behavior. Professional programmers must be able to interact directly with the classes in a foundation framework. The tool must provide a method editor that makes it easy to edit and customize methods within a class hierarchy. A *part wizard* can help programmers find what they're looking for. The rest of us will customize the control's behavior using scripts. So we also need *scripting wizards* to help us deal with the semantics of the scripting language.

- ■ ***An open palette***. In addition to its built-in controls, the tool's palette must be able to import both OpenDoc parts and OLE OCXs. This makes it easy for the tool to construct components from large pools of existing parts or OCXs. The tool's palette is used for both the construction of new parts and for assembling parts from existing components. *Views* are typically constructed by assembling low-level controls—push buttons, entry fields, and so on. *Visual containers* and *visual notebooks* are used to group multiple views to approximate a *business object*. The palette must be able to contain business objects and views as well as low-level controls.

- ■ ***A part packaging wizard***. The tool should help you package the components you construct as parts that are ready for resell. The packaging wizard should help you package the part and describe its licensing information and other attributes—including advertisement information, what suites (or Open-Doc extensions) a part supports, its attached scripts, and so on.

- ■ ***A Bento browser.*** The browser should allow you to navigate through Bento containers; find data by its attributes, type, or part ownership; display links and embedded relationships; and display data streams in the most appropriate visual representation. At a minimum, a tree view of the contents of the OpenDoc document's data elements must be presented.

- ■ ***SOM-level Spy.*** The tool should include a Spy system for displaying, tracing, and capturing SOM method invocations and OpenDoc semantic events. This feature is also useful for debugging scripts.

- ■ ***CORBA class browsers***. The tool should include intelligent browsers that can display both class inheritance and part relationships (containment and linking). It must also be able to view the insides of any object—including public and private methods, attributes, class information, version number, instance data, and the event-handling code. The browser must display outline and tree views of the things it knows about. It must work hand-in-hand with the SOM Interface Repository to get that information.

OpenDoc tools will be differentiated by how much cross-platform support they provide. The best tools will be able to create parts that run on Mac, OS/2, Windows 3.1, Windows 95, Windows NT, and Unixes. This means that the tool must be built on top of a cross-platform framework that provides a portable OpenDoc runtime—including a portable rendering engine, portable threads, memory management, printing, national language support, help, and CORBA communications. The tool must also include a multiplatform OSA-based scripting language. Ideally, the tool itself would be built on top of OpenDoc. This would provide an open environment for add-on editors and utilities. Now all you need to do is call your favorite tool vendors and ask when they plan to deliver such a tool. ❏

Chapter 21

OpenDoc: The Compound Document Model

---

*T*he IT industry is in the midst of a fundamental redesign of the desktop to support an information-centric environment featuring, in effect, "borderless" applications.

— *IDC*
Computer Industry Report
(December, 1994)

In this chapter, we cover the visual rules of engagement of OpenDoc (see Figure 21-1). We first go over creation OpenDoc style: How does an OpenDoc document bootstrap itself? How do parts find their editors? What's the shared environment in which all these parts live? If everything is a part, who provides the "application" that binds these parts together? We then go over the visual collaboration protocols: Who gets how much space on the screen? How do parts interact with their nested parts? What happens when parts move around? Who keeps track of what? Finally, we go over the arbitration rules: Which part gets the keyboard and menu? How are events routed? How do parts negotiate for shared resources? Remember, these parts are very independent; they do not know anything about each other. As you will soon find out, there's quite a bit of protocol behind that seamless look.

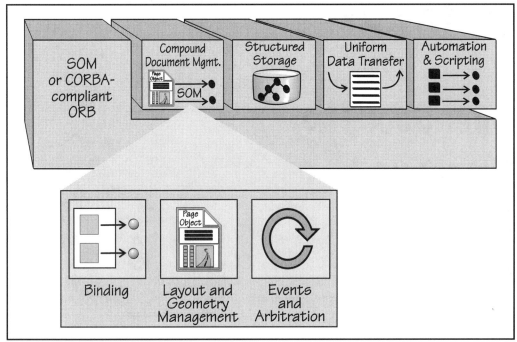

Figure 21-1. OpenDoc: The Compound Document Model.

BINDING: CREATING THE OPENDOC ENVIRONMENT

OpenDoc lives in the spaces between editors, not within them.

> — *Jens Alfke, Apple OpenDoc Developer*
> *MacTech Magazine*
> *(May, 1995)*

Compound documents are significantly different from application-centric GUIs. In a traditional GUI, the document is owned by an application. It is loaded into the application's address space, and manipulated by the GUI program. In a compound document, the document owns the process and is responsible for interacting with the operating system. OpenDoc calls this document-owned process the *document shell*.

Because part editors are not complete GUI applications, the document shell must provide an environment for dispatching events from the operating system to the proper part handler. It must arbitrate ownership of shared resources such as menus. And it must provide a shared address space that editors can use to manipulate the document content. OpenDoc provides this environment via a set of instantiated objects that belong to the document shell process. Each opened document has its own shell process.

The Document Shell: OpenDoc's Run-Time Manager

The document shell is responsible for handling document-wide operations. It is the closest thing in OpenDoc to a conventional application. OpenDoc creates an instance of the document shell environment whenever a document is opened. The shell provides the following services:

- *Creates and initializes an ODSession object*. The session object instantiates globally available OpenDoc *service* objects and maintains references to them. Parts find and gain access to most of the OpenDoc environment via the session object. Each document shell process has its own session object. Hanging off the session object are various service objects.

- *Opens a document from storage or creates new documents from stationery.* The shell reads the document into memory and reconstructs the document windows on the desktop by reading saved *window state* information. OpenDoc provides an **ODWindowState** object that keeps track of open windows and the state of the user interface. The shell also reads in the *root part* of the document, which it uses to reconstruct the rest of the embedded parts and make them visible.

- *Binds and loads the part editors, as needed.* *Binding*, in this case, means assigning the correct part editor to a given part. We explain how this is done in the next section.

- *Accepts user events and passes them to the OpenDoc* **ODDispatcher** *object.* OpenDoc also uses an **ODArbitrator** object to negotiate the ownership of shared resources among parts. We explain how this is done in later sections.

- *Allows the part editors to access global variables*. A part editor is a dynamically linked code module that is loaded in memory once and then shared by multiple parts in one or more documents. The document shell runtime allows dynamically linked code to access global variables.

Factories and Reference-Counted Objects

All OpenDoc objects are instantiated via factory methods; the C++ *new* operator is never used. Factories make it possible to distribute objects across address spaces and networks. Factories also help with *garbage collection*—meaning that they reclaim memory when an object no longer needs it. During an OpenDoc session, many objects with complex interobject relationships are created. How do the factories know when it is safe to delete an object from memory?

OpenDoc helps factory objects with their memory management by providing *reference-counted* objects derived from the **ODRefCntObject** class. Descendants of this class include all part editors as well as OpenDoc system objects. Reference-counted objects are aware of how many other objects are making use of them at any one time. An object has a reference count of one when a factory first creates it. Each *IncrementRefCount* method invocation increments the count; each *Release* method invocation decrements it. When an object's reference count goes to zero, it is responsible for notifying its factory object, so that OpenDoc can delete it from memory. Of course, all components have to play by these rules for this to work.

Binding: How Part Data Finds Part Editor

A part is an object because it encapsulates both state and behavior. The part data provides the state, and the part editor provides the behavior. When bound together, they form an editable OpenDoc component. As with any object, only the data (or state) is stored when the part is stored. And as with any object, you only need one copy of the editor code in memory regardless of the number of separate parts that it edits. So how does an OpenDoc part find its editor at run time?

OpenDoc accomplishes this task with the help of a matchmaker-like object of class **ODBinding**. To find the right editor, this matchmaker juggles three balls: information provided by part editors, preferences specified by users, and part kind information stored with parts. If there are no suitable editors for the part, OpenDoc will bind the part data with an *editor of last resort* that displays a gray outline of the part's frame. The lack of an editor never prevents the user from opening a document.

The matchmaker uses an OpenDoc object of class **ODNameSpace** to obtain the information it needs to make its decisions. This object maintains a database that maps data types to executable code; it includes the list of part editors, the preferences of users for particular part editors, and translators of part data types. In addition, each OpenDoc part maintains information on the *kind* of data the part contains and the more general *category* to which that kind belongs. Examples of CI Labs registered part categories include text, bitmap, relational database, and so on. Finally, each part editor must specify the part categories it can manipulate.

Using all this information, the matchmaker searches for "Mr. Right" part editor using the following sequence:

1. Looks for what the user considers the "preferred editor" for any given part kind.

2. Looks for the editor that created the part and makes it the default editor.

3. Looks for any editor that supports the part kind.

4. Looks for any editor that supports the part category.

5. Looks for editors that can handle translated versions of the data. It then presents the choices of part kind translations to the user. If the user picks one, the matchmaker translates the data into the new part kind and assigns it to an editor.

6. Assigns the editor of last resort.

In a nutshell, the matchmaker always looks for the editor that can provide the highest fidelity editing for a part's data contents. And the user can always change the setting. In OpenDoc, the user is always right.

LAYOUT AND GEOMETRY MANAGEMENT

OpenDoc was designed to last!

> — *Chris Andrew, Project Lead, OpenDoc for Windows*
> *Novell*
> *(February, 1995)*

OpenDoc uses four simple ideas to create compound document structures: documents, their parts, their frames, and the part editor code that manipulates them. An OpenDoc document is a persistent hierarchy of parts embedded within parts. OpenDoc also uses a separate but essentially parallel hierarchy made up of display elements called *facets*. The facet hierarchy is not stored within the document; it gets dynamically created when parts become visible. The facet hierarchy is there to expedite event dispatching to speed up drawing.

OpenDoc Container Parts

At the top of the part hierarchy, is a *root part*. This is the original part that controls the document's basic layout, page size, and how it gets printed. Figure 21-2 shows a root part with two embedded parts. All OpenDoc parts must be able to function as the root part of a document. *Containers* are parts that can embed other parts and that can also be embedded within other containers. All OpenDoc parts are embeddable in any container. However, not all parts are containers. For example, a clock part has no need to embed other parts.

Figure 21-2. OpenDoc: Parts Embedded Within Parts.

Frames, Facets, and Canvases

The OpenDoc rendering model is shown in Figure 21-3. Every document must contain at least one part—the root part—that initially owns all the document's visual real estate in a single *frame*. Frame objects—of class **ODFrame**—are used for space layout negotiations between containing parts and embedded parts. In the

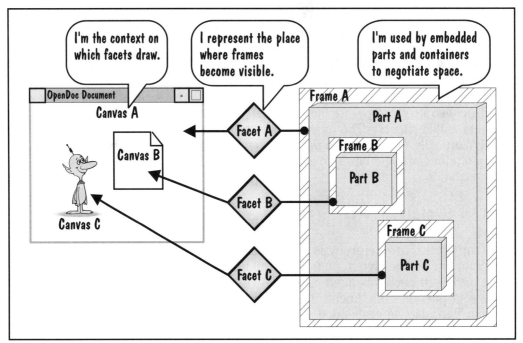

Figure 21-3. OpenDoc: Frames, Facets, and Canvases.

figure, root part A has two embedded parts: B and C. Each part has its own frame. A part can also appear in multiple frames, each showing a different view of the same part. When a document is saved, the set of frames it contains are made persistent. These frames contain the geometry information that will be used to recreate the visual look of the document.

OpenDoc needs a fast way of knowing what parts are visible in a window so that it can dispatch events to them. So how does OpenDoc avoid having to dig deep into the details of the content-oriented part and frame hierarchy to find out what needs to be displayed? It avoids doing this by requiring container parts to provide this information directly using *facet* objects of class **ODFacet**. Containing parts create a facet for each location where one of their embedded frames is visible. Facets represent a visible frame at run time. A visible part can have one or more facets.

The facet hierarchy (such as the example shown in Figure 21-3) is constructed "on the fly" for all the frames that are visible when a document is opened. Facets are only needed for those frames that are visible at any one moment. In contrast, frames must exist for all embedded parts in a document. Facets control the geometric relationships of frames with their containing frame or window. In contrast, frames control the geometric relationships of the content of a part to be displayed. Figure 21-4 shows the relationship between OpenDoc's frame and facet hierarchy.

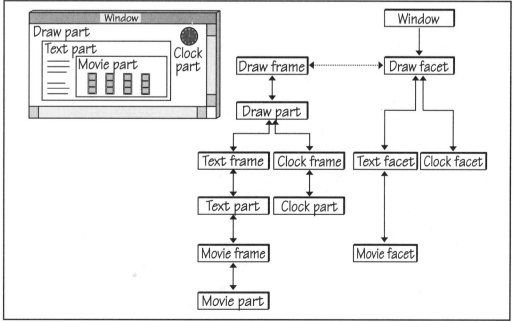

Figure 21-4. OpenDoc's Dual Frame and Facet Relationship Hierarchies.

Part 4. OpenDoc Under the Hood

The next pieces in the puzzle are *Canvas* objects—of class **ODCanvas**. They encapsulate platform-dependent presentation spaces or device contexts. The canvas is where the facets of a part render themselves. A drawing canvas is the destination of draw commands. It provides the environment for constructing a rendered image. This includes a coordinate system and state information about the drawing context—such as pen width and color.

Canvases can be either static or dynamic. A *dynamic canvas* is used for video displays that can potentially change through scrolling or paging. A *static canvas* is used for printed page displays that do not change after they are rendered. A facet is associated with a specific drawing canvas. A part editor can find out what kind of canvas its facet has, and then render itself accordingly. For example, a part editor may choose not to render adornments—including palettes and scroll bars—on a static canvas.

Finally, the *shape* object—of class **ODShape**—represents the space and coordinates of a two-dimensional shape on a canvas. A shape can have any kind of outline, even irregular ones. Shapes can be scaled, rotated, and transformed without having to know what's inside of them. OpenDoc uses **ODTransform** objects to map between content and frame coordinates.

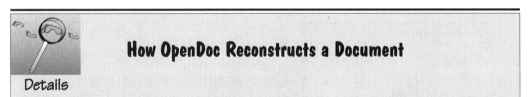

How OpenDoc Reconstructs a Document

Details

This Details box brings together the concepts described in the last sections with a detailed walk-through of how OpenDoc recreates a document from storage. When you open a document, OpenDoc instantiates a new document shell process, which then reads the document file into memory. The shell uses the window state information saved in the file to reconstruct the windows as they appeared on the screen when the document was last saved.

Once the shell has a window, it reads in the root frame and constructs the root facet. From this point on, it's all recursive magic. The root frame reads in the root part; the root part reads in its embedded frames and constructs facets for them. The embedded frames read in their own parts that in turn read in their embedded frames and create facets for them. This pattern continues until all the visible frames and parts in the document are read in from storage. After the objects all are read in, the shell asks each facet to draw itself. The part editor associated with that facet's frame draws the visible part content in the facet. If the state of the active part was saved, a part editor can even activate the palette or menus that were last active when the document was stored.

This magic happens because each part that is modified since the last draft saves its data and embedded frames in the document file. In addition, the document shell records the window state. If a user closes the document without saving changes to the current draft, the document shell throws away any changes that have been made since the last save and restores the window state from the previously saved draft. ❏

Drawing, OpenDoc Style

Each part operates within an arena of space and relies on a protocol to negotiate the use of geometric space, which may represent the display screen or the printed page. This protocol is quite dynamic, allowing objects to move and adjust "on the fly" as other objects are added or changed.

> — *Jeff Rush*
> *Dr. Dobb's Journal*
> *(January, 1995)*

Drawing the contents of an OpenDoc document is a cooperative effort between parts. No single part is responsible for the whole thing. Each part editor is responsible for drawing its own contents—including the borders of embedded frames—when OpenDoc invokes the editor's *draw* method. OpenDoc asks the part editor to draw a particular facet of a particular frame within which part contents are

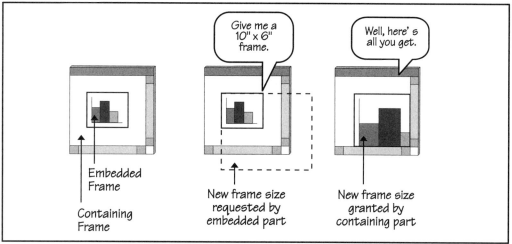

Figure 21-5. OpenDoc Space Negotiations.

displayed. The part editor is then responsible for transforming the data, clipping it so that it fits within the frame's limits, and rendering the contents.

Each container part controls the size, shape, and position of the parts embedded within it. A container can move, select, delete, and manipulate the frames of its embedded parts. The embedded part is responsible for drawing its own contents and handling events within its frame. If the embedded part needs to change its frame size or add another frame, it must negotiate for these changes with its container. The container always has the final say in space negotiations (see Figure 21-5).

Views: A Part Is a Part

OpenDoc parts can display themselves in different ways in separate frames, or in different ways in the same frame at different times. Typically, you'll want to see a part's contents within a frame. However, a part can also display itself in one of several iconic forms including regular icons, small icons, and thumbnails of the part contents. Icons are used to represent parts on the desktop and in folders, parts palettes, and tool palettes. You can think of the icon as representing a part in its closed state. When parts are opened within a document, they represent their contents in framed view types. Of course, an open document can also display parts using iconic or thumbnail views. An iconic part is not necessarily inactive. For example, an alarm part could be represented by an icon that emits a voice message.

The part is in control of its display within the borders of its frame. However, OpenDoc supports a protocol that allows a container part to specify the view type it wants an embedded part to have when it is first embedded. The container part does this by setting the *view type* value in the embedded part's frame. Typically, a part that's pasted or dropped into an open document will have a framed view type. Likewise, a part that's pasted or dropped into a folder or palette will have an iconic view.

Part Windows

OpenDoc supports *in-place editing*, which means that different parts in a document share the same window. You can manipulate the part contents "in-place" without opening a separate window for each part editor. The parts appear to be one seamless application. In-place editing is a like a piece of paper—you can directly edit anything within that paper. OpenDoc supports an unlimited nesting of embedded parts that can be edited in-place.

There are times when a user may want to run a part in its own separate window as well as within a document (see Figure 21-6). Why? Because you sometimes run into "postage stamp" sized parts that are hard to manipulate from within a document. You can blow up the part within its own window to manipulate it with more freedom. Any changes you apply to the windowed view of the part are automatically reflected in the embedded part. You're dealing with one part that has two synchronized views: a *window view* and an embedded *frame view.* OpenDoc allows any active part to be opened in its own window called a *part window.* A part window lets a part editor take a more active role. It owns an entire window in which it can display the part's contents.

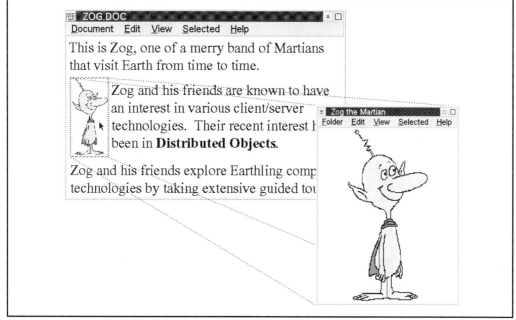

Figure 21-6. A Part Can Be Opened in its Own Window.

Controls

Controls in OpenDoc fulfill the same function as in regular applications. They provide graphic interface elements—including buttons, tool bars, entry fields, sliders, and so on—that allow a user to interact with a document. In an OpenDoc document, each part can have its own set of controls that appear and disappear as rapidly as the user activates parts. Finding space in which to display the controls may present quite a challenge. Controls can be created as independent parts or as content elements of a part. If a control is a separate part, its part editor handles events and can have attached scripts.

EVENT DISTRIBUTION AND ARBITRATION

Part editors interact with users by responding to *user events*. These events are typically sent or posted by the native operating system's event queue manager. User events include mouse clicks, keystrokes, menu commands, window activation, and others. Part editors respond to user events by redrawing their parts, transferring data, or performing menu-driven commands. Unlike traditional GUI applications, part editors do not directly receive events. So how does a user event get to the right part? It gets there via our old friend: the document shell.

The shell receives all user events from the operating system, handles most document-menu commands, and passes everything else "as is" to an object of type **ODDispatcher**. The dispatcher cooperates with an object of type **ODArbitrator** to distribute the event to the appropriate part or document. The arbitrator handles negotiations for shared resources among parts. It keeps track of what part owns what shared resource—including the selection focus, keyboard entries, the clipboard, and menus. Every part that wants to own a resource must go through the arbitrator.

The dispatcher takes "uncooked" OpenDoc events and maps them to the native event format of the target platform—that is, Windows, OS/2, and Macintosh event messages. After consulting with the arbitrator, the event dispatcher invokes *Draw* or *HandleEvent* on a target part. A containing part can set a flag in an embedded frame to receive events not handled by the embedding frame. Events that can't be handled by any of the frames are returned to the document shell.

Arbitration With Focus Sets

A part can become the target for a specific type of user event—other than mouse events—by obtaining the *focus* for that event type. A focus gives a part (or frame) ownership of a resource such as the keyboard; the part owns the resource until it decides to relinquish it. Foci may be manipulated singly or in groups called *focus sets*. Using an object of type **ODFocusSet**, parts can negotiate for a set of resources atomically; they either own an entire set of foci or none at all. After a part creates a focus set, it requests ownership of that set from the arbitrator via an atomic method invocation. This "all-or-nothing" proposition helps avoid deadlocks and makes parts thread-safe.

The arbitrator decides which part is to receive an event by consulting an object of class **ODFocusModule**. This arbitrator-owned object is used to store the owning frame (or part) for one or more foci or a list of owners of non-exclusive foci.

Mouse clicks are generally dispatched to the parts within which they occur, regardless of which part has the selection focus (or which part is currently active). The dispatcher finds the correct facet by traversing the facet hierarchy. It tries the most deeply embedded facets first.

Inside-Out Part Activation

OpenDoc allows multiple parts to concurrently work within the same document. For example, you could have clocks and ticker-tape parts within the same document concurrently updating their contents. To directly interact with a part, you must first make it *active* by clicking the mouse within its frame (more specifically, the facet's active shape). Activating a part makes it ready for editing. When one part is activated, another part is usually deactivated. The deactivated part is sent a request to relinquish its foci.

In most cases, the active part must request—from the arbitrator—ownership of a set of foci for the event types it will handle. The newly active part must then provide a menu bar, palettes, floating windows, cues, and other interface items that are part of its active state. These interface elements are in addition to those provided by the document menu. The active part typically shares the document menu and adjusts it to suit its needs.

OpenDoc uses an *inside-out* activation model that lets you activate with a single mouse click the smallest and most deeply embedded part at the location of the mouse. It's a form of in-place editing that lets you edit directly any visible part without first activating the parts that contain it (see Figure 21-7).

Figure 21-7. OpenDoc Inside-Out Part Activation.

An active part receives the *focus* for mouse, keyboard, and menu events. This means that you can edit its contents by interacting with the part editor. You can also directly interact with a part by *selecting* it with a mouse action. You can move, adjust, copy, cut, and size a *selected* part. Selected parts are manipulated as a frame by the containing part. In contrast, active parts are manipulated by their own part editor. Note that a selected part is also active. This means that you can also edit its contents as well as resize it or move it around. Figure 21-8 shows the visual differences between a part in its inactive, active, and selected states. Again, note that the part in the inactive state is not necessarily idle; it's concurrently multitasking.

Inactive   Active   Selected

Figure 21-8. OpenDoc's Graphic Cues for Inactive, Active, and Selected Parts.

Sharing Menus

To create a seamless application look, parts must learn how to share the document menu with other parts and with the document shell. The document shell handles the document-specific menu items such as open, save, and print document. The individual part editors typically handle the Edit menu. The items displayed in the Edit menu (and in the menu bar) vary with the currently active part.

To facilitate the sharing of the menu among parts and the document shell, OpenDoc provides an object of class **ODMenuBar**. This object represents a composite menu bar that consists of menu items from the shell and the active part. The OpenDoc menu bar object provides position independent identifiers for each menu item. The object encapsulation of the menu makes it easier for OpenDoc parts to share the menu among each other and with OLE 2.0 components. And, it makes it easier to write platform-independent menu handling code.

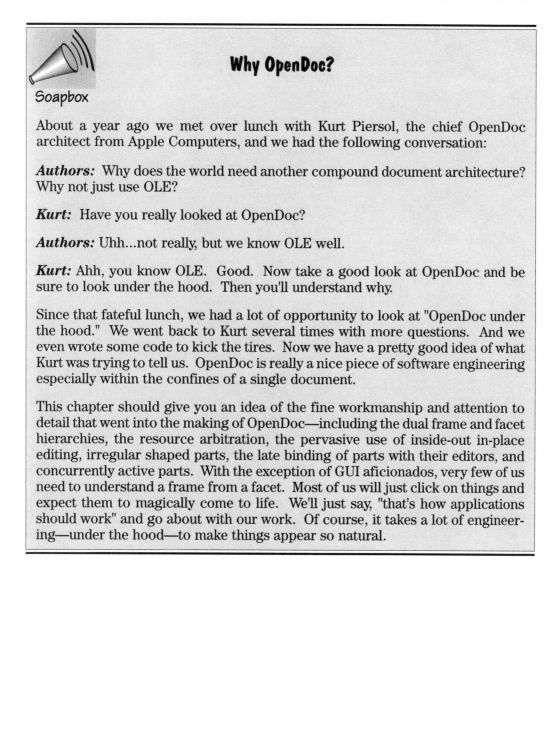

Why OpenDoc?

Soapbox

About a year ago we met over lunch with Kurt Piersol, the chief OpenDoc architect from Apple Computers, and we had the following conversation:

Authors: Why does the world need another compound document architecture? Why not just use OLE?

Kurt: Have you really looked at OpenDoc?

Authors: Uhh...not really, but we know OLE well.

Kurt: Ahh, you know OLE. Good. Now take a good look at OpenDoc and be sure to look under the hood. Then you'll understand why.

Since that fateful lunch, we had a lot of opportunity to look at "OpenDoc under the hood." We went back to Kurt several times with more questions. And we even wrote some code to kick the tires. Now we have a pretty good idea of what Kurt was trying to tell us. OpenDoc is really a nice piece of software engineering especially within the confines of a single document.

This chapter should give you an idea of the fine workmanship and attention to detail that went into the making of OpenDoc—including the dual frame and facet hierarchies, the resource arbitration, the pervasive use of inside-out in-place editing, irregular shaped parts, the late binding of parts with their editors, and concurrently active parts. With the exception of GUI aficionados, very few of us need to understand a frame from a facet. Most of us will just click on things and expect them to magically come to life. We'll just say, "that's how applications should work" and go about with our work. Of course, it takes a lot of engineering—under the hood—to make things appear so natural.

Chapter 22

OpenDoc:
Bento and
Storage
Units

An OpenDoc document can be used as an audio-enabled and animation-enabled slide show, or as a shared electronic blackboard with replicas coordinated by distributed objects, or even as an electronic voting ballot that tallies opinions as the document circulates.

— Jeff Rush
Dr. Dobb's Journal
(January, 1995)

As a container of components, compound documents are made up of wildly differing content elements such as text, images, tables, movies, sound clips, and so on. Often content is created by one application and included in documents created by other applications. Later, the content may be copied out of the document and stored in yet another document. Without standardized containers, developers must invent their own storage mechanisms for a variety of contents and work out private contracts on how they are used. These contracts can quickly become messy when documents move across networks and operating systems. This is where Bento comes into the picture.

Bento—OpenDoc's storage system—provides a persistent storage mechanism that lets multiple part editors share a single document file. Bento was designed to provide flexible storage; it allows new types of information to be defined without disrupting existing structures. Bento was also designed to handle the real-time requirements of multimedia so that sound and animation streams can be played back without interruptions. This multimedia-capable storage mechanism is implemented in a portable manner on top of the native file systems of each platform that OpenDoc supports.

Bento's self-describing storage units also provide the mechanisms for uniform data transfers across OpenDoc components. The same mechanisms and concepts are used consistently for document storage, clipboard transfers, drag-and-drop, and linking. Bento can be used to exchange data, parts, clusters of parts, and complete documents using OpenDoc's data transfer facilities. In addition, Bento provides structures for keeping track of information about parts and their storage relationships with each other. Finally, Bento itself is highly portable; it runs on existing file systems. In this chapter, we explore both Bento and storage units (see Figure 22-1). We cover Bento-based data transfers in the next chapter.

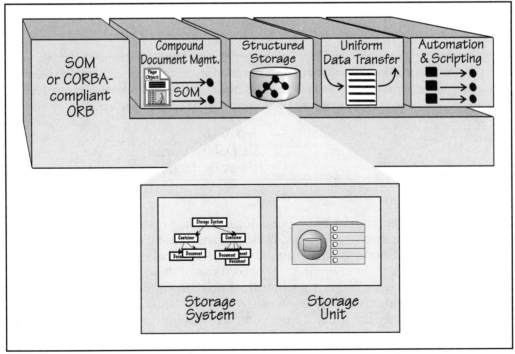

Figure 22-1. Bento: OpenDoc's Compound Storage.

THE BENTO STORAGE SYSTEM

Bento, an Apple contribution, is designed with the concept of a whole made up of distinct parts.

*— IDC, Computer Industry Report
(December, 1994)*

Bento is available in over 100 products, including Lotus 1-2-3. It provides a persistent storage mechanism that includes nested storage structures and a self-contained index, which keeps track of the part hierarchy. The storage structures reflect a user's logical construction of parts within a document. Bento provides a way for applications to exchange multiple content elements and to navigate through them. Bento objects can be as small as a few bytes or as large as 2^{64} bytes. They can be simple streams or complex structures. Bento *properties* let you keep information about objects—that is, "metadata." The content of the object is called its *value*. Bento lets you store multiple representations of the same content within each property.

Bento is not a true Object Database Management System (ODBMS). Instead, it manages both a system of structured files and references between data items. You can think of Bento as providing a file system within each file. Bento subdivides a file into a system of structured elements; each element can contain many data streams. This allows each part to have its own storage stream (see Figure 22-2). Because most existing applications use stream-based input/output, Bento is less intrusive than an ODBMS. Bento's file-based compartments of information are ideal for document (and part) interchanges across platforms. A workflow system could use Bento to ship active documents from one work location to the next.

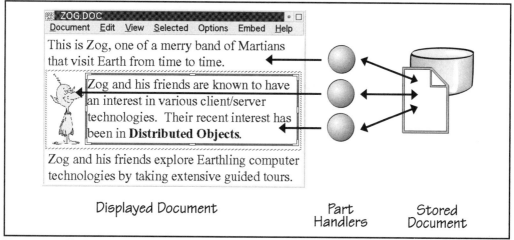

Figure 22-2. The Document as a Repository of Data Streams.

Bento, in its current incarnation, does not support multiuser concurrent access. However, its draft facility provides a built-in version control system. Drafts are created by users and maintained by the OpenDoc system. Only one user can edit a draft at a time, and only the most recent draft of a document can be edited. Associated with each draft is a set of *permissions* that specify the class of read-write access permitted. For example, a part editor cannot make changes to a draft that is read-only. Each draft object maintains a list of changes from its predecessor drafts. Drafts make it possible to do incremental updates to a document without recopying the entire document.

The Storage Containment Hierarchy

Figure 22-3 shows the hierarchy of objects that make up the OpenDoc storage system. The controlling object of class **ODStorageSystem** is responsible for instantiating and maintaining a list of *container* objects of class **ODContainer**. So what's a container? It's an object that can take on many forms—including an individual file, shared memory, or an interapplication message that contains objects. Containers are used for storing and exchanging objects. Each container object can hold one or more *document* objects of class **ODDocument**. Each document can hold one or more *draft* objects of class **ODDraft**. Finally, each draft object contains a number of *storage unit* objects of class **ODStorageUnit**.

The objects that are of most interest to OpenDoc users and programmers are documents, drafts, and storage units. A *document* object contains data for all its parts, their links, and information about frames and embedded data. *Drafts* are snapshots that represent the state of a document at a given point in time. There is always at least one draft within a document. With drafts, documents have a history that can be preserved and inspected; users decide when to create or delete a draft.

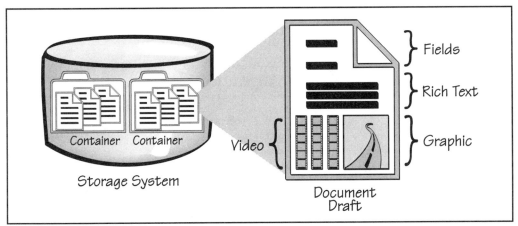

Figure 22-3. The OpenDoc Storage Hierarchy.

Drafts can have unique names and a specific set of properties—including the date they were created, the date they were last modified, and the user's name. Bento stores all drafts together in a single document file, with no redundantly stored data. Drafts provide a form of version control that let multiple users work on the same document. They can also be used for transaction control—you can always revert back to a previous draft.

OPENDOC STORAGE UNITS

A *storage unit* is where the part data lives. Storage units are the basic unit of persistent storage for a part. The **ODStorageUnit** class is an abstraction on top of Bento. OpenDoc does not expose the Bento APIs. A storage unit contains a list of *properties*; each property has a unique name within the storage unit. A property can have one or more *values*. Values can be raw byte streams or can have multiple data types. In theory, each value can contain a stream of almost unlimited length (up to 2^{64} bytes). Storage unit APIs provide random access to any point within the stream.

Properties With Multiple Values

Properties can have more than one value holding different representations of the same data. A property indicates the role of the value, not its data type. For example, a property called *my fax* could have three different types of values: *Postscript*, *plain text*, and *bitmap*. Another example is a block of text that could be created in both French and Italian and displayed to users in their language of choice. In yet another example, a property could have both encrypted and non-encrypted values. The encrypted version of the document could be shown selectively to users with the proper privileges.[1]

Just What Is a Storage Unit Anyway?

Figure 22-4 shows how storage units fit within the OpenDoc storage model. A Bento document consists of multiple drafts. Each draft contains multiple storage units; these units in turn contain properties and their values. Values can include *references* to other storage units. For example, you may want to store a reference to a movie instead of the real thing. Bento knows that this is a reference and transparently follows it to find the real movie.

---

[1] You could add a script to an encrypted document that authenticates a user and consults a capability server when a document is first opened.

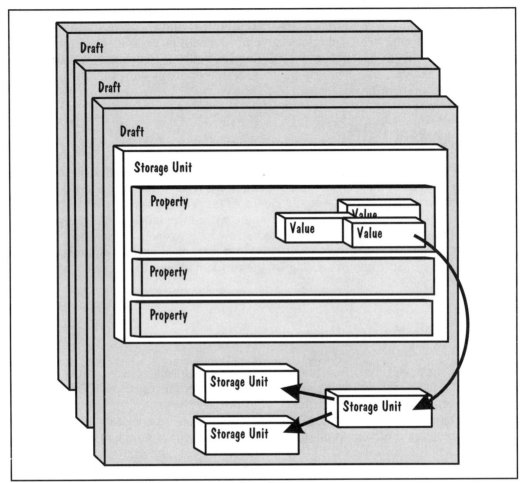

Figure 22-4. Where Storage Units Fit in the Bento Hierarchy.

In a sense, a storage unit is like a directory. Properties are like names of files, and values are byte streams. So, in essence, each OpenDoc part gets to manage its own file system within a file. Storage units can also reside in memory, on the clipboard, or as links—they are just different instances of the same class.

Navigating Through Storage Units

Storage units are *inspectable*, which means that you can selectively read in values—or data—of the various properties without having to read the entire file or part data. The **ODStorageUnit** object provides a *focus* method—not related to focus sets—to navigate within storage units and to find a specified part, property, or value. The storage unit object supports methods for creating, updating, reading, and deleting properties and their values (see next Details box). A part editor must first obtain an object reference for the storage unit object before invoking any of its methods. Once it has a reference to a storage unit, a part editor invokes the focus method to locate a particular property and value before reading or writing the data. We describe how these mechanisms work in the next sections.

Storage Units: An Inside Look

Details

A storage unit contains a list of properties and an ordered list of values. Objects of the class **ODStorageUnit** encapsulate a storage unit and provide methods to manipulate it. The factory for storage units is the document draft; a part editor calls *ODDraft::CreateStorage* to create a new storage unit. Storage units are reference counted objects derived from **ODRefCntObject**. The reference count is set to one when the storage unit is first created. It is incremented every time *ODDraft::GetStorageUnit* is called. And it is decremented when *ODStorage-Unit::Release* is called.

The **ODStorageUnit** class provides about 50 methods for manipulating the contents of storage units. It's a miniature database system. Figure 22-5 shows some of the most used methods. OpenDoc also provides a thread-safe version of this class called **ODStorageUnitView**. Finally, an **ODStorageUnitCursor** class provides thread-safe calls to all storage unit methods that would otherwise use the current focus.

A property/value combination is called a *focus*. The focus provides the context for many of the method invocations. Focusing can be absolute by passing a particular property name or value index, or relative by passing position codes. When the focus is on a particular value, the storage unit provides a stream interface to that value. A *current offset* maintains the displacement within the stream. The focus provides a navigational context that is preserved between method invocations until the focus is removed or a new focus is added.

If you frequently switch back and forth between property/value combinations, you may find it convenient to use *cursor* objects of class **ODStorageUnitCursor** to maintain focus contexts. You can create a number of cursor objects, initialize them with the storage-unit foci, and then pass them to the *ODStorage-Unit::Focus* method each time you need to switch the focus. Once you have focused the storage unit, you can read and write its data.

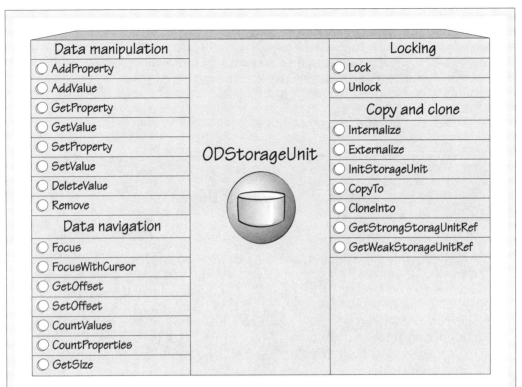

Figure 22-5. The OpenDoc ODStorageUnit Class: The Principal Methods.

To read or write data at a particular position in a value, call *SetOffset* to set the position in the value's stream. Then either call *SetValue* to write the data or *GetValue* to read it. To append data at the end of a value, call *GetSize* to get the size of the value. Then call *SetOffset* to set the insertion mark at the end of the stream and call *SetValue* to write the actual data. To delete data, call *SetOffset* to set the mark and then call *DeleteValue* to delete a block of data—of a specified length—from the stream. The *Remove* method is used to delete a property. ❑

Persistent References and Cloning

A *persistent reference* is a unique 32-bit number stored within a storage unit that points to another storage unit in the same document. OpenDoc uses these references to maintain relationships in its part hierarchy. For example, a frame maintains a persistent reference to its part. When a frame is read into memory, it can then find the part it displays. Parts maintain persistence references to all their embedded frames. Figure 22-6 shows the persistent references OpenDoc uses to maintain its document hierarchy. Notice that there are two kinds of persistent references: *strong* and *weak*. These references determine how an object is copied.

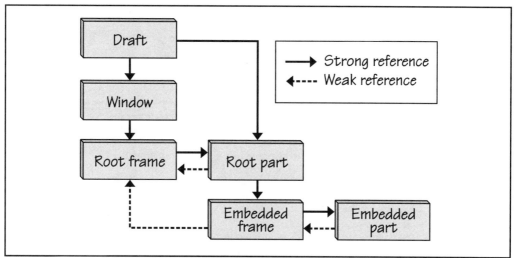

Figure 22-6. Persistent References in a Document.

To *clone* an object is to make a "deep copy" of the object. This means copying all the objects it strongly references, plus the objects that they reference, and so on. For example, if you were to clone the root part in Figure 22-6, all the embedded frames and parts are also copied. However, the root frame, window, and draft are not copied because the root part's references to them are weak. You can create strong or weak references by calling either *GetStrongStorageUnitRef* or the *GetWeakStorageUnitRef* methods of the storage unit object that holds the references.

Your part editor does not store the data of embedded parts. Their own editors take care of that. However, your part editor must store the frames of parts embedded within your part. A part editor does this by creating a strong persistent reference to the embedded frame object. OpenDoc automatically takes care of storing the frame itself.

In addition to maintaining links between the elements of a document, persistent references can be used to maintain links between content data stored in multiple storage units. Every part has a *kODPropContents* property whose values store the part's main content data. Using strong persistent links, you can create *auxiliary* storage units to store related content data. For example, each auxiliary unit can contain a separate movie.

The Persistent Elements

The OpenDoc document is a very flexible storage structure. It contains three types of information: chunks of data that "hang together"; metadata that describes the contents of the data; and references to other data. Bento defines the rules for storing this data, describing it, and finding it. Table 22-1 describes some of the typical data and metadata stored in an OpenDoc document.

Table 22-1. Contents of OpenDoc Persistent Elements.

Persistent Element	Stored Data, Metadata, and References
Draft	■ Draft name and number ■ Document name—the name of the draft's document ■ References to the root part and frame ■ Windows list—this includes all the windows that were open when the draft was written. It is used to recreate the document window and its adornments.
Part	■ Part kind ■ Part content—the actual content data for the part ■ Preferred editor—the ID of the editor that last wrote the part to persistent storage ■ Embedded frame references—pointers to all frames directly embedded in this part's frame ■ Scripts attached to this part ■ References to links and link sources in this part
Frame	■ Reference to the part displayed in this frame ■ Reference to the containing frame ■ Part info—data associated with the frame by the part editor ■ Frame shape—the boundary of the frame ■ Used shape—the area within the frame actually used ■ Internal transform—offset, scale, rotation of content within the frame ■ View type of part displayed in this frame—iconic, thumbnail, or framed
Link source	■ The content copied from the source of a link ■ Reference to the part that contains the link source ■ References to the link objects that depend on this link source
Link	■ The content to be copied to the destination of a link ■ References to the parts that contains the link destination

Standard Properties

OpenDoc specifies a set of standard properties that all part editors can recognize. This makes it easy to inspect the contents of storage units across parts, documents, and platforms. These standard properties create self-describing OpenDoc persistent elements—including documents, drafts, parts, frames, and windows. Depending on the persistent unit's state, properties can be read from either storage or memory.

A part must store its content data in the *kODPropContents* property of a storage unit; the property can contain one or more stream value representations of the data. The rest of the properties are for annotations and references, not content. Your part can also maintain persistent references to data in other storage units. Table 22-2 lists some of the more common standard properties.

Table 22-2. The More Common OpenDoc Standard Storage-Unit Properties.

Property	Description
kODPropContents	The primary content data for this storage unit
kODPropName	The name of the item (or part) stored in this storage unit
kODModDate	The date and time this storage unit was last modified
kODPropEmbeddedFrames	The frames embedded in this part
kODPropPartInfo	Part-specific information

A Day in the Life of a Storage Unit

The easiest way to understand the OpenDoc storage unit dynamics is to walk through a scenario that shows how to create a storage unit, initialize it from storage, read and write its data, and save its contents in persistent store. Figure 22-7 demonstrates how a part editor handles such a scenario:

1. *Initialize a storage unit when the part is first created*. OpenDoc invokes your part editor's *InitPart* method once in a part's lifetime—that is, when it is first created—and passes it an object reference to an empty storage unit. The empty storage unit was first created by **ODDraft**, which is its factory object.

2. *Add properties to the storage unit*. Your part editor invokes the *AddProperty* method of the storage unit object to add the required properties. At a minimum, it must add a contents property of type *kODPropContents* to the storage unit. The storage unit is now ready for business. It can read and write data. In this scenario, the document is now closed and the storage unit is stored for posterity.

3. *Later, initialize part from storage*. OpenDoc invokes your part editor's *InitPartFromStorage* method any time a storage unit within a document needs to be read into memory. One of the parameters passed in this method is a reference to a storage unit object.

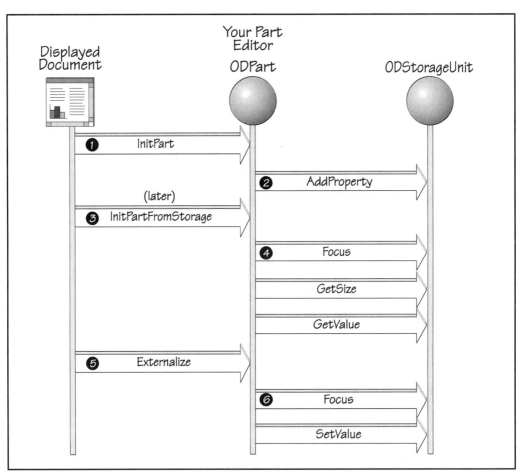

Figure 22-7. Scenario: A Day in the Life of a Storage Unit.

4. ***Read the part contents from storage***. In the simplest case, the part editor reads the contents of the storage unit object into memory by invoking three methods on that object: *Focus* to point to the start of the property value stream, *GetSize* to find out how much data needs to be read, and *GetValue* to copy the data into a memory buffer.

5. ***Externalize part to storage***. OpenDoc invokes your part editor's *externalize* method when it needs to write its in-memory contents to a persistent store. This usually happens when a user saves or closes a document.

6. ***Write the part contents to storage***. To find out if changes were made to the part's contents since the last save, the part editor invokes a *ChangedFromPrevious* method on **ODDraft**. If changes were made, the editor writes its contents to the storage unit object by first invoking *Focus* to point to the contents property and then *SetValue* to copy the data into the storage unit. The part editor should

also update the *kODModDate* property that keeps track of when the storage unit was last modified. If no changes were made, OpenDoc simply *releases* the part content from memory without writing it back to storage.

The storage unit is reactivated when the document is next opened or whenever OpenDoc needs a part's data in an opened document. When this happens, the previous scenario will replay itself starting with step 3.

CONCLUSION

This concludes the chapter on Bento and storage unit navigation objects. So what do you think of these self-describing files within files? We don't want to turn this conclusion into a soapbox but we do believe that these new compound document files systems—OpenDoc's Bento and OLE's compound files—offer tremendous opportunities for developers and system integrators. Just imagine all the good things you can do with files filled with self-describing data?

Of course, the story in this chapter is not about software opportunity, but rather about how OpenDoc provides storage for independently developed components. These components can not only share the same file but they can navigate directly to data associated with their parts and other related data. The beauty of Bento is that it is a natural container for components that need to be shipped across machines and platforms. This is another area of great opportunity especially for client/server developers.

Chapter 23

OpenDoc: Uniform Data Transfer

> For the PC to truly integrate with resources across the enterprise, it must first become proficient at integrating the many resources that reside on the desktop itself.
>
> — IDC
> Computer Industry Report
> (December, 1994)

OpenDoc's Bento-based uniform data transfers allow parts that know nothing of each other to exchange data, parts, and multiple parts. End users can orchestrate the data exchanges and use them to put any kind of media into a document. OpenDoc's three built-in data transfer mechanisms (see Figure 23-1) are:

- **Drag-and-drop** lets you directly manipulate data and parts being transferred without using an intermediary such as the clipboard. OpenDoc lets you drag-and-drop parts and data within the same document, across documents, between documents and desktops, and between documents and part palettes.

- **Clipboard** lets you transfer data and parts, just like drag-and-drop, using the familiar menu cut, copy, and paste commands.

■ *Linking* lets you copy data and parts, in the same way as drag-and-drop and the clipboard. However, unlike drag-and drop and clipboard, links are maintained between the source and destination parts. When the source data or part changes, the destination links are automatically refreshed to reflect these changes.

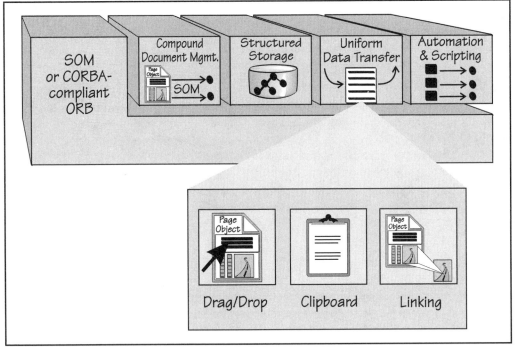

Figure 23-1. OpenDoc's Uniform Data Transfers.

At a superficial level, OpenDoc's data transfer mechanisms appear to be similar to those provided on native GUI platforms. However, OpenDoc has a lot more to offer. For starters, OpenDoc supports component interchanges as well as traditional data exchanges. When you copy a component—that is, a part—you're making a "deep copy" of the object, all the objects it strongly references, plus the objects that they reference, and so on. In addition, OpenDoc uses an intelligent form of drop or paste that can decide—subject to user override—whether to embed the data as a separate part or incorporate it as content data into the destination part. Parts can also support an *inclusion list* that specifies the part kinds that can be embedded within them. Finally, OpenDoc links can be used to refresh a local part with remote data.

OpenDoc provides a very consistent architecture for doing data transfers. All three mechanisms use storage units to carry data between source and destination parts. They all use the session object to create instances of data transfer objects. However, each mechanism requires a different class of data transfer object. If the transfer involves a large block of data, a source part can choose to issue a *promise* instead of actually writing the data to a storage unit. A promise says that the data will be supplied when a destination accepts the data. The destination part is not aware of the promise; it simply accepts data as usual. Promises can be very useful in situations where large data streams are moved around. For example, a promise can be used to make sure a destination will accept a 100 MByte movie before it is copied over. Both the clipboard and drag-and-drop can make promises.

DRAG-AND-DROP TRANSFERS

The OpenDoc drag-and-drop facility allows users to copy or move parts and data using direct manipulation. A user typically initiates a drag by first positioning the mouse pointer over some selected content and then pressing and holding down the mouse button. As the user moves the mouse pointer, an outline of the selected item is dragged to the new location. The user releases the mouse button and drops the item into a new location. Typically, OpenDoc will "drag-move" the item if it's dropped within the same document and "drag-copy" the item if it's dropped in a different document. There are also platform-specific mouse mechanisms for differentiating a drag-copy from a drag-move.

The scenario in Figure 23-2 demonstrates what happens under-the-cover when a user performs a drag-and-drop operation:

1. *Start the drag*. The user initiates the drag with a mouse-down event on the border of an embedded frame, or on a selected set of content elements within a part.

2. *OpenDoc sends a "begin-drag" event notification to the source part editor*. It does that by invoking the *HandleEvent* method on the source part editor and passing it a begin drag event.

3. *Obtain an ODDragAndDrop object*. The part editor asks the session object—remember, this is the object that creates instances of service classes—for an object of class **ODDragAndDrop**. It does this by invoking the *GetDragAndDrop* method of the session object.

4. *Get a storage unit to carry the data*. The part editor invokes the *Clear* method followed by the *GetContentStorageUnit* method on the drag-and-drop object to get an empty storage unit that will serve as a carrier for the transfer of data.

5. *Add properties to the carrier storage unit*. The part editor invokes the *AddProperty* method of the storage unit object to add the required properties. At a minimum, it must add a contents property of type *kODPropContents* to the storage unit.

6. ***Write the data to the carrier storage unit***. The part editor can copy its intrinsic contents into the carrier storage unit by invoking the *Focus* method to point to the contents property and then invoking *SetValue* to write the contents. The part editor can also clone any embedded parts by 1) invoking the draft's *BeginClone* method; 2) calling the embedded part's *CloneInto* method; and 3) calling the draft's *EndClone* method. Remember that embedded parts have their own storage units.

7. ***Start the drag***. The part editor invokes the *StartDrag* method on the drag-and-drop object. Now the control of the drag is passed to OpenDoc; it must deliver the data to the destination part. Note that the source part is still responsible for providing the user with an outline which provides drag feedback.

8. ***Track the drag***. The drag is in process while the user maintains the mouse button pressed and moves the part around. Any facet the dragged part passes over is a potential destination for a drop. OpenDoc will call a part's *DragEnter* method when the mouse pointer enters one of its facets. The potential destination part examines the dragged part's kind and displays feedback as to whether or not it will accept the dragged part. The part's frame typically contains a property that indicates if it can receive drops. OpenDoc invokes the part's *DragWithin* method continuously while the mouse is still within the facet. Finally, it calls the part's *DragLeave* method when the mouse pointer leaves the facet.

9. ***Drop the data or parts***. The user finally releases the mouse button and drops data or parts within a destination part's facet.

10. ***OpenDoc notifies the destination part editor***. It does this by invoking the *Drop* method on the destination part's editor and passing it a reference to the storage unit object that contains the drag data.

11. ***Read the contents of the dragged data or parts***. The destination part editor invokes the *Focus* and *GetValue* methods on the storage unit object to retrieve data. If the transferred data is of the same kind as that of the destination, it is embedded into the destination's intrinsic content. If the part kind is different (or if it contains an embedded frame), it is embedded as a separate part.

Note that the *Drop* method returns a value that indicates the success or failure of the operation. This value is then returned by *StartDrag* to the source part editor to indicate the success of the drag. If a drag-move is successful, the part editor can delete the source data contents. This concludes our drag-and-drop scenario. Drag-and-drop will never be the same after this. Next time you pick up the mouse to drag something think of all the poor little components that must work so hard to keep up with your mouse actions.

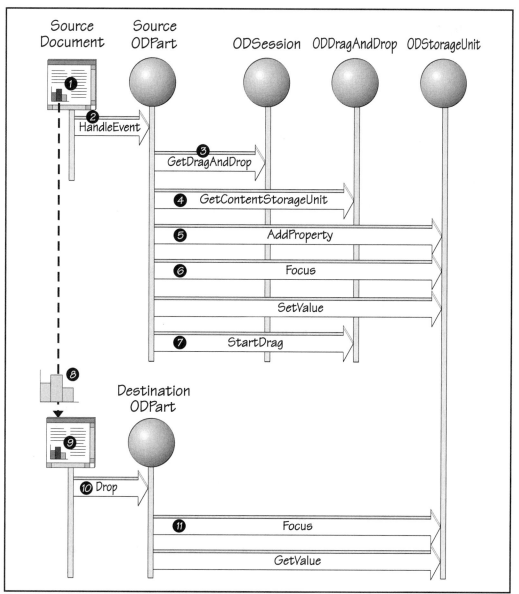

Figure 23-2. Scenario: Drag-and-Drop, OpenDoc Style.

CLIPBOARD TRANSFERS

In addition to drag-and-drop, OpenDoc lets you transfer data and parts using the clipboard's cut, copy, and paste menu commands. When a part places data on the clipboard, it can place intrinsic content data—like normal clipboard operations—

or it can place entire parts. You typically select a part or content data from a source document, select *cut* or *copy* from the edit menu, activate a part in the target document, and then perform a *paste* or *paste as* from the edit menu.

The scenario in Figure 23-3 demonstrates what happens "under the cover" when you do a cut-copy-paste via the clipboard:

1. **Activate the source part**. As part of being activated by a user selection, a part editor acquires a focus set of resources that includes the menu bar.

2. **Perform a cut or a copy.** The user selects the content in the active part and then does a cut or copy via the edit menu.

3. **OpenDoc sends a "menu command" notification to the source part editor.** It does this by invoking the *HandleEvent* method on the source part editor and passes it a menu command that includes the menu item ID for a cut or copy.

4. **Obtain an ODClipboard object**. The part editor asks the session object for an object of class **ODClipboard**. It does this by invoking the *GetClipboard* method of the session object.

5. **Get a storage unit to carry the data**. The part editor invokes the *Clear* method, followed by the *GetContentStorageUnit* method on the clipboard object, to get an empty storage unit that will serve as a carrier for the transfer of data.

6. **Add properties to the carrier storage unit**. The part editor invokes the *AddProperty* method of the storage unit object to add the required properties. At a minimum, it must add a contents property of type *kODPropContents* to the storage unit.

7. **Write the data to the carrier storage unit**. The part editor can copy its intrinsic contents into the carrier storage unit by invoking the *Focus* method to point to the contents property and then invoking *SetValue* to write the contents. The part editor can also clone any embedded parts by 1) invoking the draft's *BeginClone* method; 2) calling the embedded part's *CloneInto* method, and 3) calling the draft's *EndClone* method.

8. **Activate the destination part**. As part of being deactivated, the source part relinquishes its focus set. This allows the newly activated destination part editor to acquire a focus set of resources that include the menu bar.

9. **Perform the paste**. The user selects a destination area within the target part and performs a paste command from the edit menu.

10. **OpenDoc sends a "menu command" event notification to the destination part editor.** It does this by invoking the *HandleEvent* method on the destina-

tion part editor and passes it a menu command that includes the menu item ID for a Paste or Paste As.

11. ***Read the contents of the clipboard***. The destination part editor invokes the *Focus* and *GetValue* methods on the storage unit object to retrieve data. If the transferred data is of the same kind as of the destination, it is embedded into the destination's intrinsic content. If the part kind is different or if it contains an embedded frame, it is embedded as a separate part.

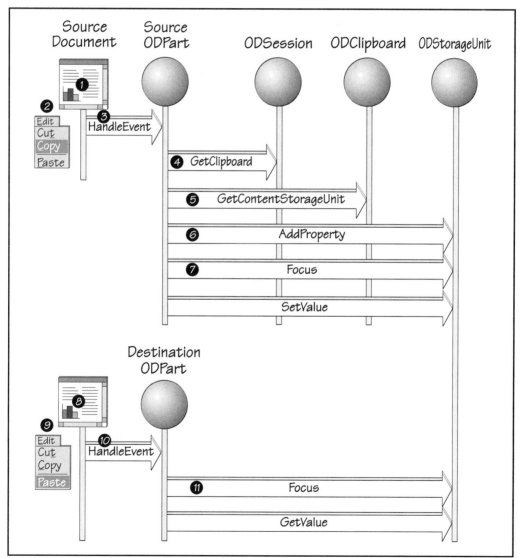

Figure 23-3. Scenario: Clipboard Transfers, OpenDoc Style.

LINKED DATA TRANSFERS

Linking is a "publish-and-subscribe" mechanism that allows information in one or more *subscriber* parts to be updated based on changes in the source information, which is the *publisher*. Unlike drag-and-drop and the clipboard, linking provides a one-to-many broadcast mechanism with automatic refresh. OpenDoc's linking mechanism uses the same data transfer mechanisms as drag-and-drop and the clipboard, but it also includes notification events for keeping the destination data synchronized with its source. OpenDoc's linking is an extension of Apple's long-standing publish-and-subscribe model.

OpenDoc's Link-Related Objects

Figure 23-4 shows OpenDoc's link-related objects. The source part must create an object of class **ODLinkSource** that contains a copy of the source data the part publishes. The link source object is stored in a shared directory so that subscribers can get to its data even if the source part is not running. In addition to a copy of the data, the link source object maintains persistent links to all the destination parts that subscribe to the source content.

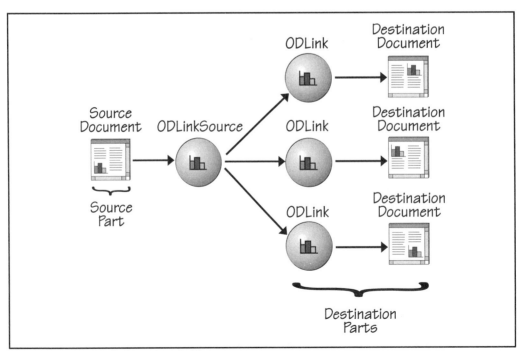

Figure 23-4. OpenDoc Linking: Meet the Players.

On the destination side, an object of class **ODLink** is created to maintain copies of the linked data for the subscriber objects within a document. In a given document, there is only one link object associated with each link source, even if the source is linked to multiple destination parts within that document.

When a change occurs in the source part, the updated contents are copied into the link source object. The link source then copies the data into the destination links in the documents of its subscriber parts. When the sources of their links change, OpenDoc informs destination parts—either automatically or whenever instructed to do so by the user. The user makes that choice, via a dialog box, when the link is created as part of a drag-and-drop or clipboard operation (see Figure 23-5).

To receive automatic update notifications, the destination part calls the link object's *RegisterDependent* method; each link object maintains a registry of dependent parts. Whenever the source part changes, the link object invokes the *LinkUpdated* method on the part editors that have registered for automatic notifications. Each destination part then copies the updated contents from the link object into the destination part itself. A single copy of the data is maintained if the source and destination parts are within the same document.

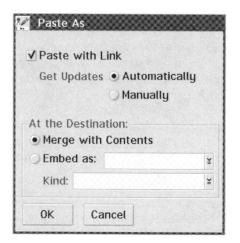

Figure 23-5. The Paste As Dialog Box.

Cross-document and networked links are transparently handled by objects of the **ODLinkManager** class. There is one link manager object per document. This manager is created by the session object and is never directly used by the part editors. The **ODLinkSource** and **ODLink** objects deal directly with their respective link manager objects to establish cross-document links.

Advertising a Link

A source part advertises its ability to create a link by writing a *link specification* within the transfer storage unit of a drag-and-drop or clipboard object. It does this in addition to copying the data. The part editor that receives the copied data sees the link specification property and displays the "Paste As" dialog shown in Figure 23-5. The dialog lets users choose whether or not they want a permanent link to the source data.

If a user chooses to create a link, the destination part editor invokes the document draft's *GetLink* method to obtain an object of class **ODLink**. The link object learns what part kinds are available by inspecting the storage unit's properties. The draft also calls the *CreateLink* method of the source part editor, which is the part that placed the data in the clipboard or drag-and-drop object. If a link source object does not exist, the source part editor requests one by calling the document draft's *CreateLinkSource* method. The source part editor must write its part-specific data into the link source by cloning or via *SetValue* invocations.

Scenario: Data Interchange Via Links

The scenario in Figure 23-6 shows what happens when a source part updates its contents. We assume that an automatic link was previously created between the source and destination parts. Here are the steps two parts must follow to exchange data using a link:

1. ***User modifies the source part's contents***. The content of a part changes in response to some event. For example, the user edits the part's contents. As a result, the part editor reads the *link status* property in the frame and discovers that the part's data is the source of a link.

2. ***Obtain a new change ID***. Each piece of linked content has a *change ID* associated with it. Because the contents of the part were changed, the source part editor must update the change ID associated with the link. It does that by invoking the *UniqueChangeID* method on the session object. The session returns an identifier that's unique to this session and unlikely to be repeated on the network. The source part editor is responsible for assigning this new change ID to all link sources affected by this change. Note that the destination part stores the change ID of the link that was current at the time the destination link was last updated.

3. ***Lock the link source object***. Before the source part editor can update a link source's contents, it must first obtain a lock to that storage unit by calling the link source object's *Lock* method. A lock is required because both the source

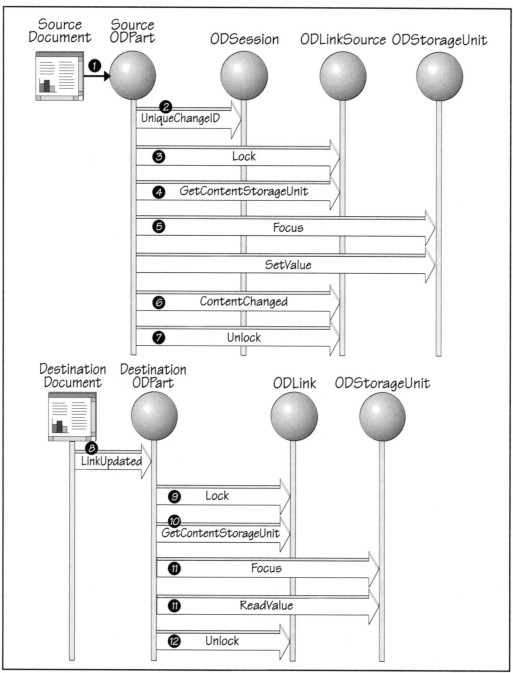

Figure 23-6. Scenario: Data Interchange via a Link Update.

and destination parts, or perhaps more than one separate destination, may attempt to access the linked data simultaneously.

4. ***Obtain an object reference to the link source's storage unit***. The source part editor does that by invoking the method *GetContentStorageUnit* on the link source object.

5. ***Update the link source's content data***. The source part editor either clones its part data or selectively writes it via *Focus* and *SetValue* method invocations.

6. ***Tell the link source that its contents were changed***. The source part editor invokes the link source's *ContentChanged* method and passes it the new change ID. The link source will send update notifications to all its linked destinations.

7. ***Unlock the link source object***. The source part editor invokes the *Unlock* method to release its lock on the link source's storage unit.

8. ***OpenDoc calls the destination part editor***. Because the destination part subscribed to automatic updates, it will be notified via a *LinkUpdated* method call that the link source contents changed.

9. ***Lock the link object***. The destination part editor calls the link object's *Lock* method to obtain a lock on its contents.

10. ***Obtain an object reference to the link's storage unit***. The destination part editor does this by invoking the method *GetContentStorageUnit* on the link object.

11. ***Replace the destination part's content data***. The destination part editor either clones the data from the link's storage unit into its own storage unit or copies it selectively via *Focus* and *ReadValue* method invocations.

12. ***Unlock the link object***. The destination part editor invokes the *Unlock* method to release its lock on the link's storage unit.

CONCLUSION

This concludes our chapter on OpenDoc's data transfer mechanisms. As you can see, OpenDoc uses the same consistent design pattern—the storage unit object—to transfer data, parts, and embedded parts using a variety of familiar desktop protocols—including drag-and-drop, the clipboard, and linking. This new protocol-independent pattern for consistently moving data and objects is light years ahead of the old ad-hoc protocols we used to move data between applications on regular desktops.

Chapter 24

OpenDoc: Automation and Semantic Events

OpenDoc scripting allows users to collaborate across space and time by explicitly writing scripts or by recording their actions and converting them into scripts.

— Jeff Rush
Dr. Dobb's Journal
(January, 1995)

It almost goes without saying that automation freaks—including scripters of all shades, power users, system integrators, and IS shops—will want to do more with parts and containers than just visual assembly. Yes, somebody will always create a "magic pushbutton" that sets into motion a complicated set of interpart commands. So how is scripting done across parts that don't know anything about each other? In OpenDoc, it is done through the *Open Scripting Architecture (OSA)*. OSA is an enabling technology for a new programming paradigm that views applications as collections of component parts. These parts can be tied together via scripts written in a variety of scripting languages.

OSA defines how containers and parts communicate with each other using an event registry, which contains lists of commands—or verbs—that evoke responses from parts. OpenDoc lets you transparently script any part within a container. In addition, a single line of script can span across multiple part boundaries. OpenDoc works with any scripting language that supports OSA. Figure 24-1 shows the three elements that provide OpenDoc's automation and scripting services: extensions, semantic events, and open scripting.

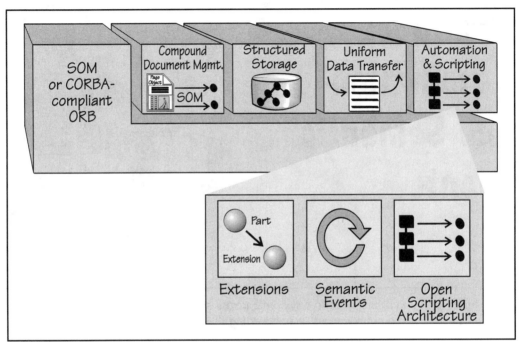

Figure 24-1. OpenDoc's Automation Services.

OpenDoc *extensions* are used by part editors to create and advertise add-on services. Clients can dynamically query server parts for the extensions they support. Extensions make it possible for programmers to create *suites* of parts that work together at an application semantic level. For example, a word processor suite could implement extensions to provide spelling checkers. A travel agency suite could implement extensions to define client/server protocols for flight schedules and hotel reservations.

Semantic events are used to manipulate a part's content model. They are similar to the user interface events—covered in Chapter 22—except that they carry messages that are meaningful to an application. Semantic events provide the basis for OpenDoc's unique *content-centric* form of scripting. With semantic events, users can act not only on parts but also on content objects within parts. Semantic events are the means by which scripting systems manipulate the contents of a scriptable part. For a part to be scriptable, its part editor must surface the list of operations on its content objects that can be invoked via semantic events.

Open scripting provides the third element of the OSA model. To support OSA, a scripting language must be able to translate human-readable scripts into semantic events. This lets a power user create scripts that fire semantic events, which result in collaborations among parts. In addition, the scripting systems must provide an OSA-defined generic interface that lets OpenDoc parts manipulate scripts, record them, and attach them to events.

A part editor can provide several levels of scripting support—including scriptability, tinkerability, and recordability. Scripts can be attached to your parts and used to fire semantic events across part boundaries. You could, for example, implement a push-button control as an OpenDoc part and have its script fire a semantic event to another part when a user presses the button.

THE BRAVE NEW WORLD OF OPENDOC SCRIPTING

The future belongs to scripting.

> — Michael Tiemann, President of Cygnus
> (February, 1995)

OSA makes it possible to design new kinds of *agent* applications that always operate in the background and can only be controlled through scripts. For example, an agent program could log on to a CORBA ORB, subscribe to a variety of services using the CORBA event service, filter the incoming events, and store them in a local database. Agents of this type do not need to provide a user interface; they are invisible. At most, they hook into the OpenDoc property editor, which allows a user to change a script or set a property.

New Age Scripting

Scripts are programs executed by interpreters. So why is there renewed interest in scripting? Haven't scripting languages and interpreters been with us since the dawn of computing? Yes, but scripts—when combined with components—are pure dynamite. They let you assemble flexible component combinations in record time. Scripts provide 10x productivity improvements over compiled languages. They allow non-programmers to automate all sorts of tasks.

Scripting provides the basis for agent technology. Agents, especially mobile ones, like to be self-sufficient. The better agents take their run-time environments with them wherever they go. Agent technology is built on scripting because the interpreters that run the scripts provide the illusion of a virtual machine. Scripts—

with the proper support environment—let you code an agent's behavior, ship it to any machine on the network, and execute it.

Using scripts, power users and IS shops can drive individual components or component ensembles across networks and operating systems. Scripts can also be used to extend an individual component's behavior. In the remainder of this section, we cover three new areas of script-based intercomponent collaborations: *roaming agents*, *disposable applications*, and *client/server suites*. OpenDoc scripts can be very effectively used in all three environments.

Roaming Agents

Agents mediate between processes and resources, which may appear, change, move and disappear anywhere within the distributed enterprise environment. Agents also are processes and resources, and they come and go just like the things they mediate.

> — *Robert Vasaly, President*
> *Peer Systems*
> *(March, 1995)*

Scripting technology provides the basis for *roaming agents*. These are interpreted programs that carry their own environment (and state) with them. Roaming agents can execute on any machine in which they happen to land. OpenDoc documents are almost the perfect carriers for these roaming agents. This is because an OpenDoc document can store—in addition to part data—scripts that can be associated with the various parts or with the entire document. In the world of OpenDoc, a roaming agent is a document with its data and scripts.

You can use scripts to create some very smart *roaming documents*. For example, a logon script can be fired every time you open a document. The script can ask a user for a password that it authenticates with a security server on a CORBA ORB. It can also obtain the access control list for that user from the security server. Then, the script can use the list to selectively unlock a set of parts in a document that the user can access. The rest of the parts can remain encrypted—OpenDoc lets you selectively encrypt individual parts in a document (also see the next Soapbox).

The logon script can also increment a counter that keeps track of how many times a document was opened. If you like, it can keep track of who used the document and for how long, and then send them a bill. It can also send you a notification every time the document is opened by a user.

The OpenDoc document can provide interfaces—via part editors—for agents to interact with users. With the help of a smart table of contents, a script can take the user directly to the parts that are of interest. Because OpenDoc supports multiple representations of the same property, a document can be displayed in French, English, or Italian, depending on a user's profile.

After the document is opened, scripts attached to parts can operate on the document contents and fire transactions against remote servers or local parts. Scripts can directly operate on a part's contents via semantic events. Upon closing a document, you can fire a script that queries a workflow server on the ORB for the next destination. If the document is routed to a supervisor's PC, a script can be used to highlight each change that was made. You can use part-annotated voice clips to verbally justify each change. The supervisor can either accept the changes or rollback the document to a previous draft's state.

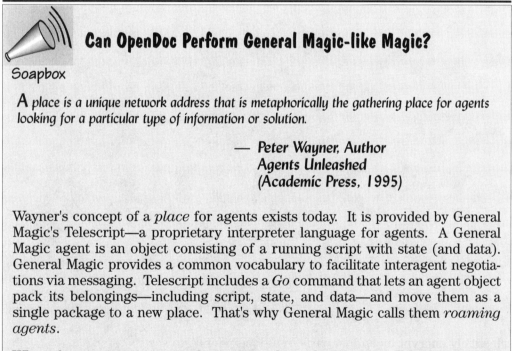

Can OpenDoc Perform General Magic-like Magic?

Soapbox

A *place is a unique network address that is metaphorically the gathering place for agents looking for a particular type of information or solution.*

> — *Peter Wayner, Author*
> *Agents Unleashed*
> *(Academic Press, 1995)*

Wayner's concept of a *place* for agents exists today. It is provided by General Magic's Telescript—a proprietary interpreter language for agents. A General Magic agent is an object consisting of a running script with state (and data). General Magic provides a common vocabulary to facilitate interagent negotiations via messaging. Telescript includes a *Go* command that lets an agent object pack its belongings—including script, state, and data—and move them as a single package to a new place. That's why General Magic calls them *roaming agents*.

When the agent arrives at a destination place, the receiving Telescript engine sets up the package as a local process that starts executing where it last stopped. General Magic provides many safeguards to ensure that the arriving agent can be trusted. The last thing you want is strange code visiting your machine without the proper safeguards. An *entering* method is executed every time a new object appears within a place. This method is typically used to authenticate an object. Each agent has an encrypted electronic signature—an identity that can be authenticated via public keys. In addition, each incoming agent can access only the objects that are within its script. It cannot directly write to memory or disk, which is how many viruses do their damage.

Because General Magic is a closed standard with a limited development environment, it would be tempting to recreate its magic using OpenDoc. There are two compelling reasons for doing this: OpenDoc can be freely distributed, and it's open. So, can OpenDoc perform agent magic? The answer must be an unqualified yes—after all, we're in the middle of a Soapbox on this topic. We already explained how OpenDoc's Bento can be used to package agents consisting of one or more parts and their associated scripts. This makes Bento an excellent container for roaming agent objects. But how does OpenDoc achieve the very granular levels of control associated with General Magic's places and agents?

OpenDoc Roaming Agents

We can create places for roaming agents using standard OpenDoc features. In this Soapbox, we assume that an OpenDoc roaming agent consists of a Bento container with a part, its associated script, and one or more part properties that maintain state persistently. You can move the Bento container across networks using CORBA's life cycle service. When it arrives at a destination machine, the part within the Bento container can be moved—using an automated "drag and move" script—into an open document that represents a "safe" place. Before a part is accepted into that safe document, it must be authenticated with a security server on the CORBA network. If everything is OK, our roaming agent will have found a new home within a local OpenDoc document.

Can You Trust Your OpenDoc Agent?

We already saw how OpenDoc can protect a part against a malicious user using scripts. So how does a workstation protect itself from a malicious OpenDoc document? The real question is: Can OpenDoc restrict the actions of a not *fully* trusted agent? OpenDoc has more than one way of doing this. First, it can cripple an unprotected interpreter by limiting its visible vocabulary of semantic events. Second, it can intercept semantic events issued from the unprotected agent's script and redirect them to a firewall where they're sanitized. Third, it can trigger a script that enforces a security policy whenever the unprotected interpreter (or part) fires a dangerous semantic event. Fourth, it can authenticate each semantic message from that interpreter. Finally, it can restrict content data access using the ORB's data-access security mechanisms. In contrast, General Magic is not ORB-aware, so it has to reinvent many of the standard services for distributed objects. ❑

Disposable Applications

Intelligent agents will eventually use scripts to assemble "disposable" applications created by wiring together parts via scripts. For example, an agent may use a script to open an OpenDoc container part, populate it with visual parts that know how to ask questions, and then ship it across a network to collect information on a topic. When the containers return with the information, the agent can tally the results and display them graphically. It can then e-mail to subscribers a perfectly formatted document that displays the results.

Is this the stuff of science fiction? Hardly. Every action you perform on OpenDoc parts can be automatically recorded in a script. This makes it easy for agents to learn "by example" how to mimic your actions. All they must do is turn on the semantic event recorder and capture all your subsequent actions in scripts. Soon, we expect to see "teach-your-agent" programs built on top of OpenDoc's script recording facilities. These programs will use recordable scripts to capture the bulk of your work. They will then ask you a few questions to create a top-level agent script that orchestrates the workflow and defines criteria for completing the different tasks. You can then set your agents loose so that they can go out and do whatever you want them to do.

Client/Server Component Suites

Increasingly, scripts will become the predominant paradigm for orchestrating inter-component collaborations on both the client and the server and between client and server parts. Most server components will be designed for scriptability. Servers will use scripting extensions to expose a set of actions and attributes that clients and system administrators can dynamically invoke, configure, and modify at run time.

OpenDoc's semantic events were designed to be distributed across documents, networks, and operating systems. They can be used to create very flexible client/server systems. Because a semantic extension can be supported by both client and server parts, you can drive server parts via client scripts and vice versa. It's also possible for system integrators, IS shops, and testers to write disposable client/server applications that can be driven by a single script (see Figure 24-2). The script generates semantic events that drive ORB-based components on both sides of the client and server equation.

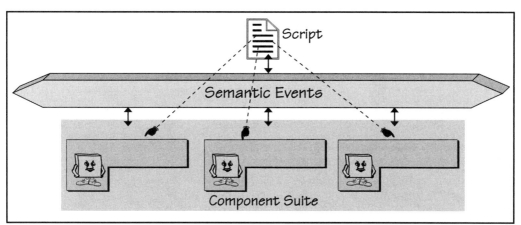

Figure 24-2. Scripts: Driving Client/Server Component Suites With Semantic Events.

THE OPENDOC EXTENSION MECHANISM

Because OpenDoc is a compound document framework, it is primarily concerned with mediating geometric relationships among parts, distributing events, and creating shared file structures. The direct communication among parts for purposes other than frame real estate negotiations or for linking and data transfers is beyond the basic function of OpenDoc. If parts need to collaborate, share information, or manipulate each other's contents they will need OpenDoc's *extension* mechanism. Extensions provide an elegant approach for adding groups of related interfaces to parts. They also provide the mechanism for parts to dynamically negotiate a protocol.

Why Are Extensions Needed?

The OpenDoc extension mechanism is used to develop "suites" of collaborating parts. The idea is for a part editor to create associated extension objects that implement the additional interfaces. For example, a part can belong to a database extension or a dental office extension. All the parts that belong to the database extension will share some common semantics and protocols that are provided through OpenDoc extensions (registered with CI Labs).

The common semantics may include common data structures defined in Bento containers. The protocols are typically implemented through predefined semantic events. OpenDoc parts must be able to respond to questions like: Which extensions do you support? Can you do database? Can you do dental office? OLE provides a similar function with the **IUnknown** interface *QueryInterface* method. Taligent

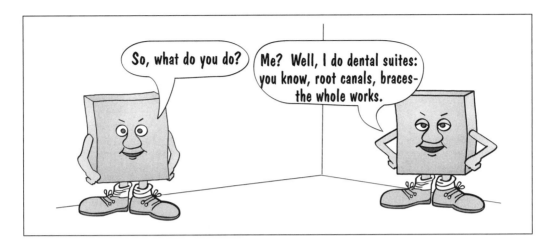

achieves suite-like collaborations by providing common ancestor classes that serve as "common DNA." Taligent components inherit their common protocols and semantics from their common ancestor classes. So with Taligent you get high semantic function right out of the box via common base classes—at the expense of tighter coupling.

In all cases, suite-like components will form the basis for collaborative desktops consisting of intelligent parts that act like horizontal suites or client/server vertical suites. At a desktop level, the suites will look like visual places in which people and things reside. For example, you should be able to purchase a desktop suite that resembles a small office with visual cabinets, fax machines, telephones, and so on. We can think of vertical places for almost every profession or activity. In addition, these places can play very well in the home.

How Extensions Work

The extension interfaces allow parts to increase their capabilities by extending their programming interfaces. At run time, your part editor registers extensions with OpenDoc to make them available to the outside world. The extension can be either private to your parts or public by standardizing it via CI Labs. The extension itself is an object of class **ODExtension** known to its part editor by an extension *category name*. An example is a "word-processor" extension.

Extensible part editors create and delete their own extension objects. They also manage their storage. The scenario in Figure 24-3 shows what a client must do to access a part's extension interface:

1. *Find out if the part editor supports the extension.* You do this by calling the part editor's *HasExtension* method, passing it an extension category name. All OpenDoc part editors inherit this method from their ancestor class **ODObject**.

2. *Obtain a reference to the extension object.* If the part editor supports the extension, the client calls the part's inherited *GetExtension* method to get a reference to it. The part editor either creates the extension object or increments the reference count if the object already exists. In both cases, an object reference is returned to the client. The part editor must call a newly created extension object's *InitExtension* method to prepare it for use.

3. *Invoke the extension object's methods.* The client directly calls the extension object's methods.

4. *Release the extension object.* When the client no longer needs the services of the extension object, it calls the object's *Release* method to relinquish it.

5. *Tell the part editor to release the object.* The extension object does this by calling the part editor's inherited *ReleaseExtension* method. The part editor either deletes the extension object immediately to recover memory or decrements the extension's reference count by one.

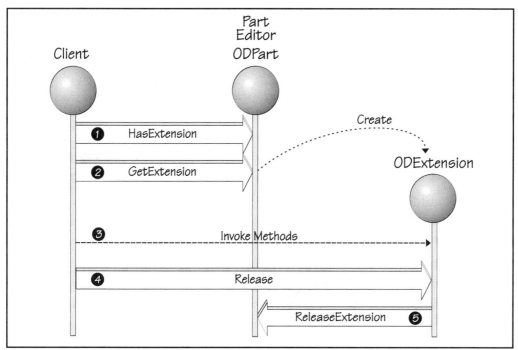

Figure 24-3. Scenario: How Clients Interact With a Part's Extensions.

SEMANTIC EVENTS

Components should communicate with each other as linguistic equals, sharing data where necessary and yielding application control to the peer that requires data for manipulation at a particular moment in time.

— Meta Group
(December, 1994)

OpenDoc supports two kinds of events: *user events* (like mouse clicks, keyboard entry, and so on) and *semantic events* that represent higher-level actions at the application level. A semantic event can also represent actions such as opening and closing documents, embedding parts, and menu commands. Most semantic events, however, are used to manipulate the contents of a part. Semantic events provide a late-binding interface to manipulate the contents of a part. They were designed to work in a world of parts.

What's a Semantic Event?

In contrast to method invocations, semantic events—also known as *OSA events* or *Apple Events*—provide a form of messaging that parts can use to dynamically request services and information from each other. A client initiates the semantic event; a server executes it. The client and server parts can reside in the same computer or on remote computers connected via a network. A part can also send semantic events to itself, thus acting as both client and server.

Semantic messages use a common vocabulary of requestable actions grouped in suites of related events. Event actions are the verbs in this vocabulary. The semantic message contains an *object specifier* that describes the target (or recipient) of the action; object specifiers are the noun phrases in this vocabulary. In addition, semantic events can have attributes and parameters. The parameters are either optional or required, and they can use either standard or private data types.

A vocabulary of publicly available semantic event *suites* is published in the *OSA Event Registry* maintained by CI Labs. Examples of suites are the Text Suite for word processors, the Database Suite, and the Core Suite. Semantic events are identified by the suite (or class) they belong to and by an event ID that uniquely identifies them within that suite. A part can support event subsets of one or more suites by collecting the individual event definitions in a placeholder suite. Placeholders use wildcards for their suite ID.

An Example

Figure 24-4 shows what happens when a standard OSA *Set Data* semantic event is sent to a part named "Summary of Sales" in the document "Sales Chart." In the example, the event also includes parameters, which are the pie-chart data. Open-Doc was able to locate the exact object reference for the "Summary of Sales" part and pass it the semantic event. OpenDoc provides the appropriate mechanisms for resolving an object specifier to the target object.

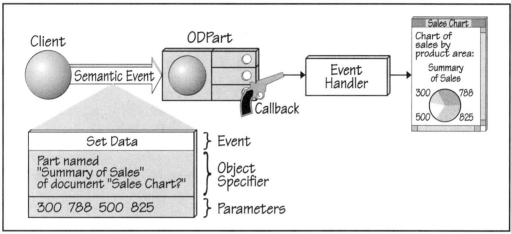

Figure 24-4. A Set Data Semantic Event.

A part should avoid defining new semantic events unless absolutely necessary. For example, you should use the generic *Get Data* semantic event instead of defining a new custom *Find* event. You can get a lot mileage out of a few predefined generic events because of polymorphism. These events behave differently depending on the part that receives them. For example, *Get Data* returns very different results when sent to a database part instead of to a movie part. It helps that parameters in semantic events can be defined as optional.

Object Specifiers Unleashed

OSA's naming scheme called object specifiers lets users treat their documents as if they were one giant object database that they can query in a natural way. The result is quite striking. Users can refer to objects, saying things like "delete seconds 5 through 30 of the first movie of paragraph 3 of my document."

— *Kurt Piersol, OpenDoc Chief Architect*
Apple Computers

Specifiers are application-specific constructs OpenDoc uses to determine the content object for the event. The specifier describes an object within a context without specifying a concrete object reference. An OpenDoc object of the class **ODNameResolver** resolves specifiers into specific objects on which the event can operate.

Object specifiers provide an extremely versatile way to describe visual objects. In many ways, they provide a higher level object model on top of the CORBA/OpenDoc object model. The model lets you specify, using ordinary terminology, objects that are consistent with the visual elements a user sees and manipulates in a compound document. For example, object specifiers can refer to lines, words, paragraphs, embedded parts, pictures, and cells within a spreadsheet. More precisely, the object specifier model provides a way to describe a hierarchical arrangement of *content objects* whose exact nature depends on the part's contents.

An object specifier can refer to any of the following target objects: an application, a document, a part within a document, a part embedded within a part, or some content element within a part. Two examples of content elements are individual rows within a table or a cell within a spreadsheet. Embedded parts are a special case of content objects. The containing part can use content operations to manipulate the frames of embedded parts, but it cannot manipulate their contents— only the parts themselves can do that.

How Semantic Events Work

Parts can send semantic events to their containing parts, to embedded parts, to linked parts, and to sibling parts. Semantic events are architected for interpart messaging across documents and across networks. Conceptually, a scripting language could send remote semantic events by providing a syntax such as *object-specifier [at internet-address]*. Examples of such scripts are: *Set to bold paragraph 3 of document 'your Doc' at orfali@ibm.com*. The presence of the optional internet address indicates that the event is to be sent on a network.

To be scriptable, a part must be able to at least receive semantic events, execute them, and reply to them; it doesn't have to send them. The OpenDoc runtime accepts the events and passes them to the correct part editor. OpenDoc uses the following objects to send, route, and dispatch semantic events:

■ **ODNameResolver** is used by the semantic message interface object to convert an object specifier to a *token* that identifies the target part and its content object (or a property of the part).

■ **ODSemanticInterface** is used by name resolver and the semantic message interface objects to help unravel part-specific object specifier information. It is derived from the **ODExtension** class. Each scriptable part must create its own semantic interface object. The object serves as a repository for the part's semantic vocabulary, including the verbs and nouns it understands. The semantic interface object also contains tables of callback functions that are used to decipher the vocabulary and execute the semantic events a part responds to. The table also points to functions that provide data *coercion*, which means they perform automatic type conversions. If there is a mismatched data type in the message, the receiver makes it right.

■ **ODDispatcher** is responsible for dispatching user interface events and semantic events to target parts; the same dispatcher object is used in both cases.

■ **ODMessageInterface** is used by part editors and scripting languages to create and send semantic events. You can specify a reply ID and a transaction ID as attributes of a message. A *transaction* is a sequence of semantic events that are sent back and forth between client and server parts. All the messages that are part of the same transaction must have the same transaction ID. You use the *CreatePartObjSpec* method to create an object specifier for interpart exchanges—the method adds a specifier representing the destination part in the message. The *CreatePartAddrDesc* method creates an address description that identifies the process in which the destination part resides.

Figure 24-5 shows the sequence of method invocations that are needed to send a semantic event. The event is delivered to the document shell's **ODDispatcher**. If the event is remote, the document shell hands it to its counterpart on the target

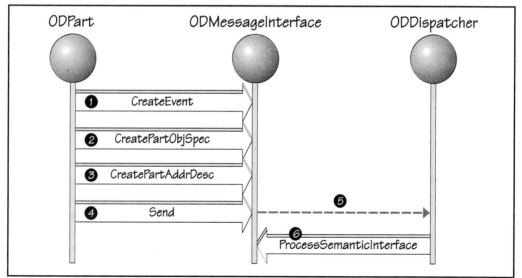

Figure 24-5. Sending a Semantic Event.

document. If the event is local, the document shell (or dispatcher) re-invokes the message interface object to resolve the object specifier (see next Details box).

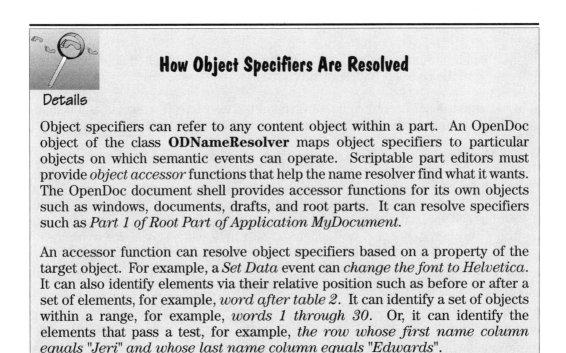

How Object Specifiers Are Resolved

Details

Object specifiers can refer to any content object within a part. An OpenDoc object of the class **ODNameResolver** maps object specifiers to particular objects on which semantic events can operate. Scriptable part editors must provide *object accessor* functions that help the name resolver find what it wants. The OpenDoc document shell provides accessor functions for its own objects such as windows, documents, drafts, and root parts. It can resolve specifiers such as *Part 1 of Root Part of Application MyDocument.*

An accessor function can resolve object specifiers based on a property of the target object. For example, a *Set Data* event can *change the font to Helvetica*. It can also identify elements via their relative position such as before or after a set of elements, for example, *word after table 2*. It can identify a set of objects within a range, for example, *words 1 through 30*. Or, it can identify the elements that pass a test, for example, *the row whose first name column equals "Jeri" and whose last name column equals "Edwards"*.

The accessor functions of a part return *tokens*—that is, descriptors that identify the content objects. If the object specifier refers to embedded parts, the name resolver does a multipart resolution by passing control from one part accessor function to another. Each returned token is used to find the next innermost element in the specifier. This cycle continues until the innermost element of the object specifier is converted to a token and returned to the name resolver. Eventually, a *final* token that identifies the requested object is returned.

The name resolver returns the final token to the message interface object. And, as a side effect of this multipart resolution, it returns a destination part—that is, the innermost target part. The message interface object replaces the object specifier with the final token in the event message. The first four bytes in a token are reserved for OpenDoc's own use. The message interface object writes the destination part ID in this reserved area. It then hands over the semantic message to the OpenDoc dispatcher. The dispatcher, in turn, calls the target part's semantic event handler, which is the callback function that executes the content-verb (or command). A part editor must provide an event handler for each semantic event it supports.

Both the event handlers and accessor functions are implemented as callback functions. They both get invoked in response to an event. And both are registered in callback tables maintained by an object of class **ODSemantic-Interface**. Each scriptable part must create its own semantic interface object; it's an extension of the part editor derived from **ODExtension**. The semantic interface object serves as a container for the nouns and verbs of the part's content model and tables that hold the callback functions. Because CORBA does not support callback functions as parameters, the callback functions and semantic-event handlers are installed and removed using an **SIHelper** utility object. ❑

Setting Up the Environment

Figure 24-6 shows some of the method invocations that are used to instantiate a part's semantic interface objects. When the part is first created—that is, when *InitPart* is invoked—the part editor creates both a semantic interface object and a helper object. Then the part editor invokes the helper method *Install-EventHandler* to install the event handlers. To install an event handler, the part editor must specify an event class, event ID, and the address of the event-handler function. Then it calls the helper method *InstallObjectAccessor* to install object-accessor functions. You install and remove these functions using the helper object, but you call them using the semantic object methods.

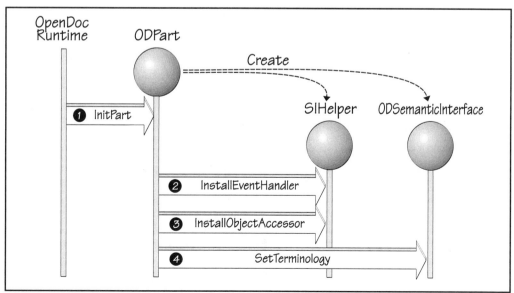

Figure 24-6. Instantiating a Part's Semantic Interface.

The *SetTerminology* method is used to register the scriptable part's terminology with the document shell. The *terminology* describes the semantic events a part supports and the corresponding human-language terminology for use in scripts. OpenDoc maintains a document-wide registry of terminology information for all parts. OpenDoc makes this registry directly available to script compilers to help their performance. Consequently these compilers don't have to deal with each part individually.

Scenario: A Semantic Message At Work

If you're still confused, a scenario should help bring it all together. So let's walk through the execution of this simple line of AppleScript, *Set the type of Part "Book Sales" to graph*. What follows are the step-by-step gory details of the scenario shown in Figure 24-7:

1. ***The script program creates and sends the semantic event***. The event is *Set Data* and the object specifier is *Type of Part "Book Sales"*.

2. ***The message interface object receives the incoming event***. But, it doesn't have the faintest idea of which part it's for. To find out, it must resolve the object specifier.

3. ***ODNameResolver is called to the rescue.*** The message interface object calls the name resolver object's *Resolve* method and passes it the object specifier.

4. ***The resolver starts an outside-in search***. It starts by invoking the *CallObjectAccessor* method on the root part's **ODSemanticInterface** object extension. It asks the part's object accessor: "Does this object specifier mean anything to you?" The root part turns out to be quite helpful. It knows how to find any part by name; it immediately recognizes its embedded part, "Book Sales." However, it knows nothing of "Type of." That's something that belongs to Book Sales—a part written by someone else. So root part returns a token with "Book Sales" that tells the resolver "go ask the Book Sales part to help you."

5. ***The resolver asks the Book Sales part for help.*** It invokes the *CallObjectAccessor* method on the Book Sales part's **ODSemanticInterface** object extension. It asks the part's object accessor: "Does Type mean anything to you?" The Book Sales part says "sure" and returns a token that identifies the content object. The token is something meaningful to the Book Sales part.

6. ***The resolver returns a final token***. The resolver writes the ID of the destination part, Book Sales, in the first four bytes of the token and then returns both the final token and the destination to the message interface object. The message interface replaces the object specifier with the final token in the semantic event message and hands it over to the OpenDoc dispatcher.

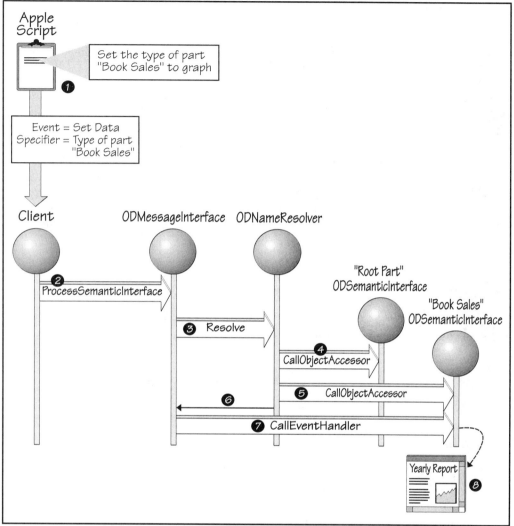

Figure 24-7. A Semantic Event Scenario: Set the Type of Part "Book Sales."

7. ***The dispatcher calls the Book Sales part's event handler.*** This is the callback function that executes the "Set Data" event.

8. ***A graph shows up magically in the document.*** The event handler changes the part content type to a graph (assume it was a table before).

This scenario should give you an idea of how the various parts cooperate to resolve an object specifier.

A Quick Review

All semantic messages are sent via the message interface object. Because an object specifier may name an embedded part or content, the message interface object needs to determine who the receiver is. It does this by enlisting the help of the name resolver and the semantic interface objects. Together, they resolve the destination part and content. The object identifier is replaced by a token that tells the dispatcher which part to invoke. The event is executed by the part's semantic event handler. A semantic event handler extracts information from the event, performs the requested action, and, in some cases, returns a result in a reply semantic message. To support semantic events, your part editor must do the following: 1) provide an event handler to respond to each semantic event it supports; 2) provide object accessor functions that direct these events to the appropriate handlers; and 3) register the events, their handlers, and accessors with OpenDoc via the semantic interface object.

SCRIPTING AND AUTOMATION

Since the parts of an OpenDoc document are actual objects and are "smart," the script verbs are handled automatically in a manner appropriate to the content type.

> — Jeff Rush
> Dr. Dobb's Journal
> (January, 1995)

A scripting system provides the third—and last—element of the OSA implementation. It lets a power user design, attach, and execute code to generate the semantic events that a scriptable part receives. OpenDoc supports any scripting language that knows how to generate OSA semantic events. A scripting language typically provides a *script editor* that lets users record, edit, save, execute, and debug scripts. Each scripting language has an OSA *scripting component* that implements a text-based scripting language based on semantic events. When a script executes, the scripting component sends semantic events to one or more parts to perform the actions the script describes (see Figure 24-8). A part editor can provide several levels of scripting support. Almost anything in OpenDoc can be scripted.

In addition to being a server to a scripting language, a part can also be a client to a script with the help of an **ODOSAObject**. A part interacts at run time with a script component to obtain a handle to a scripting program. Using this handle, the part can compile, modify, execute, save, and load the script. The part can also attach semantic events to scripts—which means that the script is executed whenever the semantic event is fired. For example, a part editor could attach a script to a specific word; the script executes whenever that word is double-clicked. The attached script

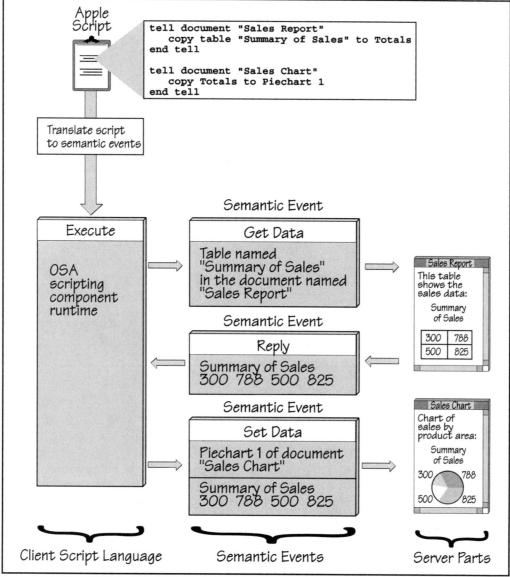

Figure 24-8. How a Scripting Language Executes a Script.

could trigger OSA events that run a movie, play a voice clip, or execute a multiserver transaction on a CORBA ORB.

In this section, we first look at the different levels of scriptability that a part can offer. We then go over the **ODOSAObject** that a part uses to connect to a scripting system. This versatile object even lets you switch between available OSA scripting systems during execution.

Beyond Just Scriptability

Because of OSA's flexibility, part editors can provide different levels of scripting support. Each level introduces an added dimension of external run-time control over a part's behavior. Each successive level requires more effort on the part of the developer, but gives the user greater flexibility and control over the part. Figure 24-9 shows a value-added spectrum consisting of three incremental levels of scripting support that parts can provide to their users: *scriptability*, *tinkerability*, and *recordability*.

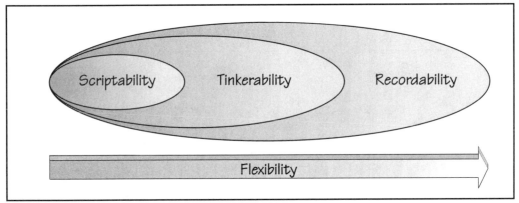

Figure 24-9. The Scriptability Spectrum.

Scriptability

Scriptability is the simplest form of scripting support. To be *scriptable*, a part editor only needs to publish a description of its content objects and operations. It must also accept semantic events. If a part editor can respond to semantic events sent by other parts, it can also respond to the same events sent by a scripting system (or what OSA calls a scripting "component").

Before it can execute a script that interacts with parts via semantic events, a scripting system must associate human-language terms used in the script with specific semantic event codes supported by a part. Scriptable part editors publish this information in an OSA *Event Terminology Extension Resource*—also known as the *Apple Event Registry*. This resource contains the list of content objects, the operations a part supports, and their corresponding human-language terminology. A scripting component uses this resource to identify the semantic event that corresponds to an action described in a human-language script form.

For a part to be *fully scriptable*, semantic events must be able to invoke any action a user is able to perform. The part editor must create a handler for every semantic event it recognizes and provide the proper object accessor functions. These callback functions are registered with the part editor's **ODSemanticInterface** extension object. So a part editor simply needs to create one semantic interface object—with all the appropriate callback functions—to be scriptable.

Tinkerability

Tinkerability is the next level of scripting support. It allows users to attach scripts to events that a scriptable part receives or generates. Events include user interface actions, editing, open, close, save, restore, and major state changes within the part's contents. The attached script is triggered when the event fires. Scripts are typically attached to human interface objects. For example, if a button part is tinkerable, you should be able to attach a script to it by simply dragging a script program's icon and dropping it on the part. The script will be triggered when a button-down event is fired. Scripts let you tinker with the behavior of a part. OpenDoc itself generates the following semantic events to which you can attach scripts: open/close document, save draft, print draft, add part, remove part, and select part.

To provide tinkerability, the part editor must check to see if a script is attached to an event. If so, it invokes the script before processing the event. To be extremely tinkerable, a part editor must allow scripts to be attached to virtually every user action. You should be able to attach scripts to parts within a document, the root part, and the document shell. A part must be able to store in its storage unit any script that a user attaches to its interfaces.

Recordability

Recordability is an extreme form of tinkerability. A recordable part editor creates a *bottleneck* that intercepts any incoming calls and events and resends them to itself as semantic events. The part editor's code is split into an interface element that accepts events and the code that actually does the work. This internal split is called *factoring*. The elements of a factored part communicate via semantic events. A factored part acts as both a client and a server for the semantic events it sends to itself in response to user actions. In a fully factored application almost all tasks are carried out in response to semantic events. Factored tasks are invoked via semantic events, regardless of what drives the user interface.

This total separation of the interface from the implementation makes it possible to record all user actions against that part. When a script editor turns the recording on, it receives copies of all the semantic events, which the part is sending to itself (see Figure 24-10). The scripting editor can convert into scripts events it receives from any recordable part within a document. The script can be replayed at a later time to reenact a user's actions.

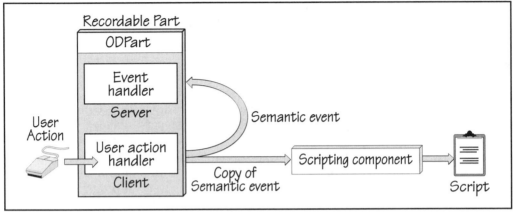

Figure 24-10. Recording User Actions in a Factored Part.

Redirecting all events through a bottleneck makes it easy to check in one place for the presence of scripts. An immediate benefit is that you get automatic tinkerability. Of course, the downside of all this redirection is a degradation in performance. Part designers should carefully weigh the benefits of recordability versus the added costs in performance. For example, most user interface actions should be recordable. But, you'll probably not want to record the tracking of a mouse; the overhead associated with recording such low-level events may not be practical.

Recording starts when you click on a record button in a script editor (or some equivalent user interface). When this occurs, the scripting system notifies the document shell, which then fires *Recording On* events to all its parts. A corresponding *Recording Off* event is fired when the user stops recording.

Recordable part editors make it possible for end users to record their actions in the form of a script. Users with little or no knowledge of a particular scripting language can automatically record their actions into some very usable scripts. More knowledgable users can edit these generated scripts and combine them with other scripts.

If you go through the trouble of factoring your part, you get—as another side benefit—a true client/server part. Factoring provides a clean split for interpart client/server distribution. The client and server sides of a factored part can run on different machines. The client provides views and the server provides the application's semantic content. If your OpenDoc platform supports it, the client and server sides of your split part can communicate using distributed semantic messages.

Scripting Systems

An OpenDoc part can connect to one or more scripting systems that use one or more scripting languages through an object of the class **ODOSAObject** (see next Details box). This object provides a universal interface to OSA-compliant scripting languages (or components). It relieves part editors from having to deal directly with the idiosyncrasies of scripting systems.

Before a part can manipulate and execute scripts, it must first connect to an OSA scripting system. Each part that needs to connect to a scripting system creates an object of class **ODOSAObject**. The scripting system enables a part to perform the following actions: load and save scripts, compile and execute them, and trigger their execution via semantic events. OpenDoc uses the CORBA Interface Repository to register scripting components and their properties.

The OSA Script-System Encapsulator

Details

Figure 24-11 shows the main methods of the **ODOSAObject** class. A part editor opens a scripting-system connection by invoking the *OpenScripting-Connection* method. It then designates itself as the target part during a script's execution by invoking the *SetDefaultTarget* method. This means the scripter does not have to specify the entire path of a part's location within the document.

The part editor can compile the script by invoking the *Compile* method. It can execute it by invoking *Execute*. And it can combine both actions by invoking *CompileExecute*. The *LoadExecute* method loads a previously compiled script from storage and executes it. The *DoScript* method compiles a script, executes it, and converts the resulting script value to text. You should use separate compile and execute commands if you expect the user to execute a compiled script several times. Use the other functions for scripts that execute once—the methods *CompileExecute* and *DoScript* will automatically dispose the script from memory after they execute.

The *ExecuteEvent* method invokes a script in response to a semantic event (the script is initiated by the semantic event). The *DoEvent* method invokes a script in response to a semantic event and also returns a reply semantic event. You can use a parameter to specify that the event is to be *continued*. This means that it should be passed to the part's semantic event handler for additional processing after the attached script completes.

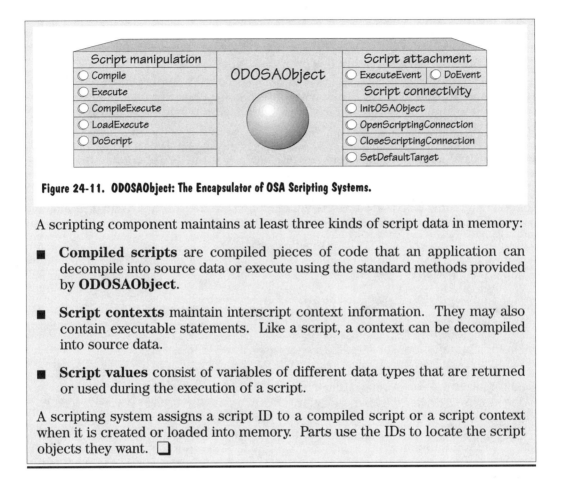

Figure 24-11. ODOSAObject: The Encapsulator of OSA Scripting Systems.

A scripting component maintains at least three kinds of script data in memory:

■ **Compiled scripts** are compiled pieces of code that an application can decompile into source data or execute using the standard methods provided by **ODOSAObject**.

■ **Script contexts** maintain interscript context information. They may also contain executable statements. Like a script, a context can be decompiled into source data.

■ **Script values** consist of variables of different data types that are returned or used during the execution of a script.

A scripting system assigns a script ID to a compiled script or a script context when it is created or loaded into memory. Parts use the IDs to locate the script objects they want. ❑

CONCLUSION

You can use OpenDoc scripting to automate the construction of very smart documents. Using scripts you can place parts in documents, play the parts, add content, add links, save the document, and ship it. OpenDoc lets you create ultra-reactive, smart documents that use semantic events to communicate changes in their environment and allow parts to collaborate. Semantic events can trigger attached scripts that react to the contents of the document and the parts they contain. OpenDoc can store these scripts in the same document as the parts they serve. As a result, it provides a solid foundation for the creation of mobile components—also known as roaming agents (or roaming documents). The OpenDoc roaming agents can be transported in Bento containers. They contain data, parts, and the scripts that can act on them.

Part 5
OLE/COM
Under the Hood

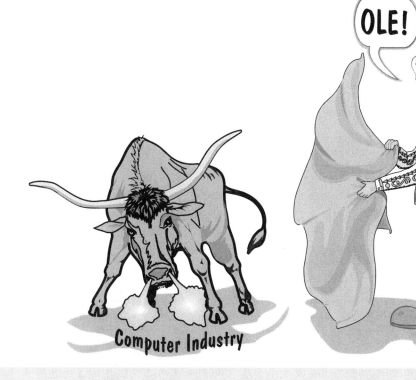

An Introduction to Part 5

But the darkest of dark sides is a thing Microsoft hastily concocted called OLE...OLE is catching on like e-mail at Al Gore's house, but unfortunately it is the deadliest possible blow to OOT—mainly because it isn't object-oriented, it isn't fully specified, it's inferior to OpenDoc, and there is little anyone can do to stop it. OLE will become synonymous with objects.

> — *Dr. Ted Lewis*
> *IEEE Computer Magazine*
> *(December, 1994)*

Are you ready for a journey into the "darkest of dark sides"? We're going to visit this "deadly" monster called OLE. To our Martian friends, don't worry—you're in good hands. Part 5 is for readers who enjoy the "dark side" and like monster movies. It's also for readers who need to understand—more than simply—what OLE is and what problems it solves. We delve deeply into what's really under the OLE hood. Are you ready?

But why bother with OLE if it's really "the deadliest possible blow to OOT"? Why should you pollute your mind with such poison and heresy? We can think of two good reasons. First, OLE is here to stay. We are absolutely certain that the future of Windows is OLE/COM. So every object-oriented system will learn how to coexist with OLE or subsume it. Second, OLE introduces some interesting new features in the area of component collaborations—especially on the desktop. In this brave new world of components, we need all the examples we can find of interaction and collaboration patterns.

OLE is more than an academic example; it's a shipping technology that forms the basis for an important segment of the component market. Regardless of where you stand, you simply cannot afford to ignore OLE. So we strongly recommend that you invest the time to go through the next five chapters. You will then understand what OLE is all about. We will help you build on what you already know by comparing OLE features to CORBA and OpenDoc, whenever this makes sense.

If OLE is so inevitable, why bother with CORBA? Why not have our industry simply accept OLE/COM as its object standard and move on to better things? This won't happen. The momentum behind CORBA is also unstoppable, especially in the area of distributed objects. OLE cannot become a *de facto* standard for distributed components even if it wanted to. *Distributed OLE* has not shipped and is not expected to ship until late 1996 (with Cairo). CORBA is currently years ahead of OLE/COM in distributed object technology. By the time distributed OLE ships, the commercial CORBA ORBs will be in their third generation. Our readers should know how long it takes to make distributed systems really work—a long time after they initially ship. So we have a stand-off: OLE/COM on the Windows desktop and CORBA/OpenDoc on the client/server ORB.

An Introduction to Part 5

The bottom line is that we have two competing distributed object technologies and both will thrive. Eventually OLE/COM and CORBA will interoperate. But because they have dissimilar object models, the components will never be able to fully collaborate across environments. Each model will have its own rules of engagement. Component providers will have to choose between these two models unless they can afford to support both.

In Part 5, we go into the next level of detail of the OLE model introduced in Part 3. Yes, this is another diehard ride. We hope you enjoyed the last one. We first cover OLE's object bus called the *Component Object Model (COM)*—it's an OLE-style ORB that runs in a single machine. After the COM chapter, we deviate from the approach we took in the OpenDoc chapters. Instead of jumping directly into OLE's compound document model, we cover the other three areas first: automation, uniform data transfer, and structured storage.

Why this detour? Because it mirrors the way OLE components are structured. In OpenDoc, a component is a *part*. All OpenDoc parts have the same basic interfaces derived from **ODPart**—of course, parts can also have extensions. In contrast, an OLE component is a group of interfaces. And it takes quite a few interfaces to make an OLE component reach the same level of sophistication as an OpenDoc part. So we must build these interfaces from the ground-up until we reach the critical mass needed by OLE's custom controls (OCXs) and their containers. Everything comes together at the OCX/container level. An OLE OCX is packaged like an OpenDoc part but it lacks some of the function—for example, an OCX cannot embed other parts.

After reading Part 5, you will really understand the OLE/COM object model and what makes OLE tick. Of course, a good OLE tool can hide some of this gore, but it also ends up hiding the object model itself. OLE tools—like Visual C++, Visual Basic, and MFC—focus on OLE automation, documents, and controls. They do not deal with key features of the object model such as monikers, persistent objects, connection points, type libraries, and the COM RPC. To understand these features, you'll have to look at OLE and COM in the raw, as we do in Part 5.

You may find the ride enjoyable in spite of the technical jargon and all the gore. From the outside, OLE/COM and CORBA/OpenDoc may appear to be very similar. But in reality, they're very different animals. We will point out the similarities and differences. If it gets heated, we may even have to jump on a soapbox. Eventually, everyone in our industry will be faced with the choice: Which component model? It's not an easy choice to make. So perhaps the next 100 pages may be worth your while. Remember, if the waters get too murky just go into "fast-forward mode" until they become clearer.

Chapter 25

COM: OLE's Object Bus

---

*T*he fundamental question COM addresses is: How can a system be designed such that binary components from different vendors—written in different parts of the world at different times—are guaranteed to interoperate?

— Sara Williams et al., Microsoft
Dr. Dobb's Journal
(January, 1995)

This is the first of a five-chapter series that covers OLE in-depth. This chapter covers the *Component Object Model (COM)*—OLE's object bus. The rest of OLE is built on top of COM. The current implementation of COM is a single-machine version of the distributed object bus that will be introduced in Cairo (or Windows 96). In addition, Digital is building, with Microsoft, something called the *Common Object Model (COM)*—not to be confused with Microsoft's COM. By the time you read this book, the two COMs may have become one and the same—unless there's a divorce. To play it safe, this chapter covers Microsoft's version of COM.

You can think of today's COM as an Object Request Broker (ORB) for a single machine environment. The COM broker only deals with OLE objects (also called

Windows objects). When it ships, the distributed version of COM will become Microsoft's alternative to CORBA. The two object models have some similarities, especially when seen from a distance. But when you look closer, these are two very different object models. OMG defines one of them, and Microsoft defines the other one. CORBA is much further along than COM in defining a distributed object infrastructure—there are more than a dozen CORBA ORBs on the market today. And by the time distributed COM ships, these CORBA ORBs will be in their third generation. The distributed COM specification is very preliminary. However, Microsoft promises that distributed COM will provide local/remote transparency without breaking today's OLE objects. Distributed COM is, in theory, simply an extension of today's COM implementation.

This chapter breaks down COM into two elements: the *object bus* and *object services* (see Figure 25-1). It's hard to draw the dividing line between OLE and COM because they're both moving targets. The object bus clearly belongs to COM. But what constitutes a COM service is currently very nebulous. As time progresses, all the non-compound document elements of OLE will be classified as COM services. For example, in late 1994, OLE custom controls (OCXs) introduced a set of new component technologies—including connectable objects, event sets, licensing, and self-registration. These technologies are now considered COM services. The same can be said of monikers, persistence, type libraries, and uniform data transfer.

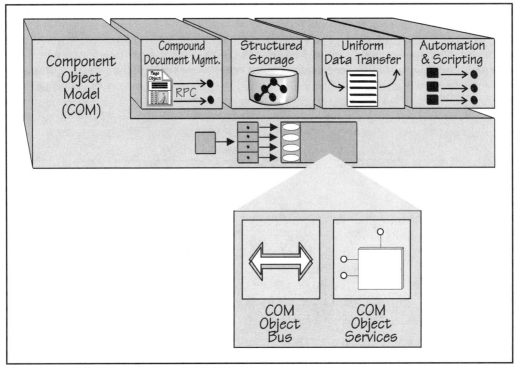

Figure 25-1. OLE's Component Object Model (COM).

COM: THE OBJECT BUS

If you come from a classical object background (or from the world of CORBA), be prepared for some culture shock. COM looks and feels like classical objects, yet it is very different. COM provides some of the same functions as CORBA, but it is done very differently. COM also introduces its own terminology and object jargon. Because we've been so heavily absorbed with CORBA in this book, we first explain in this section the COM bus in CORBA terms. Then we explore each function using COM terms. This should help ease you into the new culture. If you make it through the next five chapters, you may even start thinking like an OLE/COM objects person. Be careful though: You may forget your classical objects.

Looking at COM Through CORBA Eyes

Like CORBA, COM separates the object interface from its implementation and requires that all interfaces be declared using an Interface Definition Language (IDL). Microsoft's IDL is based on DCE—it is, of course, not CORBA-compliant (nor DCE-compliant). Microsoft also provides another DCE IDL superset called the *Object Description Language (ODL)*.

CORBA is based on a classical object model; COM is not. COM does not support IDL-specified multiple inheritance. However, a COM component can support multiple interfaces and achieve reuse by encapsulating the interfaces of inner components and representing them to a client. So with COM, you achieve object reuse via containment and aggregation rather than inheritance.

A COM object is not an object in the OO sense. COM interfaces do not have state and cannot be instantiated to create a unique object. A COM interface is simply a group of related functions. COM clients are given a pointer to access the functions in an interface—this pointer is not related to state information. A COM client cannot reconnect to exactly the same object instance with the same state at a later time. It can only reconnect to an interface pointer of the same class. In other words, COM objects do not maintain state.

Like CORBA, COM provides both static and dynamic interfaces for method invocations. The *Type Library* is the COM version of an Interface Repository. COM precompilers can populate the Type Library with descriptions of ODL-defined objects—including their interfaces and parameters. Clients can query the Type Library to discover what interfaces an object supports and what parameters are needed to invoke a particular method. COM also provides a registry and some object look-up services that are similar to a CORBA Implementation Repository.

You should note that, unlike CORBA, COM's bus does not extend to networks. It's a single-machine implementation of an ORB. Of course, one of the main functions of an ORB is to provide a cross-platform networked object bus. So, in a sense, COM is like a car without an engine. You can sit in it, but it won't take you anywhere. So are you wasting your time by reading this chapter? Not necessarily. Eventually, Microsoft will provide a fully distributed version of COM. It will have the same "look-and-feel" as today's COM. In addition, COM introduces some innovative architectural features in component design that deserve your attention—including ODL-defined outgoing interfaces, the *IUnknown::QueryInterface* function, and components with multiple interfaces.

COM Style Interfaces

A COM *interface* is a collection of function calls—also known as methods or member functions. Like its CORBA equivalent, a COM interface serves as a client/server contract. It defines functions independently from their implementation. COM clients interact with each other and with the system by calling interface member functions. Like CORBA, a COM interface is language-independent and can call functions across address spaces (but not across networks). However, unlike CORBA, COM does not provide high-level language bindings. COM does not define bindings to Smalltalk, C++, C, and COBOL that make source code portable and hide the underlying plumbing. COM simply defines a binary specification for how to access its interfaces using pointers.

A COM interface is defined as a low-level binary API based on a table of pointers. To access an interface, COM clients use pointers to an array of function pointers known as a *virtual table (or vtable)*. The functions that are pointed to by the vtable are the server object's implementation methods (see Figure 25-2). Each COM object has one or more vtables that define the contract between the object implementation and its clients (also see the next Details box).

The convention in COM (and OLE) is to represent an interface with a plug-in jack extending from an object (see Figure 25-3). These drawings are also called "bullet-and-stick" diagrams. Here, each bullet or plug-in jack represents an interface—meaning a group of semantically-related functions. It seems vtables make objects look rather intimidating. Plug-in jacks are more user-friendly; they use the metaphor of stereo system components that plug into each other.

An interface is, by convention, given a name starting with a capital "I"—for example, **IUnknown**. However, this name only has symbolic meaning (usually to a source-level programming tool). At run time, each interface is really known by its unique *Interface Identifier (IID)*. An IID is a COM-generated *globally-unique identifier (GUID)* for interfaces.

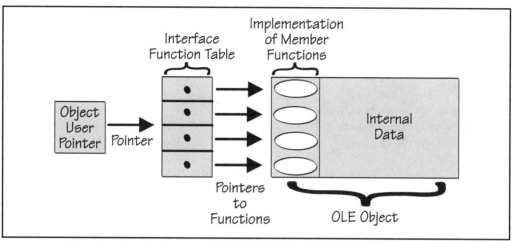

Figure 25-2. A COM Interface: The Pointer to a Vtable Representation.

GUIDs—pronounced goo-ids—are unique 128-bit IDs generated by calling the COM API function *CoCreateGuid*. This function executes an algorithm specified by the OSF DCE. If you really must know, this algorithm calculates a globally unique number using the current date and time, a network card ID, and a high-frequency counter. There's almost no chance for this algorithm to create duplicate GUIDs. The IID allows a client to unambiguously ask an object if it supports the interface. Clients ask questions using a *QueryInterface* function that all objects support through a ubiquitous interface called **IUnknown** (we cover this interface in a later section). Interfaces are meant to be small contracts that are independent of each other—they're the smallest contractual unit in COM.

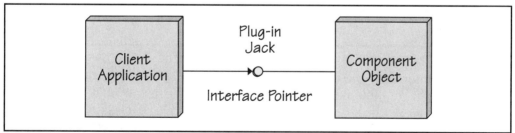

Figure 25-3. A COM Interface: The Plug-In Jack Representation.

So, What's a COM Object?

A *COM object*—also known as an *OLE object* or a *Windows object*—is a component that supports one or more interfaces as defined by that object's *class*. A COM interface refers to a predefined group of related functions. A COM *class* implements

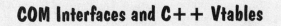

COM Interfaces and C++ Vtables

Details

A *frequent trick used by COM programmers is to use a C++ vtable as a COM method table. By strange coincidence, this works just fine with vtables laid out by the Microsoft C++ compiler. But it doesn't work with most other C++ compilers.*

— *Jens Alfke, Apple Computer*
MacTech Magazine
(January, 1995)

The COM language-neutral binary standard requires that a server object create a *vtable* containing pointers to the implementations of the interface member functions. The client's pointer to the interface is a pointer to the top of a vtable. If you're familiar with the internals of C++, you'll recognize the vtable structure as being similar to what a compiler generates for a C++ object instance. COM uses that convention to make it convenient to write OLE objects using C++.

But as Jens Alfke points out, C++ compilers use different vtable layouts and use different parameter passing techniques. So you may be OK with Microsoft's compilers, but you may be forced to lay out your method tables by hand with other C++ compilers. But, what happens if you want to create a COM interface in C or Smalltalk? You're back to laying out your method tables by hand. In addition, the client code is quite messy. Finally, if the call is made across processes, the developer must provide client and server stubs that marshal parameters across process boundaries—another messy process. The CORBA language bindings were designed to hide all these gory details and make your code portable. ❑

one or more interfaces and is identified by a unique 128-bit *Class ID (CLSID)*. A COM object is a run-time instantiation of a class. A particular object will provide implementations of the functions for all the interfaces its class supports. For convenience, the word "object" is used to refer to both an object class and an individual instantiation of a class.

Clients always deal with COM objects through interface pointers; they never directly access the object itself. Note that an interface is not an object in the classical sense. COM objects do not support unique object IDs (or CORBA-like object references). You cannot ask to be connected to a particular COM object. (Also see next Briefing box).

All COM objects must implement the **IUnknown** interface through which the client can control the lifetime of an object. Clients also use it for interface negotiations—

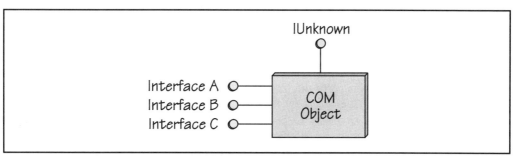

Figure 25-4. A COM Object Implements All the Interfaces Its Class Supports.

a client can ask an object what interfaces it supports and obtain pointers to them. To use the stereo system analogy, the client must have the right kind of plug to fit into an interface jack so that it can talk to an object through that particular interface. By convention, **IUnknown** is shown as a plug-in jack that extends from the top of an object (see Figure 25-4).

What? An Object With No ID?

Briefing

In a classical object system—like CORBA—each instantiated object has a unique identification (ID) that's a fundamental property of an object. The object ID— called an object reference in CORBA—is used by naming and trading services to locate a unique object. The ID is also used to track an object throughout its lifetime. Persistent services use it to save an object's state so that it can be reactivated at a later time. CORBA provides a set of APIs for converting an object ID to a string and vice versa. This allows object IDs to be passed to other objects. Clients use the object ID to connect to a particular object. So, the concept of a unique object ID is fundamental to the classical object model.

In contrast, COM does not support the concept of an object ID. With COM, clients obtain a pointer to an interface and not a pointer to an object with state. COM clients cannot reconnect to that exact same object instance with the same state at a later time. Instead, clients have transient pointers to particular interfaces of an object. COM objects with the same set of interfaces and the same implementations for each are often loosely called *instances* of the same class. However, all access to the instances of the class by clients will only be through these transient interfaces; clients know nothing about an object other than that it supports certain interfaces. As a result, object instances play a much less significant role in COM than they do in classical object systems. ❑

What's a COM Server?

A COM *server* is a piece of code—a DLL or an EXE—that houses one or more object classes each with their own CLSID. When a client asks for an object of a given CLSID, COM loads the server code and asks it to create an object of that class. The server must provide a *class factory* for creating a new object. Once an object is created, a pointer to its primary interface is returned to the client. The server is not the object itself. The word "server" in COM is used to emphasize the serving agent. The phrase "server object" is used specifically to identify an object that is implemented in a server.

So a COM server provides the necessary structure around an object to make it available to clients (see Figure 25-5). More specifically a COM server must:

- **Implement a class factory interface.** The server must implement a class factory with the **IClassFactory** interface for each supported CLSID. The class factory creates instances of a class. If a class supports licensing, then it must implement the **IClassFactory2** interface. This interface creates an object only if a valid license file is present or a license key is provided.

- **Register the classes it supports.** The server must register a CLSID for each class it supports with the *Windows Registry*. For each CLSID, it must create one or more entries that provide the pathname to the server DLL or EXE (or to both). This information is recorded using the Windows Registry APIs. Typically, the classes are registered at installation time.

- **Initialize the COM library.** The server issues a call to the COM API *CoInitialize* to initialize COM. The COM library is part of OLE32.DLL. It provides the COM run-time services and APIs. These are functions with the *Co* prefix, which stands for COM.

- **Verify that the library is of a compatible version.** The server does this by calling the API *CoBuildVersion*.

- **Provide an unloading mechanism.** The server must provide a way to terminate itself when there are no active clients for its objects.

- **Uninitialize the COM library.** The server calls the COM API *CoUninitialize* when it is no longer in use.

The implementation of the server—including registration, the class factory, and the unloading mechanism—will differ depending on whether the server is packaged as a DLL or an EXE.

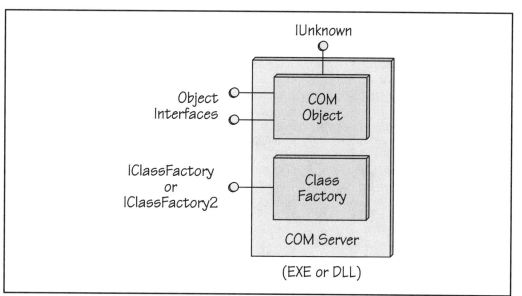

Figure 25-5. The Structure of a COM Server.

Server Flavors: In-Process and Out-Of-Process

A COM server can be implemented in one of many flavors. The actual flavor depends on the structure of the code module and its relationship to the client processes that will be using it. COM defines three flavors of servers (see Figure 25-6):

- **In-process servers** execute in the same process space as their clients. Under Microsoft Windows and Windows NT, these are implemented as *Dynamic Link Libraries (DLLs)* that are loaded directly into the client's process.

- **Local servers** execute in a separate process from their clients on the same machine (and operating system). Clients use COM's *Lightweight RPC (LRPC)* mechanism to communicate with a local server. Local servers execute in their own (.EXE) file.

- **Remote servers** execute in a separate process on a remote machine and, possibly, different operating system. Clients will use a DCE-like RPC mechanism to communicate with remote servers. Currently, COM does not implement this remote flavor.

In theory, COM enables clients to transparently communicate with server objects regardless of where these objects are running. From a client's point of view, all server objects are accessed through interface pointers. A pointer must be in-process. In fact, any call to an interface function always reaches some piece of in-process code first. If the object is in-process, the call reaches it directly; there is no intervening system-infrastructure code. If the object is out-of-process, then the call first reaches what is called a *proxy* object provided by COM itself. This object generates the appropriate remote procedure call to the other process or the other machine. The COM element that locates servers and gets involved with LRPC—or future RPC—invocations between clients and servers is called the *Service Control Manager (SCM)*—better known as "Scum."

From a server's point of view, all calls to an object's interface functions are made through a pointer to that interface. Again, a pointer only has context in a single process, so the caller must always be some piece of in-process code. If the object is in-process, the caller is the client itself. Otherwise, the caller is a *stub object* provided by COM that picks up the remote procedure call from the *proxy* in the client process and turns it into an interface call to the server object. Clients and servers always communicate using some in-process or local code (again, see Figure 25-6). The COM proxy and stub mechanism is very similar to the way CORBA implements local/remote transparency using static stubs on the client side and interface skeletons on the server side. Unlike CORBA, COM does not currently support remote calls.

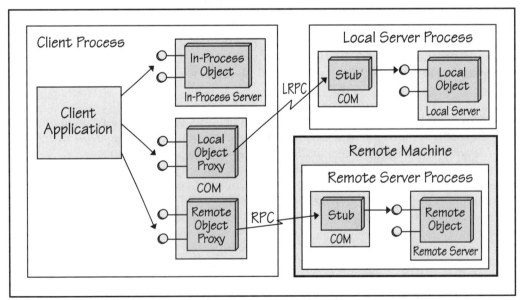

Figure 25-6. COM's Client/Server Boundaries.

Creating Custom Interfaces

The COM library provides proxies and stubs for all the standard predefined COM and OLE interfaces. To develop their own interfaces, programmers need to create a file that describes the interface's methods and their arguments using COM's *Interface Definition Language (IDL)*. They must then run this file through Microsoft's *MIDL* compiler to create the client proxies, the server stubs, and the code that marshals arguments between them. In case you forgot, *marshaling* means recreating the function's arguments in the server just as they appear in the client (see next briefing box for more information on the IDL).

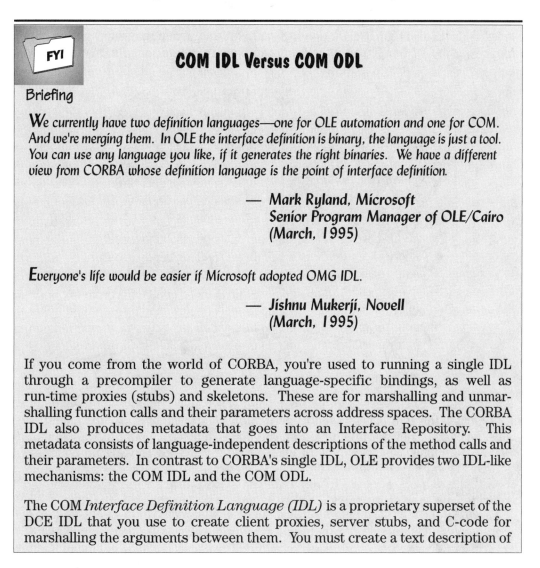

COM IDL Versus COM ODL

Briefing

We currently have two definition languages—one for OLE automation and one for COM. And we're merging them. In OLE the interface definition is binary, the language is just a tool. You can use any language you like, if it generates the right binaries. We have a different view from CORBA whose definition language is the point of interface definition.

> — Mark Ryland, Microsoft
> Senior Program Manager of OLE/Cairo
> (March, 1995)

Everyone's life would be easier if Microsoft adopted OMG IDL.

> — Jishnu Mukerji, Novell
> (March, 1995)

If you come from the world of CORBA, you're used to running a single IDL through a precompiler to generate language-specific bindings, as well as run-time proxies (stubs) and skeletons. These are for marshalling and unmarshalling function calls and their parameters across address spaces. The CORBA IDL also produces metadata that goes into an Interface Repository. This metadata consists of language-independent descriptions of the method calls and their parameters. In contrast to CORBA's single IDL, OLE provides two IDL-like mechanisms: the COM IDL and the COM ODL.

The COM *Interface Definition Language (IDL)* is a proprietary superset of the DCE IDL that you use to create client proxies, server stubs, and C-code for marshalling the arguments between them. You must create a text description of an interface in IDL and run it through the *Microsoft Interface Definition Language (MIDL)* Compiler. The MIDL is more accurately a precompiler that turns text descriptions of an interface into C code for both proxies and stubs. The MIDL compiler also creates header files that contain the interface definition. To finish the job, you must implement, compile, link, and register the server code. The MIDL compiler provides C language header files to include with any client code that uses this interface. The IDL documentation and the MIDL compiler are available in the Win32 SDK.

Unlike CORBA's IDL, the COM IDL is not language neutral—there's no concept of one IDL supporting multiple language bindings. And unlike CORBA, the COM IDL does not support multiple interface inheritance. And more unfortunately, the COM IDL and CORBA IDL do not support the same language syntax and type descriptions. The only thing they seem to have in common is the name "IDL."

In CORBA, the IDL is also used to generate and store metadata that describes interfaces and their parameters in an Interface Repository. CORBA clients can then dynamically discover how to invoke an interface by looking up metadata stored in the Interface Repository. The COM version of an Interface Repository is called a *Type Library*. To populate the Type Library with metadata, COM provides another proprietary IDL-like language called the *Object Description Language (ODL)*. The ODL is also used to describe COM interfaces and their parameters. The metadata is generated by running an ODL file through a COM utility called the *MKTYPLIB*. The end result of this process is a type library (.TLB) and a (.H) file with function prototypes for your interfaces.

The million dollar question is: Why doesn't COM use IDL to generate the Type Library metadata? It appears that because of its DCE heritage, the COM IDL is closely tied to the C language and to DCE data structures. In contrast, the ODL is more language-neutral; it has a more general structure that's suitable for describing components. The ODL introduces many new extensions to describe both static and dynamic interfaces and the overall structure of a COM class. On the surface, ODL and IDL may have a similar syntax; however, they use different keywords and they may contain different metadata. ODL describes in more detail the structure of OLE servers. In contrast, IDL describes in more detail the information needed by DCE RPCs to marshal parameters. And they each have their own precompilers.

We don't want to turn this into a soapbox, but it does seem that Microsoft—and our industry—would have been better off if COM had adopted the single CORBA IDL instead of resorting to two interface definition languages. We cover Type Libraries and ODL in more detail in Chapter 26, "OLE: Automation, Scripting, and Type Libraries." ❑

COM OBJECT SERVICES

As we said earlier, it's hard to draw the line between a COM service and an OLE service. Eventually, every object service that does not deal with compound documents will belong to COM. The traditional COM services include interface negotiations, life cycle management via reference counting and factories, component licensing, and the event service—also called *connectable objects*. Monikers, data objects, and structured storage will eventually belong to COM. What complicates matters is that every COM service was initially introduced as part of the OLE compound document model.

In this section, we go over **IUnknown**: the ubiquitous COM interface that supports interface negotiations, life cycle management, and COM's aggregation model—meaning the COM version of multiple inheritance. We also cover the **IClassFactory** and **IClassFactory2** interfaces that provide object creation services and run-time license enforcement. We then briefly introduce connectable objects—they're covered in detail in Chapter 29, "OLE: Compound Documents and OCXs." Monikers and structured storage are covered in Chapter 28, "OLE: Structured Storage and Monikers." Data objects and uniform data transfer are covered in Chapter 27, "OLE: Uniform Data Transfer."

The Ubiquitous IUnknown Interface

The **IUnknown** interface is the heart of COM. It is used for run-time interface negotiations, life cycle management, and aggregation. Every COM and OLE interface must implement the three **IUnknown** member functions: *QueryInterface*, *AddRef*, and *Release* (see Figure 25-7). **IUnknown** supports interface negotiations through *QueryInterface*. And it supports the life cycle management of an interface instance through *AddRef* and *Release*. Because all COM interfaces derive from **IUnknown**, you can call *QueryInterface*, *AddRef*, and *Release* using any interface pointer. In other words, **IUnknown** is a base interface from which all other interfaces inherit these three functions and implement them in a polymorphic manner.

```
  ○ QueryInterface        IUnknown
  ○ AddRef
  ○ Release
```

Figure 25-7. COM's Ubiquitous IUnknown Interface.

Interface Negotiations Using QueryInterface

When a client initially gains access to an object, by whatever means, that client is given one and only one interface pointer in return. The rest of the interfaces are obtained by calling *QueryInterface*, which forms the basis for interface negotiations. The *QueryInterface* function allows clients to discover at run time whether an interface—specified by an IID—is supported by a component object. If the object supports this interface, the function returns the appropriate interface pointer to the client. After the client obtains an interface pointer, COM gets out of the way and lets the client directly interact with the server by invoking member functions of its interface.

So the unit of client/server negotiation is an interface, not an individual function. All clients must first obtain a pointer to an interface before they can interact with an object's services. The object can refuse service to a client by not returning a pointer. The *QueryInterface* function returns a failure code if the interface is not supported or if the server refuses to service a client. Eventually, *QueryInterface* may be coupled with a distributed authentication mechanism that lets a single component express a different set of capabilities (interfaces) at run time based on a client's privileges.

Because COM does not support multiple inheritance, a COM component must be able to aggregate multiple interfaces to achieve a similar effect (more on that in a later section). *QueryInterface* supports the capability of returning pointers to the other interfaces a COM object supports, which is key to making aggregation work. COM requires that a *QueryInterface* call for a specific interface always return the same actual pointer value, no matter through which interface derived from **IUnknown** it is called. As a result, a client can perform an identity test to determine whether two pointers point to the same object.

QueryInterface also lets components add new interfaces and lets clients discover them. This allows new interfaces to be added to an object's class as its function evolves. A client can ask an object: "Do you support Interface X?" An old object can answer the question with a "No," while a newer object can answer "Yes." This test allows clients to invoke the function only if an object supports it. In this manner, the client maintains compatibility with objects written before and after Interface X was available. This run-time negotiation is the cornerstone of COM's version control (also see next Soapbox).

Is This Really Version Control?

Soapbox

Why does COM introduce the overhead of a *QueryInterface* call at the start of every client/server object interaction? Why not extend the IID to point to the object itself? One answer is that it is COM's way to provide a form of version control. When a component is upgraded to support a new interface, it will return a pointer to that new interface—instead of an error—the next time its *QueryInterface* is called. Because this negotiation is done at run time, new interfaces can be added without requiring a recompilation on the part of existing clients.

However, COM interfaces are immutable—you cannot change an existing interface to add new functions. For example, the COM **IClassFactory2** interface was introduced to add a new function—licensing control—to **IClassFactory**. A server cannot add a method to an existing interface, as is done in other object systems—for example, IBM's SOM, OpenStep, Newi, and Smalltalk. So, in a sense, COM solves the versioning problem by not supporting it. Servers just keep adding new interfaces and clients discover them at run time by calling *QueryInterface*. This can quickly lead to an explosion of similarly named interfaces (a la **IClassFactory**). ❑

Life Cycle Management With Reference Counts

In non-distributed object systems, the *life cycle* of objects—meaning the issues surrounding the creation and deletion of objects—is handled implicitly by the language or explicitly by application programmers. In a single program, there's always something—for example, the startup and shutdown code of a language runtime—that knows when objects must be created and when they should be deleted.

However, in distributed object systems, it is no longer true that someone or something always knows how to deal with the life cycle of objects. Object creation is still relatively easy—an object is created whenever a client with the right privileges requests it. But object deletion is another story: How do you know when an object is no longer needed? Even when the original client is done with the object, it can't simply shut the object down since it is likely to have passed a reference to the object to some other client in the system. So who's in charge of garbage collection in a distributed object system?

There are different approaches for dealing with the distributed object garbage collection issue. The first approach is to ignore garbage collection and rely on the operating system to kill objects during system shut-down. This approach may be acceptable to clients, but it is not workable on servers. The second approach is to let the ORB keep track of outstanding connections. This approach may work, especially if it is combined with ORB-mediated object caching and load-balancing. The third approach is to let an object keep track of its usage using reference counts; the clients must cooperate by telling an object when they are using it and when they are done. Both OpenDoc and COM use this third approach. This solution is based on having all objects maintain *reference counts* and having objects delete themselves when they are no longer in-use.

COM makes reference counting ubiquitous by adding that function to **IUnknown** through the member functions *AddRef* and *Release*. An interface's *AddRef* function is called when a client requests a pointer to that interface or passes a reference to it. An interface's *Release* function is called when the client no longer uses that interface. The internal implementation of the interface must increment the reference count every time *AddRef* is called and decrement it every time *Release* is called. COM implementations are required to support, at least, a 31-bit counter to keep track of reference counts.

The reference counting mechanism equates the lifetime of an object with references to it. It makes the following existential statement: "I'm being used; therefore, I exist." On the positive side, reference counting allows independently developed components to obtain and release access to a single object without having to coordinate with one another on life cycle management issues. On the negative side, it places an extra burden on every object implementation and assumes that clients are well-behaved—they must play by the rules. Reference counting is a cooperative client/server effort.

IClassFactory2: Object Creation and Licensing

Every COM class must implement a class factory that a COM server can invoke to create instances of that class. A COM class factory is an implementation of either the **IClassFactory** or **IClassFactory2** interfaces. **IClassFactory2** is an extension of **IClassFactory** that enforces licensing at object creation time (see Figure 25-8). It was introduced in late 1994 with OLE custom controls to enforce the licensing of OCXs. In addition to the ubiquitous **IUnkown** functions, **IClassFactory2** provides two member functions of the old **IClassFactory** interface and three new member functions that enforce licensing. When a COM server is initially loaded, it must instantiate a class factory for each of its classes and register them with COM by invoking the API *CoRegisterClassObject*.

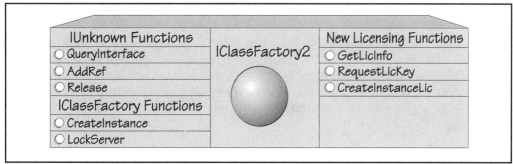

Figure 25-8. The COM IClassFactory2 Interface.

Although, the class factory is an interface, it is not the root interface of the component. Every instance of a class factory is associated with a single CLSID and exists strictly to facilitate the creation of an object of that CLSID. As shown in Figure 25-8, the **IClassFactory2** interface implements two functions for creating a new instance of a class: *CreateInstance* and *CreateInstanceLic*. These two functions are like the C++ *new* operator. They both create an uninitialized instance of the object associated with the class factory and return an interface pointer of a requested IID. The *LockServer* function allows a client to keep a server object resident in memory even when it is not being used by clients—it keeps the object from getting automatically unloaded from memory when its reference count reaches zero.

COM considers a machine to be fully licensed when a *license file* is installed on that machine. Otherwise, the client must supply a special *license key* when it instantiates the component. If the license key is not provided, the server will not instantiate the component. You can think of a license file as providing global permission to use a component on a machine, while the license key is a specific permission to use the component on another machine. License keys are used by applications that are assembled with third-party components. The development machine is fully licensed because we assume the components were purchased in the first place. The license key makes it possible to use these components on other machines. It's a piece of information that must be extracted from a component in the development environment and then provided at run time on the target machine.

The *GetLicInfo* function returns the type of licensing a component supports. It answers the questions: Is a license key required and, if so, is it available? The *RequestLicKey* function is used by a client to request a license key to use the component on a different machine. The client can use *CreateInstance* if a global license file is installed on a target machine. Otherwise, the client must invoke *CreateInstanceLic*, passing it the license key as one of its arguments. To repeat, a licensed component can only be created if a license key is provided by the client or if a global license file is available on the machine. The **IClassFactory2** implementation will validate the key or the license file before creating an instance of a component.

Compared to CORBA's licensing service, the COM implementation is very primitive. The license file is simply a text file installed with the component itself, and a license key is, typically, the first line of that text file. There's no protection against forgeries, and there's no way to meter the use of licenses. In addition, it's a system management nightmare to keep track of license files for thousands of disparate components.

A COM Object Creation Scenario

It's time to go over a scenario that shows how all these COM interfaces play together. We will assume that a class called **MyClass** was registered in the Windows registry. This class supports a single interface called **IMyInterface** and is being serviced by a local server called *MyServer.exe*. The registry will contain an entry under the CLSID for **MyClass** that looks like: *LocalServer32 = c:\MyDir\MyServer.exe*. Our scenario starts right after COM finds MyServer.exe in the registry and loads it into memory. In the scenario, a client creates an instance of **MyClass** and obtains a pointer to **IMyInterface**. Let's walk through the steps (see Figure 25-9):

1. ***The server instantiates a class factory and registers it with COM***. As soon as MyServer.exe is loaded, it must instantiate all its class factories and register them with COM. In this scenario, there's only one class, **MyClass**. This class provides a factory with an **IClassFactory2** interface. The server instantiates the factory interface and passes COM a pointer to it by invoking the API

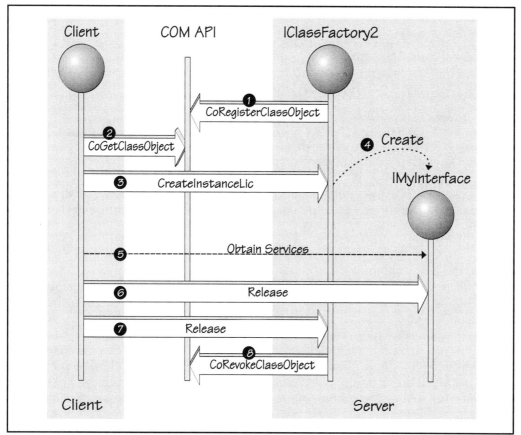

Figure 25-9. A COM Scenario: Creating an Instance of a Class.

CoRegisterClassObject. Now COM knows where to find the factory for that CLSID.

2. ***The client requests a pointer to the class factory.*** The client calls the COM API *CoGetClassObject* to obtain an **IClassFactory2** pointer for the **MyClass** CLSID.

3. ***The client requests an instance of this object.*** The client calls the *IClassFactory2::CreateInstanceLic* function to create an instance of **MyClass** and passes it the IID for **IMyInterface** as well as a license key.

4. ***The factory creates an instance of the class.*** The factory creates an instance of **MyClass** and returns to the client a pointer for the requested interface—in this case, it's **IMyInterface**.

5. ***The client interacts with the interface.*** The client can use its pointer to

IMyInterface to invoke whatever services this interface provides.

6. **The client releases IMyInterface**. The client invokes the *Release* function (derived from **IUnknown**) to decrement the reference count and release the pointer. This matches the *AddRef* count that was implicitly issued when the client obtained a pointer to **IMyInterface**.

7. **The client releases IClassFactory2**. The client invokes the *Release* function (derived from **IUnknown**) to decrement the reference count and release the pointer. This matches the *AddRef* count that was implicitly issued when the client obtained a pointer to **IClassFactory2**.

8. **The server is shutdown**. During shutdown, the server must call the API *CoRevokeClassObject* to tell COM that the previously registered class factory is now out of service.

As you can see from the scenario, **IClassFactory2** eliminates the need for clients to know the exact name of the creation function for some type of component—the client only needs to know a CLSID that can be retrieved from the registry. Also note that when clients create COM components, they're totally uninitialized—they have no persistent state. The client must help the component initialize its state by passing it a pointer to a storage unit (this topic will be covered in later chapters). Finally, the scenario shows the client interacting directly with the class factory to initialize the component. Clients must interact directly with the class factory when dealing with a licensed component. But with non-licensed components, a client can use COM-provided wrapper functions like *CoCreateInstance* that isolate it from the class factory.

Connectable Objects: COM's Event Service

Connectable objects are COM's version of a standard event service. A COM object can support ODL-defined outgoing interfaces as well as incoming ones. These interfaces provide a standard way for defining events and their parameters. Objects that support outgoing interfaces are called *connectable objects* or *sources*. COM also provides interfaces—called *sinks*—that let objects subscribe to these outgoing events. This mechanism lets source components specify events they emit via ODL. And sink components, such as event handlers, can subscribe to these events and have their event-handler interfaces invoked when an event occurs.

Sinks and sources allow clients to become servers—and vice versa. A connectable object can have as many outgoing interfaces as it likes. Each interface is composed of a set of outgoing functions; each function represents a single event or notification. These events tell whatever sink is listening that something interesting just happened to the object. Figure 25-10 shows a one-to-many relationship between a source and sinks. We cover COM's connectable objects in great detail in Chapter 29, "OLE: Compound Documents and OCXs," as part of the OCX presentation (this is where they first appeared).

In COM, producers and consumers of events are directly connected via sinks and sources. In contrast, CORBA's event service also provides an intermediary object—the event channel—to broker interactions between event producers and consumers. The CORBA approach has many advantages. The producers and consumers only have to know about a single well-known object to exchange events and notifications. In addition, because the CORBA event service is localized in a specialized event channel, event service providers can create powerful add-on features such as event filters, persistent event queues, and smart publish-and-subscribe services.

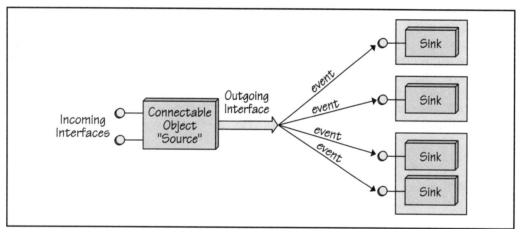

Figure 25-10. Connectable Objects: The COM Style Event Service.

COM Style Inheritance: Aggregation and Containment

Microsoft's labeling of COM as an object model has drawn jeers from some corners of the industry. To many, the definition of object oriented includes support for inheritance. The object-purists have a point: Some developers value inheritance as a way to speed development of code. However, COM is aimed at construction of interfaces, not objects.

*— **John R. Rymer** (January, 1994)*

Inheritance has become a real sticky point as far as OLE is concerned. The lack of inheritance has led object purists to denounce OLE as having "fake objects," even though end users, the ones with the money, frankly don't give a damn.

*— **Kraig Brockschmidt, Author**
Inside OLE 2, Second Edition*

Unlike CORBA, COM does not support multiple inheritance. However, a COM component can support multiple interfaces. By issuing *QueryInterface* calls, COM clients can discover at run time which group of interfaces a component supports. These two mechanisms allow developers to create outer components that encapsulate the services of inner components and represent them to a client. OLE supports two methods of encapsulation: *containment/delegation* and *aggregation* (see Figure 25-11). In both cases, the outer object controls the lifetimes of the inner objects; and its **IUnknown** represents the inner object's interfaces.

In *containment/delegation*, the outer object must reissue the method invocations it receives on behalf of its inner objects. In Figure 25-11, the outer object A contains the inner objects B and C. A's **IUnknown** knows about interfaces A, B, and C. When a client wants to talk to B or C, the outer object calls on the methods these inner objects provide—this is called *delegation*.

In *aggregation* mode, instead of re-issuing each call, the outer component's **IUnknown** directly exposes the inner object's interface pointers to its clients. In other words, the outer object exposes the inner object's interfaces as its own. So the inner object directly talks to the client, but delegates its **IUnknown** to the outer object. In Figure 25-11, inner objects B and C are part of A's **IUnknown**. However, the client directly talks to B and C without A's intervention.

What all this means is that the COM environment is inherently flat. "Inheritance" is achieved through a web of pointers that link or aggregate different interfaces. Microsoft believes that aggregation and containment provide all the reuse that's needed in a distributed environment (see next Soapbox).

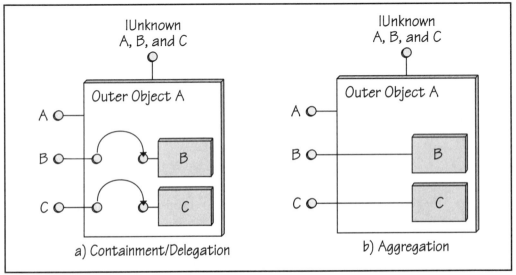

Figure 25-11. COM's Delegation Versus Aggregation.

The Multiple Inheritance Thing

Soapbox

The problem is that the "contract" between components in an implementation hierarchy is not clearly defined. When the parent or child component changes its behavior unexpectedly, the behavior of related components may become undefined.

> — Sara Williams et al., Microsoft
> OLE Technical Evangelist
> (January, 1995)

Inheritance is dangerous, so Microsoft's COM won't support it. It's like saying divide-by-zero is dangerous, so let's remove the "divide" operation from our microprocessors.

> — Cliff Reeves, IBM Director of Objects
> (February, 1995)

CORBA supports multiple inheritance; COM doesn't. COM takes the unique position that inheritance is dangerous, citing the "fragile base class problem." This means that changing a base class—for example, by adding methods—can break the code that uses the base class or inherits from it. COM's solution is to abandon inheritance—a key pillar of object-oriented programming. What you're left with is a system of vtables that you can use to encapsulate groups of procedures with an array of pointers. Paradoxically, Microsoft supports inheritance in its standalone class libraries—for example, its C++ Foundation Class Library.

For the rest of the industry, inheritance forms the basis of OO and frameworks; without it, you have simple encapsulation without object reuse. Inheritance allows an object to reuse code without duplication and without code redundancy. Inheritance also helps programmers clearly define and document reuse boundaries. Microsoft claims that to properly support subclassing, you must ship source code with the base classes—it's the documentation. Yet, NeXT has shipped three major releases of its base classes since 1989; all without disrupting subclasses that have built from them. In most cases, the NeXT class libraries were updated without requiring modification or recompilation of the client classes.

If deep inheritance is dangerous in certain situations, the programmer can flatten the class hierarchy and resort to *assembly* or *aggregation*—meaning you can combine multiple objects using encapsulation. However, we don't believe it makes sense to eliminate inheritance altogether just because it can be dangerous in certain situations. Polymorphism is also dangerous, so why not eliminate it too? Instead of eliminating key features of the object model, why not fix the problem?

For example, IBM's SOM fixes the fragile base class problem by letting you add new methods to an existing class (based on a release order). You can change an internal class implementation while retaining full binary compatibility. When users install a new SOM class, existing clients continue to work perfectly, while new apps can take advantage of the new features. SOM even lets you compose a new class at run time and add methods to an existing class. This means that you can use SOM to do run-time object composition. For example, an object factory can use multiple inheritance to create a custom class "on-the-fly" based on a client's requirements. NeXT's Objective C provides a similar solution.

In a bizarre turn of events, Microsoft and Digital announced (in April, 1995) that they plan to add base class libraries, class inheritance, and cross language object sharing to the Digital/Microsoft *Common Object Model (COM)*—remember, that's the other COM. This program, called *Pegasus*, is designed to provide advanced COM capabilities on top of Digital's *ObjectBroker*. According to Digital and Microsoft, "Pegasus enhances COM by adding the ability to use classes and multiple inheritance when creating COM software components. Developers can specialize existing COM components using inheritance, even if they do not have the component's source code." It seems that Digital may have come to the rescue!

Elements of Pegasus will become available in 1996. When all this comes together, Microsoft will provide three object models: language-based class libraries for the desktop; COM for components; and Digital's COM and Pegasus. Which do you choose? And how do they play together? We still don't know. For example, we still can't tell how distributed COM objects will be stored, located, secured, replicated, and managed. We may get a better idea after the first beta of Cairo ships in late 1996. Here is what's clear: Microsoft is putting some form of distributed objects in its next generation of Windows products and it will be based on COM and OLE. It also looks like our industry is heading for a great distributed object showdown: COM versus CORBA. Digital may provide the proverbial gateway. ❑

Chapter 26

OLE: Automation, Scripting, and Type Libraries

Since an automated task requires fewer skills to perform, a much larger number of people can effectively perform that task. Once automated, a task that was once the private privilege of a few becomes a possibility for all. Call it freedom and democracy.

— **Kraig Brockschmidt, Author**
Inside OLE 2, Second Ed., 1995

OLE automation allows client programs to dynamically invoke methods that manipulate the contents of scriptable objects. Like OpenDoc's OSA, OLE automation is not specific to any scripting language—it works with any program that can issue dynamic method invocations. The information covered in this chapter transcends automation. It explains important aspects of the OLE object model—including dynamic dispatching and how clients discover the methods that server objects provide at run time. As you know from Part 2, these are important elements of any distributed object model. Dynamic invocations are also a key technology for OLE custom controls (OCXs), which are covered in Chapter 29.

Automation services use OLE's Component Object Model (COM), but they may be implemented independently from the rest of OLE. Using OLE automation, you can create applications that expose automation objects to scripting tools and macro languages. You can also manipulate the automation objects an application chooses to expose. Finally, you can create tools—including browsers, compilers, and scripting languages—that access and manipulate these automation objects.

Figure 26-1 shows the three elements that constitute OLE's automation and scripting services. *Automation servers* are the OLE objects that a scriptable application exposes. *Automation controllers* are the tools and client programs that access these automation servers. The *type library* defines and registers the methods and properties an automation server exposes. It lets clients dynamically discover at run time automation services and their metadata. In this chapter, we cover the OLE interfaces that support these services. We also cover the *Object Description Language (ODL)* you use to describe automation servers. The ODL is used to describe all the interfaces of an OLE component—whether they're static or dynamic, incoming or outgoing.

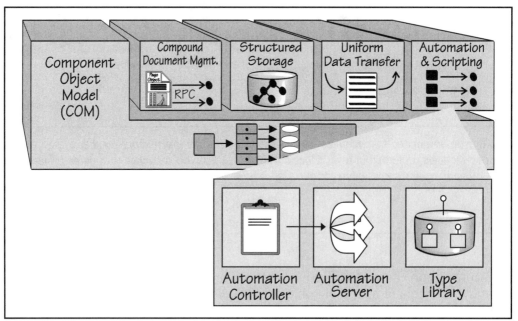

Figure 26-1. OLE's Automation and Type Library Services.

AUTOMATION, OLE STYLE

OLE automation, like OpenDoc's OSA, allows a single program to control automation servers residing in many applications. It lets system integrators assemble the best pieces from different applications to create new applications. Any scripting language or programming tool that implements OLE automation can invoke an automation server. Unlike OSA, OLE automation does not route semantic events to embedded parts and their contents; there is no equivalent of the object specifier. Instead, OLE automation is more like the CORBA dynamic invocation services—it lets clients bind at run time to an object's methods.

The OLE *type library*, like the CORBA Interface Repository, allows clients to dynamically discover the methods and properties an automation server exposes. OLE's *Object Description Language (ODL)*, like the CORBA IDL, is used to describe these interfaces. In contrast, OpenDoc's OSA not only provides late binding, but it also concerns itself with the semantics of the message. OSA looks inside a semantic message for an object specifier that it resolves to find which part should handle an event; it then dispatches the event to that part. So in this sense, OpenDoc automation does more work on your behalf.

How the Pieces Work Together

Figure 26-2 shows how the OLE automation pieces come together. An automation server must support OLE's **IDispatch** interface. The server's automation objects are described and maintained in a run-time repository called the *type library*. OLE programmers must describe their automation objects—including their method names and parameter types, as well as object properties—using OLE ODL representations. They then use OLE's *MKTYPLIB* utility to compile the ODL file into a type library.

Automation controllers—meaning clients—can learn the names of the methods and properties an object supports using the type library's **ITypeLib** interface. The type library, like the CORBA Interface Repository, lets you access this information without having to run the object. Finally, using the *IDispatch::Invoke* method clients can create or obtain automation objects; get and set the properties they expose; and execute their methods.

What's an OLE Automation Server?

An OLE automation server is an instance of a class that supports late binding. The server object exposes data and functions that get invoked dynamically at run time. A single application may provide many automation server objects. For example, an application that manages documents may expose several automation servers— including an application, one or more documents, and several windows, tables, cells, paragraphs, and characters. Each object provides unique member functions that let clients manipulate its contents. An object may expose its member functions in the form of methods or properties:

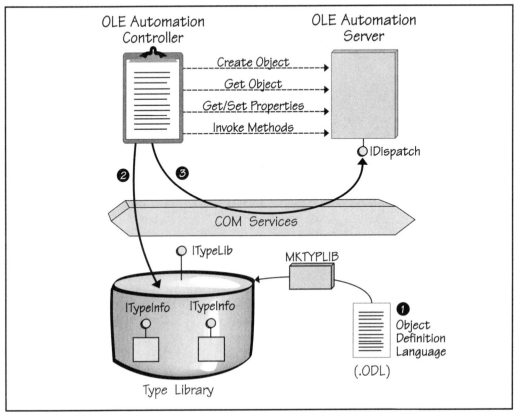

Figure 26-2. How OLE Automation Clients Find Their Servers.

■ ***Methods*** are member functions that perform an action on an object. For example, a document object might provide a *print* method.

■ ***Properties*** are pairs of member functions that *set* and *get* information about the state of an object. For example, a drawing object could have a *color* property whose value you can get or set.

OLE Guidelines for Automation Objects

OLE prescribes a set of guidelines for breaking down a large automation server. According to these guidelines, every automated application must have a top-most *Application* class. The Application class can have subordinate classes such as **Document** and **Font**. These objects are subordinate, which means that they can be reached by navigation from the Application object. OLE also defines a **Collection** class that you can use to iterate through objects. **Documents** is a special collection that combines two classes: **Document** and **Collection**.

Table 26-1 lists the standard automation classes defined by OLE, including their methods and properties. All objects must include an *application* property that returns the application class. And all objects must include a *parent* property that returns the creator of the object. All collection objects—including **Documents**—must provide a *count* property that returns the number of items in a collection. Collection objects must also provide a standard read-only property called *_NewEnum*. This property returns an enumerator object that implements the **IEnumVARIANT** interface (see next Details box). Finally, collections must also provide a standard method called *item* that takes an index as a parameter and returns a collection member—for example, *Dogs.Item(i)*. The remaining properties and methods are self-explanatory.

Table 26-1. Standard OLE Automation Objects.

OLE Automation Object	Methods	Properties
All objects		Application, Parent
All Collections	Item	Count, _NewEnum
Application	Help, Quit, Repeat, Undo	ActiveDocument, Application, Caption, DefaultFilePath, Documents, Fullname, Height, Interactive, Left, Name, Parent, Path, StatusBar, Top, Visible, Width
Document	Activate, Close, NewWindow, Print, PrintOut, PrintPreview, RevertToSaved, Save, SaveAs	Application, Author, Comments, FullName, Keywords, Name, Parent, Path, ReadOnly, Saved, Subject, Title
Documents	Add, Close, Item, Open	Application, Count, _NewEnum, Parent
Font		Application, Bold, Color, Italic, Name, OutlineFont, Parent, Shadow, Size, Strikethrough, Subscript, Superscript

The Structure of an OLE Automation Server

Except for the dynamic dispatch services and some help with collections, OLE automation consists of a set of guidelines that you should follow to expose a hierarchy of scriptable objects. Although nothing is required, OLE recommends that user-interactive applications with subordinate objects always include an **Application** object. The **Application** object identifies the application and provides a way for OLE automation controllers to navigate through an application's exposed objects (see Figure 26-3).

An **Application** object is identified by the *AppObject* attribute in the ODL (see ODL section). In addition, an **Application** object is initialized as the active object when the application starts. You can also explicitly register an active object. This lets OLE automation clients retrieve an object that is already running instead of creating a new instance of the object.

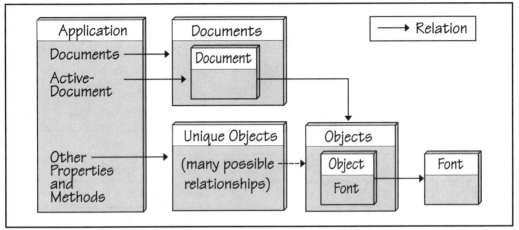

Figure 26-3. The Structure of an OLE Automation Server.

From the application object, you can navigate to embedded objects using properties as pointers. In the figure, *documents* points to a collection of **Documents**. And the *ActiveDocument* property points to a particular active document within that collection. From within a document, you can navigate to a particular subordinate object. When you finally get to a destination object, you can set its properties and invoke its methods. So in contrast to OpenDoc, where the system automatically performs navigation based on an object specifier, OLE requires that the user (or a program) traverse the different containment relationships to get to a target object.

Collection Objects

A collection object can contain zero or more items. For example, an **Application** object may have a **Documents** object that is a collection of all the documents in the application. Collection objects are usually specified using the plural form of an object. For example, the collection object for Row objects would be called Rows. All collection objects must support the *Count* property. This property returns the number of elements in the collection. For example, in a Basic language script $x = ObjVar.Rows.Count$, x equals the number of rows in the object referenced by the object variable ObjVar.

You can use an index to get to an individual object within a collection. For example, *Rows(1)* specifies the first row in an object and *Rows(Rows.Count)* specifies the last row. However, keep in mind that collection objects are not arrays. If a change is made to an element of a collection object, the position of the remaining elements may change. Even if a collection object provides a numeric iterator, there's still no guarantee that the numbers are contiguous.

So, What Makes a Collection Object?

Details

The defining characteristic of a collection object is its ability to iterate over the items it contains. OLE automation defines the **IEnumVARIANT** interface to provide a standard way for OLE automation controllers to iterate over collections (see Figure 26-4). In addition, a collection object must expose a read-only property named _NewEnum_ to let OLE automation controllers know that the object supports iteration. An enumerator object that supports the **IEnumVariant** interface is returned by the _NewEnum property.

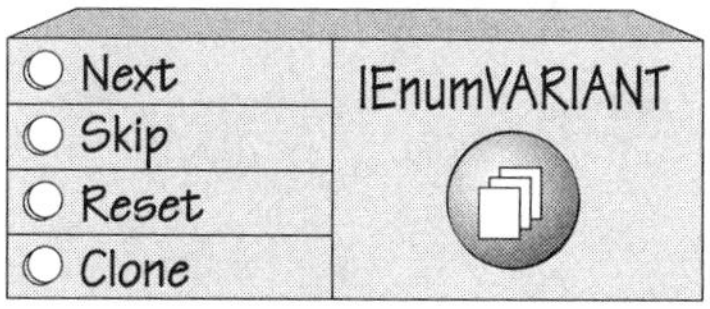

Figure 26-4. The IEnumVARIANT Collection Interface.

The **IEnumVARIANT** interface defines the following member functions:

■ _Next_ retrieves one or more elements in a collection, starting with the current element.

■ _Skip_ skips over one or more elements in a collection.

■ _Reset_ resets the current element to point to the first element in the collection.

■ _Clone_ copies the current state of the enumeration so that you can return to the current element after using _Skip_ or _Reset_.

Your collection objects must implement these member functions. In addition, they must implement functions inherited from **IUnknown** and **IDispatch**. ❑

Automation Controllers: Visual Basic and DispTest

Visual Basic—starting with version 3.0—is an OLE automation controller. It lets you create stand-alone (.EXE) files. OLE also includes a free utility called *DispTest*, which is nothing more than a crippled version of Visual Basic 3.0 used as an automation test controller. DispTest does not include Visual Basic's database access, performance enhancements, and additional documentation. But it's free and available. Visual Basic provides a complete development environment for creating stand-alone applications, while DispTest is intended as a tool for testing programmable interfaces. The snippet of Visual Basic code shown in Figure 26-5 should give you a feeling for how OLE automation can be used to create objects, get and set their properties, invoke their methods, and iterate through their internal objects.

```
' Declare variables
Dim ObjVar as Object
Dim X

' Create an object
Set ObjVar = CreateObject("MyApplication.MyObjectType")

' Write some values
ObjVar.Text = "Hello, world"

' Retrieve a property value from an object
X = ObjVar.Text

' Set the font for ObjVar.Selection.
ObjVar.Selection.Font = 12

' Test if font is bold.
X = ObjVar.Text.IsBold

If X Then
        ObjVar.Text = "The text is bold."
Else
        ObjVar.Text = "The text is not bold."
End If

' Iterate through a collection

For i = 1 to Windows.Count
        Window(i).Minimize    ' Index returns a contained object
Next i

' Visual Basic 4.0 lets you do a for-each collection iteration

For each Window in Windows
        Window.Visible = True
Next Window
```

Figure 26-5. Snippet of Visual Basic Automation Code.

BUILDING OLE AUTOMATION SERVERS

Automation is better for software developers than virtually any other aspect of OLE. It simplifies an age old problem: How to let one application communicate with another simply, easily, and elegantly.

> — *Richard Hale Shaw, Editor*
> *NT Developer*

An automation server is an OLE object that implements a specific interface called **IDispatch**. This interface provides the "late binding" mechanism through which an object can expose its functions—including its incoming and outgoing methods and properties. These late-bound functions are called *dispatch interfaces* or more simply, *dispinterfaces*.

What's a Dispinterface?

If you come from the world of CORBA, a dispinterface is the equivalent of a CORBA *dynamic skeleton interface*. The OLE server decides at run time which method to invoke based on an identifier (the dispID) that it reads from the incoming message. In contrast, OLE's regular interfaces export their functions through vtable pointers that are compiled into the client source code. This means the client must be "early-bound" to a function based on its location in the vtable.

So how do clients invoke a particular dispinterface method or attribute? They do this by calling a single function—*IDispatch::Invoke*—and passing it a *dispatch identifier (dispID)* that uniquely identifies a method or property. How are these dispIDs generated? They're specified and generated using the Object Description Language (ODL). We cover the ODL in more detail later in this chapter. But for now, the snippet of ODL in Figure 26-6 should help you understand what we mean. As you can see, the *Age* property has a dispID of 0, the *Bark* method has a dispID of 1, and so on.

```
dispinterface Dog
  {
  properties:
   [id(0)] long Age;

  methods:
   [id(1)] long Bark;
   [id(2)] long Sit;
   [id(3)] long Run;
  };
```

Figure 26-6. Object Definition Language Snippet for a Dog Dispinterface.

Only the *IDispatch::Invoke* method is compiled. The *invoke* method, at run time, uses the dispIDs to dispatch method calls and invoke gets or puts on properties. In other words, the server object must resolve at run time which method or property is invoked. In addition to the dispID, the *Invoke* method's arguments include a structure that defines the dispID method parameters and their types. Other parameters are the *locale identifier* that specifies the national language associated with the call and a structure for returning error information.

The IDispatch Interface

IDispatch provides mechanisms to access and retrieve information about an object's methods and properties as well as the *invoke* method (see Figure 26-7). In addition to the member functions inherited from **IUnknown**, you need to implement the following member functions within the class definition of each **IDispatch** object you expose via OLE automation:

■ *Invoke* maps an incoming dispID to a method call or a property access. Consequently, it lets you dynamically invoke the methods exposed by the object's dispinterface and access its properties.

■ *GetIDsOfNames* converts text names of properties and methods—including parameters—into a corresponding set of dispIDs, which may then be used on subsequent calls to *Invoke*.

■ *GetTypeInfoCount* returns whether there is type information available for this dispinterface.

■ *GetTypeInfo* retrieves the type information for this dispinterface. OLE provides a standard implementation of this function, so that you don't have to do it yourself. Type information is metadata that describes the interface.

As you can see, three of the four member functions of **IDispatch** are only there to help clients get the run-time information they need to issue the *Invoke* method.

```
○ Invoke                    IDispatch
○ GetIDsOfNames
○ GetTypeInfoCount
○ GetTypeInfo
```

Figure 26-7. The IDispatch Member Functions.

OLE provides various helper functions to implement the **IDispatch** interface including the OLE API functions *CreateStdDispatch* and *DispInvoke*. The fastest way to implement the **IDispatch** interface is to call *CreateStdDispatch*. This function is useful in situations where an OLE automation server only uses the standard dispatch exception codes and supports a single national language. *DispInvoke* allows a server object to handle special situations before or after calling the OLE API dispatch functions.

What Does an IDispatch Client Do?

By now, you should have a good idea of what an automation server does. In this section, we look at what an OLE automation client must do to obtain automation services. The best way to explain the client's role is to walk through a scenario (see Figure 26-8). Here's a step-by-step description of what an OLE automation client does:

1. *Initializes OLE*. The client must issue a standard *OleInitialize* API call to make sure OLE is present and initialized.

2. *Creates an instance of the automation server class*. The client creates an instance of the server class—represented by the specified class ID—by issuing a *CoCreateInstance* API call. The call returns a pointer to the object's **IUnknown** interface.

3. *Gets a pointer to the server's IDispatch interface*. The client issues a *IUnknown::QueryInterface* call to find out if **IDispatch** is implemented by that server. If so, the call returns an interface pointer for it.

4. *Obtains type information on this dispinterface*. The client calls *IDispatch::GetTypeInfo* to obtain information on this dispinterface. The call returns descriptions of the dispinterface's properties, methods, and their data parameters. If you want type information on all the interfaces an object supports, you must issue a *IProvideClassInfo::GetClassInfo* call (we cover this interface in the next section).

5. *Obtains a dispID for a name*. The client issues a *IDispatch::GetIDsOfNames* function call to obtain dispIDs for the properties or methods it wants to manipulate.

6. *Invokes the server*. The client must supply the proper parameters and dispID. Then it issues a *IDispatch::Invoke* function call to execute a method on this dispinterface, or to get or set a property.

7. *Decrements the reference count*. The client issues a *IUnknown::Release* function call to decrement the reference count on that object. An object with a

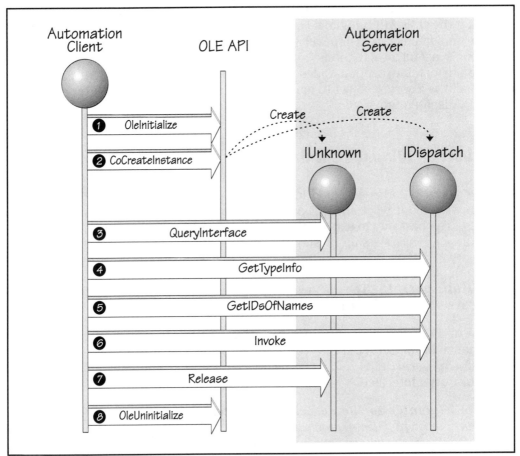

Figure 26-8. How OLE Clients Access Their Automation Servers.

reference count of zero can be safely deleted from memory.

8. ***Uninitializes OLE***. The client does this by issuing a standard *OleUninitialize* API call.

HOW OLE CREATES AND MANAGES TYPE INFORMATION

OLE's *Type Libraries* are repositories of persistent metadata that describe every object's incoming methods, outgoing methods, and the readable and writable properties they expose. This information is vital to automation servers and clients (and to OLE custom controls). The server's **IDispatch** interface uses the type library to obtain the interface descriptions it supplies to its clients via *IDis-*

patch::GetTypeInfo. In this section, we first explain how the type library is populated with metadata generated via the ODL. Then we explain how you can access the metadata using OLE's **ITypeLib**, **ITypeInfo**, and **IProvideClassInfo** interfaces.

The Object Description Language

A type library is at the heart of every OLE automation object.

> — *Richard Hale Shaw, Editor*
> *NT Developer*

As we said earlier, OLE's *Object Description Language (ODL)* is used to define the interfaces an object supports—including the automation dispinterfaces. The ODL is a normal text file that you can generate manually or through a tool like Microsoft's Visual C++. The latest version of Visual C++ provides a Class Wizard that lets you specify the methods and properties from lists of types; it then automatically generates an ODL file for you.

Figure 26-9 shows the main sections of an ODL file. Let's go over them:

- *Library* uniquely identifies and names an ODL. The library names a body of ODL—everything between the curly braces. An ODL is identified by the unique *type library* to which it belongs. A library has a name, unique global identifier (GUID), help context, and some defining attributes. The more interesting attributes include: *lcid*, the national language locale; *hidden*, meaning the library should never be displayed by a browsing tool; *restricted*, meaning the functions within the library can't be called; and *version*, which specifies a version number.

- *Importlib* brings in information from another type library (.TLB) file. To pull in automation types, servers with dispinterfaces must always import *stdole.tlb*—an OLE-provided library.

- *Interfaces* define the signatures of the member functions that are part of a static vtable. Each function must have a name, return type, and a list of parameters. The list can be void or contain a sequence of *[attributes] <type> <name>* entries separated by a comma. The more interesting interface attributes include: *hidden*, meaning the interface should never be displayed by a browsing tool; *restricted*, meaning the member functions within that interface can't be invoked; *dual*, meaning the interface is both static and dynamic; and *ODL* to distinguish it from an OLE IDL. Interfaces can also have a GUID (also called the IID for Interface ID) and help context. The attributes on each function in the interface

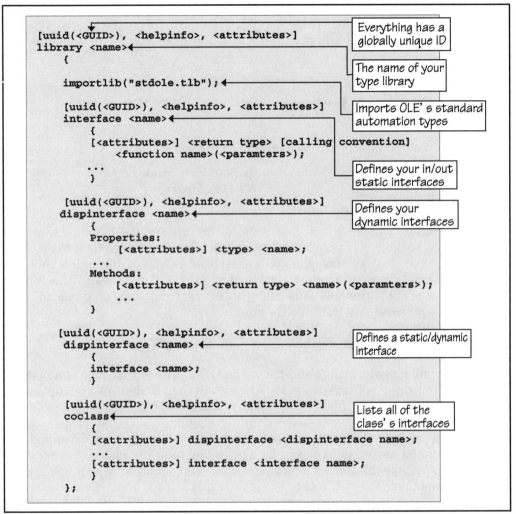

Figure 26-9. The Structure OLE's Object Description Language (ODL).

include *propget* and *propput*, which indicates a get/put property function; *vararg* indicates the function can take a variable number of parameters; and *id(n)* assigns a dispID to the member. You can also denote a hidden function with a leading underscore—for example, *_Bark*. Finally, parameters themselves can each have attributes like *in*, *out*, and *optional*.

■ ***Dispinterfaces*** define the dynamic methods and properties of a dispatchable interface. Figure 26-9 shows two formats for dispinterfaces. The first format lets you specify individual methods and properties. The second format simply picks up the functions in some interface and makes a dispinterface out of it. A dispinterface can have a GUID (also called the IID) and help context. Each property and method can have an *id(n)* attribute that specifies a dispID for that member. A property can have a *read-only* attribute. Each method and the parameters of those methods can have the same attributes as interface (see previous bullet). Note that the two formats for dispinterface were necessary before dual interfaces were introduced in late 1994. Dual interfaces let you specify that an interface is both static and dynamic using the *dual* attribute.

■ ***Coclass*** lists all the incoming and outgoing interfaces an OLE class supports. It provides the metadata that lets you enumerate all the incoming and outgoing interfaces that an OLE class supports. A class is identified by a GUID representing a unique Class ID. Coclass introduces some important new attributes: *appobject* identifies a class as an application object in the automation hierarchy; *control* identifies the class as an OLE control; and *licensed* indicates that the class must be instantiated using a **IClassFactory2**. Classes can be *hidden* and have a *version*. In addition, each interface or dispinterface in coclass can include a *source* attribute that marks it as an outgoing interface or event set. Finally, an interface may have a *default* attribute, marking it as the most important interface in a class. You typically have one default incoming interface and one default outgoing interface (also called the primary event set).

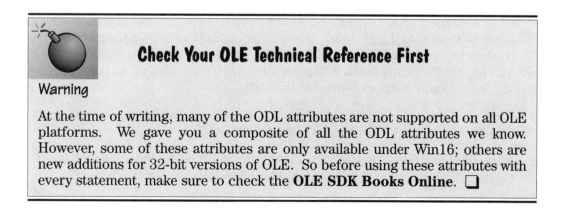

Check Your OLE Technical Reference First

Warning

At the time of writing, many of the ODL attributes are not supported on all OLE platforms. We gave you a composite of all the ODL attributes we know. However, some of these attributes are only available under Win16; others are new additions for 32-bit versions of OLE. So before using these attributes with every statement, make sure to check the **OLE SDK Books Online**. ❑

Building Type Libraries: The Hard Way

There are two ways to record information about interfaces in an OLE type library: the easy way and the hard way. The easy way is to run the ODL script through a special precompiler called MKTYPLIB.EXE (for Make type library). The hard way is to do it yourself by writing a program that uses the OLE type library creation services—including the OLE API function *CreateTypeLib* and the interfaces **ICreateTypeLib** and **ICreateTypeInfo**.

If you're a tool vendor that wants to bypass MKTYPLIB (and even ODL), you'll want to know what's involved in doing it the hard way. Figure 26-10 shows a scenario of what you must do to build a new type library:

1. ***Create a new type library***. The client calls the OLE API function *Create-TypeLib* and passes it a file name and a system identifier—Win32, Win16, or Mac. The function creates a new type library (.TLB) and returns a pointer to the interface **ICreateTypeLib**.

2. ***Set attributes of new type library***. The client calls member functions of the OLE-provided **ICreateTypeLib** interface to set the attributes of a type library. To keep this scenario short we only show three calls: *SetGuid*, *SetHelpContext*, and *SetLcid*. The interface provides member functions that let you set most of the library attributes described in the ODL section.

3. ***Create a new type info object***. The client calls the function *ICreate-TypeLib::CreateTypeInfo* to create a new **ICreateTypeInfo** instance. OLE adds a record in the library for that element and returns a pointer to the object. An element can be anything that's specified within the body of the ODL—including coclass, interface, dispinterface, typedef, and module. In this scenario, we're adding a new dispinterface description.

4. ***Set attributes of new info object***. The client calls member functions of the **ICreateTypeInfo** interface to set the attributes of the dispinterface. To keep it short, we only show three calls *SetGuid*, *SetFunctionAndParamNames*, and *SetFuncDesc*. The interface provides member functions to set most of the attributes and structures defined in the ODL.

5. ***Save your work***. The client calls the function *ICreateTypeLib::SaveAll-Changes* to save all the work in the (.ODL) file.

6. ***Register your type library***. The client calls the *RegisterTypeLib* OLE API to register the library. Now, automation clients can find it.

Building Type Libraries: The Easy Way

The easy way is to let MKTYPLIB do it all for you. It first reads your ODL and precompiles it. Then it calls *CreateTypeLib* to obtain pointers to **ICreateTypeLib** and **ICreateTypeInfo**. It then uses these interfaces to create the necessary structures based on the ODL file. The end results are a type library (.TLB) and a (.H) file with function prototypes for your interfaces and dispinterfaces.

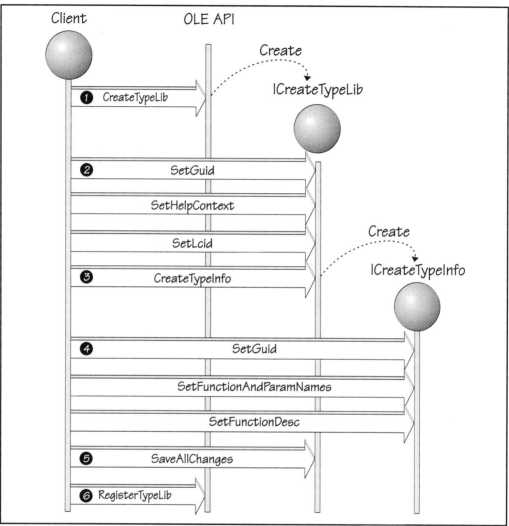

Figure 26-10. Scenario: How Type Libraries Are Really Built.

Registering a Type Library

You can ship the (.TLB) file with an object or attach it as a resource in an automation server's EXE or DLL. You can also store it inside a compound file's stream, or make it available through a shared file on a network server. Regardless of how it gets there, the information in these type libraries must be made available to automation objects and OCXs. In addition to creating registry entries for an automation server, an installation program must also create entries for the corresponding type libraries using the OLE API function *RegisterTypeLib*.

Finding and Loading a Type Library

To obtain the metadata they need, OLE automation clients must first be able to locate a type library and load its contents into memory. So how does the client find the type library in the first place? By looking for it in the registry. The client invokes the OLE API *QueryPathOfRegTypeLib* and passes it the ID of the type library it wants. The API returns the path of a registered type library. Now that the client has the library's file name, it can load it by invoking the OLE API *LoadRegTypeLib*. This function uses the registry information to load the type library. OLE also provides the function *LoadTypeLibFromResource* to extract a type library from a resource attached to a DLL or EXE. Both load functions return a **ITypeLib** interface pointer through which a client can navigate the entire library.

So, How Do I Get Information Out of a Type Library?

At this point, we know how to create a type library, fill it with information, register it with OLE, and load it in memory. So the only thing left to do is figure out how to retrieve metadata information from it. This is where the **ITypeLib** and **ITypeInfo** interfaces come into play (see Figure 26-11). You can use these two interfaces to query the details of each type within a library—for example, interface, dispinterface, or coclass.

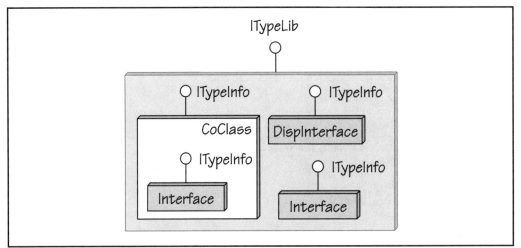

Figure 26-11. The Type Library Query Interfaces: ITypeLib and ITypeInfo.

ITypeLib and **ITypeInfo** provide a large number of member functions to help clients navigate through type libraries. A client can use these member functions to discover information about names, dispIDs, argument types, help, GUIDs, attributes, structure definitions, interface lists, and anything that's defined via an ODL. Remember, the ODL was used to capture all this information in the first place.

A Type Library Navigation Scenario

If you're getting confused, it's time for another scenario that brings it all together. Let's examine the type library from the point of view of a blind client that's looking for all the information it can get on what servers have to offer in terms of interfaces—both static and dynamic. We assume that the servers are registered and that the client knows its servers by their global Class IDs (CLSIDs). Somewhere in this universe there's a directory that keeps track of all that stuff. So let's work our way through the scenario shown in Figure 26-12:

1. ***Find the type library.*** The client calls the OLE API *QueryPathOfRegTypeLib* to obtain a path to a type library given a Class ID.

2. ***Load the type library.*** The client calls the OLE API *LoadRegTypeLib* to load the type library and obtain a pointer to a **ITypeLib** interface.

3. ***Query the type library for interesting stuff.*** The client can issue over ten member function calls to retrieve type library metadata information. In the scenario, we issue a *GetTypeInfoCount* call to retrieve the number of type descriptions in a library. We then issue a *GetDocumentation* call to retrieve the complete help file and context ID help for a library. Finally, we issue the *GetLibAttr* call to retrieve a structure containing the library's own attributes. At this point, all we're doing is looking for worthwhile metadata.

4. ***Retrieve a specified type description.*** The client now wants information on a particular type stored in the library. Let's assume it wants a particular dispinterface description. The client issues a *GetTypeInfoOfGuid* to retrieve the **ITypeInfo pointer** to the dispinterface given the Interface ID (IID). We could have just as easily asked for a pointer to an interface, coclass, or anything with a GUID specified in the ODL.

5. ***Query the type info object.*** Now that the client has a pointer to the **ITypeInfo** interface for this dispinterface, it can retrieve metadata and contractual information by calling about twenty member functions. It can even invoke a method or access a property of an object. In our scenario, the client invokes *GetDocumentation* on the dispinterface, just for fun.

6. ***Let's get some real information.*** The client issues a *GetFuncDesc* call to retrieve a structure containing information about a particular method—including its dispID, the type of function, legal return codes, the invocation style, the calling convention, the number of total arguments, the number of optional arguments, and an array of structures for each argument. Finally, it issues a *ReleaseFuncDesc* to release the structure from memory.

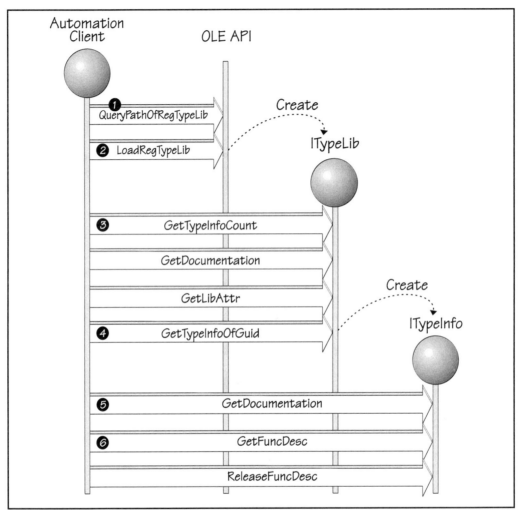

Figure 26-12. Scenario: How a Client Obtains Type Library Information.

Getting Information From IProvideClassInfo

To spare clients the pain and inconvenience of navigating through Type Libraries, server objects can do some of that work themselves and provide the information on demand. Servers can support an interface called **IProvideClassInfo** that clients can obtain through a *QueryInterface* to the object's **IDispatch** or **IUnknown** interfaces. The **IProvideClassInfo** interface has a single member function called *GetClassInfo* that returns a **ITypeInfo** for that object's class.

Of course, server objects must first obtain that information from the type library before exposing it to their clients. They do this by calling *ITypeLib::GetType-InfoOfGuid* on behalf of the clients. So it's just a convenience servers provide to relieve the clients from having to navigate a type library. **IProvideClassInfo** is the easiest way for clients to dynamically discover and learn a server object's interfaces.

Conclusion

We covered a lot of new ground in this long chapter. To explain OLE automation, we had to cover OLE's object model for dynamic interfaces. The ODL is OLE's language for capturing interface metadata and storing it in type libraries—the OLE version of an Interface Repository. OLE, like CORBA, provides interfaces that let clients discover at run time the services a component provides (the metadata). It also lets clients invoke these services dynamically. OLE automation is simply a set of guidelines for structuring scriptable applications using the dynamic services of the underlying object model.

Chapter 27

OLE:
Uniform
Data Transfer

> No matter what mechanism you use to obtain a pointer to a data object, you can treat that source of data in a very standard way, which is exactly why I coined the term Uniform Data Transfer.
>
> — **Kraig Brockschmidt, Author**
> **Inside OLE 2, First Edition**
> **(Microsoft Press, 1994)**

Like OpenDoc, OLE provides a generalized intercomponent data transfer mechanism that you can use in a wide range of situations and across a variety of media. OLE's data transfer mechanism lets you exchange data using protocols such as the clipboard, drag-and-drop, links, or compound documents. The exchanged data can be dragged and then pasted or dropped into the same document, a different document, or a different application. The actual data transfer can take place over shared memory or using storage files. Asynchronous notifications can be sent to a linked client when source data changes. Does this feel like *deja vu*? It should, if you read the corresponding OpenDoc chapter.

In this chapter we introduce the four elements that make up OLE's data transfer services (see Figure 27-1). The **IDataObject** is similar in function to OpenDoc's ubiquitous storage unit. It encapsulates the data to be exchanged and provides methods for manipulating it. The clipboard, drag-and-drop, and notification links are simply three protocols that a client uses to initiate data transfers between source and destination components. You can also initiate these transfers programmatically or from within compound documents. Regardless of how you initiate it, the data transfer part is uniform. The key point, of course, is that the transfer protocols are separated from the data exchange mechanism.

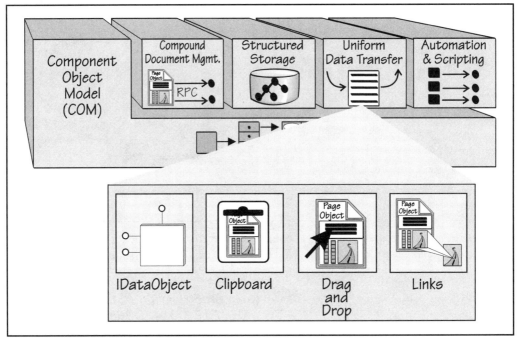

Figure 27-1. OLE's Uniform Data Transfer.

OLE'S DATA TRANSFER MODEL

A *data object* is any OLE component that implements the **IDataObject** interface. To make its data available, an OLE component sets up a data object and makes a pointer available to its **IDataObject** interface. A client can obtain this pointer directly or by using one of OLE's data transfer protocols. Once it has a pointer, the client can invoke member functions to query the availability of data in the requested formats; to send or receive the actual data; and to receive notifications about data changes. You can obtain the data in any of several supported data formats. An OLE transfer protocol is nothing more than a mechanism for passing an **IDataObject** pointer from the source of the data to the consumer of the data.

Data Transfer: Formats and Structures

A data object can represent its content data using three formats: standard, private, and OLE. *Standard* formats include the Windows clipboard interchange data types such as CF_TEXT for describing ASCII text, CF_BITMAP for describing a bitmap, and so on. *Private* formats are understood only by the applications offering the format. OLE defines two structures for describing the interchange data formats: FORMATETC and STGMEDIUM.

FORMATETC—pronounced "format etcetera"—describes a single data format that the data object makes available. The format includes a structure that contains a detailed description of what's being passed. For example, bitmaps can be full content, thumbnails, or iconic. It also contains a flag indicating what storage device is used for a particular transfer as well as a pointer to access that actual medium and get at the data. So FORMATETC is what a client uses to indicate the type of data it wants from a data source object; the source uses it to describe what formats it can provide.

STGMEDIUM describes the medium used to transfer the data. It also points to the actual variable used to access it—for example, a global memory handle or a file name. Depending on the size of the data being transferred, a client can request global memory, disk files, or OLE compound document objects. Clients can choose the most efficient exchange medium on a per-transfer basis. If the data is so big that it should be kept on disk, the data source can indicate a disk-based medium in its preferred format.

You can discover which data formats a data object provides using the *IData-Object::EnumFormatETC* call. All data objects must support this interface. However, note that the enumeration returned is not a guarantee of support. OLE recommends that you treat the enumeration as a hint of the format types that can be passed. Formats can be registered statically in the registry or dynamically when a data object is initialized. You can use the *OleRegEnumFormatEtc* API call to extract these enumerations from the registry.

The IDataObject Interface

The **IDataObject** interface plays a key role in the transferring of data. It provides member functions to retrieve, store, and enumerate data, and handle data-change notifications. The methods that provide this function—excluding the ubiquitous **IUnknown**—are shown in Figure 27-2. Because it's such an important interface, let's take a quick look at what these functions do:

■ *GetData* retrieves data in a specified format using the specified storage medium.

- *GetDataHere* retrieves data in a specified format using the storage medium specified by the client. This allows the client to provide an already allocated storage medium.

- *SetData* sends data in a specified format.

- *QueryGetData* determines whether data is available in the specified format.

- *GetCanonicalFormatEtc* returns a different but logically equivalent FORMATETC structure. This allows the client to determine whether the data it has already obtained is identical to what would be obtained by calling *GetData* with a different format.

- *EnumFormatEtc* enumerates the formats that can be used to send and receive data.

- *DAdvise* creates a callback connection between the data object and the client.

- *DUnadvise* deletes an advisory connection.

- *EnumDAdvise* enumerates the advisory connections currently established on an object.

We'll see these functions in action throughout the remaining sections of this chapter. You can use the "advisory" functions in linking situations where a consumer of data is interested in being notified of data changes in the source. Clipboard and drag-and-drop data objects will refuse any advisory connections. The rest of the functions are used by all protocols that do data transfer.

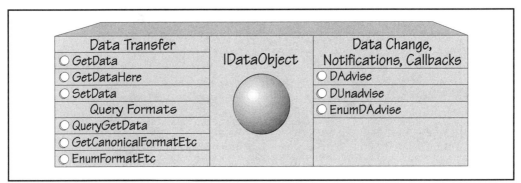

Figure 27-2. The IDataObject Interface.

CLIPBOARD TRANSFERS, OLE STYLE

With clipboard transfers, all you're really doing is passing an **IDataObject** pointer to the clipboard and retrieving it when a consumer asks for some data. OLE provides four API functions to help interact with the clipboard: *OleSetClipboard* places a data object on the clipboard; *OleGetClipboard* retrieves a data object from the clipboard; *OleFlushClipboard* clears the clipboard; and *OleIsCurrentClipboard* determines whether a data object is still on the clipboard. We'll go through a scenario that shows how you use these functions.

Delayed Transfers

Like OpenDoc's promises, OLE supports delayed transfers, a technique whereby data is not transferred until it is actually needed by the consumer. Only information about the impending transfer, such as data formats and mediums, is initially made available at copy or cut time. A source application creates a data-transfer object that holds a copy of the selected data and exposes methods for retrieving the data and receiving change notifications. When a paste operation occurs, the receiving application makes a call to get the actual data from the source application. It can request both the data format and a specific medium across which the data should be transferred.

A Clipboard Data Transfer Scenario

OK, it's scenario time. Let's bring together everything we've learned so far with a delayed clipboard cut-and-paste transfer scenario (see Figure 27-3). Let's walk through the steps:

1. ***Perform a cut or copy.*** The user selects the data content and then does a cut or copy via the edit menu. The source application creates an **IDataObject** object in which it packages the data as well as the enumerator for the FOR-MATETCs.

2. ***Pass a data object pointer to the clipboard***. The source application calls the *OleSetClipboard* API to place a copy of a pointer to the source's **IDataObject** in the clipboard. This marks that data format as being available on the clipboard without passing the actual data.

3. ***Perform a paste***. The user selects a destination area within a target document and performs a paste command from the edit menu.

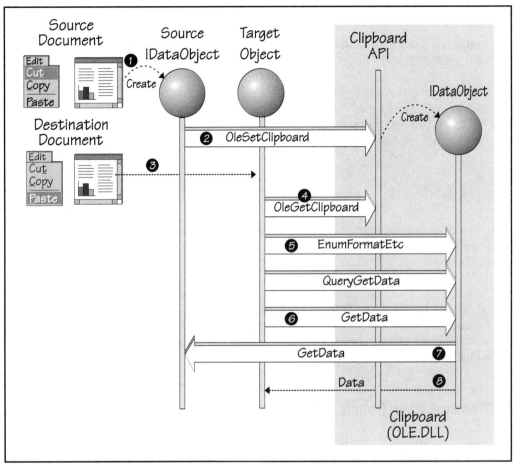

Figure 27-3. A Delayed Clipboard Transfer Scenario.

4. **Get a pointer to the data.** The target application calls the *OleGetClipboard* API to obtain a pointer to an **IDataObject** interface. The pointer returned is that of an OLE2-owned data object that represents the data on the clipboard—there's no actual data at this time.

5. **Get format information.** The target application can call *EnumFormatEtc* and get *QueryGetData* on the clipboard's *IDataObject* to find out what type of data is in this clipboard.

6. **Ask for the data.** If the target application likes what it sees, it calls the clipboard's *GetData* function to retrieve the data.

7. **Get the data from the source.** The clipboard issues a *GetData* call to the *IDataObject* that contains the real source data.

8. ***Pass the data to the consumer***. The clipboard returns the source data in the structures specified by the target application when it called *GetData*. The data is now available for pasting.

This scenario is a bit messy because we move between calls to objects and procedural calls, but it gets the job done. In addition, it illustrates how the OLE clipboard acts as a proxy data object during a delayed data transfer.

DRAG-AND-DROP TRANSFERS

*D*rag-and-drop is really nothing more than a slick way to get an IDataObject pointer from a source to a target.

— *Kraig Brockschmidt*
Dr. Dobb's Journal
(January, 1995)

Drag-and-drop is just another protocol for transferring an **IDataObject** pointer between a data source and a target destination. As opposed to the clipboard's delayed transfer, drag-and-drop is immediate—data is copied or moved from one location to another as part of the mouse action. In addition to the ubiquitous **IDataObject**, OLE drag-and-drop introduces two new interfaces: **IDropSource** and **IDropTarget** (see Figure 27-4). OLE also provides three new APIs for drag-and-drop: *RegisterDragDrop*, *RevokeDragDrop*, and *DoDragDrop*.

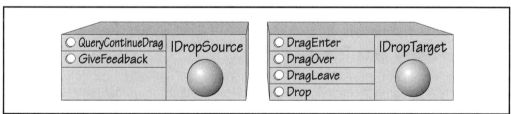

Figure 27-4. OLE's Drag-and-Drop Interfaces.

Drag-and-Drop: Who Does What?

This section gives you a brief overview of who does what during an OLE drag-and-drop operation:

■ The **IDropSource** interface is implemented by the object containing the dragged data. It provides two methods: *QueryContinueDrag* determines whether a drag operation should continue; *GiveFeedback* determines whether a drop can occur.

- The **IDropTarget** interface is implemented by the object that is intended to accept the drop—meaning the drop target. It provides four methods: *DragEnter* determines whether the target can accept the dragged object; *DragOver* provides feedback about the state of the drag operation within a target area; *DragLeave* is called when the mouse leaves the area of a given target; and *Drop* drops the **IDataObject** on this target.

- The **OLE APIs** are used to facilitate the communication between drag sources and drop targets. Every application that can be a drop target must register as such by calling the OLE API function *RegisterDragDrop* and passing it an **IDropTarget** interface pointer as a parameter. An application can "unregister" its interest in drops by calling *RevokeDragDrop*. The *DoDragDrop* API is called by the drag source to initiate a drag-and-drop operation. The API implements a loop that tracks mouse and keyboard movement until the drag is cancelled or a drop occurs.

Drag-and-drop is a cooperative protocol between source and destination objects. The source object supports the **IDataObject** and **IDropSource** interfaces. It also generates the visual pointers that provide the user with feedback during a drag. Finally, it performs any action on the original data resulting from the drop operation—for example, it can delete the data or create a link to it. The target destination object registers its drop-target interface. It also lets the drag source know whether this is a legitimate drop target. If a drop occurs, the target object is responsible for integrating the dropped data with its own content data

A Drag-and-Drop Data Transfer Scenario

In this drag-and-drop scenario, we assume the target application has already registered itself with OLE as a drop-target. The scenario starts when the user initiates a drag (see Figure 27-5). Let's walk through the steps:

1. ***Start the drag***. You initiate the drag with a mouse-down button event. The source application creates an **IDataObject** object in which it packages the data as well as the enumerator for the FORMATETCs.

2. ***The source starts the drag-drop by calling OLE***. The source application invokes the OLE API function *DoDragDrop* and passes it pointers to its **IDropSource** and **IDataObject** interfaces.

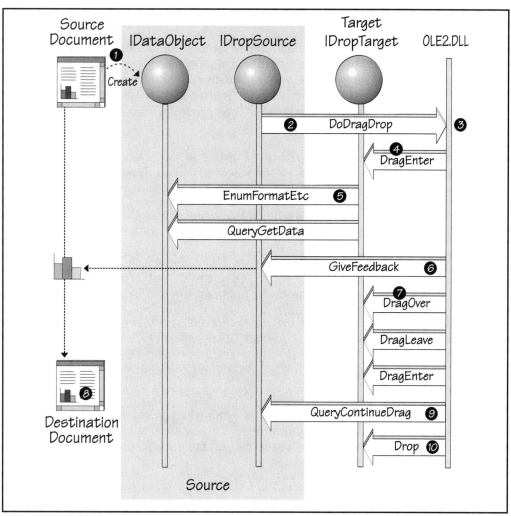

Figure 27-5. OLE Drag-and-Drop Scenario.

3. ***Start looping***. Internally, OLE enters a loop that watches for movements of the mouse. It tracks the mouse as you enter, drag over, and leave different potential target windows without releasing the mouse button.

4. ***Drag enter***. OLE calls the *IDropTarget::DragEnter* method and passes it an **IDataObject** pointer from the source.

5. ***Get format information***. The target can call *EnumFormatEtc* and *QueryGet-Data* on the source's *IDataObject* to find out what type of data is in this data object.

6. ***Provide visual feedback***. The source and target cooperate to provide you with the appropriate visual cues as you drag the data. OLE helps out by calling the method *IDropSource::GiveFeedback* according to what is happening with the mouse and the target. The target returns to OLE information on the effects of a drop at the mouse location (such as "no drop"). OLE passes that information to *IDropSource::GiveFeedback*, which is then responsible for changing the mouse cursor to an appropriate shape and providing the visual feedback that goes with it.

7. ***Continue the loop***. The *DragEnter, DragOver,* and *DragLeave* loop continues as long as the mouse button is not released or you don't cancel the drop. In our scenario, we assume a drop occurs inside the first target visited.

8. ***The mouse button is released***. OLE detects a change in the keyboard or mouse-button state.

9. ***What to do with the drag?*** OLE calls *IDropSource::QueryContinueDrag* which returns whether to cancel the operation or perform a drop. The user could have cancelled the operation by pressing the Esc key.

10. ***Perform a drop***. OLE calls *IDropTarget::Drop* to perform the drop. The target uses the source's **IDataObject** pointer to incorporate the data into the document. The *DoDragDrop* function now returns to the caller the result of the operation. The source deletes the data if the operation was a drag-move (as opposed to drag-copy).

As you can see from the scenario, OLE acts as a broker between the drag-and-drop source and destination. Through OLE, the source maintains control of the mouse's cursor and the drop or cancellation outcome. And when it's all over, the target ends up getting the source's data.

LINKED DATA TRANSFERS

How do consumers of data know when data in the source changes? By using OLE's data notification service. This service is a publish-and-subscribe mechanism through which a data object asynchronously notifies its subscribers of any changes in its data. When a subscriber (or client) receives such a notification, it can ask for an updated copy of the data. To handle data notifications of this kind, OLE introduces two interfaces: **IAdviseSink** and **IDataAdviseHolder**. This is in addition to the **IDataObject**'s notification functions that we described earlier.

What's an Advise Sink?

An advise sink is an object that implements the **IAdviseSink** interface. Simply put, it's an object that wants to be notified when a data object changes. When data changes, the "sink" receives an asynchronous callback from that data source. The **IAdviseSink** interface is implemented by the consumer of the data. The consumer invokes *IDataObject::DAdvise* to pass a pointer to its **IAdviseSink** interface to a data object—the source. When the data object detects a change, it calls the *IAdviseSink::OnDataChange* function to notify the consumer (see Figure 27-6). Think of this function as a callback. You can also use **IAdviseSink** to receive other callbacks—including *OnViewChange*, *OnClose*, *OnSave*, and others. However, the only callback that deals with linked data is *OnDataChange*—the topic of this section.

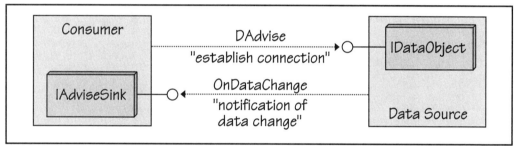

Figure 27-6. OLE Data Notification Callbacks.

Data objects can establish notifications with multiple advise sinks. This heavily burdens the data object because it must go through its subscriber list to determine whom to notify when the data changes. To help alleviate this burden, OLE provides an interface called **IDataAdviseHolder** to which the data object can delegate some of the work. It's an actual implementation instead of a specification. Figure 27-7 shows the member functions supported by **IDataAdviseHolder**. Notice that they're carbon copies of the notification functions of **IDataObject** (except these have code implementations). The function *SendOnDataChange* is new—it calls all the advisory links currently registered and sends them notifications. So all **IDataObject** has to do is delegate. Now that's a helper function!

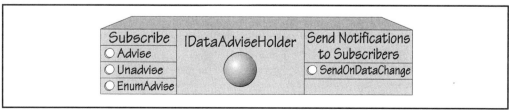

Figure 27-7. IDataAdviseHolder: The Ultimate Helper.

A Parting Scenario

Figure 27-8 is a scenario that should warm any manager's heart—it shows "true" delegation in action. Let's walk through the steps involved in passing data using advisory notifications:

1. *Create an advisory connection*. The consumer creates a connection between a data object and its advisory sink by calling *IDataObject::DAdvise* and passing it a pointer to its **IAdviseSink**.

2. *Delegate the advisory connection*. The data object delegates the connection by calling *IDataAdviseHolder::Advise* and passing it pointers to its own data and to the interested **IAdviseSink**.

3. *Enumerate the established advisory connections*. The consumer does this by invoking *IDataObject::EnumAdvise*.

4. *Ask the helper for the information*. The data object asks its helper to take care of this enumeration request by invoking *IDataAdviseHolder::EnumAdvise*.

5. *Data changed*. The data object detects a change in its data, so it invokes *IDataAdviseHolder::SendOnDataChange* and tells it to take care of business.

6. *Inform all advisory link holders of the change*. The **IDataAdviseHolder** sends *IAdviseSink::OnDataChange* notifications callbacks to all the advisory links currently registered. It also passes them a pointer to the **IDataObject**.

7. *Get the latest data*. The consumer uses the pointer it received for the **IDataObject** to obtain the latest copy of the data by issuing *IDataObject::GetData*.

8. *Break the advisory connection*. The consumer calls *IDataObject::DUnadvise* to terminate a previously established advisory connection.

9. *Always delegate*. The data object calls *IDataAdviseHolder::Unadvise* to remove the connection from its helper's list.

It would be nice if all scenarios were that sweet. This is one version of "publish-and-subscribe," OLE style. A second version uses the more generic *connectable objects* service introduced by OLE's custom controls (see Chapter 29, "OLE: Compound Documents and OCXs").

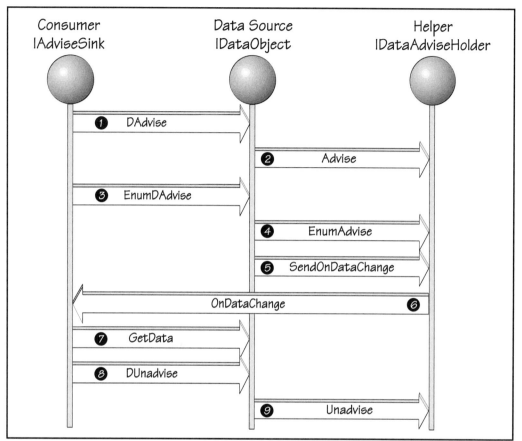

Figure 27-8. Scenario: OLE Data-Change Notifications.

CONCLUSION

This concludes our brief tour of OLE's data transfer facilities. OLE and OpenDoc share the same philosophy of separating the data transfer protocols from the data object that's being passed. However, their implementations are quite different. OLE tends to mix procedural APIs with object interfaces. In contrast, with OpenDoc everything is an object. The OpenDoc storage unit has a lot more function than the corresponding OLE data object. OLE's callbacks are elegant, especially when augmented with the more general connectable objects service. OpenDoc components can receive general notifications using CORBA's event service.

Chapter 28

OLE:
Structured
Storage and
Monikers

Masters, as we know, very often disguise themselves as servants.

— *Benjamin Wooley, Author*
Virtual Worlds
(Penguin, 1992)

Like OpenDoc's Bento, OLE provides structured storage that lets independently developed components save their contents within the same file. OLE calls it the *Structured Storage Architecture.* And like OpenDoc/CORBA, the OLE architecture provides mechanisms for components to save their state persistently and for clients to find these persistent objects and load them into memory. The commercial incarnation of this architecture is called *compound files*, also known as "DocFiles." Microsoft has strongly hinted that compound files are the precursors of the Windows 96 object-oriented file system that goes by the code name Cairo. The idea is that if you write to the OLE compound file APIs now, your investment is protected for posterity. OLE's current implementation of compound files provides a shared medium that you can use for data exchange and for storing the persistent state of components. The current implementation creates compound files on top of existing file systems. With Cairo, compound files are the file system.

In this chapter, we introduce the three elements that make up OLE's persistence and structured storage services: *compound files, persistent objects,* and *monikers* (see Figure 28-1). Think of them as persistent objects, OLE style. Some of the OLE persistent services—for example, compound files—will seem very familiar, especially if you read the chapters on Bento and CORBA persistence. Others—for example, monikers—are very peculiar to OLE. This chapter also covers scores of persistent OLE interfaces that define these functions—including **IStorage**, **IStream**, **IPersistStorage**, **IPersistStream**, **IMoniker**, and others. So fasten your seat belts; we have a lot of ground to cover.

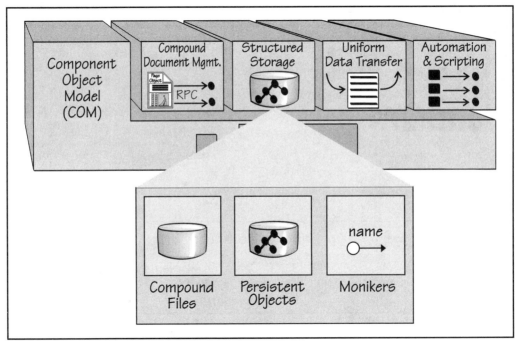

Figure 28-1. OLE's Structured Storage and Persistent Services.

OLE'S STRUCTURED STORAGE: COMPOUND FILES

OLE provides a set of interfaces (and an implementation of these interfaces) that provide a "file system within a file." The file system within a file is created by providing an extra level of indirection between a file and the applications that use it. As a result, it is possible to subdivide a single file into multiple storage compartments that the system can manage on behalf of components that know nothing of each other. If this sounds like *deja vu*, it's because you heard the same story in the Bento chapter. OLE's compound files and OpenDoc's Bento solve the same problem but with different implementations.

The Structure of a Compound File

OLE creates a hierarchy within a compound file consisting of directory-like elements called *storages* and file-like elements called *streams* (see Figure 28-2). Both storages and streams are OLE objects—they're implemented using the interfaces **IStorage** and **IStream**, respectively. A storage object can contain other storage objects as well as streams. OLE lets you create any number of storages and streams in a single compound file. Note that storages do not contain data—the data lives inside streams.

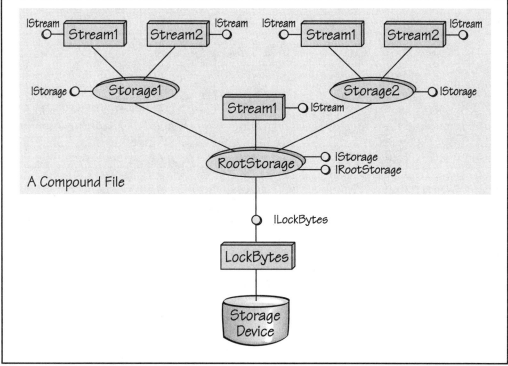

Figure 28-2. The Structure of a Compound File.

Each compound file has a *root storage* from which all other elements descend. A root storage implements two interfaces: **IRootStorage** and **IStorage**. The root storage represents the underlying file. It provides a single function *SwitchToFile* that you use to associate a storage object with a file (see Figure 28-3). If you change the underlying file by invoking this function, you also change all the enclosed substorages and streams. Finally, OLE implements a *LockBytes* object that supports an interface called **ILockBytes**. It is used to represent a physical device (see next Details box).

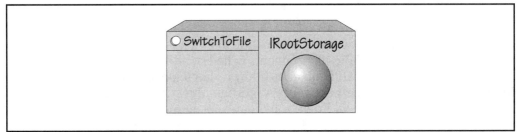

Figure 28-3. The IRootStorage Interface.

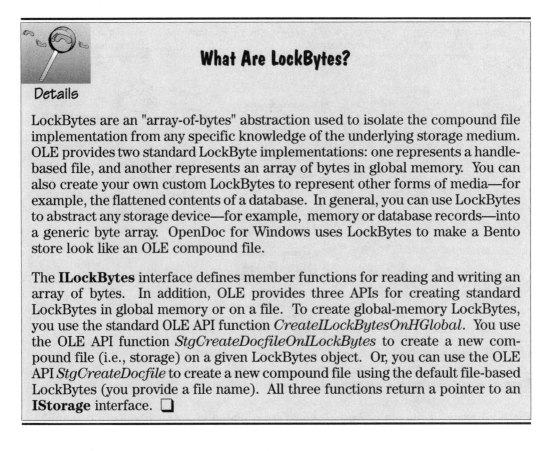

What Are LockBytes?

Details

LockBytes are an "array-of-bytes" abstraction used to isolate the compound file implementation from any specific knowledge of the underlying storage medium. OLE provides two standard LockByte implementations: one represents a handle-based file, and another represents an array of bytes in global memory. You can also create your own custom LockBytes to represent other forms of media—for example, the flattened contents of a database. In general, you can use LockBytes to abstract any storage device—for example, memory or database records—into a generic byte array. OpenDoc for Windows uses LockBytes to make a Bento store look like an OLE compound file.

The **ILockBytes** interface defines member functions for reading and writing an array of bytes. In addition, OLE provides three APIs for creating standard LockBytes in global memory or on a file. To create global-memory LockBytes, you use the standard OLE API function *CreateILockBytesOnHGlobal*. You use the OLE API function *StgCreateDocfileOnILockBytes* to create a new compound file (i.e., storage) on a given LockBytes object. Or, you can use the OLE API *StgCreateDocfile* to create a new compound file using the default file-based LockBytes (you provide a file name). All three functions return a pointer to an **IStorage** interface. ❑

The IStorage Interface

You use the **IStorage** interface to interact with storage objects. It lets you move, copy, rename, create, destroy, and enumerate storage elements. A storage object itself cannot store application-defined data. However, it does store names of elements—both storages and streams—contained within it. It's a directory. Every storage and stream object in a compound file has a specific character name to identify it. These names are used to tell **IStorage** functions what element in that storage to open, destroy, move, copy, rename, and so on. All implementations of storage objects must, at least, be able to support element names that are 32 characters in length. The root storage names must adhere to the naming conventions of their local file system because they are really file names.

You manipulate a storage through the **IStorage** interface functions shown in Figure 28-4. As you can see, a storage performs many directory-like operations. It can enumerate, copy, move, rename, and delete elements. It can also change their creation and last modified timestamps. Storages have attributes such as access rights—read-only, read-write, and so on—that you can modify and query. The create and open functions return **IStorage** or **IStream** pointers to substorages and streams anywhere in a hierarchy.

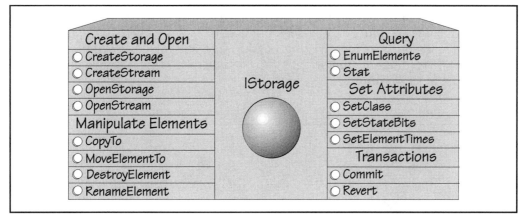

Figure 28-4. The IStorage Interface.

Transactional Storage

IStorage provides two particularly useful functions: *Commit* and *Revert*. You use commit to commit all changes made to a storage object since it was last opened or committed to persistent store. It's really a nested transaction—the changes are made visible to the parent storage and won't commit until the parent transaction commits. If the parent's transaction aborts at a later time, all the inner changes are rolled back. *Revert* discards any changes made in this storage—or any changes made visible by nested commits—since the storage object was last opened or committed.

You can access any OLE storage element in either *direct mode* or *transacted mode*. In direct mode, changes you make to an object are immediate and permanent. In transacted mode, changes are buffered so that they can be either committed or reverted. When an outermost level storage commits, the changes are applied to the underlying file on the file system. A single compound file can contain a mix of transacted mode storages and direct mode storages.

The IStream Interface

Streams are containers of user data in an OLE compound file. You use the **IStream** interface to manipulate the stream contents and access data (see Figure 28-5). Through this interface, you always view the stream as a contiguous array of bytes. Each stream maintains its own *seek* pointer into the data it holds. The **IStream** member functions let you seek to a position within the stream and then read, write, or copy a block of bytes.

Clone lets you create a new stream object that works with the same stream array of bytes but manages an independent seek pointer. *SetSize* preallocates space for the stream but does not preclude writing outside that stream. *LockRegion* restricts access to a byte range in the stream. *Commit* and *Revert* provide transaction support (see next Warning box).

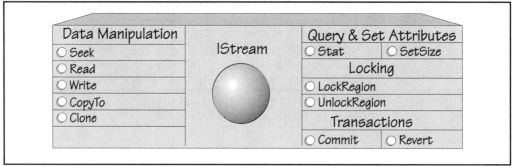

Figure 28-5. The IStream Interface.

Streams within a compound file can be very useful because they let you open file-like streams without requiring a file handle per open. Only the root storage object requires a file handle—everything else in a compound file is simply a structure in memory. Because of this important feature, you can use OLE's compound files in storage applications that require multiple open files but cannot afford the expense of all the open file handles. You can do the same with OpenDoc Bento files.

Architecture Does Not Mean Product

Warning

Compound files are an implementation of an OLE architecture called the *Structured Storage Model*. In many cases, the OLE documentation describes the architecture's features instead of the product's. As you can expect, many of the architectural features did not make it into the product. As we go to press, **IStream** objects in compound files do not support the locking functions *LockRegion* and *UnlockRegion* (they're no-ops). Nor do they support the transaction functions *Commit* and *Revert*. *Revert* is a no-op. And *Commit* does nothing more than flush an internal buffer. The bottom line is that stream objects are neither transactional or lockable.

In addition, the architecture allows streams to contain up to 2^{64} bytes but the current implementation is limited to 2^{32} bytes. This may be a problem if you plan to store "Gone With the Wind" in a stream. Finally, small streams can be inefficient because the minimum unit of allocation is 512 bytes—so you may end up with a lot of unused space. On the more positive side, storage objects completely implement all the functions in **IStorage** except for *SetStateBits* (there are no state bits defined at this time). However, some of the functions are sluggish—for example, *EnumElements* and *MoveElementTo*. ❑

A Storage Access Scenario

It's that time again. We need a scenario to pull together all these new OLE interfaces and APIs. So let's see what it takes to write "Hello World" to a stream within a new compound file (see Figure 28-6). Let's walk through the steps:

1. ***Create a new compound file and root storage***. The client calls the OLE API *StgCreateDocFile* to create a new root storage. This function opens a new compound file using the default file-based LockBytes. We'll open this compound file in direct mode by passing the STGM_DIRECT flag. If successful, the call returns a pointer to the root **IStorage** object. Note that if a compound file already exists, the client should instead call the *StgOpenStorage* API.

2. ***Create a new substorage***. The client calls *IStorage::CreateStorage* using the name "MyStorage" to create a new storage under the root storage. We'll use transacted mode by passing the STGM_TRANSACTED flag. If successful, the call returns a pointer to the "MyStorage" **IStorage** object.

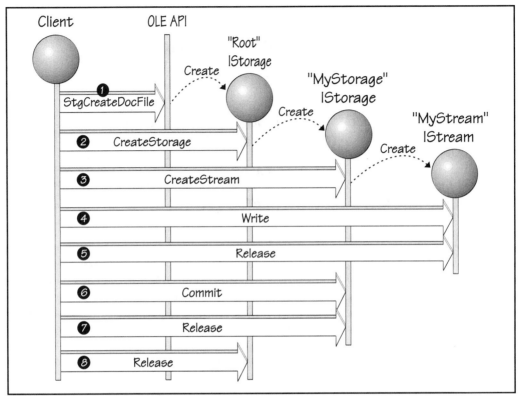

Figure 28-6. Scenario: Writing a Stream to a New Compound File.

3. ***Create a new stream***. The client calls *IStorage::CreateStream* using the name "MyStream" to create a new stream under the "MyStorage" object. The call returns an **IStream** pointer.

4. ***Write some data***. The client calls *IStream::Write* to write the data "Hello World."

5. ***Decrement the stream reference count***. The client calls *IStream::Release* (this is an **IUnknown** function) to decrement the reference count to match *IStorage::CreateStream* and close the stream.

6. ***Commit the storage***. The client calls *IStorage::Commit* to save the contents of the storage.

7. ***Decrement the "MyStorage" reference count***. The client calls *IStorage:: Release* (this is an **IUnknown** function) to decrement the reference count to match *IStorage::CreateStorage* and close "MyStorage."

8. ***Decrement the root storage reference count***. The client calls *IStorage::*

Release (this is an **IUnknown** function) to decrement the reference count to match *StgCreateDocFile* and close the root storage.

You can surely think of more productive uses of structured storage than writing "Hello World." However, the mechanisms are still the same. Remember, the idea is to let each independent component manage the contents of its own storage objects without having to involve a controlling application. Incremental access becomes the default mode of operation. In addition, any component with the proper authorization can browse the entire hierarchy of elements within a compound file by navigating using the **IStorage** interface functions.

PERSISTENT OBJECTS

OLE defines a set of persistent storage interfaces that objects can implement to save their state to storage and restore it at a later time. A *persistent* OLE object is an object that can read and write itself to storage. This section covers the persistent OLE types and how clients can control the persistence of their server objects. In OLE, clients provide their servers with **IStorage** and **IStream** interface pointers. The servers use these pointers to store and retrieve persistent data. As you may have already guessed, this section will introduce some new interfaces that define storage contracts between clients and persistent server objects.

How Persistent Is Your Object?

An object can support more than one persistence interface to suit different storage contexts. A client must first query an object—using *QueryInterface*—to discover what persistence interfaces it supports. It then obtains an interface for the level of persistence it needs. The persistence interfaces that objects can implement, in any combination, are these:

- **IPersistStorage** means that an object can read and write its persistent state to an **IStorage** object. The client provides the object with a pointer to the storage object through this interface. This is the only persistence interface that lets objects open and create storage elements and maintain the state of their pointers across API calls.

- **IPersistStream** means that an object can read and write its persistent state to an **IStream** object. The client provides the object with a stream pointer through this interface. The object reads and writes its information in a single stream within the scope of calls to this interface.

■ **IPersistFile** means that an object can read and write its persistent state to a file in the underlying file system. This interface typically does not deal with an OLE compound file. It knows nothing of **IStorage** or **IStream**. The client simply provides the object with a filename and tells it to save or load its contents.

Clients ask their server objects using the *IUnknown::QueryInterface* if they support one of the persistence interfaces just described. In effect, the client is asking the object: "Can you read persistent data from storage, stream, or file?" Even though an object may support more than one persistence interface, a client can only use one interface with any given instance of an object. Because the most complete interface is **IPersistStorage**, a client should ask for it first using *QueryInterface*. If this fails, it should request **IPersistStream**. And finally, if this doesn't work, the client should request **IPersistFile**. Of course, this priority scheme really depends on the client's own model for saving or reloading a persistent object.

The IPersist Interfaces

Figure 28-7 shows a class hierarchy diagram for the OLE persistence interfaces. What, OLE does inheritance? Yes, **IPersist** and **IUnknown** are among the few known examples of OLE's use of inheritance. It seems the designer of this interface wasn't able to kick old habits and decided to inherit one common function *Get-ClassID* from an abstract interface called **IPersist**. This function identifies the Class ID (CSLID) of the code that knows how to work with the persistent data type. In addition, an interface called **IPersistStreamInit** is a specialized **IPersistStream**. It adds a function called *InitNew* that lets a stream object know when it's first created. OLE controls needed this call to differentiate a new initialization from an initialization based on existing data.

All the persistence interfaces support a function called *IsDirty* that checks the object for changes since it was last saved. Depending on the type of persistence interface, *Load* instructs an object to load data from either an **IStream** pointer, an **IStorage** pointer, or a specified file. The client passes the pointer as a parameter of the call. *Save* saves the data in the specified persistent store. *GetSizeMax* returns the maximum size of the stream that an object would need to save this object—this allows the client to set the size of a stream before issuing a *Save*.

SaveCompleted informs the object that the client has completed a save and that the object can reopen the file, stream, or storage. *HandsOffStorage* tells the object to release all its storage pointers—including pointers passed by *InitNew* or *Load*. Finally, *GetCurFile* retrieves the path of the file currently associated with an object and makes the client responsible for the store.

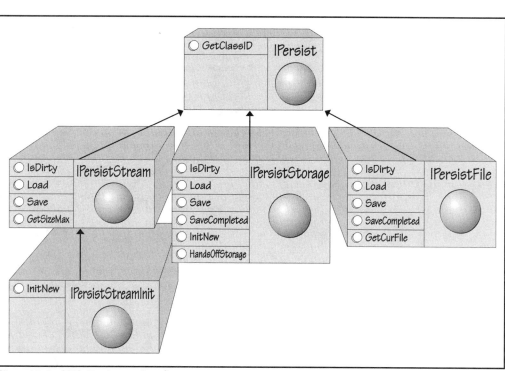

Figure 28-7. OLE's Persistence Interfaces.

A Persistent Object Scenario

We introduced four more interfaces, so it's time for another scenario to help you digest these interfaces. The scenario shows how a client interacts with a persistent object (see Figure 28-8). The scenario starts with a client in control of a root storage with a substorage called "MyStorage." The client will instantiate an object that supports the **IPersistStorage** interface and hand it a pointer to the substorage. But we're getting ahead of our story. Let's walk through the steps of the scenario:

1. ***Tell the object to load its persistent state***. The client calls the function *IPersistStorage::Load* to instruct the object to load its persistent data from "MyStorage" **IStorage**—the client passes a pointer to this object.

2. ***Increment the reference count***. Before the object can use the **IStorage** pointer, it must invoke *IUnknown::AddRef* to increment the reference count.

3. ***The object manipulates the storage***. The object can open streams within the "MyStorage" object, load its persistent state to memory, write to the streams, create and open new substorages, and so on.

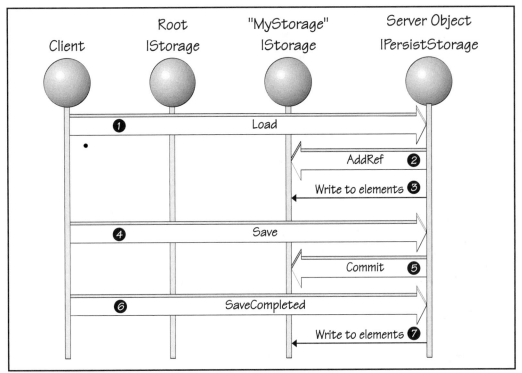

Figure 28-8. Scenario: Working With Persistent Objects.

4. ***The client says its time to save.*** The client calls the function *IPersistStorage::Save* to instruct the object to save its persistent data to the current storage.

5. ***The object saves its state.*** In our scenario the storage is transacted, so the object simply invokes *IStorage::Commit* to make its writes persistent. The object continues to hold its pointers to open elements, although it cannot write to them until it receives a *SaveCompleted* from the client.

6. ***The client says the save is completed.*** The client issues a *IPersistStorage::SaveCompleted* call to indicate that the coast is clear. Why is this call needed when the object itself performs the save? Because more than one object may be involved in a save process in which the client acts as the coordinator.

7. ***The object can use the storage.*** The object returns to normal storage mode and can again do whatever it wants with the storage.

This scenario brings together all the persistent pieces. We hope everything is now "perfectly clear." If it isn't, don't despair. Just look for a good OLE tool that hides all this nastiness from you. At this stage, it's only important for you to get some idea of how the OLE object model works. The OLE tool should take care of all the nitty details.

MONIKERS: PERSISTENT, INTELLIGENT NAMES

*M*oniker—*a person's name, nickname, alias, etc. Origin unknown and very broadly speculated upon; perhaps related to the fact that early-19th-century British tramps referred to themselves as "in the monkery." Monks and nuns take a new name when they take their vows, and monaco means "monk" in Italian...*

> — *The New Dictionary of American Slang*
> *Edited by Robert L. Chapman, Ph.D.*

*M*oniker—*an intelligent persistent name used to insulate clients from a container. Or insulate a data access provider from methods to obtain access to data, and from the parameters of the method call.*

> — *Tony Williams, OLE Architect*
> *Microsoft*

A *moniker* is an object that acts as a persistent alias name for another object. Monikers can provide aliases for distributed filenames, database queries, a paragraph in a document, a range of spreadsheet cells, a remote computer, and so on. The intelligence of how to work with a particular name is encapsulated inside the name itself. The name becomes a "moniker object" that implements name-related interfaces. In this situation, the moniker is essentially a name that identifies the source of a particular piece of data; it can even extract the data in a form that's useful to the client. This means that whenever a client wishes to perform any operation with a name, it calls the moniker to do it instead of doing the work itself. This level of indirection allows monikers to transparently provide services. In theory, a client should be able to seamlessly interoperate over time with different moniker implementations that implement these same services in different ways.

So, What Exactly Is a Moniker?

A *moniker* is simply a persistent object that implements the **IMoniker** interface. It is used to assign a persistent name to an individual object instantiation. Each different moniker class—with a different CLSID—has its own semantics as to what sort of object or operation it can reference. A moniker class defines the operations necessary to locate some general type of object or perform some general type of action. But each individual moniker object—meaning each instantiation—maintains its own name data that identifies some other particular object or operation. The moniker class defines the functionality; a moniker object maintains the parameters. So even though all monikers support the same interface, they have different implementations which are identified by their CLSID.

Monikers As Persistent Objects

The **IMoniker** interface includes the **IPersistStream** interface. This means that monikers can be saved into and loaded from streams. The persistent form of a moniker includes the data comprising its name and the CLSID of its implementation—the CLSID is used to load the moniker's implementation. The client only knows each moniker by the persistent label that is assigned to it.

The implementation of the moniker is identified by its persistent CLSID. Each moniker class can store arbitrary data; it can also run arbitrary code. These specialized class implementations allow you to create new kinds of monikers transparently to clients. OLE implements five moniker classes, each with a different CLSID. These five classes—*generic composite, file, item, anti,* and *pointer*—are simply polymorphic implementations of the **IMoniker** interface. Each different CLSID has its own semantics for what to do with a name. You can create your own monikers by implementing the **IMoniker** interface and assigning it a unique CLSID.

In a nutshell, *IMoniker* only defines the interfaces each moniker object must support. These interfaces define generic operations necessary to locate some type of object and perform some general type of action. Each moniker class—identified by a CLSID—defines the code that implements these functions in a particular manner. Each instantiation of a moniker class maintains a persistent representation of its own name data and other parameters. Finally, clients work with monikers—of any class or name—using the **IMoniker** interface.

The IMoniker Interface

IMoniker is a rather formidable interface that defines 15 member functions (see Figure 28-9). Its two workhorse functions are *BindToObject* and *BindToStorage*. "Binding" is one of the most overloaded terms in the computer industry. In this case, it means resolving a moniker name to some underlying object or data value. The rest of the **IMoniker** functions may be useful in some particular moniker implementations, but they're not as general. We cover some of the more useful ones.

The *BindToObject* function takes as a parameter the interface identifier by which the client wishes to talk to the bound object, runs whatever algorithm is necessary to locate the object, and then returns a pointer to an instantiated object of that interface type to the client (this pointer is unrelated to the moniker itself). The client can bind to an object's storage—for example, the **IStorage** containing the object—instead of to the object itself using a slightly different function called *BindToStorage*.

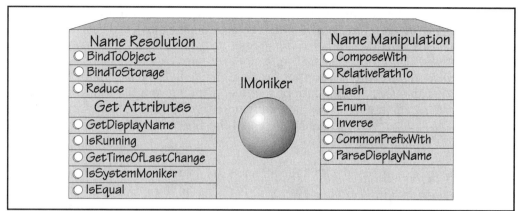

Figure 28-9. The IMoniker Interface.

The *Reduce* operation allows a moniker to rewrite itself into another equivalent moniker that will bind to the same object—usually, in a more efficient way. This function returns a new moniker that binds to the same object. You can use the reduce function to construct user-defined macros or aliases as new kinds of moniker classes. Most monikers have a textual representation that is meaningful to the user that can be retrieved with *GetDisplayName*.

Because binding is expensive and time-consuming, a client can control how long it is willing to wait for the binding to complete. To improve performance, binding takes place within a specific "bind context" that's passed as a parameter to the bind function. An example of a context is the OLE *running object table*. This is a global table that keeps track of running objects and monikers. The binding functions can access this table indirectly using the **IBindCtx** interface pointer that's passed to them. You can avoid repeated connections to the same object by first searching for the object in the running table using the *IsRunning* function.

Monikers can compare themselves to other monikers using *IsEqual*. The *Hash* function speeds up the search for monikers in the running object table. *GetTime-OfLastChange* returns the date and time when the object the moniker points to was last changed. The remaining functions are used to manage composite monikers and to parse names.

Types of Monikers

As we said earlier, monikers can have many types, depending on the information they contain and the type of objects they reference. A moniker class is really defined by the naming information it persistently maintains and the binding operation it uses. COM specifies one standard moniker called the *generic composite* moniker.

In addition, OLE implements four moniker types required for compound document linking: *file, item, anti,* and *pointer.* Here's a summary of what these five moniker implementations provide:

■ **File monikers** provide a wrapper for a pathname in the native file system. The file name can either be absolute or relative. Binding to a file moniker causes it to determine the application that can handle the file name, launch the application, and ask it to load the file by means of the **IPersist** interface. The moniker returns a pointer to the "file" object.

■ **Item monikers** are used with a file moniker to describe contents within a file that can be treated as separate "items." For example, an item moniker can refer to a range of cells within a spreadsheet. Typically, item monikers resolve a string that's only comprehensible to an application. An item moniker always works with the moniker on its left in a composite moniker. To put a file and item monikers together requires a composite moniker that can resolve hierarchical names such as *File!Item!Item,* where (!) is an arbitrary separation character in a composite name.

■ **Anti monikers**, like item monikers, only make sense within a composite moniker. An anti moniker's effect is to say "ignore the moniker that comes before me." This construct is needed because you cannot remove members from composite monikers (you can only add them). So you use an anti-moniker to negate the effects of another moniker. It's a kludge.

■ **Pointer monikers** point to something in active storage as opposed to file storage.

■ **Generic composite monikers** are collections of other monikers—including other composite monikers. You use composite monikers whenever simple monikers are not sufficient to describe a reference. The persistent data of a composite moniker is completely composed of the persistent data of other monikers. Binding a composite moniker simply tells the composite to bind each moniker it contains in sequence. The composite is generic because it has no knowledge of its pieces except that they are monikers.

Figure 28-10. A Composite Moniker Composed of Three Simple Monikers.

Figure 28-10 shows a composite moniker consisting of a file moniker and two item monikers; the structure is *File!Item!Item*. In our example, the single composite moniker *MyDoc.doc!SalesTbl!R2C2-R4C4* binds to the spreadsheet data within the SalesTbl chart inside the document MyDoc.doc. Each moniker in the composite is one step in the path to the final resolution of the bind. If OLE's standard monikers are not suitable for your naming purposes, you can create your own monikers by implementing a customized **IMoniker** CLSID. Your moniker can then be used by any application that understands how to use the **IMoniker** interface. So what makes monikers "intelligent" is that they know how to take a name and somehow locate a specific object or perform an operation to which that name refers (also see following Soapbox).

Monikers and the Rest of Us

Soapbox

There is no problem in computer programming that cannot be solved by an added level of indirection.

— **Maurice Wilkes**

The corollary: There is no performance problem that cannot be solved by eliminating a level of indirection.

— **Jim Gray**

So far, we've tried hard to give monikers a fair hearing without interjecting our personal biases. However, we've reached the limits of our endurance—we badly need this Soapbox to let off a flame or two. If you're confused by all this moniker stuff, join the club.

As we see it, monikers were first introduced to solve a major problem with OLE 1: hardcoded links. In OLE 1, links were stored using absolute pathnames and would break every time someone moved a source document around. Monikers added a level of indirection that partially fixed the problem. However, indirections can be dangerous because once they're introduced, the temptation is to use them as quick fixes for any type of problem.

So, when OLE 2 was faced with another problem—how to deal with nested data—the solution, of course, was to throw a moniker at it. We anticipate that distributed OLE will use monikers to locate remote resources and deal with local/remote transparency—just call a moniker and OLE will find what's at the other end, even if it's over a distributed network. The idea is make everything go through an extra level of indirection so that Microsoft can fix problems as they're discovered. In contrast, CORBA defines a relationship service and OpenDoc provides object specifiers for doing these kind of things in a less ad hoc manner.

The next problem monikers attempt to solve are flaws with the COM object model. In classical object models—like CORBA, OpenDoc, and C++—each object has a unique identity and state. The state can be made persistent using a Persistent ID. In contrast, with COM you get a pointer to an interface and not a pointer to an object with state. So how do COM clients instantiate an object and then reconnect to that exact same object instance with the same state at a later time? With monikers, of course—remember, monikers are persistent names. Is it a kludge? Yes. In this case, the moniker becomes a patch for OLE's lack of support for classical object identifiers.

What else could monikers be used for? Almost anything. Once you've introduced a level of indirection that lets you call some ad hoc code, the sky's the limit for what you can do with it. You can certainly use monikers to connect almost anything with anything. We're starting to see monikers used as an ad-hoc naming service—remember, the *generic composite* moniker. You can even use them as a "roll-your-own" query service.

In summary, monikers are really just a universal patch—of the "smoke and mirrors" variety—with a name that sounds very mysterious. It's a marketing term for adding fixes to the system and making them sound impressive (perhaps to cover up for the degradation in performance). So if you want to impress your friends, tell them you're in the moniker business. It's a growth business that lets you define any name, associate it with some general purpose code (the CLSID), and use it to perform some mysterious bindings. For example, you can create an "intergalactic moniker" that knows how to find Martians and connect you with them. ❑

Chapter 29

OLE:
Compound
Documents
and OCXs

There are things and there are places to put things.

> — *Tony Williams, OLE Architect*
> *Microsoft*

Like OpenDoc, OLE provides a technology that lets you create and manage compound documents. An OLE compound document mediates the interactions between two types of components: *containers* and *servers*. The containers provide the places, and the servers are the "things" that reside in these places. Or if you prefer, the container is the component that manages the document, mediates the visual layout, and manages relationships between servers that represent the content of the document. So the container is a client of the servers (the word server is used in a very broad sense). In addition to containers and servers, OLE recently introduced a newer type of server called a *custom control* (also known as an OCX). This chapter covers the three elements that constitute OLE's compound document services: containers, servers, and OCXs (see Figure 29-1).

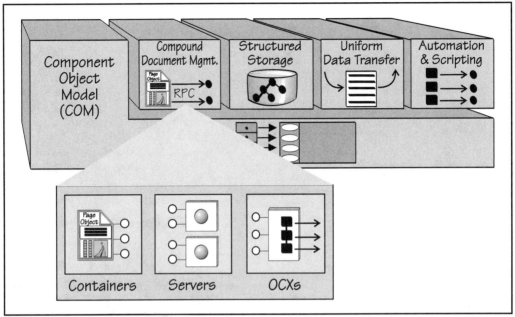

Figure 29-1. OLE's Compound Document Services.

THE OLE COMPOUND DOCUMENT MODEL

Before jumping into the details, it may help if we step back and explain how the OLE compound document model is different from that of OpenDoc's. You may recall from the OpenDoc chapters that everything in OpenDoc was a part (derived from **ODPart**). OpenDoc parts could contain other parts as well as be embedded within other containing parts. In OLE terms, an OpenDoc part is a container/server. So with OpenDoc compound documents, one interface does it all. After we described **ODPart**, we spent most of the compound document chapter explaining the underlying mechanics of the OpenDoc runtime: How it brings parts to life, how parts find their editors, how parts display their contents, and how they share resources with other parts.

In contrast to OpenDoc, the OLE model of compound documents deals with composition. We start with the idea that both containers and servers are OLE objects. Then we gradually introduce the interfaces that define the container and server functions and differentiate their roles. The interfaces define protocols between containers and servers and also define different types of containers and servers. In terms of function, an OLE OCX is the closest thing to an OpenDoc part. However, unlike OpenDoc parts, OCXs cannot act as containers.

Will the Real Container/Server Please Stand Up?

In OLE, there are not just containers and servers; there are also different types of containers and servers. The first classification is based on packaging. Some servers known as *in-process*, are implemented as DLLs that share the same address space as the container. There are three types of in-process servers: *InProcHandlers*, *InProcServers*, and *Controls*. Next are the *local servers* implemented as separate programs that reside in an EXE file. The local servers use the COM Lightweight RPC (LRPC) to communicate with their containers. This introduces a new set of constraints. For example, local servers cannot do in-place editing. Yet to come are *remote servers* that will support Network OLE using a regular RPC.

The next division is by function—meaning which interfaces are implemented. Some servers are *in-place active;* others aren't. Linking and embedding creates another set of divisions. Data can either be embedded or linked in a container. A *full server* supports both linking and embedding. A *mini server* only supports embedding. Of course, containers must provide a range of interfaces that match the capabilities of their servers, so they too have different types. In addition, a container can be *pure* or *linked* depending on whether the data is embedded within it or linked to some other container (see next section).

Are you totally confused? For all this to make sense, you must first get used to the idea that there are no universal parts, containers, or servers in OLE. There are only combinations of interfaces that grow to fit different container/server arrangements. This simple idea will help you get through this chapter and will also help you understand future types of containers and servers—they just add more interfaces. Microsoft seems to introduce these new interfaces faster than we can even write about them (see the next Soapbox).

Linking versus Embedding

OLE supports two types of compound-document objects: *linked* or *embedded*. The difference between the two types lies in how and where the actual source of the object's data is stored. When an object is linked, the source data, or link source, continues to reside wherever it was initially created, either at another point within the document or within a different document altogether. Only a reference, or link, to the object and appropriate presentation data is kept within the compound document. Linked objects cannot "travel" with documents to another machine; they must remain within the local file system or be copied explicitly. However, linking allows changes made to the source object to be automatically reflected in any compound documents that have a link.

In the case of an embedded object, a copy of the original object is physically stored in the compound document, as is all the information needed to manage the object. As a result, the object becomes a part of the document. You can transfer a compound document with embedded objects to another computer and edit it there. You can edit or activate embedded objects *in-place*—meaning that you can edit the contents of the object without leaving the compound document. On the other hand, linked objects cannot be edited in-place. Table 29-1 describes the types of embedded versus linked OLE compound document components. We cover linking versus embedding in more detail later in this chapter.

Table 29-1. OLE's Embedded Versus Linked Component Types.

Component Types	Description
Pure Container	Contains linked and embedded objects within its documents. Does not allow other applications to link to its data.
Link Container	Contains linked and embedded objects within its documents. Allows other applications to link to its embedded objects.
Miniserver	Creates objects that can only be embedded.
Simple Server	Creates object(s) that can be embedded or linked. Allows linking only to the whole object.
Pseudo-Server	Creates object(s) that can be embedded or linked. Allows linking to a whole object or to selections of data.
Link Server	Cannot create object(s) to be embedded in a container (it is not insertable). Acts as a link source only.
Full Server	Creates object(s) that can be embedded or linked and can embed or link objects within its objects. It is also known as a *container/server* object.

How Much Diversity Can Components Tolerate?

Soapbox

It finally dawned on us—after about a year of playing with OLE and OpenDoc—that the two models are superficially similar, but they're entirely different animals when you look under the hood. Their different philosophies on how to structure a compound document is a case in point. Both OLE and OpenDoc support the concept of containers in which parts live. In OpenDoc everything starts and ends with a part. Parts are very recursive—**ODPart** captures all the semantics of compound documents; it's both a container and a server (in OLE terminology).

OpenDoc parts are self-contained—you only extend a part's function to add application semantics using **ODExtension** objects. So it's a one generic part fits all concept (you simply customize the part's interface to create your components).

In contrast, OLE provides you with a construction kit for interfaces. It starts you with about a hundred standard interface definitions and then sets you loose. You're in composition heaven. You can add interfaces left and right to provide anything you want. You can implement interfaces in any way you want. You can get all kinds of strange compound document combinations by mixing and matching container and server interfaces. There's enough diversity to drive any component vendor crazy—just think of how many combinations have to be tested. OLE integrators will also face the combinatorial explosion problem. And we pity the poor users.

So the real question is this: Can our industry handle so much diversity in an open market for components? If something breaks, given the combinatorial explosion of containers and servers, who will fix it? In OLE the answer is easy: The container is always right, in practice. Why? Because most of the predominant containers are best-selling Microsoft applications—like Excel, Word, and Access. So the server component vendors must learn to live by the rules of these containers or they're just plain out of luck. We believe that, in this case, too much diversity can kill the rest of us. Or worse, it can lead to totalitarian remedies—meaning that the predominant vendor's containers will determine what's right.

So the irony is that to get diversity in an open components market, you may need a solid architecture that imposes the right level of constraints. OpenDoc may have the right level of constraints to make it manageable in the open component market—we don't have enough market data yet to tell. On the other hand, the OLE market may gravitate towards OCXs to find some level of constraint. Unfortunately, OCXs are simple servers—they cannot contain other parts. In any case, at this early stage of the open components market, we may want to follow Henry Ford's words: "You can get any color car as long as it's black." We continue this discussion in Part 6. ❑

THE MINIMALIST CONTAINER/SERVER

Container and server objects are nothing more than regular OLE objects that have particular combinations of interfaces (see Figure 29-2). The interfaces shown, form the simplest contract between OLE container and server objects. We'll go over some more complicated contracts in later sections.

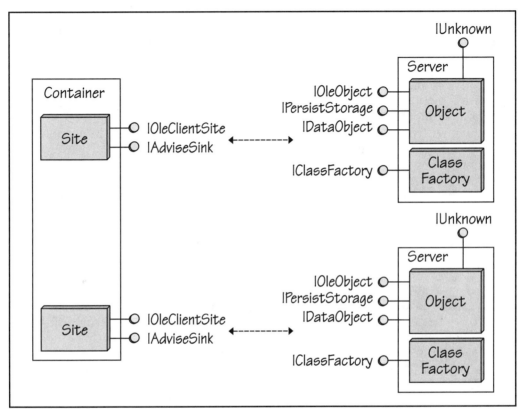

Figure 29-2. The Interfaces of a Simple Compound Document Container and Server.

The Minimalist Container

A container (see Figure 29-2) is an OLE application that can contain server objects in a compound document. A *compound document* is typically an OLE compound file that holds the container's native data as well as objects various server applications create. The container provides embedded storage or a persistent link pointer in the form of a moniker for every server object associated with it. For each server, the container creates a *site*. Think of it as the place where servers live and display their contents. Each site must implement two interfaces: **IOleClientSite** and **IAdviseSink**. The server calls the **IOleClientSite** to obtain container information. And it provides asynchronous notifications to the container via **IAdviseSink**.

IAdviseSink is the same advise sink interface we covered in Chapter 27, "OLE: Uniform Data Transfer." The "sink" receives asynchronous callbacks whenever something of interest happens to the server object. In this case, the advise sink is mainly used by a container site to subscribe to notifications of changes in the server's views. When a view changes, the site must repaint itself by calling the server's *IViewObject::Draw* function. Let us remind you that the container is interested in displaying the server's contents without getting involved in the rendering details. All containers must, at least, implement *IAdviseSink::OnViewChange*. The rest of the advise sink functions can be stubbed. However, a fancy container could also create advisory connections in order to be informed of any changes in a server's data or state. But, remember: We're only talking about a minimalist container here.

This is the first time we encounter the **IOleClientSite** interface. All interfaces that support compound documents begin with "*IOle*"; the generic OLE interfaces start with "*I*". The **IOleClientSite** is the primary interface by which a container provides services to a server object. A server object also uses this interface to discover its context—including where it is anchored in the document and where it gets its storage, user interface, and other resources.

Figure 29-3 shows the member functions of the **IOleClientSite** interface. *Save-Object* requests that the server object attached to this client site be saved. *Show-Object* tells the container to make the server object visible. *OnShowWindow* is called when an object opens or closes its own window (as opposed to in-place editing). *GetContainer* returns a pointer to the embedding container's **IOleContainer** interface. *GetMoniker* returns the container's moniker or the server object's moniker relative to the container (or a full moniker). *RequestNewObjectLayout* is called by server objects to negotiate for visual real estate; this mechanism is not supported in OLE 2.

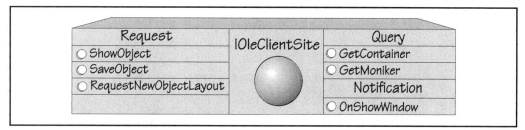

Figure 29-3. The IOleClientSite Interface.

The Minimalist Server

IOleObject looks like the interface from hell, a dumping ground for every function that just didn't seem to have a better home.

> — **Kraig Brockschmidt, Author**
> **Inside OLE 2, Second Edition**
> **(Microsoft Press, 1995)**

Server applications create and service embedded or linked objects of a specific class. These applications vary by the number of objects they can create, service, and store persistently. Microsoft Paintbrush, for example, is a single-object application. Microsoft Excel is an example of a multiobject application that provides spreadsheet and chart objects. Servers must provide user interface and editing capabilities for their objects and be able to save their contents in compound files.

In addition to the ubiquitous **IUnknown** and the class factory, a minimalist server object must implement three interfaces (see Figure 29-2). We've already encountered two of these interfaces: **IPersistStorage** and **IDataObject** (see Chapters 27 and 28). In the compound document context, you use the **IPersistStorage** interface to tell the server object about its **IStorage** in the container's compound file (or document). This is where the server object loads and saves its persistent data. The **IDataObject** interface is used to exchange data between the container and the server.

IOleObject is the interface that handles most of the container/server interactions. It provides most of the methods for compound-document object management. It is the primary interface by which a linked or embedded object serves its container. **IOleObject** has 21 member functions—excluding **IUnknown** (see Figure 29-4). It's what Brockschmidt calls the "interface from hell." The good news is that only a few of these functions really matter. So our explanation can be brief. The functions that really matter are *DoVerb*, *Close*, *SetHostNames*, and *SetClientSite* (in that order).

The most important of these functions—*DoVerb*—executes a number of predefined "verbs" that a container invokes to show, hide, and activate a server object. Many objects have an "edit" verb that displays a window in which you can edit the contents of the object. Typically, sound and video objects support a "play" verb. Verbs can

IOleObject		
DoVerb		SetClientSite
EnumVerbs		GetClientSite
InitFromData		SetMoniker
Close		GetMoniker
Update		SetExtent
IsUpToDate		GetExtent
Advise		GetUserClassID
Unadvise		GetUserType
EnumAdvise		GetMiscStatus
		SetColorScheme
		GetClipboardData
		SetHostNames

Figure 29-4. The IOleObject Interface.

be invoked on an object while it is selected in its container. A container can determine the set of verbs an object supports by calling *EnumVerbs*.

Close instructs a server object to save itself and shutdown. The container invokes *SetHostNames* to tell a server object the name of its container application and the name of the document in which the server lives. The container calls *SetClientSite* to pass the server object a pointer to its **IOleClientSite**. Another interesting function is *Advise*. It is used to pass a pointer to an **IAdviseSink** to which a server object can send notifications when it is saved, closed, or renamed.

A Container/Server Scenario

It's time to bring these ideas together again. We propose a container/server scenario that loads a single embedded server from within a compound document, activates it, and then puts it back in an inactive state (see Figure 29-5). Let's walk through the scenario:

1. **User opens a compound file.** The user launches an OLE container application and opens a compound document using the Windows File Open menu. The container calls *StgOpenStorage* OLE API, which returns a pointer to the root **IStorage** object for the document's compound file.

2. **The container finds an embedded server object.** The container calls *IStorage::EnumElements* to find out what's stored in the document. It then calls *IStorage::OpenStorage* to open a substorage where a server object resides. At this point, the server object is in the *passive* state. It's just dormant in a file.

3. **The container asks OLE to load the server object.** The container calls the *OleLoad* API passing it a pointer to an open **IStorage** from which to load the server object and a pointer to an **IOleClientSite**.

4. **OLE loads the server object.** The *OleLoad* API calls the server's *IPersist-Storage::Load*, passing it the **IStorage** pointer provided by the container. The server object calls member functions in **IStorage** and **IStream** to load its contents (we don't show all the details). The *OleLoad* function returns to the container a pointer to the newly loaded server object. The server object is now in the *loaded* state.

5. **The container activates the object.** The container calls the *IOleObject:: DoVerb* to ask the server object to execute some action. For example, "play" a wave file or "display" a window in which the contents of the object can be edited. The server object is now in the *running* state.

6. **Shutdown.** Eventually, the container issues an *IOleObject::Close* command which takes the server object from the *running* state back into the *loaded* state.

This is the simplest scenario we could imagine. It works. Now that you have a basic idea of what OLE containers and servers do in their most basic implementations, it's time to add some embellishments—meaning more interfaces and functions.

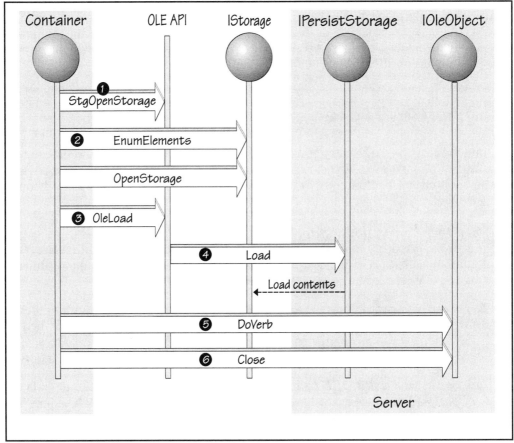

Figure 29-5. Scenario: Loading and Activating a Server Object.

THE MAXIMALIST CONTAINER/SERVER

In this section, we introduce a container/server combination with the "whole works." This means our container/server pair should be able to do linking, in-place editing, and caching. *Linking* allows the object's data to live elsewhere, while the view lives in the compound document. *In-place* editing allows views of multiple server objects to share a single document window and its menus. *Caching* provides a container access to frozen bitmap representations (or snapshots) of views that can be displayed when the server object is not active. They're just visual placeholders— they're also called "dead bits" because you can't manipulate their contents. It takes a long time to activate and launch a typical OLE local server (an EXE). So the cached bitmap representations are used as placeholders until the user decides to launch the server object. It's better than showing a gray outline.

Figure 29-6 shows all the interfaces that maximalist containers and servers can support. We will go over them in the following sections. The idea is to give you a feel for the functions they perform so that you can understand the OLE compound document model. Notice that the interfaces shown in italics are implemented only by *in-process* servers—meaning servers implemented as DLLs that live in the same address space as their container. The *local servers*—meaning servers implemented

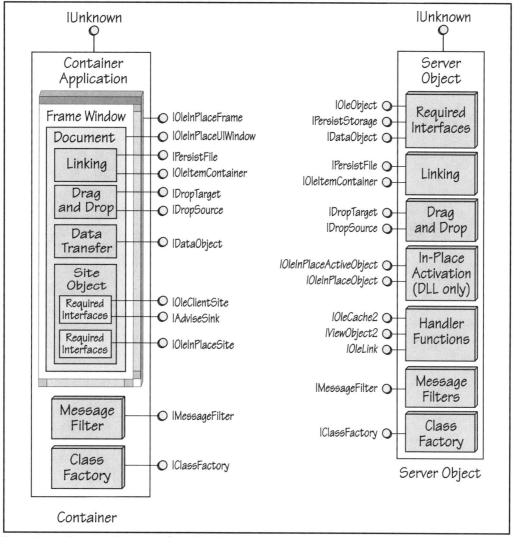

Figure 29-6. Container/Server Interfaces: The Whole Works.

in separate EXEs—rely on a local DLL called an *InProcHandler* (or *object handler*) to handle these italicized interfaces for them. In general, handlers work with local servers. Local servers cannot do *in-place* editing. They can only display their views in separate windows.

Linking and Embedding Interfaces

An *embedded object's* persistent state is totally "embedded" within the container's compound file (see Figure 29-7). OLE lets you embed the data contents of both in-process and local servers.   The container passes an **IStorage** interface to its servers to let them manipulate their data contents.   As we explained in the minimalist section, embedded objects must always implement the **IPersistStorage** interface to get to their data. OLE supports two types of *local servers*:

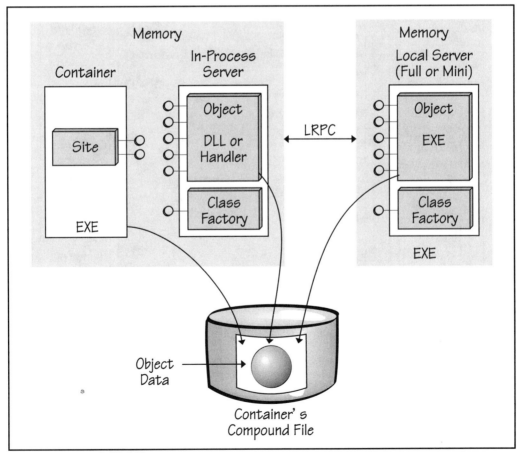

Figure 29-7. An Embedded Object.

- **Full servers** are free-standing applications like Excel or Word that support both linked and embedded objects.

- **Miniservers** only support embedded objects and cannot run as free-standing applications—the container must be running to supply the embedded data. An example of a miniserver is MS-Graph.

Both full servers and miniservers reside in their own EXE file and communicate with their containers via COM's *lightweight RPC (LRPC)*. In contrast, *in-process* servers don't require an LRPC because they're implemented as DLLs that reside in the same address space as their containers. Like miniservers, in-process servers only operate on embedded data.

The other way to share an object is through *linking*. In this case, the container document contains a moniker that refers to the location where the object's data is stored (see Figure 29-8). In most cases, the linked data is stored within the contents

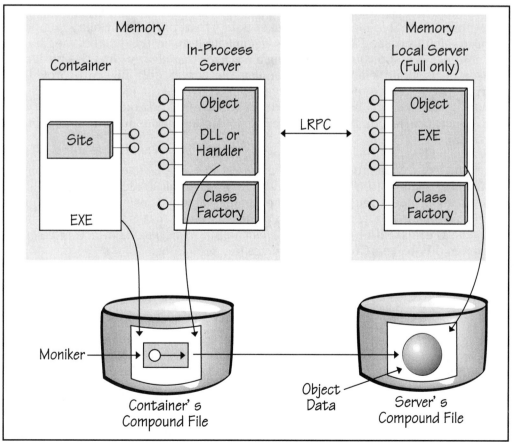

Figure 29-8. A Moniker-Linked Object.

of another document. But as we saw in the previous chapter, monikers can be very agile in locating data. You can write specialized monikers that go after data kept in the strangest of places. Only full servers support linking. You cannot link to local servers or OCXs. Note that a full server is a container/server.

So, How Does Linking Work?

Going back to Figure 29-6, you can see that linking introduces two new interfaces on the container and server sides: **IPersistFile** and **IOleItemContainer**. We already covered **IPersistFile** in the previous chapter. In the case of linking, it works with **IOleItemContainer** to resolve a *File!Item* moniker link. This means that you can link to either a file or some item within a file. Note that, in contrast to embedding, you cannot link to a compound file using an **IStorage**. The standard OLE monikers only understand files and items within a file.

So in OLE, a link is defined as a reference to a source file and sometimes items that live within that source file. A file moniker points to a source file, while a compound moniker—in this case, *File!Item!Item*—points to items within that source file. The server object is responsible for creating a moniker that clearly identifies its data. If the source is identified by a file moniker, the server only needs to provide an **IPersistFile** interface to load the linked file. If the server identifies data using a composite moniker, it must also provide an **IOleItemContainer** interface for each item. Each interface is responsible for resolving an item name into some type of object interface pointer.

A container that wants to support linking must first enable itself to create pointers to linked objects. It typically provides a Paste Link Dialog box that obtains information on the foreign source (like the file name). It uses this information to call the API *IOleCreateLinkToFile* to create an object that is linked to the foreign file. The **IPersistFile** interface resolves the file name into some other interface pointer, and **IOleItemContainer** resolves the item name.

In-Place Editing

*T*here's something compelling about seeing your own component integrated with another application. It flat out breaks through indifference and makes you go "Wow." In-place editing is without question the most important user interface feature defined in OLE.

— *Michael Fanning, Microsoft*
MacTech Magazine
(January, 1995)

You may recall from the OpenDoc chapters, that *in-place editing* consists of a set of interfaces and negotiation protocols that let container and server objects visually merge their user interfaces within the container's window. Instead of using a separate window, the server object brings its editing tools and adornments to the container's window. This includes sharing menus and toolbars. In-place objects immediately respond to mouseclicks and user interaction because their windows are in the container. Only one object at a time can be *UI active*, which means its menus and toolbars are available. A UI active object displays a hatched border and has its name in the container's caption bars.

Going back to Figure 29-6, you can see that a number of interfaces are required to make in-place editing work on both container and server objects. The interface names all start with the prefix *IOleInPlace*. The container side must support **IOleInPlaceSite** and **IOleInPlaceFrame**. The server object must support **IOleInPlaceObject** and **IOleInPlaceActiveObject**.

The container issues a *DoVerb* to activate a server object. Once it's activated, the server object initiates most of the in-place negotiations. The server is always busy trying to determine the container's capabilities and putting together the special user interface elements it needs for in-place editing. The server invokes member functions in **IOleInPlaceSite** to notify the container when the embedded object is being activated, deactivated, or when it changes size. It also uses that interface to obtain pointers to the container's **IOleInPlaceFrame** interface. This is the interface it uses to merge menus and negotiate for real estate in the container's frame window.

The container calls member functions in **IOleInPlaceObject** to deactivate and remove the user interface of an in-place active server object. It also uses that interface to notify the server object as to how much of it is visible in the container. The **IOleInPlaceActiveObject** interface is used by the container's document window to tell the server object when the container's frame or document windows are activated and deactivated. This interface is also used to notify the server object when it needs to resize its border space (also see next Soapbox).

Miscellaneous Interfaces

This section looks at the remaining container/server interfaces. They're not as exciting as the ones we just covered, but we'll quickly tell you what they do.

■ **Class Factory.** This is the COM **IClassFactory** interface that you use to create instances of a specific object class in memory. Typically applications call the *OleCreate* API, which then invokes the class factory functions. Because containers and servers are OLE objects, they must each provide an implementation of the **IClassFactory** interface.

In-Place Editing: OLE Versus OpenDoc

Soapbox

OpenDoc only uses an *inside-out* activation model that lets you activate with a single mouse click the smallest and most deeply embedded part at the location of the mouse. It's a form of in-place editing that lets you edit directly any visible part without first activating the outer (or embedding parts). In contrast, the default activation mode in OLE is *outside-in*. This means you must select the outermost frames before getting to the embedded part thus requiring many more mouse clicks. For example, to edit an OLE application that's embedded three levels deep, you must first open the top three container applications by double clicking on each one of them before getting to the application you want.

Even though the OLE default expects a server object to behave as an outside-in application, an object may register that it is capable of inside-out activation. It does this by setting two bits in the class registry. Using this registry information, an OLE container will determine whether it allows inside-out objects to handle events directly. OLE applications that are embedded more than one level deep are opened in their own window—this doesn't help with the seamless look. In contrast, OpenDoc supports an unlimited nesting of embedded parts that you can edit in-place.

Microsoft believes that ultimately "seamless inside-out containers will become more feasible as increasing numbers of OLE objects support inside-out activation." So why is it creating this schizophrenic confusion in the interim? Do end users really need to deal with two activation models? One answer is that Microsoft has legacy OLE applications like Word and Excel to protect. Without a major rewrite, these bulky applications can only support outside-in activation.

Now, here comes some real heavy soapbox stuff! We believe that the main idea behind compound documents is to let the end user directly and naturally manipulate components within visual containers. This is why OpenDoc supports irregular shapes and does not compromise on inside-out activation. The only way visual components can replace existing applications on client desktops is by providing the illusion that all the components are part of the same application. In other words, they must be totally seamless at the visual level. We cannot create this illusion with continuous compromises. It's already hard enough to make components from different vendors interoperate. It doesn't help the cause to bring these components together in clumsy visual ensembles that only emphasize their differences. So once again, we need consistency and the proper constraints to create a successful component industry. Only the consumer gets freedom of choice; designers need freedom from choice. ❑

- **Message Filters**. OLE, for the most part, hides the Windows message queue. But if you need to hook into the message queue, OLE specifies a **IMessageFilter** interface that lets a client retrieve specific messages from the queue while ignoring others. Containers and servers can implement filters by encapsulating the Windows queue with that interface. For applications that do not implement a message filter, OLE provides default behaviors—mostly first-in first-out dispatching. The ability to filter messages is useful when a lengthy operation is in progress.

- **View object**. If an object implements the **IViewObject2** interface, it can render itself on a caller-provided device context—usually a screen or printer context. This gives the object control over the rendering quality. Only in-process servers can implement this interface. Local servers (EXEs) must implement a custom drawing handler as a DLL and attach it to the container (the "2" in the name signifies that it is only for DLLs).

- **Caching**. The **IOleCache2** interface is implemented by in-process servers and DLL object handlers to maintain a cache of bitmaps and iconic representations of objects. It's like a photo album. The container uses this interface to display a frozen picture of objects when their server is not running or available. These are the dead bits we talked about earlier. The cache uses **IPersistStore** to move pictures from disk **IStorage** to memory. The **IOleCache2** interface is an extension of **IOleCache**; it is only used with DLLs.

OLE CUSTOM CONTROLS (OCXS)

OLE Customs Controls—also known as *OCXs* because of their filename extension—were introduced by Microsoft in late 1994. They provide some of the features needed to create a true components industry. Microsoft views OCXs as the replacement for their enormously popular *Visual Basic Controls* or *VBXs*. These VBXs created a very successful component industry around Visual Basic and client tools. Independent vendors offer over a thousand VBX controls that perform add-on functions, ranging from simple visual buttons to sophisticated database front-ends and report generators. VBXs sell for anywhere between $25 to $3000. Many leading tools can import VBXs into their palettes and use them to construct visual forms and client front-ends.

So, why did Microsoft disown their VBX standard in favor of OCXs? Because OCXs are true OLE components—they build on COM and OLE compound document technology. In contrast, VBXs are just kludges that are intimately tied to the Visual Basic runtime. It's a testimony to the creative energy of component vendors that they were able to get around the VBX technical limitations and create a thriving industry. In any case, Microsoft provides a VBX-to-OCX migration toolkit as part of Visual C++ 2.0. We expect that most VBXs will have been converted to OCXs and

OLE technology within a year. If that happens, Microsoft will have successfully migrated its third-party component base to a much more solid foundation.

So What's an OCX?

An OCX is a combination of an OLE in-process server and an OLE automation server. It's really an in-process server object that supports embedding, in-place editing, inside-out activation, OLE automation, event notifications, and connectable objects. In addition, OCXs support licensing, property editing, and they define standard properties and events. Finally, OCXs are self-registering; they support a new function called *DllRegisterServer*. OCXs make an excellent "grand finale" to our OLE chapters. They bring together compound document and automation technology and deal with some of the hard issues associated with component packaging.

OCXs extend the OLE compound document architecture by creating new forms of interaction between OCX server objects and their containers. OCXs are more than just editable embedded objects. They can transform end-user actions, like mouse clicks and keystrokes, into notification events sent to the container. These notifications can serve as callbacks that trigger the execution of event handlers.

OCXs introduce a new technology for creating connections between event sources and event handlers (or sinks). This new technology—called *connectable objects*—is a more generic implementation of the various "advise sources and sinks" we encountered throughout the OLE chapters. Even though the connectable object mechanisms were first introduced by OCXs, they're now considered to be a generic technology that's useful outside of controls. So connectable objects are an official part of the COM object infrastructure. Think of them as the COM event service.

It shouldn't come as a surprise that all these new capabilities are implemented with additional interfaces. The good news is that these are the last OLE interfaces we cover in this book. The other good news is that there aren't too many new interfaces because most of the new interactions are done via automation using the familiar **IDispatch** interface. So if you can bear to make it through the next few pages, you will have successfully gone through the entire OLE works. We'll have a celebration party when you get to the finishing line.

Container Meets OCX

An OCX (or a control) is a well-packaged component that communicates with whatever container it happens to land in using methods, properties, and events. Figure 29-9 shows the interfaces OCXs and containers must implement to support

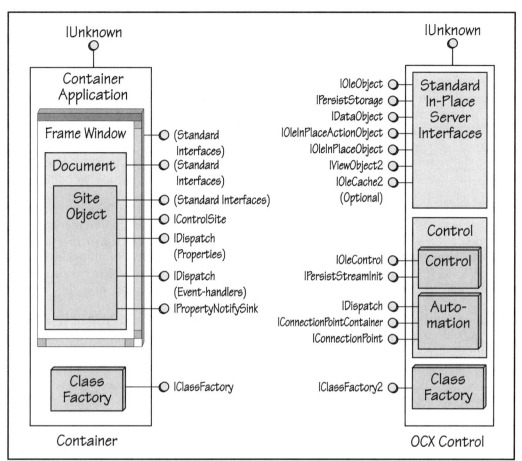

Figure 29-9. The Control Container and OCX Interfaces.

controls. A control container is a standard in-place capable embedded object container. But this is not enough. To provide a more seamless look, OCXs and their containers must do some extra work to integrate the control with the container's environment. For example, the container exposes to its OCXs a set of read-only *ambient properties* that describe the container's overall environment such as background color on a form, text alignment, and font size. This information serves as hints to the OCX on how it should set its own property values so that it appears to visually integrate with its environment. The container ultimately determines the OCX's size and position, but the control must draw its contents.

Extended properties are properties that are managed by the container itself on behalf of the control. A container maintains a set of properties on a per-control basis for each OCX within the document. For example, a container may want to associate an "enabled" property with each control and dynamically maintain the values. Of course, the OCX maintains its own set of properties called *control properties*. The container can only get to the values in the control properties by requesting them from the OCX.

OCXs and their containers must know a lot more about each other at run time. The container must be able to invoke methods on the OCX and retrieve and modify control properties. The OCX must be able to send to the control asynchronous notifications that are triggered by user interactions with the control or by other means. The control must be able to react to these incoming events and provide the right event handler. To meet all these requirements in a flexible manner, OCXs and their containers use OLE automation to implement most of their interactions.

Let's return to Figure 29-9. As you can see, for each control "site" a container implements two **IDispatch** automation interfaces. The first dispatchable interface provides access to the container's ambient and extended control properties; the second surfaces a set of event handlers to which OCXs can send event notifications. The OCX itself implements one **IDispatch** that a container uses to invoke methods and modify properties on a control by calling *IDispatch::Invoke*.

What else is new? The **IConnectionPointContainer** and **IConnectionPoint** interfaces implement the new *connectable objects* protocol (we cover this protocol in the next sections). The **IPersistStreamInit** interface allows the control to save and load its properties from an **IStream.** You also call it to notify the control when it is first created. **IClassFactory2** is an extension of **IClassFactory** that enforces licensing at creation time.

OCXs introduce a new technology called *property pages* that allows users to directly modify a control's properties through the user interface. You can add property pages into a tabbed dialog box to create a consistent user interface for manipulating properties during design time or at run time. OLE provides property pages for its "stock" (meaning standard) properties.

The **IPropertyNotifySink** is used by the control to notify the container when a control property value changes. The **IOleControl** interface is used by the container to notify the OCX when ambient property values change as well as other miscellaneous occurrences—such as when the container has loaded all its controls. The OCX obtains the changed information from the container's **IControlSite**.

OCXs also implement the standard in-place editing server interfaces that we covered in the previous section. All of these interfaces combined meet all the needs of any control. We cover the more important interfaces in the next sections. Notice that OCXs do not support linking or drag-and-drop, and the cache interface is optional.

How OCXs and Containers Use Automation

In addition to supporting the compound document interfaces, an OCX is also an OLE automation client and server. It's a client to the container's automation services, and it implements **IDispatch** to surface its own properties and methods. Because both OCXs and their containers support OLE automation, most of their interactions are through **IDispatch** interfaces. This means that the methods and properties are invoked dynamically using *IDispatch::Invoke* instead of vtables.

Like any good OLE automation object, an OCX exposes its properties and methods through *TypeInfo*, which is maintained in a Type Library. Containers—or any automation client—can dynamically access the TypeInfo using the interfaces described in Chapter 26, "OLE: Automation, Scripting, and Type Libraries." OCXs also follow a standard registry convention to give the location of their Type Library and TypeInfo. Containers that need to access type information statically can use the registry to locate and load a description of the control.

Control *properties* are named attributes of an OCX. They define object characteristics—such as the caption string, foreground color, background color—or control behaviors. The properties are managed and implemented by the OCX. A control *method* is a function that operates on a control. OLE defines a set of standard—called *stock*—properties, methods, and events for OCXs. Anything standard is identified by a well-known Dispatch ID (or dispID). The properties, methods, and events that you create are called *custom*—they too have dispatch IDs, but they're not well-known. Containers can only access properties and methods on a control via *IDispatch:Invoke*; there is no early-bound mechanism for accessing properties and methods.

OCX-Generated Events

An *event* is a notification fired by an OCX in response to some user action, such as clicking the mouse or pressing a key, or any action that changes the control. Events can also be emitted programmatically, or they can be triggered by the system. For example, the system could post an error notification.

In the OCX model, events are the opposite of method invocations. For example, an OCX method is implemented by the control and is invoked by a container. However, with a control event, the OCX does not provide an implementation. Instead, the OCX exposes the event and is very willing to call an implementation provided by some other object when the event fires; it will even pass it parameters. So an event is simply an outgoing method invocation. Individual events are gathered into *event sets*, just as incoming methods are gathered into interfaces. An OCX's event set is defined as outgoing *dispinterfaces* described in ODL.

Events are a very important part of programming with controls. Event-driven programming lets users attach scripts or programs to respond to the firing of an event. Or the event can be sent to a container, which provides the event handler. This style of programming was key to the success of VBXs and was carried over to OCXs. An event by itself is not very interesting if no one is listening. However, an event that reaches an appropriate event handler is very interesting.

In the present case, OCXs provide the events, and containers are more than happy to service these events through the **IDispatch** dispinterface they provide for just that purpose. This makes the interaction between OCXs and their containers very flexible (but there may be some performance implications). We still have to answer the question: How is the connection created between these outgoing events and the container objects that provide the event handlers? Or, how do the containers subscribe to OCX events?

You may have noticed that OLE provides many *ad-hoc* interfaces for dealing with asynchronous events and notifications. These interfaces provide a hardcoded solution for a particular form of notification. For example, the **IDataObject** and **IAdviseSink** provide object-to-client notifications when data changes. OCXs introduce a more generic approach for creating these connections called "connectable objects," which is the topic of the next section.

Connectable Objects: COM's Event Service

Connectable objects are OLE's version of a standard event service. As we explained in Chapter 26, "OLE: Automation, Scripting, and Type Libraries," an OLE object can support ODL-defined outgoing interfaces. These interfaces provide a standard way of defining events and their parameters. Objects that support outgoing interfaces are called *connectable objects* or *sources*. But how does the connectable object find the recipients of its outgoing call? Through the *connection* interfaces, of course.

A connectable object can have as many outgoing interfaces as it likes. Each interface is composed of a set of outgoing functions; each function represents a single event or notification. These events tell whomever is listening that something interesting just happened to the object. A listener implements an interface called a *sink*. So how does a sink register its interest? By calling a *connection point* object. For each outgoing interface, a connectable object creates a small object that implements the *IConnectionPoint* interface. It is through this interface that clients pass interface pointers to their sinks and ask to be connected to the event source (see Figure 29-10).

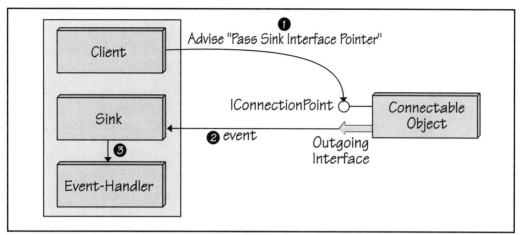

Figure 29-10. Creating the Source-to-Sink Connection.

The **IConnectionPoint** interface consists of five member functions (see Figure 29-11). A client calls *Advise* to establish a connection with an outgoing interface and passes a pointer to a sink interface. The client calls *Unadvise* to break the connection. *EnumConnections* returns an enumerator that lists all the active advisory connections. *GetConnectionInterface* returns the IID of the single outgoing interface this connection point supports. *GetConnectionPointContainer* returns a pointer to the container object that keeps track of all the outgoing connection points for the object.

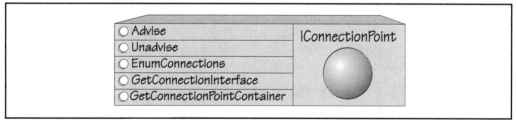

Figure 29-11. The IConnectionPoint Interface.

The **IConnectionPointContainer** interface allows a client to enumerate all the connection points supported by an object. This is how clients discover outgoing interfaces—that is, connection points. This interface defines two member functions (see Figure 29-12). *FindConnectionPoint* asks the object if it supports an outgoing interface identified by an IID. If successful, it returns a connection point for that interface. *EnumConnectionPoints* returns all the outgoing interfaces an object supports.

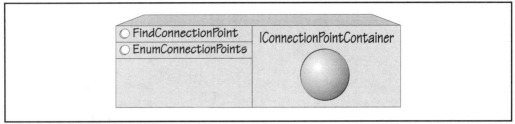

Figure 29-12. The IConnectionPointContainer Interface.

An OCX Connectable Object Scenario

You'll be happy to know that this is really the last OLE scenario. We're going to see what it takes for a container client to get an event notification from its favorite OCX (see Figure 29-13). Here are the steps:

1. ***Container to OCX: What outgoing interfaces do you support?*** The container invokes *EnumConnectionPoints* on the **IConnectionPointContainer** interface to find out what outgoing interfaces the object supports. The call returns an enumeration object through which the client can retrieve the **IConnectionPointers** for each outgoing interface.

2. ***Get the IID for this outgoing interface.*** The container can optionally invoke *GetConnectionInterface* to obtain the IID of the single outgoing dispinterface this connection point supports. This IID is only needed if the client plans to call *GetClassInfo* to obtain type information. A client can learn about all the member functions an outgoing interface supports. With this information, the client can dynamically implement an **IDispatch** sink and connect it to a connectable object. In other words, the client can wire a connection "on the fly."

3. ***Subscribe to the event set.*** The client invokes the *Advise* function to establish an outgoing connection with its designated sink. In this scenario, the container passes a pointer to its **IDispatch** interface to receive events.

4. ***An event occurs.*** Something interesting happens to the OCX.

5. ***Who are my subscribers?.*** The event source obtains the list of subscribers, which means Advise sinks, to its event set by invoking *EnumConnections*.

6. ***Dispatch the event to each subscriber.*** In this scenario, there is only one subscriber—a pointer to the container's **IDispatch::Invoke** for incoming events. The event source invokes this function and passes it the dispID that identifies the member function—an event is ultimately an outgoing function call and its parameters. The container uses this dispID to invoke the appropriate event-handler implementation.

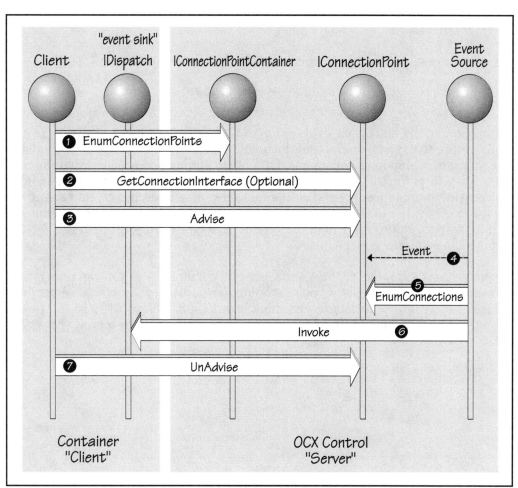

Figure 29-13. Scenario: How Containers Get Event Notifications From OCXs.

7. *Cancel the connection*. The client ends the subscription by calling *Unadvise*.

Note that **IDispatch** interfaces make great sinks because the events can be represented at run time with disp IDs. They don't have to be hardcoded into vtables. This is an example of the power of automation and late binding. OLE's newer **IProperty-NotifySink** was designed to work with connectable objects. Older sinks, like **IAdviseSink**, are tied to specific sources—in this case, **IDataObject** and **IDataView**—and they cannot be used with the new connection services.

Conclusion

It is wise to keep in mind that no success or failure is necessarily final.

— Anonymous

We've come to the end of our exploration of OLE under the hood. As you can see, OLE is more than just a compound document technology. It is an object model in its own right. Compound documents, OCXs, and automation are just what the user sees. They form the tip of an iceberg. Underneath are layers of object technology that provide persistence, events, compound files, data interchange, and so on. At the lowest layer, the COM object bus provides local/remote transparency (but not over networks), static and dynamic invocations, a type library, an ODL/IDL facility, and the QueryInterface mechanism.

In some ways, OLE is like CORBA and OpenDoc combined. So you can understand why this part is so long. But if you're reading these words, you must have survived the trek. If it's any consolation, just think how long it took to write it! So please accept our warmest congratulations and give yourself a well-deserved pat on the back.

Part 6
Component Nirvana:
Client/Server
With Parts

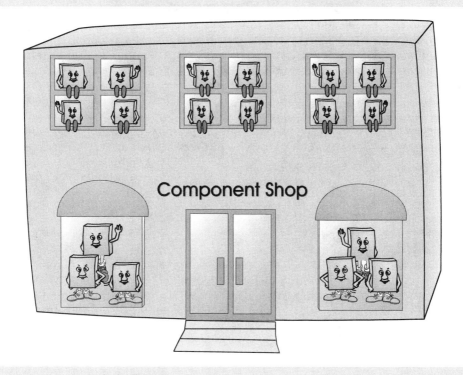

Component Shop

An Introduction to Part 6

The emerging standards for component software and compound documents signal a broad movement to spread object-oriented concepts into the mainstream of application development.

— Richard Adler, Coordinated Computing
(March, 1995)

Before components make it "into the mainstream of application development," there are still some major hurdles that we need to overcome. These hurdles are not technical in nature. You can see from reading this book that the core infrastructure for creating distributed components is almost in place. The remaining pieces can be introduced incrementally after they're developed. The beauty of object technology is that you can start with a core set of functions, and then add system-level services piecemeal to refine and enhance your system. You can do this without creating major disruptions. Yes, Virginia, encapsulation also works at the system level.

In Part 6 we answer some nagging questions this book should have stirred. The easier ones are: Which component infrastructure do I pick—COM/OLE or CORBA/OpenDoc? Can the two component infrastructures coexist? Can I write a component once and have it run on either infrastructure? Can gateways help?

These are the easy questions. We left the more nagging ones to the very last—including: What will the business side of this component infrastructure look like? How do we support these multivendor components? How do we recreate "whole" applications using components? What pieces are missing? How do I make money with components? And, how do I prepare myself for this component revolution?

It's much easier to deal with the technical merits of COM/OLE versus CORBA/OpenDoc than to answer these broad business questions. But as we discovered over the last year—speaking to thousands of developers at dozens of industry conferences—these are the foremost questions on your minds (and ours). We know that they must be answered before you sign up for this component revolution. The good news is that we have an answer to some of these questions, which we, of course, present in a Soapbox with all the accompanying pomp and ceremony. The bad news is that it takes a major cross-vendor effort to create a component market infrastructure. It's almost as significant as the effort it took to create the technical infrastructure for components.

So we hope Part 6 answers some of your questions (even ones you did not have). And, remember, you're only a few pages away from the finishing line—this is really the last part in the book. Our Martian friends will soon be able to return home to their loved ones.

Chapter 30

Which Component Model?

In any computer market there is usually room for two companies, with roughly 85% of the market going to one and 15% going to the other.

— *Cringely's Law[1]*

At most we can tolerate two component standards.

— *Christine Comaford, PC Week columnist (June, 1995)*

If we apply Cringely's Law to the component market, the two finalists—at least in "our book"—are COM/OLE and CORBA/OpenDoc. Even though two is a very small number, it introduces a huge amount of complication in the lives of component developers and component providers. As you saw in this book, the component infrastructure is more elaborate than anything we've ever seen in the software business. It's really an undertaking of intergalactic proportions. We're not talking

---

[1] This law was coined by Robert Cringely, the **InfoWorld** columnist.

about simple interoperability between component buses. We must also factor into the equation the frameworks and "insertable" system services that we need to create "supersmart" components and their suites.

Here are some of the million-dollar questions we attempt to answer in this chapter: Which of the two component infrastructures will get the lion's share of the market (Cringely's 85%)? Can the two component infrastructures converge? Can you write a component once and run it on either infrastructure? How will these two dominant infrastructures coexist? What kind of gateways should you expect? Will they help?

SHOULD YOU BET ON COM/OLE OR CORBA/OPENDOC?

Given the resources of their respective backers, OLE/COM and OpenDoc/SOM are likely to compete vigorously for the foreseeable future.

> — **Richard Adler, Coordinated Computing**
> **(March, 1995)**

If you read this entire book, you will probably agree that CORBA/OpenDoc together provide the technically superior component infrastructure for both the desktop and the client/server enterprise. CORBA is at least two years ahead of OLE in defining the distributed component infrastructure. CORBA vendors are about to launch their third-generation ORBs, while Microsoft has not even published a Network OLE specification that is stable. OpenDoc augments CORBA with a superior compound document infrastructure. It provides a more seamless look than OLE as well as superior scripting and automation facilities; *Bento* is more portable than OLE's *DocFiles*.

In this section, we provide a brief feature by feature comparison of COM/OLE and CORBA/OpenDoc for readers that have skipped over the more technical chapters. Like all top-level feature comparisons, these tables do not tell the whole story. Our readers who have gone through the detailed chapters know that there's a long story behind each of the bullets that appear in the summary tables. It's very hard to give a bird's-eye view of something that took us 500 pages to explain. But we always get asked for the bottom line, so here it is (with the noted caveats).

OLE/COM Versus CORBA/OpenDoc: The Object Models

Table 30-1 compares today's OLE/COM and CORBA/OpenDoc object models. The big difference is that CORBA/OpenDoc follows the classical object model and extends it to components. So a CORBA/OpenDoc component is a first-class object; it supports multiple inheritance, encapsulation, and polymorphism. Like classical objects, CORBA/OpenDoc components belong to classes that you can instantiate at run time. A CORBA/OpenDoc object instance has a unique reference ID. This is exactly what you would expect from a classical object. Some CORBA/OpenDoc implementations let you compose components by creating new classes and refactoring their inheritance relationships at run time. Even though OLE provides universally unique identifiers for classes, it does not do the same for run-time objects—meaning instances of these classes. When you connect to an OLE object, you obtain a pointer to an interface you can work with, but you have no way to reconnect to that exact same object at a later time.

OLE/COM components are not classical objects. You cannot extend an OLE/COM class via inheritance. An OLE/COM class is simply an encapsulation mechanism. OLE lets you compose complex classes using delegation mechanisms. For example, OLE provides a technique called *aggregation* that lets an object support multiple interfaces—including the interfaces that other objects provide. Using aggregation, you can let an outer component represent the interfaces of inner components. It's at best a poor man's inheritance. Essentially, an OLE component is a black box. You cannot extend an OLE component after you purchase it—what you see is what you get.

Table 30-1. Comparing OLE/COM With CORBA/OpenDoc: The Object Models.

Feature	COM/OLE	CORBA/OpenDoc
What does a component look like?	Black box	Black box or White box
Can a component be extended via inheritance?	No	Yes
Can a component support multiple interfaces?	Yes	Yes (via multiple inheritance)
Can a component support outgoing interfaces?	Yes	Yes (via the Event Service)
Do classes have globally unique IDs?	Yes	Yes
Do run-time objects have unique references?	No	Yes
Who owns the specification?	Microsoft	OMG and CI Labs
Which platforms are supported?	Windows and Mac (third parties may provide added platform support)	Windows, Mac, OS/2, various Unixes, Tandem, OS/400, MVS, VMS, and many others

OLE/COM Versus CORBA/OpenDoc: The Object Buses

Components had better be distributed, multiplatform, and supported by different vendors.

> — *Christine Comaford, Columnist*
> *PC Week*
> *(June, 1995)*

Table 30-2 compares the OLE/COM and CORBA/OpenDoc object buses. The big difference is that distributed CORBA ORBs have been shipping since 1993, while Microsoft has not yet finalized its Network OLE specification. In late 1994, the CORBA 2.0 specifications for heterogeneous inter-ORB communications were completed. This means that CORBA has already worked out the thorny issues of federated, heterogeneous, inter-ORB communications. The CORBA vendors also had to deal with issues such as global naming, cross-platform data representations, inter-ORB object reference IDs, inter-ORB bridging, and global Interface Repositories. This means CORBA components can discover each other, exchange metadata, and invoke each other's services across vendor ORBs and operating systems. We expect a new generation of CORBA 2.0-compliant ORBs to ship in early 1996.

Table 30-2. Comparing OLE/COM With CORBA/OpenDoc: The Object Buses.

Feature	COM/OLE		CORBA/OpenDoc	
	Local	Remote	Local	Remote
Static method invocations	Yes	No	Yes	Yes
Dynamic method invocations (Note: OLE calls it **IDispatch**)	Yes	No	Yes	Yes
Interface Repository and metadata (Note: OLE calls it Type Library)	Yes	No	Yes	Yes
Component packaging	Yes	No	Yes	Yes
Interface Definition Language (Note: OLE provides two interface languages— the ODL describes metadata and the Microsoft IDL/MIDL describes RPC linkages)	Yes (ODL and MIDL)	No	Yes (IDL)	Yes (IDL)
Implementation Repository (OLE's Implementation Repository is the Windows Registry; Microsoft is also working with TI on a future distributed object repository)	Yes	No	Yes	Yes

OLE/COM Versus CORBA/OpenDoc: Higher-Level Language Bindings

Table 30-3 compares the OLE/COM and CORBA/OpenDoc compiler-independent language bindings. As you can see, OLE only provides a binary interoperability standard; it does not provide higher-level language bindings. The binary standard defines the formats of OLE interprocess messaging and vtable calling conventions. The language bindings that generate these messages are left as an exercise to the compiler vendors or programmers (it happens that the vtable layouts map perfectly to the Microsoft C++ compiler's vtables). Microsoft provides a Microsoft IDL (MIDL) precompiler to help you generate stubs for these cross-process invocations, but it is not language-independent (it's a C-based superset of the DCE IDL).

In contrast, the CORBA IDL was designed from day one to let you port objects written in different languages to different ORB implementations. The CORBA language mappings hide the underlying middleware from your objects. This means CORBA elevates the level of abstraction from a binary standard (with pointers to vtables in memory) to higher-level language constructs. CORBA lets you invoke remote objects using familiar high-level language calls.

In addition, a CORBA component written in one language can call—across ORBs—local or remote CORBA components written in other languages and running on different operating systems. Some CORBA implementations—for example, SOM—even let components inherit their behavior from components written using different compilers or higher-level languages. No other client/server middleware provides an equivalent level of abstraction or portability.

Table 30-3. Comparing OLE/COM With CORBA/OpenDoc: The Language Bindings.

Feature	COM/OLE		CORBA/OpenDoc	
	Local	Remote	Local	Remote
Binary interoperability	Yes	No	Yes	Yes
C language bindings	No	No	Yes	Yes
C++ language bindings (Note: Microsoft matches the vtables of its own C++ compiler)	No	No	Yes	Yes
Smalltalk language bindings	No	No	Yes	Yes
Future Ada, COBOL, and Objective C language bindings (Note: These are work in process)	No	No	Yes	Yes

OLE/COM Versus CORBA/OpenDoc: The System Services

Table 30-4 compares the OLE/COM and CORBA/OpenDoc object bus services. These are the system services that go beyond simple interoperability; they let you create "supersmart" components. Again, none of the COM/OLE services are distributed. CORBA has a huge head start over OLE in the area of system services. CORBA has developed specifications for running inter-ORB transactions, interfacing to ODBMSs, and creating all types of ad-hoc relationships between components. Currently, CORBA is working on integrating security across inter-vendor ORBs. It's hard to imagine how Microsoft will single-handedly recreate this infrastructure that was developed over many years by some of the best client/server and distributed object technologists in the industry. The CORBA services will start appearing in commercial ORBs in late 1995.

Table 30-4. Comparing OLE/COM With CORBA/OpenDoc: The System Services.

Feature	COM/OLE		CORBA/OpenDoc	
	Local	Remote	Local	Remote
Events	Yes	No	Yes	Yes
Life Cycle (Note: OLE provides Life Cycle via **IClassFactory** and **IUnknown**)	Yes	No	Yes	Yes
Naming (Note: OLE provides naming via monikers)	Yes	No	Yes	Yes
Persistence	Yes	No	Yes	Yes
ODBMS integration	No	No	Yes	Yes
RDBMS integration (Note: Microsoft is working on an OLE DB specification)	No	No	Yes	Yes
Externalization	Yes	No	Yes	Yes
Transactions (Note: Microsoft is working on an OLE Transactions specification)	No	No	Yes	Yes
Concurrency Control	No	No	Yes	Yes
Relationships	No	No	Yes	Yes
Query (Note: Microsoft is working on an OLE DB specification)	No	No	Yes	Yes

Table 30-4. Comparing OLE/COM With CORBA/OpenDoc: The System Services. (Continued)

Feature	COM/OLE		CORBA/OpenDoc	
	Local	Remote	Local	Remote
Licensing	Yes	No	Yes	Yes
Properties	Yes	No	Yes	Yes
Versioning (Note: OpenDoc provides version control today; CORBA Change Management is expected in 1996)	No	No	Yes	Yes
Security (Note: Individual ORBs provide security; the CORBA Security Service is expected late 1995)	No	No	Yes	Yes
Garbage collection (Note: OpenDoc augments CORBA by providing reference counting; OLE provides reference counting via **IUnknown**)	Yes	No	Yes	No

OLE/COM Versus CORBA/OpenDoc: Compound Document Frameworks

Table 30-5 compares the OLE and OpenDoc compound document frameworks. We expect that OpenDoc will be adopted by CORBA as its compound document standard by the time you read this book. In the meantime, OpenDoc already uses CORBA as its object bus. OLE provides a compound document service on top of COM. There is no way we can recreate in this table all the nuances of the two component models and their pros and cons. If you want more detailed comparisons, please refer to the different Soapboxes in the OLE and OpenDoc parts (we tried to keep the comparisons in Soapboxes so that we could throw in some opinions).

The biggest difference is that OpenDoc lets you create very seamless looking parts with superior display capabilities. The OpenDoc scripting facilities are also very powerful. They let you operate on a part's contents via semantic messages. OpenDoc provides the mechanisms that let you deliver the message to the right content—regardless of how deeply embedded it is within a document. Most importantly, OpenDoc is very consistent—everything is a part derived from **ODPart**. In contrast, OLE fields over a dozen container/server combinations. OLE's newer OCX controls are the closest thing to a self-contained component. Unfortunately, OCXs cannot contain other parts (in contrast, an OpenDoc part is also a container).

Table 30-5. Comparing OLE/COM With CORBA/OpenDoc: Compound Document Frameworks.

Feature	COM/OLE	CORBA/OpenDoc
Compound document storage	Yes (DocFiles)	Yes (Bento)
Document drafts	No	Yes (Bento versions)
Automation and scripting	Yes	Yes
Semantic message resolution	No	Yes
Recordable scripts	No	Yes
Irregularly-shaped parts	No	Yes
Multiframed parts	No	Yes
In-place editing and inside-out levels of nesting	2	Unlimited
Bitmap caching for inactive parts	Yes	No
Drag-and-Drop	Yes	Yes
Clipboard	Yes	Yes
Linking	Yes	Yes

(Note: OpenDoc provides persistent Link IDs that
can be distributed if a networked ORB is present)

The OLE Camp: So What?

Soapbox

Many OLE proponents will take one look at the comparison tables and say, "So what?" In their opinion, Microsoft never gets it right in the first or second release—but always seems to get it right the third time. So it's always better to wait for future versions of OLE instead of going along with CORBA's "design by committee." OLE proponents may also point out that ISVs and IS shops must take on a bigger programming effort to ensure that the different CORBA products really work together.

With OLE you get all your infrastructure from one vendor. And that's *Microsoft*. These developers prefer single-company *de facto* standards like the ones the old IBM used to provide. It's a bit like making the old argument that "Mussolini may have been a dictator, but at least the trains ran on time." Of course, no one can accuse Microsoft of delivering any product on time. Distributed OLE is hopelessly behind CORBA. ❏

So, the Winner Is...

CORBA/OpenDoc is clearly technically superior to OLE. However, it takes more than a good technical infrastructure to create a winning component standard. We explain the non-technical component infrastructure requirements in the next chapter. We must first go over these requirements before declaring a winner (or, which technology gets the Cringely lion's share). Of course, we're trying to build the tension and heighten the suspense level.

COM/OLE AND CORBA/OPENDOC: CAN WE INTEROPERATE?

At this stage of the game, we do not expect COM/OLE and CORBA/OpenDoc to merge. Both sides have reached the point of no return with their installed bases. So the best the two sides can do is interoperate via gateways. We should note that a gateway is very different from a bridge. A *bridge* lets you interoperate between ORBs that share a common object model; a *gateway* lets you interoperate between ORBs that have *different* object models. A gateway must compensate as much as possible for the differences in the object models that it connects together.

Gateways Come in All Shapes

As you can imagine, many vendors are offering some type of gateway between COM/OLE and CORBA/OpenDoc. The most comprehensive gateway is Novell's *ComponentGlue*; it makes OLE look like OpenDoc, and vice versa. In addition, almost every CORBA ORB vendor currently offers a two-way gateway between their ORBs and COM—this includes Digital's *ObjectBroker*, IBM's *SOMobjects for Windows*, Expersoft's *OLE/CORBA/COM*, and Iona's *Orbix-OLE*. COM/CORBA toolkits are also available from Candle and Visual Edge. Currently, each of these vendors implements a proprietary gateway scheme. This is about to change because OMG—with Microsoft's blessing—has just issued an RFP (or two RFPs in one) for a bidirectional COM/CORBA gateway specification. In the next two sections, we briefly go over the *ComponentGlue* and *CORBA gateway* approaches.

ComponentGlue: The Deep Gateway Approach

OpenDoc doesn't assume the world is going its way and so it's also designed to support other compound document architectures, including OLE objects.

> — *Kevin Strehlo, Editor-in-Chief*
> *Datamation*
> *(November, 1994)*

CI Lab's *ComponentGlue*—it was developed by Novell—is the part of OpenDoc that encapsulates OLE. It lets OpenDoc parts play in OLE containers, and vice versa. ComponentGlue also encapsulates OLE OCXs and makes them look like OpenDoc parts. We already introduced Novell's ComponentGlue in Chapter 15, "The Open-Doc Component Model," on page 278. If you haven't done so, please review that section before continuing.

ComponentGlue achieves its magic by providing two wrapper objects:

- **OleWrapper** implements all the OLE in-place *local server* interfaces (see Figure 30-1). It encapsulates an OpenDoc part by masquerading it as an OLE server (OCX support is being added). ComponentGlue generates cached images of the part and handles shared menu negotiations. It displays the part within an OLE container by providing an in-place window that is really an OpenDoc shell application running without a titlebar or menu. It can even store an OpenDoc part using OLE's persistent storage interfaces. Readers who have gone through the OLE in-depth chapters will notice that ComponentGlue implements all the key OLE server interfaces—including **IDataObject**, **IPersistStorage**, **IOle-Object**, and **IOLEInPlaceObject**. Of course, the OpenDoc part that implements all these interfaces uses the standard **ODPart** framework; it knows nothing of OLE.

- **OlePart** allows an OpenDoc part to masquerade itself as an OLE container (see Figure 30-2). Remember that OpenDoc parts can contain other parts. This wrapper lets an OpenDoc part display OLE server objects (later OCXs) using in-place, inside-out activation. It displays a cached image when an OLE object isn't running. It also stores OLE objects inside OpenDoc Bento files.

All you need to do to turn an OpenDoc part into an OLE server (or OCX) is provide it with a GUID and an icon. You must also register the part with the OLE registry.

In addition, ComponentGlue allows OLE *Automation Controllers* like Visual Basic to drive OpenDoc parts that implement OSA-based automation, and vice versa.

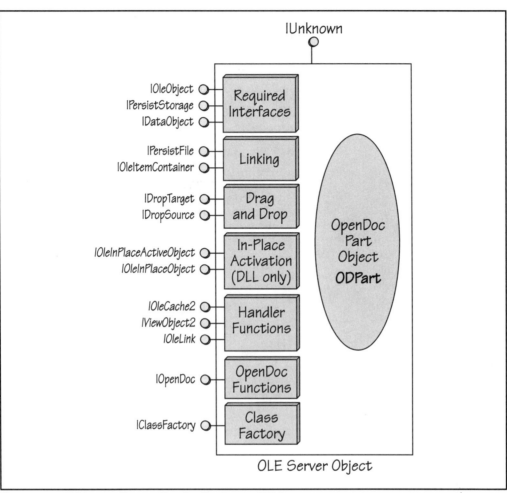

Figure 30-1. OleWrapper: Turns an OpenDoc Part Into an OLE Server.

ComponentGlue will allow OpenDoc parts to look like OLE OCXs; it will also let OpenDoc parts contain OLE OCXs.

The bottom line is that ComponentGlue provides a deep translation layer between OpenDoc and OLE. However, it neither maps OLE to other CORBA services nor does it try to reconcile their IDLs. For example, ComponentGlue cannot make an OLE object transactional using CORBA's Object Transaction Service. So ComponentGlue is really a gateway that maps between two compound document models—OLE and OpenDoc.

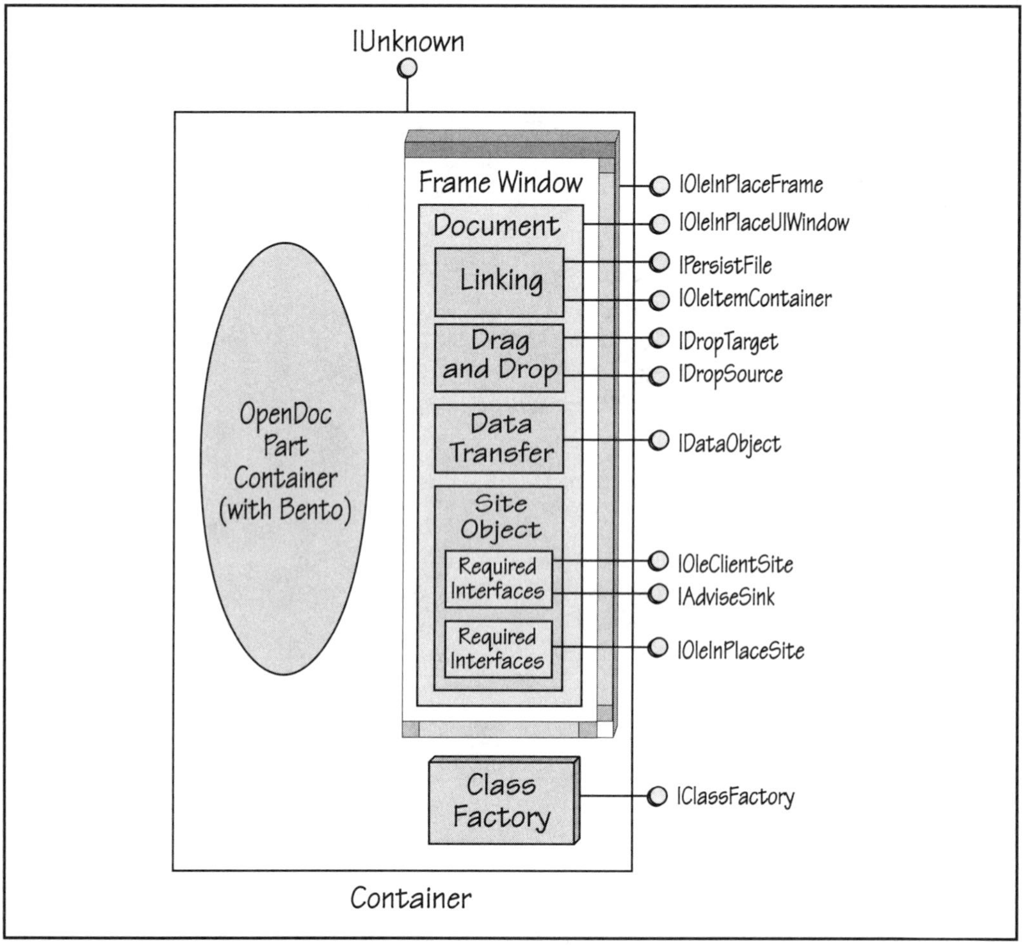

IUnknown

Frame Window — IOleInPlaceFrame

Document — IOleInPlaceUIWindow

— IPersistFile

Linking — IOleItemContainer

Drag and Drop — IDropTarget
— IDropSource

OpenDoc Part Container (with Bento)

Data Transfer — IDataObject

Site Object

Required Interfaces — IOleClientSite
— IAdviseSink

Required Interfaces — IOleInPlaceSite

Class Factory — IClassFactory

Container

Figure 30-2. OlePart: Turns an OpenDoc Part Into an OLE Container.

The COM/CORBA Interworking RFP: The Generic Gateway Approach

In April 1995, OMG issued a COM/CORBA RFP consisting of two parts:

■ *Part A* addresses interworking between local COM—as it exists today—and CORBA. Submissions are due in August 1995.

■ *Part B* addresses interworking between CORBA and the forthcoming networked version of COM. Submissions are due in December 1995. Microsoft promised to provide a final version of the distributed COM specification by October 24th, 1995.

In June 1995, 13 companies submitted letters of intent to participate in this RFP. As we go to press, it looks like most of the submitters will use the IIOP Inter-ORB protocol to provide two-way interoperability between the CORBA and COM. In the best case, these submissions will result in a gateway that provides the following interoperability services between CORBA and COM:

- **Method invocation mappings.** This means a CORBA client can invoke operations on a COM object, and vice versa. Gateways may implement this function using proxy objects that map between OLE calls and CORBA calls. The proxies must reissue the calls in a way that makes sense for each system. For example, a proxy on the CORBA side must be able to deal with OLE's **IUnknown** interface. A proxy on the OLE side must be able to invoke a CORBA method using the dynamic invocations and the CORBA Interface Repository.

- **Data type mappings.** The gateway must be able to convert CORBA data types into their OLE equivalents, and vice versa. Some data type translations are simple mappings—for example, strings. Others are more complex—for example, translating between the CORBA *any* and the OLE *variant* types won't be easy.

- **Mappings between CORBA IDL and OLE ODL (and MIDL).** A CORBA client must be able to obtain metadata on an OLE object using the CORBA Interface Repository, and vice versa. CORBA IDLs must be able to represent OLE objects with multiple interfaces and outgoing interfaces.

- **Exception mappings.** OLE and CORBA use different techniques to signal exceptions. The gateway must map CORBA's exception returns into OLE, and vice versa.

- **Initialization mappings.** The gateway must provide an environment that lets a COM client access the first CORBA service it uses, and vice versa.

- **Object factory mappings.** The gateway must allow an OLE object to create a CORBA object, and vice versa.

- **Registry mappings.** The gateway must register CORBA objects in the OLE registry, and vice versa.

- **Security domain mappings.** The gateway must map between CORBA security and OLE security, and vice versa.

This is a partial list of the mappings a gateway must implement to provide CORBA/COM interoperability. We expect that most generic CORBA/COM gateways will be implemented using dynamic invocations. This lets a CORBA server object masquerade itself as an OLE automation server. In Figure 30-3, an OLE client invokes a CORBA server. Notice that the gateway must: 1) implement the OLE **IDispatch** and **IUnknown** interfaces, 2) provide OLE-to-CORBA mappings, and 3) reissue the call using CORBA dynamic invocations on an IIOP ORB.

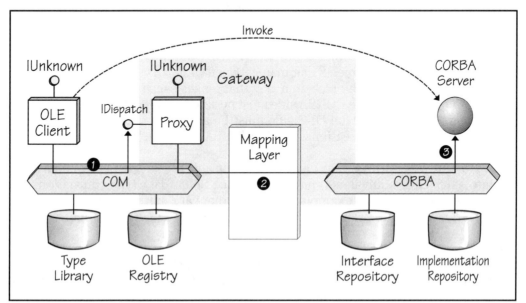

Figure 30-3. OLE-to-CORBA via a Dynamic Invocation Gateway.

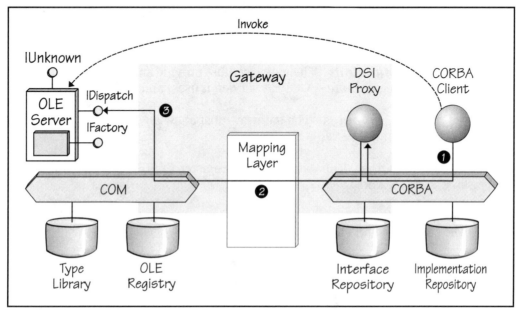

Figure 30-4. CORBA-to-OLE via a Dynamic Invocation Gateway.

In the other direction (see Figure 30-4), an OLE object masquerades as a CORBA server by using regular OLE Automation Server interfaces (meaning **IDispatch**). For a CORBA client to invoke an OLE server, the gateway must: 1) implement the CORBA Dynamic Skeleton Interface that receives the call from the client, 2) provide CORBA-to-OLE mappings, and 3) reissue the call on the COM side using OLE's **IDispatch**.

The advantage of using dynamic invocations is that they are loosely coupled and provide maximum flexibility at the gateway level. The downside is that they introduce a performance penalty because the request must be recreated "on-the-fly." Static gateways—meaning gateways that replace OLE stubs with CORBA static invocations, and vice versa—will perform better but they are less flexible. They are also more complex to implement and difficult to administer.

Conclusion

It's a hard life for an application developer to live in a heterogeneous world.

> *— Jim Archer, Director of Object Strategy*
> *IBM*
> *(March, 1995)*

COM/OLE and CORBA/OpenDoc are monumental undertakings. Both will eventually provide very complete distributed component infrastructures. We believe that CORBA/OpenDoc is about two years ahead of COM/OLE in creating a distributed component infrastructure. OLE has a head start on the Windows desktop; it is also ahead of OpenDoc in the area of desktop tools. OpenDoc's answer is to provide a better compound document framework that runs on more platforms; it also encapsulates OLE with *ComponentGlue* on Windows.

Because of CORBA's dominance on the server, even the most diehard OLE backers must support CORBA if they want to get into the client/server component business. And because of COM/OLE's dominance on the Windows desktop, the same is true of CORBA backers. This means that you must either learn two object models or depend on one of the gateway solutions to insulate you from the other object model. OpenDoc's *ComponentGlue* offers the most isolation for CORBA backers because it implements almost the entire OLE component model using OpenDoc; it minimizes OLE's impact even on the Windows client. You can write all your client and server components using CORBA/OpenDoc without ever having to deal with OLE.

The *CORBA/COM generic gateway* provides a "live and let live" solution between CORBA and OLE. But, because of the performance hit of going through a gateway, each side will stay within its own object model. They will only traverse the gateway boundaries when it's absolutely essential to do so. To be effective, the gateways must compensate for the all the differences in the object models—including security, events, transactions, persistence, and so on. It's a Herculean task because both sides are introducing hundreds of interfaces every year to augment their object models.

Because of these dissimilar object models, components will never be able to fully collaborate across environments. Each model will have its own rules of engagement. Component providers must make some hard choices. The real question is: Which interfaces do you primarily write to—CORBA/OpenDoc or COM/OLE? Remember, we're talking about several hundred interfaces each with dozens of method calls (or operations).

The CORBA ORB vendors will use their considerable headstart with distributed components to lace desktops with CORBA ORBs and services. They will try to do this before Microsoft ships its Network OLE. The OpenDoc camp will go even further. They will attempt to put CORBA/OpenDoc/ComponentGlue on both clients and servers. Microsoft will counter by building OLE/COM into the Windows desktop, their application suites, and their popular tools—for example, Visual Basic 4.0. With the OLE/COM interfaces deeply buried inside the operating systems and applications, it becomes harder to encapsulate them with gateways or replace their function. So it's a race between CORBA's superior distributed technology and Microsoft's proliferation of the COM/OLE interfaces via its applications, operating systems, and tools. Isn't it wonderful to live in such interesting times?

Chapter 31

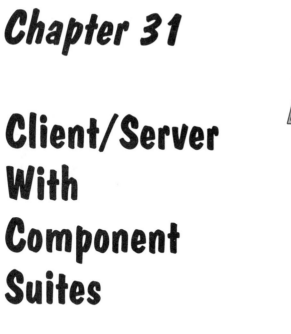

Client/Server With Component Suites

Nearly everyone agrees that the issues of cost, distribution, and support will have to be worked out before a software components market can really thrive. The technical foundations are being laid, but the business model is still up in the air.

— Jon Udell, Senior Technical Editor
BYTE Magazine
(May, 1994)

This is the last chapter in a long book. Before we say farewell, we need to answer three last questions: What will the business side of this component infrastructure look like? What's missing? And, how do I prepare myself for this component revolution? These are the most difficult questions, which is why we left them for the very last. It's much easier to write about the technical infrastructure than to worry about these collateral issues. However, we all know that these market-related issues are really the ones that eventually carry the day. This is even more true in the case of components, where the market infrastructure is just as important as the technical infrastructure. It takes an act of faith to create components—or parts. You totally depend on other complementary parts (and containers) being available to recreate the whole. This is where market dynamics must come into the picture to make sure this happens.

CLIENT/SERVER WITH COMPONENT SUITES

How are we going to recreate the functional wholeness of today's applications with components that were developed independently by different organizations that know nothing of each other? The answer is through *suites* (or *ensembles*) of components that have enough smarts to collaborate at a semantic level to get a job done.

Suites: The Sum Is More Than the Total of the Parts

A component alone is mildly interesting. A component that plays with other components is like a musician in an orchestra. It takes an orchestra to play symphonies. The conductor, as we explained in Part 3, is the application framework. A framework organizes groups of components to act like a suite. For example, a component can support an *airline reservation* suite. All the components that belong to the *airline reservation* suite share common semantics and protocols. The common semantics typically consist of common data structures, custom events, common services, and shared rules of engagement. The framework will typically enforce the rules of engagement and provide common services that make the component parts behave like a whole. A component that plays in a suite can be an extremely valuable commodity.

Suites of Pluggable Places

Frameworks will form the basis for collaborative desktops consisting of "very smart" components that act like horizontal suites, vertical suites, or client/server business applications. At a desktop level, the suites will look like "visual places" that contain people, things, tools, and business objects. For example, you should be able to plug into your desktop a vertical desktop suite that looks like a small office with visual cabinets, fax machines, telephones, and so on. We can think of a pluggable vertical place for almost every profession or activity. In addition, these pluggable places can play very well in the home. Just imagine: visual suites for cooking, entertainment, education, toddler games, and so on. Taligent's *People, Places, and Things* provides the best example of an architecture for places where we conduct activities (see Chapter 17, "Taligent's CommonPoint: Frameworks Everywhere").

Suites of Client/Server Parts

The same principles that let components play together in desktop suites apply to client/server environments. Server components are just like any other component, except that they reside on distributed ORBs. They typically control a shared resource that interests one or more clients. Client and server components must agree on common semantics that let them behave like a whole. If you think about it, this is exactly what we've been doing to create client/server applications from day one. The difference is that the frameworks do more for us. Another difference is that the units of distribution are much more fine-grained than entire applications running on the client or the server. The component is the unit of distribution. So a client/server component suite is simply a suite that runs on distributed ORBs.

Cafeteria-Style Suites

So where will these suites come from? In the world of component software, suites are simply factory assembled parts. Suites will be purchased cafeteria-style to suit all needs:

■ *Preassembled suites* are wired components prepackaged for vertical turn-key applications—for example, a *dental office* suite. These suites will be listed in catalogs.

■ *Built to order suites* let you choose your parts, places, and the platform they run on from a multivendor parts catalog. Value-added resellers will then assemble and test a suite to your specifications and ship it within hours.

■ *Client/server suites* can be assembled from networked parts and tested for a customer's environment. It's a great value-added service.

THE COMPONENT MARKET INFRASTRUCTURE

How will component vendors compete when a few hundred dollars buys you a whole application or even a suite?

> — *Jeffrey Tarter, Publisher of Softletter*
> *(May, 1994)*

An entire new marketing infrastructure is required to address issues such as component packaging, specification, pricing, distribution channels, support, and quality certification.

> — *Richard Adler, Coordinated Computing*
> *(March, 1995)*

Over the last year, we reached the same conclusion as Richard Adler—without a new marketing infrastructure there will be no component revolution. This is especially true for the CORBA/OpenDoc camp. COM/OLE already has a component marketing infrastructure that totally revolves around Microsoft's popular applications and tools. We expect a thriving OLE component business for add-ons to Visual Basic, Excel, Word, Access, and Windows 95. These applications serve as frameworks (or OLE containers) that specify the rules of engagement for add-on components. If you play by the rules of the containing application, you'll do fine. Of course, extending monolithic applications with parts is not exactly the component vision we've been espousing throughout this book.

The Open Component Market Vision

One of the obstacles to the widespread availability of high quality components is the nature of existing distribution channels. These channels are dominated by single-vendor suites.

> — *Dave Thomas, President*
> *Object Technology International*
> *(March, 1995)*

Our vision is that of an open component market with vendors offering thousands of *designer containers*. These containers are *places* in which we can plug-in business objects that represent people and things. We envision places for every industry and parts that play within them. Examples of these places are football stadiums, theaters, airplane bodies, database front-ends, factory assembly lines, building floor plans, offices, homes, desktops, garden plots, and any visual representation that can be used as a container of parts.

Parts and places will work together "hand-in-glove." For example, a *theater place* can be populated with parts representing seats and customers.   Many of the components that come together to play in places will reside on a distributed ORB. You'll be able to create client/server applications by just dragging distributed parts into places and letting them collaborate with other parts. Most of this book is on how parts obtain their collaborative smarts to play in their places.

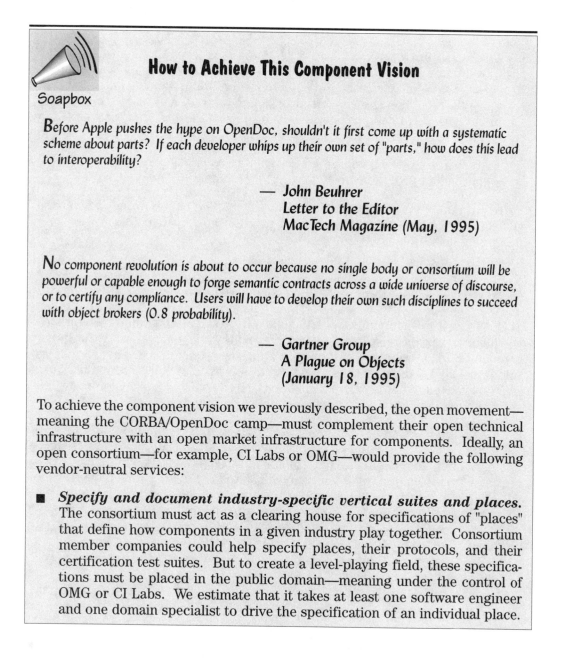

How to Achieve This Component Vision

Soapbox

Before Apple pushes the hype on OpenDoc, shouldn't it first come up with a systematic scheme about parts? If each developer whips up their own set of "parts," how does this lead to interoperability?

— John Beuhrer
Letter to the Editor
MacTech Magazine (May, 1995)

No component revolution is about to occur because no single body or consortium will be powerful or capable enough to forge semantic contracts across a wide universe of discourse, or to certify any compliance. Users will have to develop their own such disciplines to succeed with object brokers (0.8 probability).

— Gartner Group
A Plague on Objects
(January 18, 1995)

To achieve the component vision we previously described, the open movement—meaning the CORBA/OpenDoc camp—must complement their open technical infrastructure with an open market infrastructure for components. Ideally, an open consortium—for example, CI Labs or OMG—would provide the following vendor-neutral services:

■ *Specify and document industry-specific vertical suites and places.* The consortium must act as a clearing house for specifications of "places" that define how components in a given industry play together. Consortium member companies could help specify places, their protocols, and their certification test suites. But to create a level-playing field, these specifications must be placed in the public domain—meaning under the control of OMG or CI Labs. We estimate that it takes at least one software engineer and one domain specialist to drive the specification of an individual place.

We also recommend using a graphic artist to sketch out the place and its visual components. This means that it will take quite a bit of resource to specify hundreds of vertical places and standardize their interfaces. But this is what it will take to meet the Gartner Group challenge. Note that OMG has already started working on different CORBA vertical frameworks, but they're not visually integrated. In addition, the specifications are driven by volunteers and are moving very slowly. OMG can accelerate the process with full-time people on loan from the different member companies.

■ ***Run certification tests.*** The consortium must provide a certification lab for validating that components work within a suite (or place). If a component passes the validation tests, it can then use the brand name for that suite (or place). Of course, the consortium can subcontract its member companies to run the certification tests, but it must own the branding process (and names).

■ ***Evangelize the component program.*** The consortium must make its suite and branding program widely known to the industry.

We're not done yet. All we covered so far is what we expect from CI Labs and OMG. The member companies must also actively participate in this process. We describe this in the next section.

So How Does a Company Setup a Parts Business?

So what is left for companies to do? Some of the larger companies will provide a full-service parts business; smaller companies will partner with the larger companies to distribute their parts. In a sense, smaller companies act as traditional ISVs, except that they provide parts instead of complete applications. They also have better distribution channels. Here's a list of what a company that starts a parts business must provide:

■ ***Component distribution and sales channels.*** Components will be sold using part catalogs, the Internet, mail order, CD-ROMs, direct sales, telemarketing, and so on. The distributor must document the components in a catalog by function, platform, and the suites and places they play in. The catalog may also contain some turnkey applications that bundle together a number of components. To use a hardware analogy, catalogs from semiconductor vendors—such as Intel—list discrete Integrated Circuits (ICs), boards, and subsystems. In the software world, ICs are discrete components, boards are places (and frameworks), and the subsystems are turnkey applications (or assembled suites).

- *Support.* When a component breaks, who do you call? You call the distributor that sold you the component and certified it as working within a suite. Support is very important in a heterogeneous component world. Without it, there will be rampant fingerpointing. Of course, support can be very profitable—if it is run like a business. Distributors must always provide direct first-level support for any component they sell. They can subcontract their providers of parts for second-level support. But the customer must see a single face.

- *Component assembly and system integration.* System integration using components is also very profitable. Suite vendors can provide pretested client/server suites, made-to-order suites, turnkey suites, multiplatform suites, and so on.

- *ISV recruiting and partnerships.* No single vendor, however large, will be able to develop enough components to provide a full catalog of part offerings. Vendors running a parts business will develop certain parts in-house, and then obtain the rest through partnerships with ISVs. An ISV can either sell a part to a distributor or make it available on consignment. In a sense, ISVs (and part developers) are like book authors. We look for a good publisher that can sell the most books and pay us the highest royalties (and advances). ISVs will do likewise with their parts. With standard components, an ISV has a wide choice of distributors, and vice versa.

- *Consulting, education, and tools.* The distributor must provide hands-on consulting—including education on how the components in their catalog play together, as well as the tools you can use to assemble them.

We anticipate that large vendors—like IBM/Lotus, Apple/Claris, HP, Tandem, Arthur Andersen, and SunSoft—may become distributors and developers of components. These vendors already have large distribution channels and associations with large numbers of ISVs. Their entry in the distribution business will provide some level of assurance to customers. Most big customers do not want to buy their mission-critical components from "fly-by-night" vendors.

This is a very big business with considerable potential for profit. However, it's important to maintain a level playing field, which is why the suite specifications must be controlled by CI Labs or OMG. If we let the largest distributors control the specifications, we're back to the Microsoft model. Of course, it would be nice if the large distributors took on the work of specifying the suites under the control of CI Labs and OMG. Another alternative is to pay OMG royalties for developing suite specifications and for their branding efforts.

Based on our discussions with thousands of developers, ISVs, and IS people, we are convinced that this is the most important Soapbox we wrote in this book. Without a vibrant parts business, the open component movement is doomed. OMG very successfully created a multivendor technology infrastructure for distributed components. It remains to be seen whether the OMG members (and CI labs) can create the market infrastructure that complements this great technology.

So is it COM/OLE or CORBA/OpenDoc?

I have some good news: The operating system wars are over, as are the language wars, as well as the application-framework wars. The bad news is that nobody won. Instead, the struggle has moved over to the arena of interoperable objects.

> — **Ray Valdes, Senior Technical Editor**
> **Dr. Dobb's Journal**
> **(January, 1995)**

Component software has become one of the industry's primary battlegrounds.

> — **John R. Rymer, Editor**
> **Distributed Computing Monitor**
> **(January, 1995)**

In the last chapter, we explained—one last time—why CORBA/OpenDoc is technically superior to COM/OLE. But we avoided answering the million-dollar question: Who gets the Cringely 85% market share? The reason we deferred answering this question is that we first wanted to cover the market infrastructure requirements. Now that we've covered them, you'll agree that there's more to picking a winner than analyzing the technology. The outcome will be influenced by whether the CORBA/OpenDoc camp builds this market infrastructure or simply chooses to ignore it.

If they build it, CORBA/OpenDoc may own over 85% of the server component market—including ORBs. OpenDoc may end up owning over 50% of the client component market. OK, we all understand the server story, but how did we get this number for the client? With the right market infrastructure, OpenDoc will be the predominant component platform on OS/2 Warp, Macintosh, and Unix. OpenDoc may even gain a sizeable piece of the Windows component market if Novell stays on course with *OpenDoc for Windows* and *ComponentGlue*. Lotus can greatly help the OpenDoc cause if it quickly moves its applications to the OpenDoc platform. Of course, the OpenDoc camp must provide at least one *great* visual-builder tool to help developers create multiplatform parts.

If the CORBA/OpenDoc camp chooses to ignore the market infrastructure issue, it will initially still get 85% of the server component market—at least until Network OLE ships. However, their presence on the desktop will be marginal (15% if OS/2 Warp sells well). Eventually Microsoft will set standards for vertical component suites like it does today for horizontal desktop suites. It then becomes a matter of time before Microsoft gets to the 85% dominant share on the server (and the ORB). If this happens, Microsoft will impose on the industry its ORB and component standards.

So the message to the CORBA/OpenDoc camp is: *Don't ignore the component market infrastructure issues.* Notice that we disagree with Gartner's prediction. A component revolution *will* occur either way. The question is: Which component vision will carry the day—Microsoft's or CORBA/OpenDoc? ❏

Getting Ready for Client/Server With Components

Planning and construction will be guided by a process which allows the whole to emerge gradually from local acts...based on a communal pattern language that forms the basis for a shared agreement in the community.

> — **Christopher Alexander et al., Authors**
> **The Oregon Experiment**
> **(Oxford, 1975)**

Existing systems will not be replaced wholesale with object components. They'll be augmented gradually. If you already made the move to client/server, the transition to components will be smooth—the object bus is just another level of client/server middleware. Objects are simply the next level of evolution in the client/server ladder. Here are some of the steps you can take to prepare yourself for the object component phase of client/server:

- ***Think parts***. Carve out components from existing applications. At one extreme, an entire monolithic application can be encapsulated with CORBA IDL interfaces and treated as one giant part. At the other extreme, the entire application gets scrapped and recreated as collaborative parts. To get the maximum benefits of part reuse and modularity, you will need to decompose your applications into smaller parts, but you can get there gradually.

- ***Think compound documents on the client side***. Start by reorganizing your front-end applications into task-specific places. Decide on the business objects, things, and people that will live in these places. Then create (or purchase) components that match these entities. Then decide which data is going to be embedded in the document and which will be accessed via links. Which functions will your users tinker with via scripts? Make sure to expose these functions. The *place*—built as a compound document container—is the heart of the client application.

- ***Think CORBA on the server side***. Encapsulate all existing services on the network with CORBA IDL-wrappers. Use the CORBA Interface Repository and Naming Service to keep track of all the functions your servers export. Objects are additive, so start with what you have and add new components whenever you want. These pieces must be built from the start on top of an enterprise-wide distributed object infrastructure such as CORBA.

- ***Think script***. Increasingly, scripts will become the predominant paradigm for orchestrating intercomponent collaborations on both the client and the server and between clients and servers. Design your components for scriptability— ensure that your components expose a set of actions and attributes that can be invoked, configured, and modified at run time.

- ***Think resell***. Use the emerging component distribution channels to resell some of your parts and suites in the open parts market (see previous Soapbox). If you're an IS shop, reselling components should help you recover some of your costs. It also encourages your programmers to create smaller, nimbler, and more competitive pieces of software that play in an open component bus.

- ***Think suites***. Take advantage of the component bus to break applications into components, and use suites as the integration mechanism. New applications should be architected as parts and suites—from desktop to enterprise server components.

- **Think frameworks**. Use frameworks and object-oriented tools to build your new parts. Why build anything from scratch if you can avoid it?

Eventually all new applications will be assembled from component parts and suites, and then purchased through part catalogs. Part vendors and system integrators will use the catalogs as their main distribution channel. Customers will be able to browse, test drive, and purchase their parts online. Entire multiplatform client/server systems will be created on demand in a matter of days. From our reading of the technology tea leaves, it looks like 1996 may be the first year of the client/server component suites.

It's Time to Say Farewell

We define organic order as the kind of order that is achieved when there is a perfect balance between the needs of the parts and the needs of the whole.

— **Christopher Alexander et al., Authors**
The Oregon Experiment
(Oxford, 1975)

It's been a long journey and, surprisingly, we've actually reached the end. Yes, there are no more pages to turn. Writing this book was a long and personal journey. The dream of two of your authors is to one day make a living developing and selling these client/server components as small independent software vendors. But we can't do it alone. The infrastructure must be there to support us. This book is about the state of this infrastructure. It forced us to think very clearly about the options and the technology.

After writing this book, we're more convinced than ever that components are the most sensible approach to distributed systems. But we've become a lot more sensitized to the obstacles that still need to be overcome for the component vision to be realized. After reading this book, we hope you'll join the movement and work on overcoming the remaining obstacles (there are quite a few left). The reward is that components will bring the fun back in software; the current systems have become too large, unwielding, and monolithic for mere mortals to handle.

To our Martian friends, we hope you have a safe trip home and start building this intergalactic ORB that will connect us all. We hope you enjoyed your guided tour—and please tell your friends on Mars about it! We also left you pointers to resources that will help you continue your search. So farewell until the next book.

Where to Go for More Information

CORBA, OpenDoc, OLE, and components are currently the hottest topics in the computer trade press. Together they generated over 2300 articles in the last 12 months. So you'll always be able to get the latest and greatest information by reading the trade press. In addition, we compiled the following list of resources to help you find more information on the topics we covered in this book.

CORBA

CORBA: The OMG Publications

OMG recently published three new books that come in three ring binders to make them easier to update:

- **CORBA: Architecture and Specification** (August, 1995). This book covers the CORBA 2.0 ORB, IDL, Interface Repository, and inter-ORB communications. It sells for $68 ($199 with update subscription service).

- **CORBAservices** (April, 1995). This book includes the first eight CORBA services. It sells for $68 ($199 with update subscription service).

- **CORBAfacilities** (August, 1995). This book covers the CORBA Common Facilities Architecture. It sells for $68 ($199 with update subscription service).

In addition, OMG publishes a bi-monthly 28-page news magazine called **FIRST CLASS**. A one-year subscription costs $50. Call the OMG at 1-508-820-4300 to order any of the above.

Current CORBA Standards Work

The OMG meets every two months (usually in attractive locations) to continue the standards work. If you can't attend, the best way to find out what's happening is to download the list of draft documents and minutes of the meetings from the OMG FTP server (ftp.omg.org\pub\docs\doclist.txt).

CORBA Online Resources and Information

- *World Wide Web Site:* http://www.omg.org
- *FTP Site:* ftp.omg.org
- *Internet Address:* info@omg.org

Books on CORBA

- Thomas Mowbray and Ron Zahavi, **The Essential CORBA: Systems Integration Using Distributed Objects** (Wiley, 1995). This book is on object methodology and design using CORBA. Tom Mowbray is the current chair of the CORBA Common Facilities Task Force. So you will get a dose of valuable CORBA insights from reading this book.

- Roger Sessions, **Object Persistence** (Prentice Hall, 1996). This forthcoming book contains everything you need to know about CORBA's Persistent Object Service (POS)—Roger Sessions was one of POS's key architects. The review manuscript was fun to read and full of good technical information.

CORBA ORB Vendors

- *AT&T Global Information Solutions*, West Columbia, SC
  Phone: 1-803-939-7774
  Contact: randy.volters@columbiasc.ncr.com (Randy Volters)
  Product name: Cooperative Frameworks

- *Black and White Software Inc.*, Campbell, CA
  Phone: 1-408-369-7400
  Product name: UIM/X

- *Digital Equipment Corp*, Nashua, NH
  Phone: 1-800-DIGITAL
  Contact: Cooley@naszko.enet.dec.com (Al Cooley)
  Product name: ObjectBroker

- *Expersoft*, San Diego, CA
  Phone: 1-800-366-3054
  Contact: mktg@expersoft.com
  Product name: XShell

- *Hewlett-Packard*, Open Systems Software Division, Cupertino, CA
  Phone: 1-408-447-4722
  Product name: ORB Plus

- **IBM**, Austin, Texas
  Phone: 1-512-823-1706
  IBM Home Page: http://www.austin.ibm.com/developer/objects
  Contact: Anthony Brown
  Product Name: SOMobjects

- **International Computer Limited (ICL)**, DAIS Product Centre, England
  Phone: 44-161-223-1301
  Contact: D.A.I.S.User@man0506.wins.icl.co.uk (Colin Stretch)
  Product name: Distributed Application Integration System (DAIS)

- **ILOG Inc.**, Mountain View, CA
  Phone: 1-415-390-9000
  Product name: BROKER

- **Iona Technologies Ltd.**, Dublin, Ireland
  Phone: 1-800-672-4948
  Contact: info@iona.com (Colin Newman)
  Product name: Orbix

- **NEC Corporation**, Tokyo, Japan
  or NEC Systems Lab, Inc., San Jose, CA
  Phone: 1-408-433-1266
  Contact: zen@syl.sj.nec.com (Zen Kishimoto)
  Product name: NEC-ORB

- **NetLinks Technology Inc.**, Nashua, N.H.
  Phone: 1-603-891-4177
  Product name: ORBitize

- **Object Oriented Technologies Ltd.**, England
  Phone: 44-926-313-133
  Contact: chris@rtc.co.uk (Chris Nugent)
  Product name: Distributed Object Management Environment (D.O.M.E.)

- **PostModern Computing Technologies**, Mountain View, CA
  Phone: 1-415-967-6169
  Product name: ORBeline

- **SunSoft**, Mountain View, CA
  Phone: 1-800-227-9227
  Contact: larry.rice@eng.sun.com (Larry Rice)
  Product name: Distributed Objects Everywhere (DOE)

■ *Tivoli Systems Inc.*, Austin, Texas
Phone: 1-512-794-9070
Contact: info@tivoli.com (John Hime)
Product name: Tivoli Management Framework (TMF)

OLE and COM

The OLE Documentation

■ **Visual C++ 2.2 - Books Online** (Microsoft, 1995). This hypertexted book is part of the Visual C++ documentation. It is the best source of information on MFC and OLE. Note that this book does not cover OCXs.

■ **32-bit OLE Custom Controls - CDK Books Online** (Microsoft, 1995). This hypertexted book—also a part of the Visual C++ documentation—is the best source of information on OLE custom controls (OCXs). It covers the newer OLE/COM interfaces and provides a sample tutorial and Programmer's Guide.

OLE Online Resources and Information

■ *World Wide Web Site:* http://www.microsoft.com
■ *FTP Site:* ftp.microsoft.com
■ *Internet Address:* msdn@microsoft.com

Books on OLE

OLE is covered indirectly in about a dozen Visual C++ books that are on the market. The only book that really covers OLE well is the forthcoming:

■ Kraig Brockschmidt, **Inside OLE 2, Second Edition**, (Microsoft Press, 1995). We were fortunate to review an early copy of Kraig's second edition. When it comes out, this book will become the OLE programming bible (like its predecessor). The second edition reads much better than the first one. It is also more complete in some places than the "official" Microsoft documentation on OLE.

OpenDoc

The OpenDoc Documentation

The OpenDoc documentation includes a technical reference, programmer's guide, a class reference, user interface guidelines, and OSA documentation. The documentation is included with the programmer's toolkit for each platform (it comes on CD-ROM).

OpenDoc Online Resources and Information

- *World Wide Web Sites:* CI Labs—http://www.cilabs.org; Apple Computers—http://www.apple.com; IBM—http://www.ibm.com; and Novell/WordPerfect—http://www.novell.com.

- *FTP Sites:* CI Labs—ftp.cilabs.org; Apple Computers—ftp.info.apple.com; IBM—ftp.ibm.com; and Novell/WordPerfect—ftp.wordperfect.com.

- *Internet Addresses:* CI Labs—info@cilabs.org; Apple Computers—opendoc@applelink.apple.com; IBM—opendoc@austin.ibm.com; and Novell/WordPerfect—opendoc@wordperfect.com

NeXT and OpenStep

The OpenStep Specification

The OpenStep specification is freely available from ftp.next.com.

OpenStep Online Resources and Information

- *World Wide Web Site:* NeXT—http://www.next.com
- *FTP Site:* NeXT—ftp.next.com

Taligent CommonPoint

Taligent Online Resources and Information

■ *World Wide Web Sites:* Taligent—http://www.taligent.com

Books on Taligent

■ Mike Potel and Sean Cotter, **Inside Taligent Technology** (Addison-Wesley, 1995). This timely book is an excellent introduction to CommonPoint written by one of its top architects.

■ **Taligent's Guide to Designing Programs** (Addison-Wesley, 1994). This has become a cult book among C++ programmers. It has very little to do with Taligent. It gives you tips and guidelines for writing "well-mannered" C++ programs. The guidelines on mixins are excellent.

Newi

Newi Online Resources and Information

■ *Internet Addresses:* Integrated Objects—NewiINFO@ios.softwright.co.uk

Books on Newi

Oliver Sims, **Business Objects: Delivering Cooperative Objects for Client/Server**, (McGraw-Hill, 1994). This book provides a general introduction to Newi and to business objects. Oliver Sims is the principal architect of Newi and an early pioneer of business objects. You should read this book, even if you have no interest in Newi.

Background Reading on Objects

Reports and Publications

- **Distributed Computing Monitor.** This monthly Seybold publication is an invaluable source of information on distributed objects—mainly because of its editor-in-chief, John Rymer. A yearly subscription costs $495. To subscribe call (800) 826-2424. The Internet address is psocg@mcimail.com.

- **Object Analysis and Design: Description of Methods**. This OMG report examines 21 different analysis and design methods currently in use. It's the result of a survey (price $50).

- **The Object-Oriented Methodologies, Databases, and Languages Report**. This report is published by Cambridge Market Intelligence in cooperation with OMG. It provides reviews of relevant object technologies and tools. It also deals with management issues and how to transition to object technology, and so on (price $725—Ouch!).

- **Object-Oriented Strategies**. This monthly report published by Paul Harmon (for Cutter Information Corp.) contains market data on object technology and product reviews. A yearly subscription costs $495. To subscribe call 1-617 648-8702. The report is also available online on NewsNet. Contact 73352.1625@compuserve.com

- **Object Magazine**. This is a monthly SIGS publication. Refreshingly, the editor—Marie Lenzi—keeps the publication focused on distributed objects and CORBA. The magazine sells for $4.50 on the newsstands (a yearly subscription sells for $39). To subscribe, send e-mail to subscriptions@sigs.com. Note that SIGS also publishes the **Journal of Object-Oriented Programming**, which focuses on methodologies and languages. You should also check the SIGS Web-page at http://www.sigs.com. It contains a good OO resource index and information on upcoming SIGS conferences, books, and articles.

Books

This is a very short bibliography of books that we found very useful:

- David Taylor, **Object-Oriented Information Systems** (Wiley, 1992). This book is still the most approachable introduction to objects.

- Grady Booch, **Object-Oriented Analysis and Design (Second Edition)** (Benjamin-Cummings, 1994). This second edition of Booch's book is superb reading. It's also an introduction but with more emphasis on language constructs, methodology, and notation.

- Ivar Jacobson, **Object-Oriented Software Engineering** (Addison-Wesley, 1993). This book contains an early introduction to components and business objects. But it's mostly about methodology.

- Erich Gamma, et al., **Design Patterns** (Addison-Wesley, 1994). This book looks at object interactions through patterns. It's a good design reference.

- Rick Cattel, **The Object Database Standard: ODMG-93** (Morgan Kaufmann, 1994). This is the published ODMG standard. To get more information on the Object Database Management Group (ODMG) contact http://www.odmg.org.

Background Reading on Client/Server

This is a huge topic in its own right. The best place to get started is with our **Essential Client/Server Survival Guide** (Wiley, 1994). This book is still very current. If you're interested in transaction processing, you should also take a look at:

- Jim Gray and Andreas Reuter, **Transaction Processing Concepts and Techniques** (Morgan Kaufmann, 1993). This book is the Bible of transaction processing.

Recent Articles by the Authors

- Bob Orfali and Dan Harkey, "The Server Side of CORBA," **OS/2 Developer**, Jul/Aug 1995

- Bob Orfali, Dan Harkey, and Jeri Edwards, "Client/Server Components: CORBA Meets OpenDoc," **Object Magazine**, May 1995

- Bob Orfali, Dan Harkey, and Jeri Edwards, "Intergalactic Client/Server Computing," **BYTE**, April 1995

- Bob Orfali and Dan Harkey, "Client/Server With Distributed Objects," **BYTE**, April 1995

- Jim Gray and Jeri Edwards, "Scale Up with TP Monitors," **BYTE**, April 1995

- Bob Orfali and Dan Harkey, "Close Encounters With SOM," **OS/2 Magazine**, April 1995

- Bob Orfali and Dan Harkey, "Object Component Suites: The Whole is Greater Than the Parts," **Datamation**, February 15, 1995

- Bob Orfali and Dan Harkey, "Building a SOM OpenDoc Part," **Dr. Dobb's Journal**, March, 1995

- Bob Orfali and Dan Harkey, "Opening Up OpenDoc," **OS/2 Magazine**, November, 1994

- Bob Orfali, Dan Harkey, and Jeri Edwards, "OLE vs. OpenDoc: Are All Parts Just Parts?", **Datamation**, November 15, 1994

- Bob Orfali, Dan Harkey, and Cliff Reeves, "A Distributed Object Roadmap for Developers," **OS/2 Developer**, Sep/Oct, 1994

- Bob Orfali and Dan Harkey, "Client/Server Programming with CORBA," **OS/2 Developer**, Sep/Oct, 1994

Trademarks

Apple Computer, Inc.—Apple; Apple-Script; AppleTalk; Bedrock; Bento; MacApp; Macintosh; MacOS; ODF; Open Scripting Architecture (OSA); OpenDoc; System 7

American Telephone and Telegraph—AT&T

Black and White Software—UIX/MX

Borland International, Inc.—Application FrameWorks; dBase; Delphi; FoxPro; OWL; Paradox

Cahners Publishing—Datamation

Candle Corp.—Candle

Canopus Research—Canopus Research

Club Med Sales, Inc.—Club Med

Component Integration Laboratories—CI Labs

CompuServe, Inc.—CompuServe

Digital Equipment Corp.—Common Object Model (COM); DECnet; Digital; ObjectBroker

General Magic—General Magic; Telescript

Groupe Bull—Groupe Bull

Expersoft—XShell

Hewlett-Packard Corp.—Hewlett-Packard; HP; HP-UX; ORB Plus (ORB+)

HyperDesk—DOMS

Informix, Inc.—Informix; INFORMIX

ILOG—BROKER

Integrated Objects—Newi

Intel—Pentium

Iona—Orbix

IBM Corp.—AIX; AS/400; CICS; CPI-C; CSet++; CUA'91; IBM; ICLUI; MVS; NetBIOS; OS/2; OS/2 Warp; ; OS/400; Presentation Manager; SOM; SOMobjects; VisualAge; VisualAge C++; Win-OS/2; Workplace Shell; cc:Mail; DataLens; dBASE; Lotus; Lotus Link; Lotus 1-2-3; Lotus Notes; Lotus VIP

MaGraw-Hill—BYTE Magazine

Massachusetts Institute of Technology—Kerberos; X Window

MetaWare—MetaWare

Microsoft Corp.—AppWizard; Component Object Model (COM); ClassWizard; MS DOS; Microsoft; Object Linking and Embedding; MFC; OCX; ODBC; OLE; OLE DB; OLE for the Enterprise; OLE Team Development; OLE Transactions; Visual Basic; Visual C++; Windows 95; Windows; Windows for Workgroups; Windows NT; Windows NT Advanced; Win32; XENIX

Miller-Freeman Publishing—Dr. Dobb's Journal

NEC—NEC-ORB

NetLinks, Inc.—ORBitize

Novell, Inc.—NetWare; NetWare Management System; NetWare for UNIX; Novell; UnixWare; WordPerfect

Object Design, Inc.—Object Design; ObjectStore

Object Management Group—CORBA; Object Management Architecture

Open Software Foundation, Inc.—DCE; Motif; OSF; OSF/1

Oracle, Inc.—ORACLE; Oracle8

PostModern Computing—ORBeline

Santa Cruz Operations, Inc.—SCO UNIX

Silicon Graphics, Inc.—IRIX

Sun Microsystems Inc.—DOE; ONC-RPC; RPC; SUN; SPARC

Sunsoft, Inc.—Distributed Object Mangement; Network File System; Network Information System; OpenLook; Open Network Computing; Solaris

Sybase, Inc.—Sybase; Sybase SQL Server; Transact-SQL

Symantec—Symantec

Taligent, Inc.—CommonPoint; People, Places, and Things; Taligent

Tandem Computers—NonStop SQL; NonStop Guardian; Pathway; Serverware

Time-Warner, Inc.—Time Magazine

Tivoli Systems Inc.—Tivoli Management Environment; Tivoli Management Environment

Transarc Corp—Transarc

University of California at Berkeley—Berkeley Software Distribution; BSD

UNIX International, Inc.—UI; UI-Atlas

UNIX Systems Laboratories, Inc.—OpenLook; Tuxedo; UNIX

Visual Edge—Visual Edge

Watcom—Watcom

Xerox Corp.—ethernet

XVT Software, Inc.—XVT

X/Open Corp.—X/Open

Index

I

IBM 49, 89, 143, 166, 189, 196, 202–203, 206–208, 252, 272, 295, 298, 337, 557, 565
   PSP 208
IBM CSet++ 347
ICL 196, 202, 213, 565
ICreateTypeInfo 467–468
ICreateTypeLib 467–468
IDAPI 150
IDataAdviseHolder 484–486
IDC 340, 357, 375, 387
IDispatch 472
IDL
   See Interface Definition Language (IDL)
IID
   See Interface Identifier (IID)
IIOP 211
   See Internet Inter-ORB Protocol (IIOP)
ILOG 213, 565
Implementation Inheritance 345
Implementation Repository 74, 76, 78, 80
Independent Software Vendors (ISVs) 29–30
Information Highway 4
Information Superhighway 258
Information Week 157
Informix 252
InfoWorld 535
Inheritance 23, 26, 289, 451–452
   Versus Aggregation 431
In-place editing 264, 521–522
Inside-out activation 369, 522
Instance data 24
Instrumentation 251
Integrated Objects 30, 231–232, 325–326, 329
Integration frameworks 233
Integrity 207
Intel 556
Intelligent office 154

Interaction diagrams 242
Interface 25
Interface Definition Language (IDL) 35, 48, 50, 55, 74–75, 91–107, 160–161, 235, 259, 272, 323, 330, 344, 346–347, 439–440, 539
   Ada 50
   And C++ 93
   and ODMG-93 160–161
   C 50, 69
   C++ 50, 69
   COBOL 50
   Contract 93
   Format 75
   Notational tool 93
   Objective C 50
   Precompiler 72, 75, 92–93
   Repository IDs 70
   Smalltalk 69
   Versus C++ 347
Interface Identifier (IID) 432
Interface objects 245
Interface Repository 18, 74–76, 317, 330
   Defined 99
   Describe call 76
   Federations 105
   Repository IDs 70
   Uses 99
International Standards Organization (ISO) 19, 159
Internet 4, 44, 86, 89, 200, 412
   And CORBA 89
Internet Inter-ORB Protocol (IIOP) 85
Interoperable Object References (IORs) 87
Interpreters 402
Introspection 37, 317
IOleWrapper 544
Iona 49, 124, 202–206, 295, 323, 565
IORs
   See Interoperable Object References (IORs)
IProvideClassInfo 472
IPX/SPX 208, 213

X

Z